Building the Skyline

Building the Skyline
The Birth and Growth of Manhattan's Skyscrapers

Jason M. Barr

OXFORD
UNIVERSITY PRESS

OXFORD
UNIVERSITY PRESS

Oxford University Press is a department of the University of Oxford. It furthers
the University's objective of excellence in research, scholarship, and education
by publishing worldwide. Oxford is a registered trade mark of Oxford University
Press in the UK and certain other countries.

Published in the United States of America by Oxford University Press
198 Madison Avenue, New York, NY 10016, United States of America.

Cataloging-in-Publication data is on file at the Library of Congress
ISBN 978–0–19–934436–9

3 5 7 9 8 6 4
Printed by Sheridan, USA

To Kathy and Will

Contents

Figures

Tables

Acknowledgments

The writing of a book is seemingly a solitary task, but nothing could be further from the truth. This document is only the tip of a very deep iceberg. The rest—the vast majority of it—are the family, friends, colleagues, students, and organizations who have been so kind with their assistance and support throughout the years. Without them, I could never have completed this effort.

The seeds of this book came from two sources. First was from Carol Willis's 1995 book, *Form Follows Finance: Skyscrapers and Skylines in New York and Chicago*. Her masterful work suggested to me that one could apply the modern tools of economic analysis to study the skyscraper, though her work is not statistical or theoretical in nature. Economists have largely ignored this important phenomenon, most likely because the skyscraper is seen as a form of real estate, subsumable by the larger study of real estate markets (see the Bibliographic Note for references). Willis, an architectural historian, focuses on the architectural dimensions and the form of skyscrapers in New York and Chicago. In this regard, her focus is mostly on how the skyscraper looks and how its internal parts are organized, but her work carefully demonstrates that one cannot separate economics and architecture.

The second seed came in December 2005 when I stumbled on the website http:// www.emporis.com/, which provides a data base of the vast majority of skyscrapers constructed throughout the world. With this data, I was able to explore my dual interests—economics and New York City. As I reviewed the building information, a series of questions emerged. Specially, what were the determinants of skyscraper height in New York, and how did these determinants change over the course of the twentieth century? Unwittingly, these data launched me on a decade-long quest to understand something about New York's incredible history.

After I amassed a small body of academic publications that studied the economics of skyscrapers, I determined to put them together into book form. As I began to conceive of this project, it became clear that a book is not simply the sum of several articles. Academic articles have a very particular form. One that can be summarized as: (1) Research Question, (2) Related Works, (3) Theory and Model, (4) Data, (5) Results, and (6) Conclusions. Economists, as an academic breed, like to dispense with much of the historical and institutional context, and they simply want to see the question and results in as direct manner as possible. This is all well and good for a social science publication, but much of the interesting historical details had to be pushed aside. This book is thus my attempt to bridge the economics with the history. In particular, the first half of the book discusses the historical foundations for skyscrapers in New York and establishes the context for the economic analysis in the second part. It aims to fill in much of the details that were left out of my academic articles and to weave these papers into a more coherent narrative.

To this end, chapter 6 is largely drawn from my publication, "Skyscrapers and the Skyline: Manhattan, 1895-2004," in *Real Estate Economics*. Chapter 7 is from my paper, "Depth to Bedrock and the Formation of the Manhattan Skyline, 1890–1915," published in the *Journal of Economic History*, and co-authored with Troy Tassier and Rossen Trendafilov. Other related publications of mine are given in the Bibliography. Several chapters are based on academic works that were written simultaneous to this manuscript. Chapter 4 is based on my paper, "Population Density across the City: The Case of 1900 Manhattan," co-written with Teddy Ort. Chapter 8 is based on my paper, "The Dynamics of Subcenter Formation: Midtown Manhattan, 1861-1906," co-written with Troy Tassier. Chapter 10 is based on "What's Manhattan Worth? A Land Values Index from 1950 to 2014," co-written with Fred Smith and Sayali Kulkarni. The rest of the chapters contain the results of research performed specifically for this manuscript.

And now to the expressions of personal gratitude. I would first like to give a heartfelt thanks to Troy Tassier of Fordham University. If it were not for him, this book would not have been possible. As co-author, two of the chapters are based on research performed with him. No one can ask for a better collaborator and friend. I have been lucky to find someone who shares my interests in New York economic history, and working together has not only been productive but fun. He has enabled me to pursue this research agenda, and for that I am truly grateful.

I would also like that thank my other co-authors. Teddy Ort, as an undergraduate at Rutgers University-Newark, was incalculably helpful in assisting with the collection, processing, and mapping of the immense quantity of data about life in the tenements of New York around 1900. I also thank Brian Englemann, who, at the time, was a graduate student at NJIT. Together, Brian and Teddy created a shapefile for Manhattan circa 1900; it took them nearly a year to do this. I would also like to thank Fred Smith of Davidson College. I greatly appreciate not only his collaborative efforts that led to chapter 10 but also his willingness to share his land values data from 1866 to 1900 and his comments on chapter 9. As well, Sayali Kulkarni, as a Master's student, was very helpful in collecting and processing land values data that were used in chapter 10.

Many students at Rutgers University-Newark have provided valuable assistance. I am especially grateful to Nancy Elias, who tirelessly aided me in many ways. She proofread all the chapters multiple times and offered great comments, and she finished and edited the bibliography, which was originally begun by Kathleen Morales (a student at George Washington University). I thank Rubaa Saleh for her efforts with collecting and creating the images for this book. Eon Kim has also been helpful in several ways. She helped with geo-processing and geocoding historical data (including creating an address locator for 1852), and she has done an excellent job producing the maps in the book.

Other students have helped me collect data over the years. Everet Rummel and Robert Utzinger have been excellent research assistants, as have Sher Singh and Froozan Makhdoom. The students in my Fall 2014 Honors Social Science Seminar were very helpful in reading and providing comments on the chapters. I am especially grateful to Katherine Claypoole and Benjamin Sherer, who went above and beyond in their efforts. Amanda Friedman provided excellent comments for chapter 5. Dimitrios Ntarlagiannis, a geologist at Rutgers University-Newark, has been very helpful with creating the bedrock map; for ten months, his student, Jan Olechowski, diligently worked on the map as well. Together, they have, for the first time, brought a view of Manhattan's rock floor to the public at large.

I am also grateful to many friends and colleagues. I have had the privilege to know Alex Marshall, with whom I have talked about many of the aspects of this work. His writings on cities have been very helpful. Daniel Scheer has kindly provided feedback about several of the chapters, as has Nobuyuki Hanaki, Sara Markowitz, and Polly Cleveland. I am grateful to Eric Sanderson. His Mannahatta Project is work of both staggering and sublime beauty, and I am honored that he has been so generous with sharing his data and offering comments on chapter 1. I would like to thank Cheryl Moss for all of her excellent help about New York's geological history. Richard Shaw willingly discussed his knowledge of Manhattan soils. Donald Friedman has provided helpful information on Manhattan's engineering and architectural history. Gideon Sorkin generously offered much helpful feedback for the research that went into chapter 8. Although they have all been so kind with sharing their wisdom, any errors in the book belong to me and me alone.

I also appreciate the comments and feedback from attendees at various seminars and conferences. I thank participants from seminars at Binghamton University, CUNY Queens, Emory University, Fordham University, Hunter College, Lafayette College, and New York University. I am especially grateful to have been able to present my work to the Columbia University Economic History Seminar, and I have appreciated the opportunity to talk with the members of the group over the years, particularly Alan Dye and Gergo Baics. My work has also benefited from presentations at several conferences including the American Economic Association Meetings, the Eastern Economic Association Meetings, and the Southern Economic Association Meetings.

Several libraries and institutions proved vital. Columbia University's Avery Library contains a wealth of information on New York real estate. I thank Carol Willis and the Skyscraper Museum for providing valuable data. Without the Internet, I do not think I could have written this book. Several websites have been key, including http://emporis.com and http://skyscraperpage.com, which contains a wealth of information about skyscrapers.

I would also like to thank Rutgers University-Newark. My colleagues in the Economics Department have been very supportive throughout the years, especially Peter Loeb, who, as chair, hired me as an assistant professor in 2003. Rutgers-Newark provided a wonderful academic climate and allowed me the luxury to merge my professional and personal interests by writing this book. Much of the research in the second part of the book was partially funded by Rutgers University Research Council Grants, which have been immensely helpful and appreciated.

I also thank my colleagues Alan Sadovnik and Robert Snyder for their advice over the years. I thank my co-authors on other related works, including Jeffrey Cohen, Bruce Mizrach, and Kusum Mundra. For general moral support and friendship I thank Francesco Passarelli, Francesco Saraceno, Regan Solmo, Alexander Peterhansl, my mother, Marjorie Barr, and my sister, Stephanie Early. Bill and Ann O'Connor and Mary Jean Hughes are wonderful in-laws, and have provided encouragement throughout the years. But, of course, this work would not have been possible with the patience and love of my wife, Kathy, and my son, William, and for this reason I dedicate the book to them.

For more information about the book, including color figures and data sets, please visit my website, http://www.buildingtheskyline.org/.

Jason M. Barr
Hastings on Hudson, New York
May 2015

Introduction

Oh music in stone, poetry in sculpture, song in architectural marble, prayer in granite, an ecstasy in steel and iron and gold, singing city of the great heart, singing city, You are Manhattan!
Edwin Curran

Manhattan has generated a shameless architecture that has been loved in direct proportion to its defiant lack of self-hatred, respected exactly to the degree that it went too far.
Rem Koolhaas

This book begins with an image—the Manhattan skyline hovering like a giant thunderbolt on a bed of water. Once a lush forest (figure I.1A), today this bolt is covered in brick, steel, and asphalt; during the work day, nearly four million people work, live, and play on it (figure I.1B).[1]

The island is also an icon of the modern American republic—a symbol of the trials and tribulations of the country's economic and cultural growth and change. The buildings literally and figuratively contain the stories of countless strivers, arriving from all parts of the globe on a quest for material, political, and spiritual freedom. Its skyscrapers are the physical manifestation of this mass quest for success. Like a lightning bolt itself, the birth of skyline was a kind of spontaneous eruption: a burst of something new and electrifying made possible by the Industrial Revolution.

The skyline is greater than the sum of its parts; it is more than simply a collection of buildings on an island. It is a work of art in the same way a painting is more than the sum of shapes on a canvas, or a poem is more than the sum of words on a page. Collectively, society has created a masterpiece as great as that of Van Gogh or Picasso. But, unlike that of the sole painter shacked up in the studio, the skyline is the art of capitalism; it is the collective expression of an entire society. Yet it is not a deliberate act, but rather is an accident. There was never any master plan to build the skyline, and yet, here it is.

The skyscraper has taken hold of the public imagination because of its great symbolic significance. Nothing demonstrates the power and success of capitalism more that the Empire State or Chrysler Buildings. Al Qaeda terrorists on September 11, 2001, chose to attack the icons of American power—the seat of political power in Washington, DC, and the seat of economic and financial power in New York. The Twin Towers were arguably America's most important representation of the nation's free market economic system.[2] And yet, rising from its ashes is the new symbol—One

(A)

(B)

Figure I.1 *A*, the Mannahatta skyline in 1609; *B*, the Manhattan skyline in 2014.
Source: I.1*A*: Courtesy of Markley Boyer, The Mannahatta Project, Wildlife Conservation Society.
I.1*B*: Courtesy of Flyin' Phil.

World Trade Center—which conveys America's response to terrorism: though you can knock down a building, we can rebuild it just as easily.

But how did we get here? How and why was the skyline created, and what were the forces that shaped its history and growth? This book is an inquiry into what has driven and continues to drive skyscraper heights, locations, frequencies, and shapes since the late nineteenth century. Given all the attention lavished onto the skyscraper—its aesthetics, its symbolic meanings, and its engineering achievements—barely anything has been written about its economic history. But architecture, engineering, and symbolism are all moot without economics. The architect and engineer are clients of the developer, who is driven to build the skyscraper for profit. The consumer is willing to pay because of the needs it fulfills. Money creates the skyline and money sustains it.

The main argument here is that we cannot simply focus on the tall building as some isolated, soaring object, but we must focus on the context and the market. The history of the skyline is the result of the competition for access. It is a solution to an economic problem: how to house as many people as possible on the same geographic coordinates. The dilemma is that all locations are not equal, but rather some places afford the land user greater benefits than others.

Since the millions of people who live and work in the city cannot all be in the same place at the same time, the land market allocates space to the highest bidder; this market offers a nonviolent means among competing groups who are jockeying for position. The skyscraper offers a peaceful resolution to this "battle for place," since it can house hundreds if not thousands of people, most of whom would otherwise be excluded.

Land prices are an important part of the story, as they are both the cause and effect of the skyline. Land values, at their heart, are signals to society about which locations have the greatest demand, relative to other ones. If land values are high in a particular place, it suggests that the location has a great use to the city and its residents. High land values also suggest that more people want to be there than can be comfortably accommodated, and the price soars as a result, so that only the select few who can pay to be there are able to claim the prize in the battle for place.

The price of land in Lower Manhattan was so high in the late nineteenth century that developers tried to create new building types that were larger and taller in order to hold more people. The expensive land values were a signal that there was a land shortage. Developers aimed to solve this problem by creating "land" at that location—land in the sky, floating above the street. In the process, they created the skyline and also allowed for the building to express its many meanings. Skyscrapers then drew even more people to be in the same place, increasing land values even more.

The low-rise tenement districts of the Lower East Side and Five Points, just north of Downtown, were similar responses in the battle for place—the low-income immigrants were winning the battle in these neighborhoods—they were outbidding the financial firms and the Gilded Age millionaires to live in there. The reason is because they wanted to reside in these neighborhoods. They provided benefits that other neighborhoods did not. These places were often labelled as slums, but they were successful in their purpose—they provided homes and jobs for countless immigrants forced to leave their native lands. It was the land market that created the Lower East Side, and allowed for a place where immigrants could realize the American Dream.

During the nineteenth century, Manhattan saw a tremendous rise in its population. In 1800 the island housed about 60,000 people; by 1900, it held 1.85 million. Growth on such a small island naturally produces a very intense battle for the right to occupy a piece of real estate. The millions of immigrants who came to Manhattan to start a new life had to live somewhere, and, in the process, they helped determine the market for skyscrapers. The immigrant neighborhoods were shrinking the business districts, and they were driving up the price of land in the center of the island. Next to the ethnic enclaves were the commercial enclaves, and the size of the commercial areas was determined in part by the size of the immigrant areas. While there were riots from time to time, the fact that nearly two million people could not only inhabit the same island, but transform it into one of the most productive places on planet Earth is truly a remarkable achievement.

But the decisions about where immigrants were to live and where businesses were to have their offices were based on the earlier history of the island. The skyline begins its ascent in the late 1880s. Before then, the skyscraper was a technological impossibility, as the know-how to build one just did not exist. When the first one appeared in New York in 1889, it set off a building revolution, and established, in earnest, the market for height. In the first decade of this new market, the tall building appeared only in Lower Manhattan, but at the turn of the twentieth century it also began to appear 2 to 3 miles north of City Hall, in Midtown.

This book aims to understand why they first appeared in Lower Manhattan and then why they "migrated" to Midtown a decade later, but did not appear in between (see figure I.1B). To understand this requires a review of the history of land use on Manhattan before the 1890s. What occurred after 1900 was a result of how the battle for access played itself out in the early part of the nineteenth century, which in turn, was a result of earlier decisions, which began in 1626, when the Dutch first settled on the island.

The reason for going back to the beginning is because land-use patterns are sticky—when someone erects a structure on a piece of land for a particular purpose, surrounding lots will attract related or similar uses and so neighborhoods take on a particular characteristic—be they commercial, industrial, or residential—which persist and influence the future history of the neighborhood. If we truly want to understand today's Manhattan skyline, we must look at the key decisions made hundreds of years ago about how the land was going to be used.

MAJOR THEMES

Battle for Place

There are several major themes that unite the chapters in this book. First is that the skyline is a direct result of what I call the battle for place. In other words, millions of individuals, groups, and organizations are each trying to find a location for themselves, given that all locations are not inherently equal. Some locations, like Wall Street, are incredibly profitable for firms, but not so much for individuals. Finance-related companies have a willingness and ability to pay for these locations, and as a result, make them the exclusive province of the corporate sector. Those boxed out of those places must go elsewhere and bid for the right to occupy another location, and the battle goes on.

In the process, space—geography—becomes allocated according to which groups can outbid the others for the right to occupy a particular location. The winner of this battle determines the land's use and value. This is important because this battle drives the location of skyscrapers. As is illustrated in figure I.1B, the skyline is not a random jumble of skyscrapers, but rather, is a cluster of tall buildings, or two separate clusters of tall buildings, separated by about 2.5 miles of lower-rise structures. As will be discussed, the birth of the skyscraper in triangular Downtown was due, in part, to Lower Manhattan being "barricaded" by water on two sides and tenements and factories on the third. Midtown's rise was a result of how space was being allocated after the Civil War. Its birth, around Madison Square, was a product of the socioeconomic status of the people living nearby and was not related to the bedrock depths as has been so frequently claimed.

Midtown's subsequent migration north, from Madison Square to around 42nd Street, was also due to the evolving battle for place, since the city's economy is always changing as a response to the decisions made by residents, and what is happening within the larger economy, be it the business cycle, technological changes, or mass migrations from within and abroad.

Skyline as System

This leads to a second, but related, theme: because of this ongoing battle for place, the rise and growth of the skyline must be viewed as a system of interrelated parts. One group's decisions influence another group's, whose subsequent decisions feedback and influence the rest. To put it succinctly, the battle for place leads to a land dance, a kind of multiple-partner waltz around space. Each tries to be the leader and take the dancers in a particular direction, only to get a response to go in a different direction, and so on. The location and heights of buildings and land-use types form as a response to what is being built in other parts of the city. The micro-economy of a neighborhood is a result of a kind of economic "dialogue" with other neighborhoods throughout the city. To understand the skyscraper we need to understand its opposite: the tenement.

The growth of the skyline is a product of two tensions inherent in capitalism: the centripetal forces which draw people together, and the centrifugal forces that push them apart.[3] Buildings, infrastructure, transportation systems, and institutions are durable and semi-permanent. Once they are constructed they tend to draw people together and keep them there. This is often called lock-in or path dependence, and it is crucial to understanding the skyline, since the decisions that were made early in New York's history had the effect of locking-in or restricting the historical real estate trajectory of the city.[4]

But the city also faces a series of centrifugal forces—those that push people away—which include the forces of creative destruction, where the old and "inferior" is supplanted by the new and improved: real estate decays, incomes rise, technology advances, and these forces push people away from the old locations to the new ones to create new centers.[5] The city is a machine of constant churning, and the skyline is both cause and effect for this churning.

The next theme relates to our understanding of Manhattan's real estate history. Because aspects of this history have not been subject to rigorous analysis, there are many misconceptions or misunderstandings. One important analytical mistake is the confusion of correlation for causation. Another important error is what I call the framing problem, which is to telescope onto one particular element of a historical event, removing the important context, and therefore making a wrong or misleading conclusion.

Accounts of the city have not fully comprehended, for example, the role that the natural environment has played. In fact, the historiography takes a kind of schizophrenic view of how geology and ecology have influenced New York's economic and social history. Sometimes geology and ecology are seemingly all-powerful, such as the effect of bedrock on the skyline, or the rise of Five Points; sometimes geology and ecology are seemingly irrelevant, such as the implementation of the Grid Plan. Because geology and early ecology are so entwined with the city's history, a more nuanced view is in order. In short, the effects of geology and early ecology can only be understood in relation to how they affect the economic costs and benefits to land use and real estate development at a particular time and based on the city's earlier history and current state of technology.

As a preview of some of the important subjects revisited here, first is what I call the Bedrock Myth. The conventional understanding is that skyscrapers are constructed in Downtown and Midtown because bedrock is easily accessible there. Since skyscrapers need to be attached to the rock so they do not lean or settle, the location of the rock, presumably, has determined where they are built. But, as will be discussed throughout the book, this is simply not true. It is a case of mistaking correlation for causation. It is true that the bedrock is relatively far below the surface north of City Hall in low-rise neighborhoods like Chinatown, Greenwich Village, and the Lower East Side, but bedrock was not the reason for the lack of skyscrapers there.

Related to this is the question: What drove the creation of Midtown? The common perception is that it was either caused by the bedrock valley or by Grand Central Station. The reality is that it was neither. Rather, Midtown's development as a skyscraper district at the turn of the twentieth century is related to the interplay of Manhattan's shape, as a long narrow island, and its demographic evolution. Starting in the 1830s, the middle and upper classes "jumped" over the working-class districts and began their movement up the northern fringes of the city. Midtown's rise was a direct response to the commercial needs of these residents and not from the location of a railroad depot.

But what about Grand Central Station? The building boom of the Roaring Twenties created Midtown 2.0 around Grand Central Station. These skyscrapers were built to house the growing number of offices and businesses that wanted to locate in Manhattan. More broadly, contrary to the conventional wisdom, the skyscraper boom of the Roaring Twenties was largely a rational response by developers to satisfy the demand for space in the nation's most important metropolis. Height competition was only a small part of the larger skyscraper market during this period, and building height was fundamentally rooted in the profits that were available to developers in the late 1920s. More broadly, throughout the twentieth century, skyscraper competition has, in fact, been relatively limited.

As is a common theme throughout this book, the skyscraper is a solution to an economic problem: how to house as many people as possible on the same location of the planet. The tenements of Five Points and the Lower East Side were also solutions to a similar problem: how to house as many low-income immigrants as possible, when so many of them were choosing to live in the same place. We forget or ignore the facts that, by and large, given the economic realities of tenement building, these neighborhoods were successfully, and affordably, sheltering the immigrant classes of the city.

Here we see that the framing problem has driven people to focus on the negative or problematic aspects of the tenement neighborhoods and in the process reverses cause and effect. Five Points, for example, was considered one of the world's most notorious slums because part of the neighborhood was on top of made land, the filled-in Collect Pond. But this reverses causation. Five Points was not a "slum" because it was in an environmentally bad neighborhood, but rather, its environment was so poor because it was such a popular neighborhood, providing benefits to its low-income residents. It was the overuse of the neighborhood that made its quality so low.[6]

A last example has to do with land values. A frequently cited quip by America's first millionaire, John Jacob Astor (1763-1848), on his deathbed was that "If I could live all over again, I would buy every square inch of Manhattan."[7] But as will be shown, he was correct up to a point. Manhattan's land values have not been on a continual upward trajectory. For nearly half a century (1932 to 1977), Manhattan experienced a slow and painful, though uneven, deflation in its land values; so much so, that the real value of Manhattan at its nadir in 1977 was at the same point it had been nearly a century before.

In the last two decades, since the early 1990s, Manhattan's land values have not only recovered but have soared. This is actually problematic, since it indicates severe restrictions in building that would otherwise have caused land value increases to moderate. The New York City government, in an attempt to regulate the real estate market, has inadvertently given landowners a kind of monopoly power that has let them yield returns greater than if there were more competition for development. As will be discussed in the Epilogue, contrary to popular belief, Manhattan is not nearly built to capacity, but, under the right circumstances, can grow to hold many more people.

AN ECONOMICS APPROACH TO THE SKYLINE

What is an economics approach to the skyline? To answer this first requires a definition of economics. The standard definition, as recounted in textbooks, tends to be rather dull and has the magical gift of immediately alienating the would-be student from further inquiry. As given in a typical textbook, economics is the study of how a society allocates its scarce resources.[8] But if we pause to reflect on what this definition really means, we see that economics is simply the study of how human beings attempt to solve the material problems created by their existence—how they manage to provide for themselves the things they need to not only survive, but to live in comfort and style. In short, economics is the study of the causes and consequences of societal problem-solving.

We are all economists, to a degree, as we wake up each morning and make decisions about what we are going to do that day to secure a reasonable quality of life. Do we drive to work or take the bus? Do we take the day off from work and read a book in the park? Should we move to a new house or remain in the current one? Every moment of our lives we make decisions based on the weighing of the cost and benefits of our different options, in the hopes that these decisions will prove correct and will not only ensure our further survival but will also provide happiness or peace. The fact that you have chosen to read this book also suggests that, by and large, the problems of food, clothing, and shelter have been solved, so that you have ample time to read about the birth and growth of the Manhattan skyline, which was born from the need to solve problems of food, clothing, and shelter.[9]

As the study of societal problem-solving, economics is concerned with incentives: What are the costs and benefits of taking various actions and how do these incentives lead to decisions and outcomes? The conclusion is that the incentives for survival draw us to the marketplace, where we buy and sell the goods and services we need. Households need food, clothing, and shelter, and are drawn to supermarkets, malls, and cities to buy them. Businesses, in search of income for their employees and owners, provide these goods; and they do so in greater quantities and lower prices than we could ever do at home by ourselves. How many of us have recently milked a cow, made the clothes we wear, or constructed the computer on which we work? In the modern world, the market system is the means by which most, but certainly not all, of a society's material problems are solved.

The role of government then is to assess whether the incentives lead to "good" or "bad" outcomes. Government policy is about altering behavior to provide a better set of outcomes than the one we got, assuming that, by and large, governments aim to achieve these things. If a factory emits harmful pollution, it suggests that the incentives of the manufacturer are not in line with maximizing the greater good. Policy aims to reduce the pollution, while allowing society to still enjoy the fruits of the factory. If farmers and manufacturers cannot get their goods to consumers, then the government builds roads to connect them. If the free market does not produce affordable housing, governments step in try to rectify this.

The point I would like to make in this book is that in order to understand the built landscape, we must first understand what I call the incentive landscape. What do people want? And how does the cost of achieving these wants affect the decisions they make? Specifically, what is the relationship between the marketplace and the skyline?

More broadly, this book takes a tripartite approach to understanding skyscrapers and the skyline—theory, data, and historical analysis. First is the use of economic theory. These are economic ideas and concepts that apply to understanding land use and real estate. Every attempt has been made to avoid the use of mathematical analysis. The economic theory is described in words and is included to suggest the underlying, logical reasons as to why something occurs. That is to say, economic theory attempts to reduce some situation to a few key components—the fundamental incentives—in order to draw some conclusions about the problem being studied. If we can isolate the key incentives facing the different members of society, we can then understand why they act and the results of their actions.[10]

In economics, this approach comes under the heading of rational choice theory. The basic idea is that we assume that people and businesses have a simple objective in life, which boils down to the attempt to maximize their individual well-being. On the consumption side, the unit of analysis is the household. The key assumption here is that the household aims to choose a place to live to maximize its well-being, given a limited income to do so. Similarly, firms choose places for their offices to maximize profits. Take a minute to consider your choice of home. Clearly you weighed the costs and benefits of living in different places and chose that which seemed the best, in light of what you could afford. Or, consider the company for which you work; its chosen location was based on weighing the costs and benefits of that location versus others. This idea is then scaled up to different groups, sectors, or the city itself to see what happens collectively.

It is important to add that we do not need to make the assumption that everyone is perfectly rational in the sense that they always figure out the optimal solution to this problem; all that really matters is that we can clearly specify a set of aims or objectives for the different groups in our society, and then see what happens to the city—in this case Manhattan—when they attempt to satisfy their personal objectives.

There are two key insights that spring from these assumptions. First is that the location choices of the millions of people who work, live, and play in the city are not independent of each other. No two people can physically locate on the same exact spot on planet earth. As a result, if one person is at a particular location, then another person must move somewhere else. But, since "no man is an island," the location choice of the second person also affects the first. Scaled-up, it means the city can be viewed as a system of interrelated parts.

But if two people both desire to be at the same location, then they must figure out a way to choose a winner in this battle for place. This leads to the second key insight about how space is carved up. Land is assigned prices, and would-be users of land make offers for how much they are willing and able to pay for the right to occupy a particular location. The right goes to the highest bidder. In other words, the "battle" to occupy space is determined, in general, by the price system and the free market. The price paid is based by what the user can do at that location, which is also determined by income and preferences.

In order to understand the why, how, where, and when of the Manhattan skyline, this book offers economic theories regarding the land allocation and use process, and why builders chose to build upward toward the skies. But theories, in and of themselves, cannot stand if they are not supported by the facts. For this reason, these theories are tested using data and statistical analysis. I have avoided as much technical discussion as possible and have focused on the nature of the data collected and the results of these analyses. For the interested reader, specific details can be found in the Appendix.

Statistical analysis is helpful because it is a means by which larger patterns can be observed. Historical accounts of skyscrapers, for example, tend to focus on the biggest or most important of the species. The Empire State Building and Burj Khalifa attract the lion's share of attention. But we cannot draw conclusions about the skyscraper, as a building type, without investigating many skyscrapers. The skyline itself cannot fully be understood without looking at most, if not all, of the skyscrapers that constitute it.

Another advantage of statistical analysis is that it allows for the creation of a type of societal "laboratory." Unlike a scientist working directly in the lab, social scientists cannot directly manipulate the social environment to separate cause and effect. An economist cannot randomly change the income tax rates for a sample of 10,000 people to see how tax rates influence the number of hours worked. An economic historian cannot go back in time and change a policy on land use, for example, and see how an alternate history plays out.

Statistical analysis, specifically what is called regression analysis, allows the researcher to collect data on several important variables, and, through the statistical procedure, see how changes in one variable are related to the outcome of interest, holding the other variables constant. By including several variables in the analysis, one can more likely separate out cause and effect. Again, I have made every attempt to discuss the statistics in a straightforward way, with the objective of answering questions or testing theories, and so little details about the statistical methods are given in the body of the book.

Lastly, theory and statistics cannot exist in isolation and must be held together by the context in which they occur, for which we must appeal to the historical record and other writings on the subject. Newspaper accounts, histories, and biographies, for example, help to confirm or reject the findings of theory and data analysis. If one of these components negates the others, then it suggests avenues for further research or a revision of theories.

In my view, theory, data, and historical analysis form a kind of tripod of inquiry. They each help inform the other and they each clarify things in their own way. Our collective understanding about Manhattan's real estate is sometimes wrong, misunderstood, or misleading because one or more components of inquiry are missing. The easy road to drawing conclusions is based on simple observation; but do these conclusions hold up to the rigors of logical and statistical analysis? That is what this book aims to discover.

REVIEW OF THE CHAPTERS

The 1890s is the pivotal decade, when Manhattan enters the modern era. In these years, the technology for the skyscraper is perfected; the planning for the subway begins; the influxes of Italians and Jews are forming neighborhoods in Little Italy and the Lower East Side; the roots of Midtown have been firmly planted; and the northern Manhattan "frontier" is effectively closing, as virtually every neighborhood on the island had its main usage defined by this time. Today's skyline is a result of Manhattan's land use and economy in the last decade of the nineteenth century.

Because the 1890s is the crucial moment of transition, the book is divided into two parts. "Part I: Before the Skyscraper Revolution" chronicles Manhattan's real estate history before the 1890s to establish how the early trajectory of the city set the stage for the birth of the skyline later on. Chapter 1 begins at the literal beginning, with a tour of Manhattan's natural world as it existed before European settlement. We begin with Manhattan's most discussed geological feature—its bedrock—so that we may see later on how the skyline was and was not shaped by its geology. After that we take the "elevator" up to the next level and explore the island's soil. Dirt, it turns out, plays an important role in the city's history, both as attractor for economic activity and also as a nuisance, especially when perennially wet.

From there, we tour the topography and ecology—the hills, the trees, ponds, streams, and wetlands. From the perspective of early Dutch and English settlers, the natural environment had a vital influence on the decisions they made. Manhattan was established as commercial venture by a few dozen households. In 1626, when they settled the island they entered a vast forest, with networks of streams, and hills and valleys. Their survival depended on them making the correct choices within their environment.

Chapter 2 chronicles the history of land production—the conversion of the natural environment to a marketable commodity. Manhattan's real estate development was a product of the decisions that the Dutch and English settlers made about how to convert it to satisfy their own needs. Land—a geographical location that has market and use value—must be created. Trees must be cut down, hills need to be levelled, marshes, ponds, and streams filled in; this a necessity condition for converting the natural world to a city. This chapter details how the process unfolded on the island. It begins by recounting the key decisions made by the Dutch regarding how they developed the world they found. When the English took control of the colony in 1664, they continued building on what had already been established, though with a British twist.

We then fast-forward to the early period of the American Republic with what is perhaps the city's greatest act of land creation: the Grid Plan in 1811. No longer were streets and subdivisions to be created on an ad hoc basis; from hence forward the growth of the city would be ordered by streets and avenues which crossed at right angles, and were conveniently numbered from 1 to 155. The physical form of the city would be established as serving the needs of commerce and trade. And from this form, the skyline would emerge and grow.

Chapter 3 turns to the patterns of land use before the Civil War, asking the question: How did the decisions made by the residents, combined with population growth and technological change, influence the battle for place? The chapter begins with a discussion of the decisions about early agricultural settlements on the island. The key point is that Europeans were drawn to locations where the soil was relatively fertile and this drew later real estate developments. The two most important examples of this are Harlem and Greenwich Village. These neighborhoods not only remain important historical residential and cultural locations, but they influenced the later location of other neighborhoods and land uses. Most important for the skyline was that Harlem was a rural village that entrepreneurs connected to the city by railroad. The first rail line ran up the east side in the 1830s. The current Grand Central Station and Midtown 2.0 was a direct result of this earlier development.

The chapter then documents what I call the First Inversion. In the 1830s, Manhattan's residential land use "flipped." Before that, the wealthy lived at the lower tip, near the port and seat of government, while the poor and working classes lived on the northern fringes of the city. After the building of streetcar lines, the wealthy, perhaps for the first time in American history, "suburbanized" by "jumping" over the working classes and settling on the new northern areas of the city. Over the course of the nineteenth century, the upper classes would move up and outward. The location of these households would then drive the rise of Midtown proper in the 1880s.

Chapter 4 then turns to the patterns of land use on Manhattan circa 1900, asking the question: What were the important factors that drove the distribution of population density across the island right at the birth of the skyscraper revolution? In particular, the focus is on the locations of tenement districts. Residential land use was about 75% of developed land, which by 1900 housed 1.85 million people on 23 square miles.[11] The shape of the skyline would be dictated, in part, by where people were living, since tenements and skyscrapers occupied separate spheres.

Central Park plays a role in the story as well. First, it took 843 acres off the grid, so to speak, making land for buildings scarcer and therefore bidding up land prices, and promoting taller buildings. Also, it blocked the northward movement of the business district. Without Central Park, one could speculate that a new Midtown might have developed closer to Harlem. Chapter 4 concludes Part I.

"Part II: The Rise of the Skyline" begins with chapter 5, which chronicles the birth of the skyscraper and the economic determinants of building height. The chapter distinguishes among four types of height. First is "engineering height," which is the maximum height imposed by the physical constraints of construction and engineering know-how; second is "developer height," which is the height chosen by the developer; third is "economic height," which is the optimal height of a building from a societal point of view; and lastly is "symbolic height," which is that part of skyscraper height built to convey messages to the world, such as the power of the builder, the tenants, or the city itself. The history of the Manhattan skyline is based on the interplay of these different heights. The city's zoning and land-use regulations aimed at bringing developer height closer to economic height.

The chapter then revisits the 1929 analysis of W. C. Clark and J. L. Kingston (CK), as presented in their book, *The Skyscraper: A Study in the Economic Height of Modern Office Buildings*. Written at the height of the 1920s building boom, it provides an inside look at the economics of the tall building. The birth of the skyscraper gave rise to fierce arguments between its detractors and its proponents. One set of complaints related to their economics—that these buildings were simply monuments and not money makers. CK's analysis demonstrated that given the high cost of land, the most efficient height—the one that maximized the developer's return—was sixty-three stories.

The general economic validity of the skyscraper and the benefits it provides to society are now accepted facts. Few would say that New York would be better off if it limited building heights to say ten floors, and no one would advocate for the demolition of the Empire State Building. But the city still debates how tall skyscrapers should be and where they should be allowed.[12] Skyscraper policy in this day and age needs to be informed by their costs and benefits, just as they did when the Empire State Building made its debut in 1931. To this end, using CK's methodology, I estimate the economic height of a skyscraper as of 2013, and compare it to that of 1929 to see how things have changed over the period (or not).

The chapter then concludes with a discussion of the relationship between land values and skyscraper height. While it is true, as Cass Gilbert wrote in 1900, that the skyscraper is "a machine that makes the land pay," the real question is, under what conditions do land values become artificially high, so that the skyscrapers that result are economically too tall?[13] The conditions for this are laid out in the chapter.

Chapter 6 presents the findings of several statistical analyses. The aim is to understand the larger economic and policy-related forces that have driven the height of buildings and height cycles from 1890 to 2013. In particular, the goal is to understand the movement of two indicators of the skyline's growth. The first is the total height added to the skyline each year, which ranges from zero, when no skyscrapers were built, to a maximum of 15,682 feet (2.97 miles) in 1986. In order to make matters simple, I consider a building a "skyscraper" if it is 295 feet (90 meters, or about twenty-five stories, on average) or taller. The second measure is the height of the tallest building constructed each year since 1890, which ranges from 59 feet to 1,776 feet.

The statistical analyses make it possible to draw some conclusions about their economics. First and foremost, it confirms that the skyscraper is primarily an economic response to the problem of land shortages. That is to say, the skyscraper is supplied, fundamentally, to satisfy the demand for height. Second, symbolic, or non-economic, height rears its head in limited periods throughout Manhattan's history, and during boom times, in particular. Another finding is that income inequality in America affects the Manhattan skyline. Since New York is so important within the national economy, extreme income inequality in the United States spills over to the city's construction, with more income inequality leading to taller buildings in Manhattan.

Next, chapter 7 returns to the question of how geology influenced the skyline. This chapter aims to dispel what I call the Bedrock Myth, by demonstrating that the perceived influence of bedrock depths on the skyline is a misreading of history. The common belief is that there are no skyscrapers north of Chambers Street and South of 14th Street because there is a bedrock valley there. But the real reason is that in the late nineteenth and early twentieth century, there simply was no demand for them in these neighborhoods. It had nothing to do with developers' inability to supply them.

But this begs the question: If bedrock depths did not block the construction of skyscrapers, why did Midtown arise as a separate, parallel business district 3 miles north of Wall Street? This leads to the exploration of the reasons why people demand to be in skyscrapers, with a particular focus on the rise of Midtown in chapter 8. In short, Midtown arose first to service the commercial, retail, and entertainment needs of the middle and upper classes. After the Civil War, Broadway between 14th Street and Madison Square became the commercial and retail hub of the city.

By the 1880s, specific industries, such as newspaper publishers and architects, were leaving their historic locations Downtown to move northward to the Madison Square neighborhood. By the early twentieth century, about a decade after the invention of the skyscraper, developers saw that the real estate prices north of 14th Street passed a threshold and began to build skyscrapers there. Grand Central Station, rebuilt and electrified in 1913, in this early period, had little role in the birth of Midtown.

It was not until the mid-1920s when developers were drawn to the area around the station. And the discussion in chapter 9 turns to the cause of the great building boom of the 1920s. Despite the focus on the giant buildings of the day, such as the Empire State and Chrysler Buildings, there has been little probing into the reasons why so many tall structures were completed during this period. In this case, two "stories" have been offered to explain the rise of the giants. The first is that these building were a manifestation of the irrational exuberance of the age. The second story focuses on their financing. The invention of low-denomination real estate bonds sold to the public allowed the risk of the large projects to be shifted to naïve investors throughout the country.

After reviewing the data, however, chapter 9 concludes that, by and large, the building boom of the Roaring Twenties in Manhattan was a rational response to the needs of the city. After World War I, the city underwent a process of modernization and needed to develop a building stock that catered to the changing nature of work. America was moving toward an office-based society, and New York was the center of this revolution. Developers heeded the call by creating the tall Art Deco towers that characterize the period.

Chapter 10 revisits the issue of land values. If the skyscraper is a response to land shortages, then it would suggest that Manhattan is a very valuable place. For this reason, the chapter provides estimates on the value of the island, and how this value has fluctuated from the end of the Civil War to 2013, demonstrating long periods of land value inflation, in addition to long periods of deflation. The chapter also investigates the historical relationship between the growth of land values and the skyline. I find that over the last century and a quarter, the skyline has been a response to the growth in land values; while, on the other hand, land value growth is not directly affected by the skyline itself. While this finding might seem contradictory, it again suggests that, fundamentally, the skyscraper is a solution to a problem, rather than as a cause of other ones, such as congestion or excessive density.

The book closes with an Epilogue which offers policy suggestions for the future. Going forward, New York faces several potential hazards that could put its economy at risk. Since its inception, the city has seen a plethora of crises. Fires, depressions, epidemics, terrorism, riots, and crime all have affected the residents throughout its long history. Yet the city not only survives, it thrives. But what can it do to make sure it remains resilient and a home to anyone who wants to call it such, be they of any income level, nationality, or creed? Given the right set of policies, and the removal of some of its current bad ones, Manhattan's skyline can grow and evolve even more, making it, unlike a fresco or statue, a continually evolving work of art and beauty.

Part 1
Before the Skyscraper Revolution

1

Manhattan's Natural History

The lands they told us were as pleasant with grass and flowers, and goodly trees, as ever they had seen, and very sweet smells came from them.
Robert Juet

HELICOPTER TIME MACHINE

Imagine we are in a helicopter flying above New York. From this vantage point, we can see hints of the natural landscape that once was and why it was so attractive to the Europeans. Its numerous waterways form an aquatic highway network able to distribute the sailor to many places (figure 1.1). In 1609, Henry Hudson, an Englishman sailing for the Dutch East India Company, thought he stumbled on a direct route to China and sailed up the river that now bears his name. His crew member, Robert Juet, paused to document in his journal the things they saw: a vast land of forests, fish, fur-bearing animals, and natives with whom they could trade.[1] This is what excited the Dutch, who would come to settle New York and exploit its natural resources. Nature drew the Europeans and nature shaped the course of Manhattan's history and development.

But the helicopter we are in is special; it also a time machine and will take us back to an age back before Manhattan was real estate. Once we land, we will view the island's different natural layers. First, we will tour the literal foundation of the city—its bedrock, which firmly holds the buildings that make up the skyline. Next, we will inspect the subsoil—the sand, clay, and till that sits upon the rock floor, deposited during the Ice Age. After that, we will go up the elevator, as it were, to wander through the island's forests and marshlands before Europeans arrived.

Throughout the book, we will be returning back to Manhattan's natural environment. The skyline develops both because of, and in spite of, what nature provided. After detailing the natural world, we can then investigate how it influenced the built world. In the chronicles of the city, much has been made about the location of bedrock, marshes, and ponds, and how it influenced the city's economic and social history, but the veracity of these claims cannot be fully explored without a more detailed understanding of the original landscape.

In some cases, the geology and ecology were key—pushing human history along a particular trajectory, such as the rise of Manhattan's port. Other times the environment suggested trajectories, which required the will to "bend" the environment to human needs, such as the creation of the Erie Canal, which took advantage of rivers—up to Albany and across to the Great Lakes—though at great expense. The Grid Plan of 1811 was also a kind of dialogue with the natural world—sometimes nature's features were changed, sometimes they were left in place.

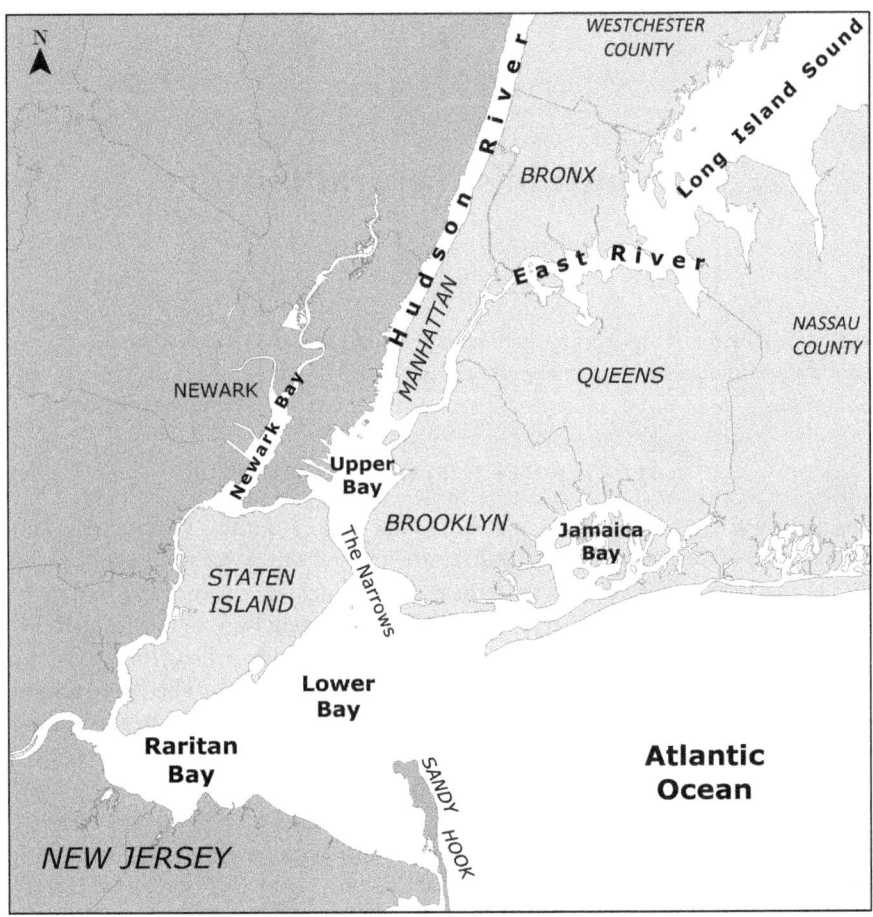

Figure 1.1 The waterways of New York.

Source: Map created by Eon Kim and Rubaa Saleh.

But we must take a more nuanced view of the role of the environment in influencing human history. Its effects occur on a sliding scale: some geological and environmental features simply cannot be ignored—they are crucial to the story—while others have more subtle effects in how they influence economic development. In other words, Manhattan, as the quintessential urban landscape, is the result of the interaction between economics and the environment. The incentives regarding where, and how tall, to build emerge within a specific environmental context. Ultimately, societies make decisions; nature does not.

A simple model is that actions get taken after considering the ratio of the perceived benefits relative to the costs (call this B/C). If the ratio is above some threshold, which is at least above one, then the action is taken. Households, developers, governments, businesses, workers, and so on are all making decisions simultaneously and (usually) independently based on what they see around them and what they think will yield the highest return.

The natural world affects B/C for the human world. The skyscraper rises Downtown, despite the geology, because the benefits of skyscraper construction were so high relative to the costs. Much historical writing on the subject of Manhattan's land use seems to forget one part of the equation, focusing only on B or C, at the exclusion of the other. At the end of the chapter I will give some examples of this.

It is important to keep in mind the difference between causation and correlation. Just because there are no skyscrapers where the bedrock is deepest does not mean that deep bedrock was the reason. Just because there were dense immigrant enclaves where the ground is damp and poorly drained, does not mean that wet ground made them slums. In order to separate cause and effect, we have to view how economic development occurred in relationship with the environment.

Before we land our helicopter, however, we take in a view of the island itself and wonder how it was created. During the last ice age, the sea level dropped so that the shorelines were 80 miles further east than they are today. After the glaciers melted and the sea began to rise, the land that remained above water was to become the New York City region. The terrain evolved from barren frozen tundra to a diverse and rich ecosystem of ponds, streams, marshes, and forests. It was the natural abundance that attracted its first native inhabitants, who arrived after the last glacier melted.[2]

When the Europeans poked their heads into the region, they encountered the descendants of these first inhabitants, the Munsees, who were part of a larger group called the Lenape, who, in turn, were part of the larger federation of Algonquin peoples, sharing similar culture and languages. For the Lenape, Manhattan was a place for hunting, fishing, and farming. While the island was not densely inhabited, small villages were dotted throughout, near bays or streams, or fertile soil.[3]

To the seventeenth-century Europeans, Manhattan was a central location in the battle for empire. It contained a series of waterways that give it entry to points in all directions and provided an ideal harbor from which the city's economy would form and grow. It was no coincidence that during the American Revolution, New York was occupied by the British Army, and that New York was George Washington's choice for the American army's first battle. Whoever controlled New York, it was believed, controlled access to the territory.[4]

The Hudson River was a road to the north and the interior—through the Mohawk River valley to the west or Lake Champlain to the north. New England was accessible through the East River and Long Island Sound; and the Caribbean could easily be reached by sailing down the coast. The southern tip of Manhattan juts into the upper New York Bay—the harbor proper—which is a veritable saltwater lake, some 4 miles wide, with the "tentacles" of the Hackensack and Passaic river systems draining into it.[5] The upper bay connects via the Narrows to the lower bay, which then merges with the sea. To the west, the lower bay connects with the Raritan Bay, which receives the Raritan River. The Narrows is a bottleneck which creates a sheltered port, protecting the upper bay from the waves of the Atlantic Ocean (figure 1.1).

Manhattan is bordered by three "rivers," though none is, in fact, a true river. On its western shores is the Hudson River, originally called the North River by the Dutch. It originates at Lake Tear in the Clouds, in the Adirondack Mountains, 315 miles north of the city, at an elevation of 4,295 feet above sea level. It is navigable from Troy, New York, 150 miles to the north. At Manhattan, the Hudson is about 1 mile wide. The majestic Palisades cliffs of New Jersey line its western banks.

The river's current path was carved by the meltwaters of the last glacier, when the sea levels were much lower. The flow cut a deep channel in the lower Hudson, allowing it to be navigable by large ships, though sadly for Henry Hudson, the glaciers carved no route to Asia.

The lower half of the river is actually a tidal estuary because it receives the saltwater from the sea. The tidal push is so strong that during high tide the flow of the river reverses and moves northward; the river is brackish as far as Poughkeepsie, New York.[6] On the eastern shore of Manhattan is the East River, which is also not a river, but rather a tidal strait connecting the Long Island Sound to the Atlantic Ocean. Along the lower tip of Manhattan, the East River was preferred as a port because it was less turbulent and more protected than the Hudson, which also had ice floes in the winter.

The third "river" is the Harlem River, another tidal strait, which connects the Hudson and East Rivers. Today, the northern part of its course is the Harlem River Ship Canal, which was constructed by the New York Central Railroad in 1895 to connect what was then a small loop of creek called Spuyten Duyvil Creek to the Harlem River proper. In the process, the neighborhood called Marble Hill was severed from Manhattan, and attached to the mainland.

THE BEDROCK: A GUIDED TOUR

Now that we have seen things from the sky, we are finally getting ready to land. Before that, though, we need to flick a few switches on the helicopter's control panel. The first activates an enormous vacuum, which sucks up all the buildings, the asphalt, the trees, the cars, the hotdog vendor carts, and so on. After that, we suck up the soil deep below the ground—the subsoil—to remove everything that stands between us and the bedrock.

Our first quest is to discover the true shape of Manhattan. Where is the bedrock relative to the sea level; what is its topography as we go from south to north, and from west to east? What are its geological properties? What, and where, is that Manhattan Schist so frequently discussed? Armed with this knowledge, we can move, in subsequent chapters, from natural history to economic history. Before we land, however, we need to flick one more switch. This one freezes the waters that surround the island, so they do not rush in and flood over the bedrock, which south of 14th Street lies below the sea level.

The contours of the bedrock began to take on great importance after the Civil War, as buildings became larger and heavier. The structures had to remain stable, and the ground below was soft and wet, and would not allow for rigid foundations. A building, if not properly stabilized, could sink several inches or feet into the soil. Or worse still, one part could sink faster than the other, causing it to crack, and perhaps split apart. Even if uneven settling did not affect the structural integrity, it presumably could affect the quality of life, as no one wants to work or live in a tilted or cracked structure.

Besides the issue of foundations, and perhaps, even more importantly, is the relationship between the natural environment and how it influenced the decisions residents made about where to put different types of buildings and the infrastructure. Every society must work with its environment. New Yorkers had to have a relationship with their bedrock.

After the vacuuming is finished, from above, we now witness the exposed bedrock—a giant Manhattan-shaped boulder—plunging downward, like a descending whale. The view looks like figure 1.2, which gives a three-dimensional map of the rock floor.[7] We land our helicopter on the southern tip. Note that we would not be in Battery Park, since all of it was made from landfill, and thus is part of the gelled waters. Our tour begins roughly at just south of Bowling Green, where the Dutch erected a fort when they first settled on the island. Looking around, we cannot help but wonder: Where did this giant rock come from? How did it form?

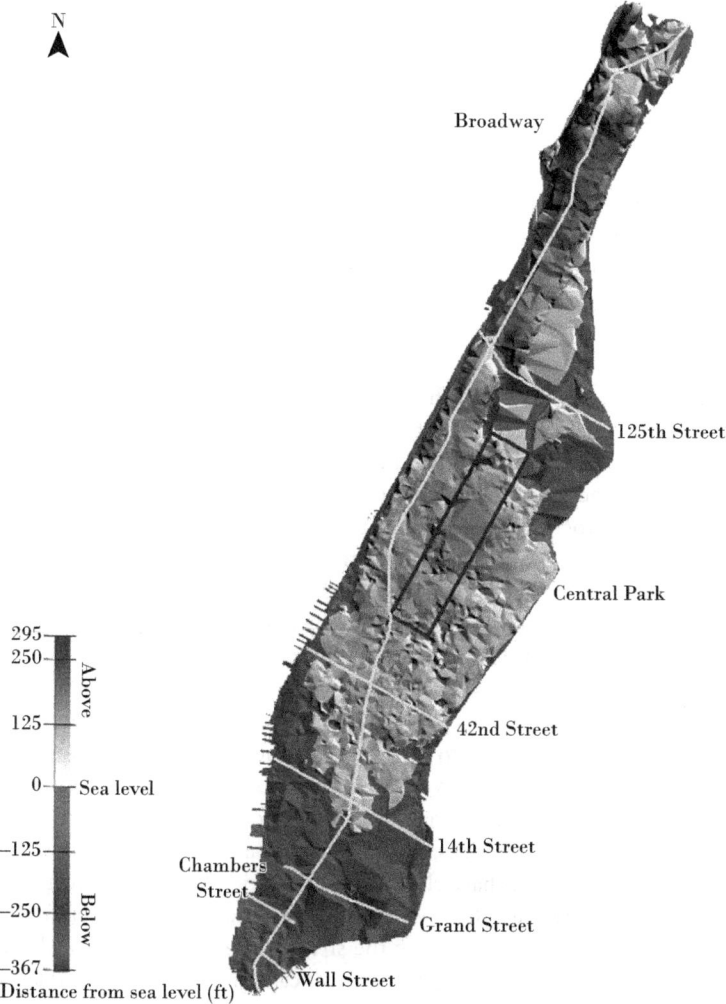

Figure 1.2 Manhattan's bedrock topography. This map shows the elevation of Manhattan's bedrock relative to sea level. The lighter areas are where the bedrock is above the water. The lower areas are where the bedrock is below the sea level. The rock floor achieves its greatest depths in the Lower East Side, around where the Bowery intersects Grand Street.

Source: Map created by Jason M. Barr, Dimitrios Ntarlagiannis, and Jan Olechowski. The streets were added by Eon Kim.

Manhattan's earliest geological lineage can be traced back at least a billion years, during the Proterozoic Age, with some of the rocks on the island being at least that old. The rock below our feet is half that age, formed in the early Paleozoic Age, some 550 million years ago when the proto-North American continent collided with the ancestral African continent. Several miles down below the ocean, as the two continental edges met, the North American plate was forced down below the African plate, in a process called subduction.[8]

As the edge of the North American plate was pushed down, it made contact with the asthenosphere, a hot liquid surface on which the continents float, causing the edge of the plate to melt and bubble up to the surface as lava, creating an arc of volcanoes in the sea—called the Taconic Island Arc—off the coast of the proto-North America. This ancient lost sea is called the Iapetus Ocean.

In these waters, the "seeds" of Manhattan were being planted. Just off the shores of proto-North America, limestone was forming from calcite precipitating out of the water and shells of marine animals piling up on top of each other over millions of years. These layers were compacted and glued together as limestone. Further out, clays, sands, and silts were accumulating in the ocean waters, forming sandstone, mudstone, and shale. While further out still, closer to the Taconic Arc, deep-water deposits of eroding rock and silts coalesced into sandstone and mudstone.[9]

During the period that these sedimentary rocks were forming, the two plates continued to move toward each other, and the Taconic Arc eventually collided into the early North American continent about 450 million years ago, during the late Ordovician period. This process of mountain building is called the Taconic Orogeny; it formed a new range called the ancestral Taconic Mountains.

Manhattan's bedrock was born out of the Taconic Orogeny, as today's rocks are metamorphosed versions of that sedimentary rock created in the Iapetus Ocean. Over millions of years, the sedimentary rocks below the Taconic Mountains metamorphosed into schists and marble from the heat and pressure deep below the surface. The island's northeast direction is due to the angle at which the Taconic Island Arc smashed into the proto-North American continent.[10] Over time, the mountains eroded, thus providing the relatively level "playing field" that is Manhattan.[11]

As the island arc moved closer to the continent, the layers were shuffled and pushed together. Some rock layers are now vertical, some are folded into each other, and some are split apart. Thus, the bedrock is not laid out in smooth horizontal bands but rather is bent into wavy valleys and ridges, called anticlines and synclines. Without any evidence to back it up, geologists have claimed that the Grid Plan of 1811 created the long north-south avenues because these were parallel to the folds, and therefore created a path of least resistance when creating the streets.[12] The historical record shows no support for this nice-sounding nugget; it seems a case of confusion of correlation with causation (more about this in chapter 2)

We now make our first cautious steps forward, ready to walk up this giant rock. We will measure our depths both relative to the sea and relative to the street level. At the southern tip, the rock rests relatively close to the surface, at about 25 feet down. But because the bedrock is about 15 feet below the sea level, the gelled sea is around us, and we feel as if we are standing inside a large aquarium, with the top of the giant bowl some 15 feet above our heads. We need to walk carefully; though our giant vacuum removed everything above it, the rock remains damp and moist, given that it was saturated by the surrounding sea.

Because of the island's geological history, our path is not smooth, and the floor can radically change direction at any moment. It is cracked in places, and the folds and deformations created small hills and valleys. Running water has eroded pockets and even created caves. The hike is like walking on a giant piece of aluminum foil that has been first crumpled up and then pulled apart again. Be careful, you don't want to trip and fall!

Walking up where Broadway would be we find a downward slope. At Wall Street, we are some 72 feet below the street; and 40 feet below the sea level. If we were to turn right, down Wall Street toward the East River, we would climb a bit, so that at Pearl Street we find we are only 40 feet below the surface. In this case, the quarter mile walk translates into a gentle slope, but then from Pearl Street to the East River, we start to descend again, so that by the time we get to the shore line, we are some 65 feet below the sea level again.

What type of rock is this below our feet? We pause to review our geologic map (figure 1.3). (We recognize, though, that it is quite imperfect. We are the first people to actually see the bedrock. The geologists who created the map were not as lucky as us. They simply had rock samples and views from various excavated building and tunnel sites.) We can see that Manhattan's rock floor is comprised of three main types of rock, mostly some form of schist, but parts have marble or gneiss. All three are metamorphic rocks formed by the heat and pressure at the base of ancient mountains. What distinguishes these rocks is their age, mineral composition, and erosion rates.

Below our feet is the famous Manhattan Schist, which is generally dark gray, but sometimes appears rusty brown. The rock was formed in the offshore area in the middle of the ocean, around the continental slope, where there were clay-rich sediments falling to the bottom of the ocean. Because of its lack of layering and its mineral composition, it is very durable and less likely to erode. Around Canal Street, the Manhattan Schist "disappears" and reappears north of about 110th Street on the west side. This is the reason for the highlands in the northwestern area of Manhattan.

But the map clearly demonstrates that Manhattan Schist is but a small fraction of the total rock floor; the rock patterns are much more complex than the conventional wisdom would have us believe. Geologists began describing and mapping the rocks on the island as early as the first half of the nineteenth century. In 1900, the geologist F. J. H. Merrill called what he saw as "Manhattan Schist" based on samples he collected.[13] In an era without sophisticated technology, the ability to make sharp distinctions at the molecular level was impossible.

"Manhattan Schist" has a nice sound to it; the term lends currency to Manhattan's exceptionalism by giving it its own rock type. But technically speaking, the type of rock that geologists actually call "Manhattan Schist" constitutes about a quarter of the bedrock. Geologists disagree on the exact boundaries of where the different schists meet, but they all agree that there are several types of it.

The conventional understanding of Manhattan's rock floor is that is comprised of Manhattan Schist, and because of this schist, we have the skyline. As an example, WNYC, the National Public Radio Station for New York, created a list of the ten most important objects "that best tell New York's story—from its first days to 2012." The idea was that if these artifacts were placed in a time capsule, then future generations

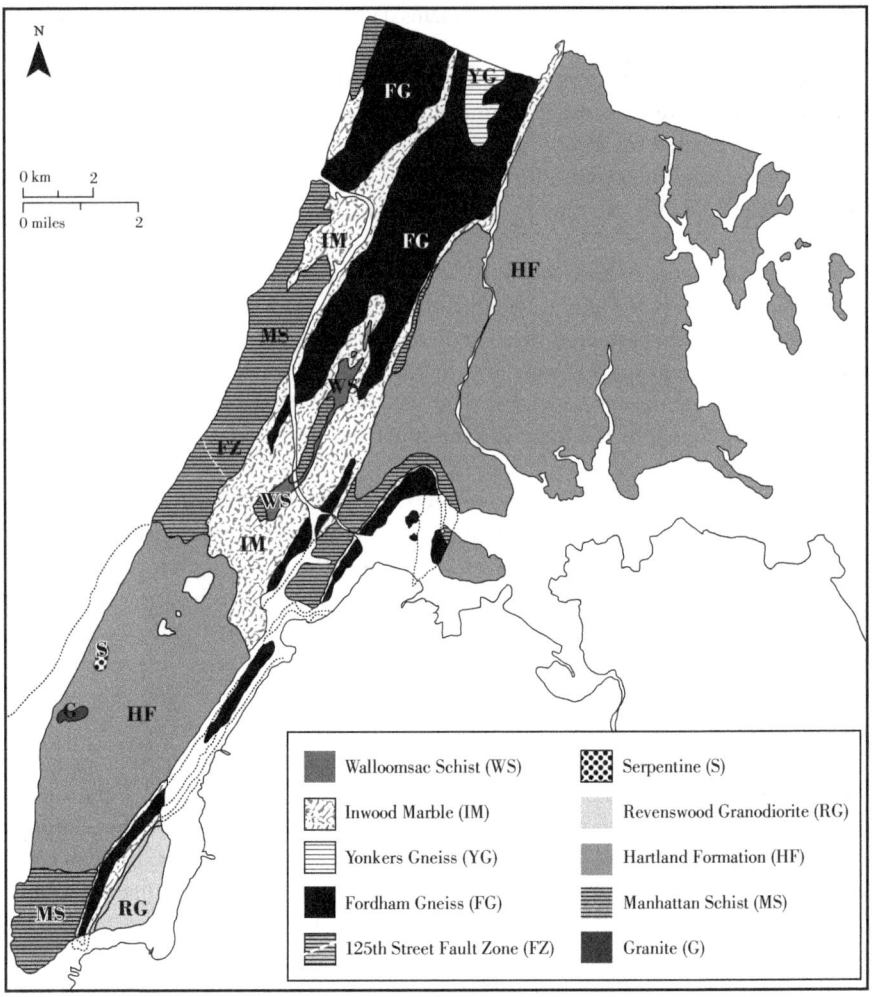

Figure 1.3 Geological map of Manhattan. While virtually all of Manhattan is comprised of some type of metamorphic rock, the term "Manhattan Schist" only applies to a fraction of the island. Three rock types dominate: Hartland Schist, Manhattan Schist, and Inwood Marble; a plethora of other types are found, though in lesser amounts.

Source: Underlying map is courtesy of the American Museum of Natural History; map was prepared by Rubaa Saleh.

who might dig it up would then understand the city's people and culture.[14] Number nine on the list was "Manhattan Schist"—the rock that created the skyline. As a short-hand phrase, "Manhattan Schist" is fine, but the geological record points to a much more diverse pattern; each rock also has different properties that are of concern to engineers.[15]

Ironically, for all of Manhattan's economic value, the rock itself has provided little of direct use. The layered schist rocks tend to be brownish gray and can be flakey; they are not ideal for building materials, as they splinter when struck.[16] The rock is aesthetically unappealing and so has no value as jewelry or for collecting; since it chips so easily it has little value as a countertop. From time to time it is used to make stone walls.[17] The rocks however, are fun to climb on, as is possible in Heckscher Playground in Central Park, or in Riverside Park, near West 83rd Street.

Some buildings occasionally use the more appealing varieties for facades, such as Shepard Hall on the City College campus on 138th Street. The building, in English Gothic style, was designed by George B. Post (also instrumental in designing early skyscrapers). The stone was quarried directly from the building site and illustrates how New York's native rock, when used at all, tends to be for Gothic-style structures, such a churches and college halls. Building facades in the city tend to be non-metamorphic rock, such as sandstone ("brownstone"), and white limestone; terra cotta and brick; and occasionally the metamorphosed marble.[18]

Now that we have the lay of the rock land, we put our geologic map away for now. We will take it out again later. Returning to Broadway, and strolling toward City Hall's location, we now find ourselves moving fast down a steeper slope. At Chambers Street and Broadway, we are about 100 feet below the surface, as the floor plummets beneath us and we sink into a large valley at Reade and Centre Streets. We turn northeast walking through this valley, which extends up through Chinatown and the Lower East Side. Here we are, at the geological bottom of Manhattan, in the famous bedrock valley, some 300 feet below the sea level, and 350 feet below the ground. If the year were 1900, thousands of Russian and Polish Jews would be out on the streets, heading off to work or home. We would be watching their world from a giant crater below their feet. Watch out! Here comes an apple that just fell off a pushcart.

At Leonard Street, we can enjoy a stroll through the bottom of the Collect Pond, which was part of old New York before it was filled in at the turn of the nineteenth century. At 5 acres, it was the island's largest body of freshwater. It was likely formed as a kettle pond, from a trapped boulder of glacial ice that melted into a pond, and remained fed by underground springs. In the seventeenth and eighteenth centuries, its depths remained a mystery—some even claimed it was bottomless—but today we can see its floor was some 140 feet below the ground. Archaeological evidence shows that the lake bed was about 70 feet above that.

We are thirsty now, and want to take a drink, so we walk a block to the southeast to the intersection of Mulberry Street and Park Row. There we see a great bubbling spring, with refreshing water coming out of some cracks in the rock. It is the old Tea Water Pump, which provided fresh water to the city, until the opening of the Croton Aqueduct in the 1840s. Ah, that's good!

We now have a choice to make; do we continue east and explore the valley or do we go north and rise out of the valley and head toward higher ground? We make note in our maps that the valley—a bowl really—runs from City Hall in a northeasterly direction to the Lower East Side, with its nadir between Canal Street, East Broadway, Essex, and Grand Streets, where Seward Park is today. We pause to wonder, could there be a relationship between the bedrock depths and the fact that this neighborhood was the densest place on planet earth in the year 1900? We will have to wait to answer this question, as we need to collect more evidence.

Back on Broadway, we have some rock climbing to do so that we can ascend from the valley. By the time we arrive at Broome Street, the floor is only about 60 to 65 feet below the surface. From here our journey is more measured; slowly the ground rises and then by the time we get to 14th Street, we realize we are looking down to see the gelled waters. It is as if we have risen from the basement to the ground floor. The rock surface is now above the sea level.

We take another quick peak at our geologic map (figure 1.3) and see we are no longer walking on Manhattan Schist. Rather, we have hit the Hartland Formation. This rock was formed mostly by deep-oceanic shale, though the rock also contains some greywacke and volcanic rock formed along the island arc.[19] The Hartland rock also has high mica content and is sometimes referred to as mica schist. Because of the Hartland's layering and mica content, it can more easily flake and crack as compared to its sister, the Manhattan Schist proper. We also see that when we toured the Lower East Side, we walked over some Ravenswood Granodiorite (which is similar to granite) and marble.

We continue on our journey up Broadway. It is a bit more rugged from here. Ridges and valleys define the contours of the bedrock on the Upper West Side. We climb and we descend and we climb and we descend. Sometimes these valleys yielded surprises to the real estate community. For example, in 1940 at 90th Street and Central Park West, developer Samuel Rudin, who was constructing an 18-story apartment building, was perhaps quite surprised when he found the bedrock there was 60 feet below ground. It was covered with clay and above that was 30 feet of water and till; the water likely emanating from an underground spring. As a result, the building had to be constructed on piles, driven down to the rock.[20] In 1963, construction of a school at Columbus Avenue and 83rd Street was halted for five months because an underground stream caused the foundation to start sinking. As a result the project's costs increased by $100,000.[21]

Now we are at Broadway and 116th Street, at a local peak in Morningside Heights. Again, we have to make a choice as the rock drops steeply in all directions. To the west, the rock falls to the river. To the east we also see another steep drop off, and we wonder why the rock to the east is a lighter color. Taking out geologic map again we see that it is mostly Inwood Marble.

These neighborhoods are nearer to sea level because marble erodes relatively quicker than the schists. Harlem was originally settled by the Dutch because it was low-lying flat lands suitable for agriculture. Down there the bedrock is also deep below the surface, the gelled waters are ten stories above the floor. Looking down at East Harlem we also see the how the bedrock is wavy and folded, almost like aqueducts running up the island.[22]

Morningside Park from 110th Street to 123rd Street marks the transition from schist to marble. It is no coincidence that the park is there, since the changeover is accompanied by a steep drop in elevation, limiting its use for real estate. We also notice a small pocket of another kind of schist, called Walloomsac, in central Harlem.

Facing north is another steep drop off, in this case because of faults in the rock. As it turns out, Manhattan's rock contains several different types of faults, where the rock has fractured or has moved relative to adjacent rocks. The complex tectonic process described above has created two major fault zones. The first is Cameron's Line, a ductile thrust fault, where the Hartland Schist was pushed on top of the Manhattan Schist. The two rock formations were sutured together when the proto-North American plate collided with the volcanic arc during the Taconic Orogeny.

The second major ductile fault system is the St. Nicholas Fault—the one we are looking down upon. It is where the Manhattan Schist was thrust over the Inwood Marble and Walloomsac Schist. Today, if you take the 1 train up Broadway, you will notice at around 120th Street, the train rises out of the ground and becomes elevated over 125th Street. The reason is that the highlands south of 125th Street give way to a valley. Along this northwest trending line is the 125th Street Fault. Similar faults appear in other areas of northern Manhattan, including at Dyckman Street and 155th Street. These fault zones produced broken rocks, and thus were more easily scoured away by glaciers to form a valley.[23]

Manhattan is considered an unlikely place for a large earthquake, but seismic activity has occurred both on the island and within the region. The most recent earthquakes on Manhattan are related to the 125th Street fault. In 2001, there was a small quake (magnitude 2.2) which resulted in some shaking but no damage. While the New York region is not nearly as active as say California, the area is at high risk of expensive damage, simply because of its density.[24] The city's building code today requires structures to withstand large earthquakes, but the problem, of course, is that older buildings, built over Manhattan's soft subsoil, are not as safe.[25]

We look over the rock cliffs of schist to the sea of marble, and then turn back to Broadway, where we descend into the deep valley at 125th Street and ascend it again. Our goal is to reach the highest peak in Washington Heights, a few blocks north of the George Washington Bridge in Bennett Park, at 183rd Street. When we arrive, exhausted from our long journey, we take in the vista: a huge 13-mile long rock jagged and cracked in parts, smoothed, folded and bended in others. Looking south, we see its long, slow plunge downward, almost like a great blue whale descending into the sea. Tomorrow, we will put back the till, sand, boulders, and clay and roam through Manhattan's subsoil.

NEXT STOP: THE SUBSURFACE

Now that we have completed our tour of the bedrock, we can move up to the subsurface. We now hit the "unsuck" button on our vacuum and return all of the subsoil that rests on the rock floor. To take this tour we are going to take a subway—the 1 train from South Ferry to 215th Street, the last stop in Manhattan. Our train, fortunately, is a glass tube that allows us to see the subsoil on all sides.

In 1895, chief engineer of the Rapid Transit Commission, William Barclay Parsons, had to choose how the New York City subway would be built given the city's particular geological conditions. He was faced with two choices: either burrow tunnels far below the surface through the hard rock, or lay down the roads just below the street.

To ensure that the tunnel remained fully under the bedrock, especially as it approached the valley near 125th Street, it would have had to be built some 200 feet below the surface. While this type of construction would have meant much less disruption to the street life above, each stop would require a series of elevators or escalators, not only increasing the cost of the project but greatly slowing down travel times. It is also likely many unexpected geological problems would have ensued from the faults and stresses on the rock. On September 25, 1915, for example, subway workers were blasting rock at Broadway and 38th Street and there was an unexpected cave in of highly irregular and fractured schist.[26] These kinds of problems would likely have multiplied if the whole system was built entirely in the rock.

Because of the varied depth and hardness of the different schists, Parsons decided tunnels were not economically viable. Instead he chose the "cut and cover" method. Subway lines would be dug 15 to 20 feet below the surface, by excavating the subsoil. After the trench was cut, and the tracks were laid down, the street would be built over the tracks, held up by steel columns.[27] Using the subway lines, we can take our tour 20 feet below the surface. Our trip will be a bit faster today, not only because we are in a subway, but because we are also viewing dark brown soil, which to us will look pretty much the same in most parts of the city. We will try to see the differences as we go northward.

Much of the subsoil was laid down by glaciers, up to 1.25 miles high. Starting about 1.6 million years ago, during the Pleistocene Epoch, New York was directly affected by at least three Ice Ages, with two larger and one minor advance during the last one, which ended only about 10,000 years ago.[28]

Glaciers affect the landscape through two types of processes—erosion and deposition. As the ice moves south it transports millions of tons of soil and rock, which it picks up along the way. The underside becomes a thick layer of mud, sand, gravel, and boulders called till. Till layers cover much of the island's rock floor.

As the glacier travels, it acts like a giant piece of sandpaper. It both smooths and polishes outcrops of bedrock, and scores deep grooves in them. In Central Park, today we can see evidence of the glaciers because of the northwest trending scrapes etched into the outcroppings. Glaciers can also carve out valleys where there are natural faults or cracks. The ice will erode softer bedrock as well, creating low-lying lands in its wake. The last glacier carved out smaller valleys in the Manhattan bedrock that run northwest to southeast, perpendicular to the folds created by the Taconic Orogeny.[29]

The front edge of the ice mountain scooped up a large mass of till and boulders, and when it finally retreated, it left a large mound, called a moraine, at the southernmost point of its advance. The last two glaciers left two moraines just south of Manhattan, called the Ronkonkoma, and Harbor Hill Terminal Moraines, respectively. They traverse Long Island, Brooklyn, Queens, Staten Island, and northern New Jersey.[30]

The Harbor Hill moraine acted as a dam, holding in the melting glacier waters, which formed several glacial lakes covering the New York-New Jersey metropolitan region. The lake bottoms were coated with the sands, clay, and silt.[31] Each spring when the region's snow and glacial ice would melt and drain, it would deposit new layers of silt and sand on top of the lake bottom. During the winter freeze, clay suspended in the lake water would settle out to form a repeating sequence of sand, silt, and clay. These layers are called varved sediments, and much of the upper layers of Manhattan's soil, just below the organic matter, are comprised of varved silts and sands.[32] It is likely that the higher ground along Manhattan's west side from 59th Street was above the level of the lake, so this area did not see much in the way of lake deposits, and the ground has a relatively thin coating of glacial till.

At least 12,000 years ago, there was a breach of the terminal moraine at the Narrows in New York Harbor, causing the glacial lakes to drain.[33] Near the Narrows nearly 200 feet of glacial strata were scoured away. The Hudson and East Rivers were carved from glacial melt, creating the island of Manhattan. While the lakes were draining, they left one final layer of silty sand.[34] The glacial till and outwash, however, are not simply layered on the bedrock like a terrarium, but the layers themselves are highly varied and jumbled together. Part of this is due to the randomness of what the glaciers picked up and deposited. Another reason is the folded and buckled nature of the bedrock, which trapped some kinds of material in some places but not others. Fissures and folds in the bedrock also created underground streams and springs, which percolate up through the subsoil. In the northern, craggy parts of Manhattan and the Bronx, there were many such springs. They are lost to us, however, by the great tide of economic development.[35]

In short, the layers covering the bedrock (from bottom up) are first unsorted glacial till comprising a jumbled mix of sand, silts, clays, and random boulders and cobblestones. In the higher elevations of the Upper West Side, there may be a thin layer of outwash sand, but, by and large, it is just till on bedrock. In East Harlem, where the elevation is lower, the till is below varved strata (silts and clays) which came from the glacial lakes; and on top of that is sand left by the melted glacial waters as they drained away.

To help us understand the subsoil types we are going to see on our journey, we pull out a handy map that shows the island's geological features along Broadway (figure 1.4). In Lower Manhattan, the street elevation is about 10 to 25 feet above sea level and our tour begins, on average, at sea level. This will make things a bit more complicated, because at that grade, the subsoil mixes with the water that seeps in from the rivers to form a gravy-like substance, known in the engineering world as "quicksand." Our worm's eye view will be a little wet as a result.

As we start our journey, a few feet above the bedrock, we see below us the glacial till, mixed with clay, boulders, and smaller rocks. Above us we see fine silt and sand. Going north, as the bedrock descends, we lose sight of the till, which hugs the rock, and now we are surrounded by the gooey quicksand. But, of course, we have to be careful to go slow; we might suddenly smash into a huge, unmapped boulder, or get stuck in a bed of hard clay.

We now approach close to the World Trade Center site (figure 1.5). Thanks to the work of geologist Cheryl Moss, we have photos of the area. They were taken during the excavation of the site in preparation for the new towers. The top two photographs show the exposed bedrock on the site, and the interesting formations that have been created over time. In figure 1.5, image A shows two large dips in the rock; while the image B shows a cave eroded by an underground whirlpool. Photograph C shows the till, which is comprised of a jumble of stones, sand, and boulders and D shows pegmatite (an igneous rock) wedged between the schist.

After leaving the World Trade Center site, our subway approaches Chambers Street where the bedrock is far below the surface. We are moving through the layers sandwiched on top of each other and which reflects the different types of material laid down over the millennia. Right above the bedrock sits a layer of gravel, above that are alternating bands of sand and clays.[36]

As we move up Broadway, we become less concerned with wet soil because we are now above the sea level. Here, we see below us a layer of hardpan (till), then dry clays, and above us, mostly sand. Starting at 34th Street and going north, the bedrock is coated with glacial till. As we move forward, the bedrock moves closer to the surface, and in fact, in some cases, it is directly below the surface so that our subway would in

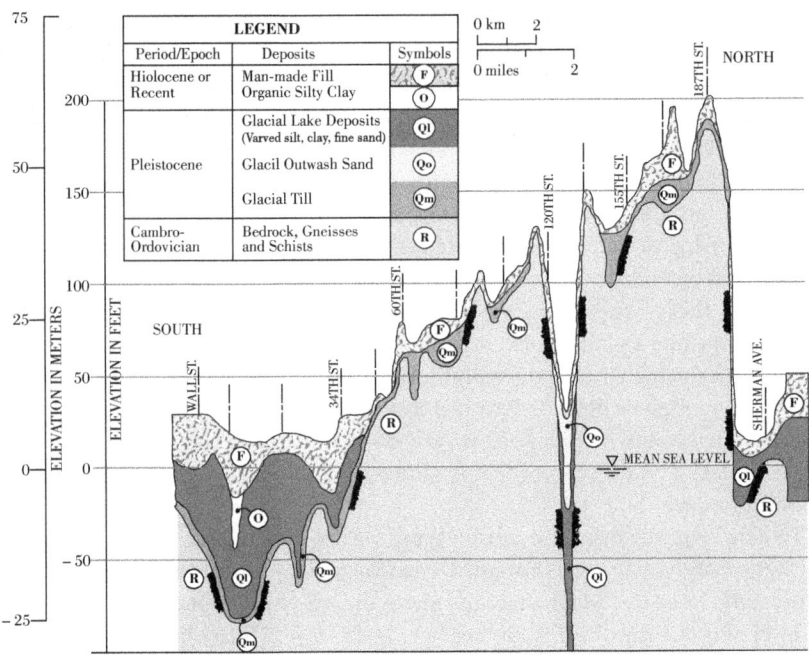

Figure 1.4 Layers of subsoil along Broadway. This figure shows the subsoil layers of Manhattan going northward along Broadway. At the southern part of the island, the rock floor is covered with layers of glacial till; glacial lake deposits, including clays and sands; and over that rest silts, manmade fill, and organic matter. The subsoil in Lower Manhattan that is below sea level is saturated by water creating a bed of quicksand. Going north, as the bedrock rises above sea level, the subsoil is mostly glacial till, manmade fill, and organic matter.

Source: Courtesy of George J. Tamaro, Mueser Rutledge Consulting Engineers.

fact come out in the open air. If we preferred to remain underground we would need to tunnel through the bedrock.

Our subway follows the elevation upward, until we come out in the open at the 125th Street valley. We proceed onward and see a similar story: till over rock, with more in the valleys, and less along the ridges; we also note along the way that some of the underground streams course through the soil. And so our journey ends. Tomorrow we take one more tour, this time of the land itself in the days before Henry Hudson and his crew first laid eyes on it. But first, a short digression.

Soil versus Subsoil: What Is the Difference?

To the geologist, the subsoil contains information about geological history, such as the stories of plate tectonics, glaciation, erosion, rock formation, and so on. To the engineer, the subsoil indicates the type of structures that can be supported. Can a building be put right on top of the sand, or does it need to be attached to the bedrock? How does the subsoil affect the construction of subways, streets, or other infrastructure projects?

To the engineer, that stuff between the ground and the bedrock is "subsoil," while the ecologist and soil expert (pedologist) refer to the same matter as "soil." To them,

(A)

(B)

Figure 1.5 Geological conditions in Lower Manhattan west of Church Street and north of Liberty Street. A, a bedrock crater; B, smooth rock created from an ancient underground stream; C, glacial till; D, the lighter colored rock on the right is an intrusion of pegmatite into the Manhattan schist, which is the darker colored rock on the left.

Source: Photos courtesy of Cheryl Moss, Mueser Rutledge Consulting Engineers.

(C)

(D)

Figure 1.5 Continued

the soil provides information about what kinds of animal and plant life can be sustained by it. The ecologist seeks to discover the ecosystem that the soil sustains, and the pedologist seeks to understand its agricultural properties. Before we tour the topography and ecology of pre-European New York, we pause to retread some old ground, as it were, and we revisit the subsoil that we toured from the perspective of the pedologist.

Although this is book is about real estate development, the soil is important, especially from the engineering and pedological perspective. Building foundations will be taken up in chapter 7. In chapter 3, we will discuss the relationship between bedrock depths, soil types, and early patterns of settlement, which, in turn, locked-in land-use trajectories that influenced the skyline.

Figure 1.6 shows a map of the location of two types of soils: those that are relatively fertile for agriculture and those that are not. The soil types were selected by Eric Sanderson, as part of the Mannahatta Project, which aims to recreate the ecology of Manhattan circa 1609.[37] Sanderson estimated a total of seventeen soil types on the island, and I reduced them to two groups simply based on their fertility.

He recreated the soil types by analyzing the local environment, slopes, and bedrock depths. To quote him,

> The trees . . . sway over territory depended on differences of soil, water, slope and fire. Soils vary with depth depending on the slope of the hill, with the thinnest soils over the crown of the hill, the mid-depth soils on the midslope, and the deepest soils at the base. Soil type depends on the rocks beneath. Soils won from nutrient-saturated rocks, like the Inwood marble, are richer, but more fiercely fought over; metamorphic schists are stingier with the nutrition they provide. Sandy soils hold water less well than the rich, loamy, black soils created by centuries of leaf fall and the slow, gentle release of summer days back to earth. Silty soils like to hold onto the water from which they were created. Soils on south-facing slopes receive more sun, are drier in summer and warmer in winter, and have their own forest type—though some woods prefer the cool, dark side of hills, saluting the north.[38]

There is close relationship between the island's geology and the types of soils resting on top of the rock. From the perspective of agriculture, the high-quality soils are loamy, which contain a majority of silt, some sand, and a little clay. These soils have good nutrients and a moderate amount of drainage, and contain fewer rocks.[39] The loamier soils tended to be found in the southern areas of the island, along the east side, and in the Harlem Flats. These soils were created by outwash sand from the melting glaciers and deposits from the glacial lakes. The shaded region in the map is what I call Fertile Manhattan. As we will see in the following chapters, Fertile Manhattan played an important role in the birth of the skyline.

NEXT STOP: THE SURFACE

Day three, we are back inside our helicopter. We hit another button, and we are instantly transported back in time. Up we go, hovering over a skyline of sorts—the skyline of

N

Figure 1.6 Fertile Manhattan. The shaded areas are those that were more suitable for agriculture due to the presence of relatively fertile soil and deeper bedrock levels.

Source: Map by Eon Kim; data is courtesy of Eric Sanderson, the Mannahatta Project, Wildlife Conservation Society.

hills and trees—and we can see what the Manhattan thunderbolt looked like centuries ago about the time that Henry Hudson arrived in 1609 (figure I.1A).[40] Manhattan is a rich and diverse ecosystem, a green rock (it is still summertime). Flocks of passenger pigeons fly in the distance. If we look carefully, we can see schools of fish down in the waters below. The smoke of a Lenape camp drifts upward in the north. There is no indication that someday tree tops would be replaced by rooftops.

The Lenape word "Mannahatta" evidently meant "land of many hills."[41] All told, the island has some 573 separate peaks, the highest of which was 270 feet high in northern Manhattan. Hills in Lower Manhattan were shorter, but still prominent. For example, Bayard's Mount rose 110 feet above sea level; we can see it from our helicopter at Canal Street west of the Bowery. These hills are made of sand deposited by the melting of the last glacier.[42]

The largest natural land use is forests and shrubs, which covers about three-quarters of Manhattan. Grasslands account for about 10% of the surface, but these likely have been produced by Lenape burning for agriculture or hunting. In the low-lying areas of southern Manhattan, there are saltwater and brackish marshes, which constituted about 8% of the land area. Freshwater marshes, swamps, and bogs are another 2%. From the helicopter we can also see evidence that the Lenape only inhabit or cultivate a small fraction of the land, using only about 2% for settlements and agriculture.[43]

We can also see the island's larger streams and brooks emptying into the rivers. Several wetlands have formed along the shores and in the heart of the island. The saltwater marshes by the banks receive water from the ocean tides; the freshwater marshes and ponds fill in low-lying areas in the center. Its hydrological diversity is due to its hilly and rugged topography, since streams and brooks drain the higher ground and run to sea level at the island's edge. Manhattan contains sixty-six hydrological networks, comprising about 67 miles of water courses. Sandy beaches line the shores, especially along the Hudson River, extending from Vesey Street to 33rd Street and then from 43rd Street to 57th Street. Beaches also wrap around Lower Manhattan and up the East River shoreline.

Our helicopter lands on the banks of the lower tip at Bowling Green so we can take our final tour. Our goal is to take a hike in the wilderness up along Broadway, treading on the lands of the Lenape, the deer, beaver, and snipe. We put our boots on and jump out, ready to begin. Fortunately, thanks to Eric Sanderson, we also have a map of Mannahatta (figure 1.7), which shows us the major water systems.[44] The letters and arrows represent particularly large and important ones and we can take notes as we walk past them.

We take one last look behind us at the upper harbor. Governors Island is just a tiny fraction of its current size—a small, rough dot floating in the sea. In the water, just off the shore to the right, is a ledge of rocks peeking up; they were eventually buried by the landfill that makes up Battery Park. The water gently laps the shore. We turn around and march forward on a path formed by the Indians, and what will someday become Broadway. We also cannot help but notice how narrow and neck-like the lower tip is compared to the present. How was it possible that Manhattan's footprint could grow so large?

The first mile or so of our walk, the path rises gently. To our left—toward the Hudson River—the land falls downward to the shore, for the Broadway path is along a ridge. All around us are woods, mostly oaks and pine trees. Walking onward, we soon see marshy wetlands to our right. Two perpendicular streams in these wetlands drain the neighborhood (A). One is a channel to the East River; someday it will become Broad Street. The other stream will become Beaver Street, named because of the fur trading that took place there.

When the Dutch colonists first arrived they found the southern tip had a familiar feel.[45] They could apply their skills in drainage engineering to recreate an environment

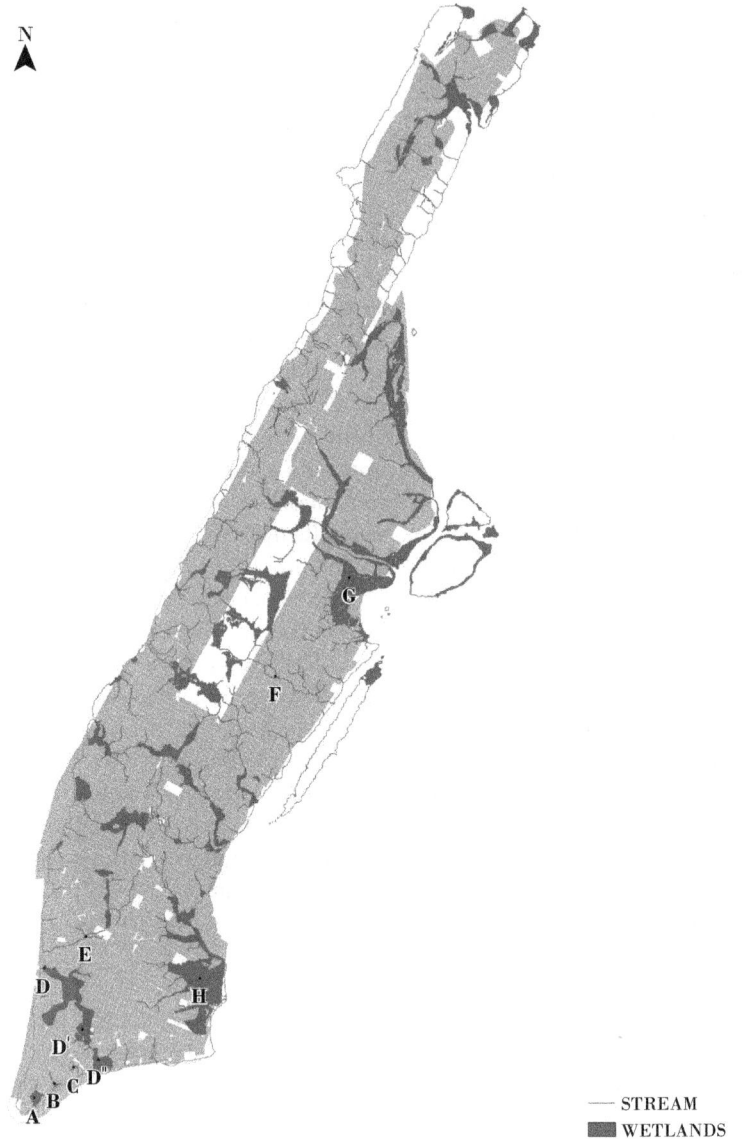

STREAM

WETLANDS

Figure 1.7 Bodies of water and wetlands of Mannahatta. The pre-European Manhattan landscape was covered in brooks, streams, ponds, and other wetlands, including both fresh and saltwater marshes. Virtually all of these bodies have been filled in or converted to sewers. *A*, an inlet at Broad Street; *B*, a stream at Maiden Lane; *C*, Beekman's Swamp; *D-D'-D''*, wetland complex from salt marshes of Lispenard Meadows to former Collect Pond to Old Wreck Brook and Wolfert's Marsh; *E*, Minetta Brook; *F*, the Saw Kill; *G*, tidal marsh south of Harlem Flats; *H*, Stuyvesant's Meadows/"The Marsh." *Source:* Map by Eon Kim; data is courtesy of Eric Sanderson, the Mannahatta Project, Wildlife Conservation Society.

like the one they knew from back home. The channels at Broad and Beaver Streets would be made into canals; the marshes were drained for pasturage. Walking northward, we drop down into a small valley, and notice that along this depression at Maiden Lane runs a small, sparkling stream (B). During the Dutch periods, the young women—the maidens—went there to wash their clothes; and the street was named in their honor. The tanners moved there in 1676 when the canal was eliminated. From there they eventually moved to Beekman's Swamp (C), and then later on to Collect Pond (D').

Once we reach the area near City Hall, the Indian path veers off to the east, toward the Bowery, and runs up the east side of the island. The Dutch would use this path to connect their farms. Several miles up north the path forks and returns to the center and then continues up the west side. Other trails lead to locations along the East River. In Lower Manhattan, these trails were important first roads for the Europeans. The Broadway trail peters out near City Hall, but we will keep going forward, through the forest.

Continuing north, about a mile into our journey as we approach Canal Street, we rise up a hill and see in the valley below us a large wetland complex (D-D'-D'') running from Canal Street on the Hudson River, southeast to Collect Pond, and then toward the East River, around Peck Slip. In rainy seasons, the freshets are deep enough to create one long channel so that a canoe can pass from the Hudson to the East Rivers. Near the turn of the nineteenth century, a plan was developed to create a canal through these wetlands from the Hudson to the East River, but it was never adopted.

Collect Pond (D') was the largest freshwater body on the island, at about 5 acres. It stood east of Broadway, roughly bordered by Pearl, Walker, and Lafayette Streets and east of Baxter Street. Just south of the main pond, was a smaller, "Little Collect," separated by a small, dry peninsula. To protect the citizens, the British constructed the City Magazine or Powder House on the strip.

Glacial drainage lines likely carved out the channel that became Lispenard Meadows (D), which we see to below us, as it winds its way to the Hudson along Canal Street, amidst a large salt marsh running from Duane Street to Broome Street.[46] The area was seen as an "extensive morass, long famous for its malaria and mosquitoes."[47] In 1732, Anthony Rutgers was given the right by the Common Council to clear and drain the swamps. He cut a channel along Canal Street; but apparently his scheme was too successful because a number of farmers petitioned the city in 1734 for him to seal part of the channel because the Collect Pond experienced a steep drop in its level. As a result Rutgers was ordered to plug the channel 30 feet from the pond.[48] In the early 1800s, the canal was covered and converted to a sewer.

The Collect is a locale for Indian life. Oyster shell middens rise around on the southwestern shore, which the Dutch referred to as Kalch Hoek (Shell Point). The English morphed the phrase into the word "Collect," and called the waterbody Collect Pond. Although the site was abandoned by the Indians after Europeans arrived, it remained far north of the city until the early nineteenth century, when it was eventually folded into the city proper. Amidst the natural beauty, we see no evidence that by the mid-nineteenth century, this area would be the teeming neighborhood known as Five Points, "the world's most notorious slum."[49]

The Collect also has an eastern outlet, called Old Kill or Old Wreck Brook, which flows to the south to Wolfert's meadow (a salt marsh) (D''), and then out to the East

River. The wetlands complex is not only a draw for humans but also for wildlife. The pond is filled with fish. The marshes to the east are the home of snipe and other water fowl.[50] The Collect is fed by a natural spring, which provided drinking water to the city, before the opening of the Croton Aqueduct system in 1842.

If we look to the southeast, a few blocks below Wolfert's Marsh, north of Maiden Lane, we can see that the area today is buried beneath the Brooklyn Bridge entrance ramp is also swampy ground (C). Parts near the shore were low enough to be wet year round, while higher areas along the interior were covered with a thick type of bramble called Kripple Bush (tangled briers). This land was part of a farm owned by William Beekman, and the area became known as Beekman's Swamp, or just The Swamp, and in the late seventeenth century, it became the home of slaughterhouses, which were banished from the city, south of Wall Street.[51] A few years later, tanners, settled there. Eventually the tanners left the city, but the wholesale leather trade developed where The Swamp used to be.

To the north of us, we can spot a chain of sand hills beginning at Richmond Hill (at Charlton and Varick Streets). This mount was the residence of Aaron Burr when he killed Alexander Hamilton in a duel in Weehawken, New Jersey, just across the river in 1804. The ridge ran northeast, up the spine, with the largest peak of over 100 feet at around 14th Street.

To the northwest, near the Hudson River, is the fertile region of what will become Greenwich Village, which is hemmed in by the meandering Minetta Brook (E) making its way down from about a mile or two to the north. This stream is formed by the confluence of two brooks originating in higher ground. The first emanated near Sixth Avenue and 17th Street, and flows south along Fifth Avenue to around 12th Street, where it is joined by the other stream, which begins near Fifth Avenue and 20th Street, running southwest and through Union Square, and also connecting with two small tributaries along the way. The Minetta stream then runs through the low, swampy ground of Washington Square Park, and then southwest, emptying into marshland nears the Hudson. By the shore where the Minetta meets the river is a small native settlement called Sapokanikan.

Moving down the hill before Canal Street and through these wetlands, we need to be very careful. Legend has it that a drunken man once tried to cross the swamp in the middle of the night and was absorbed whole, to join the occasional stray cow caught in its muddy web. Proceeding north, as we get to the area around Washington Square, we see that it is low-lying and wet. The area was a Potter's Field in the early nineteenth century. Minetta Brook was eventually buried when the park was being built, but its presence is still felt as basement floods along its path remain frequent.

If instead of going along Broadway, we had chosen to go east at City Hall Park, we would have walked along what had become known as the High Road to Boston or the Bowery Road. We would pass the Tea Water Pump, near the Collect Pond, and the road would then come to the Old Kill, which was covered by the famous Kissing Bridge, where it was customary for couples to lock lips.[52]

Just north of the bridge, the road proceeds around Bayard's Mount, until we reach Houston Street. To the east, lay 90 acres of salt marsh, bound by low sand hills. This region became known as Stuyvesant's Meadows, and it ran from Avenue A to the East River, from Houston to 12th Streets (H). Several small streams empty into the marsh. At the southern end of this area, rose a small knoll, covering about an acre. As it was cut off by creeks and marshes, and was surrounded by water during high tides; it was dubbed "Manhattan Island." On a hill, about where First Avenue and 17th Street meet, Peter Stuyvesant built his country retreat and lorded over his farms. He retired there in 1664 when the English took control of the colony.

Returning to Broadway, starting around 30th Street, we see the topography of Manhattan changes dramatically, becoming quite rocky, with the peaks underlain by the bedrock itself, rather than sand or glacial till.[53] Going north from here, our walk will be a bit more rugged. While the Upper East Side is at a higher elevation than Lower Manhattan, it is not as rugged as the west side.

As we walk through the forests of Manhattan, we spot the many different types of trees. The oaks grow on the hilltops where the soil is dryer. Pitch pine grows on the sandier soils in the south. The mid-slopes of the hills hold chestnuts. Red oaks grow in the bases between the hills. The king of the Manhattan forest, however, is the tulip tree—growing on the sides of Manhattan's hills. European settlers were drawn to these areas because they indicated good spots for agriculture.

Now we arrive at Central Park and see how rocky the Upper West Side is, with the gray-brown bedrock forming hills all around us. In the lowlands are ponds and streams, while along the slopes grow the tulip trees. Here, we can see the largest river network on the island (F). Originating in the highlands of the Upper West Side, the waters eventually wind their way downward to the East River, where they empty at around 70th Street. This stream was about 8.5 miles in total length and was called the Old Arch Brook by the English and the Saw Kill by the Dutch.

At the north of Central Park around 110th Street, we once again have a choice of topography. If we go northwest, we can continue along the rugged ridges and valley. If we go east, we can stroll along the largest wetland complex in northern Manhattan. We see there an immense tidal marsh that runs from 92nd Street to 104th Street, from Third Avenue to the river, fed by several streams, one of which originated in Central Park (G). To the north of this were the fertile Harlem Plains.

We decide to turn back and walk along the shore of the East River. Going south the journey is much less rugged than on the west side. Our map of fertile Manhattan shows that the east side was more appealing for early farms. Around 50th Street we look out over the East River and see an indentation—a nook really—in the shoreline that forms the sheltered Turtle Bay, so named, as speculation goes, for the early animal inhabitants.

Walking further south toward 37th Street we also notice a similar small bay, called Kip's Bay, another sheltered area from the swift tides of the East River. Continuing on, we walk past Stuyvesant's Meadows (H), with the cattails blowing in the breeze. Oh look, it's a black-crowned night heron hiding among the reeds! We are tired, so we head back to the tip, we ascend and descend Bayard's mount, walk past the old Collect Pond and then to the beaches of Lower Manhattan. Our long journey through the past is now complete.

Drinking Water

On our tour, we could not help but notice that while there were brooks, ponds, and marshlands all around us, there was nowhere enough water that could quench the thirst of the millions who would one day call Manhattan home. The lack of freshwater was a major problem. The constant threat of fire and epidemics drove New Yorkers to seek a large source of fresh water in Croton, New York. The system of reservoirs, aqueducts, and pipes finally reached the city in the early 1840s.

But before then, the people did what they could to extract potable liquid from the island itself. Precipitation throughout the year averages about 3.6 feet and is fairly steady from month to month so that the streams and springs are continually replenished. For the agricultural areas north of the village, farmers and locals could rely on them for themselves and their livestock. Residents of the town, however, had to turn to three possible sources: cisterns, natural springs, and manmade wells—both private and public.

The first public well was dug in front of the fort in 1677; and by 1700, there were ten throughout the town. They were not popular, however, because the water was brackish, as saltwater from the sea mixed with freshwater that seeped down. These wells did not produce enough to douse large fires.[54] If they could afford it, private citizens dug their own wells. Jacob Kip, in the 1650s, constructed one at his house at the northern end of the canal along Broad Street. In 1832, at Bleecker Street and Broadway, a well was drilled through 48 feet of earth and 400 feet into the rock; it proved to be rather generous. The water rose to within 29 feet of the surface, and the flow was estimated at 40,000 gallons per day.[55] Wells also have been dug in the twentieth century. As late as 1949, factories on the island were pumping 6.5 million gallons per day. Evidently, wells were also used for bathhouses, such as one dug for the Libby Hotel and Baths on Christie and Delancey Streets in the 1920s, which yielded 198 gallons per minute.[56]

Many of the early private wells were tapped for beer. Given the poor quality of the water, brewing was perhaps the best way to make the water drinkable. During the Dutch days, it seems, if you could find water under your property, you could easily become a brewmeister. Pieter Van Couwenhoven drew water from a well behind his brewhouse at the upper reaches of town, while his older brother Jacob had a brewhouse in the heart of town, with water from a well near the main canal. Michiel Jansen sank a well on the eastern end of the canal at Beaver Street and opened a brewhouse in 1656. Across the street was the Red Lion Brewery, also with a well in its yard.[57]

For nearly 200 years, the city sipped off what it extracted from below the ground, but, eventually it was no longer enough for a growing town.[58] Even though Manhattan was surrounded by water, it would do no good (river water was used sparingly to douse fires since the salt ruined the equipment). It would turn to upstate New York, which was awash with lakes and rivers. In 1842, the Croton Aqueduct and reservoir system was completed and showered Gotham with the clean, fresh liquid of life.

GEOLOGY TO HISTORY: BC TO *B/C*

We conclude this chapter with a few examples of how Manhattan's geological history influenced its economic history. We will return to more detailed treatments of these subjects throughout the book, but it is worth stressing that understanding the skyline's emergence and shape requires an investigation of how Manhattan's natural history did or did not influence its economic history.

First, the Taconic Orogeny, combined with the history of erosion and glaciation, produced several key geological features. Perhaps most important is Manhattan's long and narrow insularity. The fact that it was the home for not only millions of immigrants but was also the country's financial and commercial capital meant that the pressures of economic development would occur within the geological landscape produced by its natural history.

Much of the economic dynamics that unfolded in the nineteenth century would occur along the north-south axis. Since the island is so narrow, it "squeezed" together all of this action in a way that was not occurring in other cities that were more rectangular or circular. In other words, the "tubular" shape of the island would lead to its unique land-use patterns, and its particular skyline. This tubular dynamic will be spelled out in chapters 3, 4, and 8.

Second, while below the surface has good loadbearing rock, south of 14th Street this rock is difficult to reach; not just in the bedrock valley but in all places where it is below sea level. The reason is that subsoil is saturated by water, making it a wet, viscous goo. While in Midtown, the bedrock is often too close to the surface and has to be blasted away. In chapter 7, I will demonstrate how focusing on the depth to bedrock to understand the skyline is a red herring. The issue of how far it is to reach is minor compared to the economic costs and benefits of reaching it—and this was determined by society, not geology per se.

Third, the nature of erosion, glaciation, and glacial deposition created an "unequal" playing surface. Lower Manhattan was relatively loamy and fertile, and strongly suggested itself for early European colonization and agriculture. Harlem, as well, had fertile plains overlaying eroded marble and was surrounded by streams and creeks. The Upper West Side (including Central Park) was rocky and had only little ground cover, which made it of little interest to households until after public transportation allowed for the suburbanization of that part of the island. Central Park had been a convenient site as a park because it had seen very little economic development before the Civil War.

The economic and social history of specific neighborhoods can be tied to their geological properties. The Collect Pond, formed as a kettle pond from the melting glaciers, drew humans to it, and eventually led to the rise of Five Points, one of the most infamous low-income neighborhoods in the city's history. Greenwich Village is another example of a neighborhood that developed around its early agricultural attractiveness (see chapter 3). The skyline will rise within the context of these neighborhood histories. We now turn to the next subject, the formation of land and the land market: how Manhattan was manufactured from Mannahatta.

2

Mannahatta to Manhattan
Settlement to Grid Plan

The persons who instituted those suits were a few of the numerous opponents of the field of operations of the Commissioners, which included their property in the then new Plan for the city, many of whose descendants have been made rich thereby.
John Randel Jr.

WHAT IS LAND?

In 1609, the skyline was the forest. In 1859, the skyline was the ship masts and church spires. In the years before the Civil War, New York cemented its place as the nation's largest and most important commercial city. The completion of the Erie Canal in 1825, combined with the acumen of the city's merchants, promoted its intense growth. Its population in 1860, at 813,000, was 44% larger than its closest rival, Philadelphia. Its port was exporting 36% of the nation's goods, while importing over two-thirds of the merchandise entering the country.[1]

But before New York could reap the rewards of its commerce, it had to develop its land market. The business of business cannot occur without first having a way to allocate space across the city. There needed to be a way for citizens to arbitrate among themselves how land would be used given competing desires to occupy the same location at the same time. The process needed to be orderly, peaceful, and predictable. Rules must be established and people must be willing to obey them or face punishment. The battle for place—the means by which people decide who will occupy a specific location—must occur with dollars not daggers.

The rise of the skyline proper in the 1890s was a technological solution to the problem of land shortage—the creation of *artificial land*, using steel and vertical roads (elevators) to allow more people to be in the same place at the same time. But this real estate development could not have occurred without a robust property market and without the ability of developers to buy land and improve it in a way that promoted its most profitable use. In short, New York had to create land and a land market.

To reduce this to a pseudo-equation: *land = territory + access + rights*. In other words, land is a bundle of items that must be produced in order for the physical geographic location to have a social or economic meaning. Physical dirt must be bundled with a deed that confers rights to the owner (and the deed must be verified or insured in some way), and there must be access to the dirt via roads and the like. Only one part of the value of land is the territory itself.[2]

The role of government in the land markets is important. The free market generally does not call forth entrepreneurs to build streets, since they are the common property of all, and therefore must be built and maintained by the state. By extension, the government is required to plan, build (or contract to build), and maintain the city's infrastructure. The value and use of private property is wholly entwined with the value and use of public property.[3]

Land, of course, has different characteristics as compared to other things, such as pencils or automobiles. The main difference is that land does not move. People must move to it and around it, so the value of the land is determined not only by what can be done on it, but what other people are doing next to or near it. Hence, land value is determined by those three vital elements: its location, its location, and its location.

It is worth stressing that most people consider land to be a fixed and finite resource. But land is an expandable commodity like labor and capital. Economic land, defined as a lot on which to build, must be created: cleared of plants, trees, boulders, ponds, and so on; graded, subdivided, assigned rights and rules; provided with access via roads and hooked up to the infrastructure system of water, sewage, gas, and electricity. Land is the result of the production process applied to geography so that it has *use* value, which can then be sold at a *market* value.

When many people are vying for the same location, the price will rise to allocate it to the highest bidder. We can look to the price of land as a measure of the value of a particular location. If prices remain particularly high, they encourage "entry" into the land market, where developers create new land to reap the profits, which can then serve as a check on these high prices. That is to say, land, like other commodities, obeys the laws of supply and demand, and in the long run, absent hurdles to economic development, the price of land should not grow much faster than the income of the nation or region.[4]

It is also important to note the distinction between *land* and *real estate*. Land, specifically used for urban purposes, is defined as an economically viable place, a physical location or address where people can do things. Real estate, on the other hand, is defined as what they can do and is thus the specific use or uses of the place, be it for a factory, office, park, residence, museum, restaurant, and so on.

Manhattan's real estate history begins with its land creation. The decisions made by the Dutch, English, and early Americans about how to produce, allocate, and regulate the land would directly influence the growth of the skyline centuries later. Over a period of about two hundred years, New York experimented with several different approaches. The first is what can be called the Monopoly Model. Manhattan was owned by the Dutch West India Company, and it rented the land to settlers, who were expected to pay rents and sell the farm output to traders and company employees. Within about twenty years, this system began to crumble to a more decentralized, hybrid system. Because of its weak economic position, the company made concessions by granting title to the earth and letting landowners reap the gains by exchange or by what could be sold from its bounty.

The Monopoly Model gave way to what can be called the Hybrid Model, where the land was owned by several types of landlords. In the city proper, there was a fee-simple market for town lots, where owners were able to buy and sell titles to land and structures. North of that, the island was divided among two classes of landholders. First were the rentiers, who were a class of landowners with possession of large tracts of land, which they would then rent to artisans, craftsman, or yeomen for long periods of time, such as for 21, 63, or 99 years. The tenant could then improve the land and sell the remaining rental contract to the highest bidder. In this way, the large landowners, such as Trinity Church, John Jacob Astor, and the descendants of Peter Stuyvesant, could simply collect ground rents and did not need to actively manage their estates. As well, in the northern parts of the island, wealthy citizens would maintain their country retreats.[5]

Starting in 1686, the municipal corporation, as represented by the Common Council, became a large landlord, in possession of some 5 square miles of "common lands" from 23rd Street to 90th Street, between Second and Seventh Avenues. These lands were de facto private property, since the municipal corporation was considered an autonomous legal body, though its members were elected by the citizens of the city. This territory had low fertility and few roads for access, and hence, little use or market value. But the city would try to sell or rent it as was feasible.[6]

Another policy of the Common Council was the creation of new land by selling to private citizens the rights to expand the shoreline. Fill, which included excavated dirt and rocks from building construction, the soil from leveled hills, and/or waste products, was dumped into the adjacent waters and held in place with planks or retaining walls. This allowed for the city proper to expand its footprint some 30% during the eighteenth and early nineteenth centuries.[7]

New York eventually made its way to what can be called the Market Model, where buyers bought land titles outright, which allowed them to develop and use the land without restrictions and in perpetuity (assuming it conformed to the city's general laws). Starting in the 1820s, the dramatic growth of Manhattan meant that landowners could only meet this demand by increasing the number of subdivisions, and, as a result, they had to become more actively engaged in real estate development, or sell out to those who could better exploit the opportunities. Some of the earlier rentiers (such as the Astors and Trinity Church) became developers and landlords, building and renting tenement housing directly.[8]

In the first decades of the nineteenth century, New York's modern real estate market was firmly on track. By this decade, the city had developed its housing rental market and the tenement house proper, where rent was determined by the anonymous forces of supply and demand. As the economy became more industrialized and work moved to the factories, workers were no longer tied to their workshops. Merchants were no longer tied to their counting houses as mercantile business evolved into office work. The retail store was no longer tied to the small corner shop, but became a large-scale business operation. As a result of these changes, work and home became increasingly separated.[9]

By the 1830s, the city had nearly two decades of experience with implementing and living with the Grid Plan; streets were being opened at a rapid pace, and landowners were firmly aware of the rules of subdivision and auction sales. Rentiers were carving up their estates and offering them to the highest bidder, as the value of urban land surpassed that of rural land. Thus, the Grid Plan established the future growth of land and land values in the city. The rectangular, rational order of numbered streets and long avenues was a direct response to the disorganized and decentralized land market that was created during the colonial period. The Grid Plan, in effect, created hyper-order, as a response to historical disorganization.

Ironically it was the triumph of commerce over nature that gave rise to Central Park. The Grid Plan laid the framework for nature's asymmetries and complexities to be removed in favor of order and linear geometry. As the middle of the nineteenth century approached, many looked upon that decision in fear and horror—that all of nature in the city would be swept away or hidden below the ground. Amidst the juggernaut of commerce, the citizens demanded the city return to them some semblance of the natural world. It was Frederick Law Olmstead who understood how nature was to be served back to the people by creating a work of fiction nothing like Mannahatta, but rather, a real-life canvas of a nineteenth-century's artist conception of beauty on the Hudson.[10]

THE FOUNDING OF NEW AMSTERDAM

In September 1609, English navigator Henry Hudson and his crew of sixteen rounded Sandy Hook and sailed into the river. The ship—the Halve Maen (Half Moon)—had departed from the Netherlands six months earlier in search of a northeasterly route to Asia on behalf of the Dutch East India Company. But Hudson disobeyed his merchant masters and, once at sea, turned west, sailing across the Atlantic Ocean in search of a northwest passage. After approaching Newfoundland, he trolled south along the coastline looking for any sign of a portal. Somewhere near the Jamestown settlement, he turned around and went back north, where eventually he found and entered the mouth to the Hudson River.

Hudson and his crew were surprised by the beautiful vista before them. Towering cliffs stood along the New Jersey shore, almost like giant soldiers providing escort. The bounty of the region was instantly apparent. Fish of all kinds were swimming below them; the primordial oak forest was in its green glory, not yet turning to fall colors; but the abundance of fur-bearing animals excited them the most.[11]

The moment the vessel appeared in the river proper, the sailors encountered the Lenape. After some awkward pleasantries and a little violence, they proceeded to trade. The Indians offered their products: hemp, dried currants, oysters, and beans. The Dutch offered theirs: knives, hatchets, and beads.[12] Hudson then sailed northward, but soon realized that the river did not, in fact, afford a great westerly route to the orient, when navigability ceased near Troy, New York. He returned to Europe.

Almost immediately after Hudson's voyage, trading ventures from the Netherlands were organized to the region, including to the island "called Manhattes from the savage nation that dwells at its mouth."[13] In the years following, Dutch merchant vessels regularly plied the waters of the Hudson River and became familiar with its landscape.

In 1621, as a twelve-year truce with Catholic Spain was ending, there was a national cry for the Dutch to enter the battle for empire. To both reduce merchant competition in the New World and stick a craw in Spain's eye, a new plan was hatched.[14] In that year, the States General—the governing body of the Netherlands—issued a corporate charter to the Dutch West India Company (WIC). The goal would be to create permanent colonies along the expansive region running as far south as the mouth of the Delaware River and as far north as the Connecticut River. The WIC was charged with settling the territory and extracting its furs and timber.[15]

The company determined that the headquarters and port of the North American operation would be on Manhattan Island. A small colony of company employees and traders would settle there, while farms nearby would feed the population.[16] In March 1624, Captain Cornelius Jacobsen May brought thirty families on the ship *Nieu Nederlandt*. Most of the passengers were French-speaking Protestant Walloons, seeking religious freedom not available in the southern part of the Netherlands controlled by Catholic Spain.

Also on board were the agricultural tools, seeds, and the other goods for establishing the colony. Eight families (or individuals) remained on Nut Island (Governors Island), where they were more easily protected. The rest went north to settle in what is today Albany. There is no record of any settlement on Manhattan proper from this first voyage.[17] Three more ships came in 1625, with additional settlers and horses, cattle, and seeds. One of these ships deposited on Governors Island six complete families containing forty-five people.[18]

In 1626, Director Peter Minuit arrived. In one of his first important acts, he transplanted the households from Governors Island to the southern tip of Manhattan. As well, he ordered most of the settlers from Fort Orange (Albany) and Fort Nassau (Gloucester, NJ) to move there, so they could be better protected.[19] The small village on the island was to be called New Amsterdam. The larger colonial territory of New Netherland now had a population of about 200 people.

The first key decision regarding Manhattan's land use was thus made. By choosing to invest their time and resources in developing the lower tip, the WIC locked-in the northward trajectory of future growth. While nature may suggest, humans decide. The southern toe suggested itself to the Dutch as a reasonable spot for settlement. But history being what it is, there is no reason to believe that other decisions or outcomes could have prevailed.

There appears to have been a discussion that the settlement be placed along Spuyten Duyvil on the southwest corner of the Bronx, where the land was secluded and protected.[20] If this was true, it is likely that the Bronx would have developed as the center of the city. And then there were the Puritans, who in 1620 left England on the Mayflower fully expecting to settle along the mouth of the Hudson River. But, because of a host of problems, they had a late start leaving for the New World; when they finally managed to arrive, they realized they had been blown off course to Cape Cod. The coming of winter and the ill-health of the passengers forced them to remain and settle in Plymouth.[21] The subsequent waves of Puritans created Boston, near the earlier settlements.

Thus, a series of unintended events set the Puritans on a completely different trajectory than the one they thought they would have. Certainly these accidents allowed the Dutch to settle Manhattan, instead of the English. If the Dutch had arrived and saw an English settlement at the mouth of the Hudson, they likely would have focused their energies on developing the lower Delaware River or possibly the mouth of the Connecticut River instead, putting New York and the region (even perhaps even the nation) on a different historical footing.[22]

In 1626, Director Peter Minuit also concluded an agreement with the local Lenape Indians regarding how the island was going to be occupied. From Minuit's perspective, he created a contract—part deed, part treaty—which stipulated an ownership claim to the land (though the original document has been lost to history). In his view, as an agent of a corporation, he was purchasing the island, thereby giving property rights to the owner of the contract—the Dutch West India Company.

The natives had no written language, which means they had none of the institutional arrangements that a literate people take for granted. There were no documents, no records, and no need to associate physical or natural objects with a piece of paper that certifies ownership—that is, no contracts. Nor did they have a notion of property rights as did the Europeans. Rather, the agreement, from the perspective of the Indians, was on how the land was to be shared, and, also likely, an understanding that the Dutch would help with military protection, against rival tribes, if the Indians so desired. The agreement was seen as a treaty among two nations, not a market-based transaction. If anything, the Indians likely outnumbered the Dutch, so there is no reason to believe that the natives were acting from a position of weakness. It is also likely that the decade or so of trading ventures that preceded the settlement allowed the Dutch to engender a modicum of goodwill that may have made the treaty possible in the first place.[23]

Ultimately the agreement was consummated with the transfer of gifts from the Dutch to the Indians. To the Dutch, the gifts were common, household items, which because of their large supply and low cost, had low market value but high use value. To the Indians, the gifts were a symbol of the Dutch's good faith in the agreement and were novel, interesting, and useful.

In 1626, Peter Schaghen, a liaison between the Dutch government and the Dutch West India Company, wrote a letter to the States General; it contained the earliest known reference to the company's purchase of Manhattan for a price of 60 guilders. Nineteenth-century historian Edmund O'Callaghan wrote that it was equivalent to $24.[24] Thus was born the notion that the island was bought for a bargain—the greatest land deal on an island whose very name would become synonymous with real estate. But consider that this deal was only shrewd in the context of Manhattan's later success. At the time, it was likely seen by the Dutch as an expedient so that they could begin their commercial investments.

However, the reason that the Dutch would lose Manhattan to the English in 1664 was because it was not all that valuable, and there was not that much worth fighting for. Manhattan in the year 1664 had around 1,500 people and was losing money for the WIC; its people lived in constant fear of invasion by foreign powers or Indians.[25] The British wanted control of the region because it was sandwiched between their other national interests in New England and Virginia. As it happened, the English did not have to muster too many resources to take the island, sending only four warships to New Amsterdam, none of which needed to fire a shot.[26]

As Manhattan rose to great prominence in the nineteenth century, the land deal morphed into the myth about the founding of the Empire City. As Russell Shorto points out in his book, *The Island at the Center of the World*, during the colonial period, Europeans and Indians made thousands of such deals, and yet only the one for Manhattan seems to linger so strongly in the public consciousness.[27]

For the Dutch, the toe of Manhattan was a reasonable spot. Triangular in shape, it was the point where the two rivers intersected and was a natural hub for regional transportation. The East River side was calm and did not freeze in winter. The natives, on the other hand, had little use for the tip, and probably saw no harm in a small settlement of foreigners, with whom they could trade. Their settlements were scattered around the island, all north of the lower point.

Like the Native Americans in New England, the Lenape were helpful to the Dutch during the early years by providing food and teaching them about the local environment. They acted as guides and showed them how to exploit nature's abundance. In 1626, a crude fort had been constructed, but soon fell apart. An actual, workable fort was not completed in until 1635, suggesting the first settlers were not in immediate fear of the local Lenape.

Ultimately, when the Dutch colony took root and people wanted to expand their settlements for farms (*bouweries* in Dutch), it impeded on the land used by the Indians. In 1643, a war erupted between the Dutch and Indians, with great loss of life and property on both sides. By the end of the seventeenth century, the natives were gone from the region. Germs and warfare killed much of the population; and the survivors moved to the interior of the country.[28]

Over time, the colonists would settle into their Amsterdam-on-the-Hudson. Residents were given plots of land for houses and gardens. Farms were established to produce food, and traders were sent forth into the woods to get furs. In 1626, a ship returning to Amsterdam had a cargo of "7246 beaver skins, 675 otter skins, 48 mink, 36 wild cat, and various other sorts; many pieces of oak timber and hickory." In that year, some thirty houses lined the East River.[29]

EARLY DEVELOPMENT

The moment the Dutch arrived on Manhattan Island, they began manipulating the environment for their own purposes. Of most immediate concern was the provision of food, shelter, protection, and storage for furs and other products to be shipped back to the fatherland. The decisions that they would make would shape the city's future history.

The center of village life would be the fort, which was constructed at the tip of the island, where today sits the National Museum of the American Indian (formerly the Customs House). The WIC provided the settlers with a surveyor and engineer, Kyrn Fredericksz, who apparently had a plan for laying out both the fort and the town itself. Labor and resources were few, and a "poor sodded earthwork fort was constructed"; in less than two years, it was crumbling.[30]

In the beginning, land had no market value. When the settlers arrived they were only concerned with surviving and establishing trade. Lots were assigned at random. Each household was told to take as much land as they could reasonably cultivate and manage. Footpaths were created to connect the residents, and eventually, they became the streets of Lower Manhattan. As a result, the village developed along organic lines, based on the choices of settlers and the nature of the physical landscape. Any formal plan for the town seems to have been abandoned before it could be implemented.

Very early on, two main roads were created. One was the present Stone and Pearl Streets, which ran along the waterfront and was the main access to the port. The other was Broadway, which originally led northward from the fort, then cut east along Park Row and then up the Bowery, where the early farms were located. Both of these roads, however, emanated from the fort, as had been the wish of the WIC directors. Unlike other colonial cities, such as those controlled by Spain, there was to be no cathedral or religious center. It was ultimately the needs of trade and defense that promoted the initial design of the town.[31]

The location of the fort would later promote park space. The area fronting the fort was used for mustering troops. This would be turned into Bowling Green Park in 1733, when it was offered for rent at the cost of one peppercorn per year. Behind the fort, the English would construct a battery at the water's edge. In the nineteenth century, the area would be filled in and made into a park. During the British Colonial Period, the areas around the fort and Broadway would be a wealthy residential enclave.

One of the clear focal points for the early village was the inlet running from the East River to about a quarter of a mile inland, along what is today Broad Street, just south of Wall Street. In 1657, the residents living along it were ordered to improve it into a canal, by deepening it and placing vertical planks along its banks; it was given the name the *Heere Gracht*. A similar improvement was made to a small off-shoot extending northward, called *Prince Gracht*, while an inlet along Beaver Street became *Bever Gracht*. The canal allowed for the transporting of merchandise into the interior of the village. As such, after the island began to grow, Broad Street, from Pearl to Beaver Street was the commercial heart of the town. In 1653, the city tavern along the strand was converted into the Stadt Huys, the seat of the municipal government.[32]

As the neighborhood became more crowded and developed, the canal became a receptacle for waste and garbage. In 1676, the Common Council ordered it to be converted to a covered sewer; residents who lived along the canal were assessed a tax to pay for the new street. At the same time, two wet docks—large basins to accommodate cargo ships—were constructed at the foot of Broad Street, thus ensuring it would remain the center of shipping for years to come; another example of nature suggesting a location for development that would subsequently lock-in a future trajectory for the city.[33] We can only speculate that if history had taken a different turn and New York remained a Dutch city, it would have looked a lot more like Amsterdam. Much of Lower Manhattan would consist of concentric rings of canals connecting the Hudson and East Rivers.

Figure 2.1 shows a map of the small town circa 1660. It shows some of the key real estate decisions that were made that continue to have important ramifications to this day. First, the densest cluster of buildings was along the East River. The canal along Broad Street would ensure that street's place in New York's commercial history. Broadway to the west was relatively undeveloped, but its large width would draw business and residents during the English period.

The Wall, constructed in 1653, would make New York an enclosed medieval village until its removal in 1699. At the close of the Dutch period, the city had some fifteen blocks, with its greatest density at the tip between the fort and Broad Street. Much of the northern section of the town above the canal was "suburban," or rural, in that most of the blocks were taken up with large gardens. We can see the street sizes and directions were quite varied, and each was shaped by its own unique history. To this day, Lower Manhattan east of Broadway remains a tangle of narrow and crooked streets.

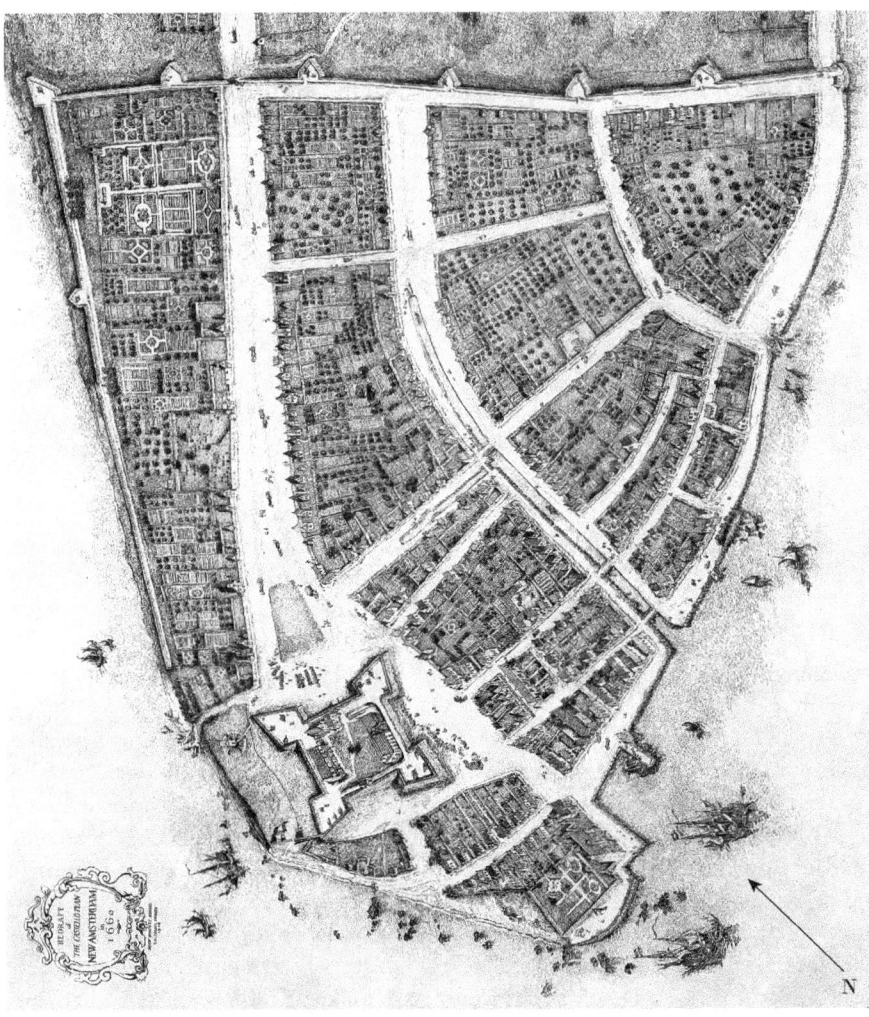

Figure 2.1 New Amsterdam circa 1660. Note how the center of town starts at the fort and goes east toward the port, and then up to the canal, what is Broad Street today. The west side remained relatively undeveloped during the Dutch period.

Source: https://upload.wikimedia.org/wikipedia/commons/0/08/Castelloplan.jpg.

DUTCH LAND GRANTS: THE BIRTH OF THE LAND MARKET

During the Dutch period, Manhattan's land market had its earliest roots. For the city, there were four components for the creation of urban land. First, earth and soil was to be processed to manufacture land; second, it was granted to private individuals so that they could buy and sell it, based on a price that reflected its value to society; third, the government (either the WIC and/or the municipal corporation) began to assert its rights and responsibilities, which included the ability to create new land; take control of private property to use for roads, docks, and commons; and to tax property to fund public works. All of these steps were taken, more or less, on an ad hoc basis through the Dutch period, and often amidst conflict between the municipality, the Director General, and the residents themselves.

Ultimately, a large reason for the successful conversion to a land market rests with an important institution: a judicial system, which allowed residents the right to have their legal grievances heard by impartial judges. These rules were imported from the Netherlands, with some local variations. More broadly, the fatherland had a long history of municipal self-rule and governance. It was these institutions, once transplanted into the New World that allowed the colony to peacefully and demo-cratically transfer land to the citizens. Complaints and remonstrance's were sent directly to the State General, which was seen as a neutral governing body, willing to enforce the rights of Dutch citizens, even if they lived abroad. While both the Dutch and English gave large tracts of land to wealthy insiders; by and large, access to land was relatively democratic and promoted the economic development of the region.[34]

The first recorded grant was in 1637. This was the "Land near Sapokanikan," which was along the Hudson River, near Greenwich Village today and was deeded to the Director General Wouter Van Twiller (1633-1638), who governed after Minuit. He intended to grow tobacco there. Another early ground-brief was for 200 acres in Harlem, dated July 20, 1638. Other grants at Turtle Bay and Harlem followed in 1639 and in Smits Vly (around Maiden Lane) in 1640. In 1643, the Director General William Kieft (1638-1647) began granting town lots. In that year, at least fifteen were given to private owners. The year 1644 saw only two grants in town, while 1645 saw several lots and farms granted to individuals.[35]

These early grants were given with a surprising degree of informality, which sug-gests how little the land was worth. They described the general location of the lots and the approximate size. The "borders" were defined relative to landmarks or other settle-ments, such as "Land on the East River, near the brook, called the Old Wreck."[36] In 1647, Director General Peter Stuyvesant (1647-1664) appointed two WIC employ-ees as a board of surveyors to "prevent a continuance of irregularities in the building and erecting of houses, such as extending lots far beyond their boundaries, setting up nuisances on highways and streets, and neglecting to build on granted lots." They were empowered "to condemn and in future to stop all unsightly and irregular Buildings, Fences, Palisades, Posts, Rails, etc."[37] No one was allowed to erect a structure without a permit. In the following year, it was decreed that residents with vacant lots were to build on them or have their grants rescinded.

In February 1650, to prevent abuses in transfer of titles, Stuyvesant ordered that no deeds would be accepted by the provincial secretary before they were reviewed and approved by Stuyvesant and his council. In 1652, the directors of the Amsterdam chamber of the WIC notified Stuyvesant that they were not pleased with how land had been distributed. They reminded him that Manhattan was wholly the property of the company and they suspected this policy was not being followed. Many people obtained land "without formality and without determination by survey as if the com-pany and its officers had nothing to say about it and had been robbed and deprived of their prerogatives."[38]

The WIC directed that Stuyvesant order that all residents apply for formal grants from the Director General himself. Grants were to be given only after acknowledgment of the company's authority and a description of how the tenants planned to populate and cultivate the lands in question. Much land from earlier grants remained unimproved, including that of van Twiller, who found his grant annulled by Stuyvesant.

After residents lodged complaints about the dictatorial style of Peter Stuyvesant, the States General decreed that the town be allowed to establish a local government to control local affairs, including land use. In 1653, Stuyvesant reluctantly issued a municipal charter.[39] Under the terms of the charter, the corporation was endowed with a schout, two burgomasters, and five schepenen; the last two positions comprised the bench of justice. The schout was an officer with the combined role of investigator and prosecutor. The schepens also acted as sheriffs. The burgomasters governed and could create administrative positions, such as weight-masters, church wardens, city surveyors, and fire inspectors. The bench of justice was to hear, examine, and rule on civil and some criminal matters. Their government's locus of control extended only as far north as the Collect Pond.[40]

In 1655, an Indian invasion drew settlers within the wall for protection. Many of them wanted to remain, and the burgomasters petitioned Stuyvesant for a plan to accommodate them. As a result, the town was surveyed, and all lots and streets were mapped. Streets were specifically demarcated and marked off with stakes. Those who lost property as a result were to be compensated. In that year, there were 120 houses and some 1,000 inhabitants. This was the first plotting of the city on a street plan that was at all systematic.[41]

In January 1658, the burgomasters passed another law that taxed vacant town lots, as, evidently earlier attempts to promote development were ineffective. In April of that year, the burgomasters decided not to grant any more lots until a new survey was created. City surveyor Jacques Cortelyou completed the survey in October 1660.

Thanks to the work of David Valentine, clerk of the Common Council during the mid-nineteenth century, we have the number of ground briefs and patents given out between 1637 and 1680; and which totaled 115 (see the appendix A).[42] If Valentine's list is accurate, it suggests that town lots were given out in spurts. The first batch of fifteen probably represented the pent-up demand; the second batch was likely due to a war with the Indians started by Director General William Kieft, which forced people in the outlying areas to seek refuge in the city, near the fort. A similar issue occurred during Stuyvesant's rule, in 1657, when there was an Indian attack, and people fled to the city. In a way, it suggests that war was good for the town's property values. By the end of the Dutch period, the land market was firmly established, as the land was widely dispersed, and being bought and sold based on market prices. Figure 2.2 shows a map of the initial distribution of town lots.[43]

THE DONGAN CHARTER AND WATER LOTS

In 1664, the Dutch surrendered the colony to the English. As part of the terms of capitulation, the Dutch residents were allowed to continue as they had before, as long

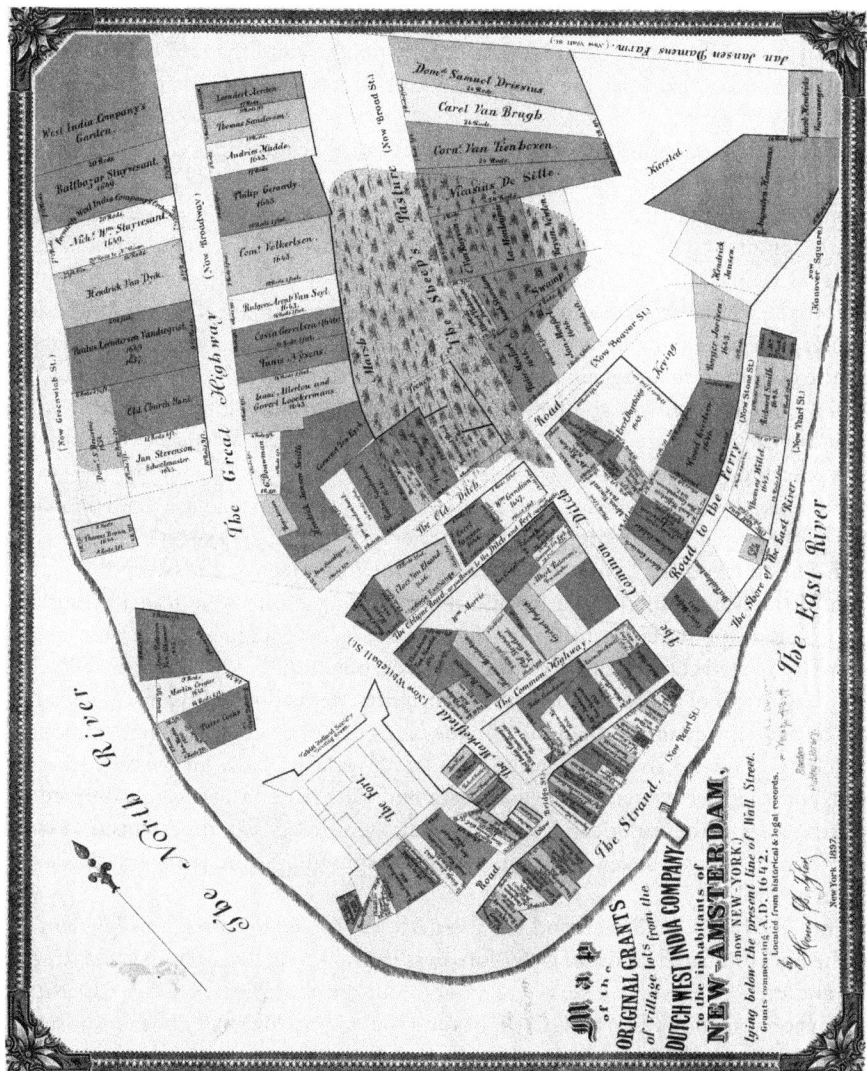

Figure 2.2 The original land grants and patents from the Dutch West India Company. This map shows that the size of the grants given to New Amsterdam residents was related to how close they were to the fort and port. It demonstrates that the standard lot sizes of 25 x 100 feet were part of the land-use patterns in New York as early as the 1650s. The Grid Plan of 1811 did not dictate lot sizes.

Source: Boston Public Library, Norman B. Leventhal Map Center.

as they swore an oath of allegiance to the King and promised to obey the English laws. Their original deeds or grants had to be submitted for certification. Only gradually did the city transform to a fully English locale.

In 1686, Governor Thomas Dongan issued a new city charter, with several important features that would greatly influence Manhattan's governance and real estate. First, the city would be divided into six wards; each was to have an elected alderman and an assistant alderman to represent each ward. Thus began the ward system that would play such an influential role in New York City politics until the mid-twentieth century. The mayor, a recorder, the aldermen, and assistants would make up the Common Council.

Second, the Common Council, as trustees of the municipal corporation, was granted the right to all "vacant, unpatented and unappropriated lands," and water bodies within the island shores as far as the "low water mark."[44] That is, the Dongan charter granted to the city the shoreline that was exposed between the low and high tides, as well as title to the docks, wharves, and the streets.[45] The council had purchased the charter from the Governor for £324 and was in need of funds. As a result, it interpreted the document to mean they could sell "water lots" to private citizens, on the condition that they fill in the land and make it level with the street grade.[46]

In 1730, the city was granted a new charter by Governor John Montgomerie; it would serve as the city's main governing document for over a century. This charter extended the city's water lots to 400 feet, or about two blocks, beyond the low-water mark. This allowed the city to sell even more water lots and extend Manhattan further out into the river. The importance of the charter for Manhattan's real estate is indicated by historian Hendrik Hartog, who writes, "In the forty-five years between the reception of the Montgomerie Charter and the beginning of the American Revolution, disposing of the water lots of lower New York City was unquestionably the major property-related concern of the officers of the corporation."[47]

The growth of the waterfront moved in spurts, depending on the fiscal needs of the city and the quantity of landfill. On the east side, for example, when the hills surrounding Maiden Lane were leveled, tons of fill were available for owners of water lots, and blocks between Hanover Square and Catherine Street were extended to Water Street.[48] The American Revolution put a temporary halt on expansion plans, but after the war, with New York City's economy growing again, water-lot sales were again possible.

In 1789, the Outer Streets and Wharves Act was passed to correct the deficiencies of the uncoordinated nature of water-lot sales. The bulkhead had become quite irregular, and the Act provided a survey to smooth out the shore lines. On the East River, expansion was allowed up to 420 feet beyond the original low-water line at Roosevelt Street and up to 590 feet at Rutgers Slip.[49]

The sale of water lots highlights a few important elements in the city's land market. First, it illustrates how land can be created, once its economic value achieves a high enough market value. Infill land manufacturing began after the issuance of the Dongan charter and continues through this day. Second, the city found it more profitable to expand outward into the sea because of limited transportation and access. The sale of water lots was an attempt to increase the size of the city, which was hemmed in by water. The port was the *sine qua non* of the city's economy and by selling the rights, along with the stipulation that the buyer produce the land and provide a street, wharf, or slip, it encouraged the growth of needed port space.[50] The sales also represented the government's early attempts to plan and design the port. It would not be until the early twentieth century, when the city was fully vested with the rights to control land use through zoning.

Third, the "water rights" market would foreshadow the emergence of the "air rights" markets in the nineteenth and twentieth centuries, which would have important ramifications for skyscraper construction. We will return to this in chapter 5, but in short, "air rights" in New York refers to two types of market transactions. First, air-rights sales include the right to develop real estate over a place that does not have land per se. This includes over railroad tracks, highways, and bodies of water. Second, the term "air rights" is also associated with current zoning regulations, which set limits on a building's bulk. A landlord with a building that has less bulk than the law allows can sell the remaining rights to this unused bulk to another developer who can then increase the density of the project. This type of right is also called transferable development rights (TDRs).

Furthermore, under English common law, a landlord owned not only the soil, but also the sky and the depths below. This was also an important legal precedent for the skyscraper, since builders in the late nineteenth century, realizing the air was theirs, felt free to build into it as they saw fit, with no restrictions from the government, and with little regard for the effects of the building on their neighbors.

Lastly, the water lots represented an interesting reuse and reallocation of the city itself. Rapid growth was producing massive amounts of rock and soil from excavated building sites, leveled sand hills, garbage, and other waste, including the burnt material from conflagrations. For example, the fire of 1835, which destroyed 50 acres south of Wall Street, provided tons of new fill.[51]

The improvement of the original water lots were left to the landowners, who had to secure their own material. It seems that as long they created something usable and at grade, nobody bothered them too much about the nature or quality of what they dumped into the river. This would come to haunt the city, as the made-land neighborhoods were often the dirtiest and least sanitary places on the island. This was due to poor sewage systems and the fact that the fill remained wet and did not drain well. Garbage and other pollution from the docks were also a constant problem. The residents living on landfill were often the sickest in the city.[52]

The process of expanding the island has continued—in spurts—up to the present and will surely continue in the future. Between 1626 and 1782, the size of Manhattan increased by 3.3%, and a total of 9.4% by turn of the twenty-first century. The lower part of the island, south of City Hall, has increased 33% since early Dutch times (see appendix B).[53] Figure 2.3 shows the growth of Manhattan until the mid-nineteenth century. As the land moved further out, the wharfs now sat in the relatively deeper waters, allowing for the docking of much larger ships. South Street Seaport was the city's primary port after the Revolutionary War, as New York was about to begin its ascendency.[54]

Battery Park City is an example of how the soil and rock from one site can be used for fill for another. It was created, in part, by the excavated ground produced to make foundations for the Twin Towers. The western half of the Word Trade Center site was originally made land created in the eighteenth century. Thus, Battery Park City was constructed with landfill landfill.[55]

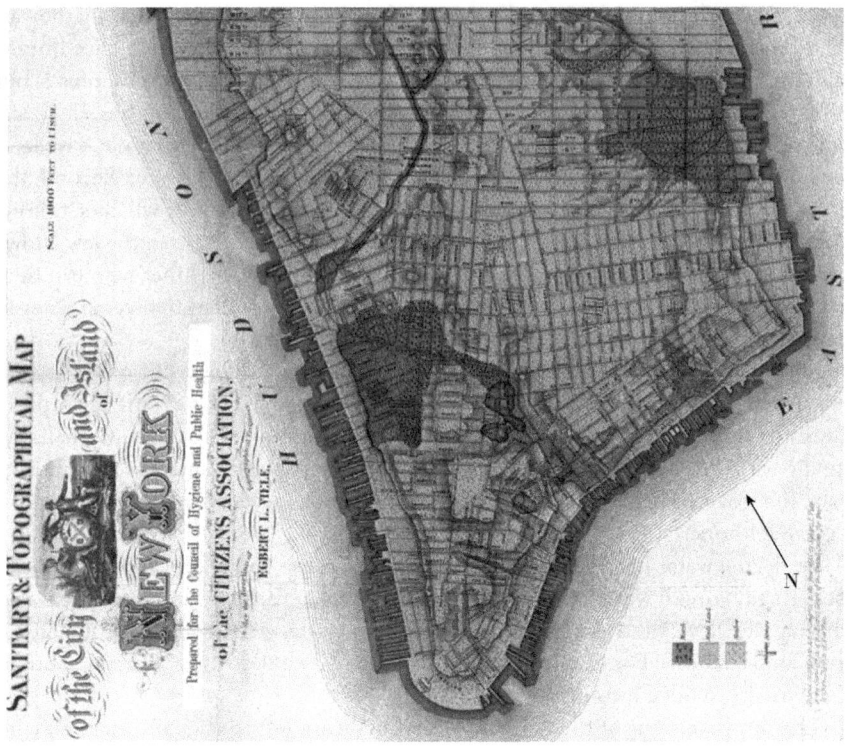

Figure 2.3 Viele map of 1865. This portion of the map published by Edgert L. Viele shows how much of Lower Manhattan was expended via infill between 1626 and 1865 (estimates range from 30% to 50%). On the east side, the original shoreline began at Pearl Street and was eventually expanded two full blocks to South Street. On the west side, the shoreline began at Greenwich Street and was extended two blocks to West Street.

Source: https://upload.wikimedia.org/wikipedia/commons/a/a3/Viele_Map_1865.jpg.

ELIMINATING NATURE

As land values and population grew, former wetlands were filled in and hills were leveled. In general, the higher the price of land, the greater B/C will be, where C is the cost of converting nature to land, and B is the market value of property. At some critical point, when economic growth hits a threshold, B becomes greater than C, and land gets produced.

In the eighteenth and early nineteenth centuries, all of the marshlands, rivers, and ponds south of Canal Street would disappear.[56] The natural beauty held no sway over the forces of economic development. Park space that was created was either squares built by private developers, or was open spaces that had formerly been used for military purposes. There was no notion that the city should create large open areas for recreation.

The swamp that formed in the low ground near what is today Beekman and Ferry Streets (about two blocks south of the entrance ramp to the Brooklyn Bridge), was known as Beekman's Swamp, and later shortened to simply The Swamp. In 1677, the slaughterhouses were banished there by Governor Andros and, soon after, the tanners arrived, having been ejected from their positions along the stream that ran through Maiden Lane.[57] The swamp (4 acres) and several acres of land were sold to a one Jacob Roosevelt in 1732 for £200. He petitioned the city to have it drained. He then subdivided the land into forty-nine lots. David T. Valentine lists the sales of two of the lots at £35 and £32, respectively. If we assume that the forty-nine lots sold for an average of £32 each, then it suggests a gross income of £1,568, likely generating a tidy profit.[58]

Another wetland, discussed in chapter 1, was the irregularly shaped, low-lying marsh and swamp of Lispenard Meadows. For about a century, this region acted as a *de facto* border for expansion on the west side. In 1732, Anthony Rutgers drained the swamps, producing about 70 acres of land. Leonard Lispenard was the renter of Trinity Farm to the south, which lay in the valley running up West Broadway. He married Rutgers's daughter in 1750, and subsequently took possession of Rutgers's land, which then became known as Lispenard Meadows.

By the end of the eighteenth century, Collect Pond had become a multiuse neighborhood. The Tea Water pump was still providing fresh water; and the lake itself was used for recreation and boating. In 1796, John Fitch, for example, tested his steamboat with paddle wheel there. Its eastern banks were lined with tanneries, which had arrived as early as the mid-1690s, but came in greater numbers starting in 1740s. In the eighteenth century, two cemeteries were established nearby. The African burial ground was located in a ravine to the west of the Collect, and a Jewish burial ground was not far to the southeast.[59]

In 1790, the city surveyed the area around the Collect in anticipation of it being folded into the urban fabric. It was concluded that, on account of the waste, dead animals, and pollution that had accumulated in the pond, "it is a desirable thing that this low ground should be filled up for both the health of the Town and also that the ground be applied to some beneficial purpose."[60] The probable source of the fill was earth removed in creating the foundation for the new City Hall as well as from surrounding hills that were leveled at the same time.[61]

The filling in of the pond started around 1803 and continued for eight years. Part of the new land was used for a prison, constructed in 1838, and called the Tombs since it resembled an Egyptian mausoleum. The building began to settle into the former lake as soon as it was completed. It was infamous for its leaks and dampness. It was torn down at the end of the century. Today, the block holds the Manhattan Detention Complex. To the east of the filled-in pond, "The resulting neighborhood, known as the Five Points, was condemned by some as 'American's first and foremost slum.'"[62]

SUBDIVISIONS BEFORE THE GRID PLAN

The 25 x 100 square foot plot size, popularized by the Grid Plan of 1811, was a mainstay of land subdivisions long before the early nineteenth century.[63] In fact, it was the de facto standard from the earliest time of settlement. This norm was never codified or existed in any legal statutes. Contrary to popular belief, the Grid Plan of 1811 said nothing about the size of the lots, only the size of the blocks. Rather, the 25 x 100 square foot size was based on the social and economic considerations of the day.

This standard emerged because there was no direct plan by the Dutch about what lots or blocks would look like. The 25 x 100 square foot plot represented the best balance between several competing considerations. A two- or two-and-a-half-story house with say a 20 to 25 foot length and 50 feet deep would be a reasonable size and would include a 20 to 25 x 50 square foot backyard, with space for a privy and a cistern for rainwater. Technologically speaking, the wooden joists used to support the floors could not be longer than 25 feet without having to add internal columns to support the floors. If a family wanted a house larger than 25 feet across, it would have added an additional expense. For most homeowners, the additional space was not worth the cost.[64]

When the Dutch settlement began to take on an urban form, and land values rose, it was natural that buildings in the densest and most valuable parts of the city would "shrink" to the smallest possible size. Higher land values would motivate people to use less land. Residents from Amsterdam were comfortable living in the narrow townhouses along the canals. By subdividing into the smallest lot sizes possible, the seller could make greater profits, since the smaller the unit the greater the price per square foot.

In short, the 25 x 100 square foot lot emerged as the most practical and saleable form of urban land. Naturally, the blocks that formed as a result were designed to be in multiples of 20 or 25 across and multiples of 100 deep. The Grid Plan of 1811 would promote this form of subdivision because it was what had been the norm for at least a century and a half.

Experiments in other cities proved that blocks with depths greater than 200 feet deep were awkward to build on, and had too much internal wasted space. In Philadelphia, where William Penn's plan created block sizes as large as 400 x 500 square feet, the residents found too much space in the center of the block. As a result, block sizes were eventually reduced by running alleys or lanes through the center.[65]

Evidence for the preference for the 25 x 100 square foot lot becomes clear if we look at the process of subdivisions before 1811. First, the map of New Amsterdam circa 1660 (figure 2.1) shows Lower Manhattan below Wall Street having around fifteen distinct blocks with a total of about 133 different plots (including the fort).

Going south from Wall Street toward the fort, there is a distinct pattern, the average lot size of the blocks becomes smaller and smaller. The lots closest to the tip were the most valuable for commerce, and the only way to allocate space for the demand was to subdivide it into the greatest number of lots. The block that is today bound between Whitehall, Bridge, Pearl, and Broad Streets was less than an acre and had sixteen different lots; this roughly corresponds to the standard 25 x 100 square foot lot.

In fact, to make this a bit more precise, figure 2.4 shows the relationship between the sizes of the granted lots, as shown in figure 2.2, and how far it was from the fort. As we can see, there is a strong positive relationship between lot size and distance from the heart of the village. On average, each one-tenth of a mile that one moved away from the fort, lot sizes would increase by 2.7%. For those parcels adjacent to the fort, the median size is estimated to be 1,850 square feet.[66]

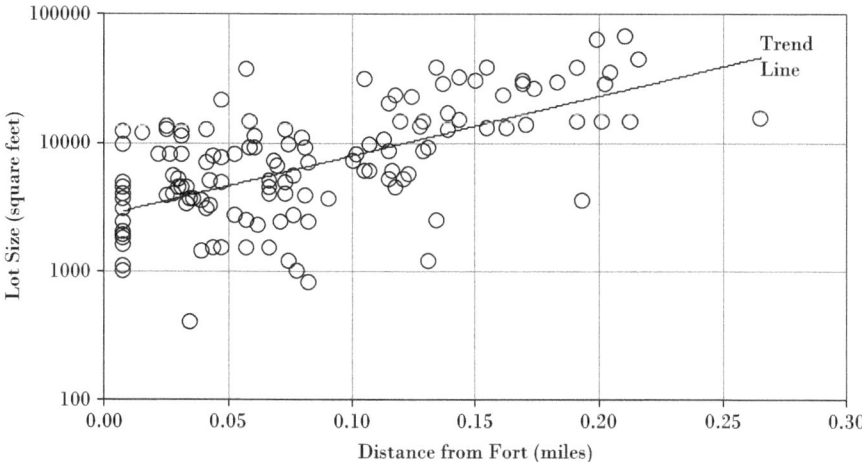

Figure 2.4 Lot size versus distance to the fort circa 1650. Each dot on the graph gives the lot size of the original grants issued by the Dutch West India Company versus the distance to the fort (see figure 2.2). This scatter plot shows that, on average, lots closest to the fort were much smaller than lots further away, and they tended to be in the 25 x 100 square foot range. These standard lot sizes would greatly influence Manhattan's real estate and architecture throughout the ensuing centuries. Note that the lot sizes are presented at a $\log_{10}$ scale. Average lots sizes about a quarter of mile away from the fort were an order of magnitude larger than those adjacent to the fort.

Source: Lot sizes were measured by the author using the Land Grants Map shown in Figure 2.2.

The roughly 17 acre area bound by Broadway, Maiden Lane, Gold, and Ann Streets was known in the seventeenth century as the Shoemakers' Pasture. In 1696, the landowners, three of whom were part of the original grantees, subdivided the land into 164 lots. The map of their plan is given in figure 2.5. While the lots with frontage on Broadway are large, 160' x 160', the vast majority of lots are roughly 25' x 100'.[67] A large block, bound by Nassau, John, William, and Fulton (then the Fair) Streets was too large for the standard lot sizes; in the middle sits "a vacant piece of ground." The existence of this vacant ground implies that it was not marketable to those who preferred the standard plot sizes; otherwise it is likely it would have been subdivided and sold.

Subdivisions in the eighteenth century also show more rationality than the original organic form. Blocks west of Broadway and north of City Hall were laid out in a rectangular or square fashion (figure 2.6). It suggests that there was a demand for more ordered blocks and lots, where a small house could be built, along with a backyard for a garden or workspace. It certainly did not approach the regularity that was to follow, but it does indicate that grid-like planning was already "in the air" during the English period.

LAND VALUES BEFORE THE REVOLUTIONARY WAR

Once land was created, allocated, and legalized with deeds, the trade in lots could begin in earnest. When the British took hold of the colony the land market was

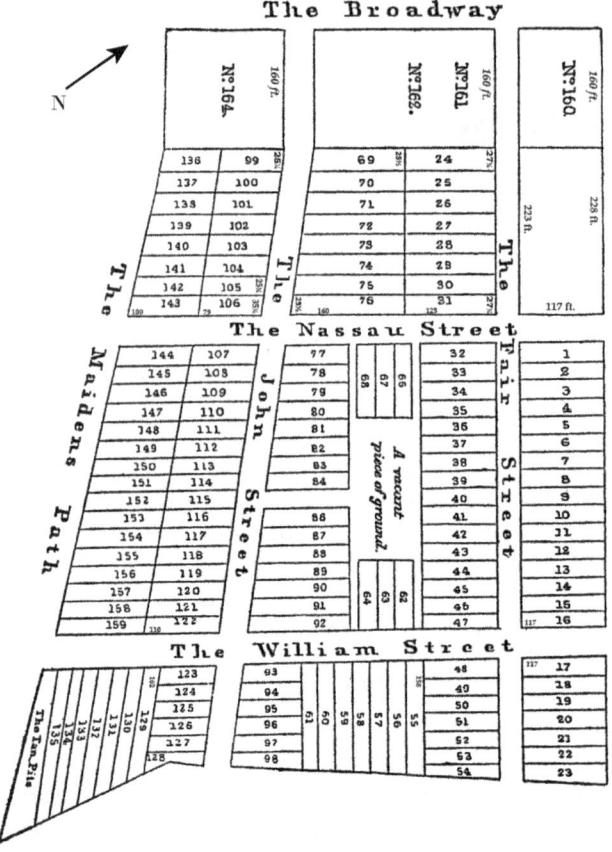

Map of the Shoemakers' Pasture,

Belonging to John Harpendinck, Heiltje Clopper, Charles Lodwick Abraham Santford and Carsten Luersen.

Figure 2.5 Map of the Shoemakers' Pasture. This parcel of land, about 17 acres, bound by what is today Broadway, Maiden Lane, Gold Street, and half a block south of John Street, was the property of five shoemakers; it was surveyed and subdivided in 1696, and lots were sold throughout the 1700s. The map shows that the subdivided properties were mostly about 25 x 100 feet, in the standard sizes favored by the Dutch.

Source: Valentine (1860).

working rather smoothly. Thanks again to the work of David Valentine, we have records for transactions that occurred during the colonial period. Valentine provides 143 market transactions that were denominated in New York–British Colonial Pounds. Each transaction gives the year, the street or intersection, the length and width of the lot, and the price. These transactions ranged from the southern tip, such as at Whitehall and State Streets, up to the area around City Hall.[68]

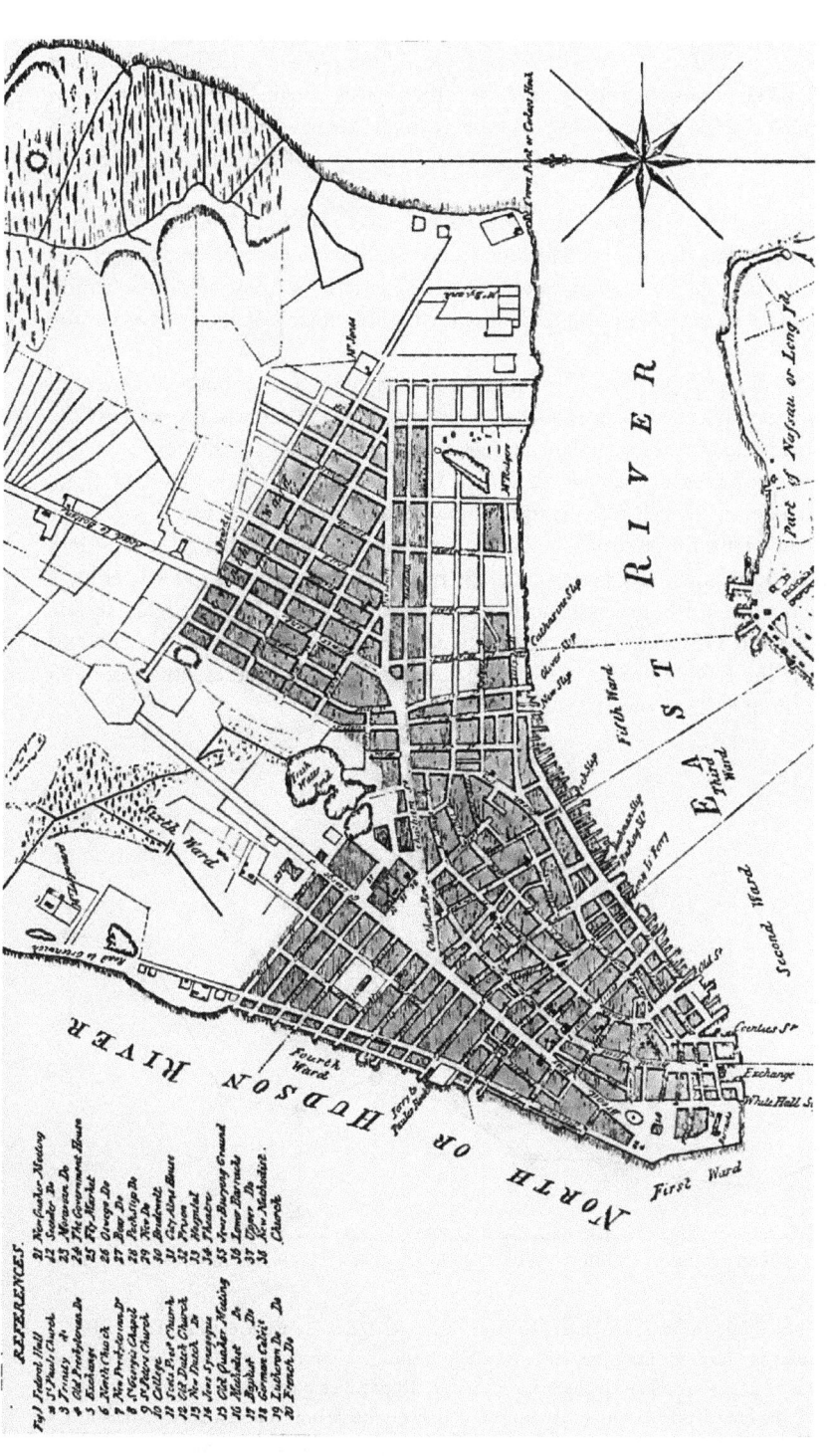

Figure 2.6 New York in 1791. This map shows how subdivisions in the outer areas of the city were created in a more orderly fashion as compared to those blocks formed during the period of New Amsterdam (1626-1664). It is clear from the map that landowners were concerned about rationally laying out their own property to maximize revenue from sales. The problem, of course, was that the various landowners were not coordinating their subdivisions; this eventually necessitated the intervention of the city and led to the Grid Plan of 1811.
Source: Valentine (1851).

The trade in town lots was by and large in "standard lots" around 25 by 100 feet (let's call them SLUs, for standard lot units). Large lots were generally sold in multiples of the standard sizes. Over the sample period the median price per square foot was £0.03, with an average price of £0.05. In other words, the median price for a standard town lot of 25 x 100 was £75.9 pounds with an average price of £139.5, though this average does not take into account both the long run upward trend of prices and the year-to-year fluctuations.

To investigate the price of land over time, I created a land price index from 1667 to 1773, though data was not available for each year. The index is recorded in nominal prices and reflects the average price of a 25 x 100 square foot plot of vacant land in the interior of a block, about one-half mile north of the fort. Results are given in the appendix C.[69]

Figure 2.7 gives the per-decade averages for land prices in the city between 1670 and 1773. Conveniently the index was about 100 in year 1715, so it measures not only the actual costs of land but also the relative values, based on 1715 prices. The horizontal line gives the average prices for each decade and the black vertical bars are the standard deviation for each decade, which is a measure of how much variation there was in lot prices. The figure shows that the price of a standard lot fluctuated widely over the colonial period.

Between 1667 and 1710, prices generally remained between £40 to £90 per lot.[70] Starting in the late 1710s, prices began to rise more dramatically, being roughly double in the 1720s and 1730s, as compared to the earlier decades. Finally, the decade and a half before the Revolutionary War saw a large run up in land values, going from an average of about £125 to over £250.

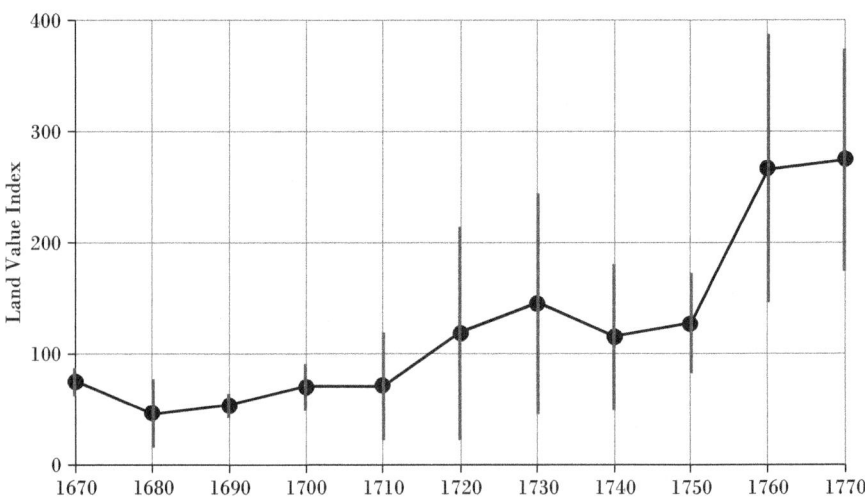

Figure 2.7 A land value index for colonial New York. The figure gives the average value of a 25 x 100 square foot plot one-half mile from the fort in New York-British Pounds from 1670 to 1770. The figure shows that land values were relatively stable until about 1710, at which point they began to rise. The 1750s, during the French and Indian war, was a particularly profitable time for New York merchants.

Source: The underlying land values data is from Valentine (1860). The index was created by the author using regression analysis.

While the detailed reasons for the fluctuations are beyond the scope of this work, the findings are consistent with the documented historical evidence. Historian Michael Kammen writes that "before about 1712, the rates at which trade multiplied, production increased, agriculture improved, and population grew were varied, erratic, and uncertain,"[71] leading to lower land values. We can see that the decade between 1710 and 1720 is when land values surpassed the £100 mark for the first time in its history. After the cessation of war in 1713, between the French and English, New York began its first period of rapid growth. Between 1720 and 1738, imports rose 255%; this was the period when the port finally came into its own and was no longer a satellite of Boston. The city was truly becoming an entrepôt, importing finished goods from England and exporting a variety of local products, the most important of which were wheat and flour.

The 1750s was a period of rapid "take-off" for the colony. During this decade, the population passed 10,000 residents, and on the eve of the Revolution, it was more than double that (see appendix G). The French and Indian War (1754-1763) encouraged New York's growth. Since the battles took place mostly in upstate New York and Canada, merchants in the city became responsible for outfitting, feeding, and arming the troops (and illegally doing the same for the French). Privateering brought in more income.[72]

The second, and perhaps more lasting, change that took place was the Industrial Revolution in England, starting in the 1740s. The rise of manufacturing and urbanization in the mother country led to economic growth and more trade with the colonies. As incomes rose, the English developed their taste for sugar. New York merchants imported it from the West Indies in exchange for bread, flour, wheat and livestock, and sent it back to Britain. Because prices of British manufactures rose slower than the price of New York's exported goods, merchants in the city saw a rise in their real incomes, and in the process, were more than happy to consume England's woolens and manufactured goods.[73]

Valentine notes—and the data confirm—that "about ten years previous to the Revolutionary War . . . real estate went up nearly an hundred percent, and those who had invested large in that species of property, such as the Rutgers family, the Bayard's and others, began to be regarded as far-sighted characters."[74] In the decades after the war, John Jacob Astor would become Manhattan's land speculator, par excellence.

How Much Was Manhattan Land Worth?

While we can see the movement of prices over the period, it is difficult for us in the present to fully judge whether a lot for £80 in 1700 or £350 in 1760 was expensive or not. Fortunately, there are a few possible ways to make this assessment, though all are imperfect. The first is to update the cost of land using a general price level index that runs from 1700 to the present. The price index tells the purchasing power of $1 over time. To make this calculation requires that we first "exchange" New York-British Pounds into dollars in 1700, and then see how much the value of a dollar has depreciated since then. In other words, we need to see how many dollars we need today to purchase the same amount of land that $1 would have bought in 1700.

The conversion rate for one New York-British pound in 1700 is somewhere between $2.50 and $2.85. Using $2.50, an £80 lot in 1700 cost the equivalent of $200 in that year. Since then, the general price level has increased by a factor of 21.4. Using this figure means that an £80 lot near Wall Street in 1700 had the 2013 equivalent of about $4,300. By 1760, that same plot of land would have been worth $25,340 in today's money, a 600% rise. But consider that over sixty years, that amounts to an average annual growth rate of only 3%. In 2012 a vacant lot on William Street sold for $7.9 million per SLU. So the "apples-to-apples" approach suggests that the real value of Wall Street has increased quite dramatically since the colonial period and was rather inexpensive at the time.[75]

A second way to compare land values is to look at wealth levels during the colonial period (see appendix D). From 1667 to around 1700, the median price of a lot was £80 pounds. Someone who had this kind of wealth would have been in the top 30th to 40th percentile. In other words, if a person had enough wealth to buy a plot, he would have had more wealth than roughly 60% to 70% of the households in the city. This suggests that lots were open to the upper middle class. By 1789, the value of a plot at £260 would have put one in the top 50th or 60th percentile. The relative price of land seems to have remained roughly constant over the period.

Furthermore the assessment roles for 1701 show which types of jobs were associated with different wealth levels. Merchants had the highest wealth, with an average of £125. Artisans, such as cordwainer, cooper, carpenter, and brickmaker had assessments between £39 and £48. The yeoman farmer came in toward the bottom, at £26.[76] Evidently farming was not very profitable on Manhattan.

We now have a measure of land values, but what was the value of water? It is a bit of a challenge to create an equivalent estimate for water-lot sales, since information about them is less complete. Generally speaking, the water lots seemed to extend some 80 feet out into the river, rather than 100 feet. Also the sales were denominated as simply "lots" so there is little sense of their widths.

Despite this, the sales data suggest that water lots, which imposed restrictions and the burden of infill on the owner, were selling for about £25 pounds per lot in the 1680s to 1690s. This was about a quarter of the price of standard lots within the city. Still, large tracts netted the city sizable incomes, as three different sale offerings generated income of about £1,100 between 1686 and 1691.[77]

THE GRID PLAN OF 1811

After the Revolutionary War, New York's population growth resumed its rapid pace. The first official census of 1790 revealed 33,131 individuals on the island. A decade later, the population was 82% larger, at 60,489. The city's northward expansion now seemed inevitable, as the population was close to doubling every ten years.

In 1807, with the population closing in on 100,000, the city set out to survey and plat the bulk of the island in order create a more orderly land market. Up to that time, the streets had been surveyed and laid out as far as Canal Street. North of that, except for several isolated hamlets and villages, such as Greenwich Village, Stuyvesant Village, and Harlem, the rest of the island was comprised of small farms, country estates, and forests.[78] The combined forces of random street development from the days of New

Amsterdam, and the individual decentralized plans of large landowners suggested that the street patterns were not promoting order or good health in a time of rapid growth. Land prices were rising, but without any "guiding hand" the process would potentially cause more randomness, confusion, and congestion.[79]

The irregularly shaped farm and country lots meant that one landholder's subdivisions would not necessarily be aligned with the adjacent properties, potentially creating discontinuities in the street patterns. Furthermore, each subdivider would choose his own street widths. In the Lower East Side along Rivington and Stanton Streets, widths were 40 feet across, which by the turn of the nineteenth century was seen as too small. But since a larger street meant less saleable land, it could potentially reduce profits. Individual subdividers generally did not create wide scenic boulevards, but rather, were more interested in maximizing frontage.

When a landowner wanted to develop his land, he would hire a surveyor who then created a plan, based on the topography, direction of the lot, and where it fit relative to adjacent properties. The surveyor, as client of the owner, would lay out the property based on his preferences, who presumably was interested in reaping the greatest return from the subdivision, regardless of whether it would produce negative or positive externalities for the community. After the plan was created, the landowner would submit it to the Common Council and petition for the streets to be added to the map of the city, at which point, the streets would become the property of the city. The Common Council did not feel empowered to take any more direct role than approving the plans of landowners.

The Ratzer map of 1776 (figure 3.2) shows the island south of today's 59th Street as a quiltwork of farms, marshes, forests, curved and winding roads. If one had the vision to see the direction of the city, it would not be too difficult to imagine the chaos that would ensue if each landowner made his own plan. Increasing property values was paramount not only among the citizens but also the Common Council itself. The government still owned more than 2 square miles of lands granted by the Dongan Charter of 1686.

After the Revolutionary War, the Council had a high debt burden and was eager to sell it.[80] The land lacked economic value for agriculture being mostly in the rocky, central part of the island, and few roads were built so there was limited access. As Manhattan began to burst beyond the seams of the lower tip, the municipal corporation stood to profit handsomely if it could create a more rational land market.

To promote development, the Common Council had undertaken a survey to plat its holdings. In 1796, Caimer Goerck, the city surveyor, mapped and subdivided the common lands into uniform 5 acre rectangular plots, all of which had access to one of three north-south roads called East, West, and Middle Road, respectively. The Goerck maps were influential in presenting a rectangular order among a large territory, but the plan did not meet with the approval of the Common Council and was rejected.[81]

In 1807, the Common Council requested that New York State establish a commission for developing a street plan. Because the powers that resided in the municipal corporation were ultimately granted by the state, it was felt that only the state had the authority to vest the corporation with the right to survey the land and create streets and parks where only private land existed before.[82] The Act of 1807 created a commission, and three prominent New Yorkers were appointed as commissioners, Governor Morris, Simeon De Witt, and John Rutherford. They, in turn, hired John Randel Jr. as the chief surveyor, who for the next three years diligently set about surveying and mapping the island. They decided that the plan was to start at the northern area of the city and would not reconfigure the streets already in use. On the east side, the plan was to start from Houston Street and on the west side at West 3rd Street in Greenwich Village.

Randel suffered many difficulties while working in the countryside. He was frequently arrested for trespassing because angry farmers feared the changes to be imposed on their lands. He writes, "I was arrested by the Sherriff, on numerous suits instituted against me as agent of the Commissioners, for trespass and damage committed by my workmen, in passing over grounds, cutting off branches of trees, etc. to make surveys under instructions from the Commissioners."[83] In 1809, the Commissioners turned to the state legislature for help in protecting their surveyor. A law was passed where landowners were to be compensated by any damage caused by the surveying teams.

After his rigorous survey work had been completed in 1810, the plan was presented to the Common Council for approval. The proposal was the now-famous Grid Plan, which divided the city into ten north-south avenues, each 100 feet wide (Lexington and Madison Avenues were added later in the 1830s). There were to be 155 east-west streets, each 60 feet wide, that connected the two rivers, with the goal of facilitating transportation between to the two ports. Blocks were 200 feet deep, from street to street, and ranged from 610 or 920 feet wide, going from avenue to avenue. At 200 feet, the blocks would naturally be subdivided into lots of 100 feet deep; there would be no room for service alleys. All the block lengths were divisible by 20 or 25, thus promoting this common lot size when subdivided by landowners.[84]

To greatly facilitate transportation, Randel's plan established a simple formula: twenty blocks was equal to 1 mile, so that at any cross street, "the proximate distance *in miles* from the City Hall . . . may be readily obtained by dividing such number by 20, and adding *one mile* to the result."[85] Wider cross streets, also of 100 feet, were placed at irregular intervals of less than a mile apart, at 14th, 23rd, 34th, 42nd, 59th Street, and so on.

By creating ordered, wide streets, Randel extolled the virtues of them now "admitting the free circulation of air through them; thereby *avoiding* the frequent error of laying out *short, narrow,* and *crooked streets*, with *alleys* and *courts*, endangering extensive conflagrations, confined air, unclean streets, etc."[86] At the time, it was considered highly ambitious, since it laid out streets as far north of 155th Street, nearly 9 miles from City Hall, and the land area in between was five times larger than the city itself.

The Commissioners issued a statement with the plan. By creating rectangular blocks, they were promoting the minimization of construction costs. As they wrote: "In considering that subject they [the Commissioners] could not but bear in mind that a city is to be composed principally of the habitations of men, and that straight-sided and right-angled houses are the most cheap to build and the most convenient to live in. The effect of these plain and simple reflections was decisive."[87] The guiding principal was to maximize the land available for real estate and to facilitate communication between the rivers.

The organization was different in this respect from Pierre Charles L'Enfant's layout of Washington, DC, which contained a series of diagonally crossing streets that allowed for ovals at their intersections. The fact that New York lost the seat of the nation's capital to Philadelphia (and then to Washington, DC), and the seat of the state capital to Albany in 1779, meant that the Commissioners felt no pressures to use the grid as an expression of political power or to advertise the glory of a democratic state. No malls or plazas were needed to situate a large government building with a capitol or lofty spires. Rather, New York was a city of merchants. The port was the vital center and the city should be organized to facilitate trade.

The gridiron style of planning had a long history, dating back at least as early as Roman times; and Randel could have drawn on many precedents. Spanish colonies in Latin America all followed a typical gridiron plan. Philadelphia's 1682 grid system was likely inspired by plans for London, after the Fire of 1666. L'Enfant's 1792 plan for Washington, DC, was being implemented while the Commissioners were doing their work.[88]

But what makes Manhattan unique is the length of its blocks. The commissioners felt the city should have an east-west orientation to more easily connect the ports on the two rivers; this combined with the desire to maximize land available for building gave New York a much different look than most other cities, whose blocks tended to be closer to square.

This design also reduced the amount of territory for public roadways. New York's plan called for streets to comprise about 35% of its land usage, which was on the low end, especially as compared to Washington, DC, at 55%.[89] A typical 200 x 800 square foot block could be divided into sixty-four lots of 2,500 square feet each; thirty-two of them would face the avenues and have more valuable frontage. Many variations were possible, especially if the developer wanted to construct townhouses that were 18 or 20 feet across.

New York City geologist Charles A. Baskerville noted an apparent relationship between the Grid Plan and the geological shape of the island. He writes, "As the ridges and valleys of Manhattan and the Bronx trend about N. 30°E, the avenues were laid out in the strike valleys, the paths of least resistance, which also run parallel to the Hudson River . . . most of the main north-south streets still follow the valleys."[90] This is another example of a correlative statement not borne out by the facts. First, there is no direct evidence from the Commissioners or Randel Jr. that they decided to lay out the avenues based on the geological paths of least resistance. The strike valleys are the low points in the bedrock folds, discussed in chapter 1 and illustrated in figure 1.3.

The Commissioners wanted streets to easily connect the East and Hudson Rivers because it would be more favorable for commerce, and, as such, streets perpendicular to the rivers would be the shortest distance between them. Also, there are several fault valleys that run in a northwest-southwest direction, and in which many of the island's streams would flow. These are illustrated in figure 1.8, which shows the direction of their flow. This map also suggests that rather than being a facilitator of the Grid Plan, the geology might have been an obstacle, since many of the ridges running perpendicular to the grid had to be eliminated. In short, despite the geologists' claims, there is no causal evidence that the shape of the strike valleys was a key influence in the layout of the streets.

WHAT THE PLAN OMITTED

The Commissioners created a relatively simple blueprint. And looking at a two-dimensional map on paper gives the impression that from the tabula rasa of rural

New York, urban order was created. But as discussed in chapter 2, the topography was an undulating system of hills, valleys, streams, and wetlands. The Grid Plan said nothing about the street grades or how the grid and topography were to work together. Rather, street slopes would be determined piecemeal, based on the need to facilitate transportation by keeping elevation changes minimal.[91] As streets were opened, if a landowner found he was above or below the grade, he was forced to make a considerable investment to match his lot to the street. The street-opening assessments plus the leveling of the property required a large investment. This forced the landlord to develop the land and bring it into the urban fabric as quickly as possible to recoup the expense. In the twenty-seven years from 1830 to 1856, Valentine records nearly 200 openings of road stretches or squares within the newly mapped area.[92]

Since the plan did not say anything about the island's drainage, there was no coordinated mechanism to account for nature's waterways. Similarly, for hills, valleys, and marshes—they would have to be leveled and filled in to make the street grades uniform. In 1865, Egbert Viele complained that the process of simply covering the rivers was dangerous. He wrote:

> I know that it is generally supposed that when the city is entirely built upon, all that water will disappear; but such is not the case. The very material which is thrown in to cover it up will form a nucleus for its increase, not only retaining a larger amount of moisture, but will have added to it the drainings through the animal and vegetable refuse which accumulates in all large cities. The fatal consequences which we have already felt are trifling compared to the suffering that will follow the entire occupation of the island.[93]

As discussed above, the Grid Plan also said nothing about lot sizes within the blocks. Over the years, the conventional understanding of the Grid Plan was that it dictated 25 x 100 foot lot sizes. It did no such thing. In most cities throughout the United States, platting schemes promoted the 100 foot depth given its "Goldilocks" properties of not being too deep (and thus not having wasted space) or being too narrow and cramped. The standard lot size was simply a convention that locked-in as the decades progressed. It also bears repeating that lot widths had a high degree of variation around a 25 foot band, ranging from 18 for modest size houses to 25 for the larger variety.

Because the plan was established and set in stone rather early, it largely did not evolve. The major deviations, in addition to Central Park, were the creation of Madison and Lexington Avenues in the 1830s. As the east side developed, landowners petitioned the city for more avenue frontage, and as a result, two of the longer blocks on the east side were cut in half. In chapter 5, we will return to one of these smaller blocks by Grand Central Station, as, by 1929, it was felt to be the ideal size for a skyscraper. Overall, little park space was provided; the Commissioners defended their decision on the grounds that the city had the "two arms of the sea" to ensure fresh supply of air.[94]

Other cities like Chicago would change the block sizes in different neighborhoods based on how the land uses were emerging. Since tracts there were laid out in 40 acre lots, different combinations of total street frontage versus block sizes were found more valuable depending whether the block would have mostly residential or businesses uses. A 600′ by 69′ block (with alley behind it) would be perfect for commercial use as it would maximize frontage. A 600′ by 124′ block would be ideal for apartment or residential use.[95] New York did not alter its lot and blocks in this way, and was more or less stuck with the 25 x 100 convention that developed from the Dutch period.

Finally, the plan said nothing about the structures that might someday sit on this land. No attempt was made to regulate density, usage, or heights. There was no mention about regulating or rationalizing the port or waterfront. The plan gave virtually no consideration to the efficient movement of people and goods on diagonal basis. Travelers to this day (both drivers and subway passengers) are victim to the perpendicular arrangement of the streets and paths of the subway lines.

From the vantage point of today, when local and state governments have more power over land use, particularly through the use of zoning rules, planning boards, and eminent domain, the limited nature of the Grid Plan seems overly limited. However, in pre-industrial times, the city government's mandate was restricted, and there was a lot of uncertainty about its power over private property.[96]

Over the two centuries since its adoption, the Grid Plan had and has many detractors. George Hill and George Waring would echo Viele in 1898 by complaining that by ignoring the topography and the water courses, the Grid Plan was wreaking havoc on the healthfulness of the citizens.[97] Because of its lack of public squares, and its monotony, in 1987, urban planning scholar Peter Marcuse would write, "Manhattan's gridiron plan . . . is generally taken to be one of the worst city plans of any major city in the developed countries of the world."[98]

But the Grid Plan emerged within a historical and social context. It was very early in the city's industrial development and it was created when the excitement with can-do republicanism was perhaps at its greatest. The plan was being developed at the same time Robert Fulton was perfecting his steamboat. It was also a time when society viewed nature as something in the way of progress and as a vector disease and death. The grid was a way to replace swamps and marshes with regularity and neatness. As historian Edward Spann writes, "For [the Commissioners], the grid was a plan for the conquest of both nature and the past in the interests of an advancing civilization."[99]

In one respect, the Grid Plan represents a great democratization. By creating uniformity and promoting subdivisions, it made the market a kind of level playing field. It standardized the land production process and made land much more like a commodity than before. Real estate developments would then be decided by how people voted with their feet and dollars—by the economic battle for place.

Despite its apparent rigidity, in the decades following its approval, the plan evolved to satisfy, to some degree, the desires of the public, both households and developers. As the blueprint was placed in action, the actual behavior of residents and developers could be observed. One issue was the desire to create small parks that could be lined with townhouses or hotels as in the case of Tompkins Square (1850), Washington Square (1826), and Mt. Morris Park (Marcus Garvey Park) (1840). The most important change to the Grid Plan was the creation of Central Park (1858-1873). Designed by Frederic Law Olmstead, it has removed 843 acres of urban land to give the city its lungs back.

In the end, if the main objective of the Grid Plan was to create a well-functioning urban land market, then it was a success. About a half century into the plan, John

Randel Jr. would have the proverbial last laugh when he wrote, "This Plan of the Commissioners, thus objected to *before its completion, is now the pride and boast of the city*; and the facilities afforded by it for *buying, selling* and *improving* real estate." And those locals who harassed him in his surveying efforts, well, many of their descendants "have been made rich thereby."[100]

Some would complain that the plan was "too successful"—that by standardizing the land it allowed for rampant speculation. A typical critique is given by historian John Reps, who writes, "As an aid to speculation the commissioners' plan was perhaps unequaled, but only on this ground can it be justifiably called a great achievement."[101] But the belief that the Grid Plan created a speculative frenzy is a bit like blaming the automobile for traffic congestion. The plan was the means by which people could develop the land; the mapping of Manhattan, as an objective of economic and social needs, was not the cause of the rampant land trading. Platting schemes in the United States were frequently followed by speculative bubbles because of the excitement they engendered, as they gave people a great sense of hope about the prospects for the future.

Speculative bubbles were not unique to New York. In the 1830s, Chicago's land values took on meteoric proportions, after the land was platted and plans for a canal were established to link Lake Michigan with the Mississippi River.[102] A land boom occurred in Florida in the 1920s, sparked by the rising interest in developing the state for tourism and vacation homes. The point is that there was nothing so unique about Manhattan's platting scheme that caused people to behave differently as compared to other land-use plans. The key is that the plan now allowed for the city to push forward its real estate development in a clear and more orderly fashion. That fact that it drove people to bid up land prices more than they might be worth is a problem of human psychology, not maps housed in municipal offices.

THE PHYSICAL CONSEQUENCE OF THE GRID PLAN

Another conventional wisdom that permeates the historiography of New York is that the Grid Plan was a great leveler, tearing the city down to a uniform topography.[103] But to what extent is this true? We can say for sure that the ecology changed. A verdant oak, pine, and tulip tree forest was paved over and turned into a brick and steel forest. All wetlands and streams were buried or removed. Collect Pond is no more. The beaver, deer, and water fowl that roamed Mannahatta are extinct or live in other places.

But how much of the elevation was changed? Figure 2.8 gives a map which shows the net changes in elevation between 1609 and 2012 for each block on Manhattan. The darker areas show where the land was raised more than 10 feet. Lighter areas are where the land was lowered more than 10 feet. The figure shows that in actuality the land changes were not as dramatic as we have come to believe. The map suggests that rather than a great leveling, the island was subject to a great smoothing. In fact, about two-thirds of all blocks had changes of less than 10 feet, and 40% of the blocks had average elevation changes of less than 5 feet. The modal change was to add between 0 and 10 feet; much of this was due to infill along the river banks. Nearly as much of the island was "brought up" as it was "brought down." The average change across all blocks, in fact, was positive, at 1.7 feet.[104]

N

Change in elevation (feet)
  -70~-10
  -10~10
  10~90

Figure 2.8 Average changes in elevation between 1609 and 2012. The map shows the average elevation changes for each block between the 1609 and the present (excluding the current-day parks). The darkest regions are where the land elevations were raised the most; while the lightest regions are where the elevation was lowered the most. Across the island the average elevation change was close to zero, since wetlands and valleys were raised and highlands were lowered. The basic topography of Manhattan remains virtually the same as nature created it, but the island has been given a great smoothing since then.
Source: Map by Eon Kim; 1609 elevation data is courtesy of Eric Sanderson, the Mannahatta Project, Wildlife Conservation Society.

This is also confirmed by a statistical analysis, which looks at what caused the average change in elevation of each block (results in appendix E). The average change was determined by a series of control variables, such as the starting elevation in 1609, whether there was a stream on the block, or whether the area was formerly wetlands. In short, higher elevation blocks were reduced, on average, by 1.5 foot per 10 feet rise in elevation. If an area was a wetland, its elevation was increased, on average, by about 3.4 feet. Despite the many images of houses perched on rocky hills surrounded by the newly created streets several feet below, the data suggest that this was not the norm. Today the general topography remains the same as it did in 1609; the highlands are still high and the low lands are low, but the transition from one area to the next is much smoother.[105]

THE ECONOMIC CONSEQUENCE OF THE GRID PLAN

What were the economic consequences of the Grid Plan? How did it affect the value of land and the economics (cost and benefits) of real estate? This turns out to be a harder question to answer. One recent study by economist Trevor O'Grady investigates the cost of Manhattan land between 1835 and 1845; he compares plots that were in the old city versus that north of the demarcation line. He finds that lots within the Grid Plan area sold for a 20% premium, all else equal.[106] So the data do suggest that land buyers found that the plan had higher value above the blocks in the lower part of the city. Anecdotal evidence also suggests that this is true, as was indicated by Randel and others.[107]

But the fact that prices were higher above the demarcation line does not tell us what, in particular, buyers found so beneficial. Here, we must enter the realm of speculation, to speak, until further research becomes available. We know that subdivisions below and above the demarcation line were roughly similar at 25 x 100 feet, so there was probably little difference in the plot sizes, though the 200 feet blocks ensured more frequent depths of 100 feet.

It might be that the shapes were more regular—that the lots were more likely to be rectangular, with corners at 90 degree angles. If this reduced the cost of construction, as suggested by the Commissioners, then this would raise land values. It might also be that the streets were wider. Businesses and residents were likely to value broader roads, since they allowed for more light and, perhaps, reduced street congestion. There was probably a general lift of land values from the wide north-south avenues. Those fronting an avenue would have more sunlight and businesses would be guaranteed greater foot traffic because they were the main thoroughfares of the city. Presumably, the flow of traffic would be more orderly and would, therefore, make lots north of the demarcation line more valuable simply because they provided easier access to other parts of the city.

However, one problem with the Grid Plan was its east-west orientation. Because of this, most residences would face north or south and would receive much less sunlight than if they were facing east or west. Looking at subdivisions below the demarcation line shows that many of the blocks were either square or ran in the north-south direction, which at least suggests, that sunlight may have been important to early residents (figure 2.6).

Another theory is health related. A large motivation for the plan was to promote "free and abundant circulation of air."[108] If residents above the demarcation line saw the street system as reducing their chances of getting sick, they would have been willing to pay a premium. The words of Viele, however, suggest that, in fact, the Grid Plan's aim of improving the general health might have, in fact, backfired, because it made no arrangements for proper drainage.[109]

Finally, the higher land prices might simply have been a result of the demographic changes that were taking place in the first half of the nineteenth century. As will be discussed in the next chapter, after the introduction of horse-drawn streetcar lines, wealthier residents began moving further north on the island; land prices were likely determined by this wealthier clientele.

Did the Grid Plan Create Artificial Land Scarcity?

When the Commissioners created the plan in 1811, they, of course, created it within the zeitgeist of the day. They did their best to anticipate the future, which to them was driven by a mercantile prerogative. They did not, and could not, have ever predicted the rise of the skyscraper, which was born of the Industrial Revolution, and the increase of population much greater than envisioned. In a city of shopkeepers, artisans, and merchants, the 25 x 100 square foot plot size was a reasonable standard. Over the course of the nineteenth century, the plan's promotion of it scattered land holdings to hundreds or even thousands citizens, so that by 1890, large lots were hard to come by.

The distribution of landholdings, it has been argued, created an artificial land scarcity at the beginning of the twentieth century, when developers preferred larger plots to build their skyscrapers. Given that tall buildings were designed to house many people, larger lots allowed for more economical construction and a more efficient layout of work space. The difficulty of assemblages, and perhaps, the higher price of land, as a result, may have caused developers to create taller but narrower towers on smaller plots of land instead. To quote architectural historian Carol Willis:

> The city's many relatively small lots created an economic logic for towers. In the financial district of Lower Manhattan . . . ownership was broken up into many parcels that for well over a hundred years were occupied by profitable lower rise buildings. Large sites were thus difficult to assemble, and unlike Chicago in 1871, no great fire conveniently cleared the way for redevelopment just at the period of rapid corporate expansion.[110]

But the question remains as to what extent this is true. First, if land values are rising, be they on the urban-rural frontier or in the business district, landowners will have the incentive to convert them to their most profitable use. As such, they should have incentive to sell out to the company that wants to build a high-rise office, increasing the size of the lots. There are no laws against multiple property owners joining together to jointly develop a skyscraper, if they should so choose, despite this being a risky prospect for all involved.

But there is, of course, the holdout problem. If a developer has, say, three out of four lots needed to erect a tall building, the owner of the fourth lot can hold out for a much higher price. If paid, it then increases the value of the land and drives the developer to add extra floors to earn back the extra costs. However, beyond the fascinating architectural books on the subject, there is no empirical evidence on the degree to which holdouts were systematically driving up the cost of construction.[111] Developers frequently use shell corporations or proxy buyers to hide their real intentions.[112]

As we will discuss in chapter 5, the logic of towers does not necessarily emerge from small lot sizes per se, but rather from the high cost of land in general, separate from available lots. Lower Manhattan was an ecology of entwined business clusters, and for one particular firm to expand, it had to compete fiercely for the right to do so.

Using data that I collected, I compared lot sizes for skyscrapers in New York and Chicago, and the analysis does not reveal any systematic differences, despite the general belief to the contrary.[113] Furthermore, an analysis of skyscraper lot sizes in New York before 1916 does not show any statistically significant differences between those in Midtown versus Downtown (see appendix F). Presumably Downtown, the home of the first skyscrapers in New York, had smaller lot sizes due to its earlier Dutch origins. Midtown, on the other hand, would have had larger lot sizes on average because the land was developed more recently. In short, there is no evidence from the data that the Grid Plan or earlier subdivision conventions systematically prevented skyscraper developers from amassing the lots they needed or wanted. We now turn to see how land use and the battle for place played out before the Civil War.

3

Land Use before the Civil War

Many of these pigs live here. Do they ever wonder why their masters walk upright instead of going on all-fours, and why they talk instead of grunting?
Charles Dickens

The Manhattan skyline has a particular shape. Skyscrapers rise at the southern tip and then just seem to disappear north of City Hall, reemerging near 34th Street in Midtown. Conventional wisdom holds that the shape of Manhattan's bedrock is the reason, but the contours of the skyline above ground have much less to do with the contours of the bedrock below ground. The depth to bedrock is a red herring; the geological roots of the skyline, rather, are tied to how it affected the initial settlement patterns on the island and economic growth from that point forward.

Skyscraper locations and heights were determined by where people were working and living at the time of their creation in the last decade of the nineteenth century; the location of these neighborhoods was determined long before that. The decisions made about where to live and work before the Civil War would lock-in a particular trajectory for the city; and the skyline would rise out of this history.

During the British colonial period, after the city began to grow in earnest, specific neighborhoods formed based on employment and class differences. The merchant and political classes were living at the furthest south, closest to the port and seat of government. Lower Broadway near Bowling Green Park was a wealthy enclave. These households were bidding the highest for the right to be there. Craftsmen and artisans were living north of them; while the least skilled were living further out still where land and rent were cheapest.

The artisans and low-skilled workers lived above the upper classes not only because they were less able to pay to be in the heart of the city but also because they were tied to the location of manufacturing, which in turn was tied to the port, and sources of fresh water for production. Shipbuilding and related activities, especially after the American Revolution, were housed along the northern port area in the Seventh Ward. Leather processing, tanning, animal slaughtering, and beer brewing were concentrated near sources of running water: namely, the marshy area to the east of Collect Pond in the Sixth Ward.

The location of different classes and jobs was due to the interplay of economics and geology. It was this early interaction that would then give rise to what I call the First Inversion. When public transportation was introduced into Manhattan, in the form of the omnibus in 1829 and the horse-drawn streetcar in 1837, it allowed the middle and upper classes to "jump" over the working classes that were previously housed on the northern fringes of the city. The working classes and the newly arrived immigrants remained in these older neighborhoods which then became the teeming "slums" housing the "other half," as so graphically depicted by Jacob Riis in 1890.[1]

In other words, public transportation gave rise to the first wave of true suburbanization in American history, with the upper classes now living on the suburban fringes and commuting to work; the lower classes were still tied to their jobs near the port and the manufacturing districts. These workers were not willing to pay for public transportation because of its expense.[2] This is especially true during the great influxes of Irish and German immigrants during the middle of the nineteenth century.

After public transportation options were available to those who could pay for it, these households moved to Washington Square Park, Gramercy Park, St. Mark's Place, and southern Fifth Avenue. These neighborhoods had several appealing characteristics for the well-to-do: they were new and undeveloped, and therefore could be built to their tastes, and they were centrally located along the spine of the city—close to Broadway—near shopping, restaurants, and entertainment.

But even when commuting became an option, there is nothing inherent in this that forced the wealthy to leave the lower, central portions of the city and move to northern suburbs. Living further north also meant being away from the amenities and institutions that made up urban life. In addition, these residents had to spend more time and money on commuting. But in this country, one universal pattern has emerged since mass transit options were implemented: higher income people have chosen to move out of the central city to the suburbs. In this sense then, "sprawl"—the residential expansion out into the hinterland—has been a common fact of life in the United States since the early nineteenth century, with the driving force being that upper income households prefer suburban living more than they mind commuting or being away from the heart of the city.[3] In other countries, with different histories and cultural preferences, the upper and middle classes have remained in the central core. Cities in France or Spain, for example, tend to show the opposite relationship between income and location: the wealthy tend to live in the center, while the poor are found in the "suburbios" around the old city.[4]

As businesses took over Lower Manhattan in the 1820s, upper income residents found they were priced out. But they could have chosen to purchase new housing in the formerly working-class neighborhoods just to the north. It would have been possible to just "push" the traditional layers of socioeconomic segregation north, so that all layers simply moved up say a half mile, keeping the low-income workers on the periphery. The wealthy could have gentrified neighborhoods near Five Points or in the Lower East Side. If developers believed there was a demand, they would have bought up lots and built higher class housing. But rather, the middle and upper classes made a decided "jump" over the working-class neighborhoods into the northern regions of the city.

This inversion, as we will see, had two very important ramifications for the skyline. First, it would create a kind of economic barrier around Lower Manhattan, around Chambers Street. When massive immigration began with the Irish and German in the middle of the nineteenth century, these immigrants would choose to live just north of the port, in the Fourth, Sixth, Seventh, and Tenth Wards; this would turn the financial district into a kind of business island, with water on three sides and warehouses and slums on the fourth. Not only would land values rise Downtown as a result, but skyscraper developers would have little incentive to build tall in the dense tenement districts. Tenement residents could not afford to pay for the high rents necessary to make the skyscraper a profitable investment; as well, likely no skyscraper developer was interested in performing the necessary "slum clearance" to have a vacant parcel on which to build.

The second implication is that Midtown would emerge as a direct response to the commercial needs of residents living on the northern fringes of the city. On the eve of the Civil War, the Manhattan suburban limits was around 42nd Street and would continually move upward throughout the century. In the 1880s, Madison Square and surrounding blocks would become the main shopping and entertainment district. Midtown's first skyscrapers would locate there.

Rapid transit would also have another effect. In 1837, the city's first rail line was designed to connect the village of Harlem with the city proper. By creating a small agricultural village to the north of the city in 1657, the Dutch were unwittingly setting the stage for the rise of the New York and Harlem Railroad. This would lead, in the nineteenth century, to the development of the east side, Grand Central Station, and the rise of modern Midtown in the 1920s.

AGRICULTURE TO REAL ESTATE

Geology influenced agriculture, which, in turn, influenced the early location of villages and farms, which ultimately helped to lock-in important land-use patterns that we see today. In other words, the *geological roots of the skyline rest with the location of fertile soil,* as well as the wetlands and bodies of water on the island. Soil fertility was due to how the Taconic Orogeny created the bedrock depths and forms, how it eroded over millions of years, and what was laid on top of the rock by the glaciers and glacial lakes. The location of streams in the valleys also helped determine land-use patterns as well, since they would be sources of freshwater for human and animal alike.

Generally, Manhattan's soil was not very fertile as compared to other locations in the state. Much of the western section of the island north of 34th Street was rocky and only had a thin coating of soil. Manhattan's most productive regions were in the areas near, and just north of, the southern tip where the bedrock was deep, and the earth tended to be a loamy mix of sand and silts. Deposits from the glacial meltwaters created hills and slopes that were less jagged and steep than those created by the bedrock to the north. As a result, the population growth of Manhattan would concentrate mostly on the east side. Manhattan's soil was not great for wheat, but was fine for buckwheat, rye, and tobacco.[5]

Figure 1.6 (in chapter 1) gives a map of "Fertile Manhattan," based on the types of soils that the Dutch would have found, though they might not have been recognized as such, as reconstructed by Eric Sanderson as part of his Mannahatta Project. The richer areas were located on the west side running from Minetta Brook north, and on the east side, from around Wall Street north to 23rd Street, from the Bowery to the east. Further, loamy soils tended to occur up the island on the east side near the river banks, until the Harlem plains, which had a wide swath of rich soil. Today, if these soil types were found below the streets, say during real estate excavation or a soil mapping project, they would be indicators of possible historical artifacts, given how attractive they would have been to previous societies.[6]

It is clear from a comparison of these soil maps to the Manatus map (figure 3.1) created circa 1639, that settlers were drawn to the most high-yielding regions on the island.[7] As a very crude map, the contours of the island are not to proper scale. But they indicate the location of early real estate and agricultural developments. From this, it can be seen that there is a strong visual correlation between the Fertile Manhattan

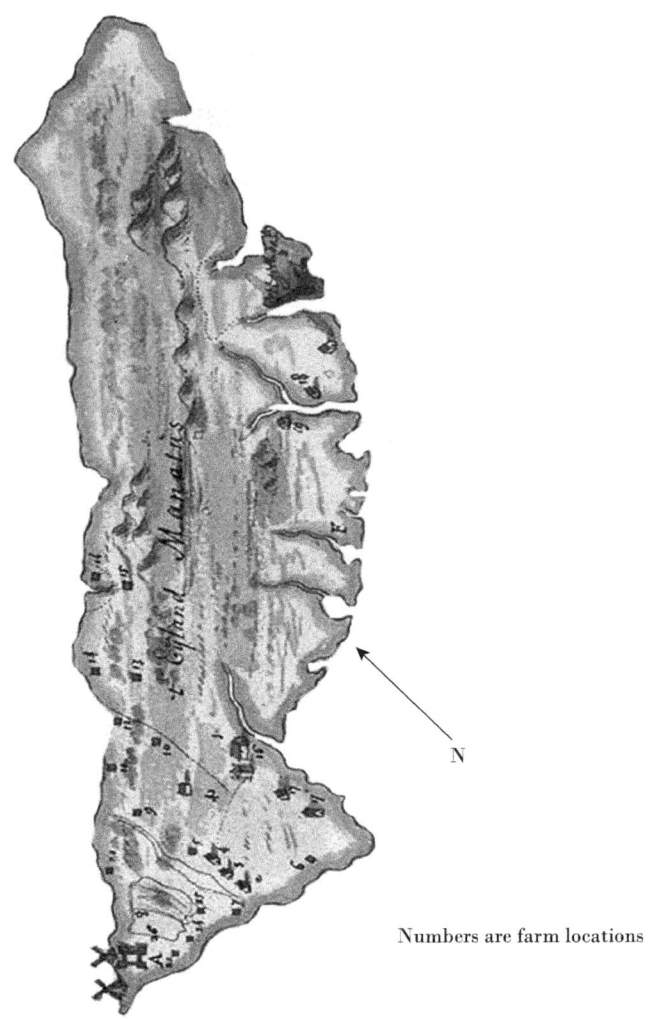

N

Numbers are farm locations

Figure 3.1 The Manatus map circa 1639. This sketch of Manhattan, redrawn from the Manatus map, shows the early location of Dutch settlements. There is a striking pattern between the location of early Dutch farms and the location of fertile soils for agriculture. It demonstrates how Manhattan's real estate trajectory and the skyline were influenced by the natural environment. The east side was developed the earliest and saw the greatest population density there. Furthermore, in the 1830s, a railroad was constructed to connect the City of New York with the agricultural village of Harlem, which would one day give rise to Grand Central Station and modern Midtown.
Source: Library of Congress (http://www.loc.gov/item/97683586).

map and early economic developments, which were clustered along the lower tip, in the loamy Greenwich Village area, the Lower East Side, and in the Harlem Flats.

Over the course of the seventeenth and eighteenth centuries, between the initial creation of farms and the beginning of the Revolutionary War, Manhattan north of the tip would be carved up into a patchwork of farms, grazing lands, and woods. By the end of the colonial period, in 1780, the area north of Canal Street had been divided into approximately 130 farms. Most of them tended to be rather small; the median size was 30 acres; while eleven were 200 acres or greater. Ownership, however, was more concentrated, since several of the farms were owned by the same family. Still farmland was no more than 7,500 acres, which was less than half the island.[8] The Ratzer map of 1767 (figure 3.2) shows how the city proper comprised only a tiny fraction of the island, with the rest being distinctly rural.

An analysis of the British Headquarters map of 1782 by Eric Sanderson and his colleague Marianne Brown shows that even after a century and a half of settlement, areas dedicated to planting crops or raising animals comprised only 10% of the island (thus the farmland above was not actively being cultivated); with developed areas making up another 6%. Even by the American Revolution, nature "controlled" some 84% of the island.[9] Rural land would not entirely disappear from Manhattan until after the Civil War. Although little food was cultivated in the nineteenth century, the 1855 New York State Census revealed some 14,000 horses living on the island; they were likely used to pull streetcars, hackney coaches, and omnibuses.

Figure 3.3 shows how the footprint of the city expanded over the course of the nineteenth century; the map is essentially a time line for the conversion of rural land to urban real estate. Before the implementation of the Grid Plan, the city's northernmost developed area remained well below Houston Street. Less than half a century later, the northern area expanded to between 42nd and 50th Streets. By 1879, nearly all of the Upper East Side was developed. The opening of the Upper West Side would happen only after the construction of the Elevated Railroads in the 1880s (see chapter 8).

As these maps demonstrate, fertile Manhattan promoted two key land-use developments during the colonial period that would directly influence the emergence of the skyline. First, several small hamlets and villages would rise to service the local needs of the agricultural communities. The two most important and lasting of these were Greenwich Village and Harlem. The lock-in factor would remain at play, as these villages were ultimately developed as residential enclaves.

Second, a network of country lanes and roads were built to connect these locales, which, in turn, would increase the economic and social interaction between village and city. These would help establish land-use trajectories that would be key in the nineteenth century, especially the road that connected the city to Harlem—the High Road to Boston—which began at the Bowery.

THE EARLY VILLAGES OF MANHATTAN

Greenwich Village

When the Dutch arrived, they found a small Indian village near where Gansevoort Street meets the Hudson River; it was called Sapokanikan by the Lenape. As one writer describes the area, "it was markedly healthful, owing to a substratum of fifty feet

Figure 3.2 The Ratzer map of 1767. Created by British surveyor, Bernard Ratzer, this map is one of the most important of early New York. It shows how the vast majority of Manhattan Island, even after a century and a half of European settlement, remained largely a quilt-work of farms, estates, woods, and other rural lands.

Source: Boston Public Library, Norman B. Leventhal Map Center.

of clear sand underlying the fertile topsoil. It was well wooded, and gave, on the river side, upon a charming beach washed by waters teeming with fish."[10] As a result, the area north of Minetta Brook was established as the company's farm. Quite soon after, however, Director General Wouter van Twiller took personal title to it and attempted to grow tobacco. No record seems to exist to indicate whether he made any money from the venture.

Van Twiller built a farm house in 1633, and over the next few years, other buildings were constructed in a cluster that would produce the seeds of the little village north of

N

Developed Area
■ 1808
■ 1833
▨ 1862
▨ 1879

Figure 3.3 Manhattan's expanding footprint. This map shows Manhattan's expanding footprint over the nineteenth century. The increase in population and the development of mass transit around 1830 allowed for a dramatic northward movement of the population. Before that, New York was a walking city and expansion occurred rather slowly.

Source: Map created by Eon Kim. Underlying data is from map reproduced in Ernst (1949) and the Taylor map of 1879.

the city. By the early eighteenth century, during the English period, Greenwich Village was a flourishing settlement of farmers and artisans, connected to the town proper by a street that followed nearly the same course as Greenwich Street today.

The marshlands to the south of the village created a natural barrier that kept the area relatively isolated until population growth in the early nineteenth century led to the paving of Lispenard Meadows and real estate development north of Houston

Street. The village streets, similar to the lower tip, formed along more organic lines; and today, the tourist wandering the neighborhood finds herself easily disoriented, as street names and directions clash with the formal grid pattern which surrounds it.

Given that the village was isolated but close to the city, in the late eighteenth and early nineteenth centuries, it became an escape for wealthy merchants and government officials when yellow fever outbreaks hit. These mass migrations caused the village to develop its character of brick and wooden townhouses. By the mid-nineteenth century, it was a WASP enclave surrounded by tenement districts.[11]

Greenwich Village's effect on the skyline was twofold. First, its early existence as a farming village promoted it as a middle and upper class suburban district during the First Inversion, especially around Washington Square Park. As such, it created the early seeds for Midtown's rise. Upper class residents would live around the park, and the neighborhood's northward growth centered along lower Fifth Avenue, where the rich would build their mansions, clubs, and churches in the decades before the Civil War.

Second, the neighborhood is currently landmarked in order to preserve its original character. As such, it is essentially closed off for high-rise development; the area will never become part of the skyline proper. But this has the additional effect of producing higher land values on the rest of the island, which again influence the incentives for tall building construction elsewhere.

The Bowery Road and Bowery Village

In 1655, fighting with the Indians broke out and devastated the farmlands on the east side. As a result, Peter Stuyvesant required that farmers north of the city establish hamlets or villages to where they could seek protection during times of war. The farmers in the area of the Bowery established a small hamlet on the western edge of Peter Stuyvesant's farm. There he helped build the chapel of St. Mark's in the Bouwerie in 1660, though the current church dates back to 1799. The hamlet also contained a tavern, blacksmith, and wheelwright shop, and a few other structures.[12]

Perhaps more important, a road formed to connect the farms (bouweries) and town; it was given the name Bowery Road. In 1671, it was decreed that a road should be completed up to Harlem. In the next year, Governor Lovelace established mail runs between New York and Boston, promoting the Bowery as a main thoroughfare in and out of the city.[13] To the west of the Bowery was Collect Pond and the industrial activity was attracted to its eastern shores. During the Revolutionary War, a line of fortification was constructed from the East River to the Hudson, along Grand Street. British troops were stationed along the Bowery near the fortification. As a result, the Bowery developed as a place to service the needs of the soldiers, which included several pubs, the type of which would later be characteristic of the street in the nineteenth century. The neighborhood "the Bowery," the area east of Five Points, would become infamous for its gangs, nightlife, and overall debauchery.

Since the Bowery Road was the principal road from the city, it also led to several recreational diversions, including botanical gardens and taverns. Vauxhall Gardens, for example, situated along Bowery and Astor Place, was a manicured garden. In 1803, the greenhouse was converted to saloon, "so that in course of time it became one of the most popular places of resort in the city."[14]

Harlem

The Town of New Harlem was officially created by Peter Stuyvesant in 1658. It began as a small agricultural settlement of about twenty families in the Harlem Flats. The residents were given the right to buy, sell, and distribute property; elect officers; build churches; and govern themselves. Thus began what would be the isolated village of Harlem situated some 7 miles north of the southern tip.

Attempts to settle Harlem had taken place even earlier than that during the Kieft administration when he granted 200 acres of land to a one Dr. Johannes de La Montagne in 1636 in the area from 109th to 124th Street east of St. Nicholas Avenue. De La Montagne and other settlers were attracted to the area because of its fertile soil and the hopes of establishing profitable plantations. In the years immediately following de La Montagne's arrival, Jonas Bronck would establish his farm on the other side of the Harlem River. William Kieft's war destroyed all that had been created. Some settlers were killed by Indian raids, and the rest fled to New Amsterdam for safety. After peace was restored, settlers returned and began rebuilding. Kieft issued several more land grants, and a number of farms were established in the 1640s and 1650s.[15]

However, for the sake of their protection, Stuyvesant ordered the settlers to form a village, with common pasturage and common farms, as distinct from the isolated settlements that had already been developed. Settlers would each get ownership of 36 to 48 acres of farmland and 12 to 16 acres of meadowland. The village was established roughly between 111th Street to 125th Street, bound by Lexington Avenue and the Harlem River.[16]

Governor Nicolls, after formally taking charge of the new English colony, affirmed Harlem's town status by issuing the Harlem Patent or Charter in 1666. The boundary line ran from 129th on the Hudson River to East 74th Street on the East River. Subsequently, Harlem would lose its political independence and be folded into the City of New York.[17]

Over the succeeding decades, the increasing connection between the two locales would be directly responsible for the rise of modern Midtown in the 1920s, after railroads connected them in the 1830s. By the end of the nineteenth century, the village of Harlem and its southern neighbor of Yorkville would also develop as tenement districts. Starting in the 1910s, Harlem would, of course, become the home for thousands of African Americans who migrated from the rural South.

THE THEORY OF LAND USE AND LAND VALUES IN THE WALKING CITY

Looking at the main features of land use before the Civil War shows that early settlement patterns were tied to the geological and geographic benefits they provided. The city proper was tied to the port; while the agriculture was tied to the fertility of the soil. The early northward growth of the city was on the eastside, where port activity dominated and where there were fewer geological barriers to expansion. Population increase was also driving greater density given the difficulty of transportation.

Chapter 2 provides evidence on the value of land in colonial Manhattan. The data suggest a few conclusions. First, market-based trade in urban land emerged relatively early in the colonial period; when the British took control, lots were being bought and sold based on their economic value; second, for most of the colonial period, land value growth was relatively slow, only showing a rapid rise in the second half of the eighteenth century, during the French and Indian War; and third, land values in the lower tip, relative to future values, were quite modest. Town lots during the colonial period were open to those in the middle classes, such as skilled artisans, merchants, and government officials.

As a small trading town still in a pre-industrial age, the fierce battle for place, and the dramatic rise in land values, would not take place in earnest until two major events took place: first was the tremendous influx of population, and second was the production of public transportation, which began in the first half of the nineteenth century. These two factors would push Manhattan on its modern land-use trajectory. But the modern trajectory, of course, develops out of the pre-modern history of the walking city.

How can we understand the interrelated patterns of land use and land values in this period? Here, I provide a theory, which has been the cornerstone of urban economic analysis for the last fifty years. It was originally developed by three economists William Alonso, Richard F. Muth, and Edwin S. Mills (AMM) in order to explain how competition for land creates segregated land-use patterns, and how this competition determines the value of land, where "segregated" specifically refers to land-use types, such as for offices or residences.[18] The theory begins by itemizing the key incentives that different groups face, and how these incentives affect their decisions about where to locate.

First, let's begin with businesses, specifically merchants. The job of a merchant is to match the supply from producers with the demand from consumers, each of whom is located at different places on the planet. Local consumers, in early New York, for example, were dependent on other countries to supply goods that they wanted. Household items, such as textiles and furniture, were manufactured in England and were imported for the local market. Rum and sugar were imported from the Caribbean; tobacco from Virginia; grains from the hinterland, and so on. Similarly, the merchant buys the surplus products of the city and hinterland, such as wheat and timber, and ships them to other places where there is a high demand.

As a result of the nature of the import-export business, the merchant is tied to the port itself. He must locate his business within a few minutes' walk of the docks. Imports are coming in by ship and he must be there to inspect the goods, pay customs duties, and so on. Furthermore, since these imports and exports are distributed primarily via ship, the goods themselves are stored in warehouses adjacent to the port. To warehouse these goods far away from the port is simply too expensive because the goods are heavy and transportation is inefficient. Goods are generally loaded and unloaded by stevedores, who carry the merchandise to the local warehouses.

All of this is to say that any movement of the merchant and his counting house away from the port would mean a loss in revenue or an increase in costs. The merchant also needs to be near the shipbuilders, who also line the riverbanks, and he needs to be near other merchants for the myriad of reasons that merchants cluster: they engage in business ventures together, provide valuable information about prices, products, business conditions, sources of labor; and they provide valuable services to each other, such as a ready markets for their wares, insurance, and credit. Other industries cluster around the merchants, the sea-based industry of captains, sailors, shipbuilders, chandlers, blacksmiths, and so on to form a port-based economic ecology.

But the fundamental problem is that all of these businesses cannot simultaneously occupy the same place at the same time. In pre-industrial New York, there were technological limits to how intensely the land could be used. In particular, buildings were either made of wood or masonry, and their heights were constrained to be no taller than a few floors, since virtually nobody wanted to climb more stairs than was necessary, and there were no steam or electric powered elevators.

The AMM model offers a theory as to how land gets allocated. Let's say there are two businesses, the merchant importer-exporter and the blacksmith, who makes products for the shipbuilding industry. If a prime site, adjacent to the wharfs, comes up for bidding, who would bid more money for the site? Most likely, the merchant would win this bidding "battle." Why? Because the merchant finds that each few blocks he moves away from the port, his profits decline substantially, because moving away from the wharfs and docks and other merchants puts him at competitive disadvantage. Near the port, his business is very profitable; a few blocks away, not so much. Thus, the merchant outbids the blacksmith for the right to occupy a spot by the port simply because the profits of being close to the port are far greater for him. On the other hand, the blacksmith, in essence, wins the battle for place further away from the port. If a lot comes up for bidding a little further out of town, the smith would be the one to place the higher of the two bids.

Figure 3.4A gives a graphic representation of this battle, showing what the merchant and blacksmith are willing to pay for the right to occupy particular locations relative to the port. These lines are called the bid rent lines, since they capture what each is willing to offer. The lines have downward slopes because the further each group is away from the port the more time and money must spent on transportation costs, and thus, the less is leftover to pay for rent.

The horizontal axis is the distance to the port (called location 0), and each unit is, say, the number of blocks away. The vertical axis is the amount each of the two businesses is willing to pay for the right to occupy a location at each distance. Most important, a merchant's willingness to pay line (say in pounds per square foot) has two features different than the blacksmith. First, at location 0, the merchant has a higher ability to pay. Being close to the port is so profitable that he can outbid the blacksmith for locations adjacent to the ships.

Second, the merchant has a steeper willingness to pay line; meaning that if he moves his business away from the port, his profits would decline precipitously. The reason is that as he moves away, the costs rise dramatically—especially the cost of moving his merchandise. Further, let's make the simplifying assumption that merchants and artisans live in the same place they work. In the colonial period, this is reasonable because the level of business, in general, was not so great that the value of upper floors would "price out" use for residences.

Now the blacksmith's willingness to pay to be at location 0 is less than the merchants, simply because his business is less profitable. But as he moves away from

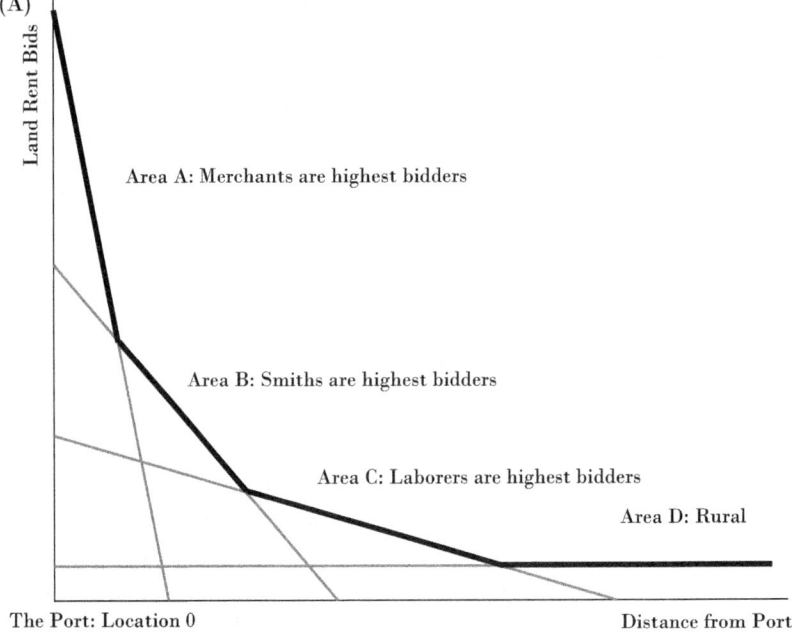

(A)

Land Rent Bids

Area A: Merchants are highest bidders

Area B: Smiths are highest bidders

Area C: Laborers are highest bidders

Area D: Rural

The Port: Location 0

Distance from Port

Figure 3.4A Hypothetical bid rent curve. This figure depicts what four classes of residents would be willing to pay for the right to occupy different locations in a walking city; that is, the rents that they would bid to occupy specific parcels (separate from what they would pay for housing), in relation to the distance to the port, the heart of the city. The steepest line belongs to the merchants; the next steepest line to the smiths and artisans; the next line is the laboring class; after that are the farmers. In colonial New York, the merchant class would have the highest bid rents closes to the port, since they prefer to live close to where they work and they have the highest incomes. After that, the smiths and artisans would occupy locations just north of the merchants. Further north would reside the laboring classes, since they have the lowest income. North of them would be the agricultural areas of the city. The thick black line is the bid rent envelope and represents the bid rent being paid at each location based on which class has the highest willingness to pay at each location.
Source: Graphic by Jason M. Barr.

the port, his willingness to pay does not fall nearly as fast as the merchants. The reason is due to the fact that the blacksmith is not moving as much product in and out of his workshop. The volume of his business in pre-industrial New York is relatively modest, and the cost of moving his ironware from the port to his workshop is not as high as that facing the merchant. In the graph, Area A is the part of the city where merchants tend to live and work, since this is the region in which they win the battle for place. Area B is the region where the smiths win the battle, several blocks north.

The third line is the rent bids of the laborers and domestics. They earn the least amount of money and therefore cannot bid very much for locations near the center. However, because the only "merchandise" the laborer or domestic moves is his or her body, the cost of moving it is not so high. This is why the laborers willingness-to-pay line has a flatter slope. Area C is where the laborers outbid the smiths, and where they

(B)   D

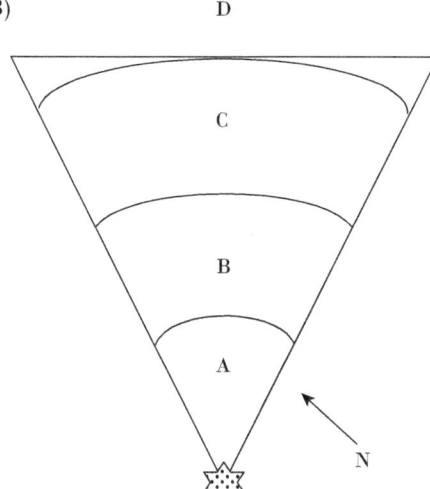

Figure 3.4B Land-use "map" for a stylized version of Lower Manhattan. This figure represents a stylized map of what land uses would emerge in the walking city. The star represents the fort. The lower part of the triangular would be occupied by the merchants (A), next would be smiths and artisans (B), and above that would be the laboring classes (C); farmers would be to the north (D). The key point is that the economics of the "battle for place" will determine a very specific ordering of land-use patterns; and these would one day influence the location of skyscrapers.

Source: Graphic by Jason M. Barr.

will reside. Finally the flat line is the price of rural land, assumed to be fixed across space and to be the lowest value. Area D is the farmland, on the northern fringes.

The prices paid to occupy each location are called "land rent," and it is determined by the winner in the battle for place; it is the envelope of each of the bid rent lines shown in figure 3.4A. Land rents are higher close to the port because the merchants pay more to be there.[19] They fall off from there because the bidders have less money "left over" to bid for land because they must pay greater transportation costs. Another stylized graph is given in figure 3.4B, which imagines that Lower Manhattan can be depicted as a triangle; the lower tip is where the fort was located, and it was just a short walk to the port on the East River. The inner circle (A) is the merchant locations; the next circle (B) is the location of artisans; and further out (C) are the unskilled laborers; above that is rural (D). In 1800, Area D would begin at about Grand Street (this can also be seen in the map in figure 3.3).

What does this model mean for land use in early New York? There are two major implications. First, even in the walking city, there will be a segregation of land uses, with merchants hugging the port, the artisan class north of that, and laborers and unskilled workers north of that. The second major implication has to do with land values. The value of land at a particular location is determined by the flow of land rents over time. In the battle for place, the way that land gets allocated is by auctioning it off to the highest bidder, who pays a fraction of his/her income. Thus, we would predict land values to be much higher near the port, where the income is the greatest, and then it would fall off from there.

Keep in mind we get these predictions from the model without any discussion of ecology or geology. The only "geological" phenomenon is the location of the port, created by the Taconic Orogeny and Ice Ages described in chapter 1. We do not include the location of ponds or hills or anything else that might subtly alter the choice of locations. The point of the model, however, is to understand how land gets used based on the underlying economic motivations. Once we have a model, we can bring it to the data.

The model also gives a reason for the gradual conversion of northern areas from rural to urban land. As the population of the city grows, it increases the demand for space among the city dwellers. Along the northern fringes, when a piece of land becomes available, the right to use it is auctioned off to the highest bidder. Over time, those highest bidders will be residents tied to the city proper: those who are "priced out" of the southern portions of the city. As discussed above, however, in the walking city, the footprint will not expand at the same rate as the population because of the difficulties in gaining access to the city itself. But at some point, the rural landowners will find that the cost of holding the land for relatively low-value uses is too high relative to the profit that can be earned by having it surveyed and brought into the urban fabric. Another way of saying this is that as the city grows, the bid rent lines in figure 3.4A move outward, and as a result, city dwellers outbid rural residents.

LAND USE IN THE CITY UNTIL THE EARLY NINETEENTH CENTURY

The question remains: Does the AMM model help explain New York City's history? For this, we now turn to land use in the colonial period and early Federal period. During these years, as the population grew and the economy developed, residential neighborhoods become increasingly differentiated by wealth and occupation.[20] The location of neighborhoods was tied to the costs of moving people and goods, but as discussed above, until the first quarter of the nineteenth century, the foot was the most common form of mobility. This meant that most of the city's real estate growth would be within the city itself via infill and subdivisions, rather than on the fringes.

What makes the Grid Plan so remarkable is that in 1807, when it was first conceived, the multitudes of people pouring into the city had no other means of getting around except by walking. The footprint of the city in 1808 encompassed only 1.3 square miles; and nearly 21 square miles of the island was effectively off limits. The belief that the whole island would someday be taken up by urban land use appears incredibly visionary from this perspective. The Upper West Side could have been in Canada, as far as the typical resident was concerned.

Research performed independently by historians Carl Abbott and Bruce Wilkenfeld provide concrete evidence for the AMM model, and how income and occupation determined the geography of economic activity during this period. Figure 3.5 shows the location of different neighborhoods in 1760s New York, based on the historical research of Carl Abbott. The map shows the location of different neighborhoods, clearly demonstrating a relationship between income, employment type, and location relative to the fort.

Figure 3.5 Neighborhoods of New York City before the American Revolution. This map
was created by historian Carl Abbot, who researched the locations of residents based on their
employment: (1) commercial activity and upper class residences; (2) upper class residences; (3) artisanal
manufacturing and residence; (4) manufacturing; and (5) slums. The map provides strong evidence for
the economic theory regarding the battle for place. The upper class residents, including merchants and
government officials, were found to be living at the lower tip (1 and 2). The wealthiest neighborhood
was west of Broadway (2). North of that, the artisans and craftsmen were found (areas 3 and 4). The
individuals in the lowest class were found in area (5) either at the very north or along the docks.
Source: Map courtesy of Carl Abbot and Margery P. Abbott.

First, the city's political classes were tied to the southernmost part of the island,
because in the eighteenth century, the seat of the King's colonial government was
housed in and by the fort. The municipal government ran its operations from the
Stadthuys (City Hall) along Broad and Pearl Streets, until 1700, when the City Hall
moved to Wall Street, where the Federal Sub Treasury building is today.

North of the core was a belt of relatively well-to-do artisans and craftsmen.[21] Because of the difficulty in moving goods (either inputs or outputs), industry was tied to port or the source of inputs. Ship builders lined the northern sections of the port along the East River, and their workers lived in neighborhoods nearby. Tanning was tied to the location of water, needed for softening and curing hides. Slaughterhouses were also located away from the city so as to keep their noisome activity separate from the population.

The commercial quarter, along Pearl and Water Streets, was where merchant activity was most evident. The trading houses were located a block inland from the river. Dealers in staples, such as sugar, clothing, and groceries lined Queen and Dock Streets (near Hanover Square and Water Street today).[22] A little further to the west, at the lower end of Smith Street (today William Street near Hanover Square) was the center of retail trade.

Hanover Square was the business center of the city. The Customs house, at different times, was located on lower Broad Street and near Whitehall Slip. The Exchange, a market and meetinghouse, was located at the foot of Broad Street, the Exchange Coffee House was at the foot of Broad Street, and Merchant's Coffee House was at the foot of Wall Street. Coffeehouses along Wall Street would drive the street's rise as a financial capital, as they were where merchants met to conduct business and catch up on the news.

The homes of wealthy merchants were near the commercial activity of Hanover Square, and the houses of the city's most well-to-do were along Queen, King (Pine Street), Wall, Smith (William Street north of Hanover Square), Broad, Duke (Stone), and Dock Streets. The most fashionable area, however, was near the fort and the Governor's mansion—at the "court end" of town, directly east of the fort. Houses on lower Broadway had views of the Hudson, and the wide street was lined with trees. Thus access to trade and government were the key criteria which the upper classes used to locate their residences.

The working classes lived further north of the tip, in the geographic center of the city. Of the roughly 250 retailers, makers of consumer goods, and craftsmen in the city, Abbott finds that about 60% lived in the areas bound by Wall Street, Broadway, and Beekman Street to the north. The poorest citizens lived in the northern half of the Out Ward, beyond the palisades line which had been erected in 1745 as protection against the French. This wall extended from Warren Street on the Hudson River to James Street on the East River, and remained standing until into the 1760s.[23] North of the wall were some of the city's least desirable areas. The gallows for executions was located at the base of hill to the west of Collect Pond, as was the potter's field, and slaughterhouses. As well, in the upper West Ward was one of the city's centers of prostitution, near and around Kings College, where the Word Trade Center site is today.

The roughest and dirtiest neighborhood, however, was along the East River waterfront. The wharves that lined the river were filled with floating debris, timber, and garbage, and noxious odors abounded. It was crowded with taverns and boarding houses for sailors, known for their excessive drinking, fighting, gambling, and whoring. This transient population, ironically, could outbid other uses since they were likely paying "hotel" rates for shorter periods of time.

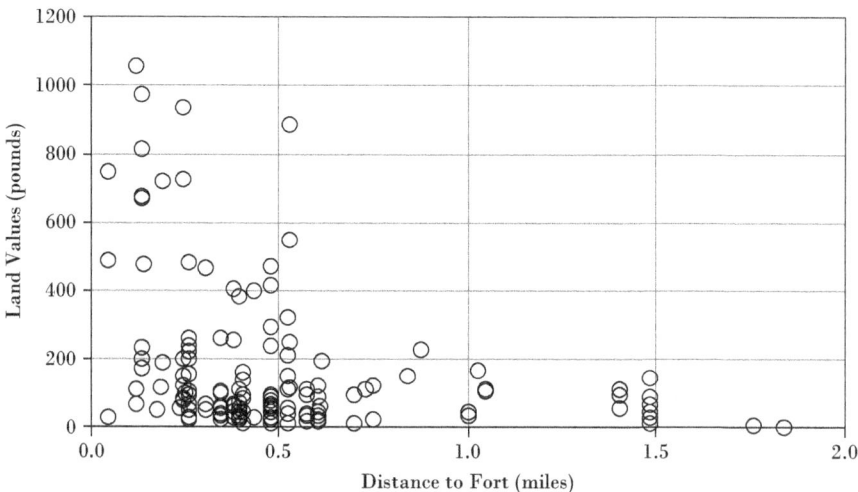

Figure 3.6 Land prices versus distance to the fort in colonial New York. This figure shows how land prices were highest closest to the fort, providing evidence that the upper classes and businesses were willing to pay the most to live in the heart of the city. Land values near the fort were orders of magnitude greater than those just a half mile away. Each dot is the inflation-adjusted price of a standard lot of land (25 x 100 feet) from 1667 to 1773 in New York-British Pounds.

Source: Data is from Valentine (1860).

During the Revolution, the city's economic fortunes experienced seven years of decline, since it was the headquarters of the British operations for the war. There was a mass exodus of non-Tory residents, and much of the city's trade came to a halt. During the occupation, two major fires destroyed large swaths of the city. British soldiers were garrisoned in the area between the Collect Pond and the Bowery Road.

After the war, when residents returned and trade began to reassert itself, the city picked up where it had left off. Enclaves before the war, returned to enclaves after the war. As the nation's first capital, the political elite were also tied to the lower tip. City Hall on Wall Street was converted to the Federal Hall. The city's importance as a political center would wane when Albany became the capital of New York State in 1797, and the Federal Government moved to Philadelphia a few years after that. But these early roots as a political seat would help lock-in the lower tip as the commercial and political center of the city.

Land-use patterns in colonial and Federal New York were consistent with the first set of predictions given by the AMM model. But the second prediction relates to the value of land. The battle for access and the right to occupy space based on the willingness to pay would suggest land values fell with distance from the city—in this case, the fort. Figure 3.6 shows the real (inflation adjusted) value of standard lots relative to the fort in the colonial period. The figure demonstrates how land values, on average, dropped precipitously with distance from the lower tip.[24] It thus provides further evidence for the AMM model. The most valuable lots were those nearly adjacent to the fort; by about 1 mile away, lots were worth orders of magnitude less than those in the heart of the city.

As figure 3.3 shows, between 1833 and 1862, the physical size of the city increased by 2,240 acres. The reason was the introduction of mass transit. Starting in 1829, a man named Abraham Bower launched omnibus service along Broadway.[25] The omnibus was an enlarged stagecoach fitted for urban transit by combining the functions of the hackney and the stagecoach. The omnibus was an instant success. By 1833, New York had 80 licensed coaches, and 683 coaches by 1853, with twenty-two separate firms competing against each other for passengers. At one intersection on lower Broadway, a coach was said to pass every 15 seconds.[26]

While the omnibus represented a revolution in urban travel, it was no panacea. The cars were overcrowded, and the condition of the streets—paved with uneven cobblestones—made the going hard on the spine. Coaches often moved at speeds of less than 5 miles per hour (consider that brisk walking occurs at about 3 to 4 miles per hour). Even by 1850, however, the omnibus was limited to a small fraction of the urban population who could pay for it; only about 25,000 people or about one resident in thirty used it in that year.[27]

The omnibus's problems promoted the search for a more pleasant form of travel. The answer came with the invention of the railroad. The first railroads in the United States were originally designed for the long haul of people and freight, but in 1832, the New York and Harlem Railroad was chartered to offer service from Lower Manhattan to 125th Street in Harlem. The Common Council granted the company the rights to the median along Fourth Avenue. Within two years, the cars operated from Prince Street up to 84th Street, with the tracks laid on open ground from 42nd Street northward. A single track ran from Prince Street to Union Place (Union Square East), and a double track ran north from 23rd Street. Within a few years, the road was allowed to run as far south as City Hall.[28]

The New York and Harlem (NYH) introduced a steam locomotive in June 1834, but an engine explosion increased the fear of this type of engine. After that, the railroad was required by city law to use horse power below 32nd Street and intermittently up to 42nd Street until 1876. North of 42nd Street the railroad used steam power starting in 1837.[29] It was the horse-drawn streetcar that would truly make mass transit possible.

Because the coaches were embedded in rails, it dramatically increased their efficiency. Now, each car only needed one horse to pull up to forty passengers.[30] Over the ensuing decades, beside the NYH, several parallel lines were built, including along Second, Sixth, and Ninth Avenues, in addition to several east-west lines.[31] By 1856, there were 23 miles of laid track, and the Second and Third Avenue lines reached as far north as 60th Street. Interestingly, omnibuses remained the only form of mass transit on Broadway until 1885, as merchants fought to keep rails off the avenue.

The introduction of the omnibus and horse-drawn streetcar created an inversion of land-use patterns. As business activity grew in the southern tip, it caused households to be priced out of their neighborhoods and promoted the separation of work and home life. Since land values rose so high in the lower portions of the city, only those businesses that were willing and able to pay the rents remained. However, rather than simply moving to the areas just above the business districts, the upper classes "jumped" over the lower income neighborhoods—the slums and the manufacturing districts that were on the northern fringes of the commercial area.

The upper classes moved directly to the northern fringes of the city, commuting to Downtown for employment and shopping. This is what I call the First Inversion, and it would have significant consequences for the skyline at the turn of the twentieth century. As will be discussed in chapter 8, the people living in the upper and middle-class neighborhoods in the northern suburbs would be the cause of Midtown's rise, not the bedrock valley.

Those neighborhoods that were working class before the 1820s would remain as such, and would then become attractive to the thousands of immigrants pouring into the city, starting in the middle of the nineteenth century. These earlier patterns would shape the land use in the second half of the nineteenth century, when even more immigrants poured into the city. The tenement districts described by Jacob Riis in 1890 had historical precedents that pre-dated the Revolutionary War. These population swells would also "trap" the expansion of Lower Manhattan, driving up land values there even more than would be the case otherwise. The upper classes would choose to live in the area roughly bound by Sixth and Third Avenues, so that as the population swelled, movement up the island would occur in vertical "bands" from east to west, with Broadway and Fifth Avenue as the home to the wealthiest residents and higher end commercial business. Income and occupational status moved down as one went closer to the river.

In order to investigate and provide evidence for the theory of the First Inversion, I collected data samples from New York directories in 1827 and 1849. The directories listed residents' names, occupations, and where they lived. For each year, I collected the residential locations of three groups: merchants, smiths, and laborers. Their addresses were then geocoded and mapped.[32] These three jobs were chosen because they are representative of three income classes, upper, middle, and lower, respectively.

Figure 3.7 shows a map of their residential locations for 1827. The graph shows that the merchants (gray dots), by and large, were living in the lower regions of the city; the laboring classes (circle-dots) remain on the northern areas, near the smiths (triangles). The modal distance for the merchants was about 0.6 miles from the tip, while the modal distance for laborers and smiths is between 1.8 and 2 miles north of the tip. Barely any laborers were living in the lower portion of the city (see the appendix H for more graphs). The data show that laborers and smiths generally lived equally far from the tip, with no clear differences in their location choices.

Figure 3.8 shows the northward movement of population as a whole in 1849. But within this movement, we see a change in the relative distributions of the population. The merchant classes now show three distinct patterns of land use. First, a large fraction of them still remain Downtown, within walking distance of their jobs. Second, another cluster formed to the west of City Hall, in the area where the World Trade Center site is today and up to St. John's Park, a wealthy enclave developed by Trinity Church. Third, another cluster of merchants is in the northern areas of the city, mostly congregated in the central regions, living between Greenwich Village and Tompkins Square Park. These are the suburban crowd, who "voted with their feet" and demonstrated their preferences for suburban living.

Between 1827 and 1849, the laborers also shifted their relative position, moving toward the outer portions of the city. As the city grew north and as business expanded up Broadway, the land values rose along the central corridor of the island, the laboring

N

Residence Location
⊙ LABORER
▲ SMITH
● MERCHANT

Figure 3.7 Home locations of merchants, smiths, and laborers in 1827. This map shows the residential locations of merchants, smiths, and laborers in 1827, collected from *Longworth's American Almanac, New-York Register* (1827). The map shows that as late as 1827, the merchant class was still living in the lower tip of Manhattan, followed by the smiths and followed by the laborers.
Source: Map by Eon Kim.

classes were priced out of their formerly central locations, and they moved toward the riverbanks where housing was more affordable.

Land-use patterns between the two periods show stark differences. First, the modal location for merchants was now about 2.6 miles from the southern tip, as compared to 1827, when it was 0.6 miles. Second, the laborers and the smiths showed little change in their modal locations, which were now at 2.2 miles, as compared to 1.8 and 2.0 for

N

Residence Location
- ⊙ LABORER
- ▲ SMITH
- ● MERCHANT

Figure 3.8 Home locations of merchants, smiths, and laborers in 1849. This map shows the residential locations of merchants, smiths, and laborers in 1849, collected from *Doggett's New York City Directory* (1849). The map shows "the First Inversion." After the introduction of the omnibus and streetcar in the 1830s, the merchant class "jumped" over the other classes, in order to live in the northern suburban fringes of the city. This was perhaps the first example of suburbanization in the United States. This northward movement of the upper classes would eventually contribute to the rise of Midtown. The areas occupied by the smiths and laborers would remain working-class districts and would attract the thousands of European immigrants pouring into New York starting in the mid-1840s.
Source: Map by Eon Kim.

laborers and smiths, respectively, in 1827. In other words, we see a clear "jumping" of the merchants over the laborers and the smiths.

In summary, we can witness the First Inversion by mapping the location choices of laborers, merchants, and smiths, three important classes of residents on Manhattan in the first half of the nineteenth century. While all groups showed a general northward trend over the first half of the nineteenth century, the merchants showed a decided "jump" over the laborers. The merchants, as representative of the upper classes in Manhattan, were on the vanguard of suburbanization in the second third of the nineteenth century. The laborers, however, remained in the historical working-class districts; though then tended to move outward away from the center, likely reflecting the rising rents toward the central spine.

THE IRISH AND THE GERMANS DURING THE FIRST IMMIGRATION WAVE

At the same time the First Inversion was taking place, New York began to experience a wave of mass migration never seen before in its history. In particular, Irish and Germans began pouring into the city by the thousands (see appendix I). The Irish were pushed by the Great Potato Famine, and the Germans sought relief from political and economic problems in their homelands. Between 1843 and 1856, 1.46 million Irish and 1.19 million Germans arrived in the United States. A large fraction of them settled in New York.[33] By 1855, a majority of the city's residents were born outside of the United States.[34]

The inflows of immigrants would have profound effects on the city, not the least of which was the battle for place. These groups represented the first set of non-British European immigrants to create intense competition with the resident population. This battle for place also occurs within the context that immigrants preferred living in ethnic enclaves. In 1860, there were approximately 200,000 Irish-born residents living in Manhattan, and they were concentrated in only a handful of wards.

To understand the land-use patterns at the turn of the twentieth century requires an investigation of these two groups and where they chose to locate throughout the first half of the nineteenth century. When the Italians and Russian Jews started arriving in the late nineteenth century, their residential choices were based on the locations of historical tenement districts, areas that had been primarily Irish and German.

Figure 3.9 shows the wards with the densest concentrations of Germans and Irish based on the 1855 New York State Census. The heaviest cluster of German immigrants was in Little Germany (Kleindeutschland), which was bound by the Bowery on the west and running from Houston to 12th Street. More broadly Germans were concentrated in the Tenth, Eleventh, Thirteenth, and Seventeenth Wards. The Irish clusters were mostly in the Fourth, Sixth, and Fourteenth Wards, with a large contingent in the Seventh Ward. A large pocket of Irish could be found in the Five Points neighborhood in the Sixth Ward.

The location choices of the Irish and Germans had to do with their socioeconomic status when they arrived in the country. The Germans, on average, had higher skills and greater incomes. They were also concentrated in artisan and manufacturing industries,

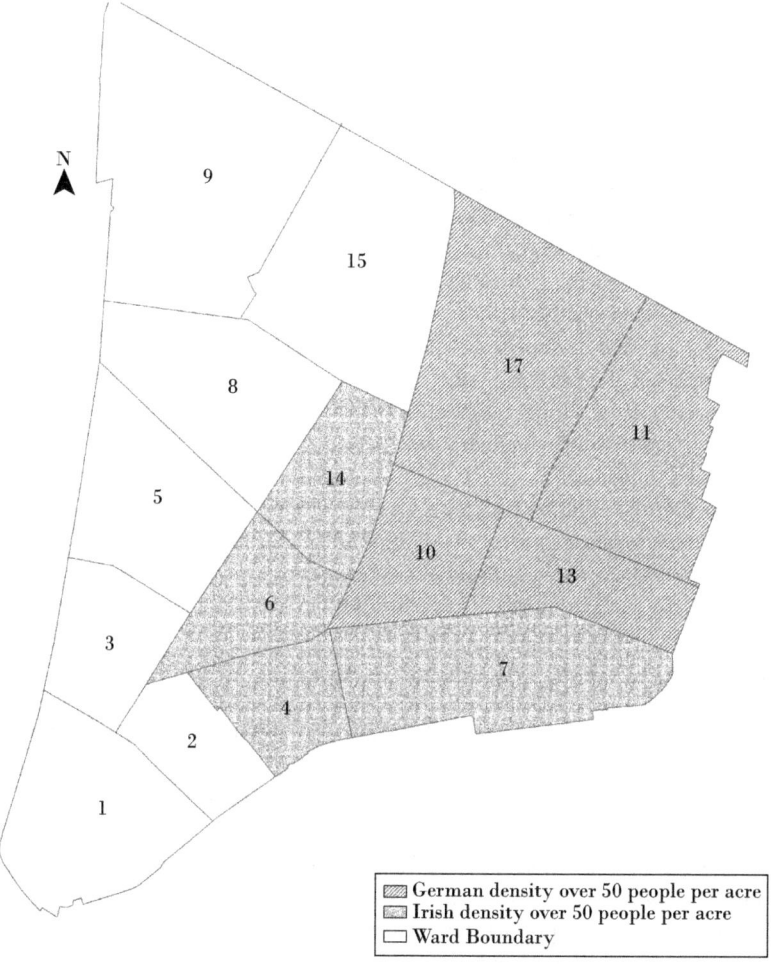

Figure 3.9 Irish and German population density by ward in 1855. This map shows the locations with the greatest concentration of Irish and German immigrants. By and large, the Irish concentrations were in the Fourth, Sixth, Seventh, and Fourteenth Wards. While the Germans tended to concentrate in what is today the East Village, Wards Ten, Eleven, Thirteen, and Seventeen. The map illustrates several important aspects of New York's land-use patterns. First, the Irish and Germans that migrated to this country tended to settle in the historical working-class districts. Second, the relatively less-skilled Irish clustered closest to Lower Manhattan where the housing was less expensive and access to work was easier. Third, the immigrant neighborhoods would form a kind of barrier around Lower Manhattan, putting upward pressure on land values there in the nineteenth century which would encourage the development of skyscrapers. Further this demographic barrier around Lower Manhattan would influence the rise of Midtown in the late nineteenth century, and which was not related to the depth of bedrock north of City Hall.

Source: Map by Eon Kim. Data from Ernst (1949).

which were less directly tied to the port, per se. About a quarter of the German work-force was employed in the clothing industry; only 11% were laborers or domestics.[35] The German choice of the relatively northern wards was an indication of their better position vis-à-vis the Irish. Tailors and craftsmen were settled in this area starting in the 1820s, and the area was likely "seeded" by earlier generation of craftsmen of similar European origin. Jewish immigrants, who had been settling in the city since the days of Peter Stuyvesant, had been living in the Lower East Side since the 1820s.[36]

The Irish immigrants had mostly come from rural backgrounds. As a result, they tended to work in low-skilled jobs. In 1855, the top employment categories of the Irish were domestics and laborers (55% of total employment). After that, they tended to cluster in semi-skilled occupations, such as in the clothing and shoemaking industries, which employed 12% of the Irish workforce. Cartmen (garbage haulers), painters, and masons constituted another 10% or so (see the appendix J).[37]

The Irish needed to choose an enclave that had lower cost housing and a central location between the port and construction and domestic jobs in the houses of the wealthy, mostly above Houston Street. For them, the natural draw was the Sixth Ward, which had been a historic manufacturing district and which had a large stock of older, working-class housing.

But the Germans and Irish were competing with businesses and the wealthy for the right to occupy locations in the city. Commercial and retail operations were moving up Broadway and crowding out residences along the side streets, and the wealthy were congregating in enclaves north of Houston Street. The "bulge" of the Lower East Side allowed for an accommodation of these immigrants, since it was the widest part of the city north of the port. The Irish, on the other hand, remained in the old northern fringe.

These patterns of land use would have several important ramifications for the rise of the skyline in the 1890s. First, the Irish and Germans established the main parts of the island that would be reserved for immigrant enclaves. In particular, the Jewish Lower East Side would begin where the Germans "left off" and the Italians would move into the old Irish neighborhoods. Little Italy and the Lower East Side would remain a wall against the northward movement of Downtown and its skyscrapers.

Second, the massive population influxes into the city would then move based on a particular land-use flow. Newly arrived immigrants would pour into the heart of the old working-class neighborhoods, making them some of the most overcrowded places on the planet. Over time, as these residents achieved a certain level of social mobility, they would fan upwards, along the areas between the central spine and rivers. The next generation of arrivals would move into the neighborhoods where the older groups were leaving. Midtown would form in the central pocket between 14th and 42nd Streets, hemmed in by the immigrant and working-class communities.

THE RISE OF FIVE POINTS: SEPARATING MYTH FROM REALITY

Perhaps no other neighborhood in nineteenth-century New York has a more infamous reputation than Five Points. To be sure, there was plenty of poverty, vice, and crime, but its reputation as a low-down, no-good slum clouds our ability to see its positive aspects. It was also a place of strivers and social mobility; a source of comfort and protection to the immigrants who came there, albeit at a greater density and dirtier than most neighborhoods.[38]

Five Points was centered at the intersection of three streets, Worth, Baxter, and Park; the Five Points neighborhood more broadly ran from Centre Street to the Bowery, and Pearl Street and Park Row to Canal Street. Today, Five Points proper no longer exists, but the area is part of Chinatown. In 1842, writer Charles Dickens chronicled his experience in his *American Notes for General Circulation* based on his tour through its streets (see the epigraph for this chapter). In the book, he describes the poverty and the foul conditions. Herbert Ashbury's *Gangs of New York*, published in 1927, wrote of the violence and moral depravity, and did little to change the people's perceptions.[39]

The historiography, however, has been based on several implicit and explicit assumptions about income and land use. Most important is the idea that the poor were essentially forced to live in the most environmentally degraded neighborhoods because they were locked out of the more salubrious environments by the middle and upper classes. Five Points, it is believed, was caused by its being on low marshy ground, and that further, no self-respecting person would dare to live in a neighborhood with wet ground, bad sewage, and the "miasmas" produced by decaying garbage and organic matter. A typical modern quote summarizes this thinking: "A recently filled-in pond below Canal Street became an area known as The Five Points—the worst overcrowded slum in the United States, if not the world, with inadequate services for sanitation, health and welfare. Those unwilling to commit their families to the misery of the Points or unable to afford the tenement rents, settled on vacant land north of the city."[40]

Its mythical status as the "world's most notorious slum" has replaced some important realities. Regardless of the environmental factors, Five Points is exactly where one would predict a low-income dense residential settlement to be in a developing city.[41] Its historical location on the fringes of the city then became a central, older location after the First Inversion. The AMM model would predict it to be a working-class neighborhood based on the battle for place. In addition, the effect of the Collect Pond on the neighborhood is misunderstood.

The conventional understanding is that the pond created an environmentally terrible neighborhood. But the truth is just the opposite. The reason it was so environmentally poor was because it was so attractive. That is to say, it was not a high population neighborhood because the environment was so bad, but rather, it was environmentally poor because it was overcrowded with people who wanted to live there, despite the poor conditions of the streets, and the rapid spread of illness. As will be discussed more in chapter 4, there is no evidence that the lower classes were systematically living in the environmentally worst areas across Manhattan, as there is no relationship between the environmental quality of the neighborhoods and the population density, once other important variables are controlled for.

Second, neighborhoods with rapid population growth indicate that the area is attractive; that is, it literally attracts people. Lower density areas are ones where people have chosen to avoid. Five Points contained some of the highest populations in the city because it was a place where people wanted to reside.[42] Flip this idea on its head: when New York in the 1970s was losing population, it was because people—rich and poor alike—did not want to be in there.[43] The city's manufacturing base was disintegrating, and housing abandonment was rampant. In the nineteenth century, with population bursting at the seams and rents rising, housing abandonment was likely nonexistent. Rather, landlords were continually trying to figure out how to produce more units of housing on a given lot to accommodate the rising demand.

The array of options for poor people is more limited, but they do have choices. There was no law that said the poor Irish immigrants coming into the city had to live in Five Points. Immigrants could choose other locations on the island, in the metropolitan region, or, like countless other folks, they could come to New York, save a few dollars and move on to other parts. There were also areas of the city that were undeveloped and allowed for less dense living. If an immigrant was trying to save money, squatting in the north would have been the cheapest thing to do.

In regard to housing, the poor must live tightly clustered, simply because they cannot afford to pay for bigger apartments. Poverty also means that the services provided will be limited because amenities, such as running water, mean higher rents, which were generally beyond the means of the working poor. Antebellum New York had a robust rental market, where, even within tenement buildings, there were a variety of apartment types and rents, which aimed to match households with the types of apartments they wanted. As will be documented later in this chapter and in chapter 4, this market was providing affordable housing, which cost about 25% to 30% of a household's income.

Poverty and density combined, however, can contribute to a host of unintended neighborhood problems, such as the under-maintenance of the housing stock. The poor are renters, and as such, they were not responsible for, and have little incentive to invest in, the maintenance of their residences. This is a simple economic fact that is an example of the classic externality problem: Why should one individual or family spend too much of their time and resources to keep a tenement hallway neat, for example, when a hundred other people are going to enter with their muddy shoes and dirty it up anyway? If renters in a dense building underinvest in maintaining the building, it will depreciate quite rapidly. Expecting that buildings are going sour fast also means that people will not bother to maintain it, thus speeding up its depreciation, and thereby making rapid depreciation a self-fulfilling prophesy. The owner, knowing this, participates in the "milking" of the property to preserve the return on his investment.

The Pond and the Points

For much of the city's early history, Collect Pond was a source of natural beauty and recreation. Until the turn of the nineteenth century, the pond was on the outskirts of town. In the winter, skaters could be found there, and during the summer, fishing offered relaxation. Peter Stuyvesant encouraged two small settlements to form there to protect the farmers who lived outside the wall. The first settlement was established on the northeastern banks of the pond near the Bowery. A second hamlet further north called the "Negro Coast" was made up of freed African Slaves, who worked for the Dutch West India Company. Taverns, saloons, and inns lined the eastern banks, and along the road leading to the city, thus establishing the area around Chatham Square as an early commercial district. Day trippers would come from the city for the beer gardens or cock fighting.[44]

The area to the east of the pond began to see industrial development in the 1690s, when the tanners were forced to move their operations out of the city proper.[45] Tanning requires both still water for soaking the hides and running water for washing them. Over the course of the eighteenth century, the blocks east of the Collect became the center of the city's tanning industry. Workers would scrape clean the hides, rinse, and soak them, in order to soften and tan them into soft, pliant leather that has many so many useful applications.

Because of the water and the tendencies of businesses to cluster near each other, the neighborhood became a successful industrial area. Several other animal-processing industries developed alongside the tanners, such as slaughterhouses, rending plants, and bone-boiling operations, as well as two large ropewalks. Here, we see the rise of an industrial ecology, emerging from the symbiotic relationship across firms and workers. These firms were not only drawing the water from Collect Pond but were also buying and selling each other's products. The slaughterhouses would sell their carcasses to the tanners. The tanner would sell their scraps to rending plants, and so on.[46]

All of these industries, however, produce a lot of waste, such as offal, blood, and decaying carcasses, and there was no sewage system proper until well into the nineteenth century. These businesses were supposed to dump their waste offshore into the East River, but much of it was just thrown into Collect Pond, despite the prohibitions from doing so.

After the Revolutionary War, the city's footprint was expanding, and the tanning industry around the pond was no longer in the outer regions. The Common Council decided that the most expedient plan would be to fill it and create urban land for real estate; the streets over the pond were opened in 1811. The hills to the west were leveled; the canal draining Lispenard Meadows was covered over and became Canal Street.[47]

The tanners were forced out of the area; they moved to the west side and were joined by the harness and saddle makers; though the shoemakers remained. The area became attractive to other artisans, sellers of dry goods, brewers, and bakers.[48] The conversion to urban land was a success from a real estate point of view, as a profitable industrial and commercial neighborhood emerged in the first decades of the nineteenth century.

Archaeologist Rebecca Yamin and her colleagues have done extensive research on the place. In particular, they have chronicled the history of tax block #160, which was in the heart of Five Points. The block no longer exists, but it was bounded by Pearl, Baxter, Park Streets, and Park Row. Current federal and state laws require that if a construction site is deemed likely to have important historical artifacts, then an anthropological study must precede construction. In the early 1990s, the federal government wanted to construct a courthouse on the block. As result, a research team under the direction of Dr. Yamin was assembled to perform an archaeological dig and artifact analysis. From this, the team was able to reconstruct the missing history about the neighborhood and in the process, debunk myths about the residents' lifestyles.[49]

In 1790, block #160 had 18 male heads of households with a total of 64 people on the block. For these household heads, ten jobs were listed; five were leather-related: three tanners, one shoemaker, and one saddle/harness marker. Two were food related: baker and granary operator, the other three were house carpenter, merchant, and mariner.[50]

By, 1820 the population was 404 and the professions listed were a variety of retail and industrial trades, including smiths, shoemakers, grocers, and masons. The evidence suggests a working-class neighborhood; and is consistent with the directory data discussed above. White male adults were 29% of the population; white females were 24%; white children were 29%; 5% were black males; 8% black females; and 5% were black children (likely slaves). There was certainly nothing in the census record as of 1820 to indicate the neighborhood was a slum. Rather, the block had a mix of professions. The 1830s shows a very similar picture.

But the industrial character and the income and composition of the labor force in the neighborhood did produce smells and waste products that lingered in the streets. The real problem was that the success of the neighborhood was generating more waste than could be removed. There was no sewage system or running water. There was decreasing space for privies and a larger population that depended on them. Gravity sewers had been installed to remove rainwater and waste from the streets, but some lots on the former Collect Pond had sunk below the street grades, and the sewers no longer worked, as they were now below the level of the other pipes. Yards would flood on rainy days.

The demographics of block #160 and the Sixth Ward were soon to change drastically when the Irish starting pouring into the city. Between 1820 and 1860, the population of the ward would double, and the population of block #160 would more than triple. When the Irish arrived, they, of course, had to find places to live. For them, Five Points would be a natural focal point, given its historical location of employment and the relatively affordable housing stock.

Dr. Yamin finds that the stereotypes of Five Points do not hold up upon closer inspection. Her data support that the neighborhood around Five Points was one of social mobility. The ratio of males to females, and the age and marital profiles mirrored the city as a whole. The archaeological work also demonstrates this, where the residents owned objects consistent with those striving for a middle-class existence, including dolls, flower pots, china, and figurines.[51]

To date, no specific statistical research exists on the degree to which Five Points was directly promoting social mobility; there are, however, several suggestive pieces of evidence that low-skilled Irish immigrants were improving their life outcomes by residing in the neighborhood. The most detailed work to date is by historian Tyler Anbinder.[52] He researched the outcomes of destitute Irish peasants who emigrated from the Lansdowne Estate in southwestern Ireland during the Potato Famine and settled in Five Points. Once there, many of them eventually opened up bank accounts in the Emigrant Savings Banks. Anbinder collected data on the amount and frequency of deposits. His findings prompted him to write,

When I began investigating the history of Five Points, I assumed that the prevailing, gloomy picture of the famine-era immigrants would be borne out on its mean streets. Given that Five Points' residents were the most impoverished in antebellum New York, I expected to find them barely scraping by from payday to payday. But the bank balances . . . [of] . . . Landsdowne immigrants force us to reconsider such long-held preconceptions.[53]

About half of the Landsdowne households living in Five Points had enough savings to open a bank account by the mid-1850s; the average value of these accounts were $102 (unskilled wages at the time were about one dollar per day). Of all the accounts opened by this group about half were able to increase their holdings by more than 50%. While we cannot say for certain that living in Five Points was the cause for their accumulated savings, Anbinder concludes, "The bank ledgers suggest that, even while living in Five Points, the Landsdowne immigrants saved far more money than one would have imagined given their wretched surroundings and low-paying jobs."[54]

As we will see in the next chapter, by the end of the nineteenth century, the Irish living in Five Points had experienced a significant amount of geographic mobility which was consistent with economic mobility. In particular, the Irish enclaves made a decided shift northward; while the old Five Points gave way to the poorer Italian immigrants arriving in the 1890s.

Housing Prices in Five Points

We now turn to the question of how successful, in fact, were the tenements in providing affordable housing for the lowest income residents in the city? In an age with little government involvement, the real estate market had to function on its own based on the demands and incomes of the residents.

Over time, in the absence of restrictions imposed by say zoning or rent control, the price of housing and the cost of replacement should move together. If an influx of immigrants causes the prices of housing to spike, then housing construction becomes more profitable, and developers will rush to add extra units to reap the higher returns; the price of housing should then fall back down to a level that is close to its replacement costs.[55] Clearly, every resident would prefer an apartment with running water and sunlight in every room. But whether they could pay for it was another matter.

In the mid-1850s, nearly half of Irish immigrants were either domestic servants or laborers. The average weekly salary of a laborer or unskilled worker was about $5.00.[56] If we use as a rule of thumb that an upper limit for the cost of housing is 30% of income, then the evidence suggests that, on average, the tenement landlords were, in fact, providing affordable housing, as average monthly rents for small apartments were about $5.00.[57] That is, builders were constructing the level of housing that the income of the residents would dictate. Further, the evidence also suggests, and we will look into this in more detail in chapter 4, that tenement landlords were providing a range of housing sizes and qualities, even in the "slums," to cater to the tastes and incomes of the residents.

Thanks to the efforts of economic historian Robert Margo, we have data on the cost of housing in antebellum New York. Figure 3.10A shows the monthly average cost of renting a two-room apartment in Five Points from 1831 to 1860, along with the growth of the population during the same period. The rents were adjusted for inflation using 1860 as the base year. In 1831, rents averaged in the $5.00 per month range, when Sixth Ward population was 13,000. From 1831 to 1847, the population showed steady increases, yet the price of housing showed no upward trend, just fluctuations around the $5.00 range. After the financial panic of 1837,

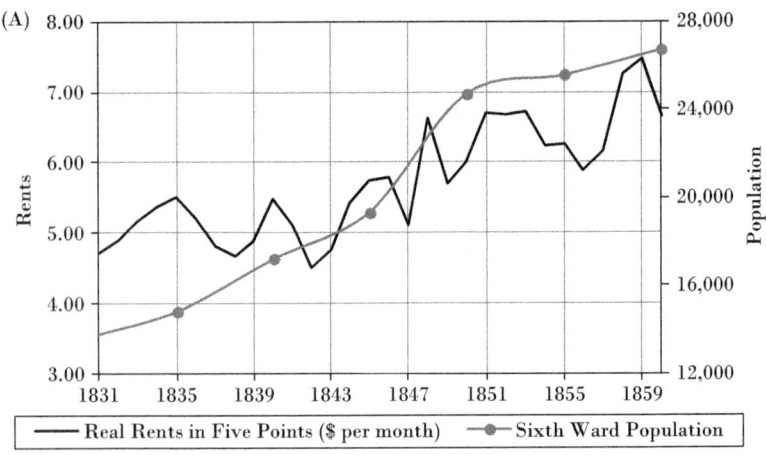

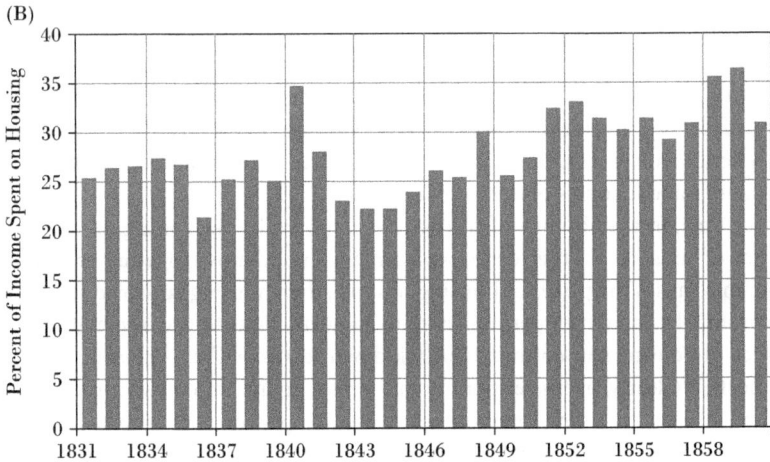

Figure 3.10 Rents and population in Five Points from 1830 to 1860. Figure *A*, shows (inflation-adjusted) apartment rent prices in the Five Points neighborhood for a two-room apartment of average quality. Rents averaged in the $5 range until the great influx of Irish immigrants and then they began to rise. Also provided is the population of the Sixth Ward. The graph shows that, by and large, during the period, the population of the Sixth Ward grew faster than average rents. This suggests that builders were able to provide relatively affordable housing for this set of the population seeking to live in New York. Figure *B*, shows the percentage of income spent on housing for laborers in Five Points during the period. The graph shows that, on average, laborers spent 25% to 30% of their income on housing over the period.

Source: Underlying rent data is from Margo (1996). Population data is from Ernst (1949). Wage data is from Wilentz (1984), *Engineering News Record* (1948), and *Historical Statistics of the United States* (2014).

rents fell to a low of nearly $4.25, which suggested that as incomes fell, rents fell with them, given the limited ability of workers to pay; this was occurring despite the fact that the city and the Sixth Ward continued to show large population gains after the panic. [58]

Starting in the mid-1840s, as Irish and German immigration began in earnest, the population of the Sixth Ward shot up from about 19,000 in 1845 to 26,700 in 1860,

Figure 3.11 Constrained Manhattan, 1865. This map shows that Lower Manhattan was relatively land-constrained. Looking at the larger circle, we can see that within a 1-mile radius of City Hall, only about 25% of the land was available for residences. The rest was used for commercial activity and the remainder of the area was water. That fact that Manhattan was so constrained meant that land values were higher, which promoted skyscraper construction Downtown and dense tenement districts north of City Hall. The waves of European immigrants needed to live within walking distance of their jobs and so they had little choice but to cluster near Downtown. But, because of Manhattan's peninsula-like nature, this generated much greater population concentrations than would have otherwise if more land were available.
Source: Map created by Eon Kim. The population density data was geocoded by Carlos Villarreal from the 1865 map in Metropolitan Board of Health (1867).

an increase of 38% in fifteen years or about 2.1% per year. Yet, the real price of housing peaked at $7.50. In other words, the population of the Sixth Ward doubled in thirty years, yet saw only a 50% increase in rents, on average. The evidence also suggests that wages were rising in this period as well, so the cost of living was more or less tracking income.[59]

Figure 3.10*B* shows estimates for the relative cost of an apartment for laborers from 1831 to 1860 in Five Points.[60] The graph shows the percentage of monthly income spent on housing for this group for the period. Between 1831 and 1847, housing costs hovered around 25%; and then, when the neighborhood experienced the influx of Irish immigrants it moved up to an average of 31%.

As the demand for tenement living drove higher prices, developers were trying to create housing as best they could, but there were severe constraints on what could be provided. First, no tenement landlord would build more than five or six stories, since even the poorest individuals would not pay rents on those floors to make it profitable. Second, the island of Manhattan was constricted by its long and narrow geography.

Looking at a stylized map of Manhattan shows this. Figure 3.11 presents a circle with radius of 1 mile from City Hall. The land-use model predicts concentric bands of land uses emanating from the center. After the First Inversion, the inner band became mostly commercial; the next band was the immigrant classes, and the next outer band was middle-class housing, and so on. But Manhattan presents a special case since the tip is triangular in shape. Within a 1-mile radius of City Hall the vast majority of the area was "off limits" for housing. Nearly half was water and, another quarter was the financial district and port. This left about one-third to one-fourth of the land available for housing. This is a severe restriction on the supply of land for the tenement classes. Yet, despite this restriction, the price of housing rose only quite modestly before the Civil War. Given how little land was available for tenements near the business district, it is a wonder that prices were as reasonable as they were.

4

The Tenements and the Skyline

All about you to the south blink the frowsy, scaly, slatternly, bleary, decayed, and crumbling old houses, leering from dirty windows like old drunkards through bloodshot eyes; the broken shutters awry like deformities, the doors agape like old, toothless mouths.
Charles Edward Russell

LAND USE AND THE TENEMENTS

Every city is a patchwork of neighborhoods. Each is defined by its types of architecture, the economic and demographic profile of its residents, and its history. But just as important, a neighborhood is embedded in an urban system and is defined by what surrounds it and how it affects, and is affected by, the city in general. Residential areas emerge based on the location of employment, shopping, parks, public transportation, and other amenities. Commercial and office districts, in turn, develop based on the access to employees, transportation routes and ports, industrial districts, and so on. The city is an interconnected web of neighborhoods and micro-economies.

At each place, developers will build the types of structures that will generate the highest return. They will not build housing when offices would be better. And if they are going to build housing, the quality, height, density, and style will depend on who will occupy them. The occupants, in turn, are determined by the neighborhood characteristics, the level of income, and access to other important places.

The decisions about where to locate are also related to the lock-in process. Once a neighborhood is selected for a type of activity, it tends to stay that way because of the agglomerative forces that draw households and businesses together. Law firms, for example, rely on the host of related firms and other law firms to remain profitable. This causes a positive feedback loop between old firms and new, cementing a location's use over time. Similarly with ethnic enclaves; the first few settlers from a particular nationality "seed" the neighborhood and make it attractive for other people from that part of the world.

Figure 4.1 gives a neighborhood map of Manhattan circa 1912, as produced by the *New York Record and Builder's Guide*.[1] The map neatly divides the city into mutually exclusive polygons of land-use types. It shows how the city can be carved up like the different cuts of beef on a cow. This chapter will discuss the emergence of this pattern, with a particular focus on the tenement districts at the turn of the twentieth century.

The choices for work, home, and play made in the last decade of the nineteenth century gave rise to the shape of the skyline we see today. This is demonstrated in figure 4.2, which shows the relationship between skyscraper height and population density in 1900. Each Manhattan block north of Chamber Street was

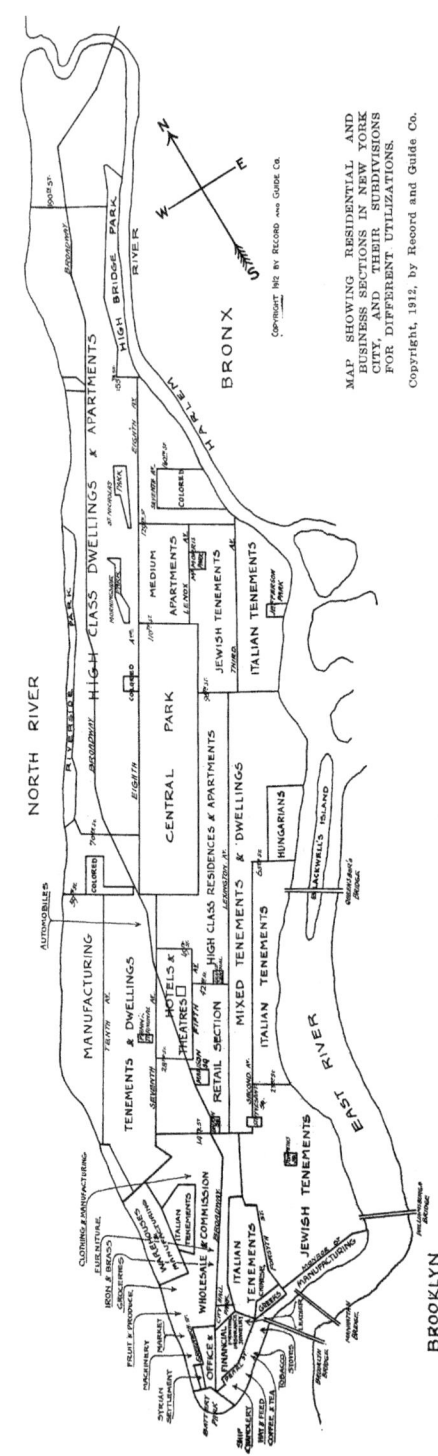

Figure 4.1 Carved Manhattan, 1912. This map, originally printed in the *New York Record and Builders' Guide*, shows how New York in the early nineteenth century could be carved up into distinct neighborhoods based on land use or ethnic composition of the residents. We can see how the streets closest to the rivers were used for industrial and transportation-related activity. Next inward were the ethnic enclaves. In the center spine we find upper class residents and commercial activity. This graph shows how the battle of place causes economic activity to segregate based on what each group is willing and able to pay to be at various locations.

Source: New York Record and Builders' Guide (1912).

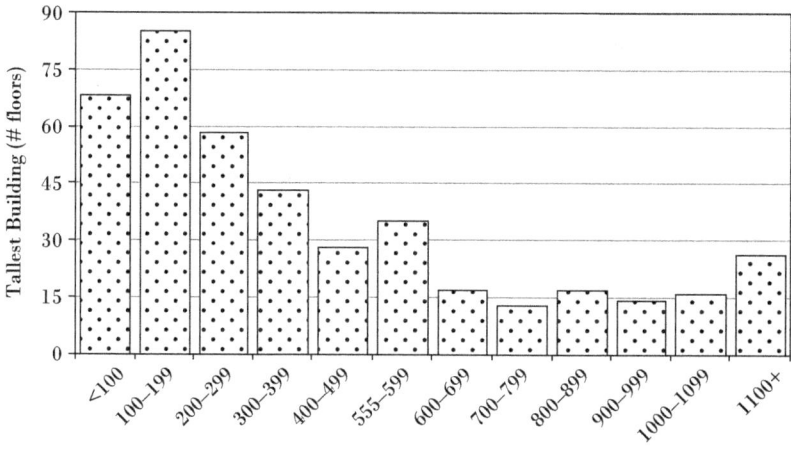

Population Density in 1900 (people per acre)

Figure 4.2 Height in 2013 versus population density in 1900. On the horizontal axis are the different levels of block-level population density in 1900. In other words, the population density of each block was put into one of the categories. I then looked at the tallest building as of 2013 among the blocks in each category. We can see that today the highest buildings were constructed in areas that had relatively low population density in 1900. In other words, the location choices of immigrants at the turn of the twentieth century would have important ramifications for the location of skyscrapers in the twenty-first century. *Source:* Underlying data is from MAP PLUTO (2013) and *First Report of the Tenement House Department* (1903).

put in one of several bins based on its 1900 population density. I then identified the current tallest building (as of 2013) in each of the density bins. That is to say, the aim is to see the relationship between population density at the turn of the twentieth century and building height today. The figure shows a clear pattern: the tallest buildings in the city reside in the neighborhoods that had the lowest density over a century ago. It demonstrates that skyscrapers and tenements did not mix. Where the tenements located, the skyscrapers did not and vice versa.[2] It also shows the lock-in principle—land uses over a century ago continue to influence land uses today.

In 1916, the city regulated real estate by introducing the nation's first comprehensive zoning law, which would legally establish what types of development could occur on each lot in the city. Starting in the mid-1960s, historic preservation would significantly reduce the amount of new development that could occur in landmarked neighborhoods, such as Greenwich Village and the Upper East Side. Today, much of the pattern of real estate types has been "frozen" by these regulations, as one of the key aims of zoning and historic preservation is to slow down or prevent the rapid change of a neighborhood's density and land uses. In this regard, the regulations have been quite successful.

The battle for place between tenements and skyscrapers was fought in very constrained territory. When the Skyscraper Revolution began in the 1890s, Manhattan housed nearly 1.5 million people on a narrow island of 22.7 square miles. This figure, however, dramatically overstates the amount of available land, since much of it was used for streets, parks, and other non-real-estate uses. Central Park, for example, removed 1.3 square miles from the grid.

Certain sections of the island were de facto off limits because the lower classes were simply unable to compete there. Lower Manhattan, south of Chambers Street, was reserved for firms who needed to be near the port and Wall Street. The streets north of 155th street were not yet accessible to most residents in the 1890s, before the subway. The blocks along the shorelines were also blocked for large-scale residential development because factories, gas works, slaughterhouses, shipbuilding, and other port activity needed to be there. Finally, commercial, retail, and the wealthy were winning the battle to occupy the spine of the island along Fifth Avenue and Broadway.

This meant that tenement districts were just outside the central districts: just north of Downtown and just east or west of the spine. Figure 4.3 provides a stylized "map" of Manhattan. The white areas were available to lower income families, or rather were the places where they would win the battle for place. The gray parts are where businesses and upper income residents outbid the lower income households. The middle rectangle is "Central Park" and the circle is the "financial district." The striped regions along the edges were port or industrial areas that needed to be near the water for shipping or other reasons.

It was along the margins of the neighborhoods where the battle was particularly fierce. The tenement builders could never compete to be in the center, but going

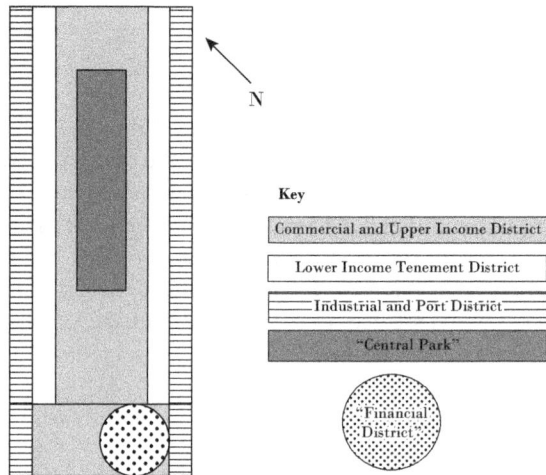

Figure 4.3 Stylized Manhattan, 1900. This figure is a stylized depiction of land-use patterns on Manhattan and how the island's narrow but long shape influenced these patterns. The light gray areas in the middle are those parts with commercial and upper classes residences (the rectangle in the middle is "Central Park"). The white areas were the location of middle-class and tenement districts. The striped areas along the edges were the location of shipping and manufacturing districts. Because of Manhattan's shape, the location of the border between the white area and the light gray areas would determine how much space was available for offices. Because of large influxes of immigration, the business districts were smaller than otherwise, putting pressure on land values and promoting the rise of skyscrapers around the turn of the twentieth century.

Source: Figure by Jason M. Barr.

outward toward the rivers from say Fifth Avenue, tenements and other uses would pay roughly the same amount for the right to be there. The question then becomes: By the end of the nineteenth century, where was the border between the commercial and tenement districts?

This border had been moved inward, toward the center, because the massive immigration waves over the nineteenth century meant that so many people were looking for housing. That is, the demand for tenements was so great that they were bidding up land rents, which in turn meant that tenement building could outbid other uses. The tenement neighborhoods, from about 1830 to 1910, crowded with the "huddled masses yearning to breathe free," moved upward and outward on the island, and filled in much of the available land for housing.[3]

The economics of low-income housing led directly to the five-story walk-up as virtually the only possible response to the massive immigration occurring in the nineteenth century, in light of little government intervention. The poorer classes, despite their poverty, were not willing to pay to live in an apartment above the fifth floor. Elevators would have made the buildings unaffordable and not a practical investment for the tenement builder.

As the population grew, it increased the size of the residential neighborhoods at the expense of businesses, which had less area to expand; thus increasing land values in the remaining business areas and putting pressure on developers to build even taller buildings for office tenants who were willing and able to pay to be in these buildings. Business, unlike low-income residents, had both the interest and income to build up. In fact, they had no choice, given how constrained Manhattan was, both because of its insular and narrow shape, and also because so much of the land was used for tenements. In effect, Midtown was created because the immigrants were winning the battle for place along the competitive margins—they were moving in toward Third Avenue on the east and toward Seventh Avenue on the west, leaving a much more constricted business district. Every acre of land devoted to tenements, removed that acre for some other use.

Another important component of the battle for land use is the ethnic enclave. Foreign immigrants preferred living among their fellow compatriots. This desire influenced land-use patterns in two important ways. First, the greater the influx of a particular group in any period meant a larger enclave. Because newer immigrants tended to be poorer, this further put pressures on land values around the enclave on which they depended. Second was the social mobility of each group. The longer the time in the country the more income they had, which influenced the kinds of housing and locations they could choose.

Since the Irish and Germans came mostly in the middle of the century, by 1890 they were relatively more decentralized than the newer immigrants, such as the Russian and Polish Jews and the Italians, who began their massive influxes after 1880. While the Irish experienced economic gains over the nineteenth century, they still remained tied to less-skilled occupations, such as those in construction and dock work. The Germans, on the other hand, saw much greater mobility and they tended to live the farthest north on the island; having re-formed their Kleindeutschland in Yorkville.

The Italians were the poorest of the late nineteenth-century immigrants, and they clustered in the oldest and most centrally located parts of the island, the Sixth and Fourteenth Wards, like the Irish before them. The Jews, similar to the Germans who preceded them, clustered in the Lower East Side because they were closely tied to the tailoring trade, and the housing stock was a little bit better. Plus, the Jewish immigrants clustered around their neighborhood institutions, such as synagogues, kosher food stores, and the host of other services related to their religion and culture.

The 1890s was the pivotal decade when the trajectory of the skyline was established, as by then the Great Battle for Place was being concluded among the different classes, ethnicities, and businesses. By 1910, because of the new subway system, higher incomes, and the Tenement Housing Act of 1901, the population of Manhattan peaked at 2.33 million people (see appendix G). The 1916 zoning rules would formalize the neighborhood characteristics formed before the turn of the twentieth century.[4]

THE THEORY OF POPULATION DENSITY AND LOCATION CHOICE

What drove the location choices of residents across the island? In particular, where and why did the immigrants choose to live, and how did these choices affect the growth of the skyline at the turn of the twentieth century? To investigate these questions, we now turn to the economic theory of land use, as it pertains to the location of residences.[5] The fundamental assumption is that different groups are each competing for access to the "best" locations, and each has a different willingness and ability to pay for these locations. The winning group for a particular area is the one that pays the most at a particular place. In this sense, we revisit the Alonso-Muth-Mills (AMM) model discussed in chapter 3, but now the focus is on housing and population density.

The key assumption of the model is that households have to pay to commute to the central business district. If they live further away they pay more for commuting, since living close to work means much less time and expense spent on daily travel to work. The more time and money paid for commuting, the less is left over to pay the rent. The fundamental insight then is that housing prices will be higher at locations with easier access to employment. The closer the household is to work, the more money it has to pay for this right, since it saves on commuting expenses. Housing is cheaper, per square foot, further away from the center because people have less money to pay for it, and so the cost of housing falls as one moves away from the center. The price of housing, in turn, affects the economics of population density.

Density, say on a given block, is measured as the total population divided by the size of the block; that is, by people per acre. But to better understand the economic and social forces that drive population density across the city, we can divide density into three different parts. Part one is how much physical shelter is provided on the block, part two is how much housing is rented per household, and part three is the average household size (see the appendix K for the equations that show this).

First, the total shelter per acre is also called "structural density." Imagine two identical apartment buildings side by side, except one has four floors and the other five. The second will have greater structural density because it more intensely uses the land. Second is the average amount of housing rented per household, which is called "housing density." If we take two identical households, but one rents 500 square feet of space and the other rents 1,000 square feet, then the first has a greater housing density, since it rents less space per household. Third is average household size; the larger the average family size, the greater the density, all else equal.

Holding housing quality and income constant for now, the higher the price per square foot that consumers have to pay, the greater the density will be. A high rental price will motivate developers to use the land more intensively, either by building more floors, or by building more structure on the property, or both, since they can get a greater return from this additional housing; this is the law of supply as applied to housing. The higher the rental cost of housing means the more tenants will have to pay. As a result, they will rent smaller apartments; this is the law of demand as applied to housing.

But returning to the fact that being close to the central business district means higher housing prices, it also means that population density will be much higher there too. As we move toward the center, a higher price, because of better access, means households consume less housing, and developers will build more intensively. Moving further away, population density drops off relatively steeply, and neighborhoods become more suburban; since housing is cheaper per square foot, families consume more of it, *even when income and household tastes are identical.* This simple model can explain the near-universal pattern in the structure of cities across the world, where density falls moving away from the center.[6]

The Income Effect

In a world with equal income, prices and density rise closer to the center simply because of lower transportation costs. In other words, there is nothing in the model that drives the segregation of rich and poor. Houses in the suburbs are larger because they are cheaper per square foot. But what does income do to this process? Let's say we follow a family living on the Lower East Side as it experiences economic and social mobility. The household—a husband, wife, and three children—successfully pass through Ellis Island and rent a tiny apartment on Ludlow Street in the 1890s. After a few years of scrimping and saving, the family begins investing in real estate, while continuing to work in the clothing and tailoring industries.

With their small nest egg, they put down a deposit, and borrow the rest, to buy a tenement building in which they live, act as landlord, superintendent, bill collector, and so on. It does well for them. With the earnings, they buy another building, and it does well. Then they sell the buildings to finance the construction of a new tenement, which they then flip for a tidy profit and so on. They continue in the real estate business for years to come. Now, the family finds itself firmly in the middle class. To quote one nineteenth-century expert on immigration,

> Many tenements in Jewish quarters are owned by persons who formerly lived in crowded corners of others just like them; and from this population comes many and many a Broadway merchant and professional men in plenty. It is a common saying that from Hester Street to Lexington avenue [sic] is a journey of about 10 years for any given family.[7]

When a household finds itself with a higher income, it introduces a new set of trade-offs. If they move out of the neighborhood to one a bit further away, they not only have to pay for commuting, but they also spend more time doing so. Staying put is desirable in that sense. But if we assume, and as stands to reason, that a wealthier family would like more space—a larger apartment—it is best to move, since they can get one for less money per square foot a bit further away from their current location.

So the question becomes: If a family moves further out from the center, do the benefits of more suburban living compensate the household for the time it must spend commuting? In chapter 3, we showed that the answer is "yes," and many other studies across cities in the United States also confirm this to be true: middle and upper income households consistently vote with their feet by moving to the suburbs when given the chance.[8]

The end result of this process is that the wealthy and poor will segregate in different parts of the city, concentrating poverty even more, which creates the additional problems mentioned in chapter 3. The free market for residential locations generates the "slums." That is, those who leave the tenements when they have money, exacerbate the problems of those who stay behind.[9] It is not just the rich "other half" in their Fifth Avenue mansions avoiding the downtrodden foreigners creating the "slums"; it is also the cycle of economic churning as the immigrants and their children move out of the neighborhoods when their incomes rise.

Amenities and Land Use

But there is something else that needs to be considered besides commuting and income: the location of amenities—those things that vary across neighborhoods that are determined by the history of the neighborhood, and that residents value or want to avoid (disamenities). Some neighborhoods are near parks, some are near elevated railroads, while others are made of poor quality landfill, and so on. The location of these amenities can have important impacts on where people live.[10]

But how these amenities affect population density depends on the interaction of income and the amenity's utility. If everyone universally prefers the amenity, there will be a positive relationship between closeness to the amenity, housing prices, and density. But if the rich strongly prefer the amenity, there can be a negative relationship between density and how close one is to the amenity, since the wealthy will not only outbid the other classes to live there, but will also consume more housing space with their higher incomes.

Nearly everyone values having greater access to transportation, and so naturally, housing prices will be higher closer to railroad or subway stations. But take the case of an opera house. It would seem that the wealthy would value being close to the opera house, all else equal, simply because wealthy people are more likely to afford the tickets and are more eager to attend the performances.

In this case, the rich outbid the poor to be close to the opera house—that is, they pay an "opera house premium." But then what is the relationship between the opera house and population density? This is not easy to answer. On one hand, prices are higher in that neighborhood because of the amenity, and so higher prices are associated with greater density. But, on the other hand, the wealthy are living in these neighborhoods, and so they use their larger incomes to live in bigger apartments. The net effect of the opera house on density could, in theory, be positive or negative depending on two things: how much the rich value being close to the opera house (how much they bid up prices) and how wealthy they are. The increased density associated with the opera house can be called the "amenity effect"; the reduced density from wealth can be called the "wealth effect." So ultimately the question becomes which is higher: the amenity effect or the wealth effect?

In some cases, the high price will encourage high structural density but low housing density. This can be called the "Central Park Effect." All along Central Park East and West, we see block after block of large, high-rise apartment houses for the wealthy. Living adjacent to the park affords great views, reduces congestion, and, of course, allows easy access to the park itself. As such, many wealthy families outbid lower income ones for the right to live next to the park. A similar pattern of land use can be seen along Riverside Park adjacent to the Hudson River. In these neighborhoods, we see many buildings but expansive apartments. Bigger housing units reduce density, but taller buildings increases density. Ironically, Central Park was designed as a people's park—the lungs of the city. Yet, its location, combined with the battle for access, meant that only the privileged could, in fact, live adjacent to it and have greater access to its green fields, rolling hills, and peaceful ponds.

Historical Lock-in

As discussed in chapter 3, the historical lock-in process is very important. That chapter demonstrated that the eighteenth- and early nineteenth-century working-class neighborhoods were those that were formerly on the fringes of the city. In addition, fertile Manhattan drew early settlers to those regions and promoted real estate investment in small hamlets, such as Greenwich Village, Harlem, and the Bowery. These early real estate investments then became crucial to land-use patterns at the end of the nineteenth century. In particular, the area north of City Hall and the Lower East Side drew the massive waves of Irish and Germans starting in the 1840s. They moved there not because the environment was so poor, but rather, because of the locational benefits, and their income and skill sets. The environmental roots of the Lower East Side was the combined effects of good soil, easy access to both the port and Broadway, and the land bulge of Alphabet City, the neighborhood south of 14th Street and east of First Avenue, which gave room for the immigrant classes to form their enclaves. Thus there is a long, but direct, relationship between the early settlement patterns during the colonial period and the rise of the tenement neighborhoods in the nineteenth century.

In summary, in a competitive housing market, the cost, quality, and location of housing will be determined by the willingness to pay at various locations. Without any distinction between income groups, housing will be more expensive closer to the center and hence there will be more density. But when we add amenities, early real estate decisions, immigration, and income to the mix, the density patterns become more complex, though not without specific patterns, to which we turn now.

DEMAND FOR DENSITY CIRCA 1900

The Tenement House Act of 1901 was New York's first housing law that had teeth. For several decades prior to that year, the city attempted to regulate tenements by limiting their structural densities and banning their worst features. But these laws were frequently evaded given the incredible demand for low-income housing, combined with corruption of public officials, the inadequate staffing of the relevant departments, and/or builders taking advantage of loopholes. The 1901 law created a Tenement House Department to enforce the new regulations (discussed later).

In one of its earliest acts, the Department undertook a detailed study of the tenement population and the quality and quantity of tenement houses. They issued a two-volume report in 1903.[11] Rather than collect the data itself, the Department obtained information, at the block level, from the 1900 U.S. Census. Data included the total population living on each block, whether the head of household was foreign or native, and the birth country of the parents of the heads of household. The report also listed the number of families and their sizes. This work contains arguably the most comprehensive data set about the Manhattan population density at the turn of the twentieth century.

Based on this data, figure 4.4 shows a newly created three-dimensional map of density across the island, north of the Third Ward and south of 155th Street. The greatest density is in the Lower East Side. But other pockets of density existed, particularly up and down the east and west sides.

This rich data set allows for a testing of several theories about the demand for density across the island. In particular, the goal is to see how the combined forces of immigration, neighborhood amenities, and early Mannahatta ecology influenced the battle

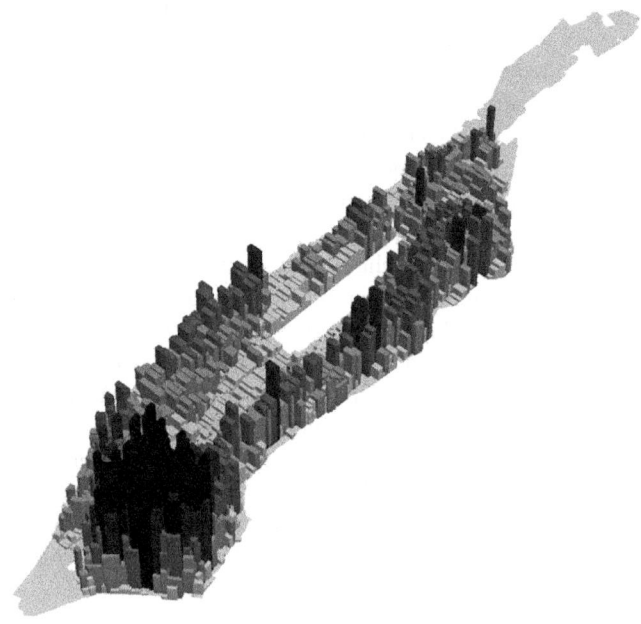

Figure 4.4 Population density in 1900. This map shows a 3D rendering of population density across Manhattan north of about Chambers Street and south of 155th Street. The greatest concentration of population was in the Lower East Side and the wards just north of City Hall.
Source: Map created by Eon Kim. Underlying data from First Report of the Tenement House Department (1903).

for place and the location of the tenement districts. In particular, in the next section, I will be discussing the results of several statistical (regression) analyses that use this and other data. Here I layout the important components that informed the statistical study.[12]

Immigration and Land Use

As discussed in chapter 3, the period between 1840 and 1865 was the first great wave of non-Anglo immigration. These newcomers were mostly Irish and German. By the 1880s, two new groups would become the majority of new arrivals: the Russian and Polish Jews and Italians. Their numbers passing through Ellis Island peaked between 1905 and World War I (see appendix I), with one final spike of Italian immigration in the early 1920s.

By 1900, these four major ethnic groups constituted the majority of the immigrant population. The Germans and Irish made up nearly 45% of the foreign-born living in Manhattan, while the Russian/Polish Jews and Italians were close to 30%.[13] Because these groups preferred living in enclaves, there would be a battle for place among each one. Immigrant communities would have their own willingness and ability to pay to reside in specific locations, and they each would have different preferences about living close to or far away from the others. This would produce a kind of enclave "dance" across the island.

So what were the factors that determined how this ethnic battle played out on the island? What does the economic theory predict about their location choices? The first relates to the economic characteristics of the group, which includes their incomes, social mobility, and employment profiles. The greater a group's income and social mobility, on average, the more likely its members would live further north on the island, since they can take advantage of better housing opportunities. Second, and relatedly, are the most common industries that employ an ethnic group. Those tied to the port, or port-dependent industries, were likely to be living closer to the rivers. On the other hand, those tied to clothing manufacturing jobs were likely to live closer to Downtown or closer to lower Broadway.

The Italians mirrored the Irish in terms of their skill levels and general poverty levels; while the Jews tended to mirror the earlier German socioeconomic profile, since they had more skills and were concentrated in manufacturing rather than menial labor. They seemed to have a greater predilection for rapid social mobility and by acquiring education to facilitate the process.

So the question becomes: How did immigration affect land use across the island at the turn of the twentieth century? Figure 4.5 presents some evidence. It shows the map of Manhattan based on the concentrations of the major ethic groups (the Big Four).

As the nineteenth century progressed, both Irish and Germans saw a degree of social mobility (though higher for Germans than Irish); they would "scatter" from their original ethnic enclaves. The Irish would fan upwards along both the east and west sides from their original locations in Five Points and the Seventh Ward. The Germans, on the other hand, would make a mass migration up to the Yorkville neighborhood, taking advantage of the streetcars and elevated railroads. The newer Germans who came toward the end of the nineteenth century would have their ethnic enclave in the

N
▲

Immigrant Population Concentration

▨ More than 40% Irish

■ More than 40% German

▯ More than 40% Italian

▨ More than 40% Polish and Russian Jew

Figure 4.5 Ethnic enclaves in 1900. This map shows the location of ethnic enclaves in 1900. The Italians were living in the most central area that had the lowest-cost housing. To the east was the Russian-Jewish enclave. The Irish had formed two enclaves, one on the east side and one on the west. There were two German enclaves: the new immigrants were living north of the Jewish wards in the historic Kleindeutschland, and a newer, higher income German enclave existed in Yorkville, just south of Harlem, which also had Jewish and Italian neighborhoods. On average, the location of an enclave was determined by time in the country, income levels, and occupation choices.

Source: Map by Eon Kim. Underlying data from *First Report of the Tenement House Department* (1903).

older Kleindeutschland in the East Village, centered on Tompkins Square Park. The Jews were concentrated in the Lower East Side in the Seventh, Tenth, and Thirteenth Wards. The Italians were concentrated in Little Italy along east of Broadway and also in the tenement district on the West Side between Canal and East 3rd Street.[14]

Each of these groups not only segregated into different parts of the city but also chose locations based on their relative incomes and time in the country. The poorer groups or those newly arrived were living closer to Downtown, where the housing was cheaper and residents were less in need of public transportation to commute to work. The Italians lived closest to the City Hall, followed by the Jews, then the Irish, and finally, the Germans. Furthermore, the Irish and Germans were much more spread out and this was likely due to the fact that they had been in the country longer, had larger incomes, and demanded newer and better housing.

The Mannahatta Effect

The natural environment could affect the location decisions of residents in several major ways. First is that the decisions of the earliest settlers could influence the desirability of urban locations centuries later. This is the lock-in principle, where earlier real estate and infrastructure development draws population growth to that area, promoting more growth and so on, so that a land-use type propagates itself throughout the centuries. Thanks to the herculean efforts of Eric Sanderson, we can use the information he collected on Mannahatta to test theories about the relationship between the early ecology—which was influenced by geology—and how this may have impacted land use at the start of the twentieth century, and therefore, the shape of the skyline.

One way to infer the early desirability of early agricultural locations is to look at the important ecological variables that may have influenced the decision of early settlers. First was the location of the tulip tree forests. These trees grew on the island's gently sloping hillsides, which were particularly good areas for agriculture.[15] On hilltops, the soil would be too dry, since the water would run down. The gullies would contain streams and wetlands; as a result, the soil was likely to be too wet for crops. The heaviest density of tulip trees was on the west side from Greenwich Village, north to around 40th Street, on the east side in the Lower East Side, and north to about 23rd Street. Two other variables of importance were included in the analysis. First was the availability of fertile soil, as discussed in chapters 1 and 3. Fertile Manhattan would be a natural draw for early real estate development. Second, the locations of stream and ponds would also likely be important, since they were sources of freshwater.

Another set of environmental variables, apart from those that help determine lock-in, would likely have a more direct influence on the health of the residents. In particular, the lower lying areas were likely to be wetter. Most important were the Lispenard Meadows-Collect Pond watershed and the filled-in salt marsh in the East Village, known as Stuyvesant's Meadows. One would suppose that these areas were particularly prone to flooding, wet basements, and to act as vectors for water-borne diseases. As discussed in chapter 2, much of the shoreline around Lower Manhattan was made from landfill. These areas were considered bad because the quality of fill was poor, and they were likely to have poor drainage.[16]

Given the claims that the poor were somehow forced into the worst environments, we can use the data on the location of wetlands, marshes, and made land to see what the population density was like in these areas, controlling for historical lock-in factors. If density was low in the worst areas, it would suggest that even the poor were likely to choose better areas. On the other hand, if density is highest in the worst environments, it would suggest evidence for a "Five Points Theory," where the poor were trapped into these neighborhoods by discrimination or other social and economic pressures.

Neighborhood Amenities

To understand the location choices of households on the island, we need to also investigate the amenity landscape as of 1900. Every location came with a certain bundle of neighborhood benefits, such as parks, mass transit stops, and other institutions. Those amenities that were of interest to all would likely increase density, as competition would bid up the value of housing close to these amenities (and the amenity effect would dominate the wealth effect). On the other hand, those amenities that were of particular interest to the rich would likely reduce density, since they would pay a premium to keep out residents not in their income class. Three amenities in particular were investigated: the distance to mass transit (the Els), distance to parks, and the relative location of houses of worship.

Turning first to the elevated railroad (Els), the earliest short road was introduced along lower Greenwich Street in 1868; and throughout the 1870s, the Els were expanded so that there were several parallel lines running up and down the island (see chapter 8). On the east side was the Second and Third Avenue Els, and on the west side was the Sixth Avenue El, which ran up Sixth Avenue until 55th Street, at which point it merged with the Ninth Avenue (Columbus Avenue) El, which ran up the rest of the west side. At 110th Street, it curved eastward and then ran up Eighth Avenue from there. The system was largely completed by 1879.[17] Els were much faster, since they did not have to contend with street traffic, but they ran on steam, which caused pollution. As well, many of the avenues containing the roads were in shadows and caused lower real estate values. Regardless, living close to an El was likely seen as a valuable amenity, as it gave residents easy access to the rest of the city.[18]

Next is the location of parks. Parks were obviously an important neighborhood benefit, since they are aesthetically pleasing; they reduce neighborhood congestion or the possibility that new development might block the light of surrounding buildings; and they allow for recreation and relaxation. Some parks, of course, are more valuable than others. Small parks offered less of the above. In particular, larger ones like Central and Riversides Park were lined with tall apartment buildings that housed the upper classes. This suggests that the demand for these locations among the rich was high, and this raised land values and thus the height and density of the buildings. Smaller neighborhood parks would presumably be less valuable to the rich, but valuable overall. The appendix L lists the parks as of 1900, their size, and the wards in which they resided.

Next are houses of worship. Closeness to a church or synagogue is an important factor for many people. Being near a house of worship makes practicing religion that much easier, but it also provides other benefits, such as socializing and catching up on news of the home country. We can hypothesize that the more houses of worship constructed prior to 1900 in a neighborhood, all else equal, the greater the residential density.

Access: Broadway, Downtown, and the Rivers

In 1911, economist Edward Pratt reported the results of a study that investigated the reason for such extreme concentration on the Lower East Side.[19] One of his findings was that hyper-density was tied to both the length of the working day and wages. The longer the work day and/or the lower the wages, the more likely workers were to cluster near their factory jobs in Lower Manhattan and along Broadway between Chambers and 14th Streets. Pratt's report highlighted the fact that there is a direct relationship between density and access to employment, especially among the lower class workers who could not pay for mass transit. As a result, living close to both Lower Manhattan and Broadway provides key benefits. The competitive battle for place and the segregation of workers by income is likely to generate higher density near these locations.

But also consider that being in Lower Manhattan or along Broadway is incredibly expensive because businesses pay the most to be in these locations, since locating in the center generates the most foot traffic and reduces travel times for clients and customers. Further, the wealthier residents are likely to cluster just off Broadway in order to have access to the commercial and retail districts along the boulevard. For this reason, we would expect to see low density on and near Broadway and rising density moving east or west away from it.

The final variable investigated is the distance to the rivers. On one hand, the port is a vital source of jobs. Not only did the city employ a vast number of workers in transportation, as stevedores, dockworkers, and shipbuilders, but industries that relied on the ports also lined up along the river. This is especially true for slaughterhouses, breweries, gas works, and coal yards. Their product was coming in through the port, either via ships or railroads.

In the Lower East Side, at the end of the nineteenth century, for example, between East Eighth Street and East Fourteenth Street, the East River and adjacent blocks were lined with factories and gas works. On two whole blocks (bound by Avenue D, East 8th, East 10th Streets, and the East River) was the Morgan Iron Works, a manufacturer of marine steam engines. North of the iron works, on East 10th Street, were several large industrial concerns. A tobacco works (B. H. M. Alpine) faced Avenue D, while the William T. Uptegrove & Brother Mahogany Saw Mill took the center of the block and the National Ice Company had a large facility adjacent to the East River. North of that, on the entire block bound by Avenue D, as well as East 11th and 12th Streets, was the New York Mutual Gas Works, with a large gas holding tank fronting Avenue D.[20]

Industrial companies outbid the poor to be there, since they required access to the river because of the expensive costs of importing and exporting their product. Those companies that had especially heavy products, were reliant on the port, or were engaged in selling for the regional, national, or international market were more likely to use these locations. The point is the density is going to be low along and near the river simply because residents are outbid there. However, being close to the jobs is important and we would expect rising density moving away from the rivers. However, there is likely to be low density near the rivers because of the pollution and so on.

DENSITY AND THE DATA

Recall that population density is determined by the supply and demand for housing. Thus we can view density as the result of several forces that might determine this demand and supply. For example, if a neighborhood amenity is in great demand, it will cause the price of housing to rise, and people will reduce the amount they consume, and this will increase density in a particular neighborhood. If a block is far away from the central business district, housing prices will be lower, and therefore density will fall since households consume more housing.

We now turn to the results of a statistical study aimed to discover what caused population density to vary across the island. To this end, I used the statistical procedure of regression analysis. A more detailed discussion of regression analysis appears in chapter 6, but the key idea is that the analysis allows for a "chopping up" of population density into different parts; it allows for a testing of the economic theories discussed earlier by seeing which demand and supply factors affected the number of people living on each block throughout the city. How much was influenced by the pre-European ecology, how much was influenced by the location of parks, and the Els, as well as historical density patterns? Given these results, we can see what was driving the immigrant and working-class communities to win the battle for place in their respective locations; and this would suggest what areas were then "left over" for skyscrapers.

The specific variable of interest is the block-level population density—that is, the number of people on a particular block divided by the area of the block (in acres). The blocks ranged from north of the Third Ward to 155th Street, since the 1903 Report excluded blocks that were in the lower tip (Wards One, Two, and Three) and those in the very north because of the very low density in these areas.

The greatest density in the city was 1,281 people per acre in the 17th Ward on the block bound by Allen, Orchard, Stanton, and Rivington Streets (the block was reduced to half its size when Allen Street was widened in the early 1930s). Consider as a modern benchmark a "typical" suburban residence with five people in a house on a quarter acre lot. This would yield 20 people per acre. The average block in 1900 Manhattan had 226 people per acre.

Two sets of regressions were performed.[21] The first set excluded characteristics of the immigrant population. The key question from these first analyses was to see if 1900 population density across the island could be explained, at least in part, by the three sets of variables: access, amenities, and the environmental factors. In the second set of regressions, prior immigrant densities (either in 1890 or 1855) were considered to see how they affected land-use patterns in 1900.

Overall, the analysis in the first set reveals that about 30% of the variation in density across the island can be explained by location, amenities, and Mannahatta. Another way to say this is that access, amenities, and the environment were important and significant determinants of the pattern of residential land use. But, they were not as important as the location of immigrant clusters, as will be discussed below. In other words, the number of immigrants, and their decisions about where they were going to cluster was more important than the other set of variables by 1900, though immigrant locations were influenced by the geological history of the island, and the historical lock-in process.

But perhaps most important for the first set of regressions is that the location of tulip trees in 1609 was a significant indicator of population density in 1900. The results suggest that if a block had tulip trees on it in 1609, its 1900 population density was about 25% higher than those blocks without the tree. Keep in mind that there were very few tulip trees left on the island at the dawn of the twentieth century.[22] These findings provide evidence that the skyline pattern was influenced by the environmental and geological factors discussed in previous chapters, at least in an indirect sense, in that it influenced early residential locations. Similarly, the location of freshwater sources in 1609 is positively related to population density at the early twentieth century, with density being about 8% higher on the blocks on average, all else equal.

The effect of fertile soils on 1900 density is a bit more complicated. In a regression that includes only the effects of the Mannahatta variables on density, fertile soil shows a positive (and statistically significant) effect. These locations were likely to have about 20% more people on them than non-fertile soils, all else equal. But, then, when the amenity and location variables are included, its importance goes away. In particular, it turns out the location of houses of worship and fertile soil was, statistically speaking, highly correlated. When measures of the number of religious buildings nearby were included in the regression, the fertile soil variable ceases to determine population density. This finding also lends support to the lock-in theory. Houses of worship were constructed near the early settlements, which attracted other buildings of the same type. So that by 1900, there was a strong relationship between the location of churches and synagogues, and where the fertile soil had once been.

Landfill neighborhoods—those neighborhoods that were once underwater during the days of Mannahatta—were avoided. They had population densities that were 40% to 50% less than the other regions, all else equal. This suggests that, to some degree, even among the poorest of the poor, the quality of the neighborhood was important. It offers a statistical rebuttal to the "Five Points Theory," which says that the worst environmental environments were reserved for the lowest income classes.[23]

The access variables show that density fell off moving north on the island, all else equal, and this provides evidence for the basic land-use model, which predicts higher densities closer to the center because it allows people to save money and time on transportation. The battle for place naturally created dense pockets like the Sixth and Tenth Wards simply because of their locational benefits to the lower classes. These places would have been tenement districts, regardless of whether the Potato Famine or the Russian Pogroms hit the European continent. Would Jacob Riis, a Danish immigrant himself, have written his book about the "other half" if migration patterns from Europe were different? Who is to say? But as long as the city attracted those with lower skills to work in the factories or at the port, the tenement districts would have been there just the same, though Manhattan's density would likely have been less.

The Lower East Side in the 1890s was the densest neighborhood on planet earth. Sanitation District A (a subdivision of the ward) in the Eleventh Ward had a population density of 968 people per acre. The northern European cities at the time did not come close. The densest neighborhood in Paris had a mere 434 people per acre, London's most crowded neighborhood had 365 people per acre, and Glasgow's most populated area had 350 people per acre.[24] Perhaps that is what the Lower East Side would have looked like if the city's migrants were mostly coming from the American hinterland.

The crowded tenements of the Lower East Side were squeezed in the area east of Broadway and west of the East River, just above the central business district. Broadway itself had the lowest populations, but moving east or west away from the center, population density peaked, on average, about a half mile away. In the opposite direction, moving from the shoreline inward, density was lightest but increased. The "sweet spot" is the region about a quarter mile from Broadway to a quarter mile in from the shores. This is where the "competitive borderlands" were located and where the willingness to pay of firms and residents were about equal.

Regarding transportation, distance to the El was important and valuable. The results show that, on average, moving a half mile away from an El stop was associated with a 25% drop off in density, all else equal. Parks were also an important amenity. Bordering a park was associated with lower density, as the wealth effect appears to have dominated the amenity effect. But nearby, density increased closer to parks. In other words, lower income families could not live along the parks, but they could live close nearby, but they paid more for the right to do so.

Immigration by Numbers

The statistical analysis also tells the story of immigrants and gives clues about the things that mattered most to them, in terms of where they chose to live on Manhattan. To understand how immigration influenced density, a two-stage statistical approach was taken.[25] The first stage aimed to understand the location choices of immigrant groups, and then, the second stage looked at total density, conditional on the immigrant locational choices. The results of the second stage show two things. First, the results discussed earlier on location and amenities still apply, even after controlling for immigrant location choices. Second, immigrant location decisions could explain an additional 35% or so of the variation in density across the island, which suggests that the location of enclaves was just as important as the location of Broadway or Lower Manhattan.

The first set of regressions reveal particulars about what mattered to each immigrant group, in terms of what each location across the island had to offer to them. In particular, I investigated the location choices of the heads of households of five categories: Germans, Irish, Russian/Polish Jews, Italians, and an umbrella "Other" category, which was all the other immigrant groups lumped together. The aim is to see how each of these groups were influenced by prior immigration and population densities, neighborhood demographics, and the Mannahatta variables described above. Each of the 1890 neighborhoods was a Sanitation District, where each ward was divided into one or more smaller units that comprised several acres (more about the Sanitation Districts later).

So how did Mannahatta 1609 affect the choices of immigrants at the end of the nineteenth century? The results confirm the findings discussed above. All immigrant groups were more likely to be living where the tulip tree once held sway. All immigrant groups, including the Irish and Italians, were less likely to be living over made land. Fertile soil was a positive indicator of all immigrant groups but one (the Italians).

The regressions also allow us to tease out each group's preferences about the others. Likely there was an inter-group dynamic, where some ethnic groups preferred living near others, while others preferred living apart. To this end, I investigated how each group's block-level 1900 density was influenced by the group and the other groups' presence in the neighborhood as of 1890. As would be expected, all groups were attracted to neighborhoods that had higher concentrations of their own group already there. However, for the other groups, the Germans were considered a type of neighborhood amenity—all the ethnicities showed increased density in the neighborhoods that had higher concentrations of Germans in 1890. Perhaps because of their higher wealth and skill sets, living close to them gave the other groups access to more resources.

The Germans, on the other hand, showed indifference toward living with the Irish and Italians, but they preferred to avoid the Jews, as there is a negative relationship between German and Jewish density. A neighborhood that had a 10% higher density of Jews in 1890 was associated with about a 1.4% reduction in Germans in 1900, all else equal. This confirms the findings of historians who describe how the older Germans, especially the older German Jews, looked down on the newer Jews, since they were seen as putting Judaism in a bad light for the Christian population.[26]

All immigrant groups preferred neighborhoods that were conducive to family life. The more children under five there were in the neighborhood in 1890, the more immigrants of all groups were likely to be there in 1900. Furthermore, by 1900, neighborhoods with high death rates (deaths per 1,000 residents) were avoided to some degree. The Italians had the lowest "avoidance rate"; while Jews had the highest avoidance rate. A neighborhood that had a 10% higher death rate was associated with 4.6% fewer Jewish heads of household in 1900.

One other variable of interest was explored: the width of the island. While immigrant groups preferred living with their own compatriots, the island's narrow geography could potentially constrain the size of the enclaves. Ethnic enclaves would presumably form along parts of the island where there was more room for them to exist. To this end, in the immigrant regressions I also included the width of the island at the same latitude as each block, to see if longer spans were associated with more density. This is a way to test what I call the Bulge Theory. The Lower East Side was likely attractive for immigrants, beyond the reasons discussed so far because from Broadway to the East River was a kind of bulge (Alphabet City). Did having this extra room draw more immigrants to the area? The results suggest the answer is "yes". For all groups, their densities are positively associated with long spans along the island. This implies that all else equal, the shape of Manhattan influenced where the immigrants would reside.

In summary, immigrant densities were based not only on the historic location of ethnic enclaves but also by the quality of the neighborhood. High-quality neighborhoods (dry soil, low death rates, and many children) drew greater population densities, as compared to those with lower quality. This, again, suggests that despite the relative poverty of the immigrants, they were not without choices about where to reside. Collectively they were choosing more favorable locations.

While thousands upon thousands of immigrants were pouring into the city each year, the ability of developers to provide housing was limited by their underlying economics. Tenants, no matter how poor, were unwilling to pay to live above the fifth floor. The additional expense of building taller did not generate enough income to make it profitable (and the cost of elevators was out of the question). In 1900, over 90% of tenements were five stories or less, with the majority at five stories, and 30% were four stories. A miniscule amount was taller than six stories, and it is likely that they were middle-class houses with elevators (see appendix M).

Given the tremendous demand for low-income housing, there were only a few ways that builders could provide it. The first approach was to use each plot more intensely. Such methods included renting cellars, erecting rear structures, or by not providing air shafts or other unusable space. The other method was building more housing. This could be done within particular neighborhoods by tearing down older, less dense structures and building newer ones with more rentable space, and with more lot coverage. The other option was to expand outward from a neighborhood by outbidding other uses. In the face of such huge demand from immigration, the response of developers was to do an "all of the above" strategy.

As the demand for housing rose because of immigration, prices would increase. This caused households to take in lodgers or boarders and to reduce the size of the apartment they rented; and thus increasing housing density. But the high price also drew developers into the market because of the profit opportunities. If building taller than five stories were in their economic interest, they would have done so. But the inability to build tall placed a constraint on the supply. In 1864 there were 15,511 tenements housing about half a million people. By 1900, there were 42,700 tenements housing nearly 1.6 million people. The number of tenements grew by 175% while the population increased by 230%.[27] Although this statistic does not account for the fact the newer tenements used more of each lot and were able to accommodate more people per building; there are no measures regarding the per capita space usage over time.

The builder was faced with the problem of how to squeeze the most profit out of the land, given the willingness and ability to pay of the residents. Furthermore, the builder found himself operating in a particular market structure that encouraged rapid and low-quality construction and was less concerned about light and air for residents. The tremendous demand for housing meant that there was more of an incentive to provide space than quality units.

There were no tenements proper in the early part of the nineteenth century. The wealthy had their townhouses Downtown, while the artisans and shopkeepers typically lived where they worked in two-story houses. As the population grew, older, private houses were subdivided to hold more people. The 1830s saw the first tenement house proper—a low-income dwelling specifically designed to house several families.[28]

In the ensuing decades, tenement structures became increasingly dense, taking up a larger fraction of the plot and having more floors. Figure 4.6 shows the evolution of tenement design between the 1820s and 1890s. In cases where the early buildings used only a small fraction of the total lot, rear apartments were added to increase rental income.

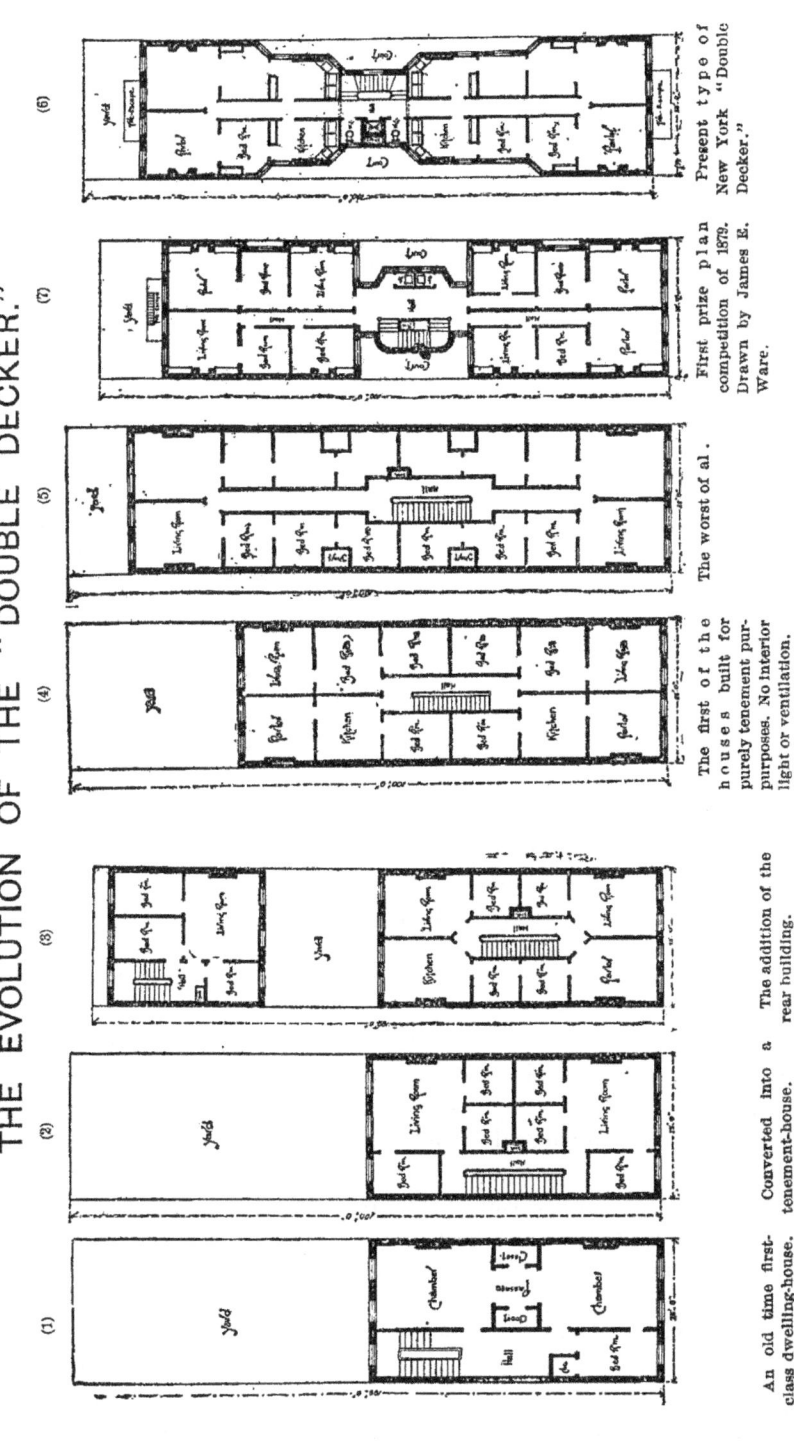

Figure 4.6 The evolution of tenement house design. The earliest tenements in the 1830s were single-family houses subdivided to hold multiple families. To satisfy the demand, some landlords added rear structures. The mid-nineteenth century saw the rise of the tenement house proper. Starting in 1867, New York began regulating tenements and this influenced their design and bulk. In 1879, based on a competition for tenement house designs, the "dumbbell" (*on the right*) became the standard for the remainder of the nineteenth century.

Source: Tenement House Committee (1895).

From the perspective of tenants and reformers, the late nineteenth-century tenement building suffered from many problems. The rooms were cramped; they provided little light and air; and buildings lacked running water. A privy would be provided in the back, but it was shared by many, many people.[29]

The first tenement house law was enacted in 1867. A "tenement" was now formally defined as any rental structure that had more than three independent families, doing their own cooking, and sharing common halls, stairways, and yards.[30] The law established a laundry list of requirements. The most important of these included that all rooms had to have a window to the outside or a transom so that air might flow. All buildings required fire escapes, and at least one water closet was to be provided for every twenty occupants. If there were sewer lines on the street, the tenement had to hook up to it. Cellars were now prohibited as residences, unless a permit was obtained from the recently-formed Metropolitan Board of Health, which was authorized to evict tenants from buildings that "were unfit for habitation by reason of being infected with disease or likely to cause sickness among the occupants, or dangerous from want of repair."[31]

The one major omission was that there were no limits to how much of a lot could be occupied by the building, and new tenements could occupy up to 90% of the lot. In 1879, the law was modified to require that there must be at least 10 feet between every new tenement and the rear lot line. In 1887, the law was amended to require one water closet per fifteen occupants. In 1891, the law was changed to require that buildings only occupy 65% of the lot, but a loophole ultimately allowed builders to use 75%.[32]

To improve tenement design, in 1878, the editors of the magazine, *Plumber and Sanitary Engineer*, held an architectural competition for tenement plans on a 25 x 100 square foot plot. The aim was to find a standard design that would be able to house the tenement population and provide air and light, and still be profitable for the tenement builder. Although 190 submissions were received, the judging committee was pleased with none of them. In the end, they awarded the top prize to architect James E. Ware, who designed what has come to be known as the "dumbbell" (or double decker) since air shafts were placed in the middle of the building, with apartments in front and back, giving the building the shape of a dumbbell. Because of his winning entry, it became the standard design until 1901. Critics claimed that it institutionalized the major flaws in dense tenement structures, making them "the curse of the city."[33]

In 1901, the city enacted the strictest and most reform-minded legislation to date. The law was largely a result of the efforts of housing advocate Lawrence Veiller, who worked with Governor Theodore Roosevelt to enact the legislation. The key objective of this "new law" was to eliminate the standard dumbbell design on the 25 x 100 square foot lot. [34]

The narrow air shafts were particularly odious to reformers, since they provided little light and air, and were receptacles for garbage. The law restricted the heights of buildings to be no higher than 1.5 times the width of street. The backyards were required to be at least 13 feet deep. And perhaps most important, air shafts had to be much larger. Instead of 28 inches wide, new shafts had to be at least 12 feet wide (half the standard lot width) and 24 feet long. Further, no room could be less than 70 square feet. Each apartment now had to have its own water-closet. The law, while not outright banning the dumbbell on the 25 x 100 square foot lot, made it economically impossible.

From the reformers' point of view, the law was an unqualified success, since housing quality was improved. But from the consumers' side, it was a mixed-bag. The new space was great, if you could afford it. But historian Anthony Jackson argues that the regulations backfired. The old law buildings, which were allowed to remain, were now in such great demand, due to the unaffordability of the new law tenements, that their rents were bid up even higher.[35]

TENEMENT DEVELOPMENT

Blame for the housing and health problems was sprayed on all sides. On one hand, the landlord was a greedy chiseler, hunching over his money pile, while the poor tenement dweller suffered from lack of air, light, or running water. On the other hand, the poor, slovenly immigrant was prone to vice and moral decay, and was only too happy to wallow in filth not fit for pigs. The tenement buildings were dens of disease and depravity, and were faulted for creating a listless population that was dragging down the vitality of the city.[36]

Fundamentally, the tenement housing problem was caused by the interaction of poverty, the market provision of housing, the overwhelming demand to live in Manhattan, and the geological constraints of the island. On one hand, the market was left to provide the shelter for the immigrants and working classes, yet the only way for this to be done profitably was for the developer to maximize the lot coverage and skimp on the amenities like hot water and views. Veiller concluded from his investigations that the typical return on tenement apartments was 5.81% with no mortgage and 7.03% with 60% mortgage. For 3% or 4% the model tenement builder could provide a better structure with less density.[37] But 7% was about as low as one could expect as a reasonable return when considering the return on other investments and the risks associated with providing housing for the poor. Calls for "model" tenements to be built by philanthropic organizations or by those generous enough to accept lower returns were met with specific building projects. But despite their good intentions, builders of model tenements largely failed to make a dent in the problem, and they sometimes made it worse.[38]

The tenement builders before the turn of the twentieth century were, by and large, immigrants who constructed low-income housing as a way to climb the economic ladder. They could leverage their small savings as starter capital and then borrow the rest. In many cases, the developer had no prior knowledge of the business but was a shopkeeper or tailor, who saw others around him making money in real estate. Many of them built them as purely speculative projects, where they would buy the land, construct the building as rapidly as possible, then fill it with tenants and sell it for a profit. Others would try to live off the income or use it to engage in more real estate construction. Veiller claimed that nine out ten tenements constructed were built simply to be flipped, though this assertion has never been proved.[39]

Many of those who learned the real estate trade as tenement builders would go on to larger projects of offices and skyscrapers. And so, we can say that there was another relationship between the tenements and the skyscrapers: in the 1920s, the skyline was built, in large part, by those who grew up in the tenements. Tenement construction was like the "minor leagues" of Manhattan real estate, as it was a training ground for more ambitious entrepreneurs.

New York developed its own particular real estate institutions and players. The process generally involved five different parties. First was the "building loan operator," who sold plots of land and gave loans for land and construction. Second was the builder/developer, who erected the structures for speculative profits. Third was the building purchaser; fourth was the "leaster"; and fifth were the tenants themselves. The leasters were essentially rent farmers, who lived in the building. They would pay the building owner a fixed fee for the right to collect the rent and live on the premises. For the enterprising family, it was a way to earn some extra money, while relieving the owner of the duties of rent collection and superintendence.

Veiller paints a dark picture of the real estate development market. He saw it as a kind of greater-fool scheme: the loan operator rips off the builder, who, in turn, rips off the buyer, who, in turn, rips off the tenants. And the process continued year after year, since every day, a new crop of immigrant suckers arrived from Ellis Island. It is hard to know how true this theory was, in fact, but it seems unlikely that misinformation was as widespread as he indicates.

Once the builder is ready to construct a tenement, he reaches out to a loan operator, who helps get him started. As Veiller writes,

> Having almost no capital, his [the builder's] first necessity is to borrow sufficient money to enable him to purchase the land and carry on his building operations. As tenement houses are seldom erected singly—such buildings generally put up in rows of three to twelve buildings at a time—and as the value of an ordinary 25-foot interior lot on the Lower East Side is from about $18,000 to $20,000, and the cost of each ordinary tenement house at the present time is about $18,000 to $20,000, it becomes apparent that he must have a capital of $36,000 to put up one house, and to put up four houses, a capital of $144,000.[40]

This is where the loan operator comes in. His business is to scout the city looking for lots that are prime for development. The operator purchases them and then finds a buyer/developer. The lot is sold at a markup. Then the operator will agree to provide a construction loan, normally at 5.5% to 6% interest. The loan is distributed in several installments, over the construction process. The first payment is made after the first tier of beams is laid. The second installment comes when the third tier of beams is installed and so on. The last payment is made when the building is ready for occupancy. By making payments over the construction cycle, the operator minimizes his risk, since money is loaned only after the project has already begun. Since the operator has the first mortgage, if the developer should walk away from the project, the operator benefits from the work already put into it. If he so chooses, he can complete the project himself, with much of the cost already born by the defaulter.

The developer, once in possession of the property, hires an architect, who prepares blueprints and gets a construction permit from the city. The plans are standard tenement designs that require little new effort. Next the builder locates and hires the subcontractors who do the actual construction work. The contractors are paid from the money from the loan operator. The developer acts as general contractor, hiring and overseeing all of the various subcontractors.

Upon completion the builder aims to secure a mortgage on the property from a bank or insurance company. This builder, in apparent collusion with insurance companies and banks, inflate the value of the completed project in order to secure a larger loan. This also means that potential buyers think the building is worth more and will therefore pay a higher price.

As soon as a permanent mortgage is secured, the builder seeks a buyer. "Such investors are often small tradesmen or persons who have saved from $5000 to $15,000, and who have heard that tenement house property pays a large rate of interest, and who are anxious to accumulate money quickly."[41] But the seller has a trick up his sleeve. He uses stratagems to fill up his building; luring new tenants with promises of a free month's rent or a signing bonus. As long as rental contracts are signed, he can show that the building will pay nicely. It would seem though that competition among sellers was, at least once in a while, yielding perks to the tenants. A free month's rent is an 8% discount.

To Veiller, this inflated profit came at the expense of the tenants, who had to pay for the return of the operator, as well as the deception of the seller. He writes,

> There is no reason why investors cannot directly build tenement houses as investments and thus do away with the profits of two middlemen, the "Building Loan Operator" and the speculative builder. [T]he "Operator" obtains from this enterprise, in case it has been successful, a profit of $6,000, and the speculative builder obtains a profit of about $5000; thus the cost to the purchaser or investor has been increased by $11,000 beyond what it should have been.[42]

While operators may have been sharks, there is no reason to believe their services were not important. In the tenement development business, legitimate banks were likely reluctant to finance the risky business of low-income housing construction. Furthermore, the builders, as immigrants themselves, were in need of information about investment possibilities. The operator was performing a brokerage service of matching the sellers of land with buyers. Furthermore, it was naïve of Veiller to expect the free market to produce housing simply based on philanthropy. As Adam Smith wrote in 1776, "It is not from the beneficence of the butcher, the brewer, or the baker, that we expect our dinner, but from their regard to their own interest."[43]

Rental Income

Thanks to Veiller's data collection efforts, we also have a sense of what residents on the Lower East Side were paying for housing.[44] Specifically, he collected rent data for virtually every building on the block bound between Chrystie, Forsyth, Bayard, and Canal Streets (tax block #291), in the Tenth Ward. A model of the block was also presented in the 1899 Tenement House Exhibition (see figure 4.7) organized by Veiller, though today it does not exist, since the land is used for an on-off ramp for the Manhattan Bridge, constructed from 1901 to 1912.[45]

In 1900 there were forty-five different structures on the block. Almost all were tenements, though one was a hotel, two were just for stores, one was under construction, and one was a private house with a store. There were nine rear tenements. Compared

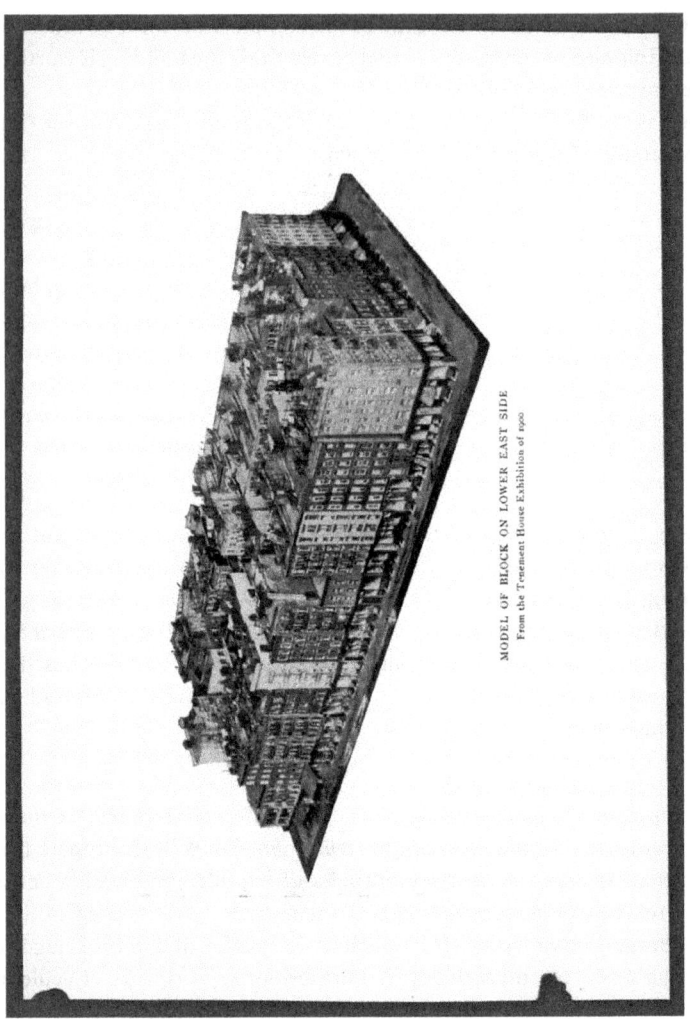

Figure 4.7 Model of block circa 1900. In 1900, housing reformer Lawrence Veiller organized the Tenement House Exhibition to highlight the plight of tenement house residents, which showed a model of one of the densest blocks on the Lower East Side block.

Source: https://repository-cache.cul.columbia.edu/images/ldpd:139599/scaled/1200.jpg.

to the blocks directly to the east and west, there were no large structures devoted to commercial or cultural purposes. The block to the west, for example, had the Windsor Theater, and the block to the east had a synagogue and a Methodist Episcopal church.

Based on the work of the Tenement House Department, we also know that in 1900, 2,862 people were living there, giving a density of 1,078 people per acre. Russians were the majority, but some were Italian and Polish. This put it in the top 99th percentile for population density on the island. In fact, there were only ten other blocks in the city that had more people per acre.[46] We can see why Veiller chose to highlight it for the exhibition.

Nearly half of the apartments had two rooms (47%), while three-room apartments were another 31% of units. Five- and six-room apartments were available, but they constituted only about 4% of units. But what was being charged for these apartments? Figure 4.8 shows the average cost per room per month on each of the different floors. The first floor above the street rented for the highest amount, at $4.00 per room per month, and the values declined from there with each floor. On the fifth floor, rents were nearly 25% less than the first floor (about $3.00). The ground floor apartments were mostly in rear buildings. The most common apartment type had two rooms and cost $8.00. But some apartments with five rooms would fetch as much as $27. The average rent per apartment was about $10 per month ($120 per year); but there was a considerable amount of variation in what households were paying. The range was much more limited as compared to the city as whole (see appendix N). On average, there were no apartments renting for less than $5 per month, suggesting that the block did not contain the worst housing in the city.[47]

A more detailed statistical analysis reveals the willingness to pay for different features (see appendix O). In particular, I looked at those characteristics that determined the monthly per room rent as a function of the apartments' characteristics, such as what floor the unit was on, how many rooms it had, whether it was a rear tenement, whether the building was on a corner or not, and whether the apartment faced the street or the back.

Perhaps the most important conclusion from this is that the 1900 tenement rental market was quite banal. It looks a lot like the market for rental housing today; the tastes of renters were not all that different than what we would expect. Front-facing units rented at about 19% higher than their rear counterparts. Corner units, with

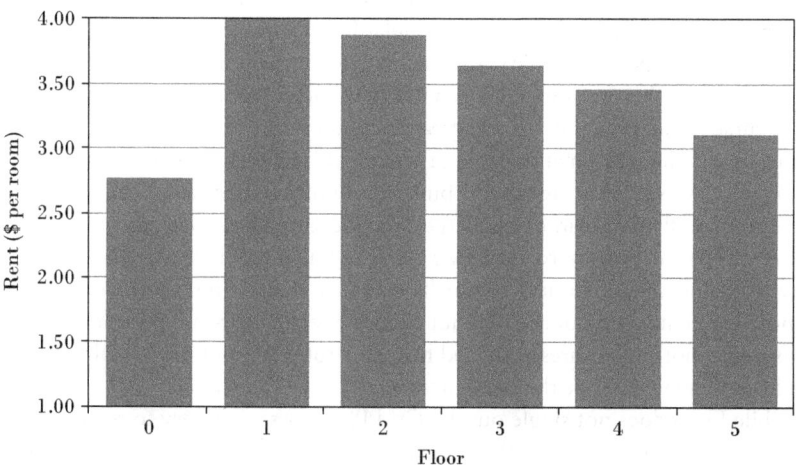

Figure 4.8 Average tenement rents versus story in 1900. Tenement reformer Lawrence Veiller collected data on rents being paid for virtually every apartment on a block on the Lower East Side (see figure 4.7). The graph shows that average rents were highest on the first story and fell after that. The graph demonstrates that the economics of tenement construction did not favor building taller than five stories, since few were willing to pay to live on the upper floors.
Source: Veiller (1903d).

double views, rented for about a 16% premium. Tenants especially did not like walking up stairs. The results confirm that the highest paying floors were floors one and two.

Rear tenements cost about 14% less to rent. There was also substantial variation across buildings themselves, with a building quality premium as well. The rents in the highest quality building (114-116 Canal Street) were fetching double the rents as the lowest quality building (13 Forsyth Street), all else equal. In short, the results of these statistical analyses suggest that, despite much of the rhetoric about the evils of the slums, tenement dwellers were quite rational in their preference for housing; and they were especially unwilling to pay to live on the upper floors.

Residents in this neighborhood were paying between $7 and $12 per month for an apartment. In terms of wages, this represented about a quarter of income (and compares favorably with low-income housing costs today).[48] In 1900, the typical daily wage for a carpenter was $4, or about $22 per week; a common laborer earned $1.40 per day, or $7.70 per week; and manufacturing workers earned between $10 and $17 per week.[49] The tenement builder was providing a range of units that were affordable given the tastes and incomes of the immigrant classes.

THE GRID PLAN AND DENSITY

As discussed in chapter 2, the Grid Plan created relatively expansive blocks, as compared to those in the original city below Houston Street, though the convention of the 25 x 100 square foot plots remained throughout. To the reformers, the small lots were the root of the tenement problem because they created unnecessary concentration. Try as they might, reformers could do nothing to combat the trade in the small lots. In 1894, architect Ernest Flagg, who went on to design the Singer Building skyscraper a decade later (see chapter 5), voiced a popular belief when writing, "The greatest evil which ever befell New York City was the division of the blocks into lots of 25 x 100 feet. . ... for from this division has arisen the New York system of tenement-houses, the worse curse which ever afflicted any great community."[50]

He argued that the unwillingness of tenement builders to erect a single structure on larger lots was driving the horrific building conditions. He calculated that building four dumbbell flats instead of one large apartment building increased total costs by 12% and reduced court yard sizes by 50%. The four dumbbells each had their own party wall, and they included minimally sized air shafts. The larger building could be more efficiently laid out and did not need the wasted expense on thicker walls. In his example, both structures provided the same total amount of rentable space, and should, in theory, generate the same income.

While Flagg does not single out the Grid Plan per se, it is easy to see how people came view the Grid Plan with the standard lot sizes, since it simply perpetuated the tradition. Flagg's analysis also begs the question: Why didn't tenement builders take advantage of the cost-savings by amassing larger lots? Veiller and Flagg both stated that tenement builders usually purchased multiple lots and built dumbbells on each one. If this is true, then they could have just as easily built one larger structure rather than a few smaller ones. So why didn't they?

There are a few possible explanations, though definitive answers need to come from future research. First is that maybe larger lot sales were actually much rarer than

Veiller and Flagg were willing to let on. It might be that most of the trade, through the operator, was in single lots. In this case, the developer would not likely have access to the larger lots needed for a better structure.

Second is that if developers were mostly "flippers," then creating four units, say, instead of one was likely more profitable, despite the additional costs. Given the buyers were likely tenement households, it was probably easier to locate four buyers each willing to pay $25,000 than one buyer willing to pay say $100,000. Another reason was that the institutional structure was so deeply formed about the 25 x 100 lot that few were likely willing to move away from it.[51]

Tenement structures on that lot size were built in the thousands for over half a century. The architectural plans were of the off-the-shelf variety. The workers and contractors were all likely familiar with the construction process and were able to move much quicker than if the design were more complicated. Lot prices were denominated in the standard lot unit (SLU) variety, and the market was structured around these SLUs. In addition, the lots would not need to be combined legally and would not present any more bureaucratic hassles in this regard.

Simply put, it is likely that both the economic and institutional forces were aligned against combining lots in the immigrant neighborhoods. One could only speculate that if there were, in fact, a "free lunch" for the developer, someone would have taken advantage of combining lots, were there not too many hurdles preventing it.

It is also possible that given the lock-in of the 25 x 100 square foot lot, it is likely that the Grid Plan, in fact, reduced overcrowding by making it easier for builders to amass the larger lots that Flagg promoted. To test this idea, in the regressions described above, I also included two variables that measure the effect of the Grid Plan on population density. First is the average block size within a quarter mile radius of each block. This was a measure of the average block size in the neighborhoods. The blocks in the Grid Plan would have much larger blocks than those below the demarcation line. Another measure was if the lot was south of the demarcation line or not.

The statistical results support the idea that the Grid Plan, in fact, was promoting reduced density. I find that south of the demarcation line, density was about 30% higher, than north of it, controlling for all the other variables that influenced density. Further, larger blocks were associated with less density. If two blocks, for example, were the same in every respect, except one was 1 acre larger, it was likely to have 14% few people per acre, on average. So in a way, the Grid Plans seems to have helped reduce the problem of overcrowding, relative to the old city.

DENSITY AND THE SKYLINE

The tremendous population growth on Manhattan had two effects on the skyline. First, it defined the zones where skyscrapers would be constructed. In 1900, 1.85 million residents chose Manhattan as their home, and their residential locations were, as described above, based on their nationalities, incomes, and the land uses determined before the Civil War. This meant that in the battle for place, the skyline could grow in two possible places: south of Chambers Street in the historical commercial district, and somewhere north of 14th Street along the main spine of the island.

Immigration and the rise of the tenement neighborhoods also had an unintended consequence. Outside of these neighborhoods, it made land for other uses more expensive since the battle for place shrank the size of the commercial and industrial neighborhoods, which raised land values and increased building height in these areas. This battle would likely be fiercer where there was less room for east-west expansion given the narrow form of Manhattan Island.

To test this theory, I performed a statistical analysis of land prices during the years 1885 to 1900. Since skyscraper construction is a response to high land values (see chapter 5), then immigrant neighborhoods would likely cause higher land values for the business districts when less land was available for commercial development. I investigated the determinants of average (inflation-adjusted) land prices in each of the 108 Sanitation Districts on the island. Each Sanitation District (SD) was akin to a large neighborhood; most were between 50 and 75 acres. The goal was to see if land values were higher on parts of the island where land was less available. Presumably in these places the tenement neighborhoods were shrinking the areas for business.

In particular, I focused on the width of the island going from south to north. The theory is that on narrow parts of the island, all else equal, we would likely see higher land values because of the restrictions imposed by Manhattan's insular nature. Presumably wider sections would have lower values, since it would allow the population to "spread" out along that the east-west corridor. For each SD, I measured the width of the island, as it runs through the center of the SD, from river to river. For example, the first two SDs in the First Ward are along the narrowest part of the island, the widths from river to river are approximately 0.60 miles across as the crow flies. Going north, the width increases. A bulge on the east side is met with an indentation on the west side, but, by and large, the island's variation north of Canal Street is within a band of 1.5 to 2.0 miles across.

And then there is Central Park. At about a half mile wide, the park from 59th Street to 110th Street, in essence, shrinks the width of the island by this much because the land is removed from possible real estate development. Consider that Central Park is 843 acres. As a comparison, the four wards on the east side above the Seventh Ward (Tenth, Eleventh, Thirteen, and Seventeenth) comprised 757 acres, and in 1900 housed a population of nearly 440,000. This was more people than the entire state of Rhode Island and was more people than the states (or states-to-be) of Alaska, Arizona, Hawaii, Nevada, and Wyoming combined.[52] When calculating the span of the island, I subtracted the width of Central Park in that part of the city.

The results show that the width of the island was a factor in determining land values at a particular east-west line; in particular, I find land values were the greatest along parts of the island that were "latitudinally challenged" (see appendix P for regression results). For areas to the east and west of Central Park, for example, land prices were 20% higher than they would have been if Central Park was not blocking development.

Toward the end of the nineteenth century, the 23-square-mile island was as cramped as it could possibly be. Not only was it well on its way to holding two million residents, but it was the financial, industrial, and transportation capital of the United

States. The island's real estate was reaching its capacity, as the swells of residents and workers pushed into what its buildings could hold. Perhaps never before in the history of humanity did a city see such an intense battle for place. In order to grow and accommodate the millions who wanted to call Manhattan home, New York would need to devise a real estate solution: the skyscraper. This is the subject to which we now turn in Part II of the book.

Part II
The Rise of the Skyline

5

The Economics of Skyscraper Height

One day the idea came upon me like a flash that an iron bridge truss stood on end was the solution to the problem.
Bradford Lee Gilbert

It was a cold and dreary Sunday morning in June 1888. Lower Manhattan was quiet and the streets were empty but for the fierce winds blowing around the stoic buildings. A small crowd was forming in front of an office building under construction on Lower Broadway. The walls were in place, but no roof existed; it was shrouded in a web of scaffolding.

Fear took hold of the crowd; at any moment the strong winds were going to push over this new, strange structure, this scraper of the sky. Suddenly, one man separates from the mass; sprinting into the building, he climbs ten flights of stairs to emerge out in the open above the crowd. Seeing a ladder left in place by the workmen, he fearlessly ascends another three stories of scaffolding. The crowd jeers that he is a fool. His companion, who had joined him up to the 10th floor, abandons him there, unwilling to climb further.

At the top of the ladder, he jumps onto the scaffolding and crawls on his hands and knees, surrounded by tornadoes of air. When he positions himself firmly into place, he pulls out from his pocket a small, but heavy, object held to a string—a plumb line—which he dangles into the space below him. There, before his eyes and to his great satisfaction, he sees nothing—the awesome nothingness of a steady plumb line, with not a single vibration. The man—Bradford Lee Gilbert, the engineer of New York's first skyscraper, the Tower Building—proved to the world that his eleven-story high-rise was sound and wind resistant.[1]

In 1905, Gilbert recounted this story to demonstrate his faith in his design for the city's first skyscraper, approved by the Department of Buildings in April 1888, despite the fear that it was a dangerous monster that would unleash more harm than good. The structure, while the first of its kind in New York, was not some random, freak occurrence. Rather, its appearance marks the birth of the Skyscraper Revolution that would forever change Manhattan's landscape and history. It emerges after several decades of engineers trying to solve the problem of how to make buildings both taller and profitable in the face of rising land values and economic growth.

The purpose of this chapter is to discuss the technological and economic determinants of the skyscrapers and their heights over the twentieth century by documenting the key incentives faced by developers and how these incentives have evolved as the century progressed. When studying the economics of skyscrapers, however, there are two possible perspectives. The first, as will be discussed in this chapter, is to directly track the costs and benefits from high-rise construction. In other words, this perspective is from the point of view of the developer: the nature of real estate investment given the economic, legal, and political constraints. This can be called the *return on investment (ROI) approach*. The problem faced by the developer is how to construct a building that will maximize the profits or returns from the investment.

The following chapter takes the second perspective, which is called the *economic approach*. This method first provides a simple supply and demand model of the economics of skyscrapers and then looks at the statistical correlates of skyscraper heights and their numbers with important variables such as population growth, gross domestic product, and income inequality, to see how these broader demographic and economic factors have driven heights.

Each of the two approaches has their own costs and benefits, as it were. The ROI approach allows for an investigation of the specific incentives facing developers. It affords a kind of bird's eye view of the real estate process, and how these incentives have changed over the decades. It enables us to answer such questions as the following: What are the key costs and revenue factors that determine how high a developer will build? Why has office construction been a decreasing share of total skyscraper construction in the last fifty years? What is causing the construction of super-slim, supertall towers in Manhattan in the twenty-first century?

The economic approach, on the other hand, is broader and provides a means to estimate the effects of important variables that have driven the *market for height*. In other words, it looks at those things that determine skyscraper supply and demand— and sees how changes in the national and regional economy affect this market. The advantage of this methodology is that specific theories can be tested. The economic approach can say something about the collective motivations of the developers in the height market, since it is generally impossible to get directly into their heads to see what they are thinking.

THE BIRTH OF THE SKYSCRAPER

Lower Manhattan in the 1890s was a kind of economic island. The financial district, running from Broadway to the East River and south from City Hall Park and Spruce Street, was hemmed in on all sides. To the west, along the Hudson, were seedy hotels, run-down tenements, and port and rail facilities. North of that were the city's warehouses and to the northeast were the tenement districts. Water was everywhere else.

This "island effect" meant that the major corporations that made Lower Manhattan their homes were limited to a very small amount of space (see figure 3.11). As such, the combined desire to cluster together and the limited room for geographic expansion meant that land values were the highest there. Figure 5.1 shows the (nominal) price per square foot for forty land sales between 1880 and 1890 versus the distance from the southern tip. Land values in the financial district averaged between $75 and $150 per square foot.[2] A 10-minute walk northward would reveal values closer to $15 per square foot, translating into a drop of $0.50 per 10 feet.

During the recovery from the Financial Panic of 1873, land values began a dramatic ascent in Lower Manhattan, more than doubling during the 1880s (see chapter 10). This rise suggests that the demand for land and office space was increasing much faster

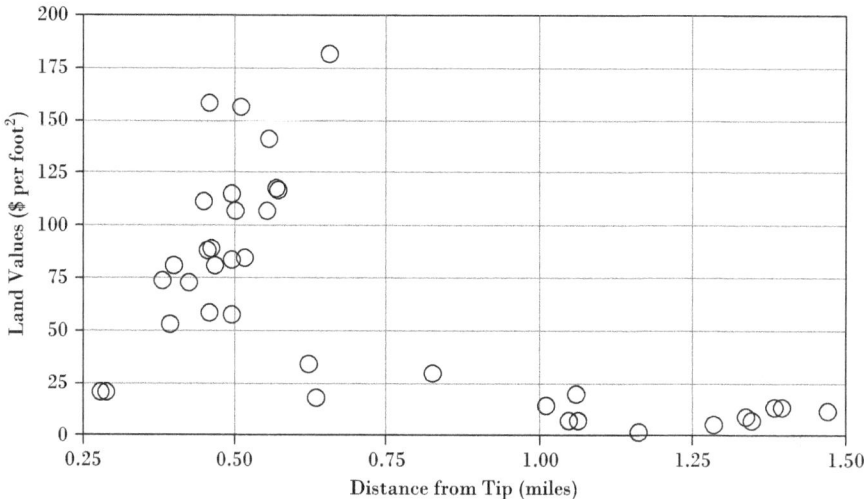

Figure 5.1 Land prices in Lower Manhattan between 1880 and 1890. This graph shows that land prices in Lower Manhattan at the end of the nineteenth century were averaging around $100 per square foot and were even $200 per square foot in some cases. Only a few blocks away, land values were an order of magnitude less. These tremendous land values promoted the rise of skyscrapers south of City Hall. Also note how the pattern of land values is similar as that from two-centuries prior (see figure 3.6).

Source: Underlying data is from *Record and Guide* (1898) and courtesy of Fred Smith, Jeremy Atack, Robert Margo, and Carlos Villarreal.

than could be adequately supplied; the only way to allocate the shortage of office space was through rising prices. But these higher rents meant that developers could increase their profits by building more or taller. But prior to the late 1880s, the technology and know-how to build taller *and earn a profit* just did not exist.

In this case, there are three possible solutions, two of which lacked appeal to the business community. First was to accept ever higher prices. Second was to spread outward into the port or tenement neighborhoods. Third was to find a technological solution. While there has been a vigorous debate about which building is the first true skyscraper, it can be said for sure that all of the components required for this revolution emerged in the mid- to late 1880s—just when the pressure on land prices was the greatest.

The rise of the office building as a distinct type of real estate can be traced back to the years immediately following the Civil War. Before then there was no building that could specifically be referred to as an "office." Rather, buildings had combined functions for warehousing, production, and administration. But the Industrial Revolution changed that. As the size and scope of business increased so that corporations operated on a national or international scale, buildings were used just for acquiring, processing, and making decisions about the vast quantities of information with which management had to deal. Thus was born the office and the demand for high-rises to house a white-collar workforce (see chapter 7).

The other side of this equation is the supply side, and for this there are two important elements. First is the engineering component. Can the tall building actually be created using the technological know-how and available materials? And, if so, can the technology be implemented in a cost-effective manner? The answer to both these questions became "yes," but only by the mid-1880s. At this time, the supply and demand forces merged to produce a revolutionary building form: the skyscraper.

In New York, at eleven stories, the Tower Building became the city's first "skyscraper," in 1889, at 50 Broadway. The developer, a silk merchant named John Noble Stearns, wanted to build a large office structure on a very narrow and oddly shaped plot of land, only 21.5 feet wide on Broadway and about 110 feet deep (see figures 5.2A and B). But thwarted in his ability to acquire additional lots, he turned to architect Bradford Lee Gilbert to devise a solution.

If Gilbert had followed the building code at the time, the load-bearing masonry walls at street level would have needed to be 3 feet thick, leaving only 15.5 feet of interior space, of which half would be used for stairs and elevators. In other words, if Gilbert designed the building to code, out of 21.5 feet of frontage, a mere 7.25 feet of rentable width would have been left. The estimated loss of rental income was $10,000 per year.[3]

Gilbert's solution was to erect an iron frame, like a bridge truss, on the bottom floors, but constructed vertically. By using it to hold up the building, the walls were mere "curtains," only needed to keep the elements out, and not for supporting the building loads. Thus, the use of iron would not only save valuable space, but would also cost less per square foot.

Despite its innovative design and its economical use of land, it was revolutionary, and as such, people did not quite know what to make of it. Protests followed the plans' release. Many were worried that it might collapse or topple over by a gust of wind, especially on that windy day described above. Masonry walls were the standard and had been used since the dawn of civilization. Iron supports to bear the main load were too risky. Gilbert soldiered on and in April 1888, the City issued a building permit.

The Tower Building represented the shoots of a new species of plant. The giant buildings that followed were the flowering of the Skyscraper Revolution, the offspring of the larger Industrial Revolution, which began in the United States after the birth of the Republic.

This revolution was bringing forth new products, and engineering and manufacturing methods were being applied to a whole host of areas, including urban real estate. The Industrial Revolution not only created the demand for skyscrapers via urbanization and the rise of big business, but it also allowed for its supply by creating the materials, methods, and expertise. Throughout the next quarter century, the city would create a sophisticated skyscraper industrial complex, which would bring together developers, engineers, architects, bankers, and brokers into a smooth functioning skyscraper industry.

HEIGHT TYPES

Before we proceed with the determinants of skyscraper height and their locations, we need to distinguish more specifically about four types of building height. The first type is *engineering height*.[4] This is the tallest height that is currently feasible from a technological standpoint. It represents the highest building that can be constructed to house

(A)

(B)

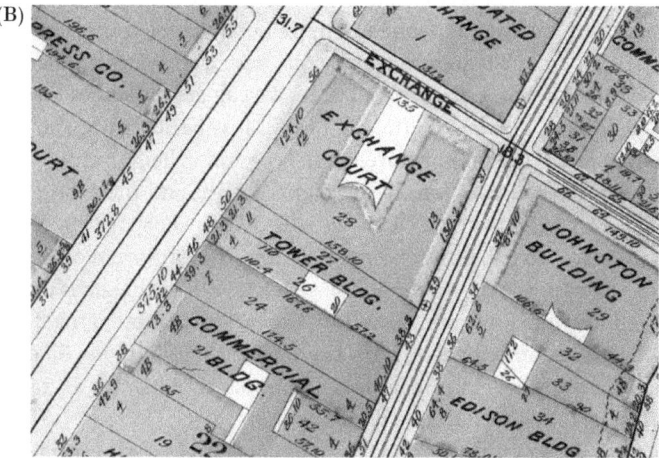

Figure 5.2 New York's first skyscraper. *A*, the Tower Building (1889) and *B*, its plot. Silk merchant and developer, John Noble Stearns, wanted to build an office building at 50 Broadway. Given the narrow lot, however, a building with thick, load-bearing masonry walls would have been unprofitable. Stearns turned to architect Bradford Lee Gilbert, who came up with the idea of using iron truss-like framing to reduce the wall-thickness and increase the rentable space, thus creating New York's first skyscraper.

Source: Image of Tower Building: http://41.media.tumblr.com/163ad6ed50c3cfe2e8a141152e47e166/tumblr_mxistoDEUD1sdzmuoo1_1280.jpg, Lot Shape: Bromley and Bromley (1899).

people and circulate them throughout the building in a comfortable, safe, and efficient manner, regardless of the costs of constructing such a building.

A convenient gauge for engineering height is the world's tallest building. If we focus only on habitable buildings constructed since the Skyscraper Revolution, engineering height has grown from about fifteen stories in 1885 to about two hundred stories in 2010, which gives an average annual growth rate of about 2%.[5] As of this writing, the Burj Khalifa in Dubai is the world's tallest building, at about one-half mile high. While there are those who dream of the mile-high building, we are still not there yet from an engineering perspective.[6]

Despite the ongoing race across the globe to build the world's tallest building, the problem of engineering height is much less directly relevant to our society. The reason is that the demand for these buildings does not exist in a way that would justify their mass production. Another way of saying this is that historically the maximum feasible engineering height generally exceeds its economic need by many years. Of course, engineering height will always be important in that eventually, our economic needs will catch up to our engineering capabilities, but we have tended to solve the engineering problems long before we need them—mostly because it is not profit-maximizing impulses that propel us forward.

The next type of height is what I call *developer height*. This is the height that a developer chooses, and is the final, completed height of the building, based on the decisions made by the developer (be it individual, group, or corporation). The developer normally chooses a height that is believed to give the greatest return on investment.

The third type of height is *economic height*. This is the height decision that is most efficient for society (as will be defined in more detail later). In a relatively free market where developers make personal decisions based on what is best for them (or what they believe is best for them), sometimes we can get outcomes that are not best for society, according to some metric of "best." Most importantly, some developers choose a height that is too tall compared to the economic height.

Lastly, the difference between the developer height and the economic height—when the former is taller than the latter—is what I call *symbolic height*. When a building is economically too tall, it is done so to convey some information to the public at large and thus takes on symbolic importance. Thus, symbolic height is the extra height added that reduces the direct net profit from the building, though the developer may feel it provides some other benefit, such as enhanced status, goodwill, or reputation. Even though the extra height might yield additional revenue, the increased costs of providing this height will reduce the profits overall.

Symbolic height emerges from several different sources. First is from the developers themselves who may compete against each other to have a taller building, especially if there is a social benefit for claiming "the world's tallest" or the "city's tallest" title. Second, an extra-tall building might confer social or corporate status to the occupant if the building stands out in the skyline and has a recognizable or unusual form. For example, a corporation may design a taller and/or architecturally novel building in order to signal its economic strength. The building can serve as an icon and can be used for corporate logos. [7] Third, height can be used as part of an urban (re)development strategy, when the government and developers work together on a planned, subsidized project to advertise the city itself and increase commerce and tourism, such as in the case of the Twin Towers or the reconstructed World Trade Center.

In general, the notion of "best" in economics refers to a specific set of principles as applied to the developer that relate to the efficiency of resource allocation and has little to do with the architectural merits of a project.[8] First, that by choosing a particular height, the developer does not impose additional costs on society that must be paid by the public at large—most specifically in the form of extra traffic and pedestrian congestion or by blocking the sunlight on the streets or neighboring buildings.

Second, he does not squander resources; that is, he does not take a profit drop or loss to satisfy his ego. A loss of income by building too tall suggests that if the money were spent elsewhere, say on building a factory or buying new textbooks for students, society as a whole would be better off, since reallocating the money would reduce the economic loss from the building and provide a greater benefit somewhere else. Thus, being too tall can impose a cost on society by lowering its overall well-being—too much was spent on the skyscraper and not enough on other, more important things.

However, the notion of what is best or most efficient for society can be a tricky concept. The Empire State Building is a good example of this. By a pure economic standard, the Empire State Building was economically too tall, in the sense that the additional height added to beat out Walter Chrysler's building was not justified by the additional rents.[9] The developers were willing to reduce some of the expected profits simply to win a height contest. Presumably, height competition is wasteful in that those resources could have been spent in a more productive manner.

Yet, having said that, economic efficiency seems too narrow a concept. The Empire State Building is one of the great wonders of humankind. It is a global icon in the pantheon of "wasteful" projects, such as the Great Pyramids of Egypt, the Eiffel Tower, and the Washington Monument. But collectively we are better off for having them. They are aesthetic wonders which give us pleasure and bind us together by providing symbols that all of humanity share in common. In short, we derive large non-economic benefits from these monuments, despite the fact that they were economic losses.

The tragedy of 9/11 illustrates this as well. The terrorist attacks were specifically aimed at striking the greatest symbols of capitalism and American economic power: the tallest buildings in the country. The Twin Towers' replacement is a new, even taller structure with even greater symbolism—a height of 1,776 feet—and has virtually no regard for a height that maximizes the economic profits of the developer. Yet, New Yorkers and the country believe that the site should be rebuilt—if only to memorialize the victims and show that mustering the replacement resources is relatively easy.

The idea of economic efficiency is narrow in other ways, and I will only note that there are other criteria on which to judge the merits of skyscrapers, such as their aesthetic characteristics, their larger cultural significances, or how they affect the quality of day-to-day life in the city.[10]

THE ENGINEERING PROBLEM

One of the big debates within the skyscraper historiography has been about which building and city were the first.[11] The reason for this argument is that, like most revolutions, change builds slowly and incrementally until, suddenly, there is a tipping point, and then the world is fundamentally different. So there is never one clear moment that defines an economic revolution, since it was in the making for several years.

The Skyscraper Revolution required a new system of integrated parts. Each component evolved at its own speed, according to its own "technological imperative," until suddenly, all the parts are in place to radically change the urban landscape. Thus, the debate about the first skyscraper is really about focusing on one part of the system that was there before the revolution and then arguing that it was really the key component.

Fundamentally, what makes a skyscraper a skyscraper from a technological point of view is the elimination of the barriers to engineering height. Prior to the use of steel skeletal construction, buildings used their walls to bear the building's load. However, the taller the building, the thicker the walls needed to be in order to hold the weight. Ultimately, that would cause the bottom floors to become much less valuable, as the masonry walls ate into otherwise usable space. With masonry walls, the builder faced a trade-off: a taller building with less space on the ground floor or a shorter building with more rentable space.

In an era without elevators and when humans relied on their own calorie-produced energy to climb stairs, this trade-off was irrelevant. No one is interested in climbing more than six stories to work or live. The top floors of these early buildings were the least desirable and commanded the lowest rents (see chapter 5).[12] But the elevator solved the problem of vertical transportation. The first practical elevators came to market in the second quarter of the nineteenth century. With the development of the safety break in 1851 by Elisha Otis, widespread elevator use for office and residential buildings became a reality. The earliest commercial buildings in New York to have an elevator were the five-story Haughwout Building at 488 Broadway (1857) and the Fifth Avenue Hotel (1859) at Madison Square Park. The first generation of elevators was inefficient and slow, and were powered by steam.[13]

At the time of the Tower Building's completion, electric models were becoming the industry norm. Technological progress was driven by the building owner, who had a competitive advantage with an elevator that improved the quality and speed of moving people and goods. In other words, the elevator represented a radical improvement in transportation and people were willing to pay a premium.

After the elevator, the problem of how to erect tall structures was solved with the use of the skeletal design. The skeleton of the structure was built with steel beams (which replaced the earlier use of iron), and the walls no longer had their weight-bearing function. Facades were mere "curtains," whose job was to keep out the elements and project the aesthetic tastes of the architect. Steel skeletons were also very practical because they maximized the amount of space for windows. Historian Carl Condit writes,

> The utilitarian advantages of steel framing were enormous and immediately obvious to architects, builders and owners. First was the possibility of getting rid of a supporting wall, with a consequent reduction in weight and an immense increase in height. The steel necessary to carry a tall building weighs only one-third as much as bearing masonry for an equal number of stories. The virtually unlimited increase in glass area, up to 100 per cent of coverage, allowed the maximum admission of light. The slender columns and wide bays offered greatly increased freedom in the disposition of interior space. Economy in cost

of materials together with speed and efficiency of construction convinced even the most skeptical owners of the superiority of steel or wrought-iron framing.[14]

History does not provide clear evidence as to the inventor of the skeleton. The conventional story attributes it to architect-engineer William Le Baron Jenney, who designed the Home Insurance Building in Chicago (1885), which is usually considered the first real skyscraper. Yet the Home Insurance Building was but one building around that time to use the technology.[15] After reviewing the evidence among the competing claims, Landau and Condit write, "The only fair conclusion to be drawn is that architects, engineers and builders in New York, Chicago and Minneapolis were simultaneously and independently developing the iron skeleton system."[16]

While the steel skeleton and elevator are perhaps the sine qua non of the skyscraper, it would be wrong to exclude a host of other necessary innovations. In total, there are about a dozen or so systems that go together to create the whole skyscraper machine. Necessary is the technology for wind bracing; anchoring the structure to the ground (see chapter 7); fireproofing; heating, cooling, and ventilation; plumbing for fresh water and sewage removal; and finally, lighting and electrical wiring, for making work possible at all hours of the day. All of these systems needed to be fully operational before tall buildings were feasible and habitable. Based on his research, skyscraper historian Carl Condit concludes, "If we are tracking down the origins the skyscraper we have certainly reached the seminal stage in New York and Chicago around the year 1870."[17]

THE DEMAND FOR HEIGHT: A CASE STUDY OF THE PRINT MEDIA INDUSTRY

Skyscraper engineering, however, would be irrelevant without the need for such buildings. Within this context, one fact of city life has always been the clustering of firms in the same industry. Even the fiercest of rivals tend to gravitate to the same neighborhood. This is certainly true for the print media business, which rose up in New York during the second half of the nineteenth century. The Industrial Revolution created the possibility for the efficient collection, production, and distribution of news and advertising to a mass audience. As a result, between 1850 and 1900, US readership of daily newspapers increased from 758,000 to 15.1 million.[18]

Since the 1830s, the Manhattan media industry was centered along Park Row near City Hall, at what became known as Newspaper Row. Here, publications of all kinds from *American Agriculturist* to *Young Scientist* set up their offices.[19] We can get a sense of the location and density of the print media companies by looking at figure 5.3. Figure 5.3A shows the locations of the 409 newspapers listed in the 1881-82 edition of *Phillip's Business Directory*, which includes 44 dailies and 193 weeklies. The vast majority of the addresses were located in Lower Manhattan, between City Hall and Wall Street. However, the map does not give a good sense of their density. The graph in figure 5.3B shows for each firm (square), the number of other firms that are within 100 feet of it. This number is plotted versus miles from the tip (i.e., from south to north). Firms in the same building (which could include multiple publications by the same publisher) were also included.

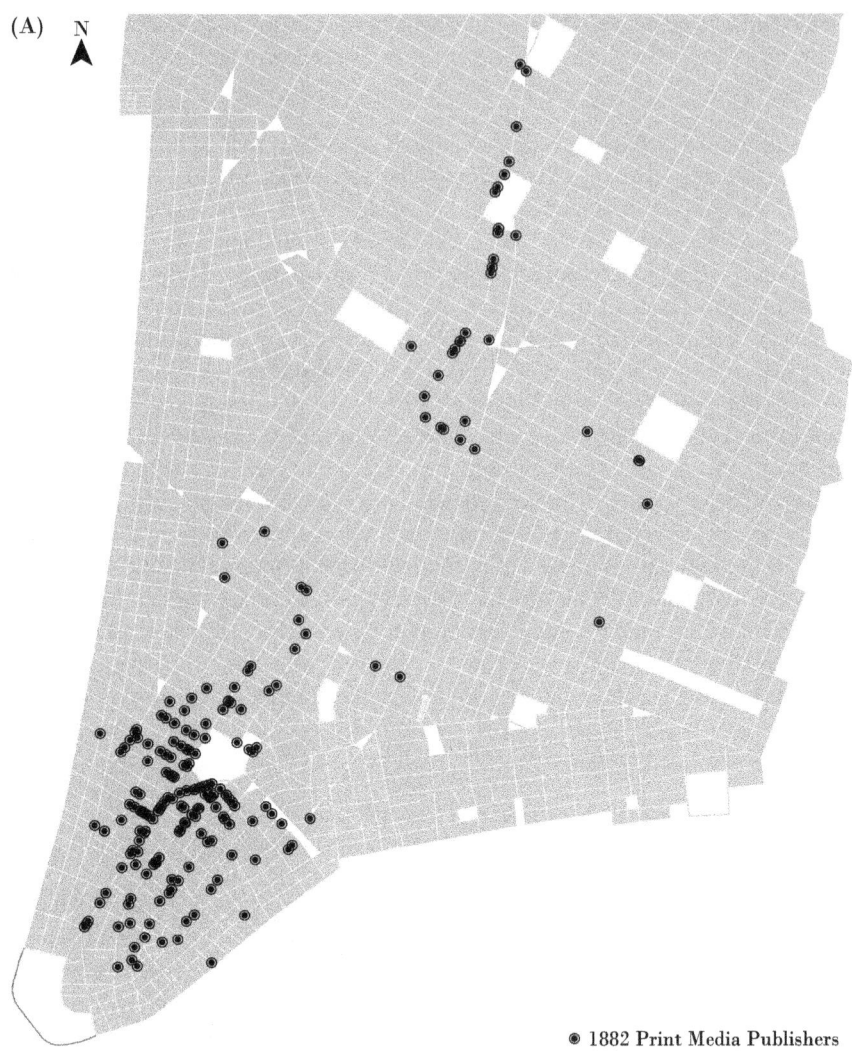

(A) N ▲

● 1882 Print Media Publishers

Figure 5.3 The location and concentration of newspaper and magazine publishers in Manhattan in 1882. *A*, the map shows the location of newspaper and magazine publishers in Manhattan in 1882. *B*, the graph shows the relative concentration of these publishers going north from the southern tip. Despite the fact that they were competing against each other, the forces of agglomeration were quite strong, and they were mostly attracted to the area to the southeast of City Hall, called Newspaper Row. Such intense clustering bid up land values, which caused developers to build tall as a response. Newspaper publishers were perhaps the first to use building height a "strategic weapon," to signal their economic strength and the power of the press.

Source: Map by Eon Kin. Data take from the 1882 edition of *Phillip's Business Directory.*

(B)

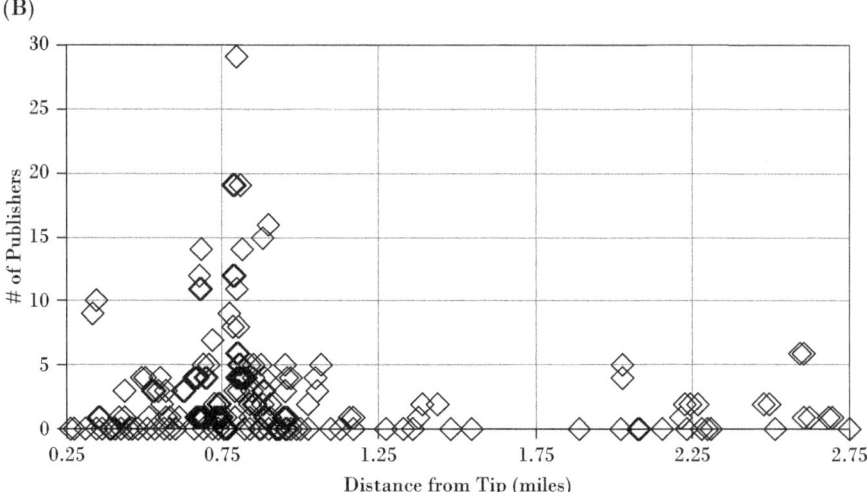

Figure 5.3 Continued

The greatest density was twenty-nine firms within 100 feet of 34 and 35 Park Row. These addresses included the dailies *World* and *Evening Mail*. The extreme concentration of publishers along Newspaper Row suggests that land values around City Hall were quite high, and further, that competition among firms would produce some kind of fitness display, as a way to stand out among the crowded field of competitors.

Newspaper publishers became the first developers in the city to use height as a "strategic weapon." Media studies expert, Aurora Wallace, writes, "In early newspaper buildings, architecture reasserted itself in monumental tributes to the power of the printing press and its most assertive masters, New York City newspaper publishers."[20] The first of these displays was provided by the *New York Tribune*, which completed its massive structure in 1875, among the density of Newspaper Row at the northeast corner of Nassau and Spruce Streets. The office (see figure 5.4) was originally commissioned by publisher Horace Greeley, though he died before its completion. The *Tribune* was founded in 1841 and over the ensuing decades, it became a major American institution. Architect Richard Morris Hunt, trained at the École des Beaux-Arts in Paris, was commissioned to create the design.

Wallace writes,

> The nine-story height ensured that the tower would be taller than any existing New York office building and was thus neither an arbitrary choice of height nor one based on the functional space requirements of the newspaper. The design and size of the Tribune building was primarily governed by the enhanced public image that would be garnered for the newspaper and only tangentially by the potential economic benefits of building tall.[21]

The building pre-dated the use of skeletal construction and depended on load-bearing masonry walls. Given its height, the exterior brick walls had to be extremely

Figure 5.4 Early skyscrapers in Newspaper Row. Since media firms felt compelled to cluster so closely to each other, it created a dramatic battle for place near City Hall, where Manhattan's earliest skyscrapers appeared. On the left is the World Building (1890), built by Joseph Pulitzer to house his newspaper. At 349 feet, it was the tallest office building in New York when it opened. The middle structure is the Tribune Building, begun by Horace Greeley and completed in 1875 after his death. Greeley began the height arms race with this structure, which originally had nine floors (several more floors were later added). Technically, it was not a skyscraper in that all of its walls were load-bearing masonry. The front building on the right was the thirteen-story New York Times Building (1889), which the newspaper left to move to Times Square in 1904. Behind it is the American Tract Society building (1905), built by the publisher of Bibles and religious materials; it was one of the earliest steel skeletal-frame skyscrapers in the city.

Source: https://en.wikipedia.org/wiki/New_York_World_Building#/media/File:Newspaper_Row,_1906.JPG.

thick: 6.5 feet wide at the basement level and 5 feet 2 inches at grade level. Nearly half of the first floor was taken up by walls. Despite the loss of space and some early warnings that people would be afraid to work in such a tall building, it proved a modest economic success. The top floors were rented first, and by 1883, the building was paying between 6% and 7% of the initial investment (including the implicit rental value to the *Tribune*, which occupied its space rent free).[22]

Figure 5.4 shows the building (third from the right), with its tower jutting out from the bulky base. The J-shaped building hugged the rival *Sun*'s building, a mere five stories, and enveloped in the shadow of its rival. However, as dominating as the Tribune Building would seem at the time, it was soon dwarfed by real skyscrapers built after 1889. The most famous of these was the World (or Pulitzer) building (first from the left), completed in 1890, which sat at 99 Park Row, at Frankfort Street, just a short block north of the Tribune Building. Designed by George B. Post, it also used masonry walls but was combined with wrought-iron columns to reduce the thickness of the stone, which would have otherwise taken up virtually all of the ground floor. Technically speaking, it did not use a steel skeleton frame.[23]

The *World* was founded in 1860 and purchased by Joseph Pulitzer in 1883, whose prowess turned the paper into a huge success. At 349 feet, the World Building was the world's tallest office building and was the city's first structure to surpass the 284-foot spire of Trinity Church which, at the time, was the benchmark height for the city's skyline. Pulitzer aimed to use the building as a way to express the triumph of journalism, justice, and democracy.[24]

In summary, the newspaper industry provides a case study about the rise in the demand for skyscrapers. Tremendous increases in readership throughout the country generated huge sums of revenue for the many media firms in New York. Their desire to cluster together placed intense pressure on land values, which made skyscraper height more economical. Given the new technology, publishers also took advantage of the symbolic nature of tall buildings to express their corporate power and egos, which put more pressure on land values as it increased density and competition between firms.

SKYNOMICS: SKYSCRAPER ECONOMICS

The objective of the developer is to choose a building height that will maximize the return on her investment. To do this, she must consider both the revenues and costs from varying heights, and choose one where the difference between the two is the greatest. A shorter building will have less revenue but also lower costs. A taller building will have more revenue but larger costs. The best height will depend on the relative balance of the two.

The developer also has to make calculations in the present based on guesses about the future. She has to make several assumptions about the growth of rental income, taxes, and other expenses. If she is bullish on the future, she will add more height; otherwise she might remain a bit more conservative. Predicting the future, however, is not an exact science, and human psychology can be influenced by the current economic climate; if today is good, tomorrow will be good too. Or, if a developer sees a rival project in the works, she may add extra height to have her building stand out.

Developer psychology can contribute to the boom-bust cycles we see in real estate. When times are flush it is often hard to imagine that the good times will end, especially when banks are lending money and tenants are relatively easy to find. It is unlikely that Al Smith and Jacob Raskob thought their monument to New York City, the Empire State Building, would obtain the moniker, the Empty State Building, because the worst depression in US history was right around the corner. In fact, it is unlikely they even envisioned that rents would slow down their upward trajectory or that New York would cease to be a hot real estate market (see chapter 10).

Then there is developer competition. Since there are such long lags between when a builder actually has an assembled plot in hand and when the first tenants move in and start paying rent, the developer has an incentive to move quickly. If other developers complete their buildings first, then it can saturate the market and cause rents to drop. Developers need to rush while the "gettins' good" or there might not be much to get. While developers may talk about their projects and coordinate to some degree through organizations like the Real Estate Board of New York, individually, no developer wants to be left with lower income due to lower rents from a glut. Competition will often force the hand of developers to bring their building online at the same time, which, ironically, can cause the very problem that they feared in the first place.[25]

Finally, there are the unintended consequences of government policy. For example, in May 1988, a zoning bonus program by the Koch administration came to an end. All projects in the designated Midtown district that were started before then would qualify for a density bonus. The looming deadline caused a flurry of construction, and two years later, the office market was saturated with new office skyscrapers. The *New York Times* reported that the Midtown zoning bonus prompted the construction of sixteen high-rise buildings with more than 9 million square feet of rentable space. In October 1989, ten of the buildings were completed but had 38% vacancy and six were still scheduled to be completed by the spring of 1990.[26]

Ultimately, the builder has to make a decision, so she needs to make some simplifications. To do so she stipulates what she knows about the current costs and revenues and what she believes will unfold in the near future. The first item is the land costs, and in New York, it can represent a substantial fraction of the total investment. But until the new building is operational, land is basically a dead weight, and the builder has to pay ongoing "carrying charges," namely the interest on the loans and the property taxes.

The next item is the cost of creating the building itself. Once the developer has the land, she works with an architect to design it according to the developer's specifications and the architect's aesthetic tastes. Together, they work with engineers who create plans for the bones of the structure—the kind of foundation will be used, how thick the steel will be, what type of wind bracing is necessary and so on.

Next comes the request for construction bids. Over the twentieth century, several large construction firms have come to dominate the industry. Today, same as a century ago, skyscrapers are still built "from scratch." Each one is uniquely designed for the site and is, literally and figuratively, built from the ground up. Despite the use of mass production for most products in our society, we have yet to develop a method to produce skyscrapers in a factory (though structures built from pre-fabricated parts are starting to be seen).[27]

The firms that erect them act as general contractors, overseeing the construction and subcontracting out specific jobs to more specialized firms. In the early period, George A. Fuller Co. was the pioneer in skyscraper general contracting. Trained as an architect, Fuller moved to Chicago in the early 1880s, where he established the George A. Fuller Co. in 1882. He spearheaded the "cost-plus" system of contracting, where the company was paid a fee (usually some percentage of total costs) to hire subcontractors and manage the work, while the developer paid the actual construction costs. In this sense, his business promoted the professionalization of large-scale building construction.[28] Today, there are a handful of firms that can operate at the scale and complexity needed to build a skyscraper.

While all of this is going on, the developer seeks to acquire a building permit and possibly negotiate with the city to obtain additional height and/or a subsidy.[29] When everything is arranged, the project begins. The site is cleared, the foundation is prepared, and the steel or cement is put in place, floor by floor. The "organs" are then inserted—the water and sewage pipes, the heating systems, the elevators, and so on.

Next the building is enclosed, in glass, masonry, or metal. The interior is finished, and the building is open and ready for tenants.

Once the structure is open for business and collecting rent, the owner must attend to the needs of the tenants by hiring staff to run and maintain the building. The owner then must pay the interest on the mortgage and any taxes. The income flows minus the costs of operation (including an allowance for depreciation) generates the net income. If the developer or new owner has done the job properly, the net income flows will be large and positive. That is not always the case, of course, as sometimes things do not go as hoped, especially when the economy goes sour and the building remains largely empty. Defaults on skyscrapers have wiped out the fortunes of many a builder who was overly optimistic.

The Revenues

No developer would be willing to invest in the project if it did not produce a decent stream of revenues. While it is true that many developers have aimed to use their buildings for advertising or ego displays, the great cost would not be worth it without some monetary compensation. At the most fundamental level, consumers must have the income to pay for height in the form of office or apartment rents or sales. The developers look at the prices per square foot to determine the revenues from possible projects.

This income is largely driven by the health of the economy and the number of jobs in the city. Employment is the most important driver of the height market because it affects not only the demand for office space but also the demand for other types of skyscrapers, such as apartments and hotels. In addition, when workers agglomerate, it increases their productivity and wages, further enhancing the growth of the city.

Interestingly, no research has attempted to measure the degree to which skyscrapers, in particular, increase worker productivity. Some research has tried to look at how agglomeration benefits drop off as workers are separated, but no study looks at workers within buildings, such as the Empire State or the Citicorp Center tower.[30] The reason this is difficult to investigate is that it is nearly impossible to disentangle worker "selection" effects from worker "treatment" effects. That is to say, it is hard to measure the degree to which more productive workers cluster together in skyscrapers because they may prefer working with each other versus the degree to which workers become more productive from being in a skyscraper. Unfortunately, we cannot simply randomize workers across buildings and measure their productivity improvements. Businesses are interested in maximizing revenues from their employees and not in testing the theories of economists, so data of this kind is not available. Yet the suggestive data there are show the skyscraper to be a productivity enhancing tool.[31]

Although we can understand what drives the health of the height market in general, this still leaves the question about what determines the value of height *at the building level*. Research that I performed on condominium prices in New York and Chicago in the 1990s and 2000s demonstrates the existence of a height premium; that is, people are willing to pay more to be on higher floors. Controlling for the quality and size of the apartment, on average, people are willing to pay about 1% more for a unit on a higher floor. Thus, the cost difference between living on the 10th floor and the 35th floor can be as high as 25%. Similarly, in the New York City office market, rents tend to increase at the rate of 0.06% per floor.[32]

Clark and Kingston in 1929 estimated that the average rents for an eight-story building would be about $2.42 per square foot, while a seventy-five-story building would have average rents of $3.54 per square foot—an increase of 46%. This shows that office rents on the top floors were higher than those on the bottom floors and were thus increasing the average rents of the larger buildings. Also, ground-floor retail rents were higher because of greater foot traffic.

But why are people and firms more willing to pay for height? There has been no systematic research on this topic, so we can only speculate. First, the height premium is partly due to the increased productivity it confers upon workers who are all clustered in the same building and can get access to each other much quicker than if they had to travel to a different building. Firms are willing to pay for this increased productivity.

For the height consumer, living or working on higher floors provides more pleasant views. Evidently, the human species is programmed to find wide open vistas more enjoyable and are willing to pay for this extra value. Height also provides amenities, such as a reduction in street noise, pollution, and pollen.[33] On the other hand, being too far up, could make it more likely that you will be working in the clouds and have to spend more time travelling up and down from your office to the lobby.

Then there is the sociological and symbolic nature of height. Working on a higher floor (or the highest floor) conveys social meaning. It broadcasts to others that the occupant is placed in a higher position within the social hierarchy. If you are on the top floor, you are clearly a VIP with greater resources at your command, and you pay to announce this. In other words, people may be willing to dissipate some of their resources to place themselves in a favorable social position.

The Costs

Clearly, the larger the project, the greater the costs; but for analytical purposes, it is the per floor costs that matter. There are two major types of per floor costs: the average cost and the additional or marginal cost. The average cost per floor is simply the total building cost divided by the number of floors. The marginal cost is the additional cost a builder must pay to add one more floor to the building.

Some per-floor costs stay the same no matter how many floors are built; some, in fact, decline with height. But, most important, some costs rise quickly as more floors are added. It is these costs that impose the greatest limits on height, since after some point, the cost of adding an extra floor is greater than the additional revenue that it would generate. In essence, while there might be a rent premium on the higher floors, after some floor level, the additional costs of adding new floors are greater than the higher rent. If this were not the case, the entire city could efficiently and comfortably be housed in one mega-tall structure, rising miles into the atmosphere.

First, a taller skyscraper needs more and stronger materials. In particular, it will need thicker steel or cement, especially on the lower floors, to support the taller structure. More height also generates a need for greater foundation supports and more piers to hold it to the bedrock. Further, the higher building must also be braced against the wind. The speed of the wind is greater higher up, and wind pressure increases at a rate of the speed squared. A 1,500-foot tall structure, for example, must be fifty times stronger against wind than a 200-foot one. In very tall buildings, up to 10% of the structural weight of the building and its costs goes into wind bracing. It is often economically infeasible to perfectly stiffen a skyscraper. Under a strong wind, the tops of the Twin Towers, for example, would swing like pendulums as much as 3 feet from their normal vertical position. During a hurricane, they could swing as much as 6 feet.[34]

A more disastrous effect could be that the skyscraper itself could fall over, something only imaginable in a Hollywood film. However, for the fifty-nine-story Citicorp Center (1977/8) at Lexington Avenue and East 53rd Street, the possibility seemed real. The structural engineer on the project, Bill LeMessurier, needed to construct the building over a church on one corner of the property. LeMessurier's solution was to build the skyscraper on four columns toward the center of the plot that would rise nine stories over the ground.

After the building was completed, however, LeMessurier realized the building was not properly braced and could, during a once-in-one-hundred-years hurricane, fall over. Citicorp then had to surreptitiously stiffen the frame while the building was in operation. The building also has a massive damper installed at the top. The damper is essentially a 410 ton pendulum that sways in the opposite direction of the building keeping the building stable, though it was never designed to be a substitute for proper bracing.[35]

Another important set of costs are those for material and labor. Developers have a few options when material and labor prices go up. They can reduce the size of the project and/or they can substitute relatively cheaper goods and workers for the more expensive versions. New York City is notorious for its steep construction costs. Wages tend to be higher because of the higher cost of living and high unionization rates. Bringing materials to the worksite is often very expensive because of traffic congestion. But despite these higher costs, New York City is quite efficient at building skyscrapers. As journalist Karl Sabbagh writes,

> This ability to build tall and fast in New York results from two factors. First, in a city with a new multi-million-dollar construction project every month, the support structure of subcontractors and suppliers is immediately available as soon as the go-ahead is given. There is a labor force with all the necessary skills, and there are materials. . . . The second factor is the need to borrow money for as short a time as possible.[36]

The Elevator Problem

Elevators create a particular problem. On one hand, adding more floors to the building will produce more space from which the developer can collect more money. But at some point, a new shaft and set of elevators need to be added to handle the additional traffic. This then eats into the rentable space. Hence the dilemma: Do the additional floors on top generate enough rents to cover the loss of space from the new elevators? Part of it depends on the value of these lofty new perches, and for what will they be used.

Clark and Kingston (CK) estimated that a seventy-five-story building would have 16,000 people who needed to use the elevators each day. In 1929, a modern elevator could travel at a maximum speed of 750 to 1,000 feet per minute. Elevators need to leave the ground floor not more than once every 30 seconds to be of practical use. In CK's example, an eight-story building would require eight passenger elevators. Moving to fifteen stories would require another elevator bank and six more elevators, which added 66% to the cost of elevators (not to mention lost value of space). When the building rose to twenty-two stories, the extra elevator cost rose 63% but only generated 22.5% more rentable area. In general, skyscrapers must devote about 30% of the total space to elevators, including their shafts, hallways, and machine rooms.[37]

In the 1920s, 2,000 feet was considered the maximum technological height because of the elevator technology. Beyond that, elevators cables were not strong enough, and furthermore, the human eardrum could not withstand the vibrations of an elevator travelling too quickly.[38] Over the twentieth century, technological improvements have allowed maximum elevators speeds to increase.

In New York, the Woolworth Building, the tallest in the world at the time of its completion in 1913, ran two cars at 700 feet a minute. Starting in 1931, express elevators at the Empire State Building could travel at 1,200 feet a minute. In the Twin Towers, express cars could travel at 1,600 feet a minute. The new One World Trade Center will have the fastest cars in the Western hemisphere, operating at a top speed of 2,000 feet a minute, though a relative snail compared with the Burj Khalifa, which can deliver its tenants to any of its 164 floors at a rate of 3,543 feet per minute. Since 1931, elevator speeds have increased by a factor of 3.5. Maximum speed has increased at any average annual rate of 1.7% since 1913.[39]

Financing and Leverage

Most developers do not have the money to pay for a skyscraper themselves; and even if they did, the power of leverage reduces the incentives to do so. If the developer finances the project himself, then his profits will be the revenue from the project minus the costs. However, if he puts only a small amount of his capital into the project and borrows the rest, he stands to increase his gains (and, of course, he increases the risk of losing the property if he cannot make his interest payments).

To take an example, say the developer needs one billion dollars to build a skyscraper. Say, also, that he expects to earn $100 million a year from rental income. In other words, the developer can expect to earn 10% on his cost of $1 billion. Now say he puts down $300 million and borrows $700 million at 7% interest. Each year he now receives $100 million − $49 million = $51 million. The interest costs eat up 49% of the money he would otherwise get to keep. However, he only puts down $300 million. Now his annual return is $51 million/$300 million or 17%. Plus, if land values increase over the years, he will get to the sell the building for much more, walking away with a hearty capital gain. With his "meager" investment, he can multiply his earnings on the project.

The major point is that the access to and availability of funds will directly impact the construction of skyscrapers. The more money that is available, the more skyscrapers that can be built. While rising interest rates can increase the cost of construction, they can also increase their supply, since real estate is often seen as an investment that protects against inflation because rents can be increased with the general price level. When interest rates rise, developers often reduce the size of the loan and find more equity investors.[40]

The Profits

Profits—the difference between the revenue and costs—ultimately determine the height and frequency of skyscrapers. Figure 5.5 shows a graph of what I call the Skyscraper Profit Index (1960 = 1.0) and how it correlates with the total height added to the skyline since 1963. This Profit Index is the ratio of the Midtown asking office rents divided by the Turner Construction Cost Index, which is a measure of the relative construction costs of large-scale buildings.[41] When the ratio is equal to one, the statistics reveal that two years later, on average, 5,400 feet will be constructed. As the figure shows, there is a very strong relationship between the *relative benefits (B/C)* to building and the number of buildings completed. It demonstrates that, by and large, the developers are responding to the economic climate. Also note that since the 1960s, there has been no upward trend in the Skyscraper Profit Index, but rather, long cycles that reflect changes in the city's fortunes (see chapter 6).

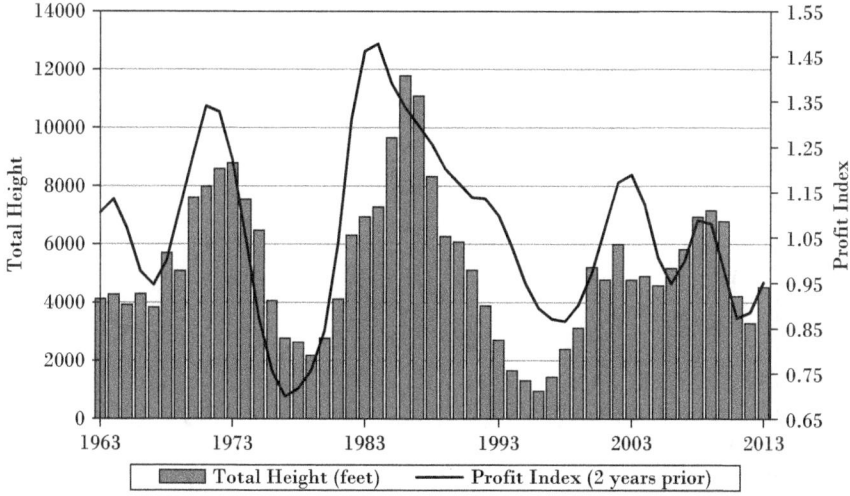

Figure 5.5 Total height and the Skyscraper Profit Index from 1963 to 2013. The Skyscraper Profit Index is created by dividing average Midtown asking office rents by the Turner Construction Cost Index. It is a measure of the relative profitability of office construction in Manhattan. The figure shows a two-year moving average of the value for two years prior. The reason is that there are long lags between when a project is started and when it is completed. Also presented is the total height of all skyscrapers completed each year (of all types, not just offices). As the graph shows, total height is strongly correlated with the Profit Index, suggesting that builders begin construction when the economic environment is favorable.

Source: Data collected by Jason M. Barr.

Why Don't Developers Build Offices Any More?

The types of buildings and their locations will be determined by the amount that consumers are willing and able to pay; developers will accordingly follow the money.[42] Figure 5.6 shows the proportion of skyscrapers that have been offices, as compared to residential buildings and hotels since 1960.[43] On average, offices have been a declining share of skyscraper construction. The reason: office rents have essentially been flat since 1960. Total city employment peaked in 1969 and remained below that level until 2011! It is only in the last few years that employment across the city has surpassed its prior historical peak.

However, the ratio of condominium prices to asking office rents has widely diverged since 1995 (the first year that a condominium price index was created for New York City). In the late 1990s, the two prices moved in tandem, but, since 2002, there has been a wide divergence, and in the last decade relative condo prices have been 55% higher than office rents, on average (see appendix Q).[44]

In short, the greatest recent growth in skyscraper demand for Manhattan has been in luxury rental apartments, and this has driven the boom in supertalls. Having said this, in the next five years, New York is likely to add sizable quantities of office space, as rents are finally rising. In addition, the Hudson Yards Project to the west of Penn Station (see chapter 8) will add up to 12 million square feet of Class A office in the next decade. Plans are also afoot to rezone the Grand Central neighborhood to promote the construction of new and taller office towers.[45]

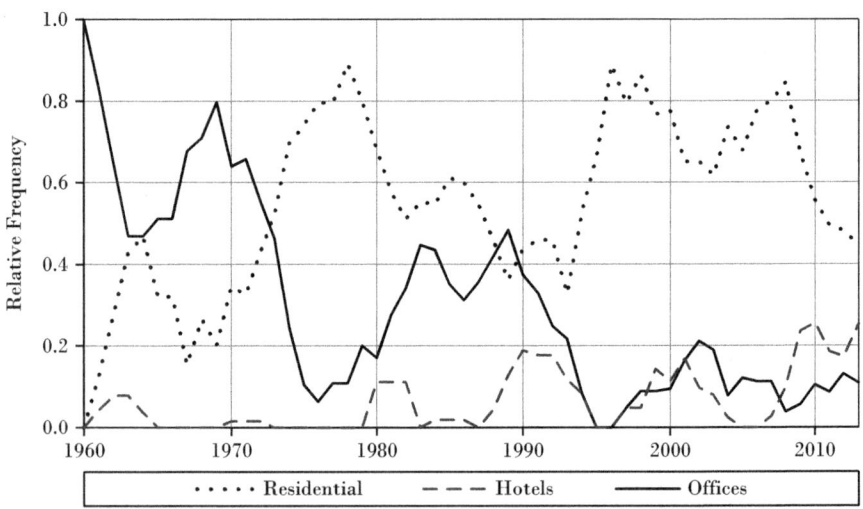

Figure 5.6 Skyscraper building types since 1960. This graph shows percentage completed of three types of skyscrapers: office, hotel, and residential (as a moving average of three years). As we can see, the fraction of office buildings completed since 1960 has fallen. The reason is that office employment has been relatively flat since 1960, while the demand for hotels and high-rise apartment buildings has been much greater. In essence, developers have "followed the money" by constructing the types of buildings that have the greatest demand.

Source: Data collected by Jason M. Barr.

ZONING AND THE SHAPE TAX

Before 1916, the lack of regulations on the shape or bulk created a specific economic calculus for a developer. Small plots suggested straight towers, with elevators

Figure 5.7 Skyscrapers before zoning. This photo illustrates the common building form for skyscrapers in the early twentieth century, before the zoning. On small lots, developers tended to construct straight towers, with a traditional tripartite construction of base, shaft, and capital. For larger lots, architects designed a "U" or "H" shape that allowed sunlight to enter the internal parts of the building. On the left is the twenty-nine-story Bankers Trust Building (1912) at 14 Wall Street. In the middle is the Hanover National Bank building (1903) at twenty-two stories. The right-most structure is the Equitable Building (1915), rising forty-two stories at 120 Broadway. Although not apparent from this photo, at the time, many felt the Equitable Building was overly bulky, and it helped provide justification for the zoning rules of 1916.
Source: http://www.nyc-architecture.com/LM/LM053-BANKERSTRUST.htm.

banks in the center and offices around the perimeter to maximize access to natural light and efficiency of use.[46] The architectural fashion was modeled on the classical Greek column with its tripartite system: base, shaft, and capital.[47] Figure 5.7 shows a row of typical skyscrapers for the pre-zoning period, located on Nassau Street between Wall and Cedar Streets. The leftmost (southern) building in the photo is the Bankers Trust Company Building, completed in 1912, with twenty-nine floors at height (540 feet). The plot size is of 6,871 square feet, which gives 184 floors per acre.

The Bankers Trust building replaced the Gillender Building (1897), which was twenty stories, on a plot of 1,828 square feet, giving a density of 477 floors per acre. The Gillender had the dubious distinction of being the first skyscraper to be torn down. At the time, Bankers Trust paid the highest amount for a plot of New York City real estate, paying $1.25 million for the site in 1910, which amounted $675 per square foot.[48] Consider that Clark and Kingston estimated land costs of $200 per square foot for Midtown in 1929. Typical land values Downtown before 1900 were around $100.

The next building to the right is the Hanover National Bank Building (1903). It had twenty-two floors on a plot of about 11,100 square feet, giving it a density of eighty-six floors per acre. Presumably, by going "first," the Hanover Building set the stage for an increase in property values on that block, which by 1912, drove Bankers Trust to build seven stories taller, and with much greater density. The next to follow was the Equitable Building, completed in 1915, constructed while the zoning regulations were being written. The Equitable Building has forty stories on a plot of about 50,000 square feet (1.13 acres), giving it a density of thirty-five floors per acre.

Because the plot was so large, it was necessary to provide as much light to the office spaces as possible; the architect placed light shafts about midway along the building. After 15 feet from the window, the value of the office space dropped off considerably because of lack of usable light.[49] The Equitable Building is generally considered the most intensive building of the period, with a gross rentable area of 1,736,513 square feet. Ironically, for a building that created so much controversy at the time, it was not that tall for the size of the plot.

In 1913, F. W. Woolworth completed his eponymous tower, on a plot of 29,411 square feet. Like the Equitable Building, it rose straight up, creating a twenty-seven-story continuous wall and had a horse-shoe design—the shaft is in the back. But, unlike the Equitable Building, the Woolworth Building faced City Hall Park and did not block as many buildings. In addition, the rest of its fifty-five stories were built as a tower, providing relatively more light on the street.

About a quarter century into the Skyscraper Revolution, the city decided it was time to regulate bulk and height. Many felt these new supertall structures were increasing congestion, throwing shadows on the streets, and driving height "arms races" between builders who aimed to preserve their access to the sun.

The objective, in theory, was to create a type of height tax that penalized excessive bulk to reduce the negative externalities. The idea was that the loss of revenue to the owner from the "tax" would be outweighed by the improved land values and working conditions that would ensue. Specifically, the Comprehensive Zoning Plan of 1916 created distinct zones of three major types: use, bulk, and height. For use, there were three districts: commercial, residential, and unrestricted; while the bulk regulations limited how much of the plot could be taken up by the structure. But most relevant for skyscrapers were the height rules, which stated how tall a building could rise before it had to be set back from the street line. The districts were given in terms of multiples of the street width, such as 1.25, 1.5, 2, and 2.5.

For example, in a "two times" district, the resolution stated that "no building shall be erected to a height in excess of twice the width of the street, but for each one foot that the building or portion of it sets back from the street line four feet shall be added to the height limit of such buildings or portions there."[50] There were no limits on the heights of a tower, as long as its floor area was no more than 25% of the lot size and was set back from the street.

The plan represented the outcome of negotiations between the real estate industry, business owners, city planners, and government officials. No regulations that were too strict would be approved by the real estate interests, but at the same time, they realized that some government regulation could benefit property values. There were two committees charged with writing the law; the Commission on Building Districts and Restrictions, and the Heights of Buildings Commission (HBC), and both were headed by Edward Basset, a lawyer, public servant, and leader in the planning movement.[51]

The zoning laws essentially locked-in the existing land-use patterns. Office districts would be officially designated as such, as would residential and manufacturing districts. As historian, Keith Revell writes, "The ordinance stabilized those patterns, giving official sanction and legal protection to the *status quo*."[52] Therefore, it likely had the effect of increasing land values Downtown and Midtown by promoting these areas as the main commercial neighborhoods of the city. If a developer was going to go tall, he would have to do it in the 2 and 2.5 times districts, and this would increase the demand for office space there.

The effects of the law, however, were not apparent for almost a decade, since the nation soon became involved in the Great War, followed by an economic depression that lasted from January 1920 to July 1921.[53] In the second half of the 1920s, Manhattan underwent a skyscraper building boom and the law's effects would become apparent (see chapter 9). The most visible manifestation was the new building style. By forcing developers to set their buildings back from the street line after a certain height, the law promoted the "wedding cake" form of architecture, popularly known as the Art Deco style (see figures 5.8A, B, and C.).[54]

By placing limits on the shape of the building, the rules produced a de facto "shape tax." The setback requirements were based on a basic geometric principle of a right triangle. Let's say that a building was in a two times district and was on a street that was 100 feet wide (a relatively wide street such as 42nd Street). Starting at the middle of a street, a triangle would be drawn so that the base ran 50 feet to the property line. From there, another line would rise at a right angle to the street four times that to 200 feet, because the total street width was 100 feet. Thus, the triangle with base of 50 and height of 200 would be completed. This gives a height-to-base ratio of 4 to 1, and hence, the setback requirement for all building space above 200 feet. Figure 5.9 gives an illustration of the zoning "envelope" which literally shaped construction.

(A)   BARCLAY VESEY BLDG., NEW YORK CITY.

Figure 5.8 The Art Deco Period. After the implementation of the zoning laws in 1916, architects had to keep their buildings within a specific zoning envelope, determined as some multiple of the street width (see figure 5.9). Thus, after going straight up until a certain height, the building had to be set back from the street. A tower of unlimited height could be built as long it occupied 25% or less of the lot area. These rules gave rise to the Arc Deco style of skyscraper, also called the wedding-cake or ziggurat style. Figure 5.8*A* is the Barclay-Vesey Building (today the Verizon Building); completed in 1927, at thirty-two stories, it was one of the earliest pure Art Deco buildings in the city; it was designed by Ralph Walker. Figure 5.8*B* is the Daily News Building (1929). It rises thirty-seven stories and was designed by Raymond Hood. Figure 5.8*C* is the fifty-seven-story building, formerly known as the City Bank-Farmers Trust Building (1931), at 20 Exchange Place; it was designed by the firm Cross and Cross.
Source: Collection of Jason M. Barr.

The HBC calculated that based on the new regulations, for "plots of normal" size, on an interior part of the block, on a 60-foot street the economic height limit will be between fourteen and seventeen stories. On a corner plot on a 100-foot street, they estimated the height limit to be "probably 16 to 20 stories."[55] In hindsight, this was overly conservative.

(B)

Figure 5.8 Continued

The Equitable Building, on 1.12 acres of land, had about 1.7 million square feet of space. According to Bassett's calculations, if it was built according to the setback requirements, it would rise nine stories before being set back, then it could rise again to eighteen stories; after that, a tower would rise to give thirty-six stories. The calculations show the building would have lost 483 square feet of space per floor from the second to twenty-second floor, 11,109 square feet from the twenty-third to thirty-fifth floors, and 36,261 square feet on the thirty-sixth floor.[56] This translates into an 11% loss of gross space, which seems a reasonable estimate for the "tax" level.

In 1926, Bassett complained that the new skyscrapers were still too big and that builders were gaming the system.[57] The shape tax could be mitigated by acquiring a larger plot, which gave the developer more flexibility to arrange the space within the

(C)

City Bank Farmers Trust
Building
New York

Figure 5.8 Continued

envelope and could still build a larger tower.[58] There has been no study of whether the zoning rules systematically drove builders to acquire large plots. However, based on my analysis of skyscraper lots sizes before and after 1916, the data do not reveal much difference between the two periods (see the appendix R). [59]

THE 1961 ZONING LAWS: HOW FAR CAN YOU GO?

As the 1920s unfolded, the original critics of tall buildings remained disappointed. The 1916 plan was designed to mollify the excesses of the early twentieth century, but little of this appeared to have been achieved. For example, between 1920 and 1932, 150 skyscrapers of 295 feet or taller were added to the skyline, with 85% of those

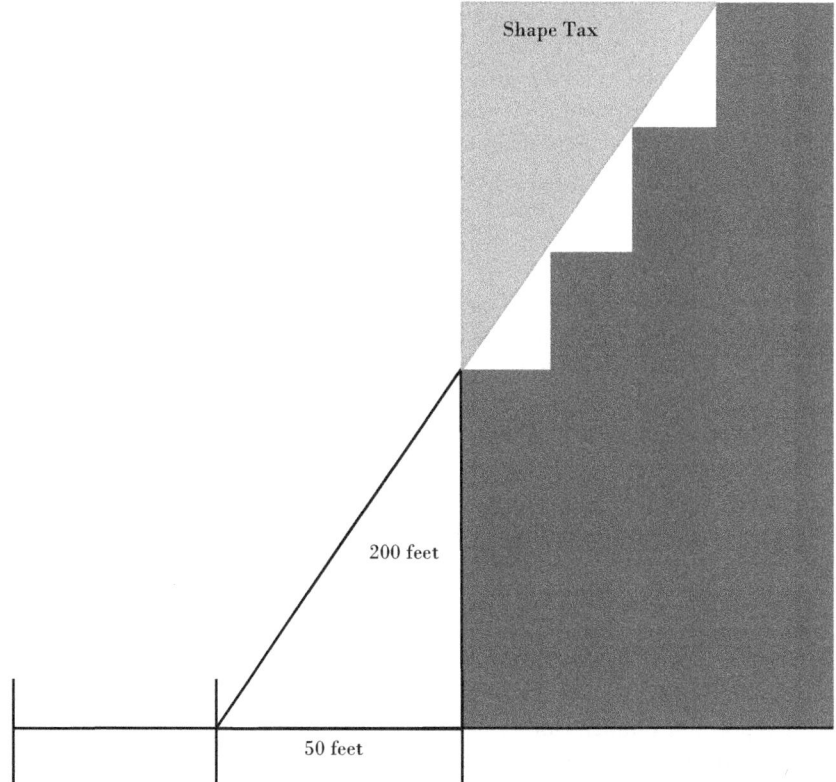

Figure 5.9 The zoning envelope and the "shape tax." The 1916 zoning rules specified how tall a building could rise before it had to be set back. The figure (not drawn to scale) shows an example of this for a 100-foot wide street, in a "two times" district. In this case, a building could rise 200 feet (about sixteen to twenty floors) and then had to set back 1 foot for every 4-foot rise in the structure. A tower could rise to an unlimited height as long as its floor area was 25% or less of the lot. The effect of these rules was to create a "shape tax," that essentially taxed away part of the building (shown as the upper triangle); this amounted to about a 10% to 15% tax in total.

Source: Graphic by Jason M. Barr.

completed between 1926 and 1931. By 1929, New York City was estimated to have 2,479 buildings that were ten or more stories. Chicago, the next highest city, had 449 buildings in this category.[60]

Bassett demanded even stricter limits, believing that urban congestion problems would go away if there were stricter rules on height.[61] But the increase in the skyline reflected the phenomenal growth of the city (see chapters 6 and 9). By limiting height even more, New York might have damaged its future by promoting greater decentralization, congestion, and sprawl.[62]

But then came the Great Depression and World War II and discussions of zoning changes were moot. It was not until the 1940s that the city began contemplating the next iteration of land-use rules, which would reflect the realities and culture of postwar

New York. Important architectural thinkers, such as Le Corbusier and Mies Van der Rohe, influenced the process. They saw the modern building as a utopian machine. A slender tower of glass placed in an open green would foster happiness and harmony among the urban citizens.[63]

Two skyscrapers, in particular, foreshadowed the future. The Lever House (1952) at 390 Park Avenue, and the Seagram Building (1958) at 375 Park Avenue introduced New York to the International Style of skyscraper. The facades were dark glass and suggested the tower-in-the-park form that would be codified in the 1961 rules.

A report, completed in 1950 by the architecture firm of Harrison, Ballard & Allen, suggested a new set of zoning rules.[64] It began by listing the major flaws of the 1916 Plan. First, it did not sufficiently separate economic activity. For example, about half of the city's residents lived in non-residential districts. Second, the regulations promoted too much bulk and density. Third, by dictating shape and design, it reduced the builder's flexibility, and therefore profitability. Fourth, the 1916 laws were never conceived to guide very large-scale projects, which might cover multiple blocks or superblocks; as such, they provided little useful regulation in these situations.[65]

Between 1916 and 1948, there were 1,439 amendments to the city codes, which gave the regulations an ad hoc flavor. The report states, "The structure of the Resolution, while complicated, can be mastered by any intelligent man or woman who has the time; but the language—full of negatives, double negatives, exceptions and qualifications—often cannot."[66]

The report's recommendations, passed in December 1960 and put into effect in 1961, created new rules on land use and building density. The use zones were modified by having finer distinctions. For example, under the 1916 zoning code, there was only one commercial zone and within it, bulk and setbacks were determined. Under the 1961 zoning code, there were eight commercial districts ranging from C1 to C8, where, for example, C1 and C2 were zones for local shopping areas, and C5 and C6 were zones for Downtown office development.

There were no limits to height per se, but the new rules regulated bulk by establishing maximum floor area ratios (FARs), which placed caps on building volume. In Manhattan the FAR in the densest areas were generally fixed between 10 and 15. For a FAR limit of 10, the developer had the choice to provide ten floors on the entire lot, fifteen floors on two-thirds of the lot, twenty floors on half the lot, or forty floors on a quarter of the lot. As another way to look at it, with a FAR of 15, for example, 1,500 square feet of floor space could be provided for every 100 square feet of the plot. The distribution of the square feet between larger floor areas or more floors was up to the builder. A FAR bonus (called incentive zoning) of up to 20% is allowed if the developer provides open space, affordable housing units, or other permitted amenities.

The postwar building boom, under the influence of the 1961 zoning rules, saw a proliferation of the glass box. Like the Art Deco buildings before them, their construction represented a confluence of three different forces: the zoning code, the zeitgeist of architecture, and the economics of tall building. The code removed the shape restrictions and builders could once more return to the rectangular-shaped buildings they built before 1916. However, unlike the towers of old, the new towers were black and the curtain walls were mostly glass.

Glass had several appealing characteristics; it was cheaper, provided better light and views, and it made the builder lighter, reducing the need for extra steel. The technological innovations of florescent lighting and air conditioning made the glass box feasible, because they had the tendency to act like greenhouses. This was not a major problem, as long as energy costs were relatively low. The Arab Oil Embargo of 1974 brought this issue to the fore when electricity costs skyrocketed.[67]

Figure 5.10 illustrates the evolution of skyscraper form. In 1908, on the south west corner of Broadway and Liberty, the Singer Tower (figure 5.10A) was completed. Designed in the Beaux Arts style by Ernest Flagg, the forty-seven-story building first rose twelve stories, with a long, goose-necked tower rising from the middle. In 1964, the Singer Sewing Machine Company sold the building to US Steel, who also acquired the rest of the properties on the block. Despite cries to landmark the building, the Landmarks Preservation Commission chose not to get involved.[68] In 1973, US Steel completed its new forty-seven-story, glass box headquarters, with 1.8 million square feet of space (figure 5.10B). Across the street is the small public space, Zuccotti Park. US Steel worked closely with the city to create a design that would promote a well-planned neighborhood, in exchange for more bulk.[69]

Twenty years into its existence, the zoning code was getting some of the same complaints as its earlier iteration. In 1981, Paul Goldberger, in the *New York Times* wrote, "As far as Manhattan skyscrapers are concerned, the 1961 ordinance has so frequently been amended and altered—and even in special cases—put aside—that it has almost ceased to exist."[70]

As government became increasingly involved with development issues, more agencies arose to focus on specific concerns. The Department of Buildings maintained its historical role over issuing permits. The New York City Planning Commission has the power to modify zoning laws for large projects. The Board of Standards and Appeals were charged with granting variances, in cases of hardship. Local community boards could review variances and contest decisions. And finally, the now-defunct Board of Estimate, as an executive branch, had the final say over negotiated projects. Through the second half of the twentieth century, large projects were negotiated with the city, as the city sought to extract some value from the developer in exchange for the right to build bigger.

By offering FAR bonuses for amenities, the code promoted direct involvement by the city government in negotiating with builders. Unlike the 1916 plan, the 1961 plan morphed into an *instrument of planning policy*, rather than simply limiting externalities. The developers were eager to negotiate for the right to build taller, while the city aimed to use the zoning rules to improve the quality of life more broadly.

A 1978 study investigated the additional square footage of office space that was created due to these greater incentives. The report estimated that about 80% of offices built between 1966 and 1975 took advantage of some kind of bonus, either as of right or negotiated. The report concluded that these additional incentives contributed to the overbuilding of the late 1960s, by adding an additional 12.6 million square feet of office space.[71] A review in 2000 of the plazas and public spaces created under the incentive zoning plan showed the majority to be underutilized, poorly maintained, or not well-planned.[72] The city's incentive zoning did not work as it was intended.

As another example of using zoning to promote development, in 1982, Mayor Koch created special Midtown zoning regulations to encourage offices on the west side of

(A)

Figure 5.10 Before and after: The Singer Building and US Steel Building. Figure 5.10A is the Singer Building (1909), which at the time of its completion was the world's tallest building. It was constructed during a period when architects were experimenting with new styles for skyscrapers. The building was demolished in 1968 and replaced by the building shown in figure 5.10B, constructed as a headquarters for US Steel and designed in the standard glass box form popular after World War II; today the building is called One Liberty Plaza.

Source: Singer Building from https://upload.wikimedia.org/wikipedia/commons/c/c9/Singer_Building_New_York_City_1908.jpg. One Liberty Plaza photo courtesy of Marshall Gerometta, CTBUH.

Midtown by allowing FAR bonuses of up to 20%. The provision was also accompanied by restrictions on how much sunlight could be blocked by the top floors of the building, requiring that 75% of the sky surrounding a new building remain open (similar to the 1916 zoning rules). The inducements contributed to the overbuilding of the 1980s.

Although proposals for a new set of comprehensive zoning regulations have been proposed over the last thirty years, nothing comprehensive has been implemented.

(B)

Figure 5.10 Continued

Under Mayor Bloomberg, there were many amendments to the zoning code in specific districts, but the rules about building height have remained essentially the same.

The Value of Air

By limiting the allowable building volume, the 1961 zoning rules created a new market: the market for air. In theory, every plot of land in Manhattan was now given a maximum allowable cube of space in which to build. An owner of an older building who had no interest in tearing it down could then sell the unused part to a developer, who then could "move" the air cube to her property. The regulations stipulated that the transfer had to occur on an adjacent property.[73] This promoted a minimum amount of light on the street, since once the rights were sold, they could never be purchased back, thus guaranteeing low-rise buildings remained so. As a policy tool, the air rights market also allowed landmarked buildings and churches to earn funds for reinvestment in their aging structures.

CitySpire Center
150 W. 56th St.

Renovation Bonus:

12 Stories

$5.5 M spent on renovation of
City Center Theater

Air Rights Addition:

26 Stories

$3 M contributed to New York City Opera
& $3 M to New York City Ballet

**Air Rights Purchase from
Five Story Building:**

297,300 sq. ft.

**Initial Height Allowable by
Zoning Law:**

34 Stories

Figure 5.11 The effect of zoning code incentives. The zoning codes implemented in 1961 offered a suite of incentives to developers, where they could build taller if they provided some public benefit in return. The CitySpire (1987) on West 56th Street is a typical example of how developers took advantage of these opportunities. As the figure shows, as of right, the structure could have risen only thirty-four stories, but the developer was able to acquire more floor area by taking three additional steps. First, Eichner Properties purchased the air rights from an adjacent property, which meant that a certain amount of sunlight would remain on the block. Next the developer acquired additional floor area by making a $6 million worth of contributions to cultural institutions. Finally, additional floor area was purchased by spending $5.5 million to renovate the City Center Theater. All told, this was enough floor area to allow the total height to be seventy-five stories.
Source: Photo by author; graphic by Rubaa Sala. Building information from Scardino (1986).

The air rights market has been a benefit to developers, allowing them to go taller than they would have otherwise done. My research shows that the purchase of air rights has allowed builders, on average, to add about seven more floors than otherwise.[74] Figure 5.11 gives an example how developers are able to build taller by the combination of providing local amenities and the purchasing of air rights. The building, CitiSpire, completed in 1987, is seventy-five stories. As of right, the building would have risen only thirty-four stories. But the developer, Ian Bruce Eichner, was able to more than double the height by agreeing to renovate the City Center Theater and by purchasing air rights. [75]

As land values have heated up in the last few years, especially in regard to luxury high-rise apartments, the value of air has risen correspondingly. The average price per square foot of air has gone from about $45 per buildable square foot in late 1990s, to about $75 per square foot in 2003 and then upward to about $305 in 2013. Air generally trades between one-third and one-half the value of the land. Consider that the median price per square foot of a newly completed luxury condo in 2013 was about $1,400 per square foot. If we assume average construction costs of $800 per square foot, then the air is certainly profitable.[76]

SUPERTALLS IN THE TWENTY-FIRST CENTURY

Figure 5.12 shows the supertall skyscrapers of the twenty-first century, all made possible by the purchase of air rights and by providing amenities. These new structures are generally ultra-luxurious apartments, meant to cater to the "inexhaustible supply" of rich foreigners or wealthy hedge fund executives (see chapter 6 on the effect of income inequality on skyscraper construction). Evidently, over the last few years, developers have been vying for title "tallest" residential tower.[77]

In figure 5.12A is Trump World Tower, completed in 2001. At the time, developer Donald Trump boasted that it was the city's tallest residential (condo) building. The tower, on First Avenue between 47th and 48th Streets is seventy-two floors and sits on a plot of 37,050 square feet, giving it eighty-five floors per acre.

When neighborhood residents heard of the plans, they did their best to stop it, claiming the building was too tall relative to the low-rise character of the neighborhood. But Mr. Trump, an experienced Manhattan developer, had done everything by the book. In late 1998, reporter Charles Bagli wrote about this in the *New York Times*.

> To obtain the site of his latest project, Mr. Trump outbid a raft of other developers 18 months ago, paying $50 million for the L-shaped property, which was owned by the United Engineering Trustees. In an uncharacteristically quiet manner, Mr. Trump began buying unused development rights from neighbors to the west on 47th Street, including the Japan Society and the Church of the Holy Family. The city also allowed him to build a larger building after he promised to include a public plaza in the project.[78]

(A)

Figure 5.12 Rise of the supertall residential building. An important set of buildings being added to the skyline in the twenty-first century are the supertall structures that are constructed for the wealthy. Developers are able to use amenity bonuses and the purchasing of air rights to acquire the necessary floor area to build tall. Because many of these structures are residential, wealthy residents are willing to pay large sums to have fantastic views and enjoy the social prestige that comes with owning or renting in these structures. Figure 5.12*A* is Trump World Tower (2001) with seventy-two stories. Figure 5.12*B* is 8 Spruce Street (2011), at seventy-six stories, which took over the mantle as the city's tallest residential building. It was designed by star architect Frank Gehry. Figure 5.12*C* is 432 Park Avenue, still under construction. When completed it will be eighty-nine stories and the tallest residential building in the world.

Source: Trump World Tower photo courtesy of Marshall Gerometta, CTBUH; 8 Spruce Street is from https://upload.wikimedia.org/wikipedia/commons/c/c3/Gehry_8_Spruce_fr_BB_Pk_Pier_1_jeh.jpg, and 432 Park Avenue is from https://upload.wikimedia.org/wikipedia/commons/d/d1/432ParkAvenueJuly2015.JPG.

(B)

Figure 5.12 Continued

The next building (figure 5.12B) is 8 Spruce Street in Lower Manhattan, completed in 2011, it took over the mantle as the city's tallest residential (rental) building. It is seventy-six stories, on a plot of 41,370 square feet, which gives eighty floors per acre. It was designed by star architect Frank Gehry and is one of the rare examples of an unusually designed building in the city, though it has the usual boxy shape. Because the lower floors contain an elementary school, the developer, Forest City Ratner, was also able to obtain a low-interest loan from the city. In addition, the developer was able to achieve its record height by the purchase of air rights from adjacent Downtown Hospital.

(C)

Figure 5.12 Continued

Figure 5.12C is 432 Park Avenue (at 56th Street). It is currently under construction and is expected to come in at 1,400 feet, with eighty-nine floors containing 147 condominium apartments. Its plot size is 4,280 square feet, which will give it a density of 160 floors per acre. At completion, it will be the tallest residential building in the Western hemisphere. Air rights were purchased from nearby properties as well.[79]

SKYSCRAPERS IN THE BALANCE: REVISITING CLARK AND KINGSTON

In 1930, at the height of the skyscraper construction boom, Clark and Kingston (CK) published their analysis of the economics of skyscraper height in Manhattan. In particular, using the return on investment (ROI) approach, they performed a cost-benefit analysis of skyscrapers of different heights on a large plot directly across the street from Grand Central Station, on the south side of 42nd Street, running 405 feet across by 200 feet deep, or 81,000 square feet. Their aim was to rebut the claim that skyscrapers were not profitable investments, and they were inefficient monuments that harmed the urban fabric more than it helped. They did their analysis on a large parcel in order to "give a very tall building a *fair chance.*"[80]

They itemized the different costs associated with creating buildings of differing heights, and which included the costs of land and construction. Then they calculated the rental income (retail on ground floor and offices everywhere else) and subtracted out the cost of real estate taxes, maintenance, and depreciation. Then they determined the return on the investment by the formula: the first year's net income (profit) divided by the total cost of land and construction. One way to think of their methodology is that it was designed to answer a very specific question: If you outright "bought" the land and the structure (that is, paid all of the costs), how many years would it take you to get your money back?

After analyzing the profits from possible buildings on the site, they conclude that, using 1929 rents, costs, and zoning rules, a sixty-three-story structure would be the one with the highest return; a structure that was very tall, even by 1920s standards (see chapter 9). That is to say, the sixty-three-story structure would pay for itself at the fastest rate. They estimated that the return on investment was 10.24%. Assuming that the rate stayed constant from year-to-year, it would take 9.8 years for the developer to recoup the cost.

How have the economics changed since then? To answer this question, I performed a repeat-version of their analysis, using 2013 rents, costs, and zoning rules to estimate the economic height of a skyscraper on the same hypothetical plot of land, using CK's cost-benefit methodology. The aim was to do a type of apples-to-apples comparison.

However, before we proceed to the results, several caveats are in order. First, the CK approach, one common for 1929, is completely outdated today. It simply takes the net income for a building, assuming 100% occupancy, and divides it by the total cost of the project. As such, there is no consideration of time; in particular, there is no inclusion of the capital gains that can be achieved in the future. Second, their analysis omits several important expenses. First is the demolition cost. They assume the site is clear and ready to build. I too omit demolition costs, but they are likely to be quite large. Further, they assume the entire (vacant) lot is available for purchase. Again, this is not realistic. The assemblage problem on such a large lot can take years, if not decades, which generates additional costs, such as the transaction costs (brokerage fees, taxes, etc.) and an "opportunity cost," which is the unrealized income from a project due to waiting until the whole lot is assembled.

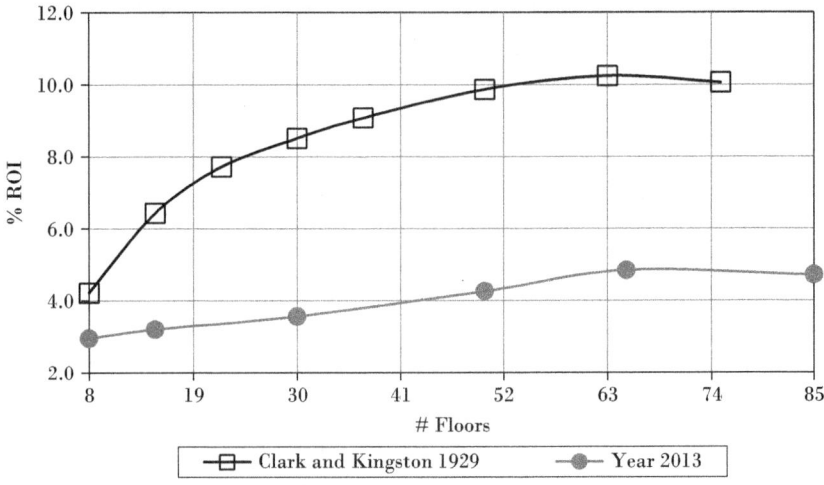

Figure 5.13 Returns to skyscraper construction in 1929 and 2013. The black line is the return to office buildings of different heights for a plot across from Grand Central Station using 1929 rents, costs, land values, and zoning rules. The gray line is the returns to buildings of different heights on the same lot using 2013 prices and zoning rules. The height that gives the greatest return is the same for both years, though the returns in 2013 were much lower overall, and reflect the fact that the late 1920s was an unusually profitable period.

Source: Data from 1929 are from Clark and Kingston (1930). Data from 2013 are from calculations made by Jason M. Barr.

Also, financing is missing from the picture. The only financing component that CK add in is a short-term loan to buy the land and finance construction. Their building does not have a mortgage, and thus there are no interest payments. Lastly, they use a simple depreciation formula: calculated as 1/50th of the cost of building; that is the building has an assumed 50-year life span. Today, depreciation practices are much different, as they are tied to tax policies.

With all this said, figure 5.13 presents a graph of the return of various heights from Clark and Kingston and my analysis. The results show that under typical building conditions, using current zoning regulations and the assumption that air rights purchases are available, the height that maximizes the developer's return today is sixty-five stories, which is about the same height found by CK in 1929.[81] However, two important changes seemed to have occurred between the periods. First is that the returns to construction today appear to be much lower. CK's maximum return was 10.24%, while I find an analogous maximum return of 4.84% (a 20.7 year pay-back time).

Second, the "shape" of the return curve appears to have flattened. In CK's model, the returns for an eight-story building start at 4.22% and shoot up to 10.24% at the sixty-three-story building. In my case, I find that the eight-story building yields 2.96% and then moves up to a peak of 4.84% at sixty-five stories. These relatively low returns demonstrate why virtually no new major office projects have been built in the Grand Central area in last few decades. In this day and age, the profitable returns are in residential construction.[82]

An extended treatment of these differences must be left for future work, but here are a few thoughts on what is going on. First relates to construction costs; simply put, the total costs of construction in Manhattan have risen dramatically over the twentieth century. For example, the inflation-adjusted Turner Construction Cost Index has risen by over 200% between 1929 and 2013.[83] It is just more expensive to build these structures today, given the cost of materials, labor, and other fees. Technological change has not generated a net savings to creating these structures.

Second is rental income. As discussed above, between 1960 and 2013 real rents in Midtown have not shown any upward trend; compared to 1929, they are most certainly lower. This might change over the next few years as New York continues its recovery, but as of 2013, the kind of rents that were available to developers in the late 1920s, were just not there eight decades later. Finally, operating costs have significantly increased over the period, due to increased taxes and the cost of living in New York more broadly; this has helped to not only reduce the profits to construction but flatten the return curve.

LAND VALUES AND SKYSCRAPER HEIGHT

What comes first: Skyscraper height or expensive land values? In other words, are land values a cause of height or are they the result of it? The answer is "both" and "it depends who you ask." To the developer, who must purchase the land and then pay millions to clear it and construct a tall building, land is another expense that affects the height calculus. To maximize his return, he must build taller as land values rise. Thus, *developer height* is driven, in part, by the cost of land, and so to the developer, land values are the cause of skyscraper height. This is what Clark and Kingston demonstrated in their book.

To the economist, land values are an effect of skyscrapers. As discussed in chapter 3 (and also in chapter 10), land prices are determined by the flow of land rents, and they represent the residual or left-over value that goes to the landowner, after payment for the building space itself. Land prices are the measure of the value of geography. Skyscrapers emerge because they efficiently allocate a particular location; they allow many people to be in the same place at the same time. The high land values are a signal to society of this benefit. *Economic height*, however, is driven by the costs of skyscraper construction and the rents or prices that tenants pay to occupy the space. To the economist, ironically, land values play no role in how tall a skyscraper should be, though they influence the value of land, since they influence the number of people paying land rent (see more details in chapter 6).

But how can these differing views on skyscrapers and land prices be resolved? It can be demonstrated mathematically that, under a specific set of conditions and assumptions, land values generated by economic height or developer height will be the same (the model is given in the appendix S). More specifically, assuming the developer aims to maximize profits from the investment, and is not concerned with ego considerations and that no externalities are produced, then it does not matter how we view land values and skyscrapers; they are just two sides of the same coin.

The real question is not whether land values are a cause or effect of height, but rather what are the conditions that might cause developer height to move away from economic height? If economic height is the benchmark for an efficient allocation of resources, then when the types of height are not the same, it suggests there is a role for government policy to help correct this.

So under what conditions will developer height be greater than the economic height? In other words, what factors drive developers to make their buildings "too tall" from a socially efficient point of view, and which may bring more people to the neighborhood than otherwise, and which might raise land values above their efficient level? Here I itemize some of the most important factors.

Externalities: If the developer does not consider the fact that his skyscraper will impose a cost on others in the neighborhood, either by creating shadows, traffic congestion, or increased risk for conflagration, then it will be too tall relative to what is best for the collective whole. That is to say, the construction costs to the developer will be lower than the total cost to society (which is construction costs combined with the costs of congestion or too many shadows on the street). When costs are too low, the developer builds taller than is optimal. The effect of externalities on land values, however, is a mixed bag. On one hand, more people will come to the neighborhood than otherwise; this would raise land values. However, if the quality of life deteriorates as a result, then this would lower land values. The net effect likely emerges from whichever is stronger: the benefits from agglomeration or the losses from overcrowding.

Holdouts and the Assemblage Problem: Because of the small plot sizes encouraged, but not created, by the Grid Plan (see chapter 2), landownership was and is often distributed among many owners, making the assemblage of large plots more difficult. These costs include negotiating separately with each owner; the fact that the costs per square foot are higher for smaller plots; and finally a possible holdout "tax." If a developer has all but one important plot, this gives the last seller some monopoly power over his land and he can raise the price above the market rate. Developers often have to spend years, if not decades, slowly assembling plots for skyscrapers. They frequently use obscure shell corporations to keep their identities secret. There is a saying in New York City developer circles, "Never talk real estate in men's rooms or elevators."[84] In one extreme case, it took over thirty years for the Durst family to acquire a sufficiently large plot to build a skyscraper on 42nd Street and Broadway.[85]

Higher land costs will cause builders to increase heights, as a way to maximize their return on investment. This "assemblage tax" can result in skyscrapers being taller than they would otherwise, since they increase the cost of land. There is no detailed research, however, estimating the cost of this problem. So it is hard to know how large its effects have been on the skyscraper market.

Ego: In some cases, the developer aims to create a monument, usually as homage to himself and his accomplishments. When multiple developers are trying to do the same thing, they may find themselves in competition to out-build each other. Perhaps the most famous case of this was the three-way competition between the Bank of Manhattan Trust (40 Wall Street, 1930), Walter Chrysler (the Chrysler Building, 1930), and John Raskob and Alfred Smith (Empire State Building, 1931). In this case, the Bank of Manhattan building announced its intention to complete the world's tallest building. Chrysler, not one to be beat, patiently waited until the bank topped out. Then Chrysler's architect, William Van Alen, revealed to the world something he was hiding in the top floor of his building: the stainless steel spire that would be lifted in place so Chrysler could then take the prize of "World's Tallest." Raskob, not one to let Chrysler get the best of him, then outdid his rival by redesigning the Empire State Building to be tallest.

Here, several different developers wanted to claim the title of world's tallest building, because of psychological or advertising desires. In these cases, developers were willing to give up some of their monetary returns for non-economic gains. This desire can drive them to overpay for land or to pay too much for that height.

Interestingly, the issue is a bit more complex because by overbuilding these developers create monuments for the city. As such, they increase the emotional enjoyment of the skyline and they increase revenues from viewing decks and merchandising.[86] So the net effect of overbuilding depends on the trade-offs between the extra costs imposed on society versus the additional gains from the happiness and beauty that is enjoyed by posterity, not to mention the uses as backgrounds for Hollywood movies. No work to date has attempted to measure the value of the Empire State Building to the human race. In the next chapter, I discuss the degree to which ego has been the cause of overbuilding in New York City throughout the twentieth century.

Related to this is the idea that skyscraper monuments artificially raise land values by imposing density on the skyline, in some sense, against the will of the people. The idea is that the ego builder decides to build a skyscraper in a place where tall buildings would not normally go. As a result, thousands of people are "forced" into and out of the building each day. While it is true that a tall building might divert more traffic to the neighborhood than otherwise, there are limits to this argument.

The Empire State Building is a perfect example of this. Developers Raskob and Smith decided they were going to attempt to make 34th Street a new hub for class A office space by constructing the world's tallest building there. And in this regard, they failed miserably. After the Great Depression and World War II, businesses much preferred to have their offices in the area north of 42nd Street (see chapter 9). To this day, the only reason the Empire State Building is profitable is because of the large revenue from the observation deck. The rents in the building are too low because of the lack of demand.[87] This illustrates that builders cannot force density on the skyline; rather, density emerges in the places that are most convenient and profitable, where transportation and history reign supreme (see chapter 10). The market punishes the ego builder who goes against the economics.

Advertising: Because developers can use their buildings to advertise, they might build higher than otherwise. F. W. Woolworth, for example, felt that by building a tower that would be the talk of the town it would generate valuable advertising for his chain of stores.[88] The advertising issue raises a similar question as the ego component: Does advertising provide a social benefit? By using a skyscraper to signal corporate strength, it can relay information to the consumer about the quality of the company and its products. If skyscraper height signals better products, then the height signal has value. If, on the other hand, the height signal is meant simply as a way to provide information about artificial product differences, then it is wasteful. The question then becomes to what extent does the value of the extra information offset the extra congestion or light-blockage from the taller structure? Since no work has explored this component to height, we are left only to speculate about its effects.

Irrational Exuberance: Finally, land values and building height can be too high if builders have unrealistic expectations about the future. If, during boom times, current projects realize significant profits, other developers will jump into the skyscraper market. This can cause a frenzy for choice lots and force up land values above their true market values. When too many builders are chasing these lots, it can cause a land bubble, which raises building height above its optimal level. When the economy turns sour and too many buildings have been completed, the consequences on skyscraper returns can be dire.

Note, however, that developer height can actually be lower than economic height, if the costs borne by the developer are greater than what would be socially efficient. Here are a few examples that might reduce the developer's height.

Uncertainty: Ownership of the land entitles the titleholder the right to develop at her discretion. Once an owner commits to a large project, much of the expense cannot be recovered. All developers fear moving forward only to find the decision was a bad one. This fear is especially present when the economic climate in uncertain—growth is currently low or negative, a war may be looming, or inflation is particularly high—and so the value of waiting till things calm down is relatively large. This means that without some ability to see more clearly about what the future will bring, each developer waits, producing less space than might be optimal for the city than if it had a clearer vision of the future.

Taxes: Since the government imposes a real estate tax, this can reduce height relative to the efficient amount, since taxes, in essence, penalize height. If taxes are raised above the amount to curb externalities or to pay for vital public services that improve property values and economic growth, the developer will build less than the efficient height. This is especially true when more and more land is removed from the tax rolls, driving an increasing burden on the rest of the real estate community.

Height Limits: Unlike New York, other cities have placed outright caps on building height. The general goal is to reduce externalities and the feared impulses of the ego builder. But there are usually unintended consequences to this policy, as they introduce inefficiencies elsewhere. First, they raise the price of space because they limit the supply. But the effect on land value is more complex. By reducing supply, and raising prices height limits can artificially raise land values, since the landowner now has some monopoly power (see Epilogue). But, on the other hand, limits cause the city to spread out and have a wider footprint than it might otherwise have. This sprawl can reduce land values in the center, since it raises the demand for land on the outskirts of the city. In addition, sprawl introduces more city-wide traffic congestion since people now need to spend more time traveling, and as a result this can reduce citywide land values.

In conclusion, by the end of the nineteenth century, developers in New York found the "perfect storm" of factors that drove the birth of the skyscraper. By the late 1880s, the technologies needed to produce them had come together so that they could be built safely and cost-effectively. Simultaneously, the booming economy drove a fierce battle for place, especially Downtown, which caused office rents (and land values) to rise, meaning there was a great demand for the tall building. In short, supply and demand came together to create the Manhattan skyline.

The new building type, however, gave rise to a set of debates. Are skyscrapers too tall? How much should they be regulated? The answers to these questions came in the form of zoning. In 1916, the city regulated heights by creating setback rules. In 1961, the regulations were updated to limit the total floor area.

In 1930, after about forty years of skyscraper construction, Clark and Kingston felt compelled to argue for their benefits and their economic rationality; given their assumptions and prices during the boom of 1920s, they found a sixty-three-story building was best. Eighty-five years later, a similar analysis that while the profit-maximizing height is about the same, the returns are much lower (without some extra benefit like subsidies or FAR bonuses). But this conclusion is based on two observations for an office building on a particular plot across the street from Grand Central Station. More broadly, though, how have the economics of skyscrapers evolved over the twentieth century, and what accounts for this evolution? It is to this subject we turn next, in chapter 6, where we will investigate the market for height since 1890.

6

Measuring the Skyline

Manhattan has been compelled to expand skyward because of the absence of any other direction in which to grow. This, more than any other thing, is responsible for its physical majesty. It is to the nation what the white church spire is to the village—the visible symbol of aspiration and faith, the white plume saying that the way is up.
E. B. White

To what degree is height like a commodity? On the flip side, is the height market particularly special? Because the skyscraper can be used for multiple purposes, including advertising, ego, competition, and conspicuous consumption, does the market for height show systematic deviations from what we would expect in a more mundane market, such as that for wheat or steel? Are skyscrapers economically too tall? Does income inequality promote greater height? To what extent do government policies shrink or expand skyline growth?

To answer these questions, we turn to the data. The purpose is to "decompose" the heights of skyscrapers completed since 1890 into various parts related to their supply and demand. Doing this enables us to investigate the skyline from a new perspective and provide answers to questions that remain understudied or misunderstood. While some discussion of statistics, economic modeling, and data are unavoidable, I have made every effort to keep the discussion at a fairly general level.[1]

In the literature on the skyline, the tallest buildings, such as the Empire State and Chrysler, dominate the historiography. This seems natural enough, as we are drawn to the biggest or most important icons of the species. But when we look down from a plane, it turns out that these buildings are the rare birds of the breed. To make a body of scholarship from the tallest and most special buildings is to draw conclusions from a biased sample.

Based on my data collections, of the roughly 869 skyscrapers constructed in Manhattan up to 2014 which are 295 feet (90 meters) or taller, only eight are taller than 1,000 feet (305 meters) (0.9%), and only another five are between 850 and 1,000 feet. The average skyscraper is around thirty-four floors.[2] The goal here is to look at the "workaday" skyscrapers and see how they might be the same as or different from the elite crop.

As discussed in chapter 5, since the late 1880s, the problem of engineering height has essentially been solved. The issue of economic height, however, is still the key concern. Of course, technology has continued to evolve, so that buildings today are lighter, greener, and more efficient than they were a hundred years ago, but the underlying economics of height have not changed all that much.[3] That is to say, that while technology has evolved, the basic laws of supply and demand have not, and fundamentally, it is the *economic* laws, not the *physical* ones, that govern Manhattan's height market.

Despite technological advances, we do not see taller skyscrapers being built in the city. The height of buildings in New York has not followed a simple upward trajectory. Economic height moves in waves—long waves—about a quarter century on average. The reason for these waves has to do with the interplay of market and political forces which change the height calculus. And when new buildings are added to the skyline, they impact the economics for future builders. These skyscraper cycles reflect the evolving incentives facing the builders. Only by year 2014, eighty years after the Empire State Building, and forty years after the Twin Towers, do we finally see a handful of new buildings approaching those heights; one of which is the newly built One World Trade Center. At 1,776 feet its height was determined by emotions not economics.

Figure 6.1 shows the height cycles in New York City from 1890 to 2014. Figure 6.1A is the total height added to the skyline each year. The graph in figure 6.1B shows the height of the tallest building completed each year. The figures represent measures of annual skyline growth—increases in both the density and height of the skyline. The graph in figure 6.1B demonstrates how the economics of tallest buildings have changed over the 125-year period.

In figure 6.1A, I make the simplifying assumption that a building is a "skyscraper" if it is 295 feet (about twenty-five stories) or taller.[4] This allows us to see the building patterns without having to debate about whether a specific building is a "skyscraper" or not; this could become a tedious argument, if the literature about which building was the first skyscraper is any indication.[5] The graph shows for each year the number of skyscrapers times their heights (in feet). Adding up the value for each year gives a measure of how much total height comprises the skyline: 381,749 feet or 72.3 miles of height have been added to the skyline since 1890. I calculate that the total usable building space of skyscrapers in Manhattan is 30 square miles of "land"; over 100% the size of Manhattan Island. Further, for all buildings on the island, the approximate total usable floor area is 62 square miles.[6]

From the figures alone we can draw several conclusions. First, height cycles do not move in lock step with the business cycle. Between 1890 and 2014, there have been twenty-six recessions or depressions in the United States.[7] Figure 6.1A shows that there have been only five distinct height cycles. More recently, there is little evidence to suggest that in the twenty-first century that the terrorist attacks of September 11, 2001, impacted additions to the skyline. As well, the Great Recession from 2007 to 2009 seems to have had a minimal impact. Only in one year, 2012, was there a considerable slowdown. In 2013, ten skyscrapers were completed and in 2014, thirteen were finished, including the new One World Trade Center.

While there are clearly fluctuations within each cycle, the pattern of larger cycles is striking. It suggests that the construction patterns are influenced by more than just the ebb and flow of economic activity, or short run jolts to the economy. Rather, skyscraper patterns are influence by fundamental changes in the economy, as well as the business cycle. We can clearly see that from 1890 to the present, there has been an upward, long run trend in the number of skyscrapers and their heights. The measured trend line shows there has been an increase in the skyline at an average rate of 47.5 feet per year (or about four floors per year). In terms of the tallest buildings, the rate has

(A)

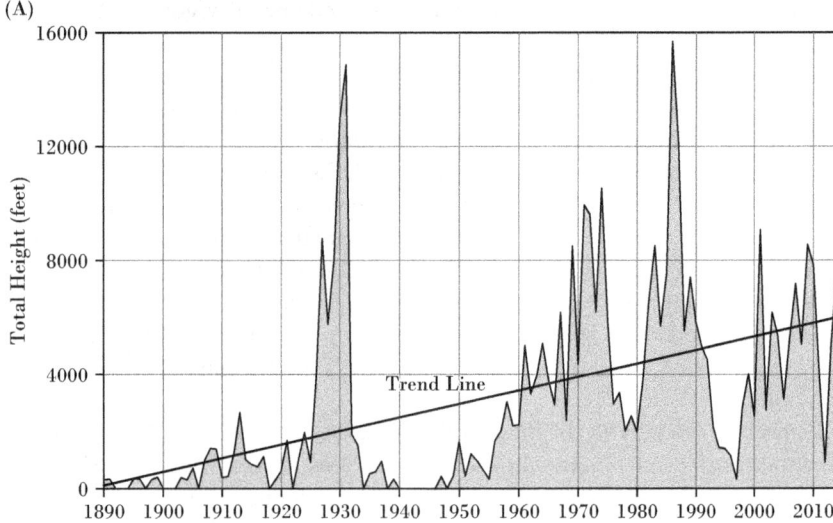

(B)

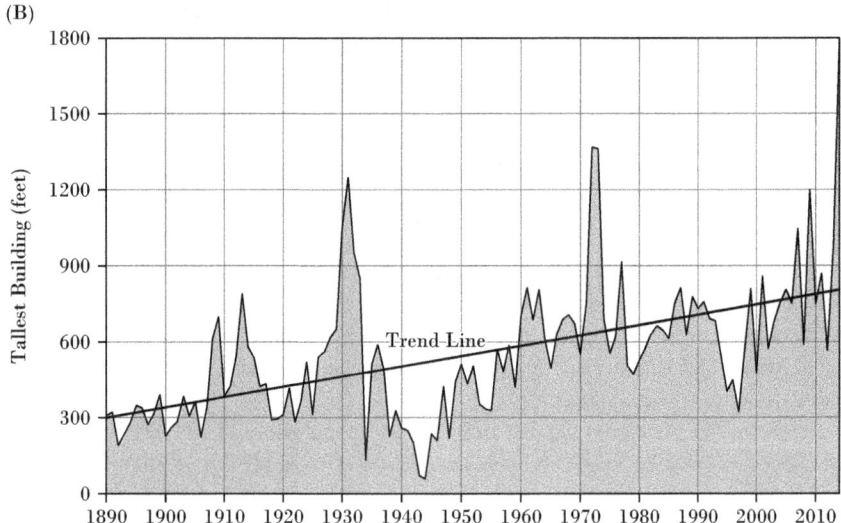

Figure 6.1 Total height added to the Manhattan skyline each year from 1890 to 2014. *A,* this graph shows the total additions to the skyline each year in feet. Note that I only include buildings that I define as a "skyscraper," which is a structure that is 295 feet or taller, regardless of use. Note how total height moves in waves that average about fifteen to twenty years. Since the birth of the skyscraper, there have been five distinct waves. *B,* height of the tallest building (in feet) completed each year in Manhattan from 1890 to 2014. During depression years, for example, the tallest building may be only at 60 feet, while during heady times, buildings can be taller than 1,000 feet.

Source: Data collected by Jason M. Barr.

been about 4.3 feet per year. In other words, on average, the tallest building completed since 1890 has grown at an average rate of about one floor every two and a half to three years.[8]

Another way to look at this is to compare the skyline growth to the economy as a whole. Since 1900 the economy, as measured by real US GDP, has grown, on average, by 3.4% per year; while over the same period, the skyline has grown by 4.4% per year. The tallest building completed each year has grown at an average rate of 0.79% each year. This compares to the population growth of the New York metropolitan region, which has grown at a rate of 0.90% per year.[9] These facts suggest that the skyline grows, more or less, in tandem with the economy.

Despite the long-run connection between the economy and skyscrapers, there is no trend if one only looks at the post-World War II period. In fact, since from about 1960 to the present, skyscraper height has shown no upward trend at all. Rather, years with large additions to the skyline are followed by several lean years. This "flattening" of height suggests that the role of technological change has not fundamentally altered the height market. The early years were ones of rapid growth and New York transitioned to the skyscraper to house this growth. The period from 1890 to 1930 represents America's adjustment to the modern economic era (see chapter 9 on the Roaring Twenties).

The flattening of height since 1960 is most likely due to the maturing of New York's economy. Its population is growing, though less rapidly as compared to the early nineteenth century. Wall Street is slowly losing its economic importance, as other cities throughout the world are increasing their competitive position. Real office rents have been flat since 1980, and today, the most frequent types of skyscrapers are hotels and apartment buildings (see chapter 5).[10]

Lastly, while the graphs do show a positive trend for heights since the late nineteenth century, this trend is actually deceiving. Once I account for the underlying economics that drive skyscraper height, the trend toward taller buildings is negative; this will be discussed later.

THE MARKET FOR HEIGHT

Fundamentally, the skyscraper represents a solution to an economic problem: how to hold as many people as possible on the same piece of land. As such, skyscraper height is a kind of economic good. Height has a value or price, and thus, it can be bought and sold in the "height market." In order to understand the economics of height I will first provide a simple supply and demand model. We can then use it as guide when looking at the data on skyscraper building patterns since 1890. That is, we can bring the model to the data and see to what extent the data support or reject this supply and demand model for height. Note that I provide the model to give some theoretical structure to the statistical results; however, what really matters is the model's conclusion: that the economic height of a building can be determined by the ratio of the net revenues (the demand side) divided by a measure of the construction costs (the supply side). So for the non-mathematically inclined, you now know the conclusion and need not be concerned about the details in this section.

Before we proceed, however, we need to lay out a few assumptions. First, is that the developer only cares about profits and is not concerned with non-economic issues, such as the manifestations of ego or height competition. Next, we assume that a skyscraper is a skyscraper is a skyscraper: the motivation for height is the same for an office or for residential building. Income is what drives height and the developer simply aims to "follow the money." The last assumption is that builders use the present as a guide for what they expect to happen in the near future. That is to say, builders use rules-of-thumb when making decisions. If the economic climate is good today, the expectation will be that it will be good in the near future and so on. I make this assumption now, but it can, in fact, be tested by seeing how well the data match this assumption. Lastly, we assume no externalities in the production or consumption of height. That is just a fancy way of saying we are not going to worry about whether skyscrapers block the sunlight of neighboring buildings, or whether they produce too much traffic congestion at the street level.

We begin with the height supplier—the developer—who constructs the project to earn a profit. As discussed in the previous chapter, this profit derives from the stream of income that flows to the owner over the life of the building. This income comes from the tenants, who pay for the right to occupy it. The owner has expenses, such as taxes and the costs of maintaining the property. So the profit of the building is the sum of income minus the costs. To make matters simpler, let's assume we are working with a fixed plot of 100 x 100 = 10,000 square feet. And by a simple shifting of units we now assume that lots come in increments of 10,000 feet, so we have a lot size of one unit. And like that, for the model, we do not need to worry about parcel size.

Let's call the sum of profits, B, which is the reward for construction. In some cases, the developer will construct a building and then flip it so that the new buyer will get the income. Other times, the developer will hold onto the building. But this is not important for now.[11] However, before the owner can start collecting his B, he has to pay a series of costs. First he must buy the land. Let's say the cost of the unit of land is given by L (i.e., L is the cost of a 10,000 square foot plot).

Next, the builder must pay the cost of creating the building, let's call this C. These costs were detailed in chapter 5, and they include the costs of creating the foundation, architects fees, steel, labor, machinery and equipment, and so on. The profit from building is given by the formula $\pi = B - C - L$, which is just the net income minus the costs of construction and land. But, what we really want to know is: How does the profit vary with the height of the building?

Another way to write this is by $\pi(H) = B(H) - C(H) - L$, where $B = B(H)$, just means that B is determined by the height, and $C = C(H)$ means that costs are determined by the height as well. We would expect B to increase with a taller building, on average. More floors mean more income. For example, we can say that $B = R \times H$, where R is the per-floor discounted expected net rent that flows over the life of the building. Here, we keep it very simple, but one could imagine that R is also determined by which floor you are on, so that R is higher on higher floors, with better views, and so on. But the fact of the matter—and what is most important for this analysis—is that *per-floor rents do not rise faster than the cost of providing extra floors* (if they did, we could house the entire city in one building).

For C, let's assume that costs rise at an increasing rate with height (given by the formula, $C = cH^2$, where c is a summary parameter that represents the costs of construction, such as the cost of materials and borrowing money). That is, we assume that as a building becomes taller, it becomes more expensive to add extra floors, due to extra wind bracing, more foundation preparation, more elevator space, and so on as described in chapter 5.

I am going to do some hand waving here for the purpose of simplicity (for more details of the model, see the appendix S). But if we make the assumption that rent per floor is the same for each floor, regardless of height, and the costs increase at an increasing rate, as above, then we can write the "optimal" economic height—the one that generates the most profits—simply as one-half the ratio of the rental flows divided by the cost parameter, c, which gives the formula,

$$H^* = \frac{1}{2}\frac{R}{c}$$

This says that the profit-maximizing height to the developer is given by the ratio of the benefits to costs. H^* is the *economic height* of the building, on the condition that this chosen height actually generates positive profits. Notice that this ratio appears similar to the Skyscraper Profit Index given in chapter 5. Here, however, we will go into more detail about what determines the relative costs and benefits of height. Also note that for simplicity I am ignoring the time dimension. In reality, there are long lags between when the height decision is made and when the building opens, and over this period conditions can change and developers can adjust their building heights to some degree. I will return to this below.

Reviewing the above formula, $H^* = R/2c$, can suggest to us why building height varies from one year to the next. R is the means by which space is allocated; it is the "referee" in the battle for place, as it represents what people are willing to pay to occupy a building. One year the economy is doing well, and people bid up R, in other years, the economy is doing poorly and R falls. If the cost materials or labor, for example, rises rapidly, it will cause constructed height to fall.

Note that the cost of land does not figure into this equation. While land costs influence the developer's costs, they do not affect the *economics* of the height decision. Economic height is determined by finding the floor count, such that the income from the last floor is just equal to the costs of providing that floor. In economic parlance, a profit-maximizing developer will find the floor count, such that at the top floor the marginal revenue from that floor just equals the marginal cost of adding it. The benefits are determined by the rent, and what tenants are willing to pay, and the costs are determined by material costs, labor, and so on.

The Economic Value of Land

Once the building is completed, what is the value of the land? Let's say a builder completes a building of H^* floors. This would give a profit of

$$\pi\left(H^*\right) = RH^* - c\left(H^*\right)^2 - L.$$

(1)

In a competitive market, the land would be valued to give the developer zero *economic* profit. Economic profits are what accrue to the builder, relative to a reasonable and fair return on his investment, assuming a competitive market for land and real estate. Setting Equation (1) equal to zero, inserting $R/2c$ for H^*, and solving for L, give value of the land, on which the building sits:

$$L = \frac{R^2}{4c}$$

This formula says that if the developer constructs a building at the optimal economic height, then the value of land is determined by, roughly speaking, the ratio of net income (squared) to the costs of construction. That is, the market will set the land price based on some function of the benefits to society, as measured by the willingness of tenants to pay at the location relative to the costs of providing the space at that location (and has a similar formula as the height determination rule). Keep in mind that if the builder overbuilds for ego or to engage in height competition, it can increase both the numerator and the denominator, and as a result, land values might not change all that much from the economic height.

The real point of this discussion is to show that under some general conditions, and assuming few externalities, land values reflect use values. If, however, c, as paid by the builder is less than c as paid by society (which includes the cost of street congestion and lost sunlight in nearby buildings), then the developer will overbuild, as compared to what is optimal for the city as a whole, and land values will be too high, as compared to what is optimal (see chapter 5).

Do skyscrapers increase or decrease land values over time? That is, what is the relationship between the battle for place and the value of place? Again, the answer depends. There are three factors that drive land values in this model. On the cost side, the Industrial Revolution caused c to fall. New technologies made skyscrapers possible because they were now cheaper to build. A lower c, means a higher L. But, on the other hand, a lower c also means more skyscrapers can be built, increasing the supply of space, and potentially reducing R, and decreasing skyscraper height and land values.[12]

However, when more people congregate together, they tend to be more productive, since they learn from each other, they communicate faster, and there is a higher division of labor and specialization. When this happens, it will increase the value of that location, by increasing R. As well, other firms will be drawn to be near that location to take advantage of the higher productivity of the place. This in turn bids up the value of the space. So, in short, by making workers more productive, skyscrapers increase land values, which in turn, causes more skyscrapers to be built.[13]

Over the long term, as costs fall and rents rise due to a growing economy, then building heights will become taller and land values will rise, on average. However, over the business cycle, when there are booms and busts, land values can fluctuate widely around these trends. Periods of rapid building will cause rapid land value rises, only to be followed by a period with too much real estate, when the economy goes into a downturn, and hence land values will fall (see chapter 10).

The goal of the model is to demonstrate the underlying economic logic of the tall building. Height is determined by the costs and benefits of construction. But it is just a model. We now turn to the data to see how well it can explain changes to the skyline and to see which factors are the most important. The first question to be answered is: To what degree is height a commodity like any other good, where the amount produced is equal to the intersection of supply and demand?

As figures 6.1A and 6.1B show, the heights of buildings have moved up and down over the course of the last century and a quarter, as, presumably, the economics of building has changed. To measure how economic variables affect height, I performed a regression analysis, which allows me to separate the different components that drive changes in height from year to year. This method is like a statistical centrifuge that separates a variable—in this case, some measure of building height—into its constituent parts.

Performing the regressions has several benefits. First, it allows for a test of the theory. One of the arguments of this book is that our understanding of skyscrapers and the skyline cannot be fully understood without investigating their economics. But this is just a claim, and therefore, the statistical analysis and the data can provide evidence for or against the validity of this claim. If the analysis finds little or no correlation between building heights or the frequency of their construction and several important economic variables, then it would suggest that we seek out other causes for the rise of the skyline—perhaps political, psychological, sociological, or aesthetic.

Second, assuming we find validity for the economic model, the statistical analysis allows us to estimate the most important factors that drive building heights, *holding the other variables constant*. In other words, the statistical procedure allows to us to understand, controlling for the other variables that effect height, what is the importance of, say, construction costs or population growth, assuming the other factors do not change?

Unlike the laboratory scientist, the economist cannot control the environment under study. The biologist looking at the effects of say a specific pill on the health of mice can control the setup to a very fine degree of precision. She can give the mice all the same food and housing; then she gives half of the mice the pill in question and the other half a sugar pill. Then if she observes a difference in the mice who took the pill, she can say with high confidence that the pill was causal.

The economist cannot force half the developers to pay one set of prices for materials and the other half to pay another set of prices to see how this determines how tall they build. The economist cannot say that on one particular block the eastern side has no zoning, but the western side does. That is where regression analysis comes in—it is a statistical method that allows the researcher to control for several explanatory variables that are changing at the same time and isolate the effects of each one individually.

Next with the regression results in hand, we can perform the exercise of *prediction*. That is, after the regression is implemented (or "run"), it can then be used to give a predicted or estimated value of skyscraper height that is determined by the list of explanatory or independent variables. We can then compare our predicted value to the actual observed value. If the two numbers are close, on average, we have high confidence that we have the correct set of explanatory variables.

The difference between the actual value and the predicted value is called the *residual*. The residual is the part of height that we have not accounted for by the explanatory variables. While the residual is, by definition, the component of height that we know nothing about, we can look at the sign and size of it to give clues about how far and frequently developers move away from the measures of economic height that comes from the regression; the residual is the measure of the degree to which non-economic factors are driving height. In particular, years in which we see particularly large residuals we can infer that part of it was due to non-economic factors, since in these years the actual heights of buildings are much larger than what was predicted from using the statistical regression procedure.

In summary, the regression analysis allows for a separation of observed heights into two parts: heights predicted from supply, demand, and other variables, and a residual part, summarized by the following three equations:

actual height = predicted height + residual height

predicted height = sum of effects from supply and demand variables.

Combining and rearranging the above equations yields:

residual height = actual heights
    − sum of effects from supply and demand variables.

There are, however, a few things to keep in mind. First, since it is virtually impossible to get expected rent or income and cost data for each building, there is no way we can see how builders have responded to the costs and benefits of building directly. For this reason, I use a series of variables that presumably affect their economics but they are not directly highlighted in the model or the ROI approach of chapter 5. These variables represent the broad market-based conditions faced by developers.

Second, when it was not possible to collect New York City specific data for the entire period, I used US level variables instead. For example, there is no consistently long-term measure of gross city product or century-long measures of New York City employment. But given New York's role in the national and international economy, the real estate market is generally based on the health of the national economy, rather than what is simply happening locally. The willingness to pay by Pfizer, Inc. for its headquarters is determined by the total number of people using their pharmaceutical products, not just the number of Viagra users in New York City. The willingness to pay by Goldman Sachs is determined by the volume of trading it does and the number of clients it has, world over, and not simply by the number of local residents who retain Goldman Sachs for financial advice.

As mentioned above, the analysis assumes a certain degree of myopia among builders. Given the lag between when construction begins and when the building is completed, I make the simple assumption that conditions this year when construction begins (such as GDP growth or population) will help us understand skyline patterns in say two years from now (when the building opens). I do not employ more sophisticated techniques that try to account for more complicated formation of future expectations on the part of the builders. However, as the results show, the simple "myopic model" works well in explaining the changes in the skyline over a century and quarter. These findings, along with other anecdotal evidence presented in chapter 5, suggest that builders use the current economic climate as an indicator that the future will be roughly similar.

The Variables

Here I describe the variables used in the statistical analysis, their hypothesized effects, and the measured effect. For this exercise, I have collected data on several different types of variables. They can be divided into four categories: (1) *Demand*: those variables that relate to the desire for height consumers to use space; (2) *Supply*: those variables that relate to the developers' costs and ability to get money for projects; (3) *Government policies*: These include measures of zoning and taxation; and (4) *Other controls*. We discuss them in turn later.

In terms of skyline variables, there are certainly a plethora of possible measures. In order to simplify the analysis, I have chosen the two particular ones shown in figure 6.1. These are the total height (in feet) added to the skyline each year (for buildings 295 feet or taller), and the height of the tallest building completed each year. The tallest building ranges from 59 feet in 1944 to 1,776 in 2014. The average across the years is 537 feet (164 meters, about forty-nine stories).

The first one is a combined frequency-density measure—how much is being added to the skyline over time; and it measures how active the market is for height.[14] The second variable is a measure of skyscraper height at the tallest levels. If non-economic motives, such as ego or conspicuous consumption, are important, then it would most likely appear in a statistical analysis of the tallest buildings completed each year. The data set includes virtually all of New York's record-breaking buildings, including the Woolworth Building (1913), the Empire State (1931), and the Twin Towers (1972/3). The only caveat is the Bank of Manhattan Trust (1930) building was completed in the same year as the Chrysler Building and is omitted from this data set (but it is counted in the total additions variable).

These two skyline measures produce two estimated equations:

Predicted total height added to skyline

$= f(demand, supply, government, other controls),$

Predicted height of tallest building completed each year

$= f(demand, supply, government, other controls).$

The part "$= f(demand, supply, government, other controls)$" is simply a shorthand way of saying height is determined by demand, supply, etc. variables. The right-hand side explanatory variables are "lagged" two or three years because of the relatively long period of time between planning and completion. In other words, the predicted total height and height of tallest building are determined by what happens in the economy two or three years prior. The idea is that decisions get made, the building then gets constructed and the final product is produced some two or three years later. The paring between what occurs two or three years prior and the height measures emerges from a statistical search procedure which aimed to find the best relationship.[15]

Another way to think about this statistical exercise is to imagine we are going to play a game with large Lego-like blocks that we can stack together to make toy skyscrapers. Let's say each block is one floor of one building. Our goal is to build out the skyline for a particular year, and we have two means to this. The first is to count the total number of blocks we use in constructing the various toy skyscrapers; the second is to see how many blocks are in the tallest one.

But in our game we cannot simply just keep putting as many blocks together as we want. Rather, we can imagine that we are handed a box with a fixed number; and further each block has a different color according to where it came from. Say, for example, the number of green blocks is based on the total population of the New York metropolitan region, and the number of yellow blocks is determined by the cost of building materials such as steel. In other words, the game to build skyscrapers based on the number of blocks in the bucket.

The statistical exercise is analogous to measuring how many blocks we have in the bucket each round, and how many of them come from different parts of the economic, political, and social environment. How many floors are added because of population growth? How many are added by growth in stock exchange trading volumes? How many floors are "taken away" because of zoning policies and so on? In short, we decompose the skyline into a series of "economic blocks."

The Results

Figures 6.2 show the results of the statistical analysis from 1894 to 2014. The figures present the skyline measures (the bars) discussed above, along with the predicted values (black lines) based on the statistical analysis (see appendix T). The lines represent the sum of all the "blocks" allocated in that year based on supply and demand variables.

Some of the differences between actual and predicted heights are due to minor, random things, such as differences in tastes or decisions among developers or architects, while other differences appear more systematic. This is especially true during peak years, in the late 1920s and early 1930s, and the mid-1980s, in particular. But the key conclusion from this analysis is that skyscraper height and frequency are largely an economically rational decision, even for the heights of the tallest buildings in Manhattan.

Consider the year 1931, widely accepted as the case of "developers gone wild"— the year the Empire State Building opened. According to the analysis, the economic height of that year for the tallest building, based on the fundamental underlying economy was 977 feet. The actual height is 1,250 feet; thus its height was only 22% too tall as compared to the prediction.[16] In other words, even the Empire State Building had a strong economic rational (see chapter 9). We now turn to a more detailed treatment of the variables that explain the height cycles.[17]

Skyline Demand

To investigate the relationship between population and skyline growth, the regression analysis included three population measures: the population of New York City;

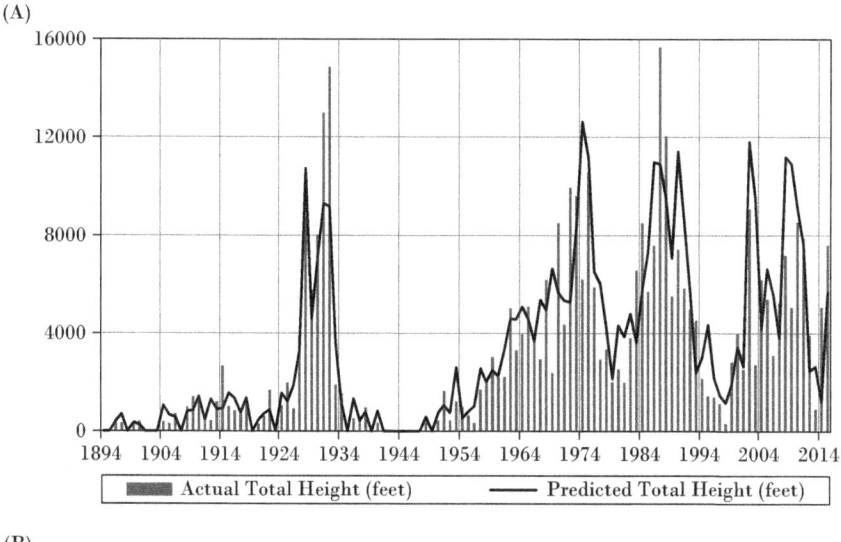

(A)

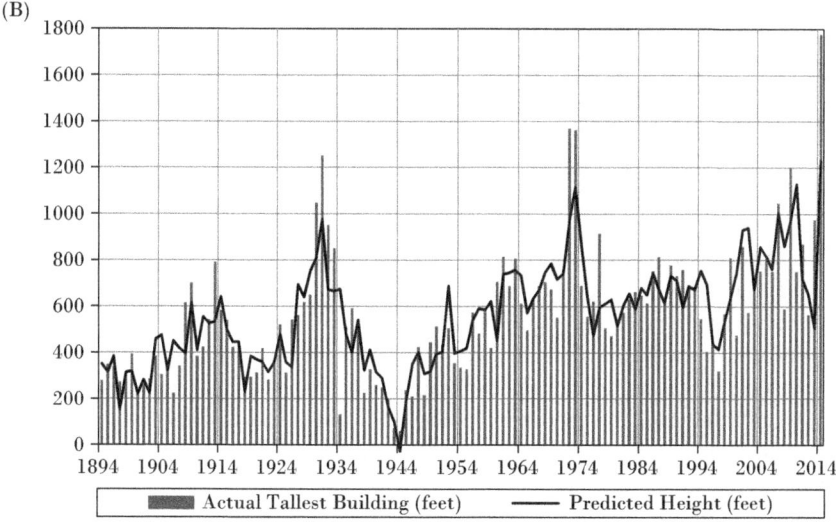

(B)

Figure 6.2 Total height versus predicted height from 1900 to 2014. *A*, the graph shows the total height added to the skyline each year as compared to the total predicted height that comes from a statistical (regression) analysis, which includes important supply and demand variables. This supply and demand-based model is able to account for the major cyclical patterns in New York's skyscraper market. It suggests that, by and large, the skyscraper is a rational response to the demand for tall buildings. *B*, height of the tallest building completed each year versus predicted height from 1900 to 2014. This figure shows how the supply and demand model can account for the major tallest-building cycles, since 1900. Again, it suggests that on average, even the tallest of the tall have a strong economic rationale. That is not to deny that some buildings are economically too tall, but these are the statistical rarities.
Source: Data and analysis by Jason M. Barr.

the population of the five surrounding counties, Nassau, Suffolk, Westchester in New York State, and Hudson and Bergen counties in New Jersey; and third is the total US population.[18]

The point of including these demographic measures is that, presumably, more people means a fiercer battle for place; and that this will be met by increasing the amount floor space and height. Clearly, the local population is likely to be influential for the demand for floor space and height, but the national population is also included because of the importance of New York in the national economy, as a destination for tourists, and as one of the main hubs of finance and commerce.

The results strongly support the idea that the skyscraper is a solution to the problem of excess demand for particular locations. Growth in the skyline is very responsive to population growth. For total additions to the skyline, growth of the New York City population by 1% increases the additions to the skyline by about 7.7% each year, on average. For the regional (non-NYC) population, a 1% increase in regional population is associated with about a 2.1% rise in additions to the skyline. Finally, increases in the US population by 1% have increased the skyline by about 8.4%, on average, since 1890! If we combine the local, regional, and national effects, we see that population growth throughout is a tremendous influence on the skyline.

Interestingly, for the tallest building completed each year, there does not appear to be an effect from the national population, but there is one from the city and region population. For example, an increase of the New York City population by, say, 10% increases the height of the tallest building by 27 feet. A 10% increase in population growth in the surrounding counties increases some 17 feet. The absence of a statistical effect from the national population is a bit mysterious; and the reason for this must be left for future work.

The results suggest a kind of multiplier effect for population growth. When a person moves into the city, she requires not only a place to live but also works in the city and consumes goods and services there. Each resident requires a buffet of local goods and services, to satisfy their needs and wants. As a result, when a person moves to the city, in an infinitesimal way, she influences the land values and the height of buildings. This logic is similar for people who live in the suburbs. Many of them work in Manhattan or come into the city for recreation and cultural events, and, again, are pushing up the value of land, which causes developers to respond by adding to the skyline. In short, the evidence demonstrates the importance of population growth for skyline growth. In fact, collectively population growth is perhaps the most important driver of the skyline.

Consider that the growth of the regional population has slowed over the twentieth century. Between 1880 and 1930, the average regional population growth was about 2.7% per year; since 1930 population growth has been closer to 0.5%, with the region losing population in the decade of the 1970s. This is part of the reason why there is no upward trend to the additions or height to the skyline. As the city's economy has matured, and as the nation has shifted its center of gravity away from the East Coast, the effect on the skyline has been felt.

Since New York is the capital of finance, I included two measures that try to capture the industry's influence on the skyline. The first variable is the fraction of US workers employed in the Finance, Insurance, and Real Estate Industry (FIRE) relative to total US employment. Presumably, the more workers in these industries, the greater the demand for space in New York (century-long measures of New York City employment in the financial sector do not seem to exist). The second variable is the average daily number of stocks traded on the New York Stock Exchange. Presumably, stock exchange volume will directly lead to profits to traders and finance firms and hence to the demand for more space.

The results show that employment in the FIRE industry has been good for the skyline. A 1% increase in FIRE employment in the United States relative to total employment translates to about a 3.3% increase in the total height added to the skyline, all else equal. In other words, the skyline growth is directly tied to the strength of the financial sector. Relative employment in the FIRE industry grew rapidly in the first half of the twentieth century, but has been flat (or slightly declining) since the late 1980s. In regard to the height of the tallest buildings, statistically speaking, the effect of FIRE growth has not played a large direct role in determining the height of the tallest building, at least relative to the other included variables.

Stock exchange volume is tied to the skyline. A 10% increase in trading volume is associated with a 5.9% increase in total height. For the height of the tallest building, an increase in 10% of the stock exchanges volume is associated with a 6 feet rise (half a floor) in the height of the tallest building, on average. While 6 feet might seem rather small, consider the twentieth-century trend for height is about 4 feet per year, on average. The combined effects of finance on the skyline have shown, in general, to be rather strong.

The last demand-side variable included is the growth rate in the economy as a whole—the percent change in gross domestic product. For this, I include the growth rate of real GDP relative to the trend growth rate of 3.3% since 1880. The idea is to see how growth relative to the norm affects the skyline. We would expect extremely robust growth to be met with extra skyline growth. Are periods of rapid building tied to rapid economic growth? Yes; skyline growth as a whole has been quite responsive to GDP growth (a 10% increase above trend leads to a 13% increase in the skyline). The effect of GDP on the height of the tallest building has been smaller, and therefore, was not included in the regression.

To summarize, the key findings from these statistical analyses is that, first and foremost, skyscrapers—theirs height and frequencies—are a response to the problem of land shortage brought on by the battle for place. Population, employment, and economic growth, as a group, represent the most important set of explanatory variables in the analysis. They are in short, the sine qua non, of the skyscraper. While non-economic factors are present from time to time, and will be discussed below, they remain secondary. The results suggest that over the twentieth century, skyscraper height behaves, for the most part, like a commodity, such as oil, steel, or wheat, reacting quite strongly to the demand side of the economy.

Skyline Supply

Cleary the demand side is not the only component that affects the skyline. Developers make decisions about what to build based on the costs of construction. To measure the supply side, I included three variables. First is an index of the real price of building materials. This is meant to capture the cost of buying physical products that go into the building itself, such as steel, wood, cement, and so on.[19] The more things cost (relative to the price level in general), the less likely a developer will add to the skyline, since it will reduce his profits.

Next, are finance-related variables that relate to the cost and access to money. Since the developer has to raise a significant fraction of the cost from the capital or money markets, the more expensive the cost of money, the less likely, one would hypothesize, a developer is to add to the skyline. For this, I include the real (inflation-adjusted) interest rate and the growth in commercial loans for real estate. These variables are meant to measure the cost and access that developers have to capital for financing their project, respectively. If banks, for whatever reason, are not supplying real estate loans, presumably, we are likely to see less construction, all else equal.

The statistical results show an important role for the supply-side variables. Building materials costs reduce the height of additions to the skyline. For example, a 10% increase in buildings materials cost is associated with 14.9% drop in the total height variable. As well, a 10% increase in building costs reduces the height of the tallest building by 34.6 feet (three floors) on average. Capital costs and access are statistically important. Increases in the real interest rate reduce the total height by a small amount (but does not seem to affect the height of the tallest building); and access to loans increases the total additions, but seems to have little effect on the tallest building.

Lastly, since skyscrapers are durable, the decisions of past builders continue to have ramifications for the market in the present. Today's builders are, in some sense, competing with those of the past because the total, cumulative amount of skyscraper space affects the current price. When builders went on construction sprees in prior years, the effects of these last a long time into the future, as it takes many years, decades even, for this new space to be fully absorbed. While new and old space can be substituted for each other, they are not perfect substitutes. New and old buildings are similar to new and old cars. Both will get you from Point A to Point B in roughly the same time, and they might even have the same gas mileage, but the new car will have a CD player, GPS, phone charging port, and a more sophisticated dashboard; the older car might have a cassette player and fewer modern features. The new car will cost less to maintain, and so on.

In the same vein, new buildings have better wiring and infrastructure for computer technology. The floor space layout will be more conducive to modern business methods; its physical plant is likely to be more efficient and provide a more comfortable environment, and so on.[20] The old building space will fetch a lower price than the new. But they are linked. If there is a lot of old space on the market, it will depress the price of the new space.

In order to measure the effects of cumulative building decisions on the skyline, all else equal, I include the net total number of skyscrapers as one of the explanatory variables; that is, I included the total count of skyscrapers constructed up to each year, minus the number demolished or destroyed. The number of demolitions of 295-feet or taller buildings is very small. By and large, once a skyscraper gets built it remains in circulation—though its use might change over time. In fact, there have only been seventeen 295-feet or taller buildings removed from New York, and three of them were due to the terrorist attacks of September 2001.[21]

The results show that the number of skyscrapers constructed in the past diminishes future construction. For every 10% increase in the cumulative total, total height falls by 27%, all else equal. For the height of the tallest building, a 10% increase in the cumulative total causes the height of the tallest building to drop by 29 feet each year. These results can also help explain the flattening of height since World War II.

Government Policies

As discussed in previous chapters, government policies play both a direct and indirect role in the heights and numbers of skyscrapers. The most important perhaps is the role of zoning. To keep things simple, the statistical analysis aims to see if the two zoning regimes (1916-1961; 1962-2013) reduced the skyline as compared to the pre-zoning years, and if so, by how much?

Recall from chapter 5 that the 1916 zoning laws restricted the shape of the building by mandating setbacks relative to the width of the street. The zoning plan created different multiples from 1 to 2.5, which, when multiplied by the street width, gave the maximum height of the building before having to be set back. An unlimited tower was permitted as long as its floor area was less than 25% of the lot size.

The 1961 zoning rules also did not limit height, but rather limited bulk by setting maximum allowable floor area ratios (FARs). In Downtown and Midtown, FARs have been capped at 15 plus 3 if an amenity, such as a plaza, was provided. A FAR of 18, means a thirty-six-story building can be built on half the lot or a seventy-two-story building on a quarter of the lot. For the sake of comparison the Empire State Building (1931) has a FAR of 30; while 30 Rockefeller Plaza (1937) has a FAR of 54.[22]

To measure how these zoning rules affected the market for height, I created variables which take on the value of one in years the respective regimes were in place and zero otherwise.[23] The interpretation of these variables is to see whether a particular zoning plan impacted the skyline *relative to no zoning*, all else equal. The results show that the two different zoning regimes had about the same effect on reducing the heights of buildings, though the 1961 rules seem to have been slightly stricter. The effect of zoning on the total additions to the skyline was quite large, by about 70% compared to years with no zoning, all else equal. Recall that in my data set, a building is included if it is 295 or taller, so the large reduction suggests that several buildings that would have been above the threshold without zoning were then reduced below it because of the regulations. Similarly, zoning has reduced the height of the tallest building between 94 feet and 129 feet, on average, over the twentieth century. For the total height equations, the 1916 and 1961 zoning rules seem to have had an equal effect on the skyline. However, the 1961 regulations have reduced the heights of the tallest buildings more than the 1916 regulations. This is likely due to the FAR caps.

Other policy variables were included. One was to measure the effect of the change in zoning rules during the Koch administration. In order to encourage development in Midtown west of Fifth Avenue, FAR bonuses were given for buildings constructed in the area, if ground was broken between 1982 and 1988. To this end, I created a "West side" variable to measure the effects of this program on the skyline during the years it was in effect.

A few other tax-related variables were included. First was the effective tax rate, which is the tax rate times the total real assessed valuation of Manhattan.[24] While the results show a negative relationship, as predicted, it is not statistically significant. Beginning in the 1970s, a series of building-related subsidies were introduced to stimulate both business and residential construction. In 1977, the Industrial and Commercial Incentive Board (ICIB) was authorized to grant tax abatements to businesses if they constructed offices (or hotels) in New York City. In 1984, the ICIB was disbanded and the program became the Industrial and Commercial Incentive Program (ICIP), which provided business subsidies "as of right," if the business satisfied a certain set of criteria. In the mid-1990s, the ICIP program was curtailed in Manhattan. I include a variable to measure its effect. That is to say, I include a variable to test for whether these programs increased the number and/or heights of skyscrapers. While they were intended to increase the amount of business in the city, they may have also had the effect of increasing investment in real estate as a result.

In terms of housing subsidies, in 1971 the "421-a" program was introduced to provide tax abatements to building developers for constructing apartments. For builders of rental units, developers would qualify for the subsidies if they agreed to charge rents within New York City's rent stabilization program. Developers of condominiums could also qualify for the abatements, and the savings could then be passed to the buyers. The program became stricter in Manhattan in 1985. Although it still exists and is used throughout the city, for the first fifteen years, its benefits were relatively more generous; for this reason, I created a variable that equals one in the years 1971 to 1985, and zero in the rest, to capture the effect of this program. In other words, did relatively generous housing tax abatements lead to more skyscrapers during this period?

Figure 6.1 shows that the decade of the 1980s was perhaps the city's most prolific skyscraper decade, and between 1982 and 1985, the three policies (the West Side Zoning, 421-a, and ICIP) were in effect at the same time. Thus, from 1984 and 1987, we would expect to see a flurry of skyscraper activity. The statistical results bear this out—policies that subsidize real estate in the city were an effective means of increasing the size of the skyline. In the years between 1984 and 1987, the combined three policies caused nearly 200% rise in the number of skyscrapers than there would have been otherwise (again, by increasing the number of buildings that were over the "skyscraper" threshold). The effect of these policies on the tallest building was a bit more modest. Only the ICIP, which was targeted to businesses, seems to have increased the height of the tallest building. On average, during the ICIP years, the tallest buildings were 147 feet (thirteen floors) taller than otherwise, on average.

The Trend

Recall from above that there has been a positive height trend since 1885 to the present, but no trend since 1960. The upward movement stems mostly from the transition from a world without skyscrapers to one with them. This growth, therefore, appears to be an artifact of the data. For this reason, a time trend variable was included in the regression; it aims to assess whether, controlling for the other factors that drive the growth of the skyline, there has been positive or negative skyline growth over the twentieth century.

The answer is that the trend, in fact, is negative. On average, the results show about an 11% drop in additions to the skyline, on average, each year, and about a 14.7 feet reduction in the heights of the tallest buildings over time, controlling for the other economic factors driving skyline growth.[25] These results appear even after accounting for those things that are moderating New York's economy and real estate market, such as the flattening of employment, population growth, zoning, taxation, and the total amount of building that has occurred in the past.

There are several possible explanations for the negative growth, but at this point, we can only speculate about what they might be, and leave a more detailed investigation for future research. One factor might be the greater regulatory burden imposed by the government over the last half-century. For example, the "zoning game" has become increasing complex, as builders negotiate with the city for FAR bonuses, or subsidies. This increases the cost of the project, and might, on the margins, reduce the number and heights of buildings, especially if it delays the time to approval for new projects.[26]

Another related issue has to do with the availability of plots. Since the Landmarks Preservation Commission was created in 1965, an increasing fraction of Manhattan has been landmarked. This means that less and less of the island is available for new construction. This is not to say that landmarking is bad, but rather its effects on the land values, real estate prices, and new construction need to be considered as one of the costs of historic preservation. Each acre taken "off the grid" due to landmark status reduces the amount of land available for new construction.

Lastly, rent control (stabilization) also has likely played a role (see the Epilogue). If tenants are getting a reduced rent, they will be reluctant to move if their life circumstances change. Landlords who might see the opportunity to teardown their older, low-rise properties and build a high-rise structure will decide the costs are too high because they cannot get their tenants to leave. They do not want to engage in lengthy eviction proceedings and court battles. As a result, new structures are not being built because price controls are reducing tenant turnover.

Income Inequality

Is there a relationship between income inequality and skyscrapers? This idea has most recently been put forth by author Alex Marshall, who speculates that the recent boom in supertall construction, both in New York and around the world is driven, in part, by the unequal distribution of wealth.[27] The nineteenth-century economist Thorsten Veblen, in his book, *The Theory of the Leisure Class*, argues that the super-wealthy feel compelled to advertise their leisure status through "conspicuous consumption."[28] In other words, if the upper classes find they have more money than can be usefully spent or invested, they will use their wealth for lavish displays, which, by their nature, have a competitive component since one person's "lavish" is only defined based on what others have or spend. High-rise apartments or extravagant offices for executives would qualify in this category.

There are two notable periods in the country's history where the relationship between income inequality and skyscraper height is apparent. The first is in the late 1920s. At the start of that decade, the share of total income going to those in the top 1%, for example, was 15%, and by the end of the decade it had risen to 22%. Then beginning in 1930, income inequality steadily declined and, in fact, continued to decline to 1976. By then, the top 1% garnered only 8.9% of the nation's income. Since the 1980s, income inequality began rising once again. By 1999, income inequality looked a lot like 1925. The recent peak for inequality was in 2007, when the top 1% earned 23.5% of the nation's income. It fell after the recession and has averaged about 20% since then.[29]

The statistical analysis discussed in this chapter allows for a test of the theory that periods of extreme inequality are associated with periods of extreme height. To this end, I included a variable that can measure the effect on the skyline from extreme inequality—in particular, from the years that the top 1% garnered more than 20% of the nation's income (1925, 1927-1929, 1999–2000, 2005-2008, 2012).

The statistical results strongly suggest that there is a relationship between the two. For a year in which the top 1% earned more than 20% of the nation's income, additions to the skyline nearly doubled. For the height of the tallest building, extreme inequality is associated with a 130-foot increase (twelve floors). These findings also suggest why New York is seeing a mini-boom in the supertall luxury condos. The demand for them has increased due to the extreme wealth being earned among the economic elite throughout the world. New York's renaissance since the 1990s has served to increase the status of the city and promote real estate as a profitable and socially important signal of wealth.[30]

WHEN DOES SYMBOLIC HEIGHT REAR ITS HEAD?

Separate from, but related to, inequality is the larger issue of the role of the ego in skyscraper height. While Freud's conception of the ego was that part of the self that interfaces with the external environment, the word has morphed over the decades to connote the psychological need of the individual to express him or herself in the public sphere, as a kind of justification for one's existence, or as a fight against one's low self-esteem. The skyscraper, because of its size, naturally presents the opportunity for grand self-expressions that can be independent of financial considerations. This form of height is referred to as "symbolic height" (see chapter 5); and is that part of the building's height that goes beyond what simple profit-maximization would dictate.[31] The skyscraper, by its very nature, conveys meaning. It cannot hide, it must be viewed, and it creates the urban fabric by its very existence. As such, the tall building produces an inherent tension between form and functionality, between symbolism and economics.

These opposing dimensions can be seen through the work and writings of architect Cass Gilbert, who was one of the key architectural pioneers in the skyscraper's early years. His buildings include the Broadway Chambers Building (1900; 226 feet) and the West Street Building (1907; 325 feet). In 1900, he apparently felt the need to argue for the skyscraper's economic existence in his article, "The Financial Importance of Rapid Building," where he states,

> The land value is established by its location, and desirability from a renter's standpoint; hence high rentals make high land values and conversely. The building is merely the machine that makes the land pay. The more economical

the machine both in construction and operation, provided it fulfills the needs, the more profitable the land.[32]

In his article, he lays out the cost of land and the cost of construction, anticipating the more detailed work of Clark and Kingston in 1930; he aims to demonstrate that when builders face high land values they must respond by using the land more intensively—simply from the logic of maximizing the return on investment.

Yet in 1910, Gilbert was hired as architect to design F. W. Woolworths' tome to himself, the Woolworth Building, completed in 1913 at 792 feet. In an interview with the *New York Times*, Woolworth confessed that he was not interested in a mere building; he wanted to provide a monument. As architect for the superwealthy Woolworth, Gilbert employed a neo-gothic style to create a "Cathedral of Commerce." Its tower shot up some fifty-five stories, making it the world's tallest building, and suggesting to society that commerce, not Christianity, was the new religion.[33]

This debate about the merits of the tall building would continue into the twentieth century, especially during the Roaring Twenties, when buildings like the Chrysler Building (1930; 1,046 feet) and Lincoln Building (1930; 673 feet) were regularly called "freak" buildings. The Great Depression laid to rest, for a while, the argument, but has recently resurfaced with the popular misconception that record-breaking buildings can be used to forecast impending financial crises. The Burj Khalif is the modern Empire State Building—built to show off the power of the builders and to claim the prize as "world's tallest building."[34]

Symbolic height, however, has a competitive or strategic component to it. Being very tall is only good when taller than surrounding buildings. If you want to claim the prize of "tallest building," then the height decision must be made relative to the next tallest. If the economic climate should bring forth several builders all seeking the same prize, then competition can become quite intense.

This seems to be what took place between the developers of the Bank of Manhattan Trust, at 40 Wall Street, the Chrysler, and the Empire State Buildings. The Bank of Manhattan and Chrysler went head-to-head in 1930. Chrysler and his architect William Van Alen waited until the Bank of Manhattan building topped out, before they revealed their building's stainless steel spire, and thus officially robbed the Bank of Manhattan from laying claim to world's tallest building.

Then within a year, the Empire State used its large plot and rosy projections to justify being taller than the Chrysler Building. The Empire State was a result of a contest between two automobile executives, who worked for rival car companies. Jacob Raskob, a former General Motors and DuPont executive, with the help of a former New York State Governor, Al Smith, was eager to take on Walter Chrysler, and win. Then the Depression came along, and the world's tallest game was put on hold, until the Twin Towers came along in the early 1970s.

The Evidence

The questions remain, however: Is the skyscraper really a "freak" building? Is the ego a dominant "partner" in the development process? We can look to the regression results to provide clues about whether developer height systematically deviates from economic height or not. That is, we can make some estimates as to when symbolic height rears its head, so to speak.

We need to keep in mind that the display of ego, however, is not without risks. First, if a developer wants to build taller than the economic height, it means he must relinquish, to some degree, profits from construction. So the question becomes: To what extent he is willing to sacrifice money for psychological satisfaction? Second, adding extra height can backfire by depressing the price of space. Building more floors for advertising or ego displays means consumers have more space to choose from and as a result the price can drop. The effect can be compounded if several builders are acting in the same manner.

We now turn to what the data say. Recall that figures 6.1 and 6.2 show the height cycles over time, and how the statistical models can account for these major fluctuations. But here we turn to a discussion of the differences between actual and predicted heights along the cycles in the most extreme years; this is called residual analysis. When there are large, positive deviations from economic height, it suggests that non-economic factors are at play. Figure 6.2 can suggest that answer to this question by showing when predicted heights rise much higher than the actual heights.

Table 6.1 shows the years with the greatest deviations of total predicted height relative to actual total height added to the skyline each year. Interestingly, 1986 had the greatest deviation, adding some 6,342 feet of additional height to the skyline above what was predicted. The year 1931 takes second place, while 1971 takes third.

Table 6.2 gives the top ten list of "too tall" buildings in New York, based on a comparison of their actual heights to the predicted heights (from among the tallest building completed each year). The regressions allow us to measure the economic height of the structures, thus the difference is a measure of the symbolic height. The top three are World Trade Center buildings. The top of the list is the new One World Trade Center. My estimates reveal that it is forty-nine stories too tall.[35] Number two is the newly rebuilt Four World Trade Center, and number three was the first of the Twin Towers, completed in 1972. Five out of ten are record breakers (if we also include the second Twin Tower), as would be expected; four out of ten are corporate headquarters (note that the Chrysler Building was built by Walter Chrysler not Chrysler Motor Company). Four were sponsored by a government agency.

The conclusion that we can draw from the analysis is that the evidence does suggest there are periods of overbuilding of skyscrapers that cannot be accounted for simply by their economics—by their demand, the costs of building them, or the supply of capital. It strongly suggests that there are periods where there is height competition and/or times when developers feel free to add heights for symbolic reasons. But notice that these periods occur during the rapid expansion of the economy. This would suggest that first and foremost the skyscraper is an "economics machine" and then, secondarily a "symbolism machine." Only after the building achieves some base profitability, can the developer chip away at this profitability to use height for non-economic purposes. The data do not suggest the skyscrapers systematically dissipate otherwise valuable capital.

Table 6.1 The Top Ten Years when "Too Much" Height Was Added to the Skyline
This table shows the years in which the predicted height from the supply and demand regression model was much lower than the actual height added to the skyline. Based on the analysis, 1986 was the top year, with 577 additional floors added to the skyline than would have been economically rational. Too much height is added when the combined forces of overoptimism and height competition take hold of the market

Rank	Year	Total height	Predicted total height	Symbolic height	Symbolic floor count
1	1986	15,682	9,340	6,342	577
2	1931	14,872	9,827	5,045	459
3	1971	9,948	5,582	4,366	397
4	1972	9,616	5,690	3,926	357
5	1974	10,542	6,791	3,751	341
6	2013	5,062	1,479	3,583	326
7	1983	8,518	5,068	3,450	314
8	1930	12,988	9,807	3,181	289
9	1969	8,504	5,531	2,973	270
10	1987	12,051	9,562	2,490	226

Source: Data and analysis by Jason M. Barr.

Table 6.2 Top Ten "Too Tall" Buildings in New York
This table compares the actual heights of buildings to the predicted heights based on the supply and demand regression model. The top "too tall" building is the recently completed One World Trade Center; at 1,776 feet, its height was a political and symbolic choice, with little regard for the underlying economics. In fact, in the top ten list, four are part of the original or newly rebuilt World Trade Center complex. Note that the results are based on the tallest building completed each year; as a result, Bank of Manhattan Trust Building (1930) did not make the list because it was eclipsed by the Chrysler Building

Rank	Year built	Height (feet)	Predicted height (feet)	Difference	Floors "too tall"	Building
1	2014	1,776	1,232	544	49	One World Trade Center
2	2013	975	507	468	43	Four World Trade Center
3	1972	1,368	975	393	36	Original One World Trade Center
4	1977	915	596	319	29	Citigroup Center
5	1932	951	673	279	25	American International Building
6	1931	1,250	977	273	25	Empire State Building
7	1913	791	533	258	23	Woolworth Building
8	1960	705	454	252	23	JP Morgan Chase World HQ
9	1973	1,362	1,117	245	22	Original Two World Trade Center
10	1930	1,047	808	238	22	Chrysler Building

Source: Data and analysis by Jason M. Barr.

There is another way to test for height competition to see to what degree building heights are affected by the heights of recently competed buildings. In economic parlance, to what degree are heights correlated across time (or serially correlated)? If developers are competing against each other, as in the case of Raskob versus Chrysler, then we would expect to see a builder "positively" respond to the height or heights of recently completed structures. As an example, if the need to stand out is important, and say, in one year, the city's tallest building for that year is 600 feet, then we might expect that next year, the tallest building completed is say 650 feet, where those additional 50 feet were added just because a developer has a need to make sure his building is taller than what is being constructed.[36]

A review of the two skyline measures discussed in this chapter does reveal that heights in one year are correlated with heights in the prior year, in the sense that taller buildings tend to be built as the economy is rising, while shorter buildings are constructed during downturns. But a more detailed look at the data shows that for the total height measure, total additions to the skyline are greater than the prior year less than half the time (46%); while for tallest structure it is more than half the time (55%). In other words, if 3,000 feet was added to the skyline in one year, there is only a 45% chance that the next year will see more than 3,000 feet.

While for the tallest building, there is a 55% chance that height in one year will be greater than the previous year; this is more frequent than a "heads" in a flip of a coin. Is this real or just chance? To test this idea more rigorously, I included the prior year's height values as explanatory variables in the regression. The idea is to see if the prior year's height can somehow "explain" the current year's height, controlling for the host of other variables that affect the total height added to the skyline. If builders are looking around them to see what others are doing, they will react by adding height. This is a test of the competition hypothesis.[37]

The results show that there is no evidence for systemic height competition in that the prior year's total height does not influence the current year's height. Last year's total height is a statistically insignificant explanatory variable. However, when looking at the tallest completed building, there is a statistically significant and positive relationship between the prior year's tallest building and this year's tallest building. The evidence suggests that for every additional 10 feet added in the prior year, a developer adds another 2 feet on, average. This positive relationship is, in some sense, hidden from view because height also moves up or down, given the state of the economy, but when we control for these factors, it suggests that developer's decisions yesterday are influencing them today; and this provides evidence for a mild form of developer competition, on average, at the highest levels, but not throughout the skyscraper market in general.[38]

WHY HASN'T NEW YORK BUILT THE WORLD'S TALLEST BUILDING SINCE 1972?

Between 1890 and 1931, New York City surpassed itself nine times with the world's tallest skyscraper, a new record about once every five years, an average. Things slowed down after that, and about forty years later, it finally beat itself once again in 1972, when the taller of the two Twin Towers opened. Two years later, the city officially yielded the top spot to Chicago with the Sears (Willis) Tower, and then the world record headed off to Asia in the 1990s.[39]

Although the extreme heights for the pre-World War II buildings might not have built at the correct economic height, they were justifiable based on the incomes that could reasonably, though optimistically, be expected to accrue. As Clark and Kingston illustrate, the optimal economic height, given the economics of 1929, and on an extremely large plot, would be sixty-three stories. Even a seventy-five-story structure in their analysis would yield a return on investment of 10.06%.

Recall that chapter 5 provided a Skyscraper Profit Index from 1963 to 2013, which ranged from 0.68 (1975) to 1.61 (1981). Calculating the index for 1929, shows for a typical new office around Midtown it was 1.88.[40] Using Clark and Kingston's numbers for their profit-maximizing building of sixty-three stories, the index value was 2.18, nearly 35% higher than the peak value after World War II. In other words, the economics of tall buildings were much more favorable in the first half of the twentieth century than in the second half.

Why is this so? First, and perhaps foremost, was that the regional population and economic growth began to level off during and after the Great Depression. The kinds of employment and population pressures that existed before the 1930s were absent after World War II. While New York retained its central role in the American economy, the realignment of economic activity away from the old "Rust belt" cities caused New York's office rents to stagnate. They would rise in good years, and fall in the bad ones, but there has been no real upward trend since 1960.[41] In the past, all of New York's record breakers have been office buildings. The economics today just do not favor this kind of construction.

Second, the growth of the skyline itself has undermined its future possibilities. Since skyscrapers are durable objects, that, with love and care, can last indefinitely, after some point, additions to the skyline are built mostly to replace the oldest and least desirable buildings as well as to keep up with population growth. Today, Manhattan has more than 500 office buildings that are 295 feet or taller. This combined with the fact that the US economy has matured, employment in New York had been on a downward trend over the years, again, suggests no private sector motivation to construct a record breaker. The most recent crop of New York's supertalls have been pencil-thin condos, which have been made possible by the purchase of air rights and the extreme wealth available for these apartments, but the economics, again, do not favor something like the Burj Khalifa, which is twice as tall as any of these new condos.

Currently, there are two approaches by which a city can build the world's tallest building. One is like the old days. A developer gets a large piece of land, calculates that the economics are in her favor and goes for it. Let's do some back-of-the-envelope calculations to see where this gets us. Today, to give the world's tallest building a "a fair chance" in New York, we would need a tremendous plot, something along the lines of an entire Midtown block, say between 52nd and 53rd Streets, between Fifth and Sixth Avenues. This block would be 900 feet by 200 feet, or 180,000 square feet. We would also need to assume that such a lot can actually be assembled.

We start with a base FAR of 15 for an office building, and let's say, by a little bit of hand waving, we can (optimistically, but very unlikely) amass a total FAR of 21, through the provision of "as of right" amenities and air rights (that is, say a FAR of 18 as of right and another FAR equivalent of 3 from air rights). So this gives us a total floor area of 3.8 million square feet (assume a gross building area of 25% more, to account for elevator shafts and physical plant). To set the record, we are going to build a pyramid-shaped building that will be 3,000 feet tall, with 250 stories.

What would it cost us to produce the structure? We would need to buy all of the current structures on the block so we can tear them down. Let's assume, that using 2013 sales prices, we pay the lowest price per square foot of land paid for a Midtown office of $4,779. In other words, in 2013, a small office building sold for $8 million on a plot of 3,526 square feet, which means we effectively paid $4,779 for the land (since we want to tear down the structure).[42]

Let's use this number and say we bought the entire block at that rate. That would cost us $860 million. (Note that if word about this project was leaked, land prices would likely be double this amount.) Next say the developer buys air rights for the project at $200 per square foot of buildable space; for a total cost $112 million (this is a very good price for air). For simplicity, round this total figure up to $1 billion, if we include demolition costs, transaction fees, and the cost of borrowing money. Further, let's assume that it would cost us $1,000 per square foot to build the structure for a cost of $4.75 billion. In sum, for the land and structure, we would need to pay $5.75 billion in total, or about $1,210 per gross square foot.[43]

If we use the ROI method described throughout the book, and assume that to make this work, we would need to have a net income of at least 6% of $5.75 billion, which translates to about $700 million per year in gross revenue, or rents at about $182 per square foot, more than double the going rate as of 2013. An office building just will not work (even if we assume current asking rates will not fall from putting so much office space onto the market at one time).

So let's say we are going to have a mixed-used structure and imagine we could sell half the building for high-end condo units (presumably we would be unable to acquire such a high FAR for a pure residential building). It cost us about $1,210 per square foot to build; as of 2013, the average price of new condos was about $1,400 per square foot, and they have been rising. So until recently, the condo portion would not have covered the loss of the office portion. But if the New York condo market continues on its rapid trajectory, the idea of the world's tallest building paying for itself might soon become a reality.[44]

The second method to build the world's tallest building is to get the government directly involved. Such strategies include being a co-developer, providing large subsidies, or acting as guarantor in some way, by using the space for government employees or providing insurance in case of loan default. Increasingly governments the world over are getting into the skyscraper game. The Petronas Towers and the Burj Khalifa are excellent examples. But the case study of the World Trade Center and its rebuilding after 9/11 show the hazards of New York doing this. The rents needed to pay for such a tall structure are nowhere near what they would need to be for a private developer to make a profit and the government would have pay for a large fraction of the project.

Government involvement would also unleash an outcry among nearly every interested party. The real estate community is likely to protest the "dumping" of all of this space on the market. And planning and neighborhood groups would cry that such a structure would create too much congestion and place too heavy a burden on the local infrastructure. In short, in today's climate, the city government would not support subsidizing the world's tallest building.

7

The Bedrock Myth

Hour by hour the caissons reach down to the rock of the earth and hold the building to a turning planet.
Carl Sandburg

THE SETTLEMENT PROBLEM

From a bird's eye view of the city, we see a distinct skyline pattern. Rising out of the ground, like so many giant stalks of steel wheat, are the skyscrapers of Lower Manhattan, which run from the Battery up to City Hall, a mile north. After that, the environment suddenly changes, the modern towers morph into older, ten- or twelve-story loft buildings, and then suddenly, after that, the district becomes decidedly low-rise near Canal Street. At around 14th Street, the skyscrapers begin to rise again, with the giants appearing from 34th Street northward. Figure I.1B shows this to be so.

This begs the question: Why are skyscrapers "missing" from the region between Downtown and Midtown? The conventional answer is bedrock. In particular, the standard story says that there is a skyscraper "dead zone" because of the nature of rock below the surface. As shown in chapter 1, the bedrock is relatively close to the surface in Downtown. Going north, say along Broadway, it begins to plunge, forming a bedrock valley (more like a bedrock bowl) with its nadir north of Canal Street. After that, the rock rises close to the surface at 14th Street, where it remains close to the surface. In several places north of 34th Street, the schist shows itself as outcroppings, such as in Heckscher Playground in Central Park. The belief is that bedrock in valley was too far down and hazardous for developers to safely anchor their skyscrapers, so they avoided building them there.

Since skyscrapers are so large and heavy, engineers have had to develop methods to secure them so they do not settle. A structure must have the proper relationship with the ground or the ground will reject it. The most famous example of this is the 179-foot Leaning Tower of Pisa.[1] The builders in twelfth-century Pisa had little knowledge of the subsurface and how it would hold the structure. After only a few levels were constructed, the tower began to lean in the soft soil below and continued to slowly settle for 800 years, until a recent foundation repair halted its movement, where it now remains 13 feet out of plumb.[2]

The first 33 feet below the surface has mixed layers of mud, compressible clay, and sand, of varying thicknesses. Below that are four layers of compressible clay, hard clay, sand, and then more clay. The third layer of sand is saturated with water. The weight of the structure on these soft layers had differing effects across the structure's footprint, which tilts in a southward direction. This suggests that the soil on the south half is relatively softer, and more easily compressed.

Begun in 1174, construction stopped after only the third terrace was finished, and did not resume until nearly a century later, in 1272, when it reached the sixth level. In an effort to counteract the leaning, the rest of the stories were built at a slight angle in the opposite direction of the tilt. The bell tower was finally added between 1360 and 1370. Ironically, the long interruption allowed the tower to settle slowly, so that when construction resumed it was in a relatively more stable position, though the building would not stop settling until the recent intervention. If it had been built in one clip, the building would likely have collapsed.[3]

The reason the building is famous is because it remained upright and serves as a monument to the failures of foundation engineering. If it had collapsed, it would have become merely a technical footnote in engineering history, rather than a wonder of the world. Giving the tower a new foundation to stabilize it in its current position was an act of historic preservation. It could have easily been made perfectly straight, but then it would no longer be the *Leaning* Tower of Pisa.

In most cities, as in New York, below the surface and manmade fill are layers of sand, silt, clay, or rocks of differing hardness, and they are often saturated with water. Many larger cities were founded on or near bodies of water before any thought was given to engineering geology; those early decisions would have ramifications far into the future. Placing a heavy structure directly on wet sand or till creates a few possible scenarios, all with hazards, if not properly considered. In one case, in Mexico City, along Alameda Square, the National Theater, after its completion in 1934, sank 6 feet below the grade, so that one had to go down a staircase to enter. The theater was originally built at the street grade, but since it was constructed on loose sand soaked by the water of ancient Lake Texcoco, it settled into the soft muck.

But fortunately, because the soil is relatively homogeneous, it compressed equally under all sides of the building, so that that structure simply moved downward at the same rate. However, after construction of several high-rises nearby in the 1950s, the building rose up 6 feet above the street. The water from the new structures was pushed out back into the soil below the theater, causing it to pop up, and, luckily, evenly across the building's footprint.[4]

More broadly, Mexico City faces a foundation problem on a colossal scale. The city is built on a bed of soft clay, above the city's aquifer, which supplies 72% of its drinking water. The thirsty, growing city is depleting the aquifer faster than it can be replenished. As a result, Mexico's capital city has sunk 30 feet in the last century.[5]

In other cases, if the composition of the subsoil is uneven at a particular site, there is the possibility of differential settlement, such as with the Leaning Tower of Pisa. In other cases, with a relatively wide structure, one part of the building can become misshapen or generate cracks in the façade, or, worse still, the structure can be torn apart and collapse.

Chicago's Federal Building (1879), for example, rested on one large concrete mat, which was meant to more evenly distribute its weight. But the unequal downward pressure across the structure caused the heavier piers to sink faster than the lighter ones. Six years after completion, repairs to the building from unequal settlement totaled $94,300. The concrete mat apparently cracked when parts of it sank over 2 feet into the soft clay. In 1896, after only eighteen years, the integrity of the building was so poor it was demolished.[6]

Another extreme example of the effect of geology is from earthquakes. Buildings placed directly on loose, wet sand are at risk for total collapse if the vibrations liquefy the soil. San Francisco has seen this problem. A large fraction of the damage from the 1906 earthquake occurred because it hit neighborhoods which were reclaimed marshlands. The fires that followed the quake were so devastating because the liquefied ground damaged the city's water system and hampered the ability to douse the blazes.[7] While New York is not along any major faults zones, the region has seen seismic activity over the last two centuries. Many older, shorter buildings in Lower Manhattan are susceptible to collapse, if a large earthquake should ever strike, because they rest on layers of sand.

But assuming, for now, that we have no concern from earthquakes, shorter buildings, as long as the building's downward pressure is evenly divided across the surface, can simply rest on top of the subsurface. Manhattan's soil generally has good load-bearing capacity for low-rise buildings.[8] But once the elevator solved problem of vertical transport, the size and height of buildings were no longer limited to a handful of floors. While it is true that per cubic foot, a steel-skeletal structure is much lighter than with load-bearing masonry walls, the skyscraper's massive size meant that they were much heavier overall.[9]

At that moment in history, when the Skyscraper Revolution was born, a new set of foundation technologies were needed to anchor the buildings and keep them secure from settlement. But the problem was difficult to solve because reaching the bedrock was not easy or cheap. As discussed in chapter 1, the ground in Lower Manhattan just below the surface is sandy and dry (unless the lot is over a historic stream or wetlands). But as one goes below sea level, the soil is going to be saturated by water. When digging, at some point, like it or not, you are going to hit a viscous sandy goo, known in the engineering world as quicksand.

To the best of my knowledge, no one in Manhattan has ever drowned in it, though at least one person came close. In 1915, a one J. Geldora, working on construction for the Seventh Avenue subway line on West Broadway, fell into a quicksand bed 37 feet below the street. According to the *New York Times*, "Before help could reach him he was up to his waist and rapidly disappearing. Workmen, dazed by the sudden accident, watched him with horror and only seized his outstretched arms as Geldora was about to become engulfed."[10]

Besides ensnaring the careless construction worker, quicksand in Lower Manhattan was a major engineering headache. Builders could not simply dig their way to the rock. If they did, the sand would ooze out of the surrounding lots into the open pit and destroy the foundations of the neighboring buildings. In addition, the wet soil meant that engineers had to devise methods of keeping the basements sealed and dry, since they were used to house the mechanical equipment.[11]

To summarize the problems faced by early skyscraper developers, in 1907, engineer Maurice Deutsch wrote

When we consider that in lower Manhattan there is a layer of 45 to 75 ft. of quicksand and other water-bearing strata overlying the rock and that a great many of the old buildings in this vicinity have very shallow foundations resting directly on the upper soil, it can be seen that the foundations for such very high buildings must go down to rock in order to safely support their enormous weights, and that to reach bedrock a method must be adopted which will not disturb the fluid material upon which the adjoining building may be resting.[12]

This quote illustrates that perhaps more important than the location of bedrock is what *exists between the ground and the rock*. In most of Downtown, south of Chambers Street, the rock is very difficult to reach. The conventional story about its effect on the skyline is misleading on several fronts. First, the assumption that bedrock is close to the surface for Lower Manhattan is true, but only *relative to the bedrock valley*, which has its nadir at over 300 feet below the street level. In an absolute sense, however, for much of Lower Manhattan, bedrock is quite deep, particularly around Wall Street, where it can be found 65 feet below the ground.

Furthermore, the bedrock, as discussed in chapter 1, is not a smooth, flat plain. The geological history of tectonic plate collisions, separations, and erosion, combined with periods of glaciation, has left the island more like a crumpled piece of aluminum foil. The surface is uneven; there are faults and cracks; and even within the same lot, the bedrock can be found at dramatically different elevations.

The conventional wisdom implies that because the bedrock was relatively close to the surface engineers could simply rest a skyscraper on the bedrock without problems. But no matter how far down or near the bedrock may be if it is below the waterline, it is going to be hard to get there. When the glaciers came and retreated, they were not so polite as to leave uniform subsoil conditions. Lower Manhattan is a kind of geological salad, with sand, till, hardpan, and boulders randomly distributed throughout. The subsoil in the bedrock valley is not qualitatively different than that of Wall Street. It was a mess throughout.

Foundation work in Midtown is also not easy. When the bedrock is close to the surface, it presents another set of headaches, mainly that of removing the rock. Blasting is dangerous and can be unpredictable, and it often needs to take place in the most crowded parts of the city. Uneven pressures on the rock can cause cave-ins or rock slides. Below ground are often a network of pipes for sewage, water, and electricity, as well as tunnels for subways and trains, all of which can be damaged by blasting. The vibrations can also cause the walls of nearby buildings to collapse. Throughout Manhattan north of 14th Street, there are pockets of quicksand or saturated soil, either from pools forming in the rock fractures or from brooks that were simply buried when the blocks were developed for urban uses. Along the rivers, the land is frequently made from fill, which has its own set of engineering issues. Even in northern Manhattan, in some places, the bedrock drops precipitously below the surface, only to reappear close to it a few feet away.[13]

That the bedrock depths were the driving influence of the skyline seems to have been first suggested by the geologist Christopher Schuberth in his 1968 book, *The Geology of New York City and its Environs*, where he writes,

South of 30th Street . . . the mica schist, however, is still accessible in deep foundations or excavations. But when one reaches the north side of Washington Square in Greenwich Village, the situation changes rather abruptly. Here, near New York University, the surface of the bedrock drops appreciably—up to several hundred feet below the street level. Farther south, near Chambers Street, it comes again to within about one hundred feet of the surface. Dividing Manhattan into the "downtown" and "midtown" districts, the low-lying area—the area where the top of the bedrock lies hundreds of feet below the street level—has been filled in and built up almost entirely with glacial deposits and, more recently, artificial land fill. That is to say, the skyscrapers of New York City are clustered together into the midtown group, where the bedrock is within several feet of the surface, and the downtown group, where the bedrock again reappears to within forty feet of the surface near Wall Street.... In any event, it is readily seen how clearly the accessibility of the bedrock has, to some degree, controlled the architectural planning of the city.[14]

Since then, the idea that the location of the bedrock was a determining factor has been accepted as truth.[15] This conventional wisdom is deeply embedded in the historiography of the city; and it is repeated by professionals and the public time and time again. The most vocal proponents of this theory, ironically, are architects or geologists, rather than engineers, developers, or economists. The reason that it is so ingrained is that the pattern—the correlation—is so strong: the deepest bedrock on the island is found north of Chambers Street and south of 14th Street, in neighborhoods such as Chinatown, Greenwich Village, and the Lower East Side, where there are generally no skyscrapers.

However, I will argue here that our beliefs about bedrock and the skyline are wrong. The bedrock story is essentially a myth—a tale about the divine powers of the earth to shape the city's destiny. This myth emerged, however, because of the confusion between correlation and causation. Like one of many typical founding myths, it connects the dots between nature and society to give us a story about the city's literal and figurative foundation. But, in fact, the bedrock depths had very little overall influence on the shape of the skyline.[16]

This is not to say that developers or engineers were ignorant of, or simply ignored, the costs of creating foundations, but rather, they were considered within the context of the overall costs and benefits of building skyscrapers in different parts of the city. The expense of creating foundations are only one part—a small part, as it turns out—of a larger story about the economics of land use in the late nineteenth and early twentieth centuries.

In cases where the subsurface is particularly soft, wet, or uneven in its consistency, engineers and developers worked together to solve the problem in the most cost-effective manner they can devise. There are a host of factors at work and there is often no one universal solution to the foundation problem. Most of it had to be based on guesswork about what is below the surface and how much weight the subsoil can support. Fortunately, despite the travails of foundation work in Manhattan, no tall building has ever collapsed.[17] In fact, many of the early engineers with little scientific research to go on often "over-engineered" the project so as to be on the safe side. Figure 7.1 shows a graphic representation of foundations in Lower Manhattan and how they had to deal with the water line.

Despite the engineering difficulties, the ultimate driver of skyscrapers, from the perspective of developers, is the willingness to pay by tenants, which is reflected in

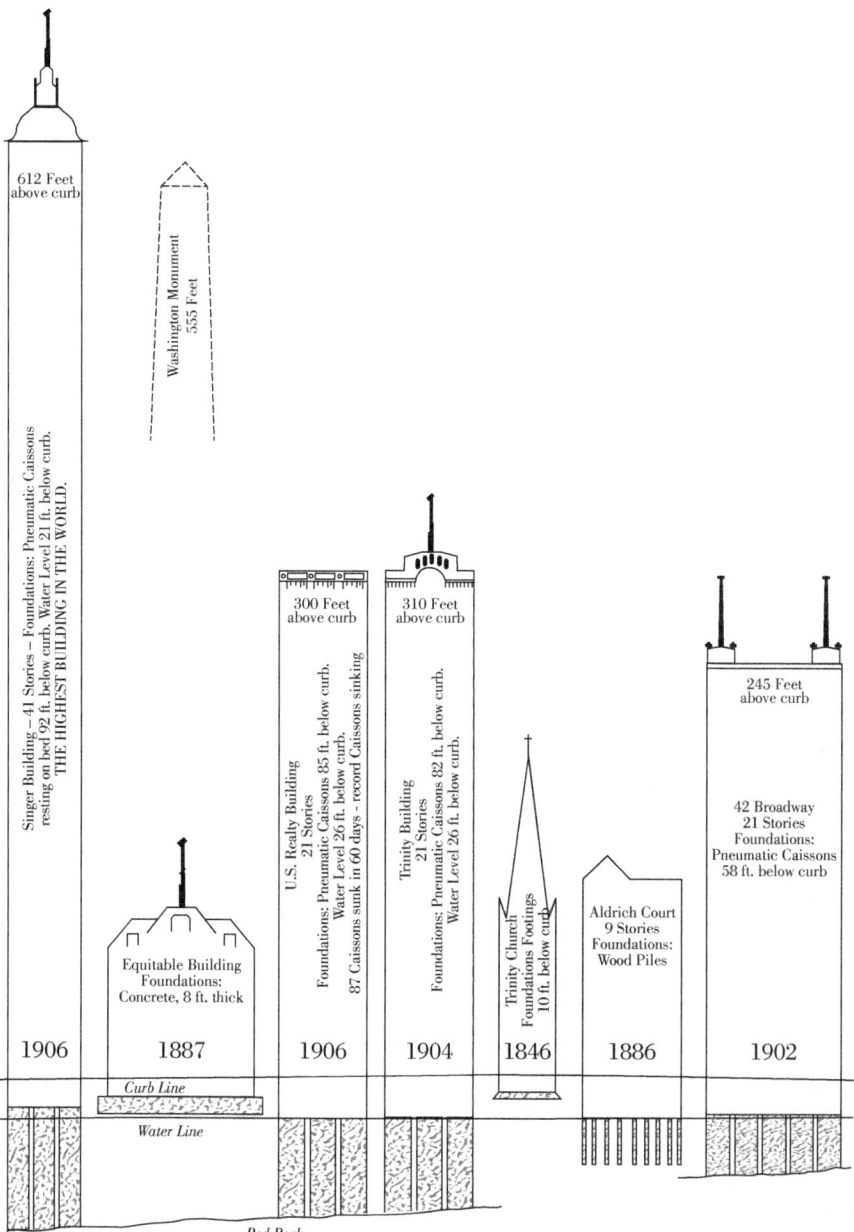

Figure 7.1 Foundations for early skyscrapers. This drawing shows the variety of foundation types for buildings in Lower Manhattan. The tallest buildings, such as the Singer Building (1906), required caissons to anchor them to the bedrock. The shorter buildings were constructed either on concrete mats, such as with the 1887 Equitable Building, or on wood pilings, such as the Aldrich Court Building (1886). Trinity Church's (1846) foundation, on the other hand, was simply built on spread footings directly on the subsoil.

Source: Deutsch (1907).

the value of land. Land values and bedrock depths are highly correlated (high land values, low depths) not because of the bedrock directly, but because of the economic decisions made by households and the history of how the city was settled. Once land values hit a critical threshold, and the general array of technologies were available, skyscrapers could be built anywhere in the city—anywhere that had the proper demand.

In other words, the location of skyscrapers south of Chambers Street and north of 14th Street was driven by the desire for tall buildings in these locations and had virtually nothing to do with bedrock depths or the inability of developers to build them in the bedrock valley. As discussed in chapter 3, it was the early land-use patterns across the city that set the stage for the skyline's shape. The First Inversion established Lower Manhattan as the city's business district, with tenements and factories directly to the north, and then, north of that, were the suburban housing and the commercial businesses that catered to the middle and upper classes. This region would give rise to the birth of modern Midtown and will be discussed in the next chapter.

NEW YORK FOUNDATIONS

Before the introduction of iron and steel for load-bearing purposes, buildings were either constructed out of wood, brick, or stone. The building codes limited wooden structures in the densest parts of the city, and so, most of the structure in the city proper had load-bearing masonry walls. Except for a subterranean spring or stream that might exist under a property, the subsoil was sufficiently compact, and the ground sufficiently level that structures could simply be built over the subsoil, using a spread footing foundation, with little concern for settling or for disturbing surrounding buildings.[18] This was done in the case of the Trinity Church, completed in 1846, at Broadway and Wall Street, which rested on sand 10 feet below the ground, far above the water line. Things were fine for over seventy-five years until modernity got in the way. The foundations began to fail during blasting work for the subway in the 1925. As a result, steel piers, mounted to the bedrock, were placed under the building.[19]

Simple foundations were of no use for the skyscraper. As the engineering limits to height were being eroded, buildings became much heavier. With little history of sophisticated foundation techniques, engineers had to resort to trial and error and guesswork, based on the current state of science and technology. Borrowing techniques from Chicago, some early tall buildings in the late nineteenth century were constructed on thick rafts of wood or concrete that were laid down on the subsoil to prevent uneven settling. Although Mexico City learned of the problems of squeezing out water from sand in the 1930s, Manhattan saw its effects much earlier. In 1897, the *New York Times* lodged this indictment:

> We dwelt lately on the fact that every new building erected to tower above its neighbor robbed the latter and the streets to a great extent of most valuable light. Another kind of injury sometimes worked has, however, been quite overlooked, though it is often of much importance and could generally be avoided. We refer to the overloading of the soil in cases where new buildings of great weight are built upon so-called "floated" or "grillage" foundations; that is, when their foundations are not built upon the rock or hardpan, but rest at a comparatively

shallow depth upon sand or silt, which they put under such pressure as to make most difficult and dangerous an excavation for deep foundations alongside or for any public purpose at a considerable depth in the street.[20]

If a large building is resting on a raft on the quicksand, and then a neighboring site is developed, and the ground is dug up, the wet sand would ooze from the adjacent lot into the excavation site, potentially causing the building to collapse and filling the site with the muck. The law increased the complexity of this problem, as owners of adjacent lots were not responsible for any soil seepage onto a new site; rather, the detritus belonged to the property onto which it flowed; and the recipient "may have to pay dearly for the improper building methods pursued next to him."[21]

Engineers had little idea what they were going to find, even after drilling for samples. Near places where the average depths were close to the surface, the rock could plunge rapidly, and unexpectedly. Borings also might give false readings if a boulder was found; engineers might wrongly conclude the bedrock was closer to the surface than it actually was. Or a pocket of hardpan clay might suddenly appear where none was expected.

Early Examples of Tall Office Buildings

The first very large office buildings that began to appear in Lower Manhattan after the Civil War were not tall by current standards. They were, however, too heavy for the old method of spread footings, but not so heavy as to require the more complicated modern technologies. In this regard, the Equitable Life Assurance Society provides a useful case study. Founded in 1859, the company grew rapidly in the newly burgeoning business of life insurance. By 1886, it was the largest life insurance concern in the world.[22]

Due to its success, the company started assembling lots in the 1860s on the southeast corner of Broadway and Cedar Street to construct a large headquarters. Equitable aimed big, constructing a massive, eight-story (142 feet) ornate Second Empire style building, being one of the first major companies to break with earlier architectural traditions, when it completed its new headquarters in 1870.

The Equitable Life Assurance Building was pivotal in the history of the skyscraper. It was the first large-scale ornate office building that was able to rise above five stories and rent out the upper stories to high-paying businesses, which were willing and able to use the building's elevators and could enjoy the great panoramic views.[23] The building contained two steam-powered elevators, which were the tallest climbing in the city. In other words, it was the first office building to create a height premium. One can say, therefore, that Equitable invented height as a marketable commodity.

As Landau and Condit write, "the new Equitable Building was instrumental in promoting the image of prosperity that would characterize insurance company buildings for at least a half-century and also inform the richness of style associated with the mature New York skyscraper."[24] All of the external walls were load-bearing masonry; the primary internal bearing partitions were brick, while throughout the structure 16-inch cast-iron columns helped carry the load. Over the next two decades, the Equitable would acquire the rest of the block to expand its operations, making it one of the largest office buildings in the world. In order to accommodate the heavy weight its foundation rested on a concrete mat 8 feet thick (see figure 7.1).[25]

Another strategy was to use a technology with a long history, the pile. Long wooden logs would be pounded into the ground until "refusal," that is, until they stopped sinking, at evenly spaced intervals throughout the plot. By pounding the piles deep into the subsoil, the friction would keep the building from settling. Once the piles were driven, a concrete mat or some form of wooden grillage would be placed on top of them.

The American Tract Society (ATS) building is an example of an early skyscraper that rests on piles. The structure was completed in 1895 on the southeast corner of Nassau and Spruce Streets. Being near City Hall, the lot is over bedrock that is 100 feet below the surface. The American Tract Society was formed in 1825 to publish non-denominational religious literature; they succeeded in their location in the heart of Newspaper Row. The building is twenty full stories plus an additional three-story tower. The subsoil below the building is clay and sand. The site was excavated 35 feet below the street level and throughout the site 25-foot piles were driven into the soft subsoil. They were capped with granite blocks on top of which were built brick piers.[26]

The West Street Building (1907), designed by Cass Gilbert, is another early skyscraper on piles. This twenty-three-story structure is over made ground. Being adjacent to the waterfront, it not only afforded excellent views of the harbor and river but was a convenient location for the myriad of port-related firms doing business along the Hudson. The bedrock was some 50 feet below the street level, on top of which was 2 to 3 feet of hardpan clay; and on top of that were layers of sand, mud, and fine silt; above that was manmade fill.[27]

Piles, however, were no longer a workable solution for buildings that were taller than about twenty stories. First, the load-bearing capacity of early piles was limited. As the weight of the building becomes greater, more piles must be used, so that, at some point, the number needed to stabilize the structure will be greater than the area of the plot itself.[28] Second, builders and engineers worried that the changing water tables could harm the piles, which had to be driven down into the wet soil and remain below the water table. If the water level fell, the piles would be exposed to air and would begin to rot. Furthermore, if the quicksand was disturbed near a site and began to flow, it could cause the piles to rotate away from their vertical position, compromising the foundation.[29]

THE CAISSON

The solution to the foundation problem, which permitted the rise of the modern skyscraper, was the caisson—a large box without a bottom. Inside were two chambers, one on top of the other. The bottomless lower chamber rested on the ground, with sharp edges. A worker—affectionately called a sandhog—entered the caisson from a hatch on top. Once inside, he then entered a lower chamber through another hatch which seals him into an air-tight compartment, large enough to hold several workers who excavate the soil at the base and pass it up through shafts that run up to the surface. As the soil below is removed, the caisson sinks downward.

Once it drops below the water-line, compressed air is pumped in to keep out the water. The two chambers inside contain an air-lock system. After the worker is sealed in the top compartment, he opens the latch to the bottom one and the high pressure air enters. When the pressure is equalized, he opens the second latch and descends, sealing the latch above him. Debris enters in the same manner, but in reverse.

When the caisson reaches the bedrock, the interior is filled with concrete and a brick or concrete pier is built up to the basement level to support the building. The caisson thus makes it possible to directly anchor the building to the bedrock, without disturbing the water or sand below nearby foundations. It was now impossible for the skyscraper to settle since the schist is firm and stronger than the weight of the structure.

Caissons were originally developed for holding bridge piers. The method was first used in the United States for the Eads Bridge in St. Louis, constructed between 1868 and 1874. The earliest appearance of caissons in New York was for the Brooklyn Bridge, built from 1870 to 1883. Caissons, however, were no magic bullet. While they represented the best method out of all those tried, they were expensive and difficult to implement. In 1912, *The New York Record and Builder's Guide* commented:

> Builders sometimes ask why foundation work costs so much in New York. The answer is: The risk is so great no matter how well trained the units of a foundation company's working organization may be, mistakes are sure to happen at times. No matter how carefully the site may have been bored, boulders or quicksand are liable to appear. . . . All perilous work is expensive, because men of robust physique and of sufficient bravery hourly to risk death are hard to find.[30]

The problems were many, and they often frustrated even the most careful of engineers. When one looks at the cost and effort required to properly create a foundation in Lower Manhattan, it is a wonder that builders just did not abandon the area altogether. One major concern was that working in the caissons could be deadly, to say nothing about the horrible conditions in a cramped, dank, overheated box with pressured air squeezing your organs. Caisson Disease (the Bends) afflicted individuals who moved from the compressed air to street level too rapidly. This happens when nitrogen bubbles suddenly form in the veins when coming to the surface. Expensive precautions needed to be taken to prevent widespread suffering. During construction of the Brooklyn Bridge, 28 cases of the bends were reported; and three resulted in death.[31]

During the construction of the Woolworth Building in the 1910s, nearly 80% of workers who applied for the sandhog positions were turned away because the medical staff deemed them not fit for the work.[32] Laborers had to be continually monitored and their working hours reduced accordingly as the box descended further into the ground. Drinking the occasional "screwdriver" cocktail during lunch breaks would exacerbate susceptibility. The Woolworth Building construction site maintained a full-time physician and nurse, and a separate steel air lock chamber as a kind of onsite hospital.[33]

Working with compressed air also made the risk of fire ever-present, since the chambers were lit with sulfur candles. A typical example occurred on December 9, 1911, and was reported in the *Washington Post*:

> Locked in a burning foundation shaft, 75 feet below the street level, six men battled for their lives . . . in the heart of New York's downtown skyscraper district. Two of them . . . probably will die; the other four are badly injured. . . . With flaring candles fastened to their caps . . . one of them placed his candle too near the wooden wall of the shaft. A few moments later flames were roaring about them. They beat upon the door for minutes before it was finally opened and they were drawn to the surface.[34]

Besides the danger to the workers, caissons could be unpredictable. In some cases they would run away or sink if the caisson hit a particularly soft patch of sand. At other times, if the unexpected boulder appeared, much effort had to be made to get rid of it. This included blasting the rock with dynamite, which would cause the obvious set of dangers. Great expense had to be incurred to deliver the caisson safely and swiftly to its final resting place.

Early Examples of Buildings that Used Caissons

The first structure in Manhattan to use caissons was the Manhattan Life Insurance Building at 66 Broadway, at New Street. Completed in 1894, it rose eighteen floors, and it was estimated to weigh 30,000 tons. The caissons contributed about 8% or 9% to the total cost. [35] Figure 7.2 shows a drawing of the foundation. One major concern was to not disturb the foundation of the six-story Consolidated Exchange building next door, which was placed on piles. While on the other side was a four-story brick building, which simply rested on soil about 28 feet above the bedrock.

The Singer Building

The Singer Building at Liberty Street and Broadway was completed in 1908 (demolished in 1968); at forty-one stories (612 feet), it was, by far, the tallest building in the world when finished. Its tower was three times taller than the spire of the Trinity Church, and was more than twice the height of the Flatiron Building (1902). The skyscraper had over 400,000 square feet of office space (about 9.5 acres) and was designed to comfortably hold 7,000 people.[36]

The structure created a load of 27 tons per square foot and required thirty-four caissons. Bedrock was found at 90 feet below the surface. However, author Otto Semsch, reports that the subsurface, "in fact . . . was so irregular that not only was the material found in one caisson no criterion for what might be expected in the adjoining caisson, but even what was found in one end of the caisson differed entirely from that in the other end."[37] Although portions of the building were rested on grillage or spread footings, caissons were used to support the tower.

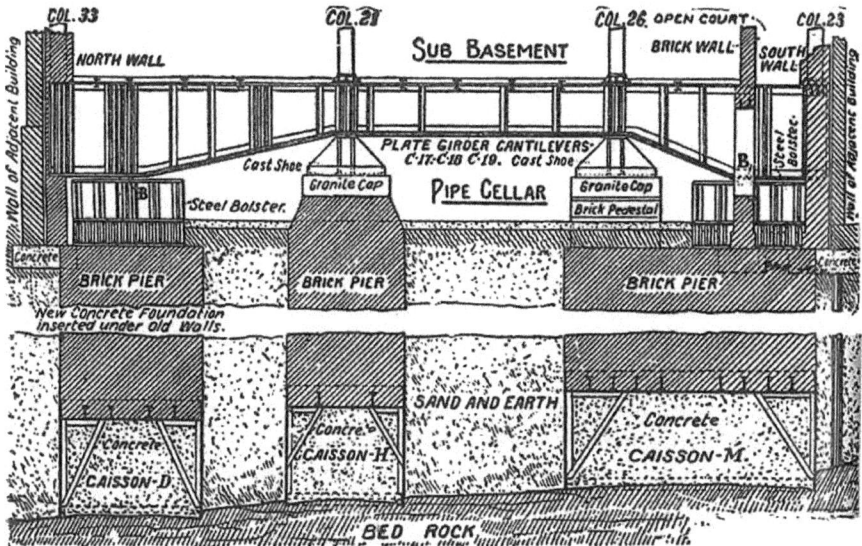

Figure 7.2 The first office building to use caisson foundations. The first structure in Manhattan to use caissons was the Manhattan Life Insurance Building at 66 Broadway. Completed in 1894, it rose eighteen floors and was estimated to weigh 30,000 tons. One major concern during construction was to not disturb the foundation of the six-story Consolidated Exchange building next door, which was placed on piles.
Source: Kidder (1920).

The Municipal Building

The Municipal Building was completed in 1914 and designed by McKim, Mead, and White; the general contractor was the Thompson-Starrett Company. This skyscraper posed the greatest building foundation challenge up to that date, as it was constructed over some of the worst geological conditions on the island. The building rises forty stories and weighs 165,000 tons. The original plans called for the sinking of caissons to rock throughout the site, until it was discovered that on part of the plot, the rock was 200 feet down, which was considered too far and dangerous. It was then decided to sink the caissons a mere 77 feet on the deepest part of the lot, where they would then rest on dry, compact sand. The rest of the caissons would drop 140 feet though quicksand, water, and gravel to rock. In total, 125 caissons were sunk to an average level of 130 feet below the street. The surrounding buildings, the Brooklyn Bridge Terminal Building, The Hall of Records, and the World Building, all had relatively shallow foundations on sand and were susceptible to perturbations at the site.[38]

The Woolworth Building

The Woolworth Building (1913), at fifty-five stories, was the next record-breaking building after the Singer Tower. Total estimated costs were budgeted as follows: land costs were $5 million, foundation costs were $1 million, and the building's cost was $7 million, making foundation costs one-eighth of total construction costs and one-thirteenth of the project's total cost. After the Municipal Building, it was the second largest caisson job for a skyscraper in the city. Like the Municipal Building, it was over some of the deepest bedrock, which was between 110 and 130 feet down. Between that rested quicksand, gravel, and hardpan. All told sixty-nine caissons were sunk; and some of them were the largest ever constructed, at 19 feet in diameter. Inside the caissons, 200 workers did their digging in eight-hour shifts. Each shaft took an average of two weeks to dig.[39]

CHICAGO'S FOUNDATION HISTORY

As the first skyscraper city, engineers in Chicago had to wrestle with foundation issues there as well. The geological problems were no less difficult than New York and were likely more so. It is thus worthwhile to take a small detour to discuss the problems faced in that city from the Great Fire of 1871 to the turn of the century. By 1900, the technology was available to render the foundation problems as solved.[40]

One key insight that comes by comparing the two cities is that engineers devise strategies based on the particular geology they encounter. Chicago's experience demonstrates that the real issue is not about geology being a barrier, but rather about discovering the most efficient means by which a developer can provide habitable space where it is most wanted. In some sense, the geological problems in Chicago's Loop can be considered comparable to those that engineers might have encountered in the bedrock valley north of City Hall, if developers had chosen to build there; certainly they are comparable to those faced during the construction of some the buildings described above. The point is that it was the demand for skyscrapers in the Loop that caused engineers to build tall, despite a geological environment that was not conducive to such an objective.

In the late nineteenth century, engineers realized in Chicago that, given the subsoil conditions, they were not going to be able to perfectly stabilize buildings; it was taken as given that they were going to settle. The object of the game was to make sure the downward movement was as little and even as possible. It bears repeating that level and slow settlement is not a problem if it can be anticipated ahead of time and properly accounted for in the building design. If the amount of compression can be predicted, the entrances simply have to be built so many inches above the ground so that when the building finally stops moving people can enter directly from the street.

The city of Chicago was founded over marshland adjacent to Lake Michigan. As a result, the original ground level was muddy silt and sand. Below that are several layers of clay, of varying hardness. The ground in Lower Manhattan, unlike Chicago, was generally dry, as it was above sea level. As Chicago grew from a small outpost to a bustling city, the decision was made in 1855 to raise the grade. This meant that stone walls were built around each block to retain the fill. After the fire of 1871, the grade was elevated once more, and the debris from the fire was used for soil. As a result, the streets of Chicago are 10 feet higher today than when it was first settled.

If you would put a shovel in the ground at say South Dearborn Street and West Jackson Boulevard you would find manmade fill for the first 10 feet. The next few feet you would see lake-bottom silts. Before you proceed, however, you need your pick axe, or a jack hammer, as below the silts is a thin layer of hard stiff clay (hardpan). Although this layer's thickness varies across the city, this was the surface that generally bore the weight of the first skyscrapers.

The issue is what you would find once you penetrated below the initial hard clay layer: several layers of softer and wetter clays that would compress under a skyscraper's weight. Below that, at say 45 feet below the sea level, began a bed of stiff clay. Finally, if you persevered in your digging, you would eventually hit the limestone bedrock, which is found between 80 and 120 feet below the street level. Unlike New York, the main issue for buildings was that the soft clay beneath the hardpan was spongy and could sink several inches under the building's pressure.

After the Great Fire, but before the invention of the skyscraper, the rebuilt structures were typically built with spread footings on the subsoil, about 5 feet above the hard clay. These foundations were created before the science of load-bearing was developed. No account was made to consider ways to prevent or minimize settlement, and there were plenty of uneven buildings as a result. But because the buildings were brick or wood, they were able to withstand the differential movement. Ironically, because the street grades were so different due to the infill process, it was hard to recognize differential settlement patterns from uneven street grades.[41]

But the taller the building, the greater is the downward pressure, and the higher is the risk from differential settlement. When the skyscraper proper was invented, a new foundation method had to be devised. The Home Insurance Building (1885) is widely considered the first skyscraper, and as such, the foundations used for this building provide a good example. In this case, each pier and interior column had its own foundation footing. In essence, each pier rested on top of a 12.5-foot pyramid of alternating layers of stone, rubble, and concrete, which rested directly on the hardpan clay. A study of the building several years after completion showed that its maximum settlement was 2.25 inches; some parts had settled an inch less. While it was a successful engineering coup, it was not a long-term solution. Each foundation base was so large and rested just below the surface that the building did not have any space for a basement.

The next solution was timber grillages. Used for the Pullman Building (1884) and Board Trade Building (1885), these grillages were layers of wood beams, each of which was rotated 90 degrees. These grillages formed a kind of raft, on which the foundations rested, and on which the weight could be more evenly distributed. The next improvement was developed by John Wellborn Root, of Burnham and Root, in 1878, for the ten-story Montauk Building (1882). He replaced the wood grillage with steel railroad beams. By using steel, the foundation footings could be reduced in size and allow for basement space, which was highly valued for the mechanical equipment and storage, and even as rentable space.

The Monadnock Building (1893) was the tallest commercial building with a load-bearing masonry exterior wall ever constructed; as a result, it was one of the heaviest office buildings in the city. The foundation was made of a reinforced concrete mat, on which spread footings would rest. The building settled 15 inches after ten years. After thirty years, the building had settled another 5 inches and likely settled a few more as time wore on.

The next innovation in Chicago was to use long piles, which were hammered into the ground until they no longer sunk, usually when they struck the hardpan below the softer clay layer. The first complete long-pile project was the Grand Central Station

(1890), on the southwest corner of Harrison and Well Streets. Its tower reached 236 feet, and each pile was about 50 feet long.

But similar to New York, as buildings became taller and heavier, piles were not adequate to the task. The ultimate solution came to be known as the "Chicago Caisson." In 1894, the owners of the Herald Building obtained an injunction against the builders of the new Stock Exchange, arguing that their plan to hammer piles next to the Herald Building might damage the structure. As a result, the Stock Exchange used this new "caisson" method, whereby a group of open wells were sunk, each about 5 feet in diameter, until hardpan, at which point they were filled with concrete and used as piers to hold up the structure. Unlike New York, compressed air was not needed, and this method eliminated the concern for differential settlement. We now turn to foundation economics to see how they affected the location and costs of skyscrapers across Manhattan.

THE ENGINEERING EVIDENCE

The conventional story is that the very deep bedrock north of Chambers Street prevented developers from building skyscrapers there. If this is the case, then there are several possible reasons why it might be so.[42] The first might be technological; namely, that engineers just did not have the know-how to anchor tall buildings to bedrock so far below the surface. The evidence, however, suggests that this was not, in fact, the case. Despite the engineering difficulty, developers constructed skyscrapers on some of the deepest bedrock in the city. In fact, the first skyscrapers were constructed in perhaps the *geologically worst places* for a skyscraper—along the bedrock valley itself—in particular with the Woolworth Building and the Municipal Building around City Hall.

Figure 7.3 demonstrates this point more broadly. On the horizontal axis are the degrees latitude for Manhattan Island, that is, movement from south to north along the island.[43] On the vertical axis is the depth to bedrock at 173 building locations that were constructed before 1915, all south of 59th Street. The graph shows data for two kinds of buildings. The triangles are the locations of 77 skyscrapers, constructed between 1890 and 1915. In this case, they were buildings that were 263 feet (80 meters) or taller since they are the earliest skyscrapers in the city. The circles are the locations of 99 other low-rise buildings randomly chosen as a comparison group.

As the figure shows, at the southern tip of Manhattan, average bedrock depths below these buildings can be found at about 25 to 30 feet below the surface; going north, the bedrock dips down into the valley, which reaches its greatest depth, in the sample, at just over 148 feet below the surface close to Canal Street. Then we see the depth decreases as one moves toward 14th Street, where, on average, it remains relatively close to the surface. The figure, of course, shows the absence of skyscrapers in the dead zone and the presence of skyscrapers again north of 14th Street. But we can also notice a few things about the patterns of tall buildings near and around the valley. First, there are skyscrapers over some of the deepest bedrock in the city, at over 130 feet below the surface. This strongly suggests that there were no strong engineering barriers posed by the bedrock.

Also note a very important pattern. Skyscrapers are not built symmetrically around the deepest part of the valley. In other words, there are skyscrapers on the south side of

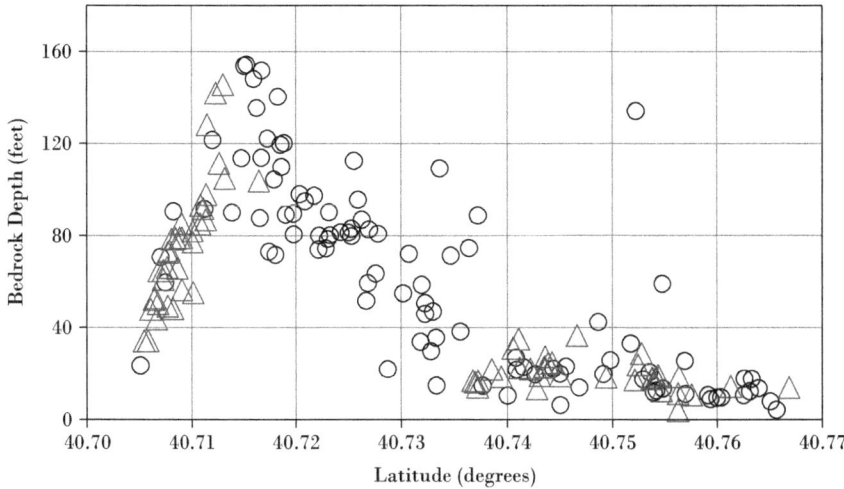

Figure 7.3 Buildings and bedrock. The horizontal axis represents the degrees latitude of Manhattan starting at the southern tip and going north to 59th Street. On the vertical axis is the depth to bedrock (in feet) relative to the street level. Each triangle is the location of a particular skyscraper that was constructed in the period 1890 to 1915. Thus, we can see how far down the bedrock lies below each one. The circles show the bedrock depths for 99 randomly chosen lots that do not have skyscrapers. The hump-shape in the figure illustrates the location of the bedrock valley, which reaches its nadir near Canal Street and the Bowery. North of 14th Street, the bedrock lies relatively close to the surface. The figure shows that some skyscrapers, most notably the Woolworth Building (1913) and the Municipal Building (1914), were constructed over some of the deepest bedrock in the city. It illustrates that bedrock depths did not present a barrier to skyscraper construction.
Source: Barr, Tassier, and Trendafilov (2010).

the valley, but none on the north until 14th Street. But if builders were eager to build skyscrapers in Lower Manhattan and the valley was a barrier, it is likely we would see them appear on the north side just where it was feasible to construct them. Yet we do not see any there. This suggests other factors are at play beyond ones related to the engineering challenges. In short, the anecdotal evidence about particular buildings and the statistical data in figure 7.3, strongly suggest that the reason for no skyscrapers in the bedrock valley was not due to technological or engineering constraints.

THE ECONOMIC EVIDENCE

Here I present four types of evidence to demonstrate that the bedrock barrier claim is false and a misreading of history. The first discusses the economics of building foundations and how they contribute to the overall cost of constructing a skyscraper. The second relates to the relationship between depth to bedrock and the heights of skyscrapers. The third part gives the theory of skyscraper locations and the tensions between business clustering and the location of bedrock. Finally, the fourth piece of evidence relates to whether bedrock depths influenced the location of skyscrapers across the island, during their first generation from 1890 to 1915.

Before I turn to each of these in more detail, let me summarize what each one shows. First, as it relates to the anchoring of buildings to the bedrock, relative to other costs, the "bedrock costs" were modest and did not rise dramatically with the depth of the rock itself. The term "bedrock costs" is used here as a shorthand term for the additional costs that must be paid to a builder to dig down deeper to anchor the building to the bedrock. In other words, the marginal or additional costs of digging caissons further into the soil did not increase the overall costs by very much. The largest costs related to the use of caissons were fixed—the costs of planning and of obtaining the equipment; these things needed to be paid for regardless of whether the caisson was to be lowered 20 feet or 100 feet.

Second, if the bedrocks costs were large and were increasing with building height, then we would expect to see a negative relationship between the depth to bedrock and skyscraper height. In other words, we would expect to see shorter skyscrapers over deeper bedrock, all else equal, since developers find it more expensive to add extra floors. But we do not see this relationship.

Next, as it relates to the logic or theory of the skyline, if bedrock depths were the cause of skyscrapers' absence north of City Hall, the skyline would likely take on a very different appearance. That is to say, if developers were prevented from constructing skyscrapers because of the bedrock depth to the north of City Hall, we would expect to see the area covered with the tallest office building possible to construct on piles (eighteen stories). But we do not see buildings of this height much further north than Chamber Street.

Lastly, the results of a statistical analysis measuring the economic and geological factors that drove the location of the tall buildings before 1916 show that once we control for other important variables, bedrock depths were not a cause for the Midtown-Downtown zones. I will, however, provide evidence, that within Downtown, developers were sensitive to the bedrock costs to some degree, and they did prefer places where the foundation costs were lower, but these places were also near Wall Street, which was the center of finance in the United States.

The point is that there might have been some "marginal" adjustments to the locations of skyscrapers within Downtown, but there was no desire to build them north of Chambers Street because of the land-use patterns that had emerged in these neighborhoods before 1890: the rise of warehouses, lofts, and factories along Broadway and adjacent streets from Chambers to 14th Street and the dense tenement neighborhoods of the Lower East Side, Little Italy, and Greenwich Village (see chapters 3 and 4). We now turn to the specifics.

The Bedrock Costs

Bedrock Depth and Construction Costs

In order to investigate the effects of bedrock depths on the costs of construction, data were obtained for fifty-three large commercial buildings constructed in Manhattan between 1899 and 1915. In particular, I obtained the construction costs from the *Cost Job Book* of the Fuller Construction Company, archived at the Skyscraper Museum in New York City. The book provides a breakdown of the various expenses for each of several Fuller projects, including the total costs, the foundation costs, the years of construction, and the developer. They ranged from three to thirty-two floors and thus contain a good sample of projects. 43% were eighteen floors or taller. The costs ranged from $117,000 to $7.5 million ($179 million in 2013 dollars), with the average project costing $1.3 million.[44] In general, foundation costs were a moderate part of the expenditures, ranging from 4.4% to 23% of the total costs, with an average of 14.6%. For each building, the depth to bedrock from the ground level was obtained from geological and topographical maps. The range of depths in this sample was similar to the range seen across the island. Some buildings were over bedrock that was near ground level, while one lot had depths 171 feet below the surface.

The goal of the analysis was to see if there was any relationship between how far down the bedrock was located and the total costs of construction. All buildings need to construct a proper foundation, so the real question is how much extra did having to dig, say, 10 feet deeper add to the total costs? In other words, what were the marginal costs of digging further down? When looking at the bedrock costs, however, one must also account for other things that are likely to affect costs in general, separate from the bedrock depth. First is the size of the building, as given by the total cubic feet of the space. Larger buildings are obviously likely to cost more since they require more time, materials, and planning. In this sample, building volumes ranged from 292,500 cubic feet (about 4,400 square feet of floor area) to 18.2 million cubic feet (roughly 69,000 square feet of floor area).

Next is the price of materials. As a proxy measure for materials costs, I created an annual index of real (inflation adjusted) brick costs. Another control variable related to the location of the building—namely, whether it was Downtown or above 14th Street—given the differing nature of the subsoil conditions. Finally, I also included a variable that indicated if the building was a skyscraper or not. Presumably, as discussed in chapter 5, the taller a building goes, the greater the additional costs. Because this is an investigation of the first generation of buildings, a building was considered a "skyscraper" if it was eighteen stories or taller, which was about 263 feet (80 meters) on average.

A regression analysis was performed to investigate how bedrock depths might influence the total costs, holding constant the other factors just discussed. The initial regression results were surprising; they actually showed a negative relationship between depth to bedrock and the construction costs. That is to say, initially it was found that the further down the bedrock, the less were the construction costs. In fact, the first regression showed, that controlling for building height, size, and brick costs, for every 33 feet lower the rock was found, there was an 8% drop in the total building cost. This did not seem correct at first blush.

But upon further analysis, the results make sense if you consider that for most buildings, there was never any need to anchor the building to rock floor. The vast majority of buildings constructed on the island of Manhattan since the day the first Dutch vessel arrived were perfectly stable on Manhattan's soil. In fact, to this day, 84% of all structures on the island are six floors or less; while 90% of structures are ten floors or less.[45]

The only buildings that required high-tech foundations are the handful of very tall buildings. Also consider that for buildings of the same volume, if one is tall and the other flat, only the tall one would need the expensive foundations because of the greater downward pressure. For low-rise buildings—the vast majority of structures on the island—anchoring the building to the bedrock is not an issue. The fact that bedrock is far down below the ground Downtown, while very close to the surface in Midtown, can explain the negative relationship. Bedrock too close to the surface is more expensive than bedrock far down, for most buildings that are sufficiently small or low, because the bedrock has to be removed to make the building level and allow for a basement. This finding then caused me to delve a little deeper into the data and the statistical relationships between bedrock and construction costs.

In the next regression equation, I added what is called an interaction term between the height of the building and the bedrock depths. In other words, I created a new variable that looks at the effect of bedrock depth and building height combined. The idea is that maybe it is the heights and depths that matter together, rather than simply one or the other. These results show in this case that the depth to the bedrock becomes a positive cost only when a building is about twenty-two stories! In other words, the depth to bedrock increases the average foundation costs only when a skyscraper is constructed; and a building greater than about twenty stories is the point when caissons are necessary to anchor the building.

So this begs the question, by how much did costs increase, on average, if a developer was going to build a skyscraper over deep bedrock? The regression results suggest that it was not very expensive at all. There are a few ways to illustrate this. Case one is that we have two twenty-five-story buildings and ask what the cost differential is if one has bedrock say 10 feet deeper than the other. In this case, the cost of those extra 10 feet adds 0.9% to the project.

Case two is to ask, what if we compare a twenty-five-story building to a thirty-story building on the same bedrock depth? In this situation, the extra downward pressure of the building might require thicker piers or additional caissons. Here, the estimates show that for the average depth of 50 feet, the additional costs for the foundation is about 4.5%; that is, going from twenty-five to thirty floors added about 4.5% to the total cost because of extra foundation work. For tall buildings, this was an expense that paid for itself with the additional rents on the higher floors.

Case three is to look at the tallest building in the data set (thirty-two stories), and estimate how much more it would cost to sink caissons in deeper soil if the building was constructed in the valley. The statistical results suggest it would increase total construction cost by about $9,000 for each additional 3 feet of depth to bedrock. If we consider about a 33-foot change in depths to bedrock from the average, we get slightly more: about a $90,000 (7%) increase in total building costs for this skyscraper.

These findings are consistent with those discussed in Francis Kidder's early textbook on building construction, which reported that in regard to the Manhattan Life Insurance Building (1893), the world's tallest building at the time, the cost of sinking caissons to the bedrock was "only 8 or 9 per cent of the estimated cost of the building."[46]

Comparing these additional costs relative to the costs of land shows bedrock costs to be quite small. Specifically, during this period, in 1905, average land values were about $72 per square foot south of City Hall, $23 between City Hall and 14th Street, and $40 north of 14th Street. The average plot size for a skyscraper in the data set is just over 25,000 square feet. If we multiply this by the land values per foot, we get the following estimates for a skyscraper lot in each area of interest: $1,800,000 south of City Hall, $575,000 between City Hall and 14th Street, and $1,000,000 north of 14th Street. Next, consider the average depth to bedrock in each of these three regions: 72

feet south of City Hall, 85 feet between City Hall and 14th Street, and 23 feet north of 14th Street.

If three additional feet of bedrock increased costs by about $9,000, then constructing a skyscraper on the average lot in the bedrock valley was only $36,000 more expensive (since the bedrock is 13 feet deeper on average) compared to south of City Hall. But the lot north of Chambers Street was less expensive by more than $1,000,000 compared to a similar lot in the heart of the business district. A developer would save substantial sums of money by buying a lot along the bedrock valley at a much lower price and paying the additional costs of digging to the bedrock.

In addition, building a skyscraper north of 14th Street would save 62 feet of digging to bedrock compared to the bedrock valley for a savings of 19 × $9,000 = $171,000. Again, the savings in terms of bedrock costs are smaller than the difference in the value of land between the two areas. The fact that developers were willing to build on lots Downtown, at greater net costs, suggests that other explanations are more plausible for the lack of skyscrapers in the bedrock valley, namely their benefits were much smaller.

In summary, a statistical analysis of the construction costs related to foundations shows that for skyscraper developers, going down to bedrock did not significantly add to the costs of the overall project during the first generation, once the initial costs were paid. Another way of saying this is that the evidence supports that once the decision to build a skyscraper was made, developers were willing to pay those extra bedrock costs because they were small relative to not only the costs of construction and land but also to the benefits of the project.

Foundation Costs and Bedrock

Another way to understand the foundation economics is to investigate those things that influenced the proportion of the total building costs that were dedicated to constructing the foundation. To investigate this, I again used the Fuller cost data, and I ran a regression that looked at how the percentage of total costs for foundations can be explained by the depth to bedrock below each building, the height of the building, how far north the building was relative to the tip, the year of completion, and a variable for whether caissons were used or not, since the cost sheets in the Fuller Cost book indicated this information (see the appendix U).

The results show that there was no statistically significant relationship between bedrock depths and the percentage of the project costs for foundations. In other words, controlling for the other factors that determined the size of relative foundation costs, bedrock depths were not a statistically significant determinant. The findings also show that the height of the building was negatively related to the percentage costs. Taller buildings had lower foundation costs on a percentage basis because the foundation costs were relatively fixed and would therefore decrease as a percentage of the project as more money was spent on steel, glass, HVAC systems, and so on. This also agrees with the findings of Clark and Kingston in their analysis of skyscraper economics in 1929.[47]

If the building required caissons, they added about 4.6 percentage points to the total foundation costs, on average, controlling for building height, bedrock depths, and location. In other words, the use of caissons in and of themselves constituted a moderate additional fixed cost. But digging down further into the subsoil, once caissons were installed, did not significantly impact the relative costs of the foundation.

In summary, an investigation into the economics of foundations for buildings constructed in the early years of the Skyscraper Revolution show there was no relationship between how far down the bedrock was located and the fraction of expenses paid for the foundation. Furthermore, in regard to the total costs, the evidence shows that foundation costs were relatively fixed, with a higher fixed cost for the use of caissons; but the marginal or additional costs of going further down to the bedrock was a much smaller fraction of the developer's total expense. The depth to bedrock was not adding very much to the total cost, and was, therefore, not a deterrent to skyscraper construction.

Height and Bedrock

If the bedrock costs were essentially fixed, and there were very low marginal or additional costs, this would suggest little relationship between skyscraper height and bedrock depths. To understand this, we must return to the height model presented in chapter 6. Recall that the profit-maximizing height (number of floors) is given by $H^* = R/2c$, where R is the per-floor income and c embodies the costs of constructing each floor. The model says that the profit-maximizing developer will choose a height, such that, at the last floor constructed, the additional cost of adding that floor just equals the additional revenue produced by it. So, the economics of skyscrapers suggests that the fixed costs of the project do not directly enter into the height decision because they influence neither the additional revenues nor additional costs of adding floors.

But given this economic theory, what do the data say? Did bedrock depths influence the height of skyscrapers in any meaningful way? To answer this question, I looked at the relationship between skyscraper heights and bedrock depths for a sample of 458 buildings that were 328 feet (100 meters) or taller and were completed between 1895 and 2004. The idea is to see if bedrock depths altered the marginal heights of the tallest of the tall across the twentieth century.

Figure 7.4 shows a scatter plot for the two variables. That is, the graph gives the height-depth pair values for each building, along with the trend line. Notice how the trend line is virtually flat; this means, for a given bedrock depth, we can say nothing about how tall a building will be at that given depth.[48]

But, again this relationship does not account for the myriad of other factors driving heights. Once I control for the other demand and supply variables, such as those discussed in detail in chapter 6, I find that for Midtown there is no relationship between the bedrock depth and heights.[49] However, for Downtown, I find the relationship is positive! That is to say, the deeper the rock, the taller are the buildings. This finding supports the fixed-cost theory mentioned above. If going tall increases the fixed costs of construction but not the marginal costs of construction, one is more likely to see a positive relationship between the two, since adding extra height is a way for the owner to make those extra fixed costs possible. A positive finding indicates that bedrock depths do not increase the marginal costs of construction and therefore do not cause heights to be reduced as a result.

Once the decision to build a certain type of building is made, the foundation costs are then fixed by the general size of the project (skyscraper, low-rise, walk-up, etc.) and

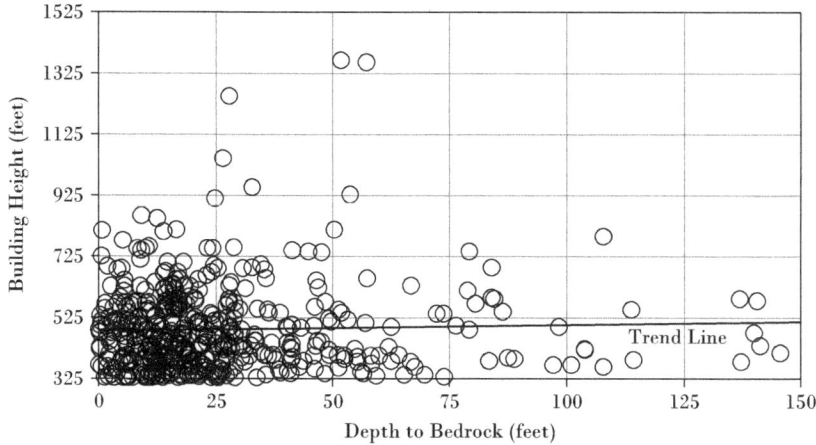

Figure 7.4 Height and bedrock. This figure shows the relationship between bedrock depths (relative to street level) and skyscraper height (for buildings that are 328 feet or taller). If developers had to pay large additional foundation-related expenses to anchor their buildings when bedrock depths were relatively deep, then we would likely see a negative relationship between the bedrock depths and building height. In fact, the scatter plot (the dots) and the trend line demonstrate that, on average, across the city, there is no relationship between how tall a building is and whether it is located over deep bedrock or not.

Source: Figure by Jason M. Barr.

have very little additional effects on the number of stories. So the idea that the depth to bedrock had an effect on the economics of skyscraper construction is not born out by the evidence. The reason for the absence of skyscrapers over the valley is neither technological nor related to their costs.

THE LOGIC OF THE SKYLINE

We now look at another piece of evidence based on the *logic* of skyscraper construction. Ultimately, what drives the decision to build a skyscraper is the profits from the project, which are determined, in large part, by what businesses and residents are willing to pay at a particular location. The rise of Downtown as the center of finance is directly related to a simple fact: clustering together improves the bottom line of firms that do so. There are many reasons for this. Being in the dense business district reduces travel costs associated when meeting with clients, facilitates the acquisition of important business-related information, and provides easier access to suppliers. The increased competitiveness from clustering has been well documented.[50]

The early growth of Wall Street as the center of finance emerged from merchants and their financial needs. Since the merchant community often sought credit to finance their ventures, which would not pay until the ships returned to port laden with goods, they developed financial instruments to support the needs of businesses, including bills of exchange, bonds, and stocks. Merchants would meet at the coffeehouses along Wall Street, such as Tontines, and discuss the news of the day, and talk with each other about their business needs. As the American economy became more sophisticated, Wall Street formed as a central location for firms that specialized in providing money and capital for the growing economy.[51]

Around Wall Street clustered the host of other specialized firms that relied on and were engaged by Wall Street firms. These included printing presses, the business and real estate media, law firms, insurance providers, corporate executives (and their headquarters), clearing houses, trading exchanges, and so on. In other words, as the Industrial Revolution spread throughout America in the nineteenth century, Wall Street developed as a kind of financial services ecology, where a host of firms and institutions created a symbiotic web to finance the growth of America.

The effect of this growth was to create tremendous pressure on land values in Lower Manhattan, where skyscrapers and business clustering became one and the same. The skyscraper would never have emerged if businesses preferred to scatter more evenly over the landscape. Since many firms and their workers all desire to reside within the small area of the city, the only way to successfully accommodate this business is to use the land more intensively. Each acre of land must generate more floor space.

But the economic limits to height, however, suggest that there must be some outward expansion of business away from the core of Wall Street, if business growth occurs at a faster rate than can be accommodated by office space growth. If the demand was so great, then northward seems like the logical place to go, given how Lower Manhattan tapers off to point at the Battery. Chapter 5 demonstrated how newspaper and magazine publishers clustered so tightly Downtown, in the vicinity of City Hall, and it is reasonable to assume that these firms would have moved north if they were being "pushed out" by other types of firms or institutions. Or if new publishers with fewer resources found that rent prices were too high in the thick of Newspaper Row, they could have considered moving a few blocks north where rents were cheaper but still in walking distance of the main cluster.

In general, when new firms are created or old firms are growing, they face a trade-off with respect to the decision of where to locate. They are naturally drawn to other firms and related industries which are of vital competitive importance; but being close means paying a very high rent for office space. But move too far away and pay a different price. The new location puts the firm out of the informational loop; or makes it more difficult to attract workers to the new, far away location; delivery and shipping times will take longer or be more expensive. Clients may be reluctant to spend the extra time travelling, when they can more easily visit a closer firm.

If new firms "jump" too far away, they are basically committing industrial suicide by abandoning their market and their support structure. This is particularly true for national or international industries, but not so much for businesses with local clients and/or local inputs, such as architects or doctors. So, firms face a trade-off during times of expansion: stay in the mix and pay high rents; move away a bit and give up a little of the agglomeration benefits, but pay lower rents; or leapfrog to a new location free of congestion and with much lower rents.

Now let's imagine, as a thought experiment, a situation where the depth to the bedrock represented a real barrier to satisfying the demand for taller buildings just north of City Hall, either because of the technological constraints or because the economic costs were so high. Now further let's assume that twenty floors is the cut-off for a skyscraper, so that any building at this height or taller would require caissons and anchoring the building directly to the rock. Imagine further that demand over or right near the valley was high enough to justify a skyscraper of twenty or more stories if the bedrock costs were not an issue.

In other words, we can imagine a scenario where the profits under "normal" bedrock conditions would produce skyscrapers like the ones along Broadway, which ranged from twenty to fifty stories. However, if bedrock costs are prohibitive above, say, at or above twenty stories, but feasible below twenty stories, because less costly foundations can be used, such as piles, then we would expect to see just north of City Hall clusters of eighteen- and nineteen-story buildings. That is to say, if developers were facing expensive land values north of City Hall because the demand from businesses was so great to be there, they would build the tallest possible building that was feasible given the nature of the bedrock depths. As we demonstrated above, this height was about twenty stories.

So moving north, along Broadway, starting at Bowling Green, we would expect to see clusters of skyscrapers, twenty stories or more, and then once we hit the bedrock valley we should expect to see clusters of buildings that are nineteen stories. That is, height should suddenly fall and plateau at the level of nineteen stories and then after that, trail off to a lower height (say five stories for tenements).

However, when we look at the actual pattern of construction, we do not see that at all. Figure 7.5 shows, rather, a sudden drop off north of City Hall, where building

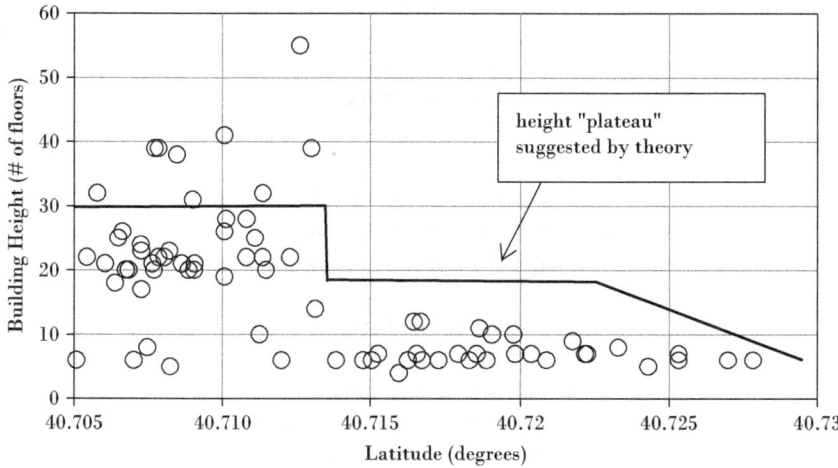

Figure 7.5 Bedrock depths and the logic of the skyline. According to the conventional wisdom, the deep bedrock north of Chambers Street acted as a barrier against skyscraper construction. The idea was that since the bedrock was too far below the surface, it made skyscraper development impossible or not cost-effective. If it was the case that developers wanted to build there, but could not, it is likely we would see a "height plateau" in the region north of City Hall, where the tallest buildings were around eighteen to twenty stories, the upper limit for which pile foundations were feasible. But, rather, we see that this is not the case. Buildings north of Chambers Street are much smaller, indicating that the issue was a lack of demand for skyscrapers, rather than a problem related to the supply side. The line represents the theoretical trend line for average heights if bedrock depths were a supply barrier. The dots represent actual buildings. We can see the actual heights do not march the theoretical average.
Source: Barr, Tassier, and Trendafilov (2010).

height goes from twenty plus stories to no more than ten and in most cases, five stories. In other words, we do not see any evidence of a bedrock "barrier" that would make builders stop at nineteen stories. If developers faced a true dilemma that the demand for tall buildings was greater north of City Hall, but they could not provide them because of the cost or engineering difficulties, we would expect to see a kind of height plateau with a cluster of eighteen- or nineteen-story buildings constructed on piles, hammered into the subsoil.

But rather, we actually see something quite different. Building height suddenly drops off north of the City Hall to a range of five to ten stories, rather than, say, fifteen to twenty stories. This strongly suggests that, again, it was not a supply issue, but rather one of demand, and the desire for firms to locate in areas that were most profitable. Presumably, they had little interest in locating within the dense tenement districts of Five Points and the Lower East Side. We now turn to the final question: What caused the absence of skyscrapers north of City Hall?

THE DETERMINANTS OF SKYSCRAPER LOCATIONS

Was the bedrock a barrier to location choice? Based on the evidence provided so far the answer is "no." The data suggest that neither technology nor costs prevented developers from building skyscrapers in the valley. Rather, the evidence suggests that it was a lack of demand that kept them away. We know that the Municipal Building and Woolworth Building were built over some of the deepest bedrock on the island. But maybe they were economic rogues as it were. The Municipal Building was built by the city government, with little concern for profit maximization, and F. W. Woolworth was eager to project his ego and corporation onto the skyline.

To investigate some of the key supply and demand variables in more detail, a statistical analysis was performed to determine the likelihood of finding a skyscraper on any given block below 59th Street. The objective was to obtain evidence on what were some of the key factors that drove developers to build skyscrapers in some locations but not others; and to see, if, after controlling for these other things, bedrock depths had any influence.[52]

To this end, we return to the data presented in figure 7.3, which shows the location, relative to the lower tip, of all skyscrapers completed in Manhattan between 1890 and 1915, and ninety-nine other randomly chosen buildings as a comparison group. The goal is do a more detailed statistical analysis to determine what drove tall buildings to be located where they were. Data for several economic and demographic variables were also collected based on the belief that they would influence a developer's decision in regard to whether to construct a skyscraper or not.

First was manufacturing worker density for the year 1905, given by the state Assembly Districts, which were similar to the wards in size, though they had different boundaries.[53] Demographic data and the amount of neighborhood park/cemetery space was also collected at the Sanitation District (SD) level for 1890, where the SDs were subsets of wards and can be considered as large neighborhoods. The SDs were used to collect data in Manhattan for the 1890 census.[54]

White-collar firms would avoid locating in districts with large recent immigrant populations but are likely to be closer to native white populations, who make up a larger fraction of white-collar employees. As well, skyscraper developers are likely to avoid dense manufacturing districts, because of the congestion and absence of other office-based firms. Park space, on the other hand, would be important for two reasons. First, presumably, the more park space the higher the quality and income of the neighborhood; second, for the first generation of skyscrapers, access to sunlight was very important, and park or cemetery space near a building would ensure greater light availability.[55]

If we look to see where some of the first important buildings were located (those not clustered in the area centered on Wall Street), blocks that formed triangles near parks or squares were natural locations for tall buildings given the abundance of light. Consider the first skyscraper north of 14th Street, the Flatiron Building (1902), was constructed on a triangular piece of land at the tip of Madison Square; the Metropolitan Life Tower (1909) was built adjacent to the park. The Times Building (1904) was also built on a triangular lot. Early buildings were specifically designed to maximize sunlight intake. In fact, the rents of office space were strongly correlated with the amount of exposure.[56]

Being close to public transportation, especially rapid transit, is likely to benefit firms, and therefore, it is likely that firms and skyscrapers would cluster near elevated rail lines (Els). I collected data on the number of elevated railway stops within a half-mile radius from each building in the data set. The more Els nearby a neighborhood, the more likely it would attract businesses and tall buildings. Lastly, land value data was collected; specifically, average land values for the different blocks on which the buildings sat. High land values, of course, are likely to mean taller buildings, as discussed throughout the book.[57]

The goal of the statistical analysis was to see to what extent bedrock depths influence the probability that a skyscraper would be constructed on a particular block as determined by the set of variables described.[58] That is to say, this approach, a form of regression analysis, maps population and employment density, amount of park space, land values, and bedrock depths to a likelihood number, between zero and one, where zero means no probability of a skyscraper at that location and one means 100% chance of seeing a skyscraper. We would conjecture that the statistical procedure would assign a value close to one in a neighborhood with low population density, a lot of park space, high land values, and moderate depths.

The results of this statistical procedure bear out these hypotheses, as they show the expected patterns for the effects of the variables. The likelihood of a skyscraper being built, however, appears to be unaffected by the depth to bedrock since holding the other variables constant there is no statistically significant relationship between the two. The results also show that manufacturing density is negatively associated with building height, while the number of transit stops is positively related. The probability of a skyscraper appearing on a block increases with the number of transit stops nearby, the percentage of native whites, and the amount of park space in the neighborhood

We can also ask the question, based on the neighborhood demographics, amount of park space, and access to transportation, what is the likelihood of a skyscraper appearing on a particular block, if the bedrock valley did not exist, and the depths were relatively close to the surface? Figure 7.6 shows the predicted probabilities of a skyscraper appearing at given location going from south to north from the statistical procedure, but *based on the assumption that bedrock depths did not vary across the city*. In this "what-if" scenario, we can see that the skyscraper dead zone appears anyway. The reason is because the area between City Hall and 14th Street, as discussed in chapters 3 and 4, contained the core immigrant neighborhoods, and, as such, they simply were not

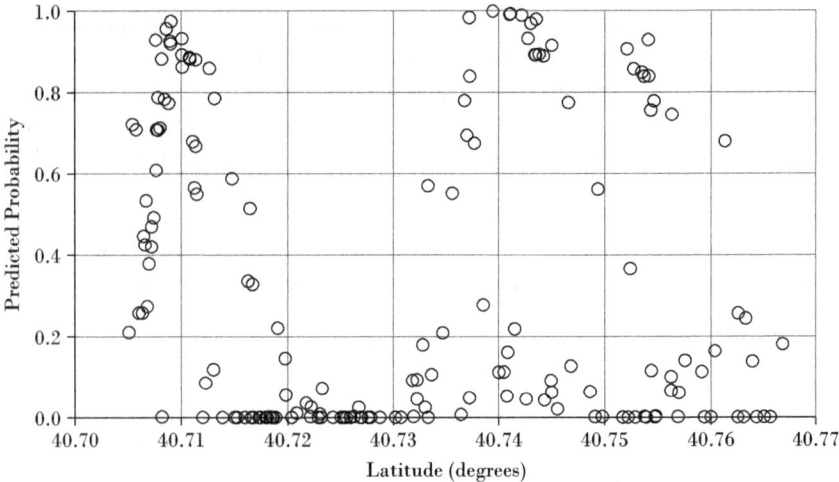

Figure 7.6 Bedrock depths and the probabilities. This figure shows the predicted probabilities of a skyscraper appearing at a given location going from south to north based on a statistical analysis, and with the assumption that bedrock depths did not vary across the city. The results show the skyscraper "dead zone" appears anyway. The reason is because the areas between City Hall and 14th Street were the immigrant and industrial neighborhoods, and there was little demand for tall buildings there. *Source:* Barr, Tassier, and Trendafilov (2010).

profitable locations for the skyscraper in the battle for place. In these neighborhoods, the tenement and the sweatshop factory were earning the most profits.

Local Bedrock Effects

But another very interesting set of results appears when bedrock depths were assumed constant throughout the city. Figure 7.7 shows the difference in the probability estimates with bedrock depths varying versus being constant. Anywhere along the graph where there are negative bars means that if bedrock depths were constant, there would be fewer skyscrapers there; conversely, positive bars indicate more skyscrapers would have been built there if bedrock depths were level.

The first item of note is that there is no change in the probabilities in the dead zone; with or without deep bedrock, no skyscrapers would be built directly north of Chambers Street. But most important is that the results suggest that fewer skyscrapers would have been built around Wall Street (these are the negative bars on the left side) and more would have been built near City Hall (the positive bars around latitude 40.715?). This unexpected result makes sense when we stop to consider it. Some of the first important skyscrapers were constructed near City Hall, such as the Tribune Building, the Times Building, and the Woolworth Building, because of the strong agglomerative forces pulling businesses there.

But as skyscrapers became heavier and taller, it is likely that developers were influenced to some degree by the additional costs of constructing them where the bedrock was so deep. It suggests that bedrock costs were not unimportant, *given the decision*

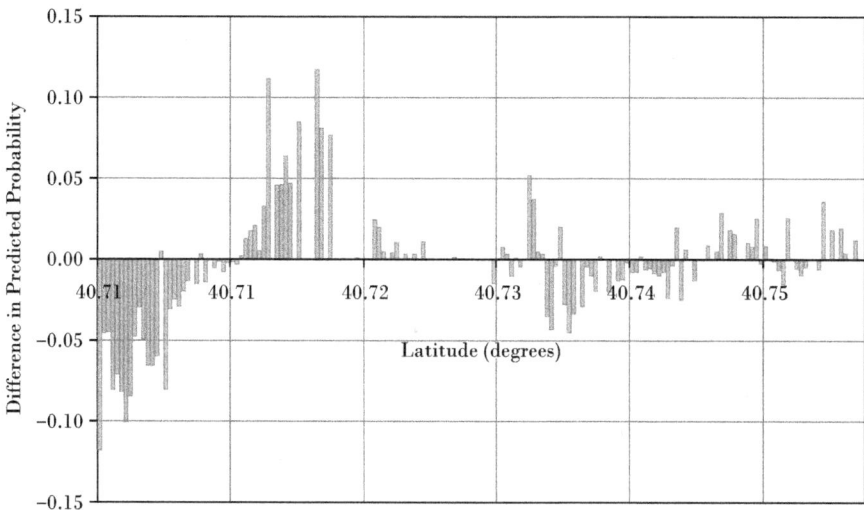

Figure 7.7 Local bedrock effects. This figure shows the difference in the probability estimates of a skyscraper being at a particular location with bedrock depths varying versus being constant. Anywhere along the graph that there are negative bars means that if bedrock depths were constant and close to the ground, there would be fewer skyscrapers there; conversely, positive bars indicate more skyscrapers would have been built there if bedrock depths were level. First, we can see that there is no change in the probabilities in the "dead zone." Second, fewer skyscrapers would have been built around Wall Street (these are the negative bars on the left side) and more would have been built near City Hall (the positive bars around latitude 40.715°). To some degree, builders south of Chambers Street appear to have preferred building over shallower bedrock. *Source:* Barr, Tassier, and Trendafilov (2010).

to construct a skyscraper. Certainly, it stands to reason that if firms want to remain in the business district, and developers were eager to provide skyscrapers, competition would drive developers to provide that space at lower cost. The data do provide evidence that builders within Lower Manhattan moved their skyscrapers to more southern locations as a response to some of the problems that were found when digging foundations near City Hall. But under no circumstances were they prevented from building them in the valley, if the demographic and economic history of the city had been different.

8

The Birth of Midtown

The ideal of quiet and of genteel retirement, in 1835, was found in Washington Square, where the Doctor built himself a handsome, modern, wide-fronted house, with a big balcony before the drawing-room windows, and a flight of marble steps ascending to a portal which was also faced with white marble.

Henry James

AGGLOMERATION ECONOMICS AND THE RISE OF DOWNTOWN

Midtown Manhattan—the area from 34th to 59th Streets—is the largest business district in the country; it contains over 241.5 million square feet (8.7 square miles) of office space; thus creating an additional 38% more "land" on the island.[1] If Midtown was the sole central business district (CBD) in the city, it would be larger than the country's next two CBDs, Chicago and Washington, DC, combined. Yet, less than 3 miles away is a second parallel district—Downtown—centered at Wall Street, which contains roughly 85 million square feet of office space.[2]

As discussed in chapters 2 and 3, Downtown was the original location of Dutch settlement, and its rise was due to its early commercial heritage. By the second decade of the nineteenth century, thanks to the city's port, Lower Manhattan, the 0.6 square mile area from City Hall to the Battery, was rising as one of the great business centers of the world. Far less understood, however, is what drove the creation of Midtown as a separate economy on the same island.[3]

As discussed in the previous chapter, the growth of Downtown as the nation's capital of finance can be understood as stemming from the positive feedback loops that occur when firms congregate together. The Dutch and English merchants had their counting houses on lower Pearl Street, adjacent the port, to facilitate the importing and exporting of goods.[4] The merchants were required to cluster for this reason; however, they also preferred being near each other to facilitate their transactions. They would talk about prices or market conditions; and they would turn to each other for joint ventures or to raise capital.

Wall Street, as the hub of finance, sprang forth from this merchant community. The buying and selling of securities was originally carried on by merchants and auctioneers as part of their regular business activity. By 1792, security trading was brisk enough on Wall Street to produce a group of specialists. When five securities auctioneers feared the loss of their business from competition, they met in front of a buttonwood tree on Wall Street and drew up an agreement for the New York Stock Exchange.[5] The rest, as they say, is history.

Wall Street's success as the go-to place for financing and securities trading promoted the emergence of a financial industrial ecology due to the need of bankers and brokers to be near each other and to have supporting firms in close proximity. Large corporations established their headquarters Downtown to be near the financiers and the legal community.[6] In the years from 1790 to the Civil War, Wall Street's financial district would blossom into the capital of capital.

Here, we see an example of a positive urban feedback loop: the port draws the merchants, the merchants draw the financing and legal community, as well as ancillary businesses, such as shipbuilders, artisans, pubs, and coffeehouses. The agglomeration of these firms and workers then has unplanned spillovers that enhance growth. Firms and workers learn from each other; they become more innovative; and they act as de facto new-firm incubators, since workers who start their own businesses draw on this pool of resources.[7] In short, success breeds more success, locking-in the district's importance.

But if agglomeration benefits are so important, why didn't Downtown simply expand, either via landfill or northward movement? Creating more land from the sea was an old practice in New York since 1686, and proposals to expand Lower Manhattan have been, and continue to be, regularly proffered. The expense of land creation is not so great if the demand is there, as evidenced by the city's early projects discussed in chapter 2, and the more recent creation of Battery Park City in the 1970s.[8]

So the question remains, why would a second, parallel office-based economy develop so close to, yet apart from, Lower Manhattan, when Downtown had such a strong pull for firms? There are two conventional answers that permeate the historiography. As discussed in chapter 7, the first reason offered is related to the bedrock valley just north of City Hall. As demonstrated in that chapter, this Bedrock Theory is not consistent with the evidence. Rather, the conventional wisdom appears to have developed because of the confusion of correlation with causation. The costs of setting foundations in deeper bedrock were a minor fraction of the total costs, and if there were sufficient demand, engineers could have created foundations for the tall buildings in the valley. In short, the rise of Midtown was not due to an inability of developers to build skyscrapers in neighborhoods directly north of City Hall.

The second belief about the rise of Midtown relates to the location of Grand Central Station.[9] Forced by the city government to keep its terminal north of Lower Manhattan, in 1871, the New York Central railroad opened a depot at its current location on East 42nd Street. The historiography holds that this area developed as a natural focal point because it created a giant transportation hub. However, the problem with this argument is that the tracks were exposed until 1913, when they were finally electrified. Before then, the neighborhood north of the station was polluted by the coal-infused steam from the locomotives. Out of the seven crosstown streets passing through the station's property, north of 42nd Street, only two were open for vehicles; the rest were for pedestrians.[10]

A closer look at building patterns reveals that the Grand Central Station neighborhood was not of interest to skyscraper (and office) developers during the earliest years. The first skyscraper north of 14th Street was the Flatiron Building completed in 1902. It was built on a triangular plot between Broadway, Fifth Avenue, and 23rd Street.[11] During the first generation of Midtown high-rises between 1902 and 1915, only four out of thirty-five were built adjacent to the station. These were built either after electrification or in anticipation thereof. These four buildings were the Belmont Hotel (1908),

Biltmore Hotel (1913), Yale Club (1915), and Vanderbilt Concourse Building (1915). Notice that only the last was an office building; it was built as part of Grand Central Station's Terminal City being constructed in the late 1910s (see chapter 9).

In terms of mass transit, the elevated railroad lines were designed to funnel as many people to Downtown as possible. The first short road began in 1868, and throughout the 1870s, the Els were expanded so that there were four parallel lines running up and down the island.[12] The Els were much faster than the streetcars, since they did not have to contend with street traffic, but they were generally run on steam, which caused pollution. As well, many of the avenues containing the roads were in shadows and caused lower real estate values. The lines all converged at the southern tip and there is little evidence of a transportation hub in Midtown. Figure 8.1 shows, for example, the number of elevated railroad stop within a half mile of each block going north from the southern tip as of the late 1880s, and before the first skyscraper was built. While there were a few blocks of Midtown where El riders had many choices, El stop concentrations were nowhere near as dense as Downtown.

The first world-record-breaking skyscraper north of Chambers Street was the Metropolitan Life Tower, completed in 1909, on the corner of Madison Avenue and 23rd Street, across from Madison Square Park. Founded in 1868, the company originally opened an office on 23rd Street and Madison Avenue in 1893. MetLife introduced the strategy of having its agents go door-to-door, collecting monthly premiums.[13] Presumably, by having their offices in Madison Square, agents were much closer to their customers. Its success at that location prompted it to construct its tower; this strongly suggests that Madison Square was the center of business and commerce north of 14th Street. The Chrysler and Empire State Buildings, further north, were completed a generation later.

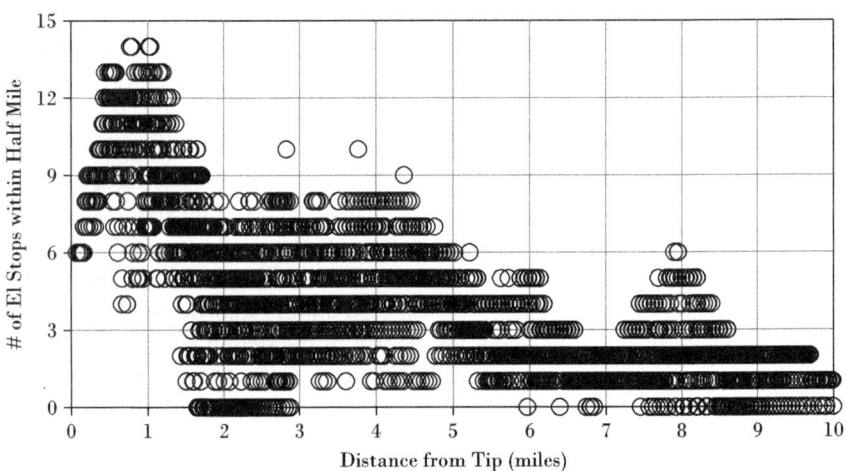

Figure 8.1 Els and hubs. This figure shows the number of elevated railroad (El) stops as of the late 1880s within a half mile of each block on the island going north from the southern tip. While there were a few blocks of Midtown where El riders had many choices, El stop concentrations were nowhere near as dense as Downtown. In essence, the elevated railroad system created a transportation hub Downtown, and less so on other parts of the island.

Source: Data collected by Teddy Ort. Figure by Jason M. Barr.

Figure 8.2 shows the pattern of skyscraper construction during this generation. Each dot represents a building that is 262 feet (80 meters) or taller. Figure
8.2A shows that during the decade or so between 1890 and 1901, all the skyscrapers were constructed Downtown, the sole exception being the tower of Madison
Square Garden. Then, suddenly, starting in 1902, there was a "jump" where skyscraper completions were evenly divided between Downtown and Midtown. The
maps indicates that around the turn of the twentieth century there was a tipping
point, where developers saw opportunities north of 14th Street that did not exist
in the decade prior, despite the fact that nothing had changed in the neighborhood around Grand Central Station, which would not be rebuilt and completed
until 1913.

The graph also reveals that Midtown construction was split between two areas. The
first was between Union and Madison Squares, from 14th Street to 26th Streets; the
second area was along 42nd Street, running west from Grand Central Station to Times
Square. Thus, the graph shows that there was no clear Midtown focal point, but rather,
there were two skyscraper districts north of 14th Street.

The corridor along 42nd Street was likely influenced by two changes occurring in
the first two decades of the twentieth century. First, as mentioned above, was Grand
Central Station. Second was the completion of the first subway line, which began at

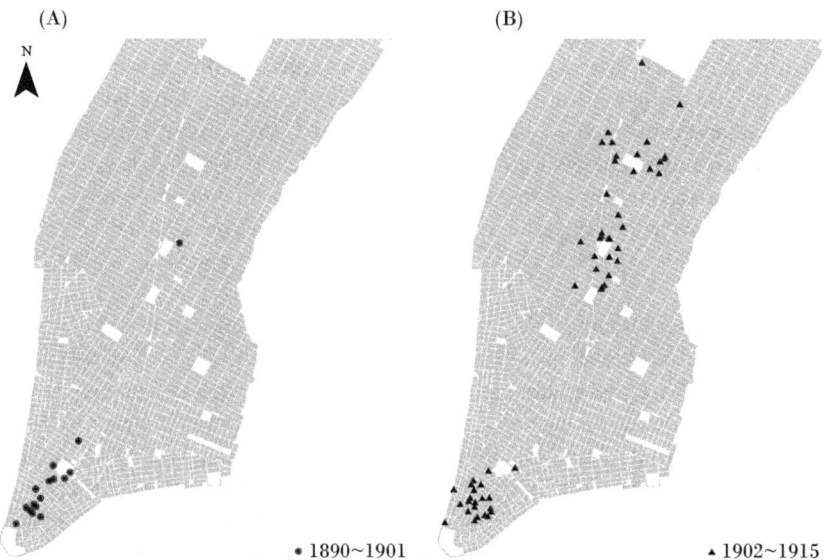

(A)

N

(B)

• 1890~1901   ▲ 1902~1915

Figure 8.2 Skyscraper locations from 1890 to 1915. Figure 8.2A shows the location of all skyscrapers
(buildings 262 feet or taller) that were constructed during their first decade. Except for the tower
of Madison Square (1890), all tall building were constructed in Lower Manhattan. Then, suddenly,
starting in 1902, there was a "jump" where skyscraper completions were evenly divided between
Downtown and Midtown (figure 8.2B). The graph strongly suggests that around the turn of the
twentieth century, there was a tipping point, where developers saw opportunities north of 14th Street
that did not exist in the decade prior, despite the fact that nothing had changed in the neighborhood
around Grand Central Station, which would not be rebuilt and completed until 1913.
Source: Maps by Eon Kim. Underlying data from Barr, Tassier, and Trendafilov (2010).

City Hall, ran up to Grand Central, then cut across 42nd Street to Times Square, and from there up Broadway. The line may have influenced the early shape to some degree, since developers and businesses saw opportunities along the lines. But as I will argue throughout the chapter, public transportation played a supporting role in the rise of Midtown, while the main force was the economic and demographic profile of the area in the decades after the Civil War.

In summary, the emergence of Midtown as a separate district cannot be explained by the bedrock valley—that idea was disproved in the last chapter; nor is there evidence that Grand Central Station was the cause of Midtown's rise either. The majority of the first skyscrapers north of 14th Street were in the area between Union and Madison Squares, and the handful that was built around Grand Central was completed around 1913. While the subway might have drawn some skyscrapers north to 42nd Street with the movement of the *New York Times* in 1904, the fact that most skyscrapers were south of that area, also suggests that the subway system was not the direct cause for Midtown's emergence. Rather the transportation investments helped nourish Midtown's growth, but only after its seeds were planted.

ECONOMIC THEORIES
OF POLYCENTRIC DEVELOPMENT

So what accounts for the rise of Midtown? Before we turn to the historical and statistical evidence, we first discuss some of the economic theories that have been used to explain the rise of polycentric urban areas, which can be used to help identify the reason for Midtown's birth. These theories emerged out of the fact that after World War II, population and businesses were leaving the central cities and spreading out within the larger metropolitan areas. The postwar period represented the beginning of massive urban sprawl, where the growth of the suburban fringes occurred at the expense of the traditional urban cores. Modern suburbia had its debutante ball, as were, in the 1950s.[14]

New York City's demographic patterns over the twentieth century demonstrate this spreading out. Manhattan—the City of New York until 1874—saw its population peak in 1910, at 2.1 million people, and then it continued to lose people until around 1980, when the population started to grow again. Today, Manhattan's population is only 70% of its peak. The population of all five boroughs grew continuously until 1950, when it peaked at 7.89 million. For the next twenty years, the city's population was essentially flat, and then, between 1970 and 1980, the city lost over 800,000 people. Today New York holds its largest population ever, at 8.4 million.[15]

In 1900, the five boroughs had nearly 2.5 times the population of the eight surrounding counties that comprised the inner ring around the city.[16] By 1950, the ratio had fallen to 2:1; and after that the ratio fell quite rapidly so that by 1980, the population ratio of these counties was roughly equal to New York City, though there has been a slight uptick since then.[17]

Starting in the 1950s, the corporate headquarters that earlier felt compelled to establish themselves in Manhattan began leaving the city. In 1956, 140 of the Fortune 500 companies had their headquarters within the city. By 1974, that number was down to 98, a drop of 30%.[18] In the same period, the city's population dropped by about 3%.[19] In 1956, there were only 16 Fortune 500 in the New York metropolitan region outside of the city. By 1974, that number grew to 46, an increase of 190%.

On December 20, 1961, International Business Machines (IBM), for example, announced that it was moving its headquarters from Madison Avenue and 57th Street to an office complex on a 443-acre woodland tract in Armonk, New York, 35 miles to the north.[20] Big firms, such as IBM, found they were both pushed out by congestion, high costs, and low quality of life, and pulled to the suburbs, to where their employees had been moving since after the war. As the *New York Times* put it, "Common talk is about 'the flight' from the overcrowded behemoth, its crime, traffic, schools and megaton-bomb peril."[21] The changing nature of work and production also affected the decision. Many firms established their research labs and plants out in the suburbs, where they could spread out with larger floor arrangements that were better suited to the new technologies.

In the nineteenth and early twentieth centuries, there was a very steep drop in density as one moved away from the center. But after World War II, a new pattern of land use emerged in metropolitan areas. First, there was a "flattening" of population density over space, as people moved out of the central cities and into the suburbs. Second, population density became "bumpier" across the region, as small cities, outside the core saw their fortunes improve. Metropolitan regions became polycentric, rather than monocentric, as the central city had to compete with other smaller centers surrounding it.[22]

But this bumpiness is not just a product of the automobile; it is not simply a postwar phenomenon. Rather, Midtown's emergence in the late nineteenth century shows that the forces that drove polycentric development after World War II were, in fact, present, in Manhattan, nearly a century before. The realignment of the urban population after World War II was rather a realignment writ large driven by the automobile, as residents voted with their feet to leave the central cities and move out the suburban rings. This was, as we shall see, the same force at work for Midtown. It is a direct result of the First Inversion that took place in Manhattan starting in the 1830s, and it drove a critical mass of the population to live on the northern fringes of the city in the decades following the Civil War.

We can see why and when the population moved north on the island, as this was done in chapters 3 and 4. But what remains to be understood is what drove businesses to "jump" to Midtown, where I mean jump in broad terms. Some firms actually moved their operations from Downtown to Midtown, and thus directly left or shrank their presence in Lower Manhattan. Other new businesses opened an office in Midtown without ever having resided Downtown. So when I use the word "jump" I simply mean that the growth of businesses in Midtown was occurring rapidly and suddenly when compared to Downtown.

To understand why firms left Downtown and why Midtown saw an explosive growth of business requires that we discuss some of the economic theories that relate to the decisions of firms to locate where they do. By laying out the theories and then comparing it to the data, we can test which theory applies to Midtown, in particular. Or, at least, which one seems most important.

We can think of firms as facing two kinds of forces: centripetal and centrifugal. The centripetal forces are those that draw businesses close to each other; while the centrifugal forces are those that push them away.[23] In New York City, these tensions became more pronounced with the rise of office-based economy after the Civil War, and with the development of mass transit. For these white-collar businesses face a constant trade-off between being close to each other and their network of suppliers versus being close to their workers or their customers, who, were moving away from the center when transportation costs fell. These trade-offs and tensions are different for different businesses and industries as well.

The theories on urban spatial structure have several approaches. The first few come under the heading of "exogenous" determinants of the location of economic activity and the next set focuses on the "endogenous" location choices. Exogenous, in this case, means determined outside of or separate from the decisions of firms and workers, in the sense that a particular location has some benefit determined before businesses decide to move there. On the other hand, the endogenous approaches focus on the properties of the urban system itself. That is, something inherent in the decisions that people and firms make eventually alter their own incentives so as to trigger a new urban configuration.

The first type of exogenous theory focuses on the presence of some bounty provided by the natural world, such as the presence of gold or oil, the location of a natural port, or being in a central geography.[24] New York, for example, was established because of its port and central location.[25] San Francisco saw its meteoric growth during the Gold Rush of 1849; and Chicago, to paraphrase the economist Homer Hoyt, was a great city before it even existed.[26] Centrally located between the Great Lakes and the Mississippi River valley, it was long known as an ideal location for commerce between the east coast and the hinterland. Once the decision was made in the 1830s to build a canal to connect the Great Lakes to the Mississippi River, Chicago's destiny was sealed.[27]

But in the case of Midtown, this natural bounty theory can be rejected on the grounds that its environment was not fundamentally different in 1900 as it was in 1600, in the sense that no gold was discovered or a new port was created there. The Bedrock Theory implicitly assumes a natural disadvantage story in the sense that north of City Hall was considered a geological barrier for builders. But, again, we can reject this theory based on the evidence presented in the previous chapter.

A second type of exogenous theory focuses on the construction of infrastructure before there is a major population swell. This theory can be thought of as the "Edge City hypothesis" based on the work of Joel Garreau who, in his book *Edge City: Life on the New Frontier*, documents the rise of subcenters on the edges of traditional urban centers, starting in the 1970s with the construction of interstate highways on the fringes of metropolitan areas.[28] In this case, governments, in partnerships with developers, first construct a "natural advantage" and then business and residents follow to take advantage of it.

By building railroads or highways, sewage and water infrastructure, local communities create natural focal points for businesses who can gain access to their clients and employees by locating near highway intersections or rail hubs. This is a kind of build-it-and-they-will-come idea, and can, in many cases, explain large suburban agglomerations.[29] As the highways emerge, new businesses move in, they hire workers, and then the ancillary businesses come to support these firms and workers, and an edge city forms as a new ecology of businesses, workers, and residents.[30]

For Manhattan, however, the data do not support this theory. First, the major transportation hubs that are believed to have caused the rise of Midtown—the electrified Grand Central Station (1913), Penn Station (1910), and the subway system (1904)—were, in fact, completed after the rise of Midtown, as will be documented below. Midtown, as a separate office district began to emerge in the 1880s, a generation before the grand railroad terminals were built.

In regard to sewage and water, while the Croton Aqueduct water system was completed in 1845, hookups to the system were haphazard and generally occurred after economic development came to a particular neighborhood. Similarly for sewage pipes; there was no master plan for their completions, and they tended to be laid down only after a majority of residents on a block requested them. In short, sewage and water infrastructure improvements tended to follow, rather than precede, real estate development in Manhattan.[31]

This also holds with the implementation of the Grid Plan, streets tended to be graded and opened in response to population growth. As the city became increasingly crowded, it put pressure on government officials to open streets. The city was not proactive in creating new streets years in advance of the population or businesses.[32] And finally, with the elevated railroads, as mentioned above, there was a steady decline in the access to public transportation going north (see figure 8.1). By and large, the elevated roads were constructed to move people up and down the island, and they were not funneling people to Midtown.

The next set of theories focuses on the endogenous emergence of polycentric spatial structure based on the balance of trade-offs for firms and residents. Within this category are several variants. The first stresses a general trade-off between the profits that come to firms when they cluster together and the problems and costs that arise from congestion and the movement of the goods and services. On one hand, firms want to be together to enhance their bottom lines. But the more they cluster, they also created greater congestion problems—at some point there are just too many firms and people, which can reduce profitability.

Some companies might realize that the costs from congestion—the delays, pollution, and frustrations from being Downtown—are too high relative to the agglomeration benefits.[33] If they move to another location, they will then have less congestion-related problems, but also fewer of the benefits from clustering. If, however, the congestion-costs-to-agglomeration-benefits ratio becomes relatively high, the move becomes worth it; a business finds that it is better to take a hit on profits by not being close to other firms, so its employees and clients can breathe and move more freely in a new neighborhood.

Another set of theories focuses on the wages that firms pay. If workers move to homes in the suburbs, then it will take them longer to get to work. Downtown companies may find they have to pay their workers more to motivate them to take the longer trip, which requires both greater expense and time. In essence, employers will find they need to subsidize their staff to make the schlep.

At some point, firms might realize that they can improve their bottom lines by moving to the suburbs and saving money on their labor costs by hiring workers who live much closer to their jobs. Imagine you are head of the Human Resources Department at XYZ International, Inc., and you find you must pay an administrative worker $65,000 to come to Downtown. But you realize, you can attract the same quality talent at $50,000 by reducing their commute from an hour and half to 20 minutes. This would give the business the incentive to move. The theory that wage savings are driving the movement of firms is referred to as the Wage Gradient Theory.[34]

In economics a "gradient" is a graph that shows how some important variable, such as land prices, population density, or wages, fall as one moves further away from the central city. As discussed in chapter 3, land values exhibit this gradient property because competition among businesses and residents to be near the best locations will bid up land values in the economic center, and they will fall moving away due to either greater transportation costs or the lost value of access to those benefits and amenities provided there.

It has also been argued that large corporations move to areas close to the residences of the corporate executives. For example, some large financial concerns moved from Lower Manhattan to Greenwich, Connecticut, and the idea offered is that it was done so the CEOs could work near their own homes.[35] But this argument confuses correlation with causation. If a CEO moved his company to the suburbs simply to save him and his fellow executives time getting to the office, it is not likely to prove a good decision, unless he can still retain a high-quality workforce.

If a wealthy CEO moves his company to horse country in western New Jersey, to be close to his horse ranch, you can rest assured that the company will go out of business, since there is no way that the business is going to get the rest of the staff to join him. Rather the CEO moves a company because his residential location in the suburbs is close to the residential locations of a large fraction of his company, and thus he can do these workers a favor by moving. Workers are happier because they waste less time in traffic and can spend more time earning money or enjoying life with their families and friends. Other firms, who also made the leap, are close by and so agglomeration effects can emerge anew in the suburban location.

Finally, a third theory stresses the role of shopping locations and traffic congestion.[36] In this theory the focus is on the rise of shopping districts. Since these businesses want to be near their customers they will tend to congregate near residential neighborhoods. Like shops in modern malls, by clustering together, stores and restaurants can attract more business than if they spread out. Shoppers know they can find many items in the same place, and this reduces transportation and search costs, and, as a result, they come more often and spend more money. If people know that other people like themselves will be there, going to the shopping centers also provides a social experience. We can think of the Broadway Theatre District or Fifth Avenue south of Central Park as examples of this type of agglomeration.

But again, we see the agglomeration-congestion trade-off with the shopping theory. Success from clustering creates new costs from congestion and pollution. At some point, firms face a trade-off: stay and lock in a steady flow of customers, or move and start fresh, and stand out apart from the dense massive crowds.

To summarize, these endogenous theories all present some form of trade-off between the benefits of clustering versus the benefits of reducing costs by moving. As a business district grows, this tension become more intense, as its success gives rise to the seeds of its moderation, like a safety valve releasing steam. This process means that after business districts hit a critical threshold, there will be an adjustment to a new "spatial equilibrium"; that is, after some density threshold is passed at the old location, it will cause people move to a new location, which is parallel to, and often in competition with, the older one. The parent gives birth to the child. Downtown gives rise to Midtown.

Of the three theories, one focuses on trade-off between business agglomeration and congestion in the crowded CBD; another focuses on wages versus agglomeration; and the third focuses on the balance between being close to customers versus traffic and traveling congestion. In order to decipher among these theories, we next turn to the history of the area between 14th and 23rd Streets, as this is where the seeds of Midtown were first planted. After that, we take a look at the statistical data. While recounting the history of the area is important and useful, the data allows us to look at the larger land-use patterns on the island during the second half of the nineteenth century.

To preview the conclusions, the evidence suggests what I call the "shopping symbiosis" theory. Over the course of the nineteenth century, the upper and middle-class residents were suburbanizing by steadily moving northward on the island and into the Bronx. By the 1870s, the neighborhood between Union and Madison Squares emerged as a commercial and shopping district to cater to the needs and wants of the residents living north of 14th Street. Retail and other local businesses had been moving northward from Downtown to SoHo and then north of Houston Street to be closer to their customers.

However, something new happened in the 1880s: some businesses that were previously located Downtown—office-based firms, in particular—found it beneficial to move to the Midtown area. These firms were, in some sense, feeding off the shoppers and retail operations by moving close to them. These businesses included architects, real estate developers, newspaper publishers, and, to a lesser degree, life insurance companies.

As these office firms moved north to be closer to their clients, workers, and the shopping districts, it triggered a readjustment of the types of business activity taking place north of 14th Street. In other words, first came the department stores, shops, restaurants, hotels, and the entertainment venues; next came office-based companies that found it convenient to be near these other businesses. This then triggered a wholesale readjustment of Midtown into an office district, based on the agglomeration benefits that then emerged when these businesses arrived in great numbers. The two decades from the 1880 to 1900 were when the seeds of Midtown began to bloom, as a new symbiotic business ecology developed that included retail, entertainment, and related office-based services.

In the third decade of the twentieth century, Midtown became that which we recognize today. Grand Central Station was completed in 1913, and after about a decade-long pause due to war and recession, the streets emanating outward from the depot, along 42nd Street and north along Fifth to Third Avenues saw the gleaming office towers of the Roaring Twenties. Penn Station, which opened in 1910, helped to trigger the movement of the garment industry from Canal to 14th Streets to 23rd to 42nd Streets along Seventh and Eighth Avenues. But this is the story of Midtown 2.0, and we leave it for the next chapter.

MANHATTAN MOVES NORTH

In 1820 the city had nearly 124,000 residents; by 1860, its population was just over 800,000, and hit one million sometime around 1875. Two million came a few years after 1900. Figure 8.3 shows the rise of New York's population from 1840 to 1910.[37]

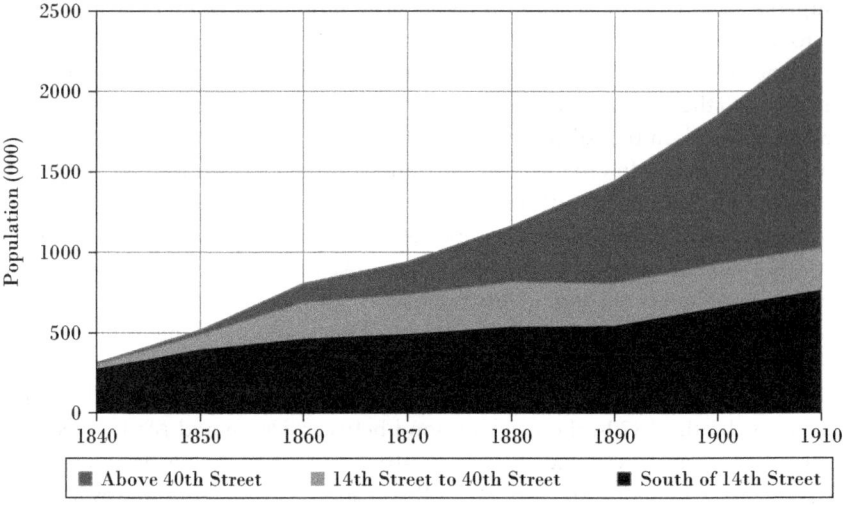

Figure 8.3 Manhattan population growth from 1840 to 1910. The graph shows population counts for three different regions. The lower area is the number of people in Manhattan south of 14th Street. The next area above that is between 14th and 40th Streets. Finally the top area is the population north of 40th street. The graph, of course, shows a rising population over the nineteenth century. By the 1870s, the majority of residents lived north of 40th Street.

Source: Barr and Tassier (2015).

The graph shows population counts for three different regions. The lower area is the number of people of Manhattan south of 14th Street. The next area above that is between 14th and 40th Streets. Finally the top area is the population north of 40th Street. The graph, of course, shows a rising population over the nineteenth century. But what is particularly important is the growth north of 40th Street from the 1860s onward, which outstripped the area to the south. By 1860 south of 14th Street comprised only about 60% of the population, with the northern suburbs being around 42nd Street. During the 1870s, the majority of residents lived north of 40th Street. By 1879, the footprint of the city on the east side extended continuously all the way up to Harlem and on the west side to 59th Street (see figure 3.3).

14 to 23: Three Squares and a Mile

As discussed in chapter 3, the 1830s was the start of the First Inversion; the period when upper and middle-class suburbanization began. The streetcar allowed for these classes to "jump" over the working-class neighborhoods and form suburban enclaves, along the central spine of the island. As population growth put pressure on land values, landowners would have their land surveyed and sold off or developed, simultaneous with the opening of new streets and avenues.

Some areas on the northern fringes naturally lent themselves to remain public spaces. The three most important examples are Washington, Union, and Madison Squares. They all had in common that they were located along the central spine of the island, and they attracted the well-to-do and the commercial business that catered to them. Also the land was available for conversion to open space based on prior decisions made by the Common Council. Union and Madison Squares were at the confluences of Broadway and some other avenue imposed by the Grid Plan. Washington Square had been a potter's field outside the city proper.

As the population was moving northward, the Common Council recognized the need to develop opens areas. In the case of Washington and Madison Squares, their first public uses were as military training grounds. However, once these fields were set aside, they became natural enclaves for upper and middle-class residents; they were converted to parks as a result.

Washington Square

Before European settlement, the area north of Washington Square was upland, and was drained by Minetta Brook (see chapter 1). The Dutch established farms to the west and south of the Minetta, while Washington Square Park was swampy and left unimproved. In 1797, the city purchased the territory for a new potter's field, and burials continued for nearly three decades. As late as 1815, farmland covered the area between Canal Street and Greenwich Village.[38]

In 1808, the Common Council ordered the high ground at the potter's field to "be drawn into the valley and levelled in such manner as to render the same more suitable for the purposes of a Cemetery," presumably to add more graves for the increasing number of deaths from the yellow fever epidemics.[39] In 1825 the cemetery was closed; as real estate development moved north, it was no longer acceptable to have a cemetery inside the city. The bodies were removed and the field was converted to Washington Military Parade Ground; it was dedicated as a public park in 1849.

The construction of townhouses around the square began with the closing of the cemetery, and about this time, New York University started offering classes at the northeast corner of the park. Washington Square's creation promoted the development of lower Fifth Avenue, which would soon be lined with mansions, churches, hotels, and clubs; firmly establishing Fifth Avenue as the boulevard of the wealthy.[40]

Union Square

The kernel of Union Square was created by the Grid Plan of 1811, which was formed by the union of Fourth Avenue and Broadway, and was referred to as "the Forks" before it was formally constructed. For several decades, however, it remained far on the outskirts of town as a collection of undeveloped lots, gardens, and shanties. The original mapping did not specify parkland, but the intersection seemed better suited for that purpose.[41]

In 1831, the city's Street Committee wrote a report stressing the need to carve out open spaces in the growing city "for purposes of military, and civic parades, and festivities, and . . . to serve as ventilators to a densely populated city."[42] At the urging of residents, the area was graded, paved, and fenced, and opened to the public in July 1839. Throughout the decade of the 1840s, Union Square developed as an attractive enclave for the well-to-do, whose row houses and mansions lined the square.

By the 1860s commerce arrived and pushed out the wealthy residents; the neighborhood would become home to theaters, hotels, and luxury retailers. By the 1890s Union Square had become a central location for the offices of publishers and banks that had moved uptown in the 1880s to be near their clients. For example, in 1868, the Institution for the Savings of Merchant's Clerks purchased a Greek Revival row house for its offices on the corner of Union Square East and 15th Street. The bank was established in 1848 and was originally located near City Hall Park. In 1904 it changed its name to the Union Square Savings Bank to reflect its association with the neighborhood; and in 1905, it built a prominent structure in the Academic Classical style with Corinthian columns and a grand entranceway. The building still stands as a reminder of Union Square's former status as an early commercial hub.[43]

Madison Square

Like Union Square, the intersection of Broadway and Fifth Avenue at 23rd Street suggested itself as a small park.[44] Unlike Union Square, which was developed based on the urging of local property owners, the area that would become Madison Square was originally mapped in the Grid Plan as a Grand Parade Grounds between 23rd and 34th Streets and Third and Seventh Avenues. But in 1814 it was reduced in size and named for President James Madison.

In the early years of its existence, Madison Square was mostly used by the US military. In 1836, the Common Council voted to create Madison Square as a public park. Funds were allocated to buy the land, drain the existing streams, and eliminate the Boston Road, which ran through it. The 6.23-acre park running from 23rd to 26th Streets, from Fifth to Madison Avenues, was officially opened in 1847, nearly a decade after Union Square. [45]

By the 1850s, Madison Square emerged as a draw for society. The wealthy lived in brownstone townhouses which fronted the park and along Fifth Avenue. Evidently, the well-to-do were opposed to having the park used for other purposes, and they lobbied against changing its use by opposing the construction of the Crystal Palace in 1853 and the construction of a new City Hall in 1855. The Crystal Palace was instead constructed in what is today Bryant Park, and it introduced to America two key innovations in building technology: iron framing and safety-breaks in elevators. Plans for a City Hall never gained traction, but the fact that proposals were floated to move it to Madison Square suggests that this neighborhood was rising as an important economic and social center.[46]

The first hotel to include a public elevator, the prestigious Fifth Avenue Hotel, opened in the neighborhood in 1859 at Fifth Avenue and 23rd Street. It was uptown from the city's other high-end hotels, south of 14th Street, but, Broadway around the park in the 1860s developed into "an avenue of great hotels."[47] The Victoria Hotel completed in 1870 and designed by Richard Morris Hunt was the first of several luxury apartment buildings constructed in the district along Fifth Avenue.

Throughout the 1870s and 1880s, the park was surrounded by hotels and commercial buildings, with stores, restaurants, and social clubs thriving in the surrounding blocks. Townhouses were converted to commercial uses, as residents moved out and upward to new suburban neighborhoods. Commercial buildings were constructed with stores at the street level and a mix of office and loft spaces on the upper floors. Initially these buildings were generally no taller than six floors, but after the widespread adoption of the elevator, the structures rose up to eight or ten stories.

Starting in the 1870s, the area became a center of night life. In 1882, electric lights were installed in Madison Square Park; by the early 1890s, Broadway above 23rd Streets to 34th Street was known as the "Great White Way" as the marquees were lit up at night. In 1890, the second Madison Square Garden, at Madison Avenue and 26th Street, was completed. It included a minaret-like tower modeled after Giralda, the bell tower of the Cathedral of Seville. At thirty-two stories, the tower was city's second tallest structure. The Garden was a playground for the upper and middle classes, hosting circuses and animal shows, as well as conventions. A large roof garden restaurant was a popular attraction. As the wealthy dined in the breezy, spring air, it is likely they gave little thought to the teeming masses jam-packed in their tenement houses just a mile to the south.

Soon offices moved in. In 1883, the Astor family moved its real estate headquarters from Prince Street to 21 West 26th Street. In the small red brick Queen Anne-style structure, John Jacob Astor (grandson of the first John Jacob Astor) managed the family's immense real estate holdings throughout Manhattan and the Bronx. Within a decade high-rise offices would emerge, such as the eleven-story 1181 Broadway (1896), at 28th Street, and 13 West 28th Street (1897) at ten stories. By the early twentieth century, wholesalers began moving in, giving the area an industrial vibe, as they followed their clients north, first occupying buildings between 14th and 23rd Streets, and then filling in the area from 23rd to 34th Street.[48]

The Ladies Mile

Along Broadway and west along Fifth and Sixth Avenues from 14th to 23rd Streets, between Union and Madison Squares, was a neighborhood that became known as the Ladies Mile because its department stores and restaurants catered to upper and middle-class women.[49] Before the district formed, high-end retail was located on Broadway, from City Hall Park northward. A. T. Stewart revolutionized the sale of dry goods with his first commercial palace on the southeast corner of Broadway and Chambers Street in 1846. Over the next decade, as rival retailers opened their stories, the shopping district crept northward.

The Ladies Mile began at A. T. Stewart's uptown store at East 9th Street and ended at 23rd Street at the Fifth Avenue Hotel facing Madison Square Park. There were large dry goods stores such as Arnold Constable at East 19th Street and Lord & Taylor at East 20th street. Other establishments specialized in household furnishings, furniture, and imported goods. Its Golden Age began after the city recovered from the panic of 1873. Sixth Avenue also saw a growth in retail after the opening of the Sixth Avenue El in 1878.

As a response to rising land values, the 1870s also saw the rise of the apartment house, known at the time as "French Flats," since they were modeled after the Parisian version. The buildings, as different from the low-income tenements on the Lower East Side, for example, were to house one family in each apartment and contained the amenities of a single dwelling.

They first appeared between Washington and Madison Squares. One of the earliest, for example, was the Stuyvesant Apartments at 142 East 18th Street (at Irving Place). Completed in 1870, it was designed by Richard Morris Hunt and built by Peter Stuyvesant's descendant Rutherford Stuyvesant. The apartment building, as a distinct building type, became the solution to a middle-class housing shortage.[50]

While lower Fifth Avenue had originally been residential, commerce from Broadway eventually spilled over. Shops first took over brownstones, and then office buildings were constructed starting in the 1880s for publishers and architects. In the 1890s, the area continued to transform with construction of large speculatively built stores and lofts, providing space for the increasing number of wholesale firms, which were part of the city's expanding readymade clothing industry.[51]

The Grand Central Depot

November 14, 1832, was a revolutionary day for New York City transportation. It was the first day of operation for the New York and Harlem Railroad, which provided horse-drawn cars on rails embedded in the streets, with the goal of carrying passengers up and down the east side of the island from the city to the village of Harlem. Within two years, the cars operated from Prince Street up to 84th street. A single track ran from Prince Street to Union Place, and a double track ran north from 23rd street. Eventually, the road ran as far south as City Hall. Its proposal to run to Wall Street was rejected.[52]

The company introduced a steam locomotive in June 1834, but, because of an engine explosion, a city ordinance required the use of horse power below 32nd Street and intermittently up to 42nd Street, where it was free to use only steam after that. By October 1837, a combination of horses and steam locomotives was able to deliver passengers from City Hall to the Harlem River at 135th Street. The railroad's presence on the east side was a powerful force for development on that side of the island. [53]

Within a few years, Harlem-bound cars left 23rd Street every 10 minutes, charging a one-way fare of six cents. The railroad built a station and produce depot at Fourth Avenue at 27th Street, at the northeast corner of Madison Square Park.[54]

In the years between 1857 and 1865, Cornelius Vanderbilt acquired control or ownership of the New York Central, the New York and Harlem, and the Hudson River railroads. He assumed the presidency of the Harlem in 1863 and New York Central in 1868. By then, he created plans for formally merging the companies and building a new terminal on 42nd Street and Fourth (Park) Avenue. The New York Central would come to operate roads from New York east to Boston and west to Chicago, Cincinnati, and Saint Louis.

In 1869, the New York State government authorized the construction of a station, and using the acquired-right of eminent domain, Vanderbilt's company purchased all the property in the five-block area extending from 42nd to 47th Street and lying between Fourth and Madison Avenues. Historian Carl Condit writes, "The location of its head house, facing 42nd Street at Fourth Avenue, its magnitude, its civic and monumental importance, as well as the obvious advantages it would confer on the traveling public, urged both state legislators and city councilmen to insist on the highest standards of design and construction."[55]

The terminal was completed in 1871, with a large train yard extending from 42nd Street to 49th Streets. A group of storage tracks turned at right angles from the main tracks between Fourth and Lexington Avenues. The entirety of tracks and buildings encompassed 37.1 acres of Midtown Manhattan. 43rd and 44th Streets were permanently blocked and the streets from 45th to 49th had bridges over the tracks, but only 45th and 48th were built for vehicles and the others were only for pedestrians. Thus, only two out of seven crosstown streets could accommodate vehicles.[56]

When the terminal opened in 1871, the steam from 85 trains per day permeated the neighborhood. However, its size and functionality caused Condit to conclude, "Grand Central was without question the first American terminal fully planned in its functional, aesthetic, and symbolic character for the needs of the rising nineteenth-century metropolis."[57]

The depot operated for about thirty years without major incident until a crash of two trains entering the station occurred in January 1902. This prompted the New York Central to electrify and rebuild the Depot, which would finally be completed in 1913. But this part of the story is left for the next chapter. The key point is that Grand Central Depot essentially created a great-neighborhood-in-waiting. Its structure announced the power of the railroad, but it remained too far north to be a draw for commercial activity, as well its northern blocks were too polluted and constricted to be of any use for high-end businesses.

In summary, the descriptive history of the city strongly suggests that the Midtown first evolved around the area between 14th and 27th Streets, from Union Square to Madison Squares. These parks become attractive to the well-to-do and then for retail and entertainment starting in the 1840s. By the 1880s, offices and warehouses moved into the district as population and commercial activity grew even more. The retail operations moved north to 34th Street, around Herald Square to follow Macy's Department Store, which opened its flagship store there in 1902 and which remains there to this day. Times Square and the Broadway theaters north of 42nd Street would begin to flourish in early twentieth century, after the subway made that region the new center.

But the question remains: What do that statistical data say? Does it support the historical chronicle? Can we pinpoint the moment when Midtown became Midtown? And, can the data decipher among the various theories discussed above, about why a second office center would emerge so close to the first one Downtown?

NEW YORK DIRECTORIES

In order to more fully understand the dynamic patterns of residential and employment locations over the nineteenth century, information about residents was collected from *Trow's New York Directories*.[58] Directories—lists of residents or businesses, and their addresses—were produced annually in the city as early as 1786. While not as systematic as a census, they contain a wealth of information about New Yorkers throughout the nineteenth century, since they tell us what kinds of jobs people had and where they were living and working.

Evidently, each year, Trow's publishing company would canvas the city and obtain from each the head of the household (usually a male, if not, then a widow or working maiden), their home address (which could be any place, not just Manhattan) and the nature of their employment. For many people, the location of the employment was also listed. The Trow's directory was primarily intended as a residential directory; we will also discuss business directories below. Also note that if an entry listed a separate work address it was somewhere in Manhattan or the Bronx, and the home address could be anywhere, though the vast majority was in Manhattan.

To investigate residents location choices, four random samples were created. Sample 1 is from 1861; Sample 2 is from 1879; Sample 3 is from 1892; and Sample 4 is from 1905/6. After each set of names and the addresses were collected, they were then geocoded. That is to say, for each address, the latitude and longitude coordinates were found so their locations could be mapped. Each sample had about 5,000 individuals working in a wide variety of jobs.

All the selected people were assigned to one of fourteen employment categories based on the nature of their work. If the job listed was for a particular good or group of goods (such as linens, furniture, or men's furnishings), the category assigned was "Goods." If a food, beverage, or drug was listed it was assigned to the "Food" category. Work related to communication (e.g., messenger) or transportation (e.g., stables) were assigned to Transportation.

Any job that indicated manual labor (i.e., use of hands), skilled or unskilled, was assigned to manufacturing (e.g., painter or blacksmith). Jobs that provided a service and generally required specialized training were assigned to "Professional Service" (e.g., lawyer, teacher, or architect). Jobs that listed a corporate position (president, vice president, secretary, or treasurer) were assigned to "Corporate Service." Jobs that provided some personal service and did not require specialized training were assigned to "Personal Service," (e.g., laundry, servant, barber, storage). Government positions (e.g., judge, police, or fireman) were assigned to "Government." FIRE jobs were those in Finance, Insurance, and Real Estate. Managerial positions were those that were specifically related to the overseeing of other workers (e.g., superintendent or manager). Finally those professions that were related to the buying and selling of goods were assigned to the "Trade" category (e.g., merchant or agent).

A further category was created that was a subset of the above-mentioned categories, that of "Office Worker." This category consisted of all those in FIRE, Corporate Service, and a set of workers in Professional Service: Accountant, Actuary, Adjuster, Advisory, Advertising, Appraiser, Architect, Auditor, Editor, Journalist, Publisher, Lawyer, and Notary. These are white-collar jobs that presumably need to have separate office spaces to perform their services and are not likely to work in close proximity to physical goods.

For each worker, three important distances were calculated. First was the straight line distance (i.e., as the crow flies) in miles for each person between home and employment location. This is a measure of commuting distance. Given the impossibility of estimating actual commuting times or distances, as the crow flies is the next best thing. Next to be calculated was the straight line distance from each person's home to the southern tip of the island, and finally was the distance of their job location to the southern tip. Since the object of the analysis is to understand the sequence of northward movement of residents and employment, distance to the southern tip for homes and jobs allows us to see how relative locations were changing over the nineteenth century. The southern tip for this analysis is where the Staten Island ferry terminal building is today.

An important note about the data is in order. The people selected were only those who gave both home addresses and work addresses. These people represent a particular subset of the population working in Manhattan (and living anywhere in the region), since presumably those without job address information were those who did not have a fixed employment address or were unemployed.[59] Given that the interest is the locational patterns of office employment associated with the rise of Midtown as a separate business district, the concern is not that the sample represents the entire population of Manhattan, but rather is representative of office workers in particular. The rise of skyscrapers in Midtown was driven primarily by those who had the greatest demand for office space: white-collar businesses. Thus, the interest is in understanding when and why the office worker became an important economic force. To this end, the sample seems to well-represent this particular group of the Manhattan working population.

The samples demonstrate the changing nature of work over the second half of the nineteenth century. The job of merchant begins as the most common in 1861, moves to number five by 1879, and then disappears from the top five after that. From 1879 to 1905/6, lawyer is in the number one position; though liquor sellers give the lawyers a run for their money, so to speak. By 1905/6, the top five jobs in the sample were lawyer, manager, liquor dealers, secretary, and president, respectively.

In regard to the job categories, Food and Goods had the largest percentages, with Manufacture, Professional Service, and Trade being the next categories. But the three categories that show the greatest increases from 1861 to 1905/6 are FIRE, Corporate Service, and Professional Service, which by the turn of the twentieth century constitute 31% of the workers in the sample, having only been 11% in 1861. These results clearly show the "office-ification" of the Manhattan workforce. But the question remains, where were these people living and working?

Analyses of the data show that over the nineteenth century there was a steady northward movement of both residential locations and employment. However, the movement of jobs was small as compared to the movement of residences. In 1861, the average person lived 2.5 miles from the tip, while the average job was only 1.4 miles from the tip. By 1892, the average person worked 2.2 miles from the tip, but lived 4.3 miles from tip. Thus, in the three decades between 1861 and 1892, the center of gravity for jobs moved north 0.8 miles; whereas the residential center of gravity moved 2.1 miles. Similarly, the 1861 distances from home to work averaged 1.3 miles; by 1892 it was 2.5 miles.[60] By 1905/6, commuting distances were 3.4 miles, on average. The residential center of gravity by this time was 5.4 miles from the tip, while the employment center of gravity was 2.4 miles from the tip.

Residential and Employment Patterns

The purpose of this section is to demonstrate where people were living and working throughout the nineteenth century. Once we understand these patterns, it can then suggest which theory best accounts for the rise of Midtown as an office and skyscraper district. Figure 8.4 shows the employment and residential locations of FIRE and Corporate Service workers over the four periods. The maps demonstrate several

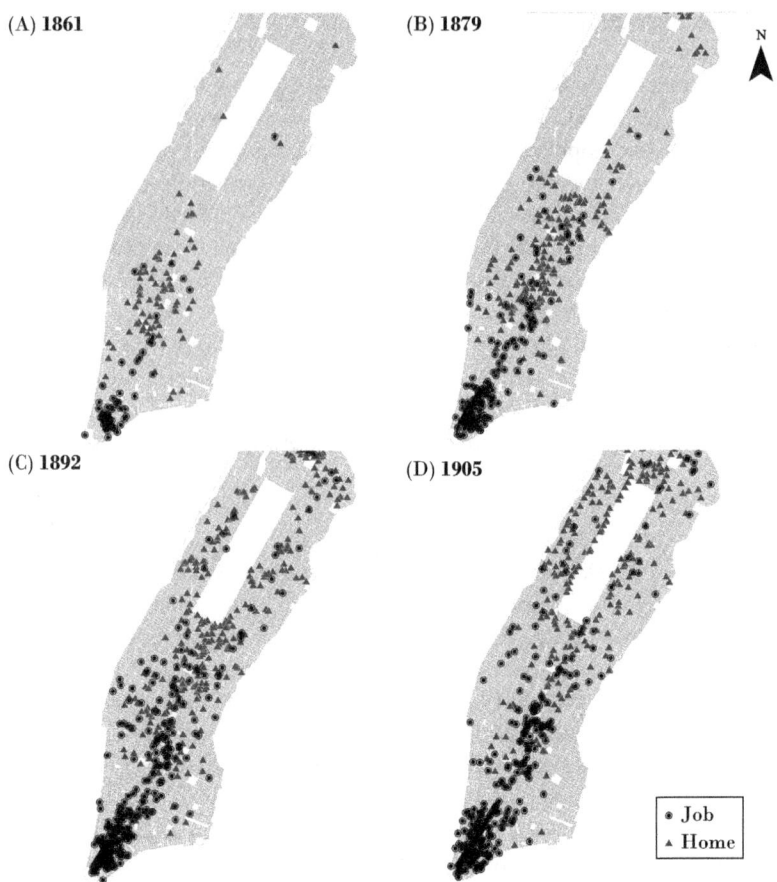

Figure 8.4 Maps of FIRE and corporate service workers from 1861 to 1906. The four maps show the northward residential movement of different samples of workers employed in the finance, insurance, and real estate (FIRE) sector, or who are corporate executives. In all four periods, employment locations remained largely Downtown. However, over the nineteenth century, there was significant northward movement of this population. The map in figure 8.4A shows that 1861 the vast majority were living in the area between Houston and 23rd Streets. The sample for 1879 (figure 8.4B) shows their residences had migrated northward to the area between 14th and 59th Streets. The map in figure 8.4C shows these workers in 1892 living mostly north of 42nd Street. By 1906 (figure 8.4D), the vast majority of these workers were living on the Upper West Side and the Upper East Side, hugging Central and Riverside Parks. *Source:* Maps by Eon Kin. Data from Barr and Tassier (2015).

things. First, the residential locations of these workers were steadily moving northward over the course of the nineteenth century. In 1861 (figure 8.4A), there was a large residential cluster around Washington Square Park. The bulk of the residences were between Washington and Madison Squares. The vast majority of job locations, however, were in Lower Manhattan.

The 1879 map (figure 8.4B) shows a steady northward movement of this population, with the majority now living between 14th Street and Central Park South in the center of the island. The job locations, by and large, remained Downtown. Figures 8.4C and D (1892 and 1905/6) again show a similar story: the FIRE and Corporate Service workers were steadily moving northward. By 1905/6 a large fraction were living on the Upper West Side and the Upper East Side. Employment locations remained concentrated in Lower Manhattan. The fact that FIRE and Corporate Service workers were not moving their offices to Midtown provides evidence against the wage gradient hypothesis, as these are the professions that would likely have the most to gain by reducing their and their employees commuting times.

Figure 8.5 shows the employment and residential densities relative to the southern tip of Manhattan (these include everyone not only Manhattan residences). These graphs are designed to show how the relative concentration of employment and residential locations evolved over the second half of the nineteenth century. Of course, population and employment were growing, but the patterns of where they were developing took on specific forms.

For each graph, the horizontal axis is the distance in miles from the tip (in 0.25 mile intervals), and the vertical axis is the relative frequency of the category. In figure 8.5, graphs A and B show all workers in the sample; graphs C and D show FIRE and Corporate Service workers only; and graphs E and F show Physicians and Dentists. Note that City Hall is about 1 mile from southern tip, Madison Square about 3 miles, and Grand Central is about 4 miles away.

Graphs A, C, and E show the employment densities, while graphs B, D, and F show the residential densities. Graph A shows that there was a general decline in relative employment density in Lower Manhattan from 1861 to 1879, but there was basically no change between 1879 and 1905/6. In other words, the overwhelming majority of employment remained in Lower Manhattan. This figure provides evidence against both the congestion theory and the wage gradient theory. If congestion or high wages were major problems Downtown, we would likely see a wholesale realignment of business from Downtown to Midtown.

Graph B demonstrates that the population continued to move their residences away from Lower Manhattan. In 1861, the modal (most common) residential location was about 1.5 miles north of the lower tip, with the vast majority living between 1.5 (Canal Street) and 3 miles (23rd Street). By 1905/6, there was a great "flattening" and de-concentration of residential location choices, so that the population was more or less evenly distributed throughout the region; distance to the tip was no longer a good predictor of where someone would be living.

Graph C shows that the Downtown concentration of FIRE and Corporate Service workers was much greater than the sample as a whole. In 1861, the modal concentration for the FIRE and Corporate Service workers was about 2.5 times greater than the entire sample. By 1905/6, it remained about 50% higher. The graph shows that throughout the second of half of the nineteenth century, no other region in Manhattan had nearly the same concentration as Lower Manhattan. Graph D shows that in 1861 FIRE and Corporate Service workers' homes were largely concentrated between Washington Square Park and Madison Square Park. By the turn of the twentieth century, they were spread much more even throughout the region.

(A)

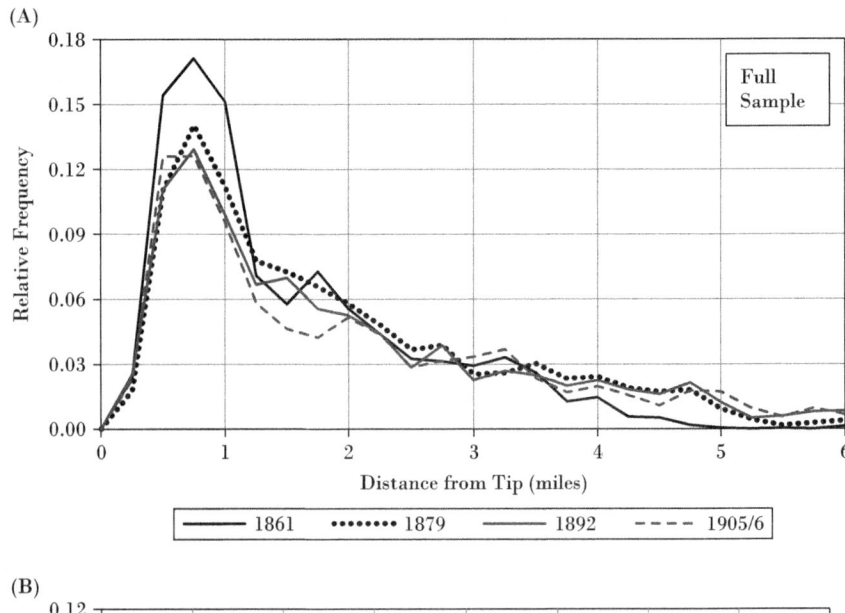

(B)

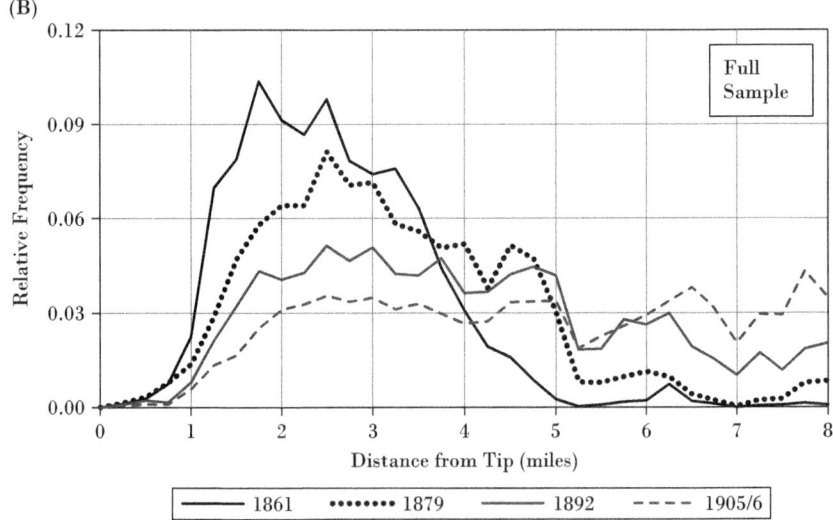

Figure 8.5 Density graphs for employment and residences from 1861 to 1906. These graphs show the employment and residential densities relative to the southern tip of Manhattan from 1861 to 1906 for three different groups. Figures 8.5A and 8.5B show the relative densities over time for employment locations (A) and residential locations (B) across the four periods for all people in the four samples taken from the *Trow's New York Directories*. Graph (A) shows that there was hardly any change in the relative employment density from 1879 to 1905/6. Graph (B) demonstrates the movements of residences over the period. Graph (C) shows that the Downtown concentration of FIRE workers and corporate executives was much greater than the sample as a whole, and remained concentrated throughout the period. Graph (D) shows the dramatic spreading out and suburbanization of these workers. Finally, graph (E) shows that physicians and dentists were already living and working relatively far north of the tip as early as 1861 and both their employment and residences continued to move north throughout the century. Taken together, these graphs provide evidence that Midtown's rise was due to agglomerative forces related to shopping and retail, rather than congestion problems Downtown, or the desire of firms to pay lower wages to their workers.

Source: Barr and Tassier (2015).

(C)

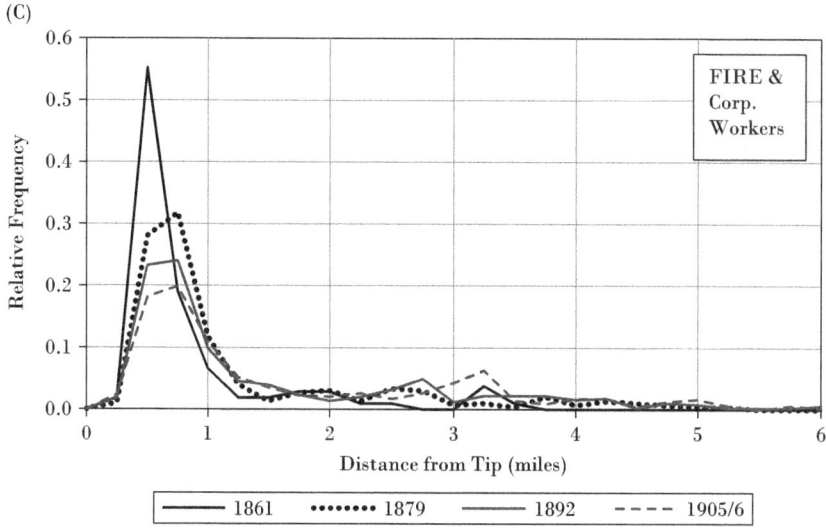

(D)

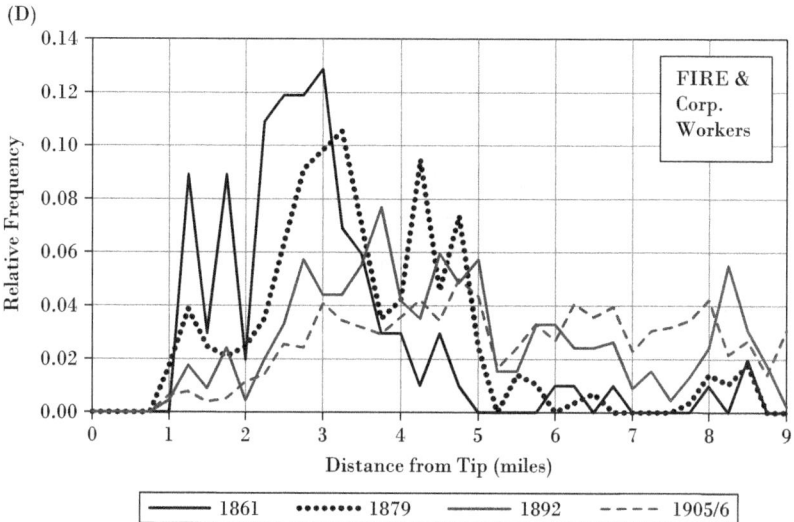

Figure 8.5 Continued

Finally, graph *E* shows the employment density for Physicians and Dentists. The figure shows in 1861 their employment locations were largely concentrated about 2 miles from the tip, which is around Houston Street. By 1879, we see a dramatic rise in their employment density near 35th Street. By the early 1900s, there are relatively few Physicians and Dentists south of 14th Street. Their residential locations (graph *F*) show similar patterns to FIRE and Corporate Service Workers. The movement of the offices of this group provides evidence for the shopping symbiosis theory. Physician and Dentists were likely following their clients, so as to reduce their travel times.

In summary, the density graphs strongly suggest that Midtown in the middle of the nineteenth century was not yet a place with dense office employment. Further, the graphs show little role for Grand Central Depot as a draw for businesses. However, by

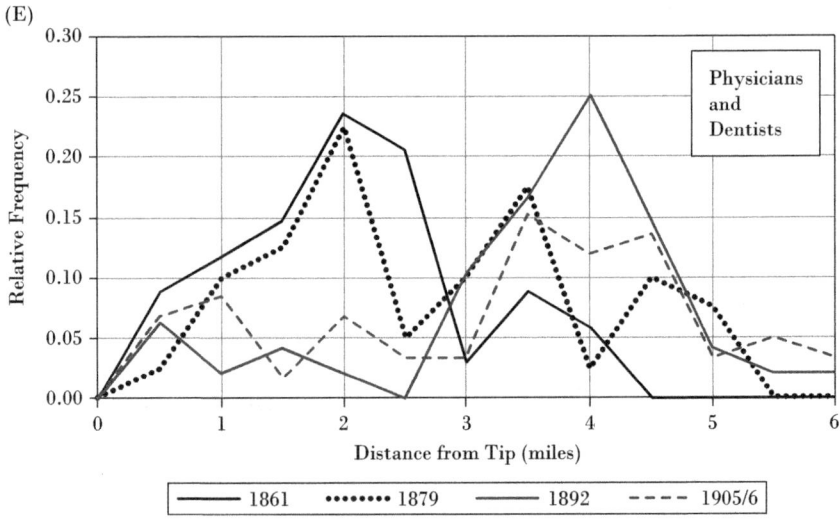

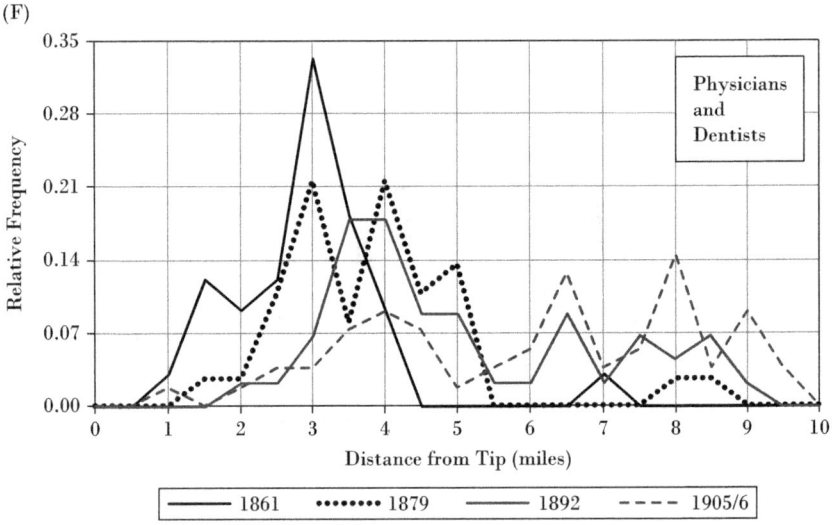

Figure 8.5 Continued

the second half of the nineteenth century, the residential density of Midtown was large. The graphs also show that unlike FIRE workers or the average worker across categories, physicians and dentists were much more likely to be working in Midtown. We do not see evidence of firms being "pushed out" of Downtown; rather Lower Manhattan continued to be a draw for professional, white-collar employment throughout the century.

EVIDENCE FROM BUSINESS DIRECTORIES

To provide further evidence on the formation of Midtown, data was collected from three different business directories: *Wilson's Business Directory* for 1866, *Phillip's Business*

Directory for 1882, and *Trow's (formerly Wilson's) Business Directory* for 1898. These directories list the addresses for either businesses or individuals engaged in certain professions. The following businesses or employment types were selected as they represent a variety of important industries: Hotels, Livery Stables, Newspapers, Lawyers, Bankers, Accountants, Architects, Advertising Agents, Dramatic Agents, and Insurance Agents.

As discussed earlier, when firms in a particular industry decide on a business location they generally have to balance several sets of trade-offs. First, they must consider how their location decisions affect access to clients, inputs, and the movement of outputs. Being close to suppliers, for example, might mean giving up being close to clients. Businesses also have to consider whether there are important agglomeration benefits that accrue when clustering with other firms in a particular neighborhood. These different forces pull firms in different directions, depending on the balance of trade-offs.

The industries chosen for analysis are ones that presumably face different trade-offs in regard to being close to customers, workers, and other firms. In addition, most of these industries are important to Midtown today and are generally office-based industries or occupy skyscrapers (except Livery Stables).

Newspaper publishers present an interesting case study as illustrated by the movements of two of New York's most famous daily newspapers: the *New York Times* and the *New York Herald*. Originally, they both resided in Lower Manhattan at Newspaper Row (see chapter 5). In 1890, the *New York Herald* left Lower Manhattan to move to 34th Street and Sixth Avenue. At the time, the *Real Estate Record and Builders' Guide* wrote, "As regards the gathering of local news we should judge the Herald will have no little advantage over its contemporaries. . . .. The upper part of the city is alive and active till past midnight. . . .. The reporters will be able to undertake more assignments, and those which are given to them can be covered more quickly, and, in case time is pressing, with greater thoroughness."[61]

Similarly, in 1904, the *New York Times* left its headquarters near City Hall to move to 42nd Street and Broadway. Its movement prompted the renaming of that area from Longacre Square to Times Square. In both cases, these newspapers felt that the loss of agglomeration benefits by not being near other publishers and printers would be offset by better access to local news.

Hotels and livery stables are presumed to be customer-close industries, because they provide retail services. Horse liveries were used to transport individuals throughout the city, and being close to their clients would be essential. For the rest of the professions, clients could be individuals or firms. Thus, it is not clear a priori which group would determine the location choices. However, these professions are also likely to benefit from being close to each other, based on the reasons that firms tend to cluster, such as sharing information and inputs, and having better access to skilled workers.[62]

Figure 8.6 shows the positions of four of these industries. The data show that Hotels (figure 8.6A) were significantly decentralized to begin with by 1866, indicating a strong draw to be near residences in Midtown after the Civil War. By 1898, the Madison Square neighborhood had the highest concentration.

Two important industries that made large "leaps" from Downtown to Midtown were newspaper publishers and architects (figures 8.6B and 8.6C, respectively). Both architects and newspaper publishers had a significant presence in Midtown by 1898, as they began transitioning to Midtown after 1882. Dramatic Agents (not shown in the figures), as an industry, emerged sometime after around 1870, and by the end

(A)

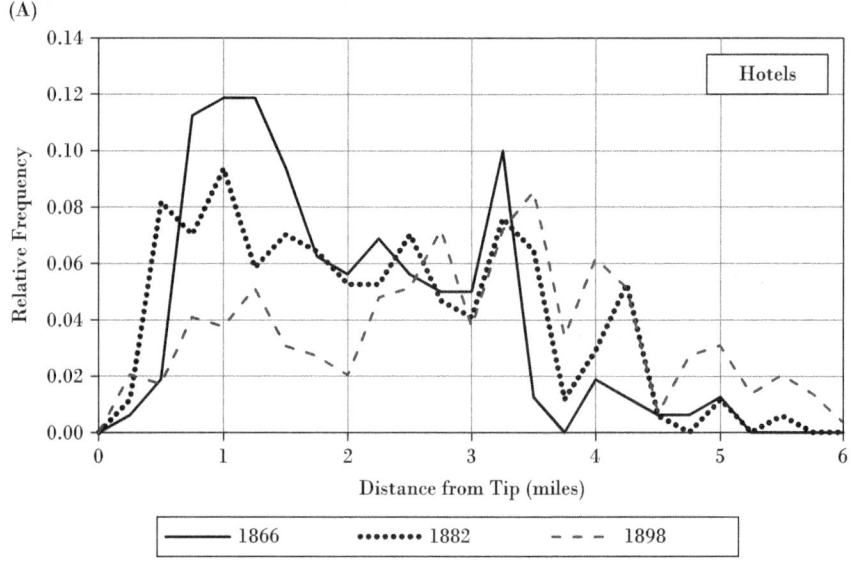

(B)

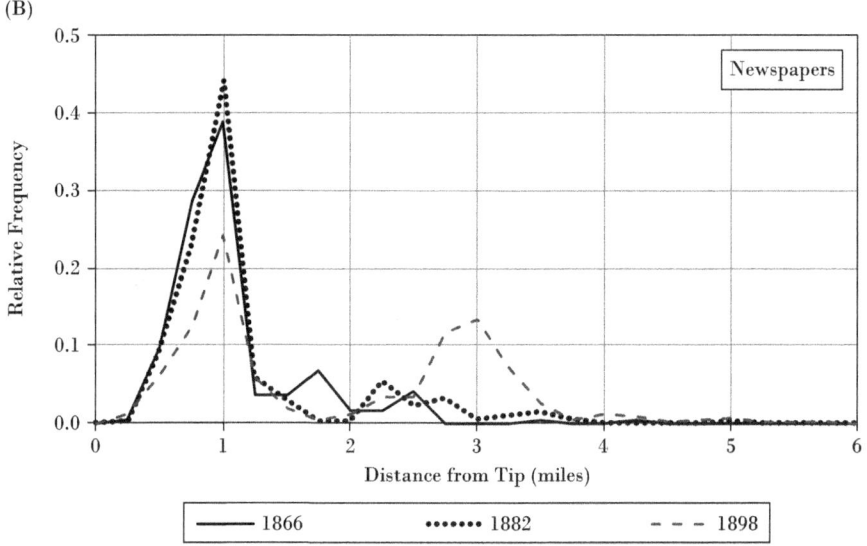

Figure 8.6 Density graphs for businesses. These graphs show the relative densities of four industries. Hotels (A) were significantly decentralized by 1866, indicating a strong draw to be near residences in Midtown after the Civil War. Newspaper publishers (B) and architects (C) made the "leap" to Midtown after 1882. Bankers (D) never left Downtown. These results provide evidence that the rise of Midtown was due to the clustering of businesses tied to local consumers, who found it convenient to shop in Midtown after the Civil War. Midtown's birth, around Madison Square, occurred after 1882, when a critical threshold of office-based firms found it profitable to move there.
Source: Barr and Tassier (2015).

(C)

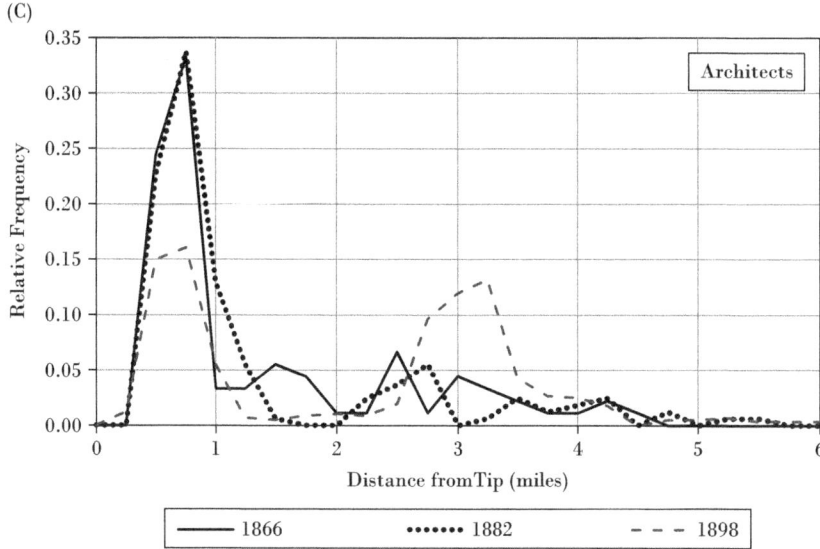

(D)

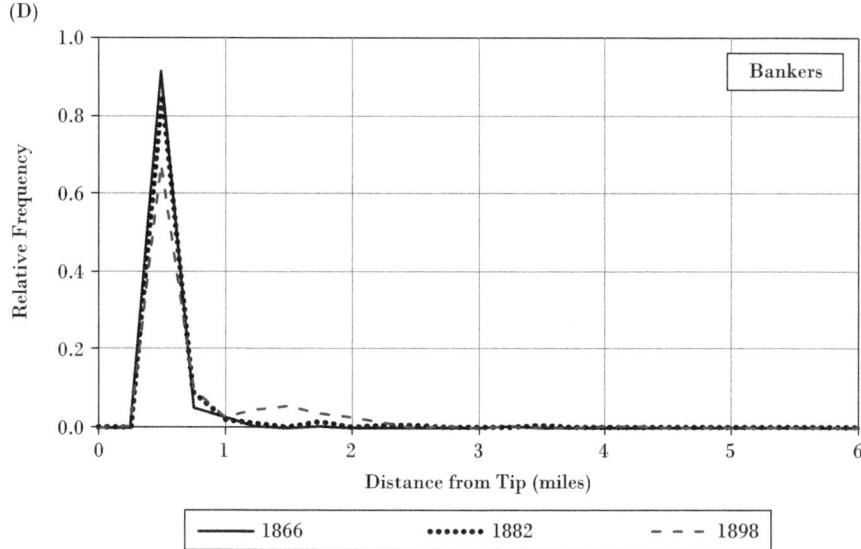

Figure 8.6 Continued

of nineteenth century were well-established in Midtown, along Broadway and 42nd Street. The other industries—Accountants, Advertising Agents, Bankers, Insurance Agents, and Lawyers—all remained clustered Downtown. Figure 8.6D illustrates this with Bankers; there was virtually no movement in their relative concentrations.

That very specific industries moved to Midtown and not others provides strong evidence for the shopping symbiosis theory, and less evidence for the other two. If all firm types were moving, it would suggest that either congestion was a problem in Lower Manhattan or that commuting times were becoming longer to Downtown. But instead

Table 8.1 Location Decisions for Several Industries between 1866 and 1898
This table summarizes the results of tracking the locations of various industries in Manhattan over the second half of the nineteenth century. The results show whether a cluster formed in Midtown or if the industry remained Downtown. As the table shows, the industries that did move tended to be those that relied on local customers for their business, while those that were more national in scope remained tied to Downtown

Industry	Location choice after 1880
Accountants	Remained Downtown
Advertising agents	Remained Downtown
Architects	Moved to Midtown
Bankers	Remained Downtown
Dramatic agents	Only were in Midtown
Hotels	Were in Downtown and Midtown
Insurance agents	Remained Downtown
Lawyers	Remained Downtown
Livery stables	Were Downtown and Midtown
Newspaper publishers	Moved to Midtown

Source: Barr and Tassier (2015).

we see firms that would particularly benefit by being near residents, who concentrating in greater numbers in Midtown and northward. Table 8.1 summarizes the results about which firm types were remaining Downtown and which were moving to Midtown.

Another important finding of this exercise is that in no case were any of these industries concentrated near Grand Central Depot. In other words, there is no evidence that the terminal was an important draw of business before the twentieth century (except perhaps for hotels and livery stables).

COMMUTING PATTERNS AND THE WAGE GRADIENT HYPOTHESIS

But perhaps rather than being close to customers these companies were moving to be close to workers to reduce their overall wage costs? In other words, is the wage gradient theory relevant for the rise of Midtown? As discussed above, this theory posits that firms could realize a savings in their wage expenses, and therefore a rise in profits, if they move closer to their employees living in the suburbs.

Since it is virtually impossible to collect wages or salaries for a large sample of workers living in Manhattan throughout the nineteenth century, it is not possible to directly investigate whether wages were lower for Midtown employees as compared to their Downtown counterparts. However, we can investigate the commuting patterns based on the data set collected from the Trow's *New York Directories*. In particular, we can see if particular professions were experiencing systematic reductions in their commuting distances. That is, we can at least look at the wage gradient theory from the point of view of workers themselves, to see if they were reducing their commuting lengths.

Based on the data on residential movement, we know there was a significant residential suburbanization to northern Manhattan, including FIRE workers and lawyers.

The maps of figure 8.6, for example, show that by 1879, virtually all FIRE workers were living at least 2.5 miles north of the lower tip. By 1892, we see a northward movement around Central Park.

The wage gradient theory would suggest a few facts about the data. First, we would expect a relatively large transition of jobs from Downtown to Midtown, especially for office-based workers, so that firms can capture the considerable savings from being close to their workers. Second, we would expect a wide variety of firms and job types to move to Midtown, since the motivation is based on the reduction of wages, rather than other factors such as agglomeration forces or reducing the search costs related to looking for high-quality workers. Lastly, we should see a wide-scale reduction in commuting distances for those who reside in Midtown or Uptown.

Figure 8.7 shows a (scatter) plot of job locations relative to the southern tip versus residential locations, also relative to the southern tip, for the four sample periods for all workers (1861, 1879, 1892, and 1905/6). The plots aim to show where people were working relative to where they live (only for people who both live and work in Manhattan). Each dot thus tells two bits of information. On the vertical axis, the location of the dot is how far north a person worked; while in the horizontal axis, the dot tells where the person lived.

Both axes start at zero (the southern tip) and go to 10 miles away. The dots in the gray horizontal "belt" are those people who work in Midtown (14th to 59th Street). The dots in gray vertical belt are those people who lived in this region. The dots in the overlapping belts are, therefore, people who both lived and worked in Midtown.

For the analysis, the graphs can be divided into four zones. The dots that run along the 45-degree line are those people who worked very close to their homes—so that the distance from the tip to work roughly equals the distance from the tip to home. In all four years, we see a large fraction of people who do not commute, though over time their fraction of the total sample is declining. Across years, office workers never make up more than 3% of the group of people who live within 0.25 miles of their jobs; office workers are inherently commuters.

The upper left section of all the graphs, above the 45-degree line, shows those who worked north of their residences. These cases are relatively few throughout the nineteenth century, so they will not be discussed further. Next are those people who worked within 2.5 miles of the southern tip; that is, those who worked below 14th Street; the majority of whom worked below Chambers Street. These are the dots below the gray horizontal belt. Generally speaking, we see no pattern between where people lived if they worked Downtown, since the scatter plot of those below the gray horizontal below has zero slope.[63] That is to say, if we were told that someone worked south of 14th Street, we would be unable to guess where they lived in Manhattan; they could live close by or far away, with equal probability.

Looking at the residential patterns for these people shows a steady northward migration, in that the right edge of the dots is moving out. By 1905/6 (graph D), we see a large cluster of workers living between 5 and 8 miles. Recall the transportation developments that were occurring in the nineteenth century. Horse-drawn streetcars were introduced in in the 1830s, and the network continued to expand over the following decades. These lines were likely influential in the northward movement of residences between 1861 (graph A) and 1879 (graph B). Then the elevated railroads were largely completed by 1879, so between 1879 (graph B) and 1892 (graph C) there was likely a reduction in

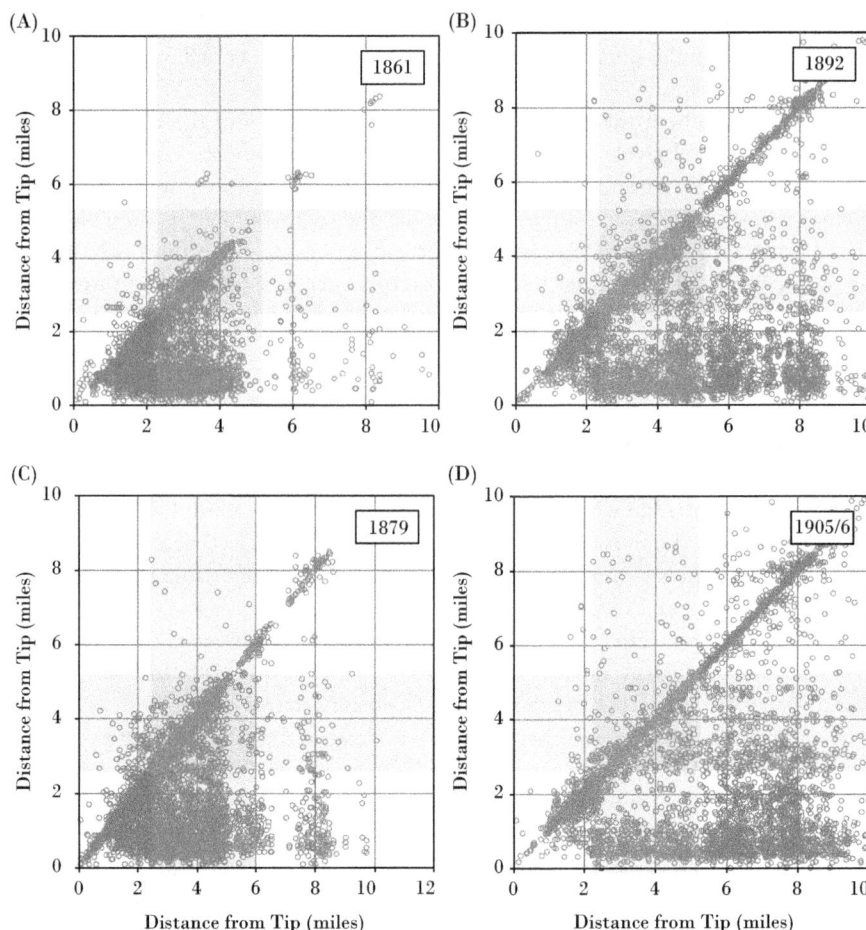

Figure 8.7 Commuting patterns in Manhattan from 1861 to 1906. Each of these figures demonstrates where people were living and working in Manhattan at different times. Each dot tells two bits of information. On the vertical axis, the location of the dot is how far north a person worked relative to the southern tip; while on the horizontal axis, the dot tells where the person lived, also relative to the tip. Both axes start at zero and go to 10 miles away. The dots in the gray horizontal "belt" are those people who work in Midtown (14th to 59th Streets). The dots in gray vertical belt are those people who lived in this region. These graphs demonstrate that employment in Lower Manhattan remained strong throughout the period, while we see a consistent northward movement of residences. In other words, the graphs demonstrate that commuting distances were getting longer for most workers; and this suggests the Els made it easier to commute Downtown. From this, we can conclude that it is not likely Midtown formed because firms were moving to be closer to their workers so that they could pay lower wages or reduce their commute times. *Source:* Barr and Tassier (2015).

commuting times for many people. Further the subway line up Broadway was opened in 1904, so there was also a further reduction in commuting times for people on the Upper West Side.

The combined facts of the increase in commuting distance to Downtown over time (as shown in figure 8.7) and that rapid transit was available after 1879 suggests that commuting times were declining, and thus would not likely spur the introduction of a wage differential on the part of firms. Or, at any rate, not one so great as to cause firms to leave the industrial ecology in which they were so deeply embedded.

Returning to the scatterplots, the fourth category is those people who work in Midtown (or north) which begins roughly 2.5 miles north of the tip. The scatter plots do not show evidence of a mass defection from Downtown. Rather the scatter plots suggest a proportionate rise in the number of people working in Midtown with respect to the number of people living north of 14th Street, which again does not show convincing proof for the wage gradient theory.

Also a review of the data shows that while we see a steady decline in the fraction of workers south of 14th Street, by 1905/6 (graph D), 60% of all jobs in the sample were still there, with only a quarter between 14th and 42nd Street. Again, this suggests that Downtown remained a tremendous draw for workers, and they were not lured to Midtown because of better commutes.[64]

In summary, based on the job and residential locations in the samples, commuting distances were becoming longer for the majority of workers, who were moving northward on the island and yet they continued to work Downtown. This suggests that mass transit developments were not making commuting times much longer, and were, perhaps, shorter. Furthermore, we see a proportionate rise in office jobs in Midtown, which suggests the area north of 14th Street was not being flooded with new workers aiming to lower their commuting times. Rather, the rise of employment in Midtown is consistent with the general rise of business there to cater to the local needs of residents.

While the wage gradient theory cannot directly be rejected, the data does not provide robust support for it as the reason for the rise of Midtown. It is likely a wage gradient theory is more relevant after World War I, when the area north of Grand Central Station took off in earnest and when workers were coming in from Westchester County and southern Connecticut.

The directory data point to one theory as the leading cause for Midtown's birth: the shopping symbiosis theory. That is to say, the data strongly suggest that Midtown did not arise due to Grand Central Depot's location or the due to transportation hubs that drew businesses to Midtown. The data do show that office-based employment largely remained Downtown, while residential locations moved uptown. From the business directories we see that very specific industries jumped to Midtown from Downtown; in particular newspaper and architects showed a sudden and massive movement northward after 1882. In other words, by the decade of the 1880s, a critical threshold had been reached in the neighborhood around Madison Square where particular office-based industries found it profitable to move there to be close to consumers, who had been coming to the neighborhood to do their shopping since after the Civil War. Once those firms moved, it triggered the rise of Midtown as an office-based district. By the turn of the twentieth century, land values had risen high enough so that skyscrapers were then profitable investments. This process unfolded at least two decades before the electrified Grand Central Station was completed in 1913.

WAS CENTRAL PARK A BARRIER TO MIDTOWN 4.0?

Midtown 1.0 was born in the 1880s in the area around Madison Square because of its central location for shopping and entertainment. The skyscrapers constructed during the first generation after 1900 were relatively traditional, with a tripartite style of base, shaft, and capital, and were built before zoning regulations dictated their shape and bulk starting in 1916.

By the beginning of World War I, the corridor from 32nd Street, between Seventh and Park Avenue, up to 42nd Street, from Times Square to Grand Central was well on its way to developing into Midtown 2.0 (see chapter 9). By the second decade of the twentieth century, Grand Central Station and Penn Station were allowing millions of commuters, tourists, and business travelers to enter into the heart of the city. This period was the triumph of Art Deco architecture.

Then after World War II, because of the rapid decentralization of population into the suburban counties, and the need for the city to revitalize its aging office stock, Midtown 3.0 was constructed in the area north of Grand Central Station from Seventh to Third Avenues, from 42nd Street to 59th Street. This period, from 1949 to 1978, witnesses the ascendency of modernism and the ubiquity of the glass box. The next period, the boom years of the 1980s, saw the rise of postmodernist architecture, and the rejection of modernism, which was exemplified by structures designed by architect Philip Johnson. The first is the Sony Tower (formerly the AT&T Building); completed in 1984, it has a top shaped like a piece of Chippendale furniture. The second is the so-called Lipstick Building (1986), which looks like its namesake, and its roundness stands in stark contrast to the myriad of glass boxes nearby.

During each of the three periods of growth (see figure 6.1), Midtown's center of gravity shifted northward. The logic of "creative destruction" has meant that developers have aimed to provide new mini-centers with up-to-date buildings that were close to, yet apart from, the older locations. Figure 8.8 shows these phases, and how the bulk of new construction takes place in a more northerly direction. The maps show the hotspots—the greatest concentration of skyscrapers—in each period, where a skyscraper is a building that is 295 feet or taller. Figure 8.8A shows the first generation of Midtown (1900-1919), where skyscrapers were evenly divided between two areas: Union to Madison Squares and along 42nd Street. Figure 8.8B shows Midtown 2.0, between Penn and Grand Central Stations, and shows a decided northward shift vis-à-vis Midtown 1.0. Figure 8.8C, shows the postwar boom—Midtown 3.0—further northward still, and forming an arc or horseshoe from 42nd Street and Third Avenue up to about 55th Street and Sixth Avenue.

While it is virtually impossible to say what Midtown 4.0—the period from 1979 to 1993—would have otherwise looked like, one cannot but help speculate that the presence of Central Park has been acting as a kind of dam for the northward movement of Midtown. During these years (figure 8.8D), Midtown expanded to the west, and grew via in-fill in the Midtown 3.0 area, with some northward movement. In fact, my statistical analysis shows that the northward movement of Midtown stopped around 1991 and has since "retreated" since then (see appendix V).[65]

In the early 1980s, Mayor Edward Koch, recognizing that office stock needed to expand beyond the Grand Central neighborhood, initiated a set of zoning and tax incentives to promote skyscraper development on the west side of the Midtown. It was feared the east side would become overly congested if the new office towers were built there instead of in another neighborhood. As discussed in chapter 6, these incentives were quite successful, as the 1980s saw the greatest number of skyscrapers constructed in the city's history. The plan caused Midtown

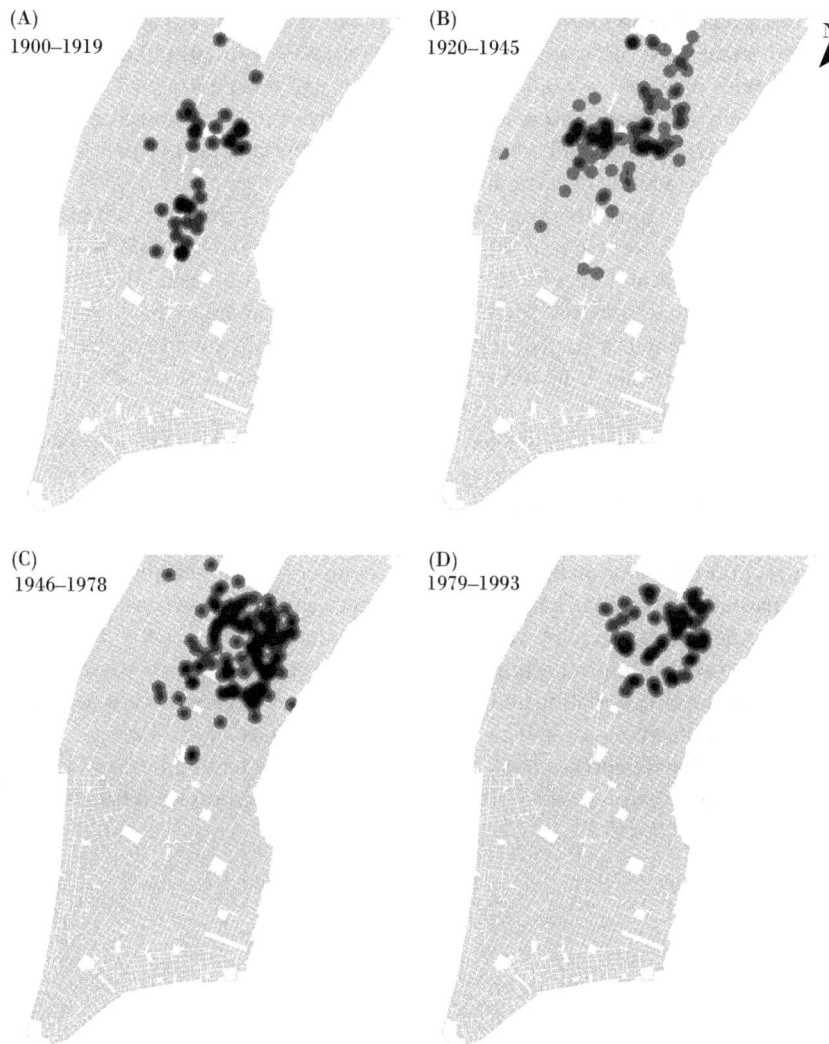

Figure 8.8 Skyscraper hotspots in Midtown from 1900 to 1993. Each map shows the skyscraper hotspots in Midtown—those areas with the densest construction—in each period. During the first generation (A), the period from 1900 to 1919, skyscrapers were mostly built near Madison Square, with a few along 42nd Street. During the second generation (B), skyscrapers were constructed from the corridor from Penn Station to Grand Central Station. Midtown 3.0, after World War II (C), was built north of the second generation, running in an arc from Third Avenue up to West 55th Street. During the period from 1979 to 1993, Midtown 4.0 (D) took a westward turn and did not shift north like the prior iterations of Midtown. It is possible that Central Park has been acting like a dam, blocking its movement up the island.

Source: Maps by Eon Kim. Underlying data collected by Jason M. Barr.

to spread to the west closer to Times Square, creating a government-promoted Midtown 4.0.

Likely, if Central Park was not in the way, Midtown 4.0 would have been in the region north of 59th Street, adjacent to the east side skyscraper district. Part of the reason Koch initiated the buildings incentives was because Times Square in the 1980s was still a seedy neighborhood, with pornographic movie theaters and drug dealers cruising 42nd Street, west of Sixth Avenue. Midtown 4.1 (1994 to 2011) has been quite subdued, with relatively few offices constructed during this period (see chapter 5). Geographically speaking, these buildings have mostly been constructed on the west side, north of 42nd Street; and in this sense, it was not the creation of a new Midtown proper, but rather a filling in of the area.

In 2013, Mayor Bloomberg announced a plan to rezone the area around Grand Central Station to promote new office construction. The reason is that New York's office stock is aging, and large-scale office construction has not taken place since the 1980s. Despite some setbacks, such as the Great Recession and Superstorm Sandy, New York's economy has started to grow again in second decade of the twenty-first century. Land values are high, office rents are up, and businesses are moving to or expanding in the city.

As a result, Bloomberg sought to incentivize the construction of new offices in the Grand Central area in order to generate Midtown 4.2. While his proposal was not passed, Mayor Bill de Blasio has taken up the mantel and, as of December 2014, his plan is working its way through the city's legislative process. Detractors fear the congestion; supporters focus on keeping New York competitive in the global economy.[66]

The reason for rezoning Grand Central is because new office skyscraper construction has no new Midtown to move to. The "ideal" Midtown 5.0 would be adjacent to Midtowns 3.0 and 4.0, given the importance of agglomeration economies, but not too far away from the transportation hubs and the institutions that exist in Midtown today. But because Midtown 5.0 cannot be created, in part because of the park and zoning restrictions north of Grand Central, government policy aims to promote a modernization of Midtown 2.0, which is comprised mostly of buildings completed before World War II.

9

Edifice Complex?
The Cause of the 1920s Building Boom

I have analyzed some of the appraisals that have been printed in advertisements of certain houses who sell bonds to the public . . . and their favorite statement is based on these values: "We are advised by legal counsel that these bonds constitute legal investment for trust funds." Gentlemen, you know perfectly well that many of these statements are not true.

Walter Stabler, Controller of the Metropolitan Life Insurance Company

The Roaring Twenties, a mythic period in our collective consciousness, was the decade when modern America was born. It was a time of great excitement and danger—the age of F. Scott Fitzgerald, Al Capone, Charles Lindbergh, and Babe Ruth.[1] Yet, despite all that has been said about the 1920s, little is known about why so many of the giant skyscrapers were created then. Much has been written about the architectural style of the time and the soaring Art Deco towers. Much ink has been spilt about the dramatic battles for the world's tallest building.[2] Yet, similar to other aspects of New York's history, there are assumptions and beliefs, but little direct evidence or inquiry.

Between 1890 and 1925, the average number of 295-foot or taller buildings completed each year was 1.6, and in no year was there more than seven. Suddenly, their numbers shot up, going from eleven in 1926 and to a peak of thirty-one in 1931. From 1915 to 1925, the average height of these skyscrapers was about 351 feet. In 1926, average height grew to 426 feet, and in 1932, average height peaked at 623 feet (see figure 6.1).

Before the 1920s, the world's tallest building was the Woolworth Building, at fifty-five stories. Completed in 1913, it represented the embodiment of the skyscraper as grand public monument; it held the record for seventeen years. But then at the end of the 1920s, within a span of only one year, New York City would shatter the world height record three times in rapid succession. First was the Bank of Manhattan Trust Building, at 40 Wall Street, completed in April 1930 at 71 stories, next was the Chrysler Building, completed in May 1930 at 77 stories, and finally, the granddaddy of them all, the Empire State Building, completed in April 1931 at 102 stories.[3]

There are two conventional wisdoms about the period which can be summarized as "the exuberance story" and the "financing story." The exuberance story is that the construction boom was a direct result of the headiness of the times; people got carried away because rationality was swept aside by the euphoria of the day. Within this, however, are two sub-versions.

The first is that builders were simply responding to the high land values, and as land becomes more expensive, buildings get taller.[4] But it is nearly tautological to say it was the reason for the boom in the 1920s. What was causing land values to rise? If it was "irrational exuberance" that was driving land values, then we can say that developers were only indirectly being irrational, since they may have been rationally responding to a wider current of irrationality in the land market.[5]

A second version of the exuberance story focuses on the role of the ego. Since the skyscraper can be used to show-off, the developer can create a monument for society to behold. The Woolworth Building of 1913 fits this category; the Chrysler Building does as well. The newly rich titans of industry were flush with cash and eager to engage in a height battle: General Motor's John J. Raskob versus Walter P. Chrysler in a race for the title "Super Automobile Mogul" of the era.

More broadly, there is a perception that during boom periods, height is driven by the ego. That is, profits from the corporate sector, and/or growth in income inequality, drive investments in non-productive uses, such as supertall buildings or lavish mansions (see chapter 6).[6] While it is true that the tallest of the tall were products, to some degree, of non-economic decision-making and height competition, it is misleading to focus on these buildings in order to make generalizations about the age. No doubt times were prosperous, and a speculative fever spread throughout the land in both real estate and stocks, but, as will be shown in this chapter, the Empire State and Chrysler buildings were anomalies.[7]

The construction of these "vanity" projects demonstrates the fact that men with money, power, and business connections were able to muster, in a relatively easy fashion, the resources to build them. They were in the loop about good real estate deals, and they were able to draw on the "skyscraper industrial complex" that was available to them—the stable of brokers, bankers, architects, engineers, lawyers, contractors, and government officials, that made the city so incredibly productive at building skyscrapers.

For the Empire State Building, groundbreaking to opening occurred in twenty months because the Starrett Brothers & Eken were chosen as general contractors. Paul and William Starrett along with Andrew J. Eken had been building skyscrapers in New York and Chicago since virtually day one, and they knew a thing or two about putting these structures up quickly and efficiently. Such logistical sophistication was feasible due to the great number of skyscrapers that had already been completed in the city. The Empire State Building's completion was at the top of a forty-year learning curve; and it immediately followed the construction of the Bank of Manhattan Trust Building, also built by Starrett Brothers & Eken, and finished in record time as well.[8]

The Empire State Building Corporation consisted of an esteemed board of New York financiers and executives. The president was Al Smith, former governor of New York and the 1928 Democratic presidential candidate. The lead developer was John J. Raskob, a former General Motors executive. The vice president of the company was Robert C. Brown, who was also the vice president at Chatham and Phenix National Bank of New York, which took title to the property when its previous purchasers defaulted on their loan payments. The other directors included Pierre S. du Pont (executive at General Motors and E. I. du Pont de Nemours and Company), August Heckscher (mining industrialist and philanthropist), and Louis G. Kaufman (president of Chatham and Phenix).[9]

The skyscraper industrial complex was in place to build structures for the needs of the city's residents. The majority of skyscrapers were neither for corporate headquarters nor "toys" made by newly rich industrialists; rather they were built to house the businesses, travelers, and residents that were living, working, and playing there. Most office buildings provided space to small firms.[10] Many of them had the equivalent of a commercial pied-à-terre because of the vital linkages between the city and the rest of the world. Any company that had aspirations to be a national company had to have an office in Manhattan. Businesses found that having a New York address improved their status. Across the Hudson River, for example, Newark, New Jersey was churning out jewelry, leather goods, and industrial chemicals; yet even as early as the 1870s, a New York Times journalist reported,

> I am inclined to think that there are few people in New-York City who are aware that Newark ranks as the third manufacturing city in the United States. . . . The reason why this fact is so little known is obvious. Nearly all the manufacturers of Newark have branch houses in New-York, where the bulk of their sales are made; and, no matter, whether it be leather or jewelry, trunks or hardware, hats, clothing, or boots and shoes, the manufacture of these goods is thoughtlessly credited to New-York by the wholesale buyers, and, of course, if they think any-thing at all about it, by the consumers.[11]

The titans of industry gravitated to New York because of its central role in the economy—the need to be near finance, transportation, and communication, and the need to be part of the in-crowd. These men knew the important players and they knew the real estate scene. The real story is not that Walter P. Chrysler wanted to build the world's tallest building; it is that Chrysler needed offices in New York City to succeed in business.[12]

Besides the ego story about the Roaring Twenties, however, there is another con-ventional wisdom about the building boom that focuses on the financing for tall build-ings. After World War I, Wall Street started issuing real estate "Gold Bonds" to raise money for construction. They were sold to investors throughout the country at rates of 4% to 7% and in relatively small denominations.[13]

Gold Bonds were popular with those eager to invest in real estate without get-ting directly involved in the construction and development process. At some point, however, as bond sales became increasingly successful, the bond houses were so eager to lend money that they sought out developers to whom they could lend, rather than the other way around. It is believed that with access to so much capital, builders had no choice but to go on a binge, and they put up speculative skyscraper after speculative skyscraper without fear of losing their shirts. Thus, easy money created a moral hazard. By issuing bonds and selling them to widespread, anony-mous investors, the risks of skyscraper speculation were shifted from the develop-ers and Wall Street to the public at large, all the while earning more fees for the bond houses.[14]

Cheap credit may have been an enabler but was it the cause of the great boom? To quote economic historian George Soule, "Money is not always borrowed just because it is available. The borrower must expect that he can make profitable use of money before he will pay the interest on the loan."[15] This applies to the skyscraper boom of the 1920s. As will be discussed below, it was a particularly good time to be in real estate in New York City, not simply because financing was available, but because the money could be put to profitable use.[16]

Note that speculation in skyscrapers is different than speculation in land or stocks. In the case of stocks or land, the speculator does nothing to the product itself. She buys and sells pieces of paper. The value of that paper, for the most part, is determined independently of the actions of the speculator. The land speculator makes minimal changes to the property—he buys it, holds it for a bit, and then flips it to a developer when the time for improvement has come. These suggest a passive relationship with the underlying asset.

Skyscraper speculation, however, is about the most active form of speculation in which one can participate. It requires the mustering of large amounts of land, people, and resources, and it requires the energy to solve big problems as they come up. The project takes several years from start to finish. Skyscraper construction is a very public display, not like the anonymous buying and selling of stocks through one of the many brokers that work Downtown.

Failure to construct and rent a skyscraper represents a very public failure; as such, builders have to be aware of their actions and how it might affect their public personae. Once built, these large buildings cannot simply be flipped to another small investor, quietly waiting to purchase the asset from behind a desk in Boise. Selling a skyscraper requires finding a buyer who can amass millions of dollars and has the credit to obtain a mortgage.

By the 1920s, developers already had a generation of experience building the skyline. Construction was not occurring based on a promise and a dream. The build-it-and-they-will-come vision of skyscrapers had already been realized for several decades, and real estate developers had good reason to build them. This was illustrated in Clark and Kingston's book. They found that the profit-maximizing skyscraper was sixty-three stories in 1929. In hindsight, this was overly optimistic, but the height reflects the balance of income and costs at the time. Land values were so high because the Grand Central District was the new, hot office district in one of the nation's busiest railroad hubs.

The conclusion here is that the building boom of the 1920s was largely a rational response to the economic climate of the day.[17] It was a period of rapid growth and modernization for the American economy, and the nature of work itself was changing; the 1920s saw the demand for office space grow dramatically. Within this national trend was New York's role as the country's economic center. Companies headquartered in New York needed space for their businesses, while other companies throughout the land required branch offices to market their wares and be close to the web of industries that helped to finance, produce, and sell their products.

In the city, the boom was driven in large part by the rise of Midtown Manhattan, or, rather, Midtown 2.0 (see chapter 8). On the east side, the land around the newly electrified Grand Central Station drew class A offices, hotels, and luxury apartment buildings. The west side, near Penn Station, which opened in 1910, saw the rise of the new Garment District, which had relocated en masse from its earlier position south of 14th Street. Connecting these two areas was the city's entertainment hub of Times Square and the retail corridor along Fifth Avenue and Herald Square.

The fact that the developers might have gone overboard, however, is, in part, based on the definition of overbuilding created by the terrible depression that followed. From the perspective of a real estate developer in the late 1920s, there was every reason to expect the new office space to be absorbed in rapid fashion. No rational investor would have ever been able to foresee the Great Depression. Ups and downs were common, but the Great Depression was something utterly new and unpredictable. We cannot hold developers to the standard of 20/20 hindsight based on the events of the

1930s to say that they were acting irrationally. Between January 1920 and November 1927, the decade had already seen three downturns and rebounds, and it was reasonable to expect that any future downturn would be no different than what occurred in the recent past.[18]

My conclusion about the rationality of skyscraper construction is based on several strands of evidence. First, the supply and demand variables discussed in chapter 6 can account for a large fraction of the growth in the 1920s skyline, suggesting an economic reason for its growth. Second, looking in more detail at the income and profits accruing to building owners shows they were rising quite dramatically. Simply put, it was a good time to be a landlord because rents were rising, and they were rising faster than the costs of maintenance. Developers were constructing skyscrapers as a response to these profits, which were driven by the economic demand for office space and apartments. There is also little evidence to suggest that Gold Bonds or easy credit was fueling over-construction. Gold Bonds, rather, were the effects of this construction, not its cause.[19] Third, a review of the developers themselves, and the types of buildings they constructed, indicates that they were reacting not only to the high rental values but also to the needs of an increasingly diverse economy, which required different kinds of spaces for different kinds of consumers. The developers, by and large, were experienced real estate men, who had been working and living in the city for all their adult lives. These men built to hold, and they were interested in creating real estate portfolios for income and funds to build more skyscrapers. They were not the Al Smiths, John Raskobs, or the Walter Chryslers of the skyscraper world. They were often men who came to the United States as immigrants and worked their way up from the tenements to the penthouses. They considered themselves respectable businessmen, who frequently received industry accolades for their entrepreneurial endeavors in the city.[20]

Many of them went into real estate as off-shoots of their work in the garment industry.[21] They rose to be part of New York's elite, and it is not likely they saw much gain by taking bond money and risking it all on pie-in-the-sky-scrapers. Many of them also found themselves, unexpectedly, in liquidation and foreclosure in the mid-1930s. For the all possible moral hazard created by Gold Bonds, many of these developers went down with the economic ship, as it were, and suffered a similar fate to many other overinvested Americans.

Lastly, the Art Deco skyscrapers were part of the second generation of skyscraper construction, and the evidence suggests that the relative costs of constructing them were declining due to technological advances and builders having moved up a steep learning curve. Thus, developers were able to provide these buildings at lower per-floor costs than they had in the past because of the experience in the industry since the 1890s. By the end of the 1920s, there was a substantial reduction in the real costs per square foot (nearly 50%). In other words, while incomes were rising, construction costs were falling, thereby, increasing the profitability of larger buildings.

But if developers were responding to rising rents, why were tenants paying so much to be in New York City? The answer lies in the structure of the economy, as a whole, and the structure of New York's economy, in particular. Business was good; corporate America was profitable. Firms needed to house their head offices in New York and were willing and able to pay for this. The high rent values were driven by the extreme profitability of firms due to productivity improvements and rising consumer demand. The profits came partly at the expense of labor, who did not see their wages rise in proportion to corporations and their owners. Some of the extreme wealth did manifest itself as a demand for excessive height, due to the high income inequality of the period (see chapter 6).

In addition, the stock market bubble spilled over into the real estate sector. Wall Street brokers and banks were generating tremendous revenues due to the rising value of stocks, the frenzied pace of trading, and the returns on call-loans made for speculation. As a result, they needed more space for their larger workforce. The new buildings were a response to the demand for offices and trading desks, and pristine headquarters.

Toward the end of the boom, however, as builders were lulled into a false sense of security about the future health of New York's economy, several projects in Midtown and Downtown were economically too tall due to height competition and an overvaluation of land values given the rampant growth of skyscrapers. Although they were not a systematic part of the market, it is the too-tall buildings that we remember the most.[22]

THE ECONOMIC CONTEXT

The 1920 census revealed that the country had finally transitioned from rural to urban, with more than 50% of the nation living in cities for the first time in its history. Agricultural surplus was so great that half of the population was no longer tied to the land. Those freed from the farm went to work not only in the factories but also the offices of America's cities. The Roaring Twenties was inherently an urban phenomena and the culmination of the Industrial Revolution.

After the end of World War I, the country faced a severe recession that lasted from January 1920 to July 1921. The war and downturn created a building shortage and pent-up demand for new products. Starting in 1922, the economy began to rebound. Profits were on the rise and the times were ripe for businesses to exploit the technological innovations that had been developed in the preceding decades.

As real incomes were growing, there was a greater desire for modern goods and services. The largest demand was for new consumer durables, many of which were purchased using consumer financing, also recently developed. The age brought forth automobiles, radios, refrigerators, and other appliances. Consumption was so great that between 1922 and 1926, the production of all durable goods (including housing and machinery) increased 51%, as compared to non- and semi-durable goods, which increased only 14% in the same period.[23]

During this time, industrial productivity, as measured by output per person employed and output per man-hour, skyrocketed. One of the greatest forces was the increased use of centrally transmitted power. In particular, factories became more dependent on electricity, moving away from steam power generated from on-site boilers. In 1914, only 30% of factories relied on electric power, by 1929, it was 70%. Much of this electricity came from local utilities, which were able to produce it more cheaply thanks to economies of scale.

The internal combustion engine also became widespread, as manufacturers and farmers increased the use of trucks, tractors, and transportation machinery. Between 1919 and 1929, horsepower per worker saw dramatic gains in manufacturing (49.5%), agricultural (62.2%), mining (60.3%), and railroads (72.2%).[24] Another large increase in productivity emerged from the development and implementation of new manufacturing equipment and processes. For example, new glass machines reduced labor time by 97% in the production of electric light bulbs (and the cost of glass to be used in skyscrapers).

The result of these gains throughout the economy was a reduction in the need for labor. Between 1920 and 1929, manufacturers eliminated the labor of 32% of workers needed per unit of output, but were able to reemploy 27% because of the increases in total production, and the growth of the economy as a whole.[25] The productivity enhancements combined with overall rising incomes drove a shift in the nature of work. Manufacturing, mining, agriculture, and transportation all saw drops in employment, while there was simultaneous growth in trade, finance, and the service sector. The economy was shifting away from producing things to performing services, which largely took place in offices.

From 1922 to 1929, real employee compensation rose about 38%, and the total number of workers increased about 23%, so workers saw their average compensation level increase about 15%.[26] The big winners of the decade, however, were the shareholders of corporations, who saw their dividends grow by 100%. This translated into a greater accumulation of wealth for those who owned the corporate sector.[27]

In addition, many larger companies had accumulated so much cash from their productivity gains, that they were able to finance their internal growth from their surpluses, instead of borrowing from banks. As a result, the amount of commercial loans made by banks declined. Corporations were depositing their reserves in bank accounts, which created a pool of surplus funds. Since banks found a low demand for corporate and industrial loans, they turned to lending the money for short-term speculation in stocks and bonds.

Between 1924 and 1927, these loans, with the securities used for collateral, increased 40%.[28] This resulted in the freeing up of money for stock market investments—both on the demand side, as dividend gains could now be used to buy more stocks, and on the supply side, as banks financed the purchasing of shares on margin. Ultimately all of this money pouring into the stock market created a massive speculative bubble, which then led to the Great Crash of October 1929.

The rise of the automobile also fundamentally changed the American economy. In 1921, consumers purchased 1.5 million automobiles; in 1929, they bought nearly 4.8 million. The total number of registered vehicles (cars and trucks) rose to 26.5 million by the end of the decade. The effects of this on industry were tremendous as well. By 1929, the value of cars represented 12.7% of all manufactured goods. The industry employed 7.1% of all manufacturing workers and paid 8.7% of manufacturing wages.[29] The demand for steel, rubber, gasoline, glass, and related products was a boom to these industries as well.

The popularization of the automobile then gave rise to massive infrastructure investments, which further stimulated the economy. Roads and highways needed to be built, and it allowed for the growth of suburban communities surrounding the traditional city centers. The 1920s saw the birth of suburban America and car culture; though suburbia's rapid take-off would not begin until after World War II.

Urban America was both the cause and effect of the rise of modern America. Agricultural workers no longer needed on the farm moved to the cities to work in the factories and the growing service industries. Big cities, such as New York provided the financing, marketing, and transportation to produce and move these goods across the globe. The millions of people living in metropolitan areas provided a huge consumer demand and a ready market for the new goods and services being produced. These consumers were, in turn, driving businesses to innovate and compete for sales.

During the period, New York's population grew from 5.6 million in 1920 to 6.9 million by the end of the decade, an increase of 20%. The eight surrounding counties saw their total population go from 2.5 million to 3.5 million, an increase of over 37%, and many of these residents were pouring into the city each morning via commuter rail or automobiles. In 1920, 1.8 million people were entering into Manhattan each work day. By 1929, that figure rose to 3.0 million.[30] Nearly 78 million passengers came through Grand Central and Penn Stations in 1920, and at the end of the decade that number was about 108 million.[31]

By 1930, the New York City metropolitan region housed a population of more than 10 million people, which constituted 8% of the total US population, and about 16% of its urbanized population. During the 1920s, New York had emerged as the nation's undisputed center of finance, commerce, and culture.

THE REAL ESTATE MARKET IN NEW YORK

Because of World War I, construction across the United States slowed down considerably. In the early 1910s, Manhattan builders requested 800 new building permits per year. During the war, the issuances decreased to below 200. Although permits started to rise after that, it was not until 1921 when the number surpassed that of 1910.[32] In 1919 construction materials prices shot up, due to supply restrictions from the war. The severe housing shortage pushed New York State in 1920 to impose rent controls.[33] After that, from 1920 to 1921, a severe postwar recession further delayed new real estate development.

However, the recession caused construction costs to fall by 41%, while the price level in general only fell by 33%. This created an incentive to build since materials for new buildings were comparatively cheap.[34] At the same time, the housing shortages that resulted from the war and recession meant that rental prices were rising. By the middle of 1922, builders found a near perfect climate for new construction. Money from the real estate bond market also greased the wheels.

Across the country, the construction of single family homes peaked in 1925 and apartment buildings in 1926. In the second half of the decade, many cities would then turn to office construction. Between 1870 and 1920, the population of the United States had doubled; during the same period, office space requirements had risen from about 1 square foot per capita to 5 square feet. The combined forces of increased population and office space needs meant that by 1920 the country needed ten times as much office space as in 1870.[35] A 1931 study by F. P. Burt of the trade magazine *Building and Building Management* calculated that cities with populations of over one million people needed, on average, 5.57 square feet of office space per capita, compared to only 3.67 for cities with 100,000 to 200,000.[36]

Overall, New York's real estate market was robust by the mid-1920s; 1925 was considered a record year for new construction in the city, and 1926 to 1929 showed continued growth. On January 3, 1926, for example, the *New York Times* printed the opinions of sixty-eight real estate professionals about the year to come. Only a handful expressed something less than hearty optimism. The overwhelming consensus was that the real estate market was in excellent shape due to the demand for houses and offices, both within city and suburbs.

A few in the real estate community, however, were concerned that easy credit and excessive optimism was driving overbuilding in the middle of decade. Walter Stabler, Controller of the Metropolitan Life Insurance, while expressing his general optimism about the New York market, was trying to avoid losses similar to what happened after the Panic of 1907. MetLife financed the construction of several loft buildings north of 14th Street in the early part of the twentieth century, but he lamented,

> We loaned a great deal of money there—we loaned it on what we thought were conservative values. At that time the maximum of our loans was not over two-thirds of what we considered the value of the properties. A few years later the garment trades decided to move further north to get closer to the Fifth Avenue retail merchants, and they swarmed out of those buildings as rats from a sinking ship.[37]

He goes on to say, "There is no question that there is an oversupply of the properties that we have under consideration," and he lays blame in part to other lenders who over-appraise the value of the property in order to justify the large loans and bond floats that brought in income to the financiers (see the epigraph above).

But surveys throughout the decade continued to show that new space in New York was being absorbed at a reasonable, if not consistent, pace. In a survey released in April 1927, the American Bond and Mortgage Company concluded that "the saturation point in building construction has not been reached," and "the rental situation in Manhattan appears normal, with the average vacancies in all types of structures about 5 per cent to 10 per cent."[38]

In the summer of 1928, the Forty-Second Street Property Owners and Merchants Association reported that, despite fears of the Grand Central area being overbuilt, it found that "on the contrary, the general feeling seems to be that the tall-building era has just commenced, and that many more skyscrapers will be need to keep pace with the growing demand. . . .. In recent years practically every manufacturing concern in the country that has passed its 'infancy' stage has established a New York connection of some sort."[39]

The Association's survey concluded that the demand for Midtown was coming from three different areas. On one hand,

> much of the space soon to be available has been taken by new industries. Practically every new invention that gets on the market in a large way is produced and distributed by a company that will maintain a New York headquarters. They include manufacturers and distributor of photographic devices, radio manufacturing concerns and corporations dealing in various phases of aviation.

The second type of demand came from growing firms, which needed more space. These firms come to or remain in the city "to keep in touch with the trade and the sources of financing." A third type of tenant moving to Midtown were the financial firms, who felt compelled to open offices closer to these other firms.[40]

In January 1929, William J. Demorest, the vice president of Cushman Wakefield, opined that, though a large amount of office space was about to come on line that year and the next, it was not a problem for the market. He writes:

A number of pessimistic prophets have been predicting during recent months demoralized market for office space in the Grand Central district. . . . A brief consideration of recent history indicates, however, that a panicky attitude toward this situation is decidedly ill-advised. All sorts of dire disaster was predicted by very much the same calamity howlers who are so busy at the present time. . . . What happened? The Graybar Building, the French Building and the Delmonico Building were all in good shape by May 1, 1927; that is, they were sufficiently rented to more than cover their carrying charges, and by May 1, 1928, all but the Salmon Tower were more than 90 per cent rented. . . . Consequently, it is my belief that although we must prepare for some growing pains within the next couple of years the owner in this vicinity will have sufficient good sense not to become panicky, and the normal growth and prosperity of the country will do the rest.[41]

Vacancy from 1925 to 1929 averaged about 5%, though there were some fluctuations from month to month.[42] But it is likely that developers saw a 5% average rate and were more than comfortable with that. At the time, the industry felt that 10% was a reasonable vacancy rate, as it allowed companies in the building the opportunity to add more space if the need arose.

In the summer of 1930, the real estate community was still seeing a hazy picture, with vacancies wildly different across the island. A Building Managers Association of New York study found the financial district's vacancy still quite low at 4.4%, though the Grand Central Station's vacancy was in the could-be-better-but-could-be-worse area of 12.0%. The Plaza District, near Central Park South, on the other hand, was suffering the most at 24.7%. Still throughout the year the sentiment was measured and the community remained hopeful.[43]

Over the next year, things had worsened, but by not so much that by the summer of 1931, the *Wall Street Journal* felt safe in printing the headline, "Office Vacancy Not Abnormal." A survey by the Real Estate Board of New York found average office vacancy across the city at 15.6%. The financial district saw a rise to healthier level of 7.7%; while the Plaza District remained a terrible 29.3%. The Grand Central district maintained an acceptable vacancy of 13.5.0% despite all of the new offices opened between 1929 and 1931.[44] The past decade's growth suggested that while there was some overbuilding, renewed growth would soon see the extra space absorbed.

By end of 1931, however, the real estate community awoke to the fact that the economic climate was truly different. The market was not recovering, citywide vacancy levels began to rise to 16%, then to 17%, and then to 18%, and so on; peaking at 25% in the middle of the 1930s.[45] The American economy was in a tailspin, and real estate construction in New York would remain at a standstill for the next decade and a half.

The completion of the Empire State Building in 1931 did not help matters. It put on the market two million square feet of space at a time when rents were on their way down. Ironically, the building suffered from a location problem. The area around 34th

Street and Fifth Avenue had developed at the turn of the century as a retail district. The growth of the Grand Central area as the center of Midtown in the 1920s made the Empire State Building's location uncompetitive, as it was just too far south to be practical for the industries moving north.

Raskob and Smith thought they could transform the neighborhood, but, the northward real estate tide was against them. The downturn that followed meant that the office market would not be revived for about fifteen years; and at that time few were interested in deviating from the lure of the neighborhood north of 42nd Street. The Empire State Building remains a monument to how hard it is to buck the forces of agglomeration.

VACANCY ACROSS AMERICA

Real estate experts, Earle Shultz and Walter Simmons in their book, *Offices in the Sky*, report the results of a study of office construction across the country. All told, between 1925 and 1931, Manhattan's office space increased by 92%.[46] But it was not the only city to invest so heavily. In the same period, San Diego increased its office space by 96%, Minneapolis by 89%, and Chicago by 74%. By and large, the building boom was trigged by the needs of the cities. Those places that had the greatest shortage of space in 1925 increased their office stock by the greatest amount.[47]

The data from Shultz and Simmons allowed me to perform a regression analysis to investigate how each city fared at the beginning of the Great Depression. The analysis looked at the change in vacancy rates from 1925 to 1931 for twenty cities across the country. The aim was to see which cities suffered the largest increases and what factors were at work. In particular, I looked at how the change in the vacancy rate was affected by the vacancy rate in 1925, the percent increase in the office stock, and the size of the city, as measured by the 1920 population (see results in the appendix W).

The analysis shows that in 1931, vacancy rates across the major cities were determined not only by their 1925 vacancy but also the amount of office stock they subsequently added and the size of the city. The higher the vacancy in 1925, the higher it was in 1931; the more office development over the period, the greater the vacancy in 1931; and most important, I find that the larger the city, the lower the vacancy in 1931; on average, a city with a 1% larger population had its vacancy reduced by 1.4 percentage points.[48]

Because of its sheer size, New York's excess stock was moderate compared to other cities. By the end of 1931, across Manhattan, office vacancy averaged 17%, which ranked 12th out of the twenty-four cities surveyed—exactly in the middle. San Diego was the worst of the group with vacancy at 30.5%. Furthermore, if we look at the predicted vacancy of each of the twenty cities (based on 1925 vacancy, population, and growth rate in office space), we see that New York's vacancy was 2.37% below what would be expected given the economic environment. Detroit's vacancy, on the other hand, was 12% higher than would be predicted, suggesting that the city was excessively optimistic in the 1920s in light of the growth the automobile industry (see appendix W).

Again, it bears repeating that no one saw the Great Depression coming. Many in the real estate community in New York remained sanguine about New York's prospects at late as the middle of 1931. Compared to other cities, New York's construction growth appears rather modest, and again, suggests that the boom was fundamentally a product of a growing city, rather than for some less benign purposes, such as height competition or ego displays.

THE RISE OF MIDTOWN 2.0

One of the key drivers of the skyscraper boom was the rise of modern Midtown. As discussed in chapters 3 and 8, Midtown proper was a product of the demographic movements that were occurring on the island after the rise of mass transit in the 1830s. Midtown's existence and growth predated the opening of Grand Central and Penn Station, but their presence was to create Midtown 2.0.

On the eve of the Civil War the city's northernmost suburbs were around 42nd Street. After the end of fighting, Manhattan would resume its northward movement, and the area between 14th and 23rd Streets would grow as the hub of commercial life for residents and visitors alike. The Rialto—the neighborhood along Broadway and Sixth Avenue, Union to Madison Square—emerged as New York's the main theater district (see chapter 8). The city's red-light district, the Tenderloin, filled in the streets from 23rd to 42nd Streets, west of the city's respectable shopping areas.

But the continued northward movement of the population and the increasing corporate nature of Madison Square pushed retail and entertainment up the island. Thus, 34th Street became the city's new shopping center, especially after Macy's moved to Herald Square in 1902. Broadway theaters crossed the 42nd Street threshold around the same time. Newspaper publishers came to the region to be close the action. The *New York Herald* arrived in Herald Square relatively early in 1890, in order better report on local nightlife and entertainment. In 1904, the New York Times Company completed its new headquarters on a lot at the intersection of Broadway and 42nd Street.[49]

The building's location was chosen not only because the triangular lot guaranteed light for newspaper editing but also because of the subway running underneath the building. The trains would stop there, and the papers would be hauled on board and distributed throughout the city. The newspaper lobbied the city to change the name of the area from Longacre Square to Times Square and initiated the ritual of dropping the ball each New Year's Eve. The *Times's* arrival was simultaneous with the northward movement of theater district, which crossed 42nd Street after the turn of the century.[50]

At the same time, the city's two major railroads both decided to modernize and construct spectacular terminals. The New York Central in 1902 began the process of tearing down its old station and creating its masterpiece, Grand Central Terminal, on 42nd Street and Park Avenue. Concurrently, the Pennsylvania Railroad (PRR) decided that it was time its roads entered the city. In 1902, the PRR began to build tunnels under the Hudson River, while simultaneously digging tunnels under the East River to connect the Long Island Railroad with Manhattan. It chose the blocks between Seventh and Eighth Avenues and 31st and 33rd as the location for its grand new facility.

After World War I, both railroads would see a dramatic rise in commuter traffic, as the metropolitan region became increasingly suburbanized. The two stations also attracted real estate development; they would both contribute to the northward movement of Midtown, though this trajectory was likely to occur regardless, simply because of the momentum of the city's economy and population growth.

The original Grand Central Depot was opened at 42nd Street and Park Avenue in 1871 (see chapter 8). By the end of the nineteenth century, the New York Central began to consider a new, modern terminal, along with the electrification of their trains. After thirty years of operation, the original station was too small and outdated to accommodate the passenger traffic. The tunnels and neighborhood were polluted from years of steam and smoke bellowing from the trains.[51]

A terrible collision forced the company's hand, when in the morning of January 8, 1902, a train rear-ended another one inside the Park Avenue tunnel at 56th Street.[52] As a result, the State Board of Railroad Commissioners in February ordered the company to end the use of steam locomotives near the terminal. The city granted the company the right of eminent domain to expand its operations.

The station, designed by Reed and Stem and Warren and Wetmore, is one of great architectural wonders of the world; and it was wisely planned to accommodate both local and intercity travelers on different levels. The company also created a planned "Terminal City" of new high-rise buildings to surround the station (see figure 9.1).[53] Some 2 miles of streets were to become available to the public by burying the tracks underground.

Perhaps most important was the opening of Park Avenue from 45th to 57th Streets. The 140-foot-wide avenue was now a blank slate for developers, particularly for office towers, hotels, and upscale apartment buildings. The railroad company invested heavily in providing the infrastructure necessary for this development, by creating a substructure of steel and masonry piers, rising from the bedrock, in order to support the new buildings over the tracks.[54]

10781-40   THE NEW GRAND CENTRAL RAILWAY STATION, NEW YORK.

Figure 9.1 Grand Central Station and Terminal City. As part of the new Grand Central Station (1913), the New York Central Railroad created a planned Terminal City over the covered tracks. The company would sell the air rights to developers who would build offices, hotels, and apartment buildings. The Terminal City drew Midtown northward during the 1920s.
Source: Collection of Jason M. Barr.

To fund its Terminal City, the company would sell the air rights over the tracks. The idea was to create a neighborhood that contained a "general harmony of architecture."[55] The Grand Central Terminal officially opened on midnight of February 2, 1913, with the expectation that 24 million passengers were to pass through the station that year.[56]

Several projects were constructed simultaneously with the depot. For example, the high-end Biltmore Hotel, at East 43rd Street and Vanderbilt Avenue, was completed at the same time as the station. Its opening caused the *New York Times* to observe,

> This notion of a hotel built in connection with a terminal provides endless diversion for the idle fancy. It has already been pointed out that when the Biltmore is a thing accomplished, your business-man from Chicago will be able to come to New York, stop here over night, attend to his business down in Wall Street, and return to State Street and Michigan Avenue without once having come out into the open.[57]

By the late 1920s, the area north of the station was cemented as an upscale neighborhood of offices, hotels, and residences. The Waldorf Astoria Hotel, for example, was completed in 1931 on one of the railroad's lots—the whole block from 49th Street to 50th Street between Park Avenue and Lexington Avenue. The Waldorf Astoria Hotel left its old site at 34th Street and Fifth Avenue, paving the way for the Empire State Building to rise in its place.

Penn Station and the Garment District

Because of Manhattan's insular nature, it created particular problems for the railroads. North-south traffic had a much easier time entering the island because the Harlem River was narrower and could be bridged at a much lower cost. Lines arriving from New Jersey, Pennsylvania, and points west and south would terminate at the New Jersey side of the Hudson River. Passengers were then ferried into Manhattan.

By the turn of the twentieth century, PRR was the primary railroad for the western and southern traffic into and out of New York City. Under the leadership of Alexander J. Cassatt, the PRR's president from 1899 to 1906, the company determined that it would find a way to directly enter Manhattan. After toying with the idea of building a mile-long bridge across the Hudson River, the company finally decided to pursue the construction of tunnels. The PRR also formally took over control of the Long Island Railroad in May 1901.[58] Like the New York Central, trains entering the station would run on electrified lines.

The PRR now had to choose a location for its station. An early proposal had the station on the east side of Fourth Avenue, near 34th Street, but the grades to safely deliver trains there would have been too steep. In the end, the company decided that the best location would be west of Seventh Avenue, in the heart of the city's red-light district, also known as the Tenderloin, just a few blocks west of the city's retail and entertainment neighborhood. After some heated negotiations, the city government passed the railroad's franchise right at the end of 1902.[59]

The PRR was the largest railroad in the nation and decided it was going to build the largest station in the largest city in the nation; the company spared no expense. It

Figure 9.2 Penn Station. In 1910, the Pennsylvania Railroad (PRR) completed its terminal on Seventh Avenue and 32nd Street. Unlike the New York Central, the PRR was not interested in engaging in real estate development. The hanging laundry in the right front shows how the surrounding neighborhood was a dense tenement area and was less amendable to upscale development as compared to the area around Grand Central Station. The terminal's effect on Manhattan, however, was equally as important, as it drew the garment industry. As railroad travel declined after World War II, the terminal became an aging giant and was demolished in 1963. The current Madison Square Garden was built over the tracks. *Source:* Collection of Jason M. Barr.

chose the architecture firm McKim, Mead and White, who, under the leadership of Charles Follen McKim, designed a Beaux Arts masterpiece (figure 9.2). Like Grand Central Station, it too represented one of the greatest architectural and engineering achievements in the country's history. Covering two entire city blocks, the terminal was designed to move a quarter of a million people per day into and out of the city. The exterior was of pink granite and surrounded by Doric columns. The main waiting room was similar in size to the nave of St. Peter's cathedral and was modeled after the Roman baths of Caracalla. To the block to the west, the PRR sold the air rights to the US Postal Service, which constructed its giant post office.[60]

After World War II, as railroad traffic declined, the station fell into decay; it morphed into an aging, unprofitable giant. In one of the greatest acts of "urbanicide," the terminal was demolished in 1963 and replaced with a skyscraper and Madison Square Garden. Its loss prompted the rise of the preservation movement in New York.

Unlike the New York Central, which buried its tracks, the PRR's roads and yards remained exposed. The PRR decided against covering the tracks, feeling it was not in its economic interests, as it would not generate the income to cover its costs. The station was simply too far west to be an economic center of gravity like its east side competitor.

The PRR was also reluctant to promote real estate investment on Seventh Avenue. This neighborhood was already built up, and the prospect of creating the type of redevelopment seen on the east side was daunting. The PRR, for example, failed in its attempts to lure Gimbels Department Store to an adjacent block. In the end, the best the PRR could muster was money to finance the construction of the Hotel Pennsylvania (1919) on Seventh Avenue across the street from the terminal.[61] For these reasons, Penn Station did not have the same effect on the surrounding neighborhood as did Grand Central Station. It would not develop into a district for class A office space or luxury apartments.

For a century, the blocks directly west of Penn Station remained open track yards. But in perhaps one of the city's greatest examples of history repeating itself, today a new Terminal City rises to the west of Penn Station. The Hudson Yards Project, a planned city within city, will be built on platforms constructed over the tracks. The city rezoned the Hudson Yards neighborhood to allow for large-scale commercial and residential development. The area now has the capacity for about 26 million square feet of office space. Consider that a large office building today will have one or 1.25 million square feet of rentable space. The plan also calls for the creation of Hudson Boulevard, the west side's answer to Park Avenue.

At the same time, two important transportation projects are in the works. The first is the extension of the #7 train west across 42nd Street and then south along Eleventh Avenue. The old James A. Farley post office behind Penn Station is likely to be converted to Moynihan Station, a new home for Amtrak and New Jersey Transit. Part of the financing will come from the sale of air rights over the station.

After the opening of the original terminal in 1910, the neighborhood did see a tremendous amount of real estate construction, as it became the largest garment district in the country. Manufacturers first moved to between 23rd and 32nd Street after World War I; and in the 1920s, they moved north once again, perfectly situated between Penn Station and the shopping mecca along Fifth Avenue and Broadway (see figure 9.3). The ladies garment manufacturers needed to have ready access to buyers and retailers to make sure they were providing the most fashionable products. By 1922, nearly three-quarters of all ladies garments were manufactured in New York City.[62]

Builder A. E. Lefcourt is an example of the type of builder who developed the neighborhood. He constructed the twenty-five-story Lefcourt-State building in 1927 on the northwest corner of Broadway and 37th Street. All of the renters, but one, were manufacturers of women's and girl's dresses. The *New York Times* claimed it was "the largest number of dress concerns that have ever been assembled under one roof since the exodus of the apparel trades from the east to the west side of the city. The only coat manufacturing concern in the building is Louis Cohen, who has taken the entire second floor of the building."[63] Even as late at 1931, the dress trade buildings were easily rented. The thirty-six-story structure at 1400 Broadway, completed in that year, on the northeast corner of Broadway and 38th Street was 90% rented upon opening. It too was claimed to be "the world's largest dress trade building."[64]

The garment district was a product of those who had come up from the immigrant classes. To quote architectural historian, Carol Willis:

Figure 9.3 Jump of ladies garment manufacturers. The figure shows the location of ladies garment manufacturers in 1900 and 1922. The industry grew from Canal Street to 14th Street along Broadway and employed the newly arrived immigrants living in the Lower East Side. In the 1920s, the garment manufacturers moved their cluster northward. Here they could be perfectly situated between Penn Station and the city's shopping hub near around Herald Square and Fifth Avenue.

Source: Committee on the Regional Plan of New York and Its Environs (1931).

Most of the high-rises were erected and owned by immigrant entrepreneurs who had begun their climb from clothing manufacturers, to builders, to real estate moguls. Some made and lost fortunes as boom turned to bust in the Depression, and their names—Lefcourt, Adler, Bricken, among others—have faded. A handful of little-known architects, all Jewish, like their clients, were responsible for nearly a hundred buildings within the district.[65]

One of the beliefs about the boom was that it was caused by a flood of money due to the creation of "Gold Bonds" for real estate construction. The appetite for these invest-ments, combined with the often-unscrupulous dealings of the bond houses gave rise to a building craze, or so the story goes.

The American real estate bond market developed in the early 1900s and started to take off after World War I. During the war, the federal government promoted sales of its Liberty Bonds, and the public became accustomed to investing their savings in this way. Advertising campaigns stressed that it was every American's patriotic duty to invest in the war effort.[66] The interest payments were redeemable in gold, which acted as a hedge against inflation.

After the war, the market for real estate bonds was promoted by bond houses such as S. W. Straus & Company, Greenbaum Sons Investment Company, and American Bond & Mortgage Company. These companies were "one-stop shopping" for the bonds, as originators, underwriters, and distributers. Originating was the process of seeking out a developer or real estate corporation that would use the money for a large construction project; it could be initiated by either the bond house or the borrower. Part of the role of the bond house was to perform due diligence regarding a venture's feasibility. But during the 1920s, bond houses were accused of trolling the real estate community looking for developers on whom they could foist a development using financing from the bonds.[67] During the Depression, bond houses were widely accused of fraudulent advertising and many of the bonds were worthless because the buildings themselves were in default.[68]

Underwriting is the process where the bond house, for a fee, guarantees to pur-chase all or some percentage of the bonds, if not sold out by the public. This shifts the risk of issuing the security away from the borrower to the financier and drives the bond house to find buyers. Lastly, bond houses would actively sell, market, and ser-vice the bonds to the public and thus acted as distributors.[69] Each of these actions generated fees.

Detailed research by the economists William N. Goetzmann and Frank Newman into 125 bond prospectuses across the country demonstrates their nature.[70] On aver-age, they were issued in denominations of $1,000 to $5,000, but several had denomi-nations as low as $100. Interest rates were generally between 4% and 7%. The bulk of the bonds were paid in gold coin. The terms of the bonds varied widely from two to forty-seven years. Many were self-liquidating; and nearly all bonds were redeemable (callable) at any time with little or no penalty by the issuer.

Concern about fraud in the bond market prompted the National Association of Real Estate Boards to create, at its 1927 annual meeting, a platform of principles. It urged that (1) speculative risks should not be assumed by bondholders; (2) money held for construction should not be used for other purposes; (3) loans made for projects be conservative and safe; (4) advertisements be truthful; (5) the title "First Mortgage Real Estate Bonds" should only be used for the first lien on both land and buildings, and leasehold bonds should be so designated; (6) mortgage houses should accept full responsibility for appraisals they use as a base for their issues; (7) the loan should be used to offset depreciation and obsolescence, and should be liquidated in an orderly manner; (8) appraisals should be conservative.[71]

But to what extent was cheap and easy credit responsible for the building boom in New York City? Between 1919 and 1928, real estate bond issues across the country went from $239.3 million in 1919 to $683.7 million in 1928, at their peak, though the years 1929 through 1931 saw a great diminution in their use.[72] Buildings in New York absorbed 46.7% of all issues; with Chicago using 25.9% and Detroit in a distance third with 6.9%.

In their research article Goetzmann and Newman conclude that:

> More buildings taller than 70 meters were constructed in New York between 1922 and 1931 than in any other ten-year period before or since... These 235 tall buildings represented more than an architectural movement; they were largely the manifestation of a widespread financial phenomena.[73]

But is this true? Perhaps, rather than being a cause, the Gold Bonds were the effect of the growth in real estate. Bond issuances might simply reflect the fact that the returns to real estate construction were high, and Gold Bonds were a convenient way to meet the demand for capital. While there is a strong correlation between Gold Bond issuances and construction patterns, causality still needs to be determined. To what extent did the Gold Bond create buildings in New York that would otherwise not have been built or would have been built at a much smaller scale?

Other evidence suggests that New York's boom was built for other reasons beyond cheap and easy credit. Even Goetzmann and Newman concede that the motivation to build was based on the profits to construction, and rising rents, through the 1920s. The authors investigate the riskiness of these bonds by comparing the Gold Bond rates to the risk-free Treasury bond rates (the spread) in 1926. A larger difference suggests that investors perceived a greater risk to owning the Gold Bonds. They find that issues for New York projects consistently had a lower spread, indicating that investors saw New York as less risky vis-à-vis other cities, such as Chicago. They also found that two bond houses in particular, S. W. Straus, and American Bond and Mortgage, who operated out of New York, had lower spreads; this meant the market perceived these houses as issuing more solid offerings.

While New York garnered almost 47% of the funds, it was not the most overbuilt city. Detroit, which attracted only 6% of the funds, was the most overbuilt city by the end of the decade. Figure 9.4 shows that there was no relationship between how much a city garnered relative to its population size and the degree to which it overbuilt or not, as based on its 1931 vacancy rate.[74] The figure shows vacancy rates in 1931 versus the dollar amount issued per million people in seven cities. If there is any relationship at all, on average, it is negative—that is, more bond issuances, on average, meant less vacancy in 1931.

Among the group, Philadelphia had the lowest amount of bond issues relative to its size and yet its vacancy rate in 1931 was 25%. Detroit had a medium amount of bond issues, yet its vacancy was close to 30%. New York and Chicago received the highest bond issues relative to their populations, yet their vacancy was not as high. San Francisco had the lowest vacancy of the group, and yet it had the third highest bond issue amount per capita. Albeit the sample size is small, it suggests that money was going to the cities with the highest need, rather than the bond issues being "pushed" on cities.[75]

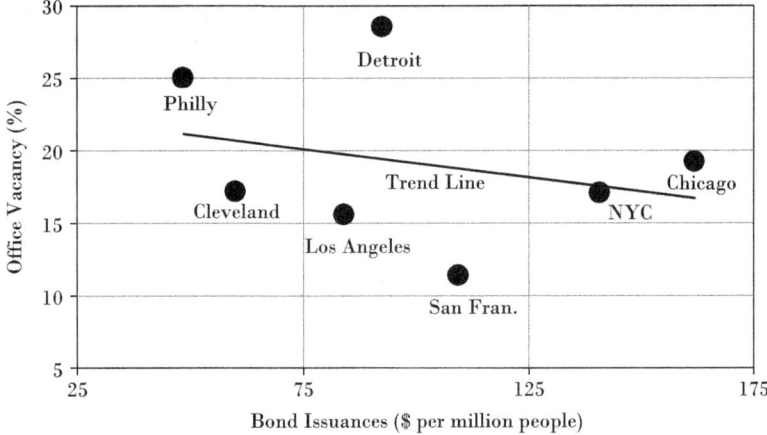

Figure 9.4 Per capita gold bonds issuances versus overbuilding. This graph shows the relationship between the amount of real estate gold bonds issued per capita (dollar value divided per million people) across seven cities and its office vacancy rate in 1931. The graph shows a negative relationship, suggesting that those cities that issued the most gold bonds per capita had lower vacancy rates at the onset of the Great Depression. These results indicate that Gold Bonds issuances, rather than being a cause of overbuilding, were an effect of rapid urban growth.

Source: Gold Bond data from Goetzmann and Newman (2010). Vacancy data from Shultz and Simmons (1959).

While Gold Bonds may have had a marginal effect on the real estate market for skyscrapers in Manhattan, their widespread use throughout the country suggests that they had larger influences in other parts of the United States. It seems that Manhattan was not, in fact, built based on a financial phenomenon.

WHO BUILT THE SKYLINE?

In order to draw some conclusions about what happened during the boom, I collected a data set on a specific group of buildings: all skyscrapers that were 328 feet (100 meters) or taller and were completed between 1928 and 1931 in Manhattan. These were the peak years, and by getting more information on who built them, where they were built, and who the tenants were, it can help shed light on what was happening at the time. All told, seventy-two supertalls were built in this period.

An analysis of their heights reveals that the majority (55%) were thirty-five floors or less. Further, the extreme buildings that were more than fifty stories were only 10% of all skyscrapers completed during this period. Even during the 1930–31 periods, most of the buildings were less than thirty-five stories; the Empire State and Chrysler Buildings were not the norm.

For each of the buildings, I also obtained information on the lead developer, and placed them into four different categories based on their backgrounds: Corporation, Real Estate Professional, Businessman, and Hotelier. The Corporation category refers to those buildings that were constructed for and by a major corporation to house its headquarters (and other businesses). The Real Estate Professional was a seasoned developer who had a record of constructing tall buildings in the city. The Businessmen did not have much experience in the New York real estate market, but rather were using their money, and business and entrepreneurial experience toward the task creating a skyscraper. Finally, the Hoteliers were those developers with experience running or building hotels or restaurants and were extending their experience to skyscraper development.[76]

Of seventy-two structures, sixty-three were offices or hotels; seven were residential apartment buildings; one was the Riverside Church in Morningside Heights, and the last was built by the Downtown Athletic Club. Table 9.1 shows that about 21% were built as corporate headquarters; 64% were built by real estate professionals for office or apartment space; 8% were built by the businessmen; finally about 4% were built by the hoteliers. The table strongly suggests that the ego theory is not a central cause for the boom, since the businessmen, like Raskob and Chrysler, were only responsible for a small fraction of these buildings.

Nearly half were built as part of the rise of Midtown 2.0. The greatest number—twenty-two (31%)—were built near Grand Central Station; while twelve structures (17%) were built in the Garment District near Penn Station. The financial district made up 18% of these supertalls. The rest were spread throughout the island, but were generally south of Central Park (see appendix X).

A review of the twelve corporations that built skyscrapers to house their headquarters shows that seven were banks and were mostly located on or near Wall Street; one was in insurance; two were in media; and two were in utilities (see appendix X). Again the list suggests these headquarters were built because business was good, and were constructed in part because of the success of Wall Street in the late 1920s. All of these companies were long established in New York City.

Table 9.1 Types of Developers during the Roaring Twenties
This table shows the types of developers that constructed the seventy-two skyscrapers built from 1928 to 1931 that were 328 feet or taller. The vast majority of them were constructed by professional developers, who generally built for the many businesses that called New York home. They were often first- or second-generation immigrants, who had grown up in the city. The next largest group was corporations, who constructed skyscrapers to house their headquarters. The businessmen were those who succeeded in some other business before investing in real estate in New York. The Hoteliers were those in the restaurant or hotel business before going into real estate. The fact that less than 10% of these builders were in the Businessmen category suggests that the "ego builders" such as Walter Chrysler were only a small fraction of those who constructed the skyline in the 1920s

Developer Type	Number built	%
Real estate professional	46	63.9
Corporation	15	20.8
Businessman	6	8.3
Hotelier	3	4.2
Other	2	2.8
Total	**72**	**100.0**

Source: Data collected by Jason M. Barr.

Table 9.2 The Real Estate Professionals in the Roaring Twenties
During the Roaring Twenties, many of the city's skyscraper builders were self-made men who grew up in New York. This table lists the names and backgrounds of those developers who constructed more than one 328-foot or taller skyscraper between 1928 and 1931

Developer	Number built	Background
A. E. Lefcourt	6	Jewish immigrant; started in garment industry
Abe Adelson	3	Born in New York; Jewish; started in garment industry
Abraham Bricken	3	Jewish Immigrant; started in garment industry
Irwin Chanin	3	Born in Brooklyn; Jewish; attended Cooper Union.
Louis Adler	2	Jewish immigrant; started in garment industry
A. M. Bing	2	Born in New York; attended Columbia Law
Total	**19**	

Source: Data collected by Jason M. Barr.

The real estate professional was responsible for forty-six out of seventy-two projects, and, of those, about 40% were built by six men, most of whom were self-made. Table 9.2 shows the real estate professionals who completed more than one skyscraper.[77] While all of them started their early careers in other areas, they all eventually moved into the real estate business full-time.

Abraham E. Lefcourt was one of the most prolific builders. Between 1910 and 1930, he had constructed thirty-one commercial buildings in the city.[78] Lefcourt is widely credited with transferring the garment district to the area around Seventh Avenue from 34th to 42nd Streets.[79] After he constructed his buildings, he retained ownership, with his organization acting as renter and building manager.

Lefcourt was born in 1877 and came to America in 1882. He started out hawking newspapers on the streets of the Lower East Side, and later worked in the garment industry. In his early thirties, he built his first structure, a twelve-story loft building for garment businesses, at 48 West 25th Street in 1910. The first two floors housed Lefcourt's own women's apparel manufacturing company. The success of the endeavor prompted him to move into the real estate business full-time. By 1930, his organization had a staff of over 200 people. His holdings in 1929 were reportedly valued at $100 million. When the Depression hit, he suffered tremendous losses. He died in 1932 in his early fifties; newspapers reported his estate was worth $2,500.[80]

Abraham Bricken was another self-made developer. He arrived as a poor immigrant from Kiev in 1905. With the first $50 he saved, he opened a tailor shop on Grand Street. Four years later, he left tailoring and turned to real estate. By the 1920s, the Bricken Construction Company was one of the most active in the city. The company built several skyscrapers, such as the forty-five-story Transportation Building at Barclay Street. For a time it was the third largest office building in the world. Between 1921 and 1927, he constructed more than $50 million worth of real estate in the garment center alone.[81]

Fred F. French was another important builder in the city. His projects included the thirty-eight-story Fred F. French Building on Fifth Avenue and 44th Street, Tudor

City, and the Knickerbocker Houses on the Lower East Side. None of his projects qualify in the list of seventy-two buildings that were 328 feet or greater constructed from 1928 to 1931. But French's story has a familiar ring in the developers' clique. The eldest of four sons, he was born into poverty in the Bronx in 1883. His father died when he was a child, forcing him to help support the family through part-time jobs. French won a scholarship to the prestigious Horace Mann School, and after high school, he spent one year in Princeton. Then after a stint working in the West, he came back and enrolled in engineering courses at Columbia University.

At age 27, he determined to go into the real estate business and started by erecting small buildings in the Bronx. He plowed his profits back into the company, and by dint of hard work and shrewd decision-making, by the mid-1920s he was one of New York's most prominent builders. His company, the Fred F. French Company, had over 300 employees during the mid-1920s. He died unexpectedly in 1936, at the age of 52, though his holdings seemed to have been in relatively better shape during the Depression.[82]

As a respected member of the real estate community, French's opinions carried weight. Expressing his continued optimism for New York's future, French told the *New York Times* in March, 1930:

> It is also plain that the next decade and the next dozen decades will show the most surprising and most enormous increases in Manhattan values. It is likewise plain that smaller investors, though lots on Fifth Avenue at $1,000,000 are no longer available to them, are nevertheless now offered the same opportunities to make profits out of Manhattan real estate as were offered in 1859.[83]

Many of his company's projects were financed via the "Fred French Plan," which had a similar flavor to real estate bonds, but relied on stock issues. For each project he would sell low-denomination stocks to the public to finance the project, and then would pay dividends from the profits. He employed a large sales force to market the securities. French, through a series of subsidiary companies, would raise the capital through security issues, then another company would construct the building, and finally a third would rent and manage them and distribute the profits to the shareholders.

In summary, while nothing can be said directly about whether irrational exuberance took hold of the market in the late 1920s, the analysis of those who built the city's tallest buildings demonstrates that the overwhelming majority were constructed by corporations for their headquarters or by seasoned real estate professionals. These builders and companies were deeply embedded in the New York City economy and they had a vested interest in promoting its future success. The notion that the skyline was driven by egomaniacal businessmen eager to leave monuments for society is not borne out by the facts.

INCOME AND CONSTRUCTION: THE EVIDENCE

Owning commercial real estate in the 1920s was very profitable. The Equitable Building, for example, completed in 1915 at 120 Broadway, saw its net income rise from $1.24 million in 1926 to $2.1 million in 1929, despite the fact that its rent was lower than not only the new buildings being constructed around it but also as compared to nearby offices of similar age.[84] Finance and trust companies were renting space in the building, and thanks to the booming stock market, they were willing to pay higher rents.

Equitable's rising rental income was not unusual. Economist Leo Grebler in his 1955 book, *Experience in Urban Real Estate Investment*, provided clues as to what skyscraper developers were seeing in general.[85] Grebler investigated the income and costs of several properties in New York City, including offices and apartment buildings. Based on his data, he created an index of net income from 1905 to 1950. Figure 9.5 presents the real index for office buildings (1905 = 100), along with the number of skyscraper completions during this period (295 feet or taller).

The figure shows that between 1905 and 1920, the inflation-adjusted income for office buildings was falling. After that, the fortunes of building owners began to improve quite dramatically. In 1920, the index value was 69.4, and by 1931, at the peak, the index was at 190.9, this represents a 275% rise in real income over the 1920s! Also notice that the indexes peaked in 1931. Over a year after the stock market crash, building owners were still realizing sizable profits. In other words, even into 1931, New York does not seem to have fully shifted to "depression mode." Rather, the stock market crash was not followed directly by a complete drop in business. In 1932, building incomes were still higher than they were in the late 1920s.

To further investigate how responsive developers were to the economic climate, I performed a statistical analysis to see how the number of skyscrapers completed each

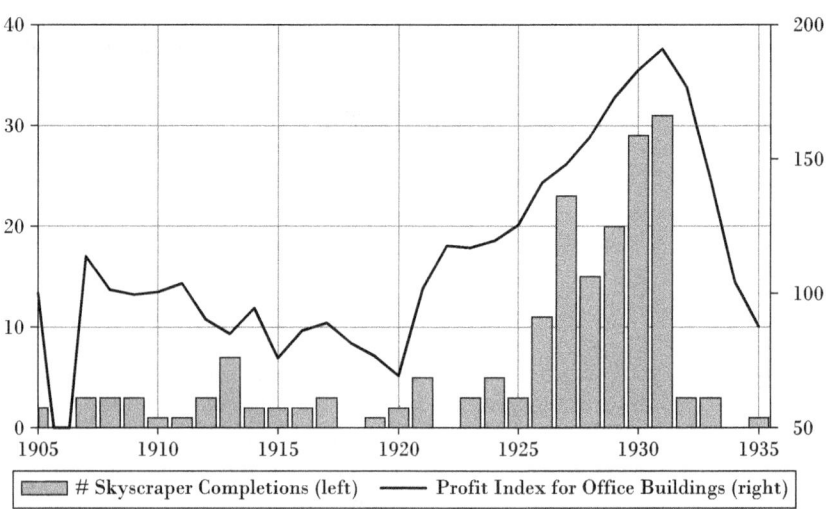

Figure 9.5 Real estate profits versus skyscraper completions from 1905 to 1935. One of the reasons that so many very tall skyscrapers were constructed during the late 1920s was because real estate profits were so unusually high. The graph shows an index of the inflation-adjusted profits from owning office buildings. Starting in early 1920s, these profits began to climb dramatically and peaked in 1931. Developers were responding to this favorable climate by constructing more skyscrapers.

Source: Index data from Grebler (1955). Skyscraper data collected by Jason M. Barr.

year between 1901 and 1950 (295 feet or taller) was determined by average incomes and access to loans. This analysis is similar to the one performed in chapter 6, but is different in that I specifically use the profit index created by Grebler. His index runs for fifty years and allows for a greater understanding of how income growth created the building boom of the 1920s.

Ideally, to test the Gold Bond Theory—that easy access to these real estate bonds fueled skyscraper construction—I would include the growth in issuances over the period. Unfortunately, data on Gold Bonds has only been collected for sixteen years. Instead, I look at the growth rate in real (inflation-adjusted) real estate loans issued in New York State.[86] For the overlapping years, the correlation in New York loans growth rate and Gold Bond issuance growth rate is 0.52, so there is a substantial positive correlation between the two, and it suggests that New York State real estate loans are a useful indicator for the supply of capital for Manhattan skyscrapers.

Two regressions were run. The first one looks at how the number of skyscraper completions between 1901 and 1950 was determined by the net income index value in the prior year, which measures the profits from construction, and the growth in real estate loans two years prior. The second regression investigates the number of completions versus the prior year's index value for gross income and the growth in real estate loans two years prior (see the appendix Y).

The results show the builders are sensitive to both the income side and financing side, but they are much more responsive to income than access to capital. For net income, a 10% increase in net income for building owners produced an 8.2% increase in the number of skyscrapers. Builders are even more responsive to gross income, which shows that a 10% increase in gross income generated a 12.3% increase in the number of completions. As for access to building loans, developers do react to the amount of additional money offered for real estate. For each 10% increase in loans, skyscraper completions increased by about 5%.

In conclusion, the results of this analysis demonstrate that builders reacted to a much greater extent to the rise in income than they did to the growth in real estate loans. While real access to financing was important, it took second place to income and profits.

THE STOCK MARKET AND THE SKYLINE

From late 1926 to October 1929, the stock market experienced an unprecedented run. The Standard & Poor's (S&P) Index, which tracks the stock prices of the largest corporations, was at 13.49 at the close of 1926. At its peak in September 1929, the index was at 31.3, an increase of 132% in just 2.75 years.[87] The Dow Jones Industrial Average, which comprised a smaller group of blue chip companies, showed a similar rise, going from 157.2 at the close of 1926 to 381.17 at its peak in September 1929. New York Stock exchange volume was 500% greater in 1929 than it had been only five years before.[88] The brokers and traders of Wall Street were truly busy.

The seeds of the boom, however, were planted by the underlying profitability of the firms themselves (see the appendix Z). Throughout the 1920s corporations in the S&P Index were consistently raising their dividends, and shareholders saw a consequent rise in the average earnings per share. But the boom morphed into a bubble because of both the demand for speculation among the public at large, and by Wall Street brokers and bankers pushing stock sales and credit. As investors made money, they were eager to plow more of their earnings and savings into the stock market. Unbridled euphoria overtook the market.[89]

But the stock market boom had an unanticipated consequence. To service the needs of the investors, Wall Street had to hire more workers. The effect on the skyline was twofold. First, it reduced office vacancy in Lower Manhattan to near-zero levels; this, in turn, drove up office rents, which then fueled skyscraper construction. Second was that given the rising rental prices in Lower Manhattan, some non-finance-based businesses saw rents rise faster than they were willing to pay; as a result, they moved to Midtown, further stimulating growth there.[90]

Based on the statistical analysis discussed in chapter 6, both New York Stock Exchange volume and changes in the S&P Index are strong predictors of skyline growth. Using these data, I find that every 10% rise in volume from one year to the next is associated with 4.7% more skyscrapers two years hence; and every rise in the S&P Index by 10% is also met with a 4.9% rise in skyscraper completions. In 1928, the S&P Index rose by 27%; while stock exchange volume increased by 66%. Over the twentieth century, stock exchange volume has increased by 11.65% each year on average; while the S&P Index increased by 6.65%. This meant that New York City added 36% more skyscrapers to the skyline in 1930 than would have otherwise occurred if 1928 had been an average year for Wall Street.[91]

TECHNOLOGICAL CHANGE AND THE COST OF CONSTRUCTION

The first skyscraper in New York was completed in 1889. Over time, as engineers and developers gained experience, the construction process became much more efficient. This can happen for many reasons. First, developers and construction companies improved their logistics to organize the process more efficiently. Additionally, builders can adapt their practices to incorporate new construction technologies, machines, and tools, specially built for the purpose of high-rise construction.

Another way is through the prices of materials and labor. The Industrial Revolution made for the mass production of important products at lower costs. For example, as the economy employed steel for railroads and buildings, the mills were able to take advantage of economies of scale, so that per ton, the cost of steel fell dramatically over the nineteenth century. In 1867, one ton of steel rails cost $166, by 1889, the (nominal) price had fallen to $17.63.[92] That is, the price of virtually the same product fell nearly 90% over three decades.

When discussing the reason for the rapid building of the 1920s, one key explanation has been omitted from the discussion: the costs of their construction, which as will be discussed below, were falling quite rapidly from 1890 to 1930. These reduced costs reflected the movement up the learning curve for developers and contractors. Another part came from the drop in costs for vital building components. Some costs, like steel, were falling rapidly, while other costs like labor were rising. But since developers and contractors could substitute less expensive inputs for more expensive ones, their experience over the three decades allowed them to figure out ways to cut costs without sacrificing quality.

Builders had to wrestle with many logistical and technological challenges; each time they faced and conquered a particular set of problems, it was added to the knowledge stock, and could be applied to the next project (see chapter 8 for how this related to foundations). The robust economy of the 1920s allowed developers to take advantage of their experience and erect structures that were both taller and less expensive on a per square foot basis.

To investigate how costs evolved in the early years of the skyscraper, I collected data on the construction costs of 109 buildings completed throughout Manhattan between 1899 and 1931.[93] The average height in this sample was 16.6 floors and the range went from 2 to 102 floors. Using this data, I ran a regression to see how real (inflation-adjusted) total costs were determined by the size of the project (the number of floors and the lot area), and other control variables, including the cost of materials and labor (and measured by construction cost indexes created by the Turner Construction Company or the *Engineering News Record*), and if the project was commercial or residential.

In this case, the key variable of interest is the year of completion, which measures the overall trend of constructions costs, controlling for a host of other things that determine the cost, including the prices of materials and labor (results are given in the appendix AA). The result show that the total costs were falling, on average, about 4% to 5% per year!

Between 1900 and 1920, the marginal or additional cost of adding another floor, holding other factors constant, averaged about 7%; between 1921 and 1931 the cost dropped to about 3%. In other words, it was getting cheaper to add extra floors. As discussed in chapter 6, the economic height of the building is one that sets the additional cost of the last floor just equal to the benefits of adding it. As the costs of building taller were going down, developers were responding by adding more floors. By the late 1920s, the construction of tall buildings was significantly less expensive per square foot or per floor than it had been at the dawn of the Skyscraper Revolution; and this helps explain, in part, the building boom of the late 1920s.

In summary, despite much rhetoric about the building boom of the 1920s, the data reveal a more stolid reason for why so many skyscrapers where constructed: the rapid growth of New York as the economic heart of modern America. The Grand Central area's boom was a response to needs of new offices for headquarters; while the Penn Station neighborhood's rise was due to the fashion and clothing industries; Downtown's growth was a product of Wall Street's ascendancy. New York needed offices and developers obliged. There is little evidence that Gold Bonds were egging them on, as it were.

The office boom likely began so late in the decade because the housing shortage after the Great War required that developers focus their energies in this area first. But when they turned to offices, they did so quite fiercely; all the while, they were innovating to reduce the costs of delivering skyscrapers to the market. Some developers, of course, could not but help get caught up in the frenzy by building taller than otherwise would have been rational.[94] But fundamentally the 1920s reaffirms the role of supply and demand in moving the American economy forward.

10

What Is Manhattan Worth?
One Hundred Fifty Years of Land Values

The ownership of land is the great fundamental fact which ultimately determines the social, the political, and consequently the intellectual and moral condition of a people. And it must be so.
Henry George

Land and height are inextricably linked. Skyscrapers house the millions of people who want to be in the same place at the same time. By allowing these people to be together, the skyscraper makes the city more productive and draws in even more residents, which creates new land shortages, which must be eliminated by the construction of more skyscrapers. As a result, the skyscraper is both a cause and effect of high land values.

The price of land represents the value of the location and is, therefore, a measure of the social benefits of place. The fact that land values are so high in Manhattan means that the island—its geography and collection of people and businesses—provide valuable services to humankind. When land values are rising, it means the benefits of geography are rising; when falling, it suggests a lower utility of that particular place relative to others. The relationship between land values and well-being holds when government land-use regulations are neither overly restrictive nor too lax.

Economist and 1886 New York City mayoral candidate Henry George argued that the landowner was a kind of leech on society.[1] He buys a plot and, figuratively speaking, sits on it, watching its value grow, while providing no contribution to society as a whole. George argued, in essence, that the landowner is a kind of monopolist, who extracts income from those who worked hard to endow the land with value, such as the workers and shopkeepers, on the assumption that the owner of the lot is different than the owner or user of the structure. [2]

George's policy recommendation was to abolish the standard property tax, where the city comes up with an assessed value of the property—on both the building and land—and then sends the owner a tax bill, based on the tax rate times the assessed value. His idea was that the buildings (the improvements) should not be taxed at all, while the land should be taxed at 100% of its value, which is tantamount to the government taking the property, and making it the full owner.

For a plot of fixed size, taxing it will not reduce the amount used for productive purposes. If you tax the improvements, it discourages people from building structures that are best for both the individual and society. Since the price of land, on the other hand, is determined by the collective actions of society, the individual landowner should not be permitted to simply sit back and reap the rewards of everyone else's efforts.

We will return to the land taxation idea in the Epilogue, where I discuss policy recommendations, but one thing that perhaps George did not fully understand was that the landowner does have competition—if prices of a location become too great, then developers can add floor space, which will reduce the price (or growth rate) of space and land. New land can also be created out of infill in the water or by grading the natural contours of the earth; or "land" can be created over highways, rail yards, and other rights of way.

The point is that in the long run, land prices, in a relatively free market, are similar to other important investments like stocks and bonds, and they should not grow faster than the value of the underlying assets or phenomena that give them value. The owner of a plot of land is like the owner of a stock, in that she really owns a piece of paper—a deed—that entitles her to generate an income or some personal benefit.

Similarly, an investor in corporate stocks is the owner of pieces of paper that entitles him to some of the profits of the company. The value of the stock is determined by the current and expected future profitability of the company. General Motors (GM) stock is only worth as much as the income it makes by selling cars. If the price of General Motors shares rises faster than the market as a whole, it suggests one of a few possibilities. First is that GM is extremely profitable because it is providing a better service to society than their competitors—that is, they make better cars.

A second reason can be that the company has some monopoly power which allows it to earn excessive profits above a normal rate of return for a car company (which is referred to as "economic profits" or "economic rents"). Past success in business, for example, gave General Motors such a large market share, that by the 1960s, it had monopoly power, simply because it was so dominant in the industry. A third reason for high valuations is that the buyers of the stock, for psychological reasons, are willing to pay a premium to own GM. Premiums can arise from "irrational exuberance" or from a speculative bubble of some kind.

All of these factors have been present in Manhattan's land market history: rational pricing, bubble mentality, and monopoly power. In this chapter, we focus on the evolution of land values in general since the Civil War. We can think of land prices like stock values, and they indicate the profitability of Manhattan, Inc. In this chapter, we begin by asking: Has the island's value moved primarily in an upward direction or are there long periods of decline or flat prices? What have been some of the major economic forces at work driving Manhattan's value?

This will lead us to the next question: What is the island worth? Imagine if we could remove all the buildings, but leave the infrastructure and the parks: what then is the total value of the island? Because Peter Minuit's $24 "purchase" of Manhattan looms large in the real estate history of the city, we can use it as a benchmark to ask the following hypothetical question. If the equivalent of $24 had simply been put in a savings account versus being invested in a diversified portfolio of Manhattan lots, which would have been a better deal? Has Manhattan, Inc. outperformed the economy as a whole?

Besides Minuit, John Jacob Astor's ghost still haunts New York's real estate history. On his deathbed, he apparently quipped, "Could I begin life again, knowing what

I now know, and had money to invest, I would buy every foot of land on the Island of Manhattan."[3] Well, what has happened to those who would follow in his investing footsteps?

It is important to keep in mind that Astor's vision related to the early growth of the city; something, in fact, that was foreseen at least as early as 1811, when the Grid Plan was established for the island south of 155th Street. While it was hard to imagine a small city of 60,000 would someday grow to occupy the entire island and hold 2.3 million people, Astor was not alone in projecting its growth. He was, however, shrewder than most in exploiting this vision. But for how long was Astor's wisdom applicable? Would owning the entire island really reap such a good return?

After the discussion of the history of Manhattan's land values, we then turn to the issue of the long-term relationship between land prices and the skyline. Have additions to the skyline moved in sync with land prices? Is there evidence that one causes the other or vice versa?

The question of causality is important because if land values drive economic height, it then means that the skyscraper is fundamentally a solution to the allocation problem. Presumably, tall buildings act like a safety valve on land prices, since the increased supply of real estate will cause rents and land prices to fall (or growth to moderate), given that there is a direct relationship between the two.

Nonetheless, in the historical debate about the skyscraper, one accusation that has been lodged is that they draw too many people to a location. If the ego builder does not care about economics, then the skyscraper will force a higher concentration of people and more congestion and neighborhood disamenities. If so, this would suggest that skyscraper height is the cause of high land values, since people are drawn to a location at which they would otherwise prefer not to be; thus making the location artificially more valuable.

My reading of the data, however, reveals that skyscrapers are responding to land values, and not the other way around. This implies that, by and large, the skyscraper is a solution to an allocation problem, not a cause of it; but, of course, government policy is important to check overbuilding or reduce the externalities.

THE THEORY OF LAND VALUES

Before we proceed to the data, we pause here to review the theory of land values. As we have discussed throughout the book, land prices are determined by what people can do at each particular location. In other words, values are determined by how much benefit the users derive at different places.[4]

A simple model proceeds as follows. Let us start with a business, located at a particular spot on planet earth, spot X; and it gains profits from its operations there:

$$profits\ at\ X = income\ at\ location\ X$$
$$-\ costs\ at\ location\ X - land\ rents\ at\ location\ X.$$

For example, take a law firm located on lower Broadway, near Wall Street. The income at location X is the money earned from its business. Being close to Wall Street, we can assume it draws a large revenue stream from its high-income clients close by.

Plus, the additional proximity to other law firms suggests that it increases its profits from the usual suite of agglomeration benefits, such as fast communication with others in the industry, easier access to workers, and so on.

The costs at location X represent the costs of paying for office rent, wages, and the expenses related to traveling to clients and so forth. The final part of the equation is what the firm pays for the right to occupy a specific geographical site on the planet. Imagine a company in Lower Manhattan pays $50 per square foot each month for its 1,500 square feet of office space. Some fraction of the $50 goes toward the shelter and building services, and the rest (between 25% and 40%, depending on the size of the structure), goes to the landowner as payment to occupy that location.[5]

The landlord purchased the lot based on the income that it would generate. She charges rent to the tenants and collects the income to get a return on her investment. Implicit in the rent cost is the money to pay for the land. These rents, in a competitive market, are determined by what is left over after the business pays for the other costs at location X. That is, land users would bid away their "economic profits" to rent the location, where economic profits are profits above and beyond a reasonable return to the business. This gives:

land rents at location X = income at location X − costs at location X.

And so how is the price of land determined? The price of the land at location X is the net economic benefit of that location over many years. Succinctly,

price of land at X = discounted flow of land rents at X over many years.

This equation says that in a competitive market the value or price of land today is worth the flow of income that it generates today and over many years into the future. The "discounted" part just means that buyers discount or reduce the rent flows from the future when calculating the value of land today, since money to be paid in the future is not as certain or as valuable as money today.

The reason land is so valuable in Lower Manhattan and Midtown is that the income at these locations is so high. Businesses find that being there gives them a competitive advantage that lets them bid a hefty sum for the right. If a company would jump to a new location, it would find that its net profits would fall. More broadly, life in the city is so expensive only partly because it costs more to deliver goods and services to consumers, but mainly because so many people want to be in the city; they spend more money there and generate a lot of income for the businesses, including stores and restaurants. The high prices are the result of the demand for city living.

For the homeowner or apartment renter, the cost of location Y is determined in a similar manner, but with a different objective than a business. The firm wants the benefits associated with being in business: profits, reputation, market share, a high stock price, and so on. The homeowner wants a good home in a good neighborhood, with access to stores and restaurants, high-quality schools, public transportation, and friends and relatives. The household tries to find a location that maximizes the economic benefits, given its ability to pay for different homes and locations, summarized as:

net benefit at location Y = dollar value of benefits of location Y
− costs at location Y − land rent at location Y.

What does the household at location Y pay to be there; that is, what is the land rent? In a competitive market, the winning bidder bids away any extra benefit for the right to occupy the spot. If the household owns the house, then it has the dual position of being both the land renter and the landlord. The economics are the same as if the roles were split, but the price of land is more indirectly embedded in cost of living in the house, since homeowners do not pay rent to themselves. Nonetheless the rent paid for land is given by the equation:

land rent at location Y = benefits of location Y − costs at location Y.

The price of the land is given by:

price of land at location Y = discounted flow of land rents at location Y.

As a thought experiment, imagine you bought a house in a nice neighborhood, and you tore it down, and sold the lot. It would still fetch a high price, even without the structure, because someone is purchasing a bundle of neighborhood amenities and the right to build a new home. The price of vacant land is then a good measure of the value of the location to businesses or households.

In theory, we can come up with the total benefit of the city by adding up the price of land at every location:

price of Manhattan = sum of land values at every location

sum of land values = sum of net benefits to the users of each location.

This model can help us understand some key events in New York's history. First is the general trajectory of land values in the city. Rising land values suggest optimism about the city's economy. When the benefits of a location become so great and the price of land increases, the response to this is to provide more "land" at a location by building a taller building.

Conversely, we can also understand why there might be wholesale abandonment and rampant arson of housing in neighborhoods, as took place in the 1970s. When the value of being at location X is less than the costs of maintaining the location, land prices, in theory, are negative; the owner would pay someone to take the property off her hands. As the real estate tax arrears mount, the owner owes a debt to the city, and which is then cancelled when the government takes title to the property.

Finally, we need to consider that the price of location X or Y is not simply based what is happening today, but the perceptions of what will happen in the near future. Land value bubbles, like other asset bubbles, occur because high expectations about the future prospects of a neighborhood increase the value of a place. This draws in investors and speculators who believe they can get profits while the "gettin's good." As prices rapidly rise, it draws in more investors aiming to cash in on the speculative frenzy. Bubbles emerge from a positive feedback loop: rising land values draw more investors, which raise prices even more, drawing in more investors, and so on. At some point the irrational investors begin to dominate the buying and trading, seduced by the siren song of easy wealth, until market prices have no rational basis. Then, like a pin to a balloon, the bubble bursts, and investors are left holding land worth pennies on the dollar.

In the long run, however, the total value of a place, such as Manhattan, must be based on its usefulness to *Homo sapiens*. But there exists one caveat: government regulations. Since the second half of the nineteenth century, government has become increasingly involved in real estate and land markets, both in a direct and indirect sense. As we will see below, New York's renaissance since the 1990s has put landowners in an advantageous position given the heap of city regulations and policies that make new real estate development quite difficult. Perhaps it is the revenge of Henry George's ghost!

Directly, land-use laws began with the tenement house laws of the nineteenth and early twentieth centuries, which ensured a minimum set of quality standards. The next set of laws established zoning rules, which limited use and bulk across the five boroughs. The first zoning laws were established in 1916 and were updated in 1961; they have become increasingly complex over the twentieth century (see chapter 5). In 1965, the city created the Landmark's Preservation Commission and a set of laws designed to preserve the city's historic architecture.

Indirectly, the city has become involved in the land market in two important ways. First is through taxation; on one hand, the actual (inflation-adjusted) real estate tax burden increased dramatically over the twentieth century. All the while, the city has a suite of subsidies and abatements that are applicable to a variety of real estate types (see Epilogue).

Second is the process of negotiation that takes place between developers and the city. In the case of zoning laws, though they were meant to reduce the externalities from overbuilding, they have morphed into planning tools, as developers have increasingly negotiated with the city for the right to build larger buildings in exchange for providing some local amenity, such as a park or a new subway station. Developers also negotiate with the city over tax abatements to make their project more profitable. This slows down or inhibits the development process, making landowning more valuable, since there is lower competition than otherwise.

Third is through the use of price controls. During and after World War II, rent control laws were enacted for the housing market; and as of this writing, the city has been unable to wean itself off of some kind of price manipulation system. Today 45% of rental units in the city remain under the rent stabilization program.[6]

The net effect of these policies on land values, ironically, is not clear. On one hand, as the model shows, anything that limits the profits to landowners will reduce land values. In this case, rent stabilization and zoning can limit the income. On the other hand, if some lots have rent stabilized buildings, then those lots and buildings without any stabilized tenants will be relatively more valuable. The restrictions placed on one segment of the market will confer an additional value on the unrestricted segment. Further, if zoning improves the quality of life in a neighborhood, then a higher land value will result. All of this is to say that regulations designed to limit land uses or manipulate prices have a complex effect across the urban landscape, and the ultimate result of this smorgasbord of policies requires much more detailed analysis. However, to the extent that these policies reduce the incentives for new construction, it means that, on average, as the demand to be in Manhattan rises, landowners will likely reap a reward, as this increased demand generates a more furious battle for place, which will manifest itself through higher land prices.

In summary, in a competitive market, land values will be set by the zero economic profit condition, which says that land users will pay landowners an amount that causes the excess profits they earn to go to zero (remember economic profits are different than accounting profits). The willingness to pay is tied to the income of the population working, playing, and living in the city. On average, rising or falling land values should be tied to the city's income levels.

Thus, in a relatively free market, if rising income bids up land values, there will be a kind of self-regulating principle at work. Higher land values increase the incentive to use the land more intensely—that is, make artificial land; this increases the total supply of real estate, which will cause the relative rents to fall, creating an equilibrium outcome, where land prices reflect the income of the population. When land values "get out of whack," and restrictions on the market are not overly burdensome, market forces will return the prices back to a more sustainable level. The more restrictions placed on the real estate market, the greater the monopoly power of the landowner who earns economic profits because of the lack of competition in the marketplace.

HOW TO MEASURE THE VALUE OF LAND?

In some sense, plots of land are like snowflakes—they may have the same basic appearance, but upon closer inspection there is something a little different about each one.[7] Be this at it may, land prices are generally determined by a set list of features, and once we account for them, we can then determine what part reflects the overall benefit to society.

The value of a particular plot of land is determined by its size and shape, its placement on a block, such as whether it is on a corner or the interior, and its proximity to other important amenities and locations, such as public transportation, the central business district, or a park. For each lot, we could, as would be done if we hired an appraiser, come up with an average price for lots in that neighborhood, and then add or subtract value based on its particular features. Unlike an appraisal of a particular property, our objective is to scale up values and create an average value of Manhattan itself. The goal is to discover the average price of land over time for the city after accounting or controlling for many of the important features that determine prices across the island.

To this end, I created an index of land values based on vacant land transactions (as was done in chapter 2 for colonial New York). In this case, I ran regressions that look at how the real (inflation-adjusted) price per square foot for these vacant land sales were determined by its location relative to the closet core (the corner of Wall Street and Broadway or Grand Central Station), its square footage, the neighborhood it is in, and the year of the sale. By investigating the real value of land, we can see how land prices have moved relative to the price level in general.

I ran a separate regression for the data collected from the years 1866 to 1900, and then another one for sales from 1950 to 2013. For the period 1900 to 1949, I used an index derived from the total assessed value of land on the island, since this was more readily available for analysis than vacant land sales. All three indexes were then adjusted so they could fit together as one long index from 1866 to 2013 (see in the appendix BB).[8]

Vacant land sales as indicators of land values have their pros and cons, but since they are the most readily available measure we have, they are perhaps the best and most easily collected indicator we have. When I tell people that I have been collecting data on vacant land sales in Manhattan, a frequent retort is "Well, the land must be vacant for a reason." Meaning, if land is vacant it must be because there is something wrong with the lot that makes it uncharacteristic for the measure of land values.

My thought is that this might be true for some parcels, but I do not think it is systematically true for all the parcels in the data sets. In this chapter there are actually three data sets. For the one from 1866 to 1900, the vast bulk data was collected by Professor Fred Smith of Davidson College, and for this period, its likely much of the vacant land was "on the way up" in the sense that it was a period of rapid growth for the economy, and as such, vacant parcels were in the process of being converted to their new, most valuable use. It is unlikely that during that time there was anything systematically problematic with these properties.

The second data set spans from 1901 to 1949. In this case, I have used the annual total assessed value of all land on the island. This data comes from the city government and was used for the purpose of real estate taxation. In particular, every year, the city's tax or finance department would evaluate the value of every property on the island, and determine how much of the value came from the land itself versus how much came from the structure.

The values were then amalgamated to determine the assessed value of the island. For the first half of the twentieth century, the assessors aimed to determine the true market value of the land. And for the most part, the evidence suggests that they were relatively accurate. The figures were widely used and published, and accepted as relatively accurate measures of land values. Because we have, in theory, a measure of the value of Manhattan in toto, I simply created an index from this data, and do not use any regression analysis.

Based on my reading of the data, the assessed values do appear reasonable, but they lag true land values by several months.[9] It is likely the assessors adjusted land values in a smoother manner than would have occurred if each plot were bought and sold each year. For example, the true peak in land values in the Roaring Twenties probably occurred in 1931, while the assessed values shows the peak 1932.[10]

In addition, each year, the State of New York creates "equalization rates" for every county in the state. Since each municipality, and, therefore, county, is likely to have different assessment methods, the equalization rates are designed to create market values from the assessed values. By and large, for every year between 1900 and 1950, the State of New York deemed the City's assessments to be between 99% and 100% of market values, suggesting that the state believed assessments were more or less accurate.[11]

From 1950 to 2013, land prices come from vacant land sales. For this data, similar to 1866 to 1900, a regression analysis was performed to construct an index. Here the issues of property abandonment and unusual lots may play a factor in determining land values, especially during the 1970s and 1980s when property owners in the old tenement neighborhoods were walking away from, or illegally burning down, their holdings. This is true particularly of East Harlem and the Lower East Side, which were hard hit by the restructuring of urban America after World War II. Landlords in the 1970s and 1980s were simply walking away from their properties rather than investing in and maintaining them.[12]

Over time, the city acquired a portfolio of vacant properties. As the economy began to rebound, they were put back on the market and sold. Despite the fact that vacant lots in low-income neighborhoods disproportionately enter into the data set, there are ways to statistically account for this. Overall, vacant land sales since 1950s have occurred throughout the island, and thus we do have a measure of the value of land for Manhattan, not just for declining neighborhoods.

MANHATTAN LAND VALUES SINCE THE CIVIL WAR

What has been the trajectory of land values since the Civil War? Figure 10.1 presents the big picture by showing the index from 1867 to 2012, which measures the relative

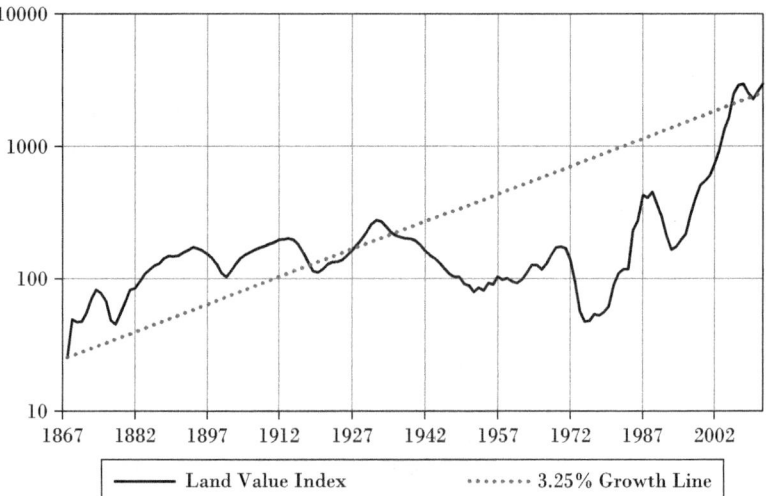

Figure 10.1 Land Value Index from 1867 to 2012. This graph shows an index of the inflation-adjusted price of land in Manhattan since after the Civil War. Land prices show a dramatic rise, on average, until the Great Depression; this was followed by a long period of deflation. Starting in 1977, land values renewed their ascent. Since 1993, prices have shown incredible gains. Note the index is a moving average of two years and is presented on a $\log_{10}$ scale, which means that each horizontal line is an order of magnitude higher than the one below it. The dashed line is the 3.25% growth line. Between 1866 and 2013, $100 invested in Manhattan land in 1866 would have yielded 3.79% by the end of 2013, after adjusting for inflation.

Source: Underlying data for 1866 to 1900 from Fred Smith. 1900 to 1949 data is from Manhattan assessed values for land. 1950 to 2013 data from Barr, Smith, and Kulkarni (2015).

value land in Manhattan over time. A few notes are in order. First, the graph shows a smoothed version of the index, a three-year moving average, in particular, but the actual index runs from 1866 to 2013. Second the index was created so that 1900 had a value of 100; lastly, the figure presents the numbers on a logarithmic scale, and thus each entry on the vertical axis represents an order of magnitude difference; the effect of using the logarithmic scale is to graphically compress the index. The dotted line is a 3.25% growth line. In other words, if you invested your money in 1868 and it grew at a real rate (inflation-adjusted) of 3.25% it shows how much you would have by 2013.

The first conclusion from the index is that since the Civil War, the long-run growth rate to Manhattan real estate has been about 3.79% per year, on average (note the 3.25% figure in the graph is lower than 3.79% because the index is smoothed over three years and has a lower value). In other words, if you have invested $100 dollars in a diversified selection of Manhattan lots, and also invested $100 dollars in another investment fund that paid a real (inflation-adjusted) return of 3.79% in 1866, by the end of 2013, you would have the same amount of value in both funds. However, you would have had to wait a long time to get that return from Manhattan land.

From the graph we can see that land values do not demonstrate a single upward trajectory. Rather, each period is marked by a different trends and cyclical pattern. From 1866 to 1895, the city experienced three decades of rapid land price growth and two major cycles. The first half of the twentieth century saw two major cycles, and hardly any net growth by the mid-century. The drop in values during the Depression and World War II was so great that land values in 1950 were where they had been in 1900. Since the war, there have been three major cycles, which occurred from 1950 to 1977, 1977 to 1993, and 1993 to 2007.

More broadly, from 1866 to 1932 the trend was strongly upward. Of course, the downturns from the business cycle caused prices to fall in periods of recession, but the overall growth rate was positive. Between 1866 and 1932 the index rose from 13 to 291, a 2,073% return, or about an average rate of 4.66% a year, in real terms. Here the vision of John Jacob Astor is confirmed. The post-Civil War period represents New York's development into a modern city.

But much of the growth in land values, which peaked in 1931/32, was wiped out by fifteen years of depression and war. A postwar boom, promoted the return to price increases, but the economic troubles of the 1970s and the fiscal crisis all but wiped out those gains, returning land values back to what they were a century before. Thus, we can say that for most of the twentieth century, Astor's vision is wholeheartedly rejected.

The mid-1970s was the low point in the city's land value history; but from there prices experienced a renaissance. In fact, the bounce back of prices since then has been nothing short of remarkable. In the late 1980s, the island achieved its highest value since the Roaring Twenties. A recession in the early 1990s caused a retrenchment, but over the last twenty years, land value prices have made huge strides; peaking in 2007, right before the financial crises and the bursting of the national housing price bubble.

Between 1977 and 2007, the index grew from a low of 44 to a high of 3,737. This represented a 460% return on land; an average annual return of 14.8%! This is perhaps better than what John Jacob Astor achieved. The foresighted investor who bought land at the bottom would have been a very rich person today. But the image of New York City in the late 1970s was bleak and it would have taken a true visionary—perhaps one greater than Astor himself—to see that better times lay ahead.[13]

Overall then, what can we say about the long return to "holding" Manhattan land? One way is to look at the average trend—that is the average, per year growth rate, that ignores the wide ups and downs of land values due to the business cycle. Using this method, I calculate that the average long-run trend of Manhattan was only 1.31% per year.[14] Consider that the long-run trend for real per capital GDP, over the same period, is 2.0%. The reason is that years or decades of feast—of rapid rise in land values—were followed by several years of famine—years of decline and stagnation.

Another approach is to ask the following, imagine you invested $100 in a piece of land in Manhattan in 1866, what would it be worth by 2013? Here the answer would be a bit more sanguine; your plot of land would be worth $26,279, which gives an average annual return of 3.79%. But the problem is: if you are the "buy and hold" type, you would have needed to hold your land for a long time to get that return.

We now turn to a review of three major eras in Manhattan's land value history: 1866 to 1900, 1900 to 1950, and 1950 to 2013. For each of them, there were two general forces at work: the trend—the average up or down trajectory—and the cyclical component, the movement around the trend. The cyclical fluctuation is largely driven by the forces of the business cycle in both the nation and the city: when the economy is growing rapidly in the city and the rest of the country, land values will move above the trend; when the economy is in recession, land values will fall below it. The trends, on the other hand, are largely driven by the structural strength of the city, that is, whether its population and employment base are growing and the level of confidence that people have in New York's future.

1866 to 1900

After the Civil War, land values in Manhattan started at an index value of 13 in 1866 and peaked in 1895 at 181, a 9.0% average annual return (see figure 10.2). The reason, of course, was Manhattan's stellar economic and demographic growth. In 1860 the island's population was 813,669, by 1900 it was 1,850,093 (see appendix G). The local economy was booming; the Industrial Revolution promoted the rise of big businesses. Wall Street's success came from supplying the financial needs of the country; while the port was the nation's largest importer. New York was also a tremendous manufacturer of goods.[15] The post-Civil War period was important for building innovations as well. The elevator began its widespread use during this time. In the 1870s, the apartment building was introduced. Developers were experimenting with new engineering and construction methods that gave rise to the large, modern office building. Ultimately, the end of the period would give birth to the Skyscraper Revolution.

The second half of the nineteenth century saw two major cycles. The first was a speculative wave from 1868 to 1873, sparked by the prospects for Upper West Side and excitement about the elevated railroads. Below 86th Street, over 25,000 lots were

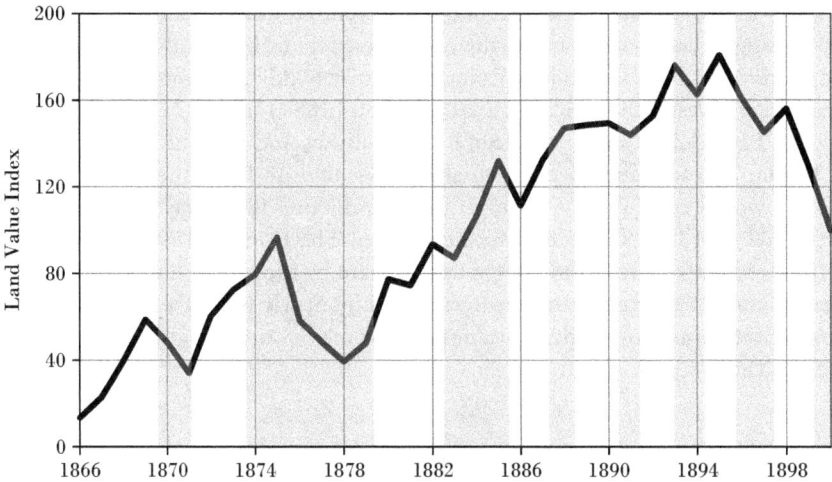

Figure 10.2 Land Value Index from 1866 to 1900. This graph shows an index of the inflation-adjusted price of land in Manhattan from 1866 to 1900. The gray bars are the approximate recession dates. We can see that, on average, land values rose quite dramatically over the period, and this was driven by the city's rapid economic and population growth. The run up in prices from 1878 to 1895 was particularly striking and was caused, in part, by the opening of the elevated railway lines and the opening of the Upper West Side for residential development.

Source: Underlying data from Fred Smith.

still vacant, and their development now seemed inevitable.[16] In 1868, the Central Park Commissioners released plans for the west side, which included Morningside and Riverside Parks. This year represented the Upper West Side's "coming out"; a speculative frenzy for lots ensued.[17]

According to one historian,

The peculiarity of this great speculative craze was that it was almost entirely restricted to dealing in lots—vacant property—lying east and west and north of Central Park. On the West Side in 1868 there were not more than half a dozen modern houses. Standing at the southwest corner of the park, stretching away to the northwest over the territory which is to-day the great residential section of the well-to-do, there was nothing to be seen by a wilderness of rocks dotted with dilapidated shanties. The region was almost as wild as at the time when Washington rallied his forces on the Heights to the north.[18]

Following a banking panic in September 1873, property prices declined as the economy went into recession. For land above 59th Street, "Choice lots that brought $35,000 in the days of the inflation were selling for $11,500, and somewhat less desirable lots for $6,000 to $8,000."[19] Real estate development on the Upper West Side was halted.

The 1880s saw New York resume its upward trajectory, and the completion of the elevated railroad system. The first line opened in 1868, and the system was built out over the 1870s. But by the end of the nineteenth century, Manhattan's "frontier" was closing as large-scale tracts in the north were rapidly being subdivided and sold for apartments and townhouses. Fancy apartment buildings began to appear along Central Park West in the 1880s, such as the Dakota (1884) and the Beresford (1889).[20]

The Els would soon be replaced by the subway, and its construction starting in 1900 promoted land speculation along its route. By 1904, the New York City subway would run to the very tip of the island along Broadway, embedding the area north of 155th Street into the city proper. The Panic of 1893 drove a major correction; land values would begin to rise again by the end of the century.[21] This second major downturn caused prices to fall by nearly 50%. Despite this, at the close of the nineteenth century, values were some 7.5 times higher than they had been in 1866.

Land Values Downtown at the Dawn of the Skyscraper Revolution

After the Civil War, land prices Downtown began to recover, with a peak right before the Panic of 1873. Eventually by 1878, land values not only began to recover but they also began to skyrocket, fueled in part by the completion of the elevated railroads, which, as shown in chapter 8, served to funnel greater numbers of workers into the lower part of the island.

During the late 1870s, the first shoots of the Skyscraper Revolution began to appear. Following the installation of elevators in the Equitable Life Assurance Society headquarters in 1870, structures grew taller. Two early proto-skyscrapers were the New York Tribune Building (1875, nine stories) and the Western Union Building (1875, ten stories). These companies used building height to telegraph their profitability. But ten stories was the practical limit this time because iron or steel framing had not been invented yet (see chapter 5).

In 1879, following the crisis of 1873, prices Downtown averaged about $25 per square foot. At their apex in 1890s they were near $200. This run suggests that the demand for office space was rising faster than what could be accommodated in masonry buildings. Starting in 1890, the ability for Downtown to grow tall in earnest was first realized. The skeleton system was deemed a reality after the completion of the Tower Building in 1889. Using steel instead of masonry walls generated a savings, reducing construction costs from $2 to $.40 per cubic foot. [22] The skyscraper, as a result, allowed builders to go tall in a way never before possible and provided the needed space at an affordable price. Between 1880 and 1897, Lower Manhattan increased the amount of floor area by 50%, growing from 2.6 to 3.9 million square feet.[23]

But the new technology created a building boom that caused a rents and land values to drop, due to both a glut of new space and loss of value in the older buildings. As one writer put it:

> The multiplication of the tall building since 1879, and particularly since the crises of 1893 . . . has placed downtown mercantile property in a crucial situation. Land values have adjusted themselves to the income producing power of the tall buildings, while the sudden accommodations, resulting from the erection

of these mammoth structures, has reduced rentals, thus increasing the pressure on the owners of antiquated properties to improve, and aggravate the competition for tenants. Building in the down-town section has unquestionably been temporarily overdone.[24]

Land Values 1900 to 1950

Unlike the nineteenth century, the twentieth century produced a much different story. After the correction in the 1890s, prices resumed their upward trajectory, but not in a way that perhaps John Jacob Astor would have imagined. Between 1900 and 1950, Manhattan saw two major land value cycles (see figure 10.3). The first was from 1900 to 1920; the second was from 1920 to the Great Depression/World War II. By mid-century, however, real land values were in the same place they had been fifty years prior.

1900 to 1920

The first twenty years of the twentieth century saw the index go from 100 in 1900 to a peak of 202 in 1914 (an average of 5.0% per year). New York experienced several key events that promoted this growth. First, of course, was the continued influx of population, especially Jewish and Italian immigrants. Manhattan's population peaked sometime around 1910 at about 2.33 million (see appendix G).

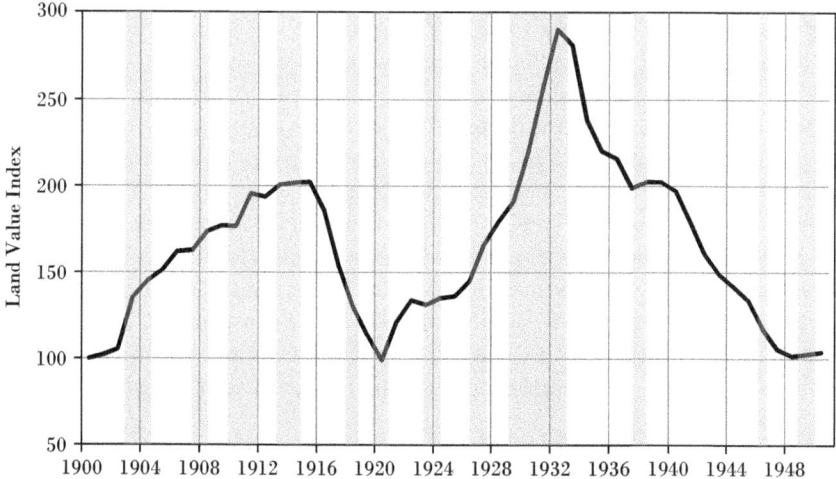

Figure 10.3 Land Value Index from 1900 to 1950. This graph shows an index of the inflation-adjusted price of land in Manhattan from 1900 to 1950. The gray bars are the approximate recession dates. The first half of the twentieth century was marked by two major cycles, one from 1900 to 1920, and another from 1920 to 1947. Unlike the previous century, land value declines during the downturns were so severe that there was no net increase in land values by mid-century. The land price growth during the Roaring Twenties was all but wiped out by the end of World War II.
Source: Underlying data from Manhattan assessed values for land.

Second was the creation of Greater New York in 1898, by the annexation of Brooklyn, Queens, Staten Island, and the eastern Bronx (the western half of the Bronx had been annexed in parts between 1874 and 1895), creating an urban colossus of 302 square miles. By uniting into five boroughs, New York was on a much greater financial and economic footing. As the population suburbanized, the city was able to maintain its tax base as residents of Queens, Brooklyn, and Staten Island continued to pay New York City real estate taxes. The merger further reduced competition between Brooklyn and Manhattan, especially for port traffic. And perhaps equally important were the psychological benefits that came to the "City of Greater New York," as large and important as any metropolis on planet earth.[25]

Lastly, was the opening and expansion of the NYC subway system. The first subway line (the "IRT") opened in 1904 and ran from Lower Manhattan to the northern tip and into the Bronx. Its tremendous success promoted a vast expansion. Contracts were soon issued for new lines running from Manhattan into Brooklyn (the "BMT"), along with more lines in Manhattan and the Bronx. A third set of roads (the "IND") was added beginning in the 1920s. By the end of the 1930s, the New York City subway system was largely complete.[26]

It is important to note, however, that the effect of the subway on Manhattan land values was mixed. On the one hand, it allowed people to leave the densest neighborhoods on the island, such as the Lower East Side. It was these overcrowded districts that saw population and land value loss; while new neighborhoods on the northern fringes of the island gained the most. On the other hand, the subway system locked-in Lower Manhattan and Midtown as the city's central business districts, since the subway lines were designed as a hub and spoke system, with very little consideration to the movement between spokes. It was Midtown, in particular, that saw the greatest land value gains after the subway lines were opened.

The early years of the twentieth century saw land values rise rapidly between 1900 and 1905 due to a strong economy and some speculative fever in the real estate market. In 1907, a banking panic put the brakes on real estate development. But fortunately for the city, the panic only moderated land value growth; it did not cause it to shrink. In the end, the effect of this particular panic was quite modest regarding land values. [27]

In 1916, New York City implemented its first zoning rules, which regulated use and bulk on every lot in the city. It remains an open question as to whether zoning increased or decreased land values in Manhattan. In one sense, if zoning improves the quality of life and reduces the harmful effects of dense construction, it can increase land values. But in another sense, if it increases the costs of construction or limits the profitability of landlords by restricting the amount of floor area provided, it can reduce land values.

The majority of Manhattan's territory was designated 1.25 or 1.5 time districts, meaning that buildings could only rise 1.25 or 1.5 times the width of the street before they had to be set back. This likely made the 2 and 2.5 times districts relatively more appealing, since they were allowed to have denser structures. One could conjecture that the rise of land values in the central business district was affected by the relative constraints placed on the rest of the island.

In the long cycle between 1900 and 1920, the peak in land values occurred in 1914, after a financial panic and before America's involvement in World War I. The mobilization for combat and the subsequent recession meant that the city saw a steep decline in its values. Prices hit their nadir in 1920, and from there begin to rise once again.

1920 to 1949

The second boom period for land prices lasted from 1920 to 1932; the index started at 99 and peaked at 291, a run up of 192% in thirteen years, or about 9% per year. The rise in the 1920s did not come from population growth itself, since Manhattan's population was falling after 1920. After World War I, European immigration was choked off at first by the war. Then the Immigration Act of 1924 limited the annual number of immigrants from any country to 2% of the number who had arrived from that country as of 1890. The Great Black Migration from the South, however, mitigated this drop, as it created Harlem as America's black economic and cultural capital.

By the 1920s, the children and grandchildren of immigrants had achieved enough social mobility to move out of Manhattan's ethnic enclaves. The subway system allowed them to take advantage of new, affordable housing in Brooklyn and the Bronx. As a result, there was a mass migration out of the Lower East Side and other older neighborhoods. The 1901 Tenement Housing Act also reduced affordable housing in Manhattan, making the outer boroughs relatively more attractive. The exodus out of Manhattan took pressure off land values in these neighborhoods. Overall, the growth of land prices was driven mostly by the rising tide of business profits and average household income.

Between 1890 and 1920, real unskilled wages rose 50%. In the same time, the real wages of manufacturing workers increased 83%.[28] For the economy as a whole, real GDP per capita rose nearly 28%.[29] These rising incomes meant a greater willingness and ability to pay for housing and office space. The growth in land values during the Roaring Twenties was fundamentally due to the fact that New York was the economic heart of modern America (see chapter 9). By the early 1920s, the United States had established itself as the only major western power still standing after World War I. The center of finance had firmly shifted from London to New York; while New York remained the cultural capital of the nation. But despite New York's key role in the American economy, it could not withstand the devastating tsunami that was the Great Depression.

Thanks to a report published in 1930 by economist Edwin H. Spengler, we are able see land values growth across the island for three different periods in the early twentieth century.[30] Spengler's report includes average land values for 2,446 Manhattan blocks in 1905, 1913, 1921, and 1929. Figure 10.4 presents the average growth rates for three periods (1905-1913, 1913-1921, and 1921-1929) versus the distance of each block from the southern tip to demonstrate how values were changing along the north-south axis of the city. If a line is above zero it means that land values were growing in a particular period, while less than zero means they were falling.

The first key insight from the graph relates to the land prices across the island. On average, growth between 1905 and 1913 was positive, though generally moderate. On the other hand, land values between 1913 and 1921 fell across the board. The currents

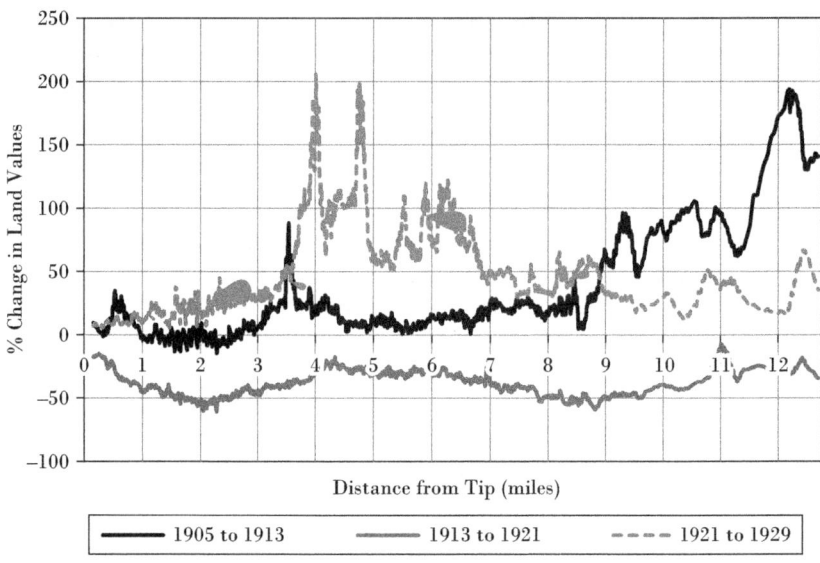

Figure 10.4 Changes in land values during three different periods from 1905 to 1929. This graph allows us to see the location of land price changes across Manhattan in three different periods. The horizontal axis is the distance from the southern tip in miles; the vertical axis is the average percentage change in land value prices at that distance. During the period 1905 to 1913, the most rapid growth occurred in northern Manhattan, as new residential development took place there, thanks to the opening of the subway in 1904. During the period 1913 to 1921, all of Manhattan experienced deflation due to economic downturns and World War I. The worst-hit areas were the tenement districts. During the Roaring Twenties, the greatest land value rises were in Midtown.
Source: Underlying data from Spengler (1930).

of war and recession were just too much to prevent the value of Manhattan from falling. From 1921 to 1929, however, land values resumed their upward momentum.

The graph also gives evidence as to where growth was the greatest. Here we see some interesting patterns for the 1905 to 1913 years. First, land value growth in Lower Manhattan was positive but moderate, while the area north of Chambers Street saw zero or negative changes. Then we see a relatively strong rise at Midtown 1.0, with a peak in values 3.6 miles from the tip, at about Sixth Avenue and 33rd Street.

But, by far, the greatest rise in land values was the area from about 9 miles to 12.5 miles north of the Battery, from Harlem around 135th Street to 220th Street and Broadway. The fact that the northernmost area was the hottest location was due to the IRT subway line. The period from 1913 and 1921 shows a very different story, however. Here we see near universal drops in land values. The older residential neighborhoods, such as the Lower East Side and East Harlem, were hardest hit, while Downtown and Midtown saw less steep drops.

The graph also shows that the rise in land values during the Roaring Twenties was driven by the emergence of Midtown 2.0, with the movement of the shopping district to Herald Square, the rise of Broadway Theatre District in Times Square, the sprouting of the Art Deco towers around Grand Central Station, and the development of the Garment District near Penn Station. Further, prices saw rapid growth around Central

Park South, and the Upper East and West Sides. In other words, despite the loss of total population during this decade, upper and middle-income households were driving the growth of property values north of Midtown, while the new commercial and business districts from 34th Street to 59th Street was lifting the island's value to the greatest degree.

Interestingly, Downtown did not experience the kind of land value growth seen in Midtown. Of course, Wall Street was hot, but other areas, further away and closer to the rivers, were not of great interest to the business community. By the 1920s, Lower Manhattan had been the city's central business district for a century. Many of the buildings were aging and the area was very congested. Lower Manhattan had already seen three decades of skyscraper construction and so land values were not likely to rise as they had in the years before the tall building was introduced.

1950 to 2013

After the end of World War II, land values began to stabilize in Manhattan. Since 1950, Manhattan has seen three cycles, ones that lasted from 1950 to 1977, 1977 to 1993, and 1993 to 2007; a fourth one is well underway. The index over this period is given in Figure 10.5.

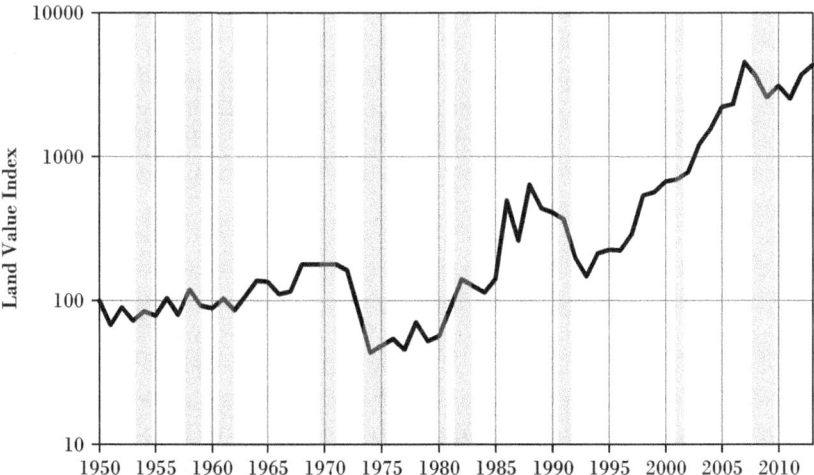

Figure 10.5 Land Value Index from 1950 to 2013. This graph shows an index of the inflation-adjusted price of land in Manhattan from 1950 to 2013. The gray bars are the approximate recession dates. After World War II, land values begin to grow, though at a relatively slow rate. However, a deep recession, falling population, job loss, and the Fiscal Crises caused land values to plummet, reaching a nadir in 1977. Since then, land values have risen, on average. There was a rapid rise in the 1980s followed by a correction, and since 1993, land values have shown a dramatic rise, with some moderation caused by the financial crises of 2007. The city's renaissance since the early 1990s has meant that land value prices have risen much faster than population growth. Note that this index is presented on a $\log_{10}$ scale. The reason is that price growth has been so rapid that a standard scale would make it difficult to see relative land value changes before 1980.
Source: Barr, Smith, and Kulkarni (2015).

The Great Depression had the effect of wringing Manhattan like a sponge, squeezing out the value of its land, so that prices began a twenty-year deflation that would last until 1950. As soldiers returned home and re-engaged with the business of civilian life, there was every reason to believe that New York would resume its place as an economic dynamo.[31] Although there were hints of problems before the war, such as the loss of port and manufacturing jobs, if you asked a man on the street in 1946, that if by the late 1960s, New York and other major cities would witness urban rioting, spikes in crime, and that by 1975, the City of New York would be on the verge of bankruptcy, he would probably have laughed at you.

But, while New York was able to remain the capital of American finance, it was battling against a tide of a wholesale realignment of resources throughout the country, generating a great shakeout of America's older urban centers. While the city's employment, in fact, grew until 1969, things took a decided turn for the worst from there. From 1969 to 1977, New York City lost over 600,000 jobs or 16% of its workforce. More broadly between 1947 and 1980, the city lost about a half million manufacturing jobs. Some of this loss was offset by growth in the service sector. From 1977 to 1980, for example, the city lost 40,000 manufacturing jobs, while adding 106,000 service sector jobs. [32] However, fifteen years of disinvestment in real estate prompted the city to go on a building spree. An office and apartment construction boom helped fuel growth in some neighborhoods while others would be hit hard by the realignment.

New York City's population plateaued in 1950 at just shy of eight million. For the next twenty years, the total population remained stable because an influx of African Americans and Puerto Ricans offset the loss of the white population. But then, starting in the early 1970s, the city's population began a dramatic decline, losing about 10% of its residents in that decade. Fortunately for the overall health of the city, the total headcount bottomed out by 1980 and has been rising since then. In 2000, the city as a whole recorded its highest population ever.

New York's single decade of population loss contrasts sharply with other manufacturing cities from Maryland to Maine, and from the Atlantic Ocean to the Mississippi River. The census for Buffalo, New York, for example, showed a peaked in 1950 at 580,000, and it continues to lose population to this day. Similarly Chicago's population peaked around 1950, and has nearly one million fewer people today compared to then. Newark, New Jersey's population also peaked in 1950, at nearly 439,000 people. Over the next several decades it steadily lost about 40% of its residents. Newark, unlike Buffalo, however has seen its population stabilize since 1990 as it benefits from being in the orbit of New York.

Land prices reflected the postwar growth and economic collapse of the 1970s. Between 1950 and 1971, the land value index went from 104 to 157, an average increase of 2.5% per year. But the recession that hit the city in 1969 would beat down land prices, so that by 1977, the index was back at 48; the same place it had been in 1880! [33]

Urban Bankruptcy

The post-World War II era followed on the heels of President Franklin Roosevelt's New Deal. Government became increasingly involved in the private lives of citizens in the attempt to relieve poverty, discrimination, and segregation. New York City was at the forefront of the American trend to fight a "war on poverty" and created government policies that aimed to improve the lives of those in the lower and middle classes.

The 1950s and 1960s were a period of great experimentation by governments at all levels. The belief in America's power, resources, and technological capabilities, led to the idea that lawmakers could develop a set of policies to eliminate poverty and increase the quality of life for the city and citizens alike. As a result, the programs for welfare, social security, food stamps, housing, and slum clearance were greatly expanded.[34]

For New York City and State, these policies were being implemented while the city's tax base was stable at best. Between 1956 and 1966, the city's budget increased from $1.74 billion to $3.88 billion. In real terms, this was an 82% increase, yet population increased by 1.5% in the same period.[35]

Historically, the city's increased government expenditures, such as the Croton Aqueduct System or the subway system were largely paid for by the economic growth it engendered. But the postwar social welfare system was created at a time when the city's fiscal resources were diminishing. As a result, Mayor John Lindsay (1966–1973) resorted to paying for expanded programs with borrowed money.[36] Short-term debt tripled in the four years between 1971 and 1974.

The city's fiscal crisis began in February 1975, when a state agency, the Urban Development Corporation, was unable to sell one-year notes to pay off expiring ones. This created a crisis of confidence, under the logic that if a state agency could not get financing, the financial health of the city itself must also be very poor. By the spring of 1975, under the mayoralty of Abraham D. Beame (1974–1977), Wall Street was no longer willing to finance the city's mounting debt, putting it on the brink of default.

To avoid this scenario, a series of reforms were instituted. The government would cut back its expenditures and eliminate budget gimmicks and deficits; in return, the state would assist with financial restructuring. One of the lasting effects of this plan was the creation of the Financial Control Board (FCB). If the city was ever unable to balance its budget, the FCB was authorized to take over the budgeting process. This credible threat for the loss of autonomy was an important means to force the city to keep its fiscal house in order. [37]

The resultant drop in services due to budget cutbacks, however, only served to promote the perception that the city was spinning out of control. Crime, poverty, and a general sense of hopelessness pervaded the streets. It warrants repeating that in the 1970s, the city lost 823,000 people, which was more the entire state of Idaho in 1970. All of this retrenchment and chaos, of course, reduced the value of the island, so that it reached its lowest point in 1977, arguably the darkest time for the city. Clearly John Jacob Astor's vision was eradicated in the 1970s. What would he have thought on his deathbed if told that his holdings might someday be worthless?

Housing Abandonment

The loss of the value of place was the direct cause of a massive wave of housing abandonment that affected the historic tenement districts of the city. As the socially mobile immigrant populations left these neighborhoods, the residents who remained were poorer and less skilled. The result was a drop in landlords' incomes, which corresponded with a large rise in costs and property taxes. This drove a downward spiral in the quality of low-income housing. Landlords would cut back on essential services and maintenance, further reducing the housing quality, and all the while neglecting to pay mounting property tax bills.

At some point, the value of the outstanding tax bills became greater than the market value of the property. When this happens, the rational behavior is to abandon the property (or burn it down to collect the insurance money), and eliminate the net loss to the landlord. As abandonment increased, it exacerbated the drop in the quality of life in these neighborhoods. Few wanted to live near abandoned properties, as they are magnets for drug users and homeless people, and they also signal that the neighborhood is depressed. This meant that areas like Harlem and the South Bronx in the 1970s and 1980s were truly slums. Their populations were dropping fast, the quality of life was terrible, and poverty, crime, and drug use were rampant.

Under Mayor Edward I. Koch (1978–1989), the city developed a plan to return the abandoned properties to the market. As the economy improved in the 1980s and 1990s, much of the land was sold, and real estate development returned. But the process was slow and uneven, and the urban ills of crime, poverty, and drugs remained.

1977 to 1992

Land values in Manhattan bottomed out in the year 1977, two years after the Fiscal Crises. Despite many of the lingering urban problems that plagued the streets, prices from there began a steady climb until their peak in 1988. The city at large was still suffering from the Great Shakeout, when it was hit by another affliction: crack cocaine. This highly concentrated form of cocaine swept through the city and devastated the poorest neighborhoods. While crime had been steadily rising since the 1960s, the crack epidemic brought crime to new heights. In 1990, 2,262 people were murdered in New York City, as compared to about 300 in 1950.[38]

Under Mayor Koch the government began to return to a more stable budgetary situation. The economic prospects of the country improved in the 1980s, after Fed Chairman Paul Volker spiked interest rates to wring out inflation. Wall Street's growth was rapid due to a great "Bull Run." In 1979, the S&P Index was at about 100, and it hit 500 by mid-1994, an average increase of about 10% per year. Consider that the index had been around 100 in 1968, so that for a decade the stock market had been flat. The run up in equities was, of course, a boom to Wall Street employment. Important innovations on the Street, such as junk bonds and leveraged buyouts, also helped fuel growth.[39] The 1980s also saw a tremendous office building boom in both the city and the United States. This boom helped push up land values.

From a low of 48 in 1977, the land value index rose to 664 by 1988, about 24% per year! New York's rebound was nothing short of remarkable. The recession that followed put the brakes on the land value growth for a few years. But then . . .

1993 to 2013

Since 1993, Manhattan has witnessed a great inflation in the price of land. Part of this is due to New York's renaissance, which can be tied to several local and global factors.

First, locally, since the early 1990s, crime rates in New York City steadily declined. Murders across the city precipitously dropped thanks to an improving economy, higher incarceration rates, a drop in the youth population, and more aggressive and proactive crime fighting strategies.[40] The city's fiscal situation remained stable because of the laws that imposed budgetary discipline. Some of the rise in real estate values across the city can be attributed to the improved quality of life and security that comes with less crime in the city.[41]

But perhaps just as importantly, after the Great Shakeout subsided, New York retained its attractiveness as a city and place to do business. The nation's largest city has been able to grow because of the tremendous forces of agglomeration, and its ability to add buildings to the skyline.

Given the renewed popularity of New York and Manhattan we would, of course, expect sharp land value growth. But, in a relatively open market extreme growth would be met by competition. A rise in prices, either real estate or land, would be met with increased building, which would then reduce prices or price growth. Instead from 1993 to 2007, the index went from 133 to 3,727, an average annual growth rate of 23.8% per year! This is much better than what we saw in the glory days of Manhattan's growth after the Civil War. For a few years, after the financial crises, land values fell, but the eventually rebounded, and by 2013, there were back where they had been in 2007; prices are poised to go to ever greater heights.

Fifteen years of nearly uninterrupted growth at such an unprecedented rate can only suggest one thing: the demand to work and live in Manhattan is far greater than developers' ability to supply real estate to meet this growing demand. In other words, the cost of housing and office space has become so profitable because of the restrictions placed upon the market, that those owners of land have reaped monopoly profits.

But what are the causes of these restrictions? First are the distortions placed on the market by rent stabilization and vacancy decontrol. New construction tends to be expensive market rate luxury condo or apartments, which are highly profitable. A set of policies has aimed to incentivize the provision of affordable housing by giving developers density bonuses or low-interest loans if they set aside or construct units for middle- and lower income households. But these policies do not systematically address the major supply problem.[42]

Second is the difficulty of the construction process itself. Over the years, city policy has placed more and more roadblocks on the market as an attempt to regulate construction. A substantial fraction of real estate is within a landmarked district, and therefore there are considerable hurdles that prevent new, large-scale construction.[43] In an attempt to use zoning for its planning goals, the city has created a very complicated and drawn-out zoning process. For large-scale projects, developers find that if they want to increase the size of their project, they have to negotiate with the city for the right to do so. The city demands some amenity in return, such as a renovated subway station or park. But this just serves to delay and draw out the process.

Furthermore, developers appear reluctant to purchase older buildings, tear them down, and redevelop these sites. First zoning rules generally limit the bulk of these buildings, plus the expense and difficulty of evicting tenants makes the process not cost-effective. The irony of this situation is that if there were more teardowns and redevelopments, tenants would be much less reluctant to leave their current apartments. So there is a catch-22 at work. Teardowns are only possible if tenants are willing to move, but tenants would only move if there were more teardowns (and redevelopments). In the Epilogue, I suggest some policy ideas to eliminate this trap.

WHAT IS MANHATTAN WORTH?

Chapter 1 asked the question, what would the island look like if we removed the buildings, roads, dirt, hot dog carts, cars, people, and all of the other things that reside on top of the island, and just viewed the bedrock? Now we turn to hypothetical question of similar style. Imagine now that we keep the streets, roads and parks, but just remove the buildings. We now have prepared vacant Manhattan for sale. How much would someone have to pay to own Manhattan? One way to think about this is to pretend that all landowners sell their ownership claims to one person or company, who then would be able to collect ground rents from all of the occupants living on or above the surface. How much would that right be worth?

Once we can come up with an answer we can then compare that value in 2013 to the fictional value of $24 (essentially zero) in 1626, a benchmark number, which indicated the approximate value to a rag tag group of settlers, randomly scattered about the lower tip, with nary a thought that someday Manhattan would be one of the world's most important locations on planet Earth. Was that "$24" well spent? Could it have been invested somewhere else and given a better return?

As described above, the statistical analysis from 1950 to 2013 investigated how vacant land sales have varied across time and across the island itself. The regression was able to determine how much of the value of each parcel was determined by its size, location, and the year. The index shows how land values have changed over time, holding constant the other things that are different from lot to lot. Thus, the index is a measure of Manhattan's relative value over time.

But what is its actual market value? To determine this I performed a similar exercise as done in chapter 7, where predicted values are created for vacant land prices based on their various characteristics. In chapter 7 we saw how different supply and demand variables could account for skyscraper heights since the late nineteenth century. Here, predicted values can be used to derive an average per square foot land costs for all of the neighborhoods across the island. This information is then used to estimate the total value of developable land in each neighborhood, which is then allows for a calculation of the total value of developable land on the island. All told, developable land constitutes about 60% of the island; the rest is used for roads, streets, docks, and parks.[44]

So what is Manhattan worth? The market value of Manhattan, as of the end of 2013, is estimated to be between $1.4 trillion and $1.8 trillion. Taking the average gives $1.6 trillion. At its peak in 2007, the island would have been valued closer to $1.97 trillion. To put this into context, the value of Gross Domestic Product (GDP) in the United States in 2013 was $16.8 trillion. But we must consider a GDP to land values comparison as a kind of apples-to-oranges situation. Land values represent wealth—the total accumulation of income; while GDP represents the net value-added of goods and services produced each year.

Nevertheless, we can ask how much it would cost to buy Manhattan or to buy every good and service produced in the United States. In 2007, the answer is about $2 trillion would either buy Manhattan or purchase 1/8th of the GDP of the United States. Or for the same money, you could purchase the entire output of Indonesia and Turkey, which each have GDPs in the $800 billion range. The GDP of New York State is about $1.2 trillion. Another way to look at this is to ask: if we assembled the world's richest people in one room, how many of them would be needed to muster all of their wealth to buy Manhattan. In 2013, it would take about fifty of the world's richest billionaires to collectively buy the island.[45]

And now the final question: What has been the average annual return on Manhattan over nearly four centuries? As of 2013, the answer is that the average annual growth rate since day one to today has been about 6.4% per annum. This is pretty good, considering, for example, since 1790, the average annual growth rate of the entire US economy has been 3.7%. The average annual growth rate of the Standard & Poor's Composite Index has been 6.0%.[46]

SKYSCRAPERS AND LAND VALUES: A LONG-RUN PERSPECTIVE

Throughout the book, we have discussed the relationship between skyscrapers and land values. One perspective is that high land values cause skyscrapers to be constructed. Since land values are a large fixed cost, real estate developers have an incentive to use the land more intensely when land values go up. Developers in this sense are land farmers, raising "crops" of steel from the ground.

But some people have argued that the skyscraper artificially increases the value of land by funneling so many people into a particular location, because of the will of the developer.[47] A low density environment suddenly becomes high density when a tall building is erected. The Empire State Building was constructed to house 15,000 workers on an average work day; and several thousand more visit the observation deck.[48] Presumably that is several thousand more people that arrive to the corner of Fifth Avenue and 34th Street than would have otherwise done so.

But the question remains: Does the skyscraper satisfy a latent demand for place or does it drive people to go where they would otherwise not be? Is the tall building a way to satisfy the needs and wants of people, or is it acting like a fishnet drawing people there simply because of the strategic aims of the developer? That was certainly the thinking of many in the early days of the skyscraper, and it is what prompted Clark and Kingston to write their book.[49]

Developers, of course, might have multiple and varied reasons for building tall, as has been documented throughout this book. The ego- or monument-based reasons attracted great attention from the 1890s until the Great Depression; and the assumption was that these buildings did not pay a reasonable profit on investment—meaning they were economically inefficient. Edward Basset, the head of the Heights of Buildings Commission, held this view when drafting the report for the 1916 zoning laws. He wrote in the report,

Few skyscrapers pay large net returns. Most of them pay only moderate returns. The cost per cubic foot of tall buildings is greater than that for low buildings. . . . [T]he very tall buildings demand many things out of proportion to their increased bulk. . . . [T]he great item of waste in the high building is the big loss of valuable renting space on the lower floors due to the dead run of the express elevators to the upper floors."[50]

There was plenty of evidence to back up this claim. In 1910, for example, F. W. Woolworth told the *New York Times* about his soon-to-be-built eponymous tower, "I do not want a mere building, I want something that will be an ornament to the city."[51] In 1928, Darwin P. Kingsley, president of New York Life Insurance, said at the opening of his company's new tower, "The skyline of New York is singularly beautiful because it expresses power; it strikes a new note of power. . . . [O]ur objective has been to express in this building the power that makes the New York skyline beautiful."[52]

To this day, the supertall structures that rise in skylines across the world are considered wasted investments, especially the ones in Asia. Economist Andrew Lawrence compares the approximate completion dates for the world's tallest buildings and offers the claim that they come online roughly at the same time that a financial crisis hits. He concludes that his timeline,

[C]ontinues to show an unhealthy correlation between construction of the next world's tallest building and an impending financial crisis: New York 1930, Chicago 1974; Kuala Lumpur 1997 and Dubai 2010. Yet often the world's tallest buildings are simply the edifice of a broader skyscraper building boom, reflecting a widespread misallocation of capital and an impending economic correction.[53]

It remains an open question as to whether skyscrapers are a cause or an effect of high land values. If skyscrapers are a result of high land values, it suggests that skyscrapers are solving the problem of land allocation. If skyscrapers are driving high land values, it suggests that skyscrapers might, in fact, be a diversion of resources away from productive uses and a cause of urban problems.

To test for the causal link skyscrapers and land values, we return to the long-run time series that was discussed in chapter 6—the total additions to the skyline and the height of the tallest building completed each year from 1885 to 2013. The goal is to see how the ups and downs of skyscraper construction over the years relate to changes in land values.

To investigate the causal nexus between the two, we employ a statistical method known in as "Granger causality." Dr. Clive Granger (1934-2009) was a Nobel-prize winning economist who developed many important statistical methods that economists use to understand the relationships between economic variables, say X and Y. With numerical information, it is often difficult to disentangle causation and correlation; thus Granger argues that if one is to conclude that X *causes* Y, then two things, at a minimum, should be present in the data. First, the causal factor will occur *before* the effect, so that changes in X should come before any changes in Y. Second, if we want to forecast future values of some important variable (such as the number of skyscraper completions two years from now), then predictions about Y should be more accurate if the statistical analysis incudes past values of X.[54]

The way to do this is to perform a regression to see if the values of Y are statistically determined not only by past values of Y but also by past values of X. If the answer is "yes," X is said to "Granger cause" Y, and it suggests the presence of causality. In this case, a set of regressions was performed that investigated changes in the skyline measures based on past values of these measures, and past values of land values growth. The idea is to see how well we can predict or forecast the future values of the skyline measures simply based on past values of the measures, versus past measures and land values growth (see appendix CC for results).

Broadly speaking, we can see from figures 10.1 and 6.1 that land value and skyscraper cycles since 1895 are roughly coincident. There were peaks in both around 1913, and then again, in the late 1920s. The postwar era has shown there are skyscraper cycles (1950-1977, 1977-1992, 1992-2013); similarly, land values have shown this cyclical behavior. It suggests that land values and skyscraper buildings move together in predictable ways.

But the questions remain: Does knowing something about past land value growth help predict additions to the skyline? And does knowing something about past skyscraper construction tell us something about land values growth? The answer from the statistical analysis is that, in fact, past land value growth is, indeed, informative about changes to the skyline. Another way of saying this is the land value growth "Granger causes" building height, or building height is statistically determined by land value growth. It passes the test for Granger causality and allows us to conclude that it strongly suggests economic causality as well: the skyscraper is a response to the land values, which are a signal about pent up demand for geography. These results occur both when looking at the tallest completed building each year, and the total additions to the skyline.

However, the reverse is not true. The statistical results show that past skyline growth does not improve the forecast of land prices. In other words, the statistical tests reject the idea that skyscraper height Granger causes land value growth and suggests little evidence that building height is creating artificially high land values. These tests indicate that developers are fundamentally responding to the demand for height, rather than imposing height on the public. In other words, it is not so much that the skyscraper is a "machine that makes the land pay," as was claimed by Cass Gilbert in 1900, but rather that the skyscraper is a machine that allows people to get paid.[55]

Epilogue
The Resilient Skyline?

London is satisfied, Paris is resigned, but New York is always hopeful. Always it believes that something good is about to come off, and it must hurry to meet it.
Dorothy Parker

It'll be a great place if they ever finish it.
O. Henry

In 2009, New York celebrated the 400th anniversary of Henry Hudson's arrival in the region. It has been the goal of this book to chronicle how the once diminutive Amsterdam-in-the-woods grew to be the skyline capital of America. One of the themes has been that not only the people, but the city itself and its buildings have always been in a constant state of flux. Since competition among the citizens-as-strivers generates an immense battle for place, the winners have the right to create something new and better on their property—to the victor belongs the spoils. The city is a creative-destruction machine; its success has been premised on embracing this concept.

But New York in the early twenty-first century faces very different challenges vis-à-vis the early twentieth century, when the skyline was in its infancy. In an attempt to preserve its rich history and to help those who were unfairly treated in the battle for place, the city has enacted a suite of policies aimed at improving the quality of life for its residents. While these rules and regulations were often designed with the best of intentions, collectively, they have not always succeeded; in fact, the city risks being choked by these very policies.

After a decade of population loss in the 1970s, New York City began to grow again. By the year 2000, it recorded its highest population ever and continues to add people; this success has caused some problems. In particular, housing prices are at an all-time high, and the city suffers from an affordability crisis. The demand to live and work in New York is outstripping the willingness and ability of the real estate community to supply the needed space.[1] Government policy has created this imbalance and only changes in government policy can rectify it.

While Manhattan's demographic path was a bit different than the city as a whole, the problems it faces today are just as great. Around 1910, the island's population peaked at 2.33 million. From there it continued to fall to a low of 1.43 million by 1980, when it started growing again. In 2013, Manhattan's population is 70% of what it was at its peak. While I am not advocating a return to the type of density seen in the Lower East Side in 1900 as described in chapter 4, it is reasonable to say that the city can hold a much larger population than the one it has. But the combined forces of rent stabilization, zoning regulations, real estate tax policy, and landmarking have perverted the real estate market to what it is today—overly expensive and unresponsive to market conditions across the income spectrum.[2]

When we consider how many major crises have afflicted New York City, it is a wonder to think how it has survived. It has suffered from major fires that destroyed substantial swaths of the landscape; it suffered repeated outbreaks of epidemics, including smallpox, yellow fever, and cholera; it has been victim to crime and drug epidemics, several major riots, and, of course, it has been victim to terrorist attacks.[3] Yet the city has not only survived, but has thrived, figuring out ways to solve these problems so that their threats are minimized. For New York, the major crises that loom large are the combined forces of sea-level rise and climate change, along with a self-created housing shortage. For these problems, the skyscraper remains a helpful and hopeful solution.[4]

POLICY RECOMMENDATIONS FOR THE TWENTY-FIRST CENTURY

No modern, market-based society is free of conflicts and crises. Once humanity tethered itself to the marketplace as the central means to organize its economic life, it meant that cities were going to be part of the solution to the material problems we face. But the city, itself, as a community of people, is a living, breathing organism—and like all organisms its survival depends on its fitness. Unlike Darwin's finches, however, this organism can adapt itself—it can evolve from within to better fit its changing environment.

The key to this adaptation toward a new fitness is to promote the type of creative-destruction that made the city so successful.[5] There was nothing inherent about New York's success. It was handed an advantage, to be sure, with an excellent and centrally located harbor; but its growth was based on the decisions made by government and citizens alike, each who played a role in its growth. The state built the canal so the merchants could trade; the government built the Croton Aqueduct system so citizens could live their lives in a healthy manner; the government regulated building height but did not restrict it, and thus allowed for New York's skylines upward growth. The future should look like this: the government should promote investments that allow citizens to unleash their creativity and their new ideas. It should not fear the new, but embrace it. The cost of these investments can be paid through the growth of the metropolis.

Perhaps the biggest and most pressing problem is that of climate change. Since 1751, humanity has released 337 billion metric tons of carbon into the atmosphere that had been formed and sequestered underground for billions of years.[6] This radical movement of carbon has caused us to deeply consider the interaction of the human species with biosphere in which it resides. Are we like a parasitic virus that will ultimately kill the host or are we likely to develop a more symbiotic relationship with the natural world? Will we make our world more sustainable and resilient?[7]

The second crisis is housing affordability. Between 2000 and 2012, for example, median apartment rents have increased by 75%, compared to 44% in the rest of the country. In 2000, renters earning between $20,000 and $40,000 (in inflation-adjusted dollars) were spending 33% of their income for housing, and by 2012, that figure jumped to 41%.[8] The loss of affordable housing has occurred despite Mayor Bloomberg's commitment during his tenure to preserve or create 165,000 units. Under Mayor De Blasio the problem is not getting better, despite the recent introduction of his ten-year plan. The fundamental problem is that new construction is constrained. Developers are unable or unwilling to build the new housing needed to reduce prices.

Affordability is also related to gentrification, the process where young, upwardly mobile, middle-class residents move into formerly lower income neighborhoods. Gentrification occurs when these residents are priced out of their preferred neighborhoods and take advantage of lower cost housing in "rising" neighborhoods. But, gentrification then bids up the price of housing in that neighborhood. In a relatively free market, however, more housing should be supplied in nearby neighborhoods as a result; if government policy disincentivizes new construction, however, then older residents who want to remain in the neighborhood will be priced out. The point is that gentrification and the loss of affordable housing do not have to go hand-in-hand. Given the current set of policies, gentrification has become a kind of urban merry-go-round. As prices rise in one neighborhood, the would-be gentrifiers move on to the next one and housing affordability declines that much more.

If we encourage new construction to keep up with the demand, it will have multiple effects. It will lower the price of building space and it will allow the older remaining structures to be used for other purposes that make the city so interesting and unique. Further, it will promote economic growth and a modernization of the city's building stock. Old buildings are charming to be sure and they help contribute to the beauty of the urban fabric, but we cannot aim to preserve the city for this reason alone. Preservation for the sake of preservation is the role of the museum, and we do not want to turn the city into a museum.

The solution contains, in part, a skyscraper solution. First, tall buildings allow for a much greater concentration of people who want to live and work in the city—they satisfy the demand for urban living. And they can do so in a much more eco-friendly way.[9] Next, because of the imperative of technological innovation, new buildings are inherently better suited to the realities of the twenty-first century. Skyscrapers are more able deal with climate change, sea level rise, and other possible disasters, such as earthquakes, as the building codes can require new safety and resiliency features. And perhaps just as importantly, they can address the housing affordability problem.

But we must also remember that no real estate policy works in isolation, since the city is a system of interrelated parts. When one policy is designed to improve the lives of its residents, it impacts the "general equilibrium" of the urban fabric in some way. The city can be thought of as a combined geography and market system, where people are making decisions about where to work, live, and play, based on the relative prices of being at, and traveling to, different locations. Changes in one part of the system affect the relative prices across the system as a whole, and, as such, change the general suite of incentives. This is a fancy way of saying that policies can often backfire by creating a set of unintended consequences that were not thought of because policymakers were simply thinking of the parts and not the whole.

A classic example is landmarking. The devastating loss of Penn Station in the early 1960s woke up the world to fact that grand civic architectural gems were not immune from the creative-destruction process (see figure 9.2). Penn Station had been an aging giant. Train ridership peaked during World War II. Postwar America was distinctly car based. By 1960, inter-city train ridership fell to 27% of passenger traffic.[10] In an attempt to make something profitable from the site, the owners sold the air rights to developers who built Madison Square Garden and a fifty-seven-story office tower above the station. Horror was met with reaction. In 1965, the city created the Landmarks Preservation Commission in order that similar structures avoid the same fate. While preservation is important, it is not without consequences. By removing a large fraction of the land for new development, it makes land scarcer and drives up the price.[11]

The key to New York's future growth is to design policies that create flexibility and promote the rapid movement of people and goods and services. A resilient and more affordable city will emerge as a result.

Recommendation 1: Expand Manhattan

In 1686, the Common Council undertook the project of expanding the island—of reclaiming land from the sea. The reason was that land was scarce. In an age when the foot was the primary means of transportation, it was convenient to build out the lower tip of the island so the city had more land and wharfage. To enact this policy, the Common Council sold "water lots" to the adjacent landowners who then had the responsibility to fill in the land and to build streets and retaining walls or docks. Water lots sold for roughly one-quarter to one-third of the price of land.

This policy should be employed once again. That is to say, the city should create new land by the process of infill and/or creating platforms into New York Bay. This idea is similar in spirit to Michael Bloomberg's 2013 proposal to build a "Seaport City" on the East River to mirror Battery Park City on the Hudson River; but the plan should be more expansive than this. The city should aim to grow itself by a thousand or more acres, such as by connecting the Battery to Governors Island, and beyond.[12] Imagine adding back for development the equivalent of Central Park.

New York City has a long tradition of not only creating new land but also selling the air rights over areas often considered off-limits for construction. Take the case of the construction of Grand Central Station in early 1900s, which was financed, in part, by the selling of air rights over the tracks. The forty-seven-story Waldorf Astoria sits on piers constructed between the networks of railroads, where scores of trains pass daily. On top of the approach to the George Washington Bridge is an entire apartment complex, built on piers over the highway. In 1960, the government sold the rights to a developer, netting over one million dollars. Today, the complex houses some 4,000 people.

Manhattan's current largest development is the Hudson Yards Redevelopment Project. In May 2010, the Metropolitan Transit Authority leased the air rights over the rail yard for ninety-nine years, and in return, it will earn $1 billion for improvements of the city's transportation infrastructure. A platform is being built above the tracks to hold sixteen skyscrapers.

New land will help solve several problems. First, creating this land will open up Manhattan to new economic development and help alleviate the housing shortage. Second, the land will generate additional sources of income. Given the high cost of land, air rights sales might, in fact, return a net profit to the city above the cost of producing the land. Also, the new development will add real estate to the tax rolls.

Perhaps more important, the creation of a new, raised land-bed in New York Harbor can help protect the island against rising sea levels and the more frequent and damaging storms due to climate change. Since 1856, water in New York Bay has risen, on average, 1.1 inches per decade, so that today, sea levels are about a foot and half higher than the middle of the nineteenth century. Some projections have sea levels in New York rising 1 to 3 feet over the century.[13]

Ironically, the land created in the seventeenth and eighteenth centuries made Manhattan more vulnerable to the effects of sea-level rise. In October 2012, when Hurricane Sandy flooded a large part of Lower Manhattan, the greatest damage was over that part created by infill or the reclamation of wetlands. Yet one area of landfill remained relatively unscathed: Battery Park City, constructed in the 1970s. Figure E.1 shows the parts of Lower Manhattan inundated by the storm, and a comparison with the Viele map (figure 2.3) shows the worst-hit areas were in the historical landfill zones, but not in the most recent ones. Figure E.1 demonstrates that new land, properly planned, can act as a useful buffer against storm surges. The project can also employ soft protection measures by constructing wetlands around the perimeter. The new skyscrapers can also have the lower floors raised several feet above the ground to minimize flood damage.

Recommendation 2: End Price Controls in the Housing Market

New York has the lowest homeownership rate of any major city in the country; renters make up nearly 70% of occupants. Today, 45.7% of renters in the city live in rent stabilized units, 1.8% live in rent controlled units, 8.8% live in public housing, and 38.6% live in units with prices set by the market.[14] In short, less than four out of ten rental units in the city are available to operate according the laws of supply and demand. Since the late 1990s, many rent stabilized apartments have been subject to vacancy decontrol, where once the units are vacant the price can float according to the market rates. But this plan has backfired in the sense that it has not encouraged the building of new middle-class housing in the city, and it has not solved the affordability problem.

The demand for living in the city is so great that when new units are decontrolled, they are still rented at the unaffordable, low-supply rates. In 2014, Manhattan's housing vacancy rate was a mere 1.64%. Ironically, the government justifies the rent stabilization program on the grounds that New York suffers from a housing shortage; but it is this very program that creates this shortage in the first place; and the program is like a perpetual motion machine.[15]

There is no reason that in the twenty-first century, the government of one of the world's most productive cities should be in the business of setting housing prices. This is not to say that there is no role for important housing initiatives, especially for those in the lowest income brackets. But rent stabilization helps the lucky few while they have the apartment, but makes the overall housing market worse for everyone else; all the while, it reduces the flexibility of those in the rent stabilized apartment because they have less incentive to move when their life circumstances change.[16]

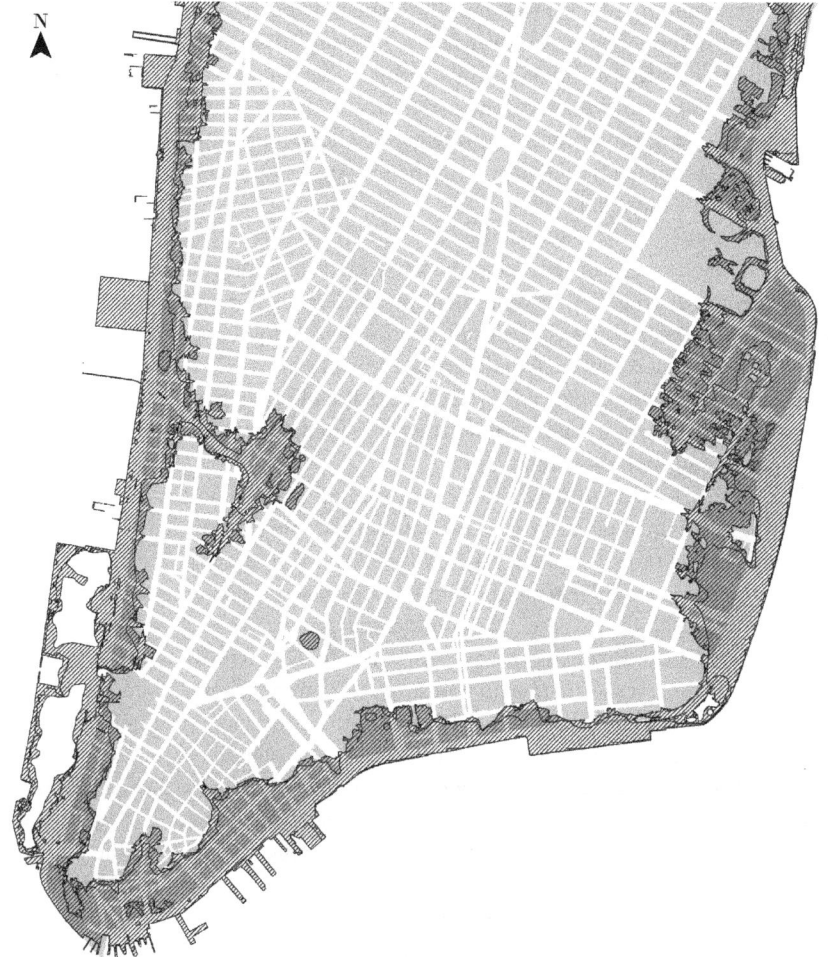

▨ AREA FLOODED BY HURRICANE SANDY

Figure E.1 The Sandy effect. This map shows the area of Lower Manhattan that was flooded by Hurricane Sandy in 2012. We can see that much of the land that was inundated was made land, filled in over the centuries since 1626. Note, however, that one area was relatively unscathed: Battery Park City, which was created from infill in the 1970s. This suggests that making new land, with climate change in mind, can protect Lower Manhattan from sea-level rise as well as damage from storm surges.

Source: Map by Eon Kim. Inundation zone data courtesy of the National Resources Defense Council.

The reason rent stabilization continues year after year is because those who stand to lose in the short run have an undue influence on the political process. If the mayor tells the current beneficiaries that their benefits will end, they will, of course, be very upset; and rightly so. No one feels that he or she should be the "sacrificial lamb" for a change in policy, nor should the city make those people pay a large price. Any change away from rent stabilization should try to not only minimize the costs but also assuage the current beneficiaries that the change is ultimately good for them and the city.

But would ending rent stabilization be a panacea? No. But, it would end some of the distortions in the housing market. If price controls did end so that all apartments were valued according to their quality and size, then empty-nesters, for example, would now have an incentive to downsize and let the apartment be occupied by a larger family or a group of recent college grads who want to share an apartment and still maintain a modicum of dignity with their living quarters. In that regard, housing allocation will be more efficient.

Because renters in stabilized units slow down turnover, they make it much less likely that a developer can redevelop the site to reflect its most profitable use. If half the tenants are getting a good deal, then the landlord is not going to want to battle with them to leave. As a result, rent stabilization implicitly reduces the growth of the housing stock. Rent stabilized tenants are not going to move to a new apartment in the city, if new units are not being added at a rate that will bring down the relative cost of housing. In order for rent stabilization to be eliminated, the city to needs to implement both a carrot and stick approach.

First, rent stabilization needs to be removed all at once and not using vacancy decontrol; but it must occur in a future time so that current beneficiaries have some time to develop alternative plans; let's say seven years. In the first five years, the rent stabilization board would meet and set rental rates growth according to the same metrics that it has used in the past: rent is increased generally based on the inflation of housing costs. Then starting in year five, rents are allowed to move to closer to market rents; similarly in year six and then in year seven, all rent price regulations are dropped.

In the meantime, the city needs to promote the construction of new housing to lower the overall prices and to increase the flexibility of renters when they lose their rent subsidies. The city needs to grease the wheels of middle-class housing construction. As a rule, I do not think the government should be using subsidies and tax abatements to promote housing construction, but it is needed in this case to undo the long-term effects of rent controls. To this end, the new middle-class housing should be given tax abatements for a fixed period of time, such as for ten years. The abatement itself must gradually fall over the period, so that at the end of the tenth year, property taxes are at the standard level. In other words, the tax abatements should be particularly generous in the early years and become less so in the later years. The point is to stimulate housing construction and not to favor one group over another with permanent tax breaks.

Ending rent stabilization, of course, cannot happen in isolation to the policies outlined below.

Recommendation 3: Reform the Land-Use Rules

By the turn of the twentieth century, all cities across the country were witnessing the effects that new technology had on the urban landscape. Arguably, the most important of these were the automobile and truck. For businesses, the truck dramatically altered the location calculus. Formerly, rail lines segregated land-use types. Factories and warehouses were tied to inter-city trunk and branch lines, while households hugged the streetcar lines.

But then, firms no longer needed to be close to the port or rail lines, but were free to choose locations where there was more land, light, and less congestion. The automobile also allowed workers to commute to these new sites. This new mobility meant that households in residential neighborhoods no longer had protections against the kinds of economic activity that would occur there. Large industrial concerns were now footloose, as it were, and could open up shop in a quiet suburban neighborhood. Residents, fearing the worst, sought protections from the state.[17]

A second effect was the rise of the tall building. Again, technological change meant that there were few engineering limits to how tall a building could go. This generated a series of unintended consequences for the urban fabric. First, a tall office building would block the sunlight on the street or of other buildings. Nearby landowners would respond by constructing their own skyscraper to gain back the lost light. This then initiated a height arms race, further darkening the streets and increasing congestion—turning lower Broadway into a canyon. Second, low-rise buildings saw their rents fall when skyscrapers opened up around them. Businesses were drawn to the new buildings and rendered the older structures less valuable. Landlords and urban planners fearing the worst sought protection from the state.

The result of this was the city's first comprehensive zoning laws, enacted in 1916, which established land use, bulk, and height rules for every single plot of land in the city (see chapter 5). There were three use zones: residential, commercial, and unrestricted. Heights were regulated by the setback rules which required buildings to be set back from the street line based on the width of the street and the height multiple set by the city. Bulk requirements were set by limiting how much of the lot could be used for the structure.

Starting in 1961, bulk and height were limited by establishing floor area ratio (FAR) limits. Each lot was assigned a FAR value which could then dictate the maximum floor area and hence building volume; and this volume could be distributed however the owner desired, such as by a short bulky building or a tall slender one. Rules were also established to create off-street parking. And the city created many more fine-grained use categories. For example, rather than one residential category, the 1961 rules created ten, and within each one were different subcategories. There were also eight commercial districts and three manufacturing districts.

In addition, for large projects in the densest neighborhoods, developers could gain extra FAR bonuses if they provided a public amenity, such as a plaza. There were two unintended effects of the law, as it related to building height. First was the creation of the air rights market (aka transferable development rights), which allowed building owners with "excess" FARs to sell them to neighboring lots so a developer could build taller. Second, in the quest for ever greater FAR bonuses, developers began negotiating with the city for high FARs in exchange for subway station upgrades, more parks, or other amenities.

After a half century of the current rules, zoning, once again, needs of an upgrade. The rules are incredibly complex and navigating the system increases the cost and time to completion.[18] The regulations also reduce the flexibility of builders by being overly restrictive on what can be built. Third, they confer an undue advantage on those with the power and knowledge to negotiate with the city. Given the time and expense needed, they encourage large, multi-lot projects at the expense of the more mundane, small site projects, which are likely to have greater impacts on the city as a whole.

The economic base of the city has radically shifted since 1961. Manufacturing is now a tiny part of the urban economy, employing less than 2% of city workers, and the threat of factory pollution in the heart of the city has all but disappeared.[19] As the service economy has taken hold, and as computerization has become deeply engrained in our daily lives, the lines between work, family life, and leisure have become increasingly blurry. The city succeeds because people are able to mix and meet and take advantage of this proximity. The zoning rules need to be less restrictive as a result.

My policy suggestion is to remove and reform the zoning rules that we currently have now. Let's start with a clean slate. These changes must also be tied to policy adjustments discussed below, especially as it relates to real estate taxes and transportation. First, the city should return to a three-use zone system, rather than the arcane and byzantine system in place today.[20] The first use type should be called "urban use" and should permit any mix of commercial, office, residential, and even light manufacturing.

To some degree, we see this now along the avenues in the skyscraper districts, but these districts are generally Class A offices with condos and mall-like stores. Jane Jacobs railed against the sterilizing effects of homogeneous land uses, and I agree— neighborhoods should be diverse and the market prices are a good way to signal to developers and to businesses the kinds of mixes that are needed.[21] If housing is in short supply, then the price will rise causing more apartments to be built, or non-housing units will be converted to housing; if office space is in short supply, then its price will rise and so on. The important thing is that the city needs to be pro-active in making sure the nuisances of multiple uses (such as noise levels or odors) in a building are kept to a minimum; the Department of Buildings needs to strictly enforce nuisance laws that unduly harm households in mixed-used structures.

The second area can be residential only. This would be more relevant for the outer boroughs, which are predominantly suburban. There is no doubt that a large fraction of the residential population prefers the suburban lifestyle and residents in these neighborhoods are entitled to protection against encroachment. But we must be mindful that by limiting the bulk and use in these neighborhoods, we are imposing constraints on the city as a whole. The more limits in one neighborhood, the more likely it is that prices will rise in surrounding neighborhoods. However, if the economic disincentives for construction are removed, this negative effect can be minimized. The third use should be an unrestricted category, where factories, power plants, and other buildings are allowed to exist unimpeded.

In short, the goal of use-zoning is that the city should protect individuals against the most annoying and pernicious externalities that exist from dense urban living. But the rules should not, however, be used to micro-manage what people can and cannot do with their property.

Landmarking

Landmarking and historic preservation is an important and necessary condition if we are to maintain our urban history and the diversity of urban architecture. However, by removing or nearly removing buildings and entire neighborhoods from possible redevelopment, it reduces the available land for new projects that are necessary for urban growth. Once buildings are landmarked they tend to remain so; as time passes, the number of landmarked neighborhoods and structures continues to increase. To this end, it is important to maintain a high threshold for what gets landmarked. Also we need to keep in mind that these buildings are less likely to able to withstand possible natural disasters like hurricanes, earthquakes, and flooding. As of 2014, about 1,300 acres of developable land on Manhattan are either in a historic district or contain a landmarked property.[22] In other words, the equivalent of 1.5 Central Parks has essentially been removed for future development.

There are two strategies to handle the problems that landmarking introduces. First, as discussed above, is to add more land to the city. While I think this is a good idea, the problem is that land creation in this day and age is slow and fraught with political dangers. Environmental Impact Statements, protests by interest groups, and the general slow pace of government decision-making means that land-use creation is not a quick fix, though it is one that can be considered as a longer run policy tool.

Second is to create a more vigorous air rights market related to landmarked structures. The city has experimented with this, such as with Grand Central Station and the Broadway Theatre District, where air rights are permitted to be sold by the owners of the landmarked buildings. Air right sales allow the owner to be compensated, since landmarking a property is a soft form of taking by the city. In this case, the government is restricting the right of the landowner to use their land as they see fit. Air rights sales allow the owner some payment for this restriction. Air rights also provide income for the owner to maintain and restore the property to something closer to its original condition.

But, the process should be simpler and more systematic. Recent research suggests that air rights for landmarked properties are difficult to use and are underutilized.[23] The best strategy would be to create a law that requires that every time a building is landmarked, air rights for that structure must be created, and without regard to how dense the structure is. I would propose the number ten. That is to say, every time a structure is landmarked the quantity of air rights available for sale is ten times the lot area size. The point is that landmarking needs to both compensate the owners for the restricted use, and, just as important, it needs to allow for more real estate investment elsewhere.

This raises the question of where and how these air rights can be marketed. The standard principal of air rights, not related to landmarking, is that the air rights must be sold to neighboring properties so that the net bulk of the block remains constant. In the landmarking case, air is being released for more development; to this end, my suggestion is twofold. First the air rights should be sold within a specified zone around the building, say within a half mile or say a four-block radius around the property. This would help distribute the bulk and also keep surrounding neighborhoods from seeing higher prices.

Second, an open market for air rights should exist. That is to say, an Air Exchange should be created, where property owners sell their Air Rights Contracts to the highest bidder on an exchange market, and they can be purchased by any other property owner that qualifies, that is, has a non-landmarked property in the fixed radius. The contract could expire in say seven years; this way, speculators would not try to game the system by hoarding air rights. There should also be upper limits on how much of these air rights purchases can be used for any one building. One could even envision the creation of an Air Rights Index that would show the average prices of these contracts over time.

Regulating the FAR

More broadly, we need to think about the FAR system in general as a means for limiting urban bulk or density. I personally have no issue with limiting FARs across neighborhoods, but we need to recognize the effects on the real estate market. Right now, as will be discussed below, the maximum bulk of the entire city is effectively capped. Since each lot has a maximum FAR, no builder, without engaging in lengthy and complicated negotiations with the city, can build more than what is allowed. This essentially puts the city under a "FAR bubble." The city as a whole, including Manhattan, is nowhere near hitting the limits of the bubble (see below), but it is important to recognize that Manhattan's maximum density is capped as a result.[24]

Air rights are valuable because of this fixed bubble, and so, people can transfer their slice of the pie to others. But once air rights are sold, it means that a piece of land is effectively removed from development. This is fine if we want to preserve valuable architectural gems, but it also discourages the redevelopment and future growth of the city.

My suggestion would be that rather than establishing many different FAR limits throughout different neighborhoods of the city, we take a simpler approach. In the "urban use" category described above, which would likely be most, if not all of Manhattan, the law should specify a universal base FAR, somewhere between 10 and 15 (say 12.5).

That is, every landowner "as of right" can build a structure with maximum FAR of 12.5. Beyond that, however, the builder must pay a "FAR tax." This tax can be thought of as a kind of Pigovian Tax, where the builder must pay based on the externalities that are being imposed on the neighborhood, such as traffic congestion, taxing the infrastructure, or increasing class sizes in neighborhood schools. The point is that city rules should encourage construction but also limit the strain on the neighborhood.

In Michael Bloomberg's 2012 plan to rezone the East Side, he essentially proposed this idea—builders pay an extra fee for extra height. Interestingly, the City Club of New York asserted that it is a kind of extortion racket.[25] But from an economic point of view, the idea is reasonable. Builders should pay for the stresses that extra height imposes on the neighborhood. The plan is a simpler version of what many developers do now anyway and it should be applied citywide.[26]

Currently, if a developer wants to build a high-rise apartment building, and the demand is high enough, he might want to build up fifty stories. Under the old zoning rules he is given a base FAR of 10. He might provide an as-of-right amenity to get him to 12. Then he might try to snap up some air rights, giving a new FAR of say 15. Then, he negotiates with the city and tries to get a FAR of 18 by providing another amenity. If the land is not zoned for residential use, he first has to go through the rezoning process (ULURP). All of this takes time and resources, and delays construction further and further down the road.

Under my proposal, the developer can build as tall as she wants using a new economic calculus. First, she is given a higher base FAR, as compared to today, to encourage new development. Second, when she goes beyond that, she must pay a fee to the city in proportion to how much additional bulk she adds to the building—a FAR tax. The tax could even be progressive in that FARs over 15 are taxed at a higher rate than those below 15.

Let's say she pays a tax equal to 10% or 15% of the additional floor area constructed. This is a one-time fixed fee that is payable at the time the building is going to be issued a certificate of occupancy. This tax money is specifically to be used to compensate the city for the additional services required. I would propose that something like half of the revenue go into the city's general coffers and the other half be allocated to the local community boards, who can then decide if the money should be spent on say new parks, bike lanes, schools, subway station improvements, or whatever public projects are deemed a priority, with the consent of the City Council.

In an era of climate change, the new zoning codes can encourage sustainability. New buildings that can, for example, produce (ideally) a zero carbon footprint could be given a large as-of-right FAR bonus. If the developer adds solar panels, wind mills, organic waste processing facilities, and/or a green roof, then it helps move the city toward a more sustainable future.

In summary, the zoning rules need to be greatly simplified. They should not be used a planning tool or to impose notions of the "good city," but they rather should be used to limit the externalities and strains put upon the city for density, and they can encourage sustainability. Architects, developers, and the people they serve should be the arbiters of beauty. The rules should be loose enough to encourage sorely needed construction, but not so loose as to overly burden the neighborhoods. In other words, the rules should be established so that infrastructure and services growth can happen in parallel to the additions to the neighborhood's building stock.

Recommendation 4: Reform Real Estate Taxes

Since virtually day one, the real estate tax has been an important means by which the city raised revenues. Peter Stuyvesant, for example, assessed residents for money to build a canal along Broad Street. Like other aspects of city policy, the real estate tax system has become complex, arcane, and arbitrary. Today, the general process works something like this. Each year, assessors come up with an assessment figure, which is loosely based on the value of the property. The assessor designates two figures: the assessed value (AV) of the land and the AV of the entire property (land and structure combined).

Before the mid-twentieth century, the AV of the property more or less reflected its true market value.[27] The intent of the law was to tax people according to the value of their holdings, and thus, rich households paid more than poorer households. But over the years, the assessment and tax process become less directly tied to the market values.

The city now has different tax rates for different kinds of property; they use different methods to determine "market values," and they use different formulas to determine the property's AV. Also complicating matters is that when assessments rise very rapidly from one year to the next, the law requires that these increases be phased in over a five- or eight-year period with a total cap. On top of this is an array of abatements and subsidies that apply to different kinds of structures.[28]

As an example, relatively smaller homes, such as one- or two-family properties (Class 1) are assessed at 6% of "market value," where, in this case, market value is determined based on recent sales of comparable properties. Annual assessment increases are limited to 6%; increases above that are phased in over five years and limited to no more than 20%. These properties must pay a tax rate of $19.191 per $100 of AV.[29]

For larger residential properties and office buildings (Classes 2 and 4), AVs are determined at 45% of "market values," where market values are determined as some function of net income. Assessment increases in any year are limited to 8%, and no more than 30% over five years for building with ten or fewer units. Large residential properties (Class 2) pay $13.145 per $100 AV; while offices (Class 4) pay $10.323 per $100 AV.[30]

Given all these rules, several problems arise. First, it is difficult to determine whether, in fact, properties are assessed to anything close to true market values, where true market values are determined by sales prices, for a given size, quality, age, and type. Second, the different tax rates combined with the different assessment methods for different types of structures means that, implicitly, the tax system is picking winners and losers, though it is hard to see how this exactly plays out.

A study commissioned by the *New York Daily News* and conducted by the impartial Independent Budget Office found that New York City property tax system, in fact, favors the wealthy over the lower classes. To quote their headline,

New York City property tax system favors the rich, hits lower classes harder, News investigation finds: Because of a bizarre method the city uses to charge residential taxes people living in upscale New York neighborhoods often pay less than those living in those living in poorer areas of New York.[31]

Another problem is that real estate taxes are paid on the total AV of the property, where the total is comprised of two parts—the value of the land and the value of the structure. As a result, it acts as a disincentive toward a landlord tearing down her structure and building a newer, taller one. If a taller building is constructed, it will generate a reassessment and the property tax bill will go up. This is problematic from two perspectives. First is that the value of the structure is determined by the entrepreneurial effort of the landowner; while the value of the land is determined by the community, and the value of the neighborhood in general. A tax on the total property penalizes the entrepreneurial efforts of the developer and disincentives the redevelopment of the property toward its highest and best use.

Lastly, over the twentieth century, private landlords have been asked to shoulder an increasing fraction of the property tax because over the twentieth century, more and more land has been removed from the tax rolls.[32] Such buildings include government-owned structures and religious and non-profit institutions. Today one-third of all properties in Manhattan receive some form of property tax exemption; about 11% are totally exempt. As more and more properties are given exemptions, this means that cost of the real estate tax is being shifted to fewer and fewer lots. One simple way to see the effects of this is to calculate the tax rate multiplied by the total AV of non-exempt land for Manhattan and then adjust it for inflation to get an estimate of the real tax impact on private property. When I do this calculation I find, that the real tax rate has increased by a factor of 14 since 1900.[33]

How to remedy these problems? Ideally, the whole real estate tax scheme should be thrown in the garbage and rebuilt from the ground up. All properties should be assessed at 100% of their true market values, and the tax rates should be uniform across all use types. This, however, is way too politically explosive. First, people fear (and rightly so) wholesale reassessments, as they fear a rise in their tax bills. Second, assessing at 100% true market values can cause too much assessment volatility. In any given, year assessment values could rise or fall by considerable amounts given the fluctuations in the business cycle and the real estate market.

The next best thing is perhaps not to disturb the assessment process and just focus on the tax rates. The real estate tax code needs to be simplified. Tax rates needs to be uniform and not favor any one group over another. The point of the tax system is to raise revenue. Since the government already calculates the AV of land separate from the AV of the structure, a remedy for promoting economic development would be to tax the land value at a much higher rate than the structure. For example, a tax rate now of $12 per 100 AV, should have say $24 per 100 AV of land and say $6 per $100 of AV of structure. The point is very simple: by taxing the land at a higher proportion, the city will not penalize the entrepreneurial efforts of real estate developers and will more fairly spread the tax across the community.

In other words, taxing the structure less will encourage more development because it will now cost less to redevelop the site. Taxing the land more will not influence the size of the structure because the land tax does not affect how much land can be supplied, as it were. This split-rate system can be set in a way that leaves the city in the same fiscal situation as before.[34]

Under rent stabilization, tenants do not want to move to give up their benefits. At the same time, developers are reluctant to tear down their structures and build taller ones, both because of the problems related to evicting tenants and because doing so would result in a higher tax rate. If developers were sufficiently incentivized, and if housing construction became robust enough, it would give rent stabilized tenants more incentives to move. Going to a split-rate system would help grease the wheels of new construction, which would reduce housing prices and demonstrate that the end of rent stabilization is not a catastrophe.

The major hurdles to implementing the split-rate are political. People resist changes to the current tax system more out of fear than rationality. Tax policy in the United States is so fraught with politics, that it is often difficult to discuss meaningful changes without creating a political free-for-all. Implementation, however, would be straightforward in New York and would require few changes in operating procedure. The city already provides AVs for both land and the structure, so, in theory, the only major adjustment is to the tax rates.[35]

Who would win and who would lose under such a scheme? The biggest losers will be those who generally have a high land-to-structure ratio. This includes businesses that have large lots, such as car dealerships, strip malls with large parking lots, and those households with small houses relative to the size of the lot. Those who gain from the system are those whose property is densely built. But, the question remains, would those who stand to lose be able to block the change? How could such a policy be implemented politically? This is also likely to pit the outer borough residents against Manhattanites, since Manhattan is already so "structure heavy." At a minimum, a split-rate system should be imposed in just Manhattan, or perhaps the oldest parts of the city, say Manhattan, the western half of the Bronx, and parts of Queens and Brooklyn that are much denser.

Recommendation 5: New Transportation Policies

All of the changes discussed above cannot be implemented without considering changes to transportation policy. When we step back to consider why cities exist, the answer lies in the fact that they exist to eliminate the barriers of geography. The city—and the skyscrapers which comprise it—are a means by which the spaces between people are reduced as much as possible: a worker is more easily united with employment; employer is more easily united with worker, and firms are more easily connected to other firms. People can more easily fulfill their social, economic, psychological, and cultural needs. The city is thus a set of structures—buildings, roads, spaces, that allow people the benefit of living their lives in a more productive way.

As such, we must consider the role that transportation serves. Buildings and places are symbiotically tied to the means that allow people to access them. Transportation should be thought of more broadly as the entire interconnected system of *routes* (roads, highways, subways, commuter trains) and *modes* of travel (foot, bicycle, car, and train). All modes in New York are linked, directly or indirectly, by the relative costs and benefits of using each mode for a given objective. In New York, people frequently alternate between modes depending on the day, time, the nature of the journey, the availability of parking, how often the trains run, and so on. And yet, despite the overall flexibility that citizens have, the system is aging and too easily gummed up.

The ultimate goal of transportation should be to give people as much flexibility to move across the city when and how they want. But the transportation system is subject to several major problems. First is congestion. When more travelers want to use a particular road than can accommodate them, movement is slowed down considerably and personal costs and frustrations mount. Second is that transportation systems are subject to network instabilities or externalities, in the sense that if one part of the system is disrupted it impacts other parts of the network. If a traffic accident occurs on a major commuting artery, it then backs up traffic on the routes that connect with the highway. If a particular subway line is taken off the grid, it causes people to move to other lines, thereby causing congestion on the other routes and so on. Third is the fact that New York's transportation system has not significantly changed in several decades. The current highway system was largely completed by 1960, with the major roads feeding into the city built under the leadership of Robert Moses. The subway system was essentially finished by the 1930s, with its three lines (IRT, BMT, and IND). While there is currently some expansion underway (the #7 line and the Second Avenue Subway), if you divided this new trackage by the total miles of road it would be tiny.[36] In 1950, when the transportation infrastructure was nearing completion, New York and the eight surrounding counties had 10.65 million people. Today, those same counties hold over 16 million people; they are travelling on virtually the same system as from that time.[37]

Commuters are rightly annoyed at the costs they must pay. Tolls and fares appear to rise faster than inflation, all the while people get stuck in traffic or idle in stopped subway cars. The total cost of commuting has risen dramatically over the last several decades because of not only the user cost but the lost time wasted away by travelling in a system that was never designed to handle so many people. At the same time, expensive land values, regulations against economic development, and cries of "not in my back yard!" have made it virtually impossible for the region's transportation infrastructure to expand to accommodate the population growth. A tour through other cities throughout the developed and developing world will show that New Yorkers need not settle for what they have.

Because transportation systems are inherently regional they need to be addressed at this level. The governors of New York, New Jersey, and Connecticut need to formulate a regional strategy, such as expanding the subways to outside of the city. This is unlikely to happen.[38] So what can New York City do to improve its own system? I propose three different proposals. First is to let the prices of traveling move up or down depending on the relative supply and demand for different modes. In other words, given the current system, make it operate more efficiently by matching supply with demand. Second is to make it more expensive to enter Manhattan via automobile. Third is to expand and upgrade mass transit options.

Prices and Transportation

Given the current transportation network in the city, user-prices must be set so that it more efficiently allocates transportation space across time and space. In other words, the entire system should operate to limit or make more expensive those things that cause the most congestion, while simultaneously encouraging those parts of the system that are underutilized or are relatively more efficient. This means that transportation prices should be set, more or less, according to the supply and demand for that mode at any given time.

While this might seem like a backhanded way of saying that tolls and fares should be increased, that is not completely true. If a certain bus route is underutilized at the same time that a certain subway line is overutilized prices should rise for the subway and fall for the bus. This means that some routes, say bus lines at a certain time of day, can be free or nearly free, while simultaneous with that the rates of a parallel, but congested, route is relatively expensive.[39] In this day and age, the technology exists so that real-time pricing, and the costs and benefits of different means of travel can be instantly calculated and provided via website, mobile phone app, or on digital signs at bus stops and subway stops.

Travelers would not only be charged according the supply and demand, but just as important, they would have as much information as possible on what the costs and travel times will be, and they thus can make an informed decision based on the balance of two. The entire network of roads, streets, subways, commuter trains and highways needs to be linked to this plan. During rush hour, people would choose between the modes that offer to them the best benefit to cost ratio.

Not in a rush? Take the cheaper but longer option. Have a meeting that you must attend? Take the quicker but more expensive option. Note that the different alternatives can have different cost-benefit ratios across days of the week and times of the day. So there is nothing inherent in the plan that would favor the wealthy over the poor. The information should also include driving times and costs, including tolls (and even options for street parking availability). The point is to increase the efficiency of the movement of people, and the costs or benefits of using automobiles is not independent of what is going on with the other modes of travel.

Reduce Automobiles in Manhattan

In 2007, Mayor Michael Bloomberg attempted to pass a congestion pricing bill to reduce automobile congestion in Manhattan. Under his plan, all automobiles entering the most congested part of Manhattan—south of 60th Street—would be required to pay a large toll.[40] Cameras and sensors would be used to charge drivers. This was a good idea from the point of view of maximizing transportation efficiency. There are too many cars in Manhattan, and they cause too much congestion. Street space, like land, is a valuable commodity and it, in effect, should be auctioned off to the highest bidder. Those most eager to pay for the right to drive in Manhattan should be required to do so.

Ultimately, however, the plan was doomed because those residents who drive into the city from Queens, Brooklyn, and the Bronx are generally able to enter Manhattan without paying bridge tolls. The city has a panoply of bridges and tunnels, and they are owned and operated by different agencies. For example, to drive across or under the Hudson River from New Jersey, the commuter must pay tolls to the Port Authority of New York and New Jersey. To cross the East River, the driver has different options. Entering by one of two tunnels requires paying a toll. Taking the Brooklyn Bridge requires no toll. Taking the Henry Hudson Parkway into Manhattan from the north requires a toll. Entering from Interstate Highway 87 into Manhattan requires no toll. Entering Manhattan from the Triborough (Robert F. Kennedy) Bridge requires a toll. To enter from the 59th Street (Edward Koch Queensboro) bridge requires no toll.

The apparent randomness with which tolls are applied makes no sense. The simplest way to reduce automobile driving in the city is to have all bridges and tunnels require tolls. These tolls should have floating prices set up according the system described above. In addition, an on-street parking system like the one in San Francisco can be implemented, where parking meter prices change according to supply and demand. A website or mobile app can tell the relative prices and the location of abundant parking.

Invest in New Transportation Routes

Again, it bears repeating that the aim of transportation is serve two functions: reduce the space between individuals and businesses, and provide flexibility in movement. All of the policies described above are based on the fact that the current transportation system is relatively fixed and, therefore, this resource should be allocated more efficiently across time and space. But more broadly, this system can be greatly improved if was expanded. For example, if the number of automobiles entering into Manhattan were reduced, then an efficient streetcar system can be built up and down and across the island, and can then be expanded outward to the other boroughs.

The transportation network that was implemented over the twentieth century is a holdover from a different era. The two major commuter rail stations, Penn Station and Grand Central, were built by two railroads that were in competition with each other. It is only now, a century later, that efforts are being made at rationalizing commuter rail by allowing Long Island trains to enter Grand Central Station. Presumably in the next few decades, there will be access to Penn Station by residents in the north.

Two out of the three subway lines were built by private companies, again, in competition with each other and the third line, the IND, was built in competition with those two.[41] The subway routes were designed to funnel many people into Downtown and Midtown. The city and the state need to take much greater steps to better rationalize the subway system. For example, to this day, it remains a huge problem for east-west travel on Manhattan and in the Bronx; north-south travel between Queens and Brooklyn is equally as frustrating. The medians of the city's highways also can be used for monorails, such as that to JFK airport from Jamaica, Queens.

If New York is committed to expanding its real estate stock and accommodating a much larger population, it can pay for these new transportation investments through the additional growth. This is how the original system was built; it was largely paid for with the nickels of the millions of strivers who moved to the city.

In an age of climate change, the system needs greater resiliency. If storms or floods take out one line or mode of transport, this should not gum up the entire transportation network. My pricing scheme above will create a more flexible system as travelers learn how to adapt their behavior according to the incentive-signals being generated by the various transportation routes. Greater density, of course, will also bring more services closer to home, which will promote more walking and bicycling, and less use of fossil fuels.

In addition, in planning for climate change, there are many sustainability-oriented policies that can strengthen not only the current level of infrastructure and urban services but also promote economic growth. Renewable energy is a perfect example. There is no reason that solar panels and/or windmills cannot be placed on the majority of building roofs for all apartment buildings or parking lots in the city. Vast swaths of open space that are not utilized are thus perfect for on-site energy production. If the city moves toward a FAR tax system, the growth in real estate will be matched by money for new transportation and sustainability-oriented innovations.

HOW MANY PEOPLE CAN MANHATTAN HOLD?

When we think of Manhattan as the ultimate skyscraper city, we ignore the fact that high-rises that constitute thirty stories or more are only 1.7% of all buildings on the island. In fact, 70% of all structures on the island have five or fewer stories; while 90% of all structures are ten stories or less.[42] Manhattan is decidedly low-rise.

In 1910, Manhattan's population was 2.33 million, with far fewer tall buildings. Today, its population is 1.63 million and yet the technology available for even greater density is here. While the common perception is that Manhattan is filled-up, nothing can be further from the truth. It is true, of course, that purely vacant land is relatively rare, but the total population that the island can hold is fundamentally a political and social decision, not an economic or technological one. Seventy percent of all structures do not have to be five stories or less.

Even under the current zoning rules, Manhattan is considerably underbuilt. Thanks to the New York City Department of City Planning's Primary Land Use Tax Lot Output (PLUTO) file, we can tabulate the current structural density on the island and compare it to the maximum structural density allowed by law. As of 2013, Manhattan contained 1.73 billion square feet (62 square miles) of usable floor area. Half of that floor area—868 million square feet—is used for residences. If built out to its fullest extent, the city could add an additional one billion square feet of residential floor area. Or in other words, the city could more than double the amount of space devoted for residential living, which could then accommodate a doubling of its population, to roughly 3.25 million.[43]

But, of course, that will never happen, though it is theoretically possible. Let's move to a scenario that is (only slightly) less far-fetched. There are about 914,000 residential units on the island, and 64% are rentals.[44] To make matters simple, let's assume that only rental buildings are available for possible redevelopment, given the difficulty of owners collectively deciding to tear down their own building in order to redevelop it. The average household size in Manhattan is two people.[45] So, this suggests that rental units contain a population of about 1.17 million people, or about 72% of the total population. Assuming, as above, that we can double the rental housing stock under current zoning rules, this would give us a maximum population of about 2.8 million people, or an increase of 72% from its 2013 figure.

In a third calculation, we can assume that lots in landmarked neighborhoods are taken out of circulation in perpetuity. The above figure of three million people assumes that the development rights are transferred to properties that can take advantage of them. Currently, some 176 million square feet—comprising 144,000 units—of residential space is within a landmarked district. Let's assume these units can hold up to 300,000 people. This means that the island's population could grow to 2.5 million people.

These calculations are made based on the current land-use regulations. Again, the question about what Manhattan can hold is fundamentally a political and social decision. We can think of the city's land-use regulations combined with its current infrastructure and level of public services as defining its carrying capacity. New York's present population is 8.4 million people, and, as of this writing shows little inclination to think big about its future. In essence, it has taken the path of least resistance, which is to grope its way to the future, destined to hug its self-imposed capacity constraints.

If the city reforms its land use and aims to encourage more high-rise living, then the true population limits are much greater. What could it hold if half of the island's developable land was used for fifty-story buildings? Assuming an average of 800 people per building, this would mean Manhattan could hold 17.8 million people, more people than the state of Illinois![46]

THE FUTURE?

What will the future of the city look like? And how can we ensure it will be better? It seems that our society, New York included, has evolved from thinking big to thinking small, from thinking civic-orientedly to parochially. Large public projects like new subways or new zoning regulations almost seem impossible today. A severe status quo bias has set in as we resist and fear the large-scale changes that were embraced to build New York into the world's greatest metropolis.

But the looming crisis of climate change might be the way to propel us to action. We need to recognize the crisis and use it as a call to action. We should look back to the big projects of the past for inspiration. There are many models: The Gridplan of 1811, the Croton Aqueduct System of the 1840s, and the subway system of the early twentieth century. The 1916 Zoning Laws represents a useful case study. The reason the city was able to enact such rules was because there were many citizens across the political and policy spectrum that had an interest in regulating land use. Residents and businesses wanted a higher quality of life; the real estate community wanted to reduce volatility; and planners wanted a more rational and healthier city. Each group was able to come to the table and agree to a larger framework that allowed for a more orderly and robust real estate market.

The city today needs to create a new plan. One that embodies all of the policy changes discussed above and one that begins by throwing out the window all the arcane and bizarre rules that govern New York's real estate market. The motivating force will be climate change: a master set of regulations and transportation and infrastructure investments that will propel the city into the twenty-first century. If we want to make the city sustainable, livable, and growable, we must think big and we must act in a big way. If not, we will suffer the consequences. The city can, of course, respond to each crisis that comes up, one by one, but it delays the inevitable reckoning that must be made to deal with the realities of a more volatile climate and higher sea levels; the ad hoc approach will cost more in lives and treasure.[47] The politics of winners and losers must be put aside to solve the major problems that face all citizens of the city.

The new plan would establish a framework for resilient transportation and infrastructure investments. It would establish the zoning rules, real estate tax policy, and the building and design codes, all in one master document. It should strive for simplicity and transparency—a document that will allow government to do its job, while allowing the citizens to unleash their creative energies. The new plan will bring to the table residents, businesses and local organizations, the real estate sector, and the transportation and planning communities. It will allow the city to think systematically about the interconnected roles that all of these different components have on the well-being of New York. It will allow the city to build its way up and into the future.

Appendices

Please note that the graphs, tables, and information about the data that appear in my research papers are not presented here. The endnotes in each chapter will refer you to the respective sources. Also note that for the various regressions, I only present one set of results for each dependent variable. Other specifications are available from the author. Data sets are also available at http://www.buildingtheskyline.org.

APPENDIX A

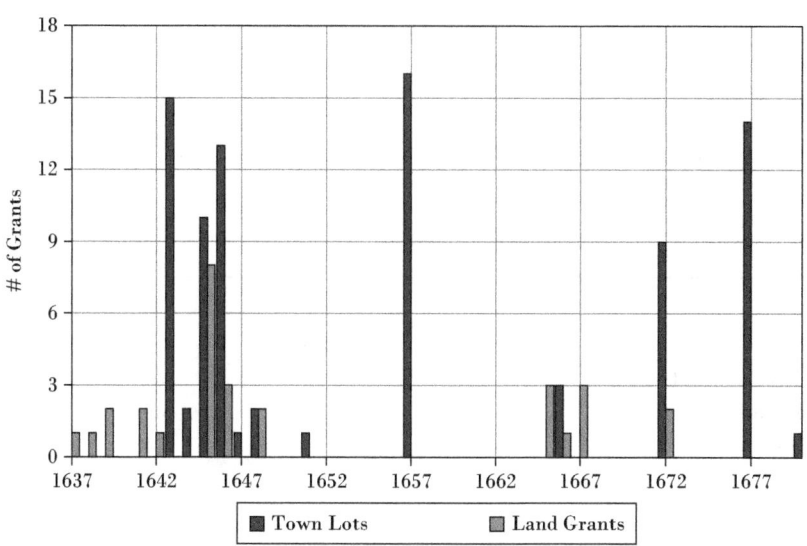

Appendix Figure A The number of Manhattan land grants and town lots distributed to individuals from the colonial authorities from 1637 to 1680.
Source: Valentine (1853).

APPENDIX B

Appendix Table B The Total Growth of Manhattan via Landfill

Period	Added landfill (acres)	Size of Manhattan (acres)	% increase
1625		10,428	
1626–1900	3,336	13,764	32.0
1900–1924	124	13,888	0.9
1924–1957	390	14,278	2.8

(*Continued*)

Appendix Table B Continued

Period	Added landfill (acres)	Size of Manhattan (acres)	% increase
1957–1994	250	14,528	1.8
Total	4,040		

Source: Walsh and LaFleur (1995).

APPENDIX C

Appendix Table C Regression Results for Land Value Prices from 1667 to 1773
The dependent variable is the natural log of real land prices per standard lot unit (2,500 square feet). *Ln(Area)* is the natural log of the plot area (in square feet). *House dummy* is 1 if the property had a house, 0 otherwise. *Corner dummy* is 1 if the property was on a corner, 0 otherwise. Each variable that begins with "Year" is a dummy variable that takes on the value 1 if the transaction occurred in that year, 0 otherwise. Note that the year 1667 is omitted from the regression, since that is the base year for the index. The land values index was calculated by taking $100*exp(year\ dummy\ coefficient)$. The year 1667 was assigned a value of 100

Linear Regression
Dep. Var.: ln(Real Pounds)
Number of obs = 143
R-squared = 0.77
Adj R-squared = 0.59

Variable	Coef.	Std. Err.	t-stat	P>|t|
ln(Area)	0.452	0.098	4.61	0.00
Distance to Fort (miles)	−0.525	0.260	−2.02	0.05
House dummy	1.013	0.183	5.55	0.00
Corner dummy	0.241	0.173	1.40	0.17
Year 1675	0.685	0.776	0.88	0.38
Year 1676	0.927	0.764	1.21	0.23
Year 1682	−0.493	0.771	−0.64	0.53
Year 1683	−0.350	0.771	−0.45	0.65
Year 1684	0.926	0.628	1.48	0.14
Year 1685	0.557	0.632	0.88	0.38
Year 1694	0.578	0.634	0.91	0.37
Year 1697	0.212	0.794	0.27	0.79
Year 1699	0.591	0.566	1.04	0.30
Year 1700	0.258	0.492	0.53	0.60
Year 1705	0.769	0.763	1.01	0.32
Year 1706	0.763	0.570	1.34	0.19
Year 1709	1.042	0.764	1.36	0.18
Year 1711	1.628	0.791	2.06	0.04
Year 1714	0.264	0.633	0.42	0.68
Year 1715	−0.556	0.773	−0.72	0.47

Variable	Coef.	Std. Err.	t-stat	P>|t|
Year 1716	0.614	0.493	1.25	0.22
Year 1717	0.801	0.625	1.28	0.20
Year 1718	0.423	0.489	0.86	0.39
Year 1719	0.879	0.533	1.65	0.10
Year 1720	1.170	0.528	2.22	0.03
Year 1721	1.309	0.569	2.30	0.02
Year 1722	0.079	0.776	0.10	0.92
Year 1723	0.699	0.584	1.20	0.23
Year 1724	0.126	0.766	0.16	0.87
Year 1725	0.100	0.790	0.13	0.90
Year 1726	1.138	0.570	2.00	0.05
Year 1727	1.039	0.627	1.66	0.10
Year 1728	2.080	0.767	2.71	0.01
Year 1729	2.223	0.764	2.91	0.01
Year 1732	2.047	0.596	3.44	0.00
Year 1733	1.750	0.763	2.29	0.02
Year 1737	0.137	0.627	0.22	0.83
Year 1738	1.000	0.763	1.31	0.19
Year 1740	1.337	0.785	1.70	0.09
Year 1741	0.733	0.641	1.14	0.26
Year 1742	0.783	0.767	1.02	0.31
Year 1743	1.071	0.541	1.98	0.05
Year 1745	1.141	0.576	1.98	0.05
Year 1746	0.670	0.636	1.05	0.30
Year 1747	1.188	0.765	1.55	0.13
Year 1748	2.131	0.589	3.62	0.00
Year 1749	1.216	0.784	1.55	0.13
Year 1750	1.179	0.647	1.82	0.07
Year 1751	0.574	0.808	0.71	0.48
Year 1757	1.534	0.645	2.38	0.02
Year 1758	1.657	0.630	2.63	0.01
Year 1759	1.401	0.556	2.52	0.01
Year 1760	1.482	0.772	1.92	0.06
Year 1761	2.423	0.539	4.49	0.00
Year 1762	2.264	0.578	3.92	0.00
Year 1763	1.797	0.635	2.83	0.01
Year 1764	2.065	0.551	3.75	0.00
Year 1767	2.573	0.636	4.05	0.00
Year 1768	1.223	0.832	1.47	0.15
Year 1770	2.355	0.563	4.18	0.00
Year 1771	1.516	0.618	2.45	0.02
Year 1772	2.376	0.643	3.69	0.00

(Continued)

Appendix Table C Continued

Variable	Coef.	Std. Err.	t-stat	P>|t|
Year 1773	1.944	0.671	2.90	0.01
Constant	0.047	0.907	0.05	0.96

Source: Underlying data is from Valentine (1860).

APPENDIX D

Appendix Table D The Distribution of Wealth in Early New York
Each column gives the value in pounds of the wealth levels for the different percentiles. For example, in 1695, a household with £150 or greater would have been in the top tenth percentile

Percentile	1695	1701	1708	1730	1789
Top 10	2,610–150	1,625–110	620–90	670–60	16,430–1,300
Top 20	150–100	110–60	90–55	55–35	1,280–660
Top 30	100–60	60–40	55–35	35–25	650–400
Top 40	60–40	40–30	35–25	25–20	400–270
Top 50	40–30	30–20	25–15	20–15	270–200
Bottom 50	30–0	20–0	15–0	15–0	200–0
Number Assessed	760	1,000	1,076	1,399	4,406

Source: Wilkenfeld (1978).

APPENDIX E

Appendix Table E Regression Results for Changes in Manhattan's Elevation (in feet) from 1609 to 2012
The dependent variable is the average elevation change for each city block. *Latitude miles to tip* is the number of miles north of the tip; *Longitude miles to 5th Avenue and 59th Street* is the number of miles east or west of Fifth Avenue at 59th Street; *Below sea level dummy* is 1 if the block was below sea level, 0 otherwise. *Stream dummy* is 1 if a stream ran through block, 0 otherwise; *Pond dummy* is 1 if block had a pond on it, 0 otherwise; *Freshwater wetland dummy* is 1 if block had a freshwater wetland, 0 otherwise; *Saltwater dummy* is 1 if block had saltwater wetland, 0 otherwise; *Tulip trees dummy* is 1 if block had tulip trees, 0 otherwise; *Distance from central spine* is the distance (in miles) from the geographic central spine of Manhattan at each latitude point. *Distance to closest shore* is the shortest distance (in miles) to closest shore line; *Collect Pond dummy* is 1 if Collect Pond was formerly on the block, 0 otherwise. Note blocks with parks were omitted from the data set

Linear regression
Dep. Var.: Elev. Change (feet)
Number of obs = 3180
R-squared = 0.31

Variable	Coeff.	Robust std. err.	t-stat.	P > |t|
Average elevation 1609	−0.15	0.01	−15.82	0.00
Latitude miles to tip	7.51	0.91	8.21	0.00

Appendix Table C Continued

Variable	Coeff.	Robust std. err.	t-stat.	$P > |t|$
Longitude miles to 5th Avenue and 59th Street	−5.29	0.47	−11.16	0.00
Distance from tip (miles)	−5.74	0.82	−7.00	0.00
Below sea level dummy 1609	11.19	0.77	14.55	0.00
Stream dummy 1609	2.77	0.47	5.89	0.00
Pond dummy 1609	−0.79	1.1	−0.72	0.47
Freshwater wetland dummy 1609	3.45	0.95	3.64	0.00
Saltwater dummy 1609	3.40	0.56	6.05	0.00
Tulip trees dummy 1609	1.37	0.65	2.12	0.03
Distance from central spine	−7.60	1.17	−6.49	0.00
Distance to closest shore	−8.18	1.31	−6.22	0.00
Collect Pond dummy	7.11	1.57	4.53	0.00
Constant	12.54	1.52	8.25	0.00

Source: Underlying data is courtesy of Eric Sanderson, the Mannahatta Project, Wildlife Conservation Society.

APPENDIX F

Appendix Table F Regression Results for Lot Sizes for Skyscrapers Constructed before 1916 Above and Below the Grid Plan Demarcation Line
The dependent variable, *ln(Area)*, is the natural logarithm of the lot area (square feet). *Below line dummy* is 1 if the lot is below 1811 demarcation line, 0 otherwise. *Latitude* is coordinate of the lot (in degrees); *Year* is the year of building completion. A building is considered a skyscraper if it is 262 feet or taller

Linear Regression
Dep. Var.: Ln(Area)
Number of obs = 35
R-squared = 0.016
Adj R-squared = −0.079

Variable	Coef.	Std. err.	t-stat	$P > |t|$
Below demarcation line dummy	−0.67	1.14	−0.59	0.56
Latitude	−17.90	27.12	−0.66	0.52
Year	0.00	0.02	0.09	0.93
Constant	734.6	1,112.09	0.66	0.51

Source: Barr, Tassier, and Trendafilov (2010).

APPENDIX G

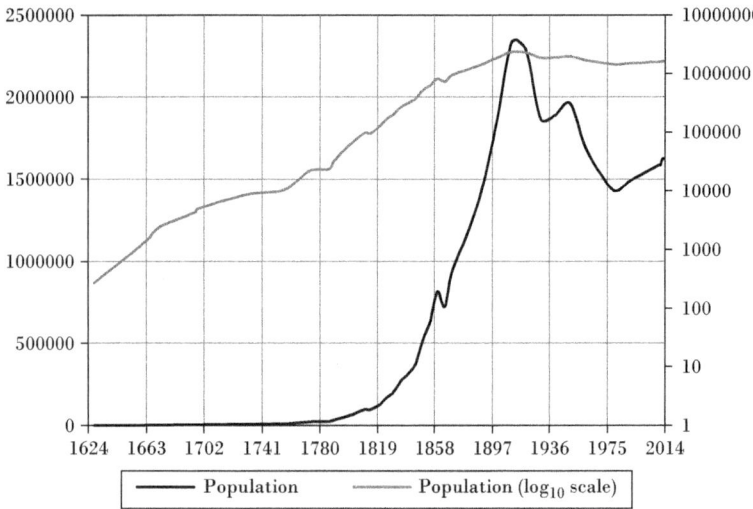

Appendix Figure G Manhattan population from 1624 to 2014. The left scale (black line) shows the population for each year. The right scale (gray line) is the same population figures but shown on a $\log_{10}$ scale. The left scale is good for showing the relative population. The right scale is good for showing growth rates. For example, the relatively steep slope of the gray line from 1780 to 1900 shows that this was the period of Manhattan's most rapid growth. Since 1900 growth rates have been negative or much closer to zero. Note that Manhattan's population peaked around 1910.

Sources: US Census; Ernst (1949); and Rosenwaike (1972).

APPENDIX H

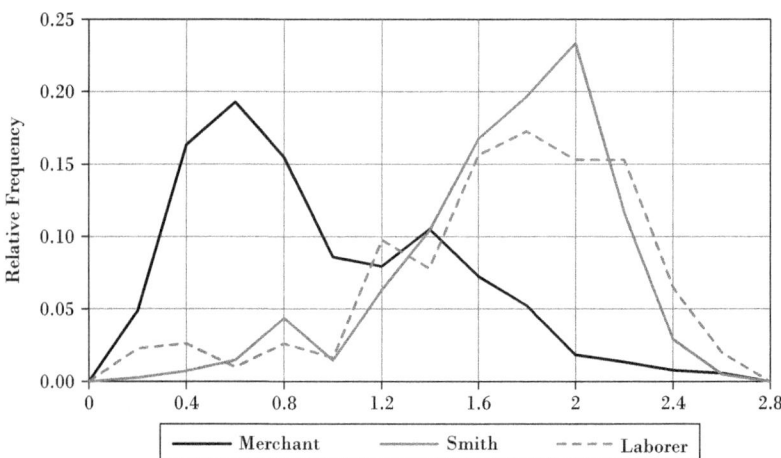

Appendix Figure H.1 Relative Densities of Three Groups, 1827. This graph shows the relative densities of each of the three groups vis-à-vis the lower tip of Manhattan. For example, the greatest concentration of merchants is found about 0.6 miles from the southern tip. Note how merchants are much closer, on average, to the lower part of the city, while smiths and laborers clustered between 1.6 and 2.2 miles away.

Source: Data was collected from *Longworth's American Almanac, New-York Register* (1827). The addresses were then geocoded using an address locator created from the 1852 Perris *Atlas of the City of New York.*

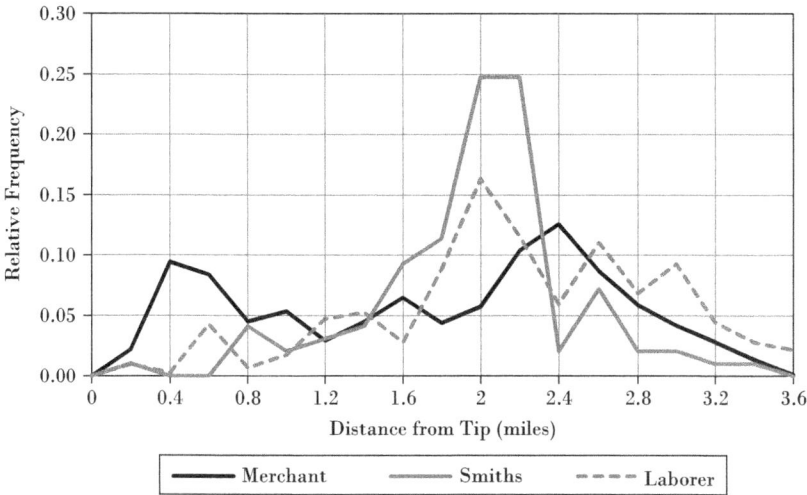

Appendix Figure H.2 Relative Densities of Three Groups, 1849. This graph shows the relative densities of each of the three groups vis-à-vis the lower tip of Manhattan as of 1849. Note how the merchants now have a bimodal distribution, with about half still remaining close to the lower tip and the rest clustered around 2.4 miles from the tip. The laborers and the smiths, however, showed locational stability between 1827 and 1849.
Source: Data was collected from *Doggett's New York City Directory* (1849). The addresses were then geocoded using an address locator created from the 1852 Perris *Atlas of the City of New York.*

APPENDIX I

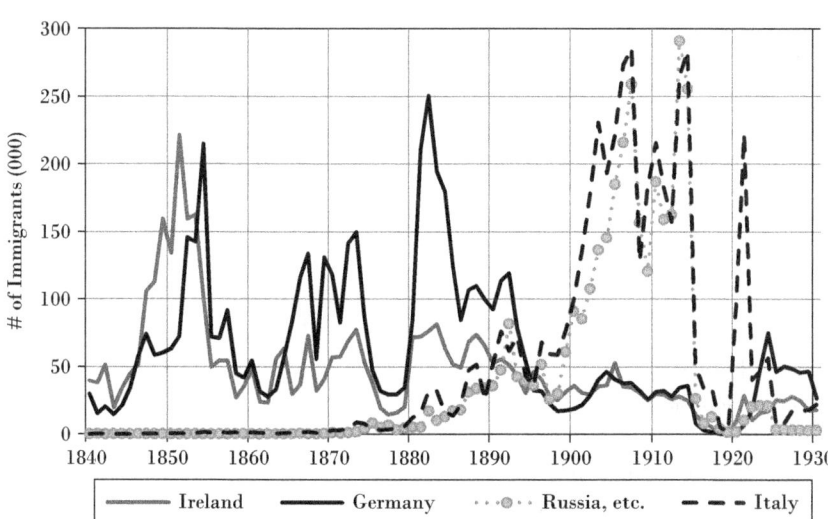

Appendix Figure I Number of immigrants (in thousands) entering into the United States for the four largest groups from 1840 to 1930. The Germans and Italians first arrived in big numbers between 1845 and 1860. German waves also occurred in the 1870s and 1880s. The Russian and Italian waves began in the 1890s and peaked before World War I, though there was one final spike of Italians in the 1920s.
Source: Historical Statistics of the United States, Millennial Edition (2014, tables Ad106–Ad120).

Appendix Table J.1 Top Employment Categories for New York Irish in 1855

Rank	Employment category	Number	%
1	Domestic worker	23,386	26.4
2	Laborer	17,426	19.7
3	Tailor/dressmaker/seamstress/shoemaker	10,851	12.3
4	Brick layer/mason/stone cutter	3,454	3.9
5	Cartman	2,505	2.8
6	Carpenter	2,230	2.5
7	Clerk	2,135	2.4
8	Food dealers	1,817	2.1
9	Blacksmith	1,339	1.5
10	Painter	1,070	1.2
	Total employment in top 10	66,213	74.80
	Total Irish employed/participation rate	88,480	50.35
	Total Irish population in 1855	175,735	

Source: Ernst (1949).

Appendix Table J.2 Top Employment Categories for New York Germans in 1855

Rank	Employment category	Number	%
1	Tailor/dressmaker/seamstress/shoemaker	11,365	24.8
2	Domestic servants	4,493	9.8
3	Food dealers/tobacco/alcohol	4,922	10.8
4	Clerk	2,249	4.9
5	Cabinet maker	2,153	4.7
6	Baker	1,987	4.3
7	Laborer	1,870	4.1
8	Carpenter	1,664	3.6
9	Pinter	905	2.0
10	Peddler	944	2.1
11	Merchant	627	1.4
	Total employment in top 10	33,179	72.5
	Total Germans employed/participation rate	45,764	46.9
	Total German population in 1855	97,572	

Source: Ernst (1949).

APPENDIX K

The Economics of Population Density

This appendix reviews the basics of the economics of population density, on the assumption that households are identical (i.e., they all have the same incomes and tastes, and that there are no urban amenities); a more detailed model is provided in Barr and Ort (2014). The only item that matters is the amount of housing consumed or supplied. Density, say, on a given block, is measured as the total population divided by the size of the block, say, in acres, which can be concisely written as:

$$Density = \frac{Population}{Acres} \equiv \frac{P}{A}.$$ (1)

Next multiply the right side of Equation (1) by $\frac{H}{H} \times \frac{F}{F}$, where H is the total amount of habitable square footage on the block and F as the number of families (households) on the block. Rearranging terms then gives:

$$Density = \left(\frac{P}{A}\right)\left(\frac{H}{H}\right)\left(\frac{F}{F}\right) = \left(\frac{P}{F}\right) \times \frac{\left(\frac{H}{A}\right)}{\left(\frac{H}{F}\right)}.$$

Renaming the new variables that result from the algebraic manipulation gives a formula for the population density on each block:

$$Density = Avg.\,Household\,Size \times \frac{Total\,Housing\,Per\,Acre}{Avg.\,Amount\,Housing\,per\,Household}$$

Total housing per acre is called "structural density." Imagine two identical apartment buildings side by side, except one has four floors and the other five. The second will have greater structural density because it more intensely uses the land. The average amount of housing per household is called "Housing Density." If we take two identical households, but one rents 500 square feet of space and the other rents 2,000 square feet, then the first has a greater housing density. In other words,

$$Density = Avg.\,Household\,Size \times \frac{Structural\,Density}{Housing\,Density}.$$ (2)

Holding quality and income constant, we can see that the higher the prices per square foot consumers have to pay, the greater the density will be. A high rental price will motivate developers to use the land more intensively, either by building more floors, or by building more structure on the property, or both, since they can get a greater return from this additional housing; this is the law of supply as applied to housing. The higher the rental cost of housing means the more tenants will have to pay (holding income constant). As a result, they will rent smaller apartments; this is the law of demand as applied to housing.

As a household moves closer to the city center, it will pay less in commuting costs, as a result it will bid up the price of housing, which, in turn will cause greater density closer to the center. Moving further away population density will drop off relatively steeply, and neighborhoods become more suburban, since housing is cheaper and families use more of it, *even when income and household tastes are identical*. Prices adjust to create a "spatial equilibrium," where housing prices exactly reflect the benefit of the location (i.e., higher prices where commuting is lower; lower prices where commuting is longer), so no family can have a net gain by moving. This simple model can explain the near-universal pattern in the structure of cities across the world, where density falls moving away from the center of the city.

APPENDIX L

Appendix Table L Parks of Manhattan circa 1900
Note that the opening dates are when the park was officially opened, but access to the parks may have been available prior to the years listed

Park name	Year opened (approximately)	Area (acres)
Battery Park	1855	23.6
Bryant Park	1847	12.5
Carl Schurz Park	1876	12.6
Central Park	1859	843.0
City Hall Park	1803	11.5
Colonial (Jackie Robinson) Park	1911	18.1
Corlears Hook Park	1905	9.3
Gramercy Park	1844	2.6
Hamilton Fish Park	1900	5.1
Jefferson Park	1905	14.7
Madison Square	1847	8.7
Morningside Park	1887	40.2
Mount Morris Park	1840	23.8
Mulberry Bend Park	1896	3.6
Riverside Park	1900	144.2
Seward Park	1903	4.3
St John's Park (Hudson Park/James J. Walker Park)	1896	2.9
St. Nicholas Park	1906	41.5
Stuyvesant Square	1850	5.9
Tompkins Square	1878	12.6
Union Square	1839	8.1
Washington Square	1826	11.7

Source: Park sizes from Manhattan shapefile and atlases. Years from various websites.

APPENDIX M

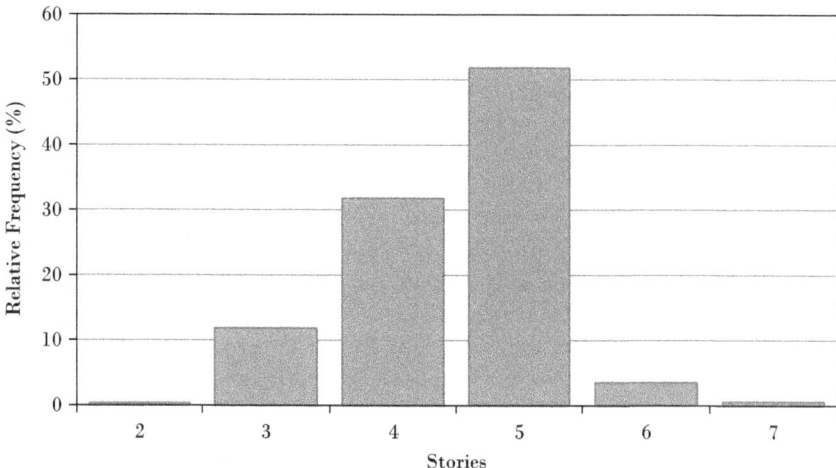

Appendix Figure M Percentage of tenements buildings of different stories in 1900.
Source: Veiller (1903a).

APPENDIX N

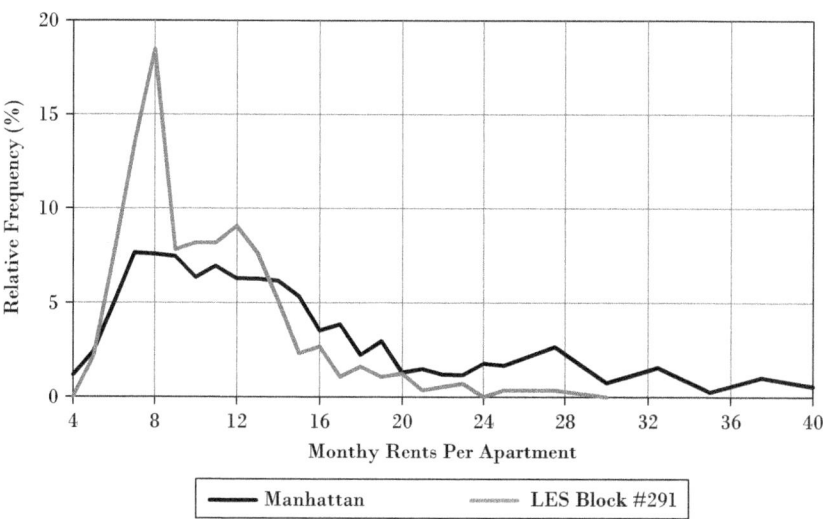

Appendix Figure N Percent distribution of monthly rents per apartment in 1900 across Manhattan and on Block #291 in the Lower East Side.
Sources: Manhattan-wide data is from Tenement House Department (1903). Data from Block #291 is from Veiller (1903d).

APPENDIX O

Appendix Table O Regression Results for Rents for Lower East Side Block #291
Note that building fixed effects were included (but not shown). Dependent variable
is the natural logarithm of cost per room. *Number of rooms* is the number of rooms
in the apartment. *Story* is the floor of the apartment. *Corner apartment dummy* is 1
if apartment is on a corner and has windows facing two directions, 0 otherwise. *Rear
tenement dummy* is 1 if the apartment was in a rear tenement building, 0 otherwise.
Facing back dummy is 1 if the apartment faces the rear, 0 otherwise. *Facing front dummy*
is 1 if the apartment faces the street, 0 otherwise, *Facing through x rear tenement
dummy* takes on 1 if the apartment is a rear tenement and it faces both front and back
of the building (i.e., the apartment takes up entire floor of rear structure). The default
apartment for the "Facing" variables is that the apartment has windows on both front
and back of building

Linear regression
Dep. Var.: ln(Cost per Room)
Number of obs = 563
R-squared = 0.85
Adj R-squared = 0.84

Variable	Coef.	Robust std. err.	t-stat	P > |t|
Number of rooms	−0.067	0.014	−4.97	0.00
Floor	0.061	0.014	4.53	0.00
Floor squared	−0.021	0.002	−9.15	0.00
Corner apartment dummy	0.175	0.026	6.81	0.00
Rear tenement dummy	−0.178	0.016	−11.06	0.00
Facing back dummy	−0.152	0.034	−4.46	0.00
Facing front dummy	−0.101	0.031	−3.22	0.00
Facing through x rear tenement dummy	−0.083	0.043	−1.93	0.06
Constant	1.618	0.059	27.33	0.00
P-value for building dummys = 0.00				

Source: Veiller (1903d).

Appendix Table P Spatial Autocorrelation Regression of Natural Log of Average Real Price per Square Foot for each Sanitation District (SD) between 1885 and 1900 This regression shows that, controlling for other features of each Sanitation District, parts of the island that are narrower have higher land values. *Island width (minus CP)* is the width of the island at the center of each SD. *Distance to tip* (miles) is the distance to the southern tip from the center of each SD. *Death rate of SD, 1890* is deaths per 100,000 people for each SD. *Distance to spine* is the distance to the center of the island at the same latitude as the center point of each SD. *SD population density, 1890* is the total people per acre for each SD. *rho* is the estimated land value spatial autocorrelation parameter. The weights matrix was a standardized binary matrix that took on the value of one for all SDs directly adjacent to each SD, 0 otherwise

Spatial lag model
Dep. Var.: ln(Price Per Square Foot)
Number of obs = 108
Log likelihood = −42.84

Variable	Coef.	Robust Std. err.	z-stat.	$P > |z|$
Island width excluding Central Park (miles)	−0.443	0.221	−2.01	0.05
Distance to tip (miles)	−0.096	0.041	−2.36	0.02
Distance to spine (miles)	−0.094	0.040	−2.35	0.02
Death rate of SD, 1890	−0.013	0.004	−2.88	0.00
SD population density, 1890	−0.001	0.000	−1.77	0.08
Constant	2.717	1.112	2.44	0.02
rho	0.581	0.243	2.39	0.017

Wald test of rho=0: chi2(1) = 5.7(p-val.: 0.017)
Lagrange multiplier test of rho=0: chi2(1) = 5.9 (p-val.: 0.015)

Sources: Land value data provided by Fred Smith, Davidson College; SD data from Billings (1894). Distance variables and weight matrix calculated by Teddy Ort.

APPENDIX Q

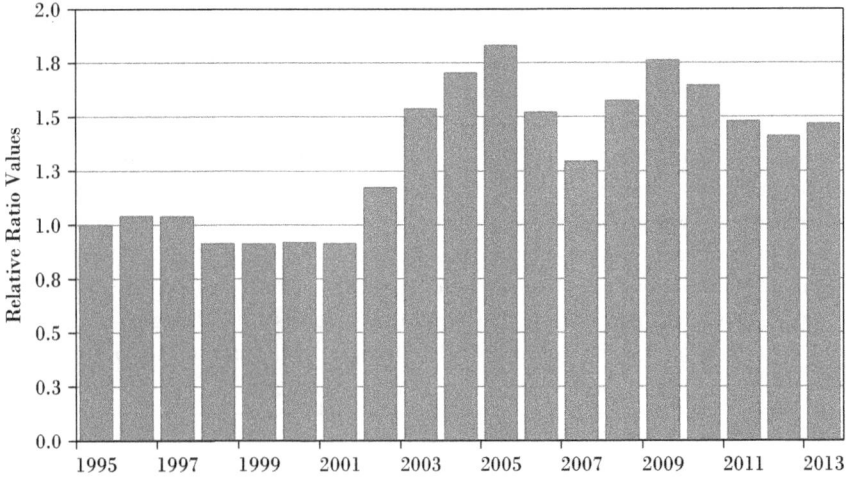

Appendix Figure Q Normalized ratio of New York condo prices to Midtown asking office rents from 1995 to 2013 (1995 = 1).

Sources: Manhattan condo price data from the S&P Shiller condo price index. Asking rents data from Kelly (2002) and various industry reports.

APPENDIX R

Appendix Table R Building Height Regressions, 1895 to 1932
The data set is office buildings that are 325 feet or taller that were constructed between 1895 and 1933. This regression shows the lot sizes were no different for the tallest buildings before and after 1916. The dependent variable is the natural logarithm of the lot area. *Year* is the year of completion. *Zoning 1916 dummy* is 1 if the building was completed after the implementation of the zoning rules in 1916, 0 otherwise. *Distance to core (miles)* is the distance of each building to the closest business core (Wall Street or Grand Central Station). *Plot irregular dummy* is 1 if the lot is irregularly shaped (i.e., is not rectangular)

Linear regression
Dep. Var.: ln(Area)
Number of obs = 96
R-squared = 0.035

Variable	Coef.	Robust std. err.	t	P > |t|
Year	0.023	0.017	1.37	0.173
Zoning 1916 dummy	−0.250	0.402	−0.62	0.535
Distance to core (miles)	4.036	17.594	0.23	0.819
Plot irregular dummy	−0.054	0.161	−0.33	0.74
Constant	−33.90	31.8	−1.07	0.29

Source: Barr (2012b).

APPENDIX S

Land Prices and Skyscraper Height

This model demonstrates that land values will be the same respective of whether developer height or economic height is chosen, assuming no externalities or ego considerations. Also, assume that land values are set by the zero profit condition in both cases. First let's start with an economic model and assume that a developer's profit function is given by:

$$\pi = RH - cH^2 - F - L, \tag{1}$$

where R is the present value of per-floor rents, H is the building height (number of stories), c is a cost-related parameter, and L is the cost of land (and assume the lot size is fixed at one unit). The first order condition (FOC) with respect to H (i.e., taking the first derivative and setting the new equation to zero) allows to us to solve for the height, $H^* = R/(2c)$, that maximizes profits (we know it is a maximum and not a minimum because the second derivative is negative). Note F is the non-land fixed costs.

If we insert H^* back into the profit function, set the equation equal to zero and solve for L, we get the land value for a lot with a profit-maximizing height:

$$L^* = \frac{R^2}{4c} - F. \tag{2}$$

A developer, on the other hand, aims to maximize the return on investment (ROI). So in this case the ROI function is:

$$ROI = \frac{RH}{cH^2 + F + L}. \tag{3}$$

Taking the FOC with respect to H generates an H that maximizes the ROI (call it H**):

$$H^{**} = \sqrt{\frac{F + L}{c}}. \tag{4}$$

Note that just land and construction costs enter into the height decision. Plugging H^{**} into equation (1), setting it equal to zero, and solving for L yields equation (2).

APPENDIX T

Appendix Table T.1 Annual Total Height Regressions
The dependent variable is the natural logarithm of one plus the total height added to the skyline, where the total height is the sum of the heights of all buildings that are 295 feet or taller, each year from 1894 to 2014. *ln(Avg. Plot Size)* is the log of average plot size. Next to each variables in the number of years it was lagged (e.g., t-2 means lagged two years). *ln(FIRE/Total Emp.)* is the log of US FIRE employment to total US employment. *ln(Cum. # Skyscrapers)* is the log of net cumulative number of skyscrapers completed up to that year. *ln(US Pop)* is the log of the US population. *ln(Pop 5 Surrounding Counties)* is the log of population of five surrounding counties. *ln(NYC POP)* is the log of New York City population. *ln(GDP Detrended)* is the log of detrended GDP. *ln(NYSE Vol)* is the log of annual New York Stock Exchange volume. *ln(Real Materials Prices)* is the log of index of building materials prices. *% change real estate loans* is the percentage change in real value of national real estate loans. *Real interest rate* is the nominal interest rate minus the inflation rate. *Zoning 1916 dummy* is 1 if the year was 1916 to 1961, 0 otherwise. *Zoning 1961 dummy* is 1 if the year was after 1961, 0 otherwise. *ICIP dummy* is 1 in the years ICIP was most generous (1977–1992), 0 otherwise. *Tax421a dummy* is 1 in the years in which 421a tax plan was most generous (1971– 1985), 0 otherwise. *Westside zoning dummy* is 1 in which west side zoning rules were in effect (1982 to 1988), 0 otherwise. *ln(Effective Tax Rate)* is the log of tax rate times real assessed value of Manhattan real estate. *Income inequality dummy* is 1 if top 99 percentile garnered more than 20% of the nation's income, 0 otherwise

Linear Regression

Dep. Var.: ln(1+Total Height)

Number of obs = 121

R-squared = 0.97

Adj R-squared = 0.96

Variable	Coef.	Std. err.	t-stat	$P > |t|$
ln(Avg. Plot Size)	0.564	0.019	29.47	0.00
ln(FIRE/Total Emp.)(t-2)	3.339	1.267	2.63	0.01
ln(Cum. # Skyscrapers)(t-2)	−2.716	0.539	−5.04	0.00
ln(US Pop.)(t-2)	8.393	4.355	1.93	0.06
ln(Pop 5 Surrounding Counties)(t-2)	2.144	1.109	1.93	0.06
ln(NYC Pop./)(t-2)	7.681	1.700	4.52	0.00
ln(GDP Detrended)(t-2)	1.364	0.949	1.44	0.15
ln(NYSE Vol)(t-2)	0.591	0.155	3.82	0.00
ln(Real Materials Prices)(t-2)	−1.489	1.117	−1.33	0.19
% Change real estate loans (t-3)	0.008	0.008	0.99	0.32
Real interest rate (t-3)	−0.028	0.017	−1.68	0.10
Zoning 1916 dummy (t-2)	−1.161	0.537	−2.16	0.03
Zoning 1961 dummy (t-2)	−1.202	0.623	−1.93	0.06
ICIP dummy (t-2)	0.820	0.293	2.80	0.01
Tax421a dummy (t-2)	0.412	0.222	1.85	0.07
Westside zoning dummy (t-2)	0.529	0.323	1.64	0.11
ln(Effective Tax Rate)(t-2)	−0.262	0.368	−0.71	0.48

Appendix Table T.1 Continued

Variable	Coef.	Std. err.	t-stat	P > |t|
Year	−0.124	0.048	−2.55	0.01
Income inequality dummy (t-2)	0.957	0.223	4.29	0.00
Constant	−8.34	69.15	−0.12	0.90

Sources: See Barr (2010) and Barr (2013) for more details on the data.

Appendix Table T.2 Tallest Building Regressions

ln(Area) is the log of the lot area. *ln(Cum. # Skyscrapers)* is the log of net cumulative number of skyscrapers. *ln(Pop 5 Surrounding Counties)* is the log of population of five surrounding counties. *ln(NYC POP)* is the log of New York City population. *ln(NYSE Vol)* is the log of annual New York Stock Exchange volume. *ln(Real Materials Prices)* is the log of an index of materials prices. *% Change real estate loans* is percentage change in real national real estate loans. *Real interest rate* is the nominal interest rate minus the inflation rate. *Zoning 1916 dummy* is 1 if year was 1916 to 1961, 0 otherwise. *Zoning 1961 dummy* is 1 if year was after 1961, 0 otherwise. *ICIP dummy* is 1 in the years ICIP was most generous (1977–1992), 0 otherwise, *Tax421a dummy* is 1 in the years in which 421a tax plan was most generous (1971–1985), 0 otherwise. *Westside zoning dummy* is 1 in which west side zoning rules were in effect (1982 to 1988)), 0 otherwise. *ln(Effective Tax Rate)* is the log of tax rate times real assessed value of Manhattan real estate. *Income inequality dummy* is 1 if top 99 percentile garnered more than 20% of the nation's income, 0 otherwise

Linear Regression

Dep. Var.: Height of Tallest Building (feet)

Number of obs = 121

R-squared = 0.67

Variable	Coef.	Newey-West Std. err.	t-stat.	P > |t|
ln(Area)	89.86	25.43	3.53	0.00
ln(Cum. # Skyscrapers)(t-2)	−287.02	123.00	−2.33	0.02
ln(Pop 5 Surrounding Counties)(t-2)	457.94	268.66	1.70	0.09
ln(NYC POP)(t-2)	815.56	251.47	3.24	0.00
ln(NYSE Vol)(t-2)	60.24	62.45	0.96	0.34
ln(Real Materials Prices)(t-2)	−346.13	255.09	−1.36	0.18
% Change real estate loans (t-3)	−0.53	3.03	−0.17	0.86
Zoning 1916 dummy (t-2)	−94.06	71.84	−1.31	0.19
Zoning 1961 dummy (t-2)	−129.69	101.98	−1.27	0.21
ICIP dummy (t-2)	146.79	53.39	2.75	0.01
Income inequality dummy (t-2)	218.99	77.40	2.83	0.01
Year	−1.70	12.32	−0.14	0.89
Height of tallest building (t-1)	0.25	0.10	2.40	0.02
Constant	−16076	20609	−0.78	0.44

Sources: See Barr (2010) and Barr (2013) for more details on the data.

APPENDIX U

Appendix Table U Regression Results for the Percentage of Total Construction Costs that Were Devoted to the Foundation for Fifty-Three Buildings Completed between 1890 and 1915

Caisson dummy is 1 if the building used caissons, 0 otherwise. *Depth to bedrock* (feet) is depth to bedrock from street level. *Number of floors* is the building height. *Distance to tip (miles)* is the location of the building relative to the tip of Manhattan

Linear Regression

Dep. Var.: % Total Costs for Foundations

Number of obs = 53

R-squared = 0.25

Adj R-squared = 0.17

Variable	Coef.	Std. err.	t-stat.	$P > |t|$
Caisson dummy	4.605	1.311	3.51	0.00
Depth to bedrock (feet)	0.010	0.020	0.52	0.60
Number of floors	−0.141	0.093	−1.51	0.14
Year	−0.250	0.144	−1.73	0.09
Distance to tip (miles)	0.899	0.481	1.87	0.07
Constant	490.1	274.3	1.79	0.08

Source: Barr, Tassier, and Trendafilov (2010).

APPENDIX V

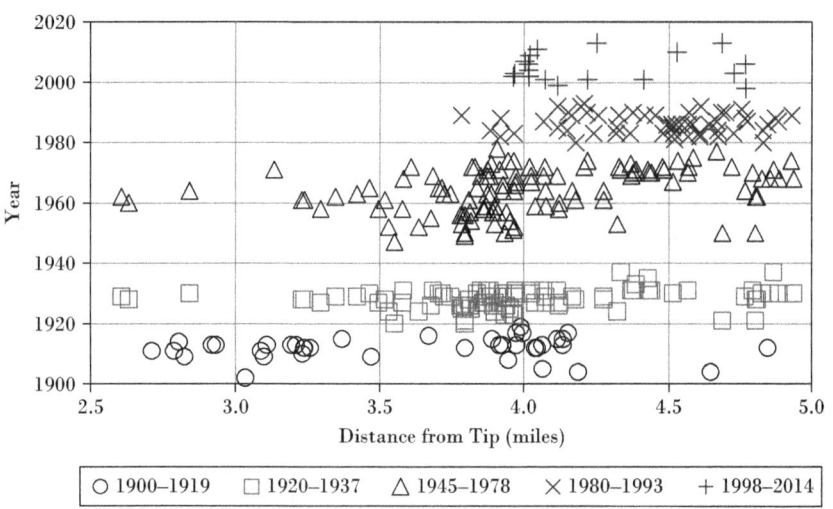

Appendix Figure V Office skyscraper construction in Midtown from 1900 to 2014 for buildings that are 295 feet or taller. The horizontal axis shows the location of each skyscraper relative to the lower tip of Manhattan. The vertical axis shows the year of completion. The graph shows that in each period, on average, there was a northward movement of offices until the last period. Note gaps are recession years when no skyscrapers were built in Midtown.

Sources: Data collected by author. See Barr (2010, 2012b, 2013).

APPENDIX W

Appendix Table W.1 Regressions for Change in Office Vacancy Rates between 1925 and 1931
Vacancy 1925 (%) is the office vacancy from 20 U.S. cities in 1925, *Office increase* (%) is
the percentage increase in office space in the period. *Ln(POP)* is the natural logarithm
of each city's population as of 1920. Note that the cities are listed in Appendix Table W.2

Linear regression

Dep. Var.: Change in Vacancy Rates

Number of obs = 20

R-squared = 0.57

Variable	Coef.	Robust Std. err.	t-stat.	$P > |t|$
Vacancy 1925 (%)	−0.63	0.19	−3.30	0.00
Increase in office space (%)	0.10	0.05	1.98	0.07
ln(Population 1920)	−1.41	1.42	−1.00	0.33
Constant	29.91	18.37	1.63	0.12

Source: Vacancy and office growth data is from Shultz and Simmons (1959). Population data is from
the US Census.

Appendix Table W.2 Change in Vacancy Rates Above or Below Prediction in 1931
Each value tells how much change in vacancy rates occurred relative to what would be predicted
from the regression shown in Table W.1. In the case of Detroit, for example, its vacancy growth
was much greater than predicted, suggested it was overly optimistic in its forecasts about the
demand for office space. New York's value suggested that its forecasts were not unreasonable

Rank	City	Vacancy over or under the average (%)
1	Detroit	12.20
2	Oakland	9.66
3	San Diego	6.58
4	Philadelphia	4.27
5	Kansas City	2.75
6	Chicago	0.10
7	Indiana	−0.69
8	Cincinnati	−0.99
9	Atlanta	−1.07
10	Los Angeles	−1.51
11	Memphis	−1.75
12	New York	−2.37
13	Minneapolis	−2.68
14	Cleveland	−2.78
15	New Orleans	−2.96
16	Seattle	−3.35
17	San Francisco	−3.48
18	Pittsburgh	−3.67
19	Denver	−3.96
20	Buffalo	−4.32

Source: See Appendix Table W.2.

Appendix Table X.1 Location of All 328 Feet (100 meters) or Taller Buildings Completed from 1928 to 1931 Notice that the Grand Central, Garment, and Financial Districts account for 65% of the total

Neighborhood	Number	%
Central Park	9	12.5
City Hall	4	5.6
Downtown West	3	4.2
Financial	13	18.1
Garment/Penn Station	12	16.7
Grand Central	22	30.6
Insurance	1	1.4
Madison Square	1	1.4
Midtown South	3	4.2
Times Square	1	1.4
Union Square	1	1.4
Upper East Side	1	1.4
Upper West Side	1	1.4
Total	72	100.0

Source: Underlying data from Barr (2012b).

Appendix Table X.2 Corporations that Built Skyscrapers between 1928 and 1931 That Were 328 Feet (100 meters) or Taller for Their Headquarters

Year	Company	Address	Floors	Neighborhood
1928	Chase National Bank	18 Pine Street	38	Downtown
1928	National City Bank	52 Wall Street	32	Downtown
1928	Consolidated Gas Co.	4 Irving Place	26	Union Square
1928	New York Life Insurance Co.	51 Madison Avenue	40	Madison Square
1929	Bank of NY & Trust	48 Wall Street	32	Downtown
1929	Empire Trust Co.	580 5th Avenue	33	Midtown
1929	NY Central Railroad	230 Park Avenue	35	Midtown
1930	Western Union	60 Hudson Street	24	City Hall
1930	Bank of Manhattan Trust	40 Wall Street	70	Downtown
1930	AT&T	32 Sixth Avenue	28	City Hall
1930	Daily News	220 E. 42nd Street	36	Midtown
1931	Irving Trust Co.	1 Wall Street	50	Downtown
1931	City Bank-Farmers Trust Co.	20 Exchange Place	57	Downtown
1931	RCA	570 Lexington Avenue	50	Midtown
1931	McGraw-Hill	330 W. 42nd Street	33	Midtown

Source: Underlying data is from Barr (2012b).

APPENDIX Y

Appendix Table Y.1 Regression Results for the Number of Skyscraper Completions from 1902 to 1950

This table shows regression results for the natural logarithm of 1 plus the total number of skyscraper completions (295 feet or greater) for each year from 1902 to 1950 on the natural logarithm of an index of real net income for office buildings (lagged one year), the percentage change in real estate loans issued in New York state (lagged two years) and the lag of $\ln(1+\#\text{Completions})$

Linear regression

Dep. Var.: $\ln(1+\#\text{Completions})$

Number of obs = 49

R-squared = 0.59

	Coef.	Robust Std. err.	t-stat.	$P > |t|$
$\ln(\text{Real Net Income Index})(t\text{-}1)$	0.815	0.283	2.88	0.01
% Δ.NYS real estate loans (t-2)	0.047	0.017	2.83	0.01
$\ln(1+\#\text{Completions})(t\text{-}1)$	0.355	0.137	2.60	0.01
Contant	−1.380	0.584	−2.36	0.02

Sources: Income data from Grebler (1955). Real estate loans data from Board of Governors (1959).

Appendix Table Y.2 Regression Results for the Number of Skyscraper Completions from 1902 to 1950

This table shows regression results for the natural logarithm of 1 plus the total number of skyscraper completions (295 feet or greater) for each year from 1902 to 1950 on the natural logarithm of an index of real gross income for office buildings (lagged one year), the percentage change in real estate loans issued in New York state (lagged two years) and the lag of $\ln(1+\#\text{Completions})$

Linear regression

Dep. Var.: $\ln(1+\#\text{Completions})$

Number of obs = 49

R-squared = 0.58

	Coef.	Robust Std. err.	t-stat.	$P > |t|$
$\ln(\text{Real Gross Income Index}) (t\text{-}1)$	1.23	0.67	1.84	0.072
% Δ.NYS real estate loans (t-2)	0.06	0.02	3.45	0.001
$\ln(1+\#\text{Completions}) (t\text{-}1)$	0.38	0.14	2.78	0.008
Constant	−5.65	3.22	−1.75	0.087

Sources: Income data from Grebler (1955). Real estate loans data from Board of Governors (1959).

APPENDIX Z

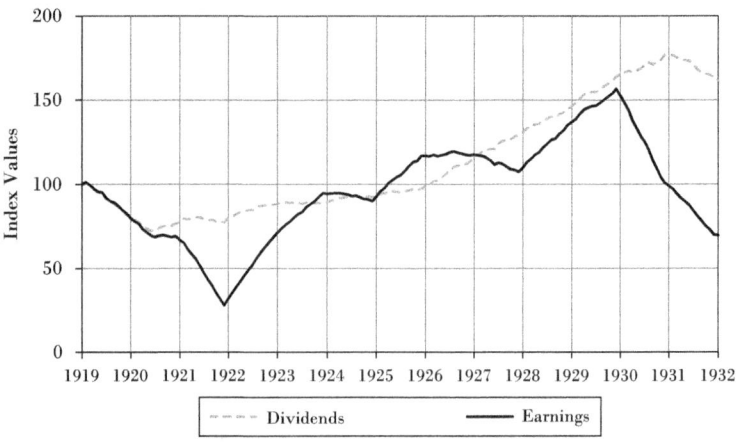

Appendix Figure Z Index of real monthly dividends and real earnings per share for the Standard & Poor's Index from January1919 to January 1932.
Source: Shiller (2014).

APPENDIX AA

Appendix Table AA Regression Results for the Natural Logarithm of Real Building Construction Costs for 109 Structures Built between 1899 and 1931
ln(Area) is the natural logarithm of the lot area (square feet). *Number of Floors* is the height of the structure, *Year* is the year of completion. *ln(Real Materials)* is the natural log of the real building materials cost index. *Commercial Dummy* is 1 if the building was used for commercial purposes, 0 otherwise. *Post-1916 Dummy* is 1 if the building was completed after the implementation of the 1916 zoning rules, 0 otherwise. Source 1 is 1 if the data were from the City Construction Co.'s cost sheets, 0 otherwise. Source 2 is 1 if the data were from the HRH cost sheets, 0 otherwise. Note that the omitted source is cost data from the Fuller Construction Co. cost sheets

Linear regression
Dep. Var.: ln(RealConstruction Costs)
Number of obs = 109
R-squared = 0.83

Variable	Coef.	Robust std. err.	t-stat.	$P > |t|$
ln(Area)	0.90	0.12	7.68	0.00
Number of floors	0.04	0.01	3.14	0.00
Year	−0.05	0.02	−2.49	0.02
ln(Real Materials)	0.20	0.54	0.37	0.72
Commercial dummy	−0.23	0.15	−1.50	0.14
Post-1916 dummy	0.41	0.46	0.90	0.37
Source 1	−0.45	0.22	−2.00	0.05
Source 2	0.14	0.24	0.56	0.58
Constant	93.87	35.93	2.61	0.01

Source: Construction cost data is from cost sheets that are housed in the Skyscraper Museum and Columbia University Avery Library Archives.

Appendix Table BB.1 Inflation-Adjusted Land Value Index for Manhattan
The index was created by combining three separate indexes (and is explained in the text). The first index (1866 to 1900) was created by using the results of the regression given in Appendix Table BB.2. The second index was created by creating an index from the real total value of assessed value of land on Manhattan from 1900 to 1950. The third index, 1950 to 2013, was created by the regression given in Appendix Table BB.3. For overlapping years, the index was adjusted so they would have the same value in that year. Then the index was normalized so that 1900 was equal to 100

Year	Index	Year	Index	Year	Index	Year	Index
1866	13	1903	135	1940	197	1977	44
1867	23	1904	145	1941	179	1978	66
1868	40	1905	151	1942	161	1979	49
1869	59	1906	162	1943	149	1980	53
1870	48	1907	163	1944	141	1981	83
1871	34	1908	174	1945	134	1982	130
1872	60	1909	177	1946	117	1983	117
1873	72	1910	177	1947	106	1984	106
1874	79	1911	195	1948	102	1985	130
1875	97	1912	194	1949	103	1986	456
1876	58	1913	201	1950	104	1987	240
1877	48	1914	202	1951	68	1988	591
1878	39	1915	202	1952	94	1989	395
1879	48	1916	186	1953	76	1990	374
1880	77	1917	154	1954	88	1991	327
1881	74	1918	130	1955	81	1992	176
1882	93	1919	114	1956	110	1993	133
1883	87	1920	99	1957	81	1994	188
1884	107	1921	121	1958	121	1995	202
1885	132	1922	134	1959	92	1996	195
1886	111	1923	131	1960	90	1997	254
1887	132	1924	135	1961	103	1998	470
1888	147	1925	136	1962	86	1999	484
1889	148	1926	145	1963	109	2000	576
1890	149	1927	166	1964	138	2001	591
1891	144	1928	180	1965	134	2002	632
1892	153	1929	191	1966	108	2003	975
1893	176	1930	220	1967	110	2004	1,187
1894	163	1931	257	1968	170	2005	1,842
1895	181	1932	291	1969	172	2006	1,899
1896	161	1933	282	1970	175	2007	3,727
1897	145	1934	238	1971	177	2008	3,015
1898	156	1935	220	1972	157	2009	2,097

(*Continued*)

Appendix Table BB.1 Continued

Year	Index	Year	Index	Year	Index	Year	Index
1899	129	1936	216	1973	82	2010	2,510
1900	100	1937	199	1974	43	2011	2,167
1901	102	1938	203	1975	48	2012	3,132
1902	106	1939	202	1976	53	2013	3,517

Sources: Fred Smith, Davidson College; reports by the New York City Tax Department; and Barr, Smith, and Kulkarni (2015).

Appendix Table BB.2 Regression used to Create the Land Value Index for 1866 to 1900 Here the natural log of vacant land prices were regressed on $ln(Area)$, the natural logarithm of the lot area (square feet); a corner dummy variable, equal 1 if the lot was on a corner, 0 otherwise; the distance to Wall Street and Broadway (in miles); year dummies and Sanitation District fixed effects (not shown). The index was created by taking the exponent of the year dummy coefficients. The standard errors were clustered by the Sanitation Districts

Linear regression

Dep. Var.: $ln(Real Price per Square Foot)$

Number of obs = 8,967

R-squared = 0.52

Adj R-squared = 0.51

Variable	Coef.	Robust std. err.	t-stat.	$P > |t|$
$ln(Area)$	−0.543	0.02	−22.50	0.00
Corner dummy	0.388	0.03	11.77	0.00
Distance to Wall Street and Broadway (miles)	−0.339	0.06	−5.40	0.00
Year 1867	0.533	0.11	4.68	0.00
Year 1868	1.090	0.11	9.57	0.00
Year 1869	1.480	0.13	11.57	0.00
Year 1870	1.284	0.13	9.96	0.00
Year 1871	0.934	0.15	6.21	0.00
Year 1872	1.504	0.14	10.92	0.00
Year 1873	1.687	0.12	13.53	0.00
Year 1874	1.782	0.13	13.96	0.00
Year 1875	1.977	0.12	16.54	0.00
Year 1876	1.472	0.14	10.67	0.00
Year 1877	1.285	0.16	8.28	0.00
Year 1878	1.080	0.15	7.24	0.00
Year 1879	1.277	0.15	8.52	0.00
Year 1880	1.753	0.13	13.97	0.00
Year 1881	1.716	0.14	12.45	0.00
Year 1882	1.943	0.12	15.61	0.00
Year 1883	1.873	0.15	12.41	0.00

Appendix Table BB.2 Continued

Variable	Coef.	Robust std. err.	t-stat.	P > |t|
Year 1884	2.074	0.13	15.88	0.00
Year 1885	2.288	0.14	16.77	0.00
Year 1886	2.120	0.13	16.19	0.00
Year 1887	2.292	0.13	17.48	0.00
Year 1888	2.396	0.15	16.07	0.00
Year 1889	2.406	0.14	16.68	0.00
Year 1890	2.412	0.13	19.04	0.00
Year 1891	2.375	0.13	18.22	0.00
Year 1892	2.435	0.14	17.76	0.00
Year 1893	2.577	0.13	19.68	0.00
Year 1894	2.498	0.14	17.54	0.00
Year 1895	2.603	0.12	21.16	0.00
Year 1896	2.486	0.15	16.89	0.00
Year 1897	2.385	0.17	14.06	0.00
Year 1898	2.456	0.14	17.21	0.00
Year 1899	2.269	0.17	13.41	0.00
Year 1900	2.011	0.17	11.55	0.00
Constant	5.515	0.33	16.51	0.00
SD Fixed Effects				
P-value = 0.00				

Source: Data from Fred Smith, Davidson College.

Appendix Table BB.3 Regression used to Create the Land Value Index for 1900 to 2013
Here the natural log of vacant land prices were regressed on $ln(Area)$, the natural logarithm of the lot area (square feet) and the natural logarithm of the area squared; a corner dummy variable, equal 1 if the lot was on a corner, 0 otherwise; the distance of the property to the closest core, either Wall Street and Broadway or Grand Central Station (in miles); a CoStar dummy equal to 1 if the data was provided by CoStar, 0 otherwise; the number of subway stops within a half mile of the lot; year dummies and Sanitation District fixed effects (not shown). The index was created by taking the exponent of the year dummy coefficients; the base year was 1950. The standard errors were clustered by the Sanitation Districts

Linear regression
Dep. Var.: $ln($Real Price per Square Foot$)$
Number of obs = 3375
R-squared = 0.70
Adj R-squared = 0.68

Variable	Coef.	Robust std. err.	t-stat.	P > |t|
ln(Area)	1.146	0.307	3.74	0.00
ln(Area) squared	−0.068	0.017	−3.93	0.00

(Continued)

Variable	Coef.	Robust std. err.	t-stat.	P > |t|
Corner dummy	0.150	0.074	2.02	0.05
Distance to Broadway (miles)	−0.318	0.417	−0.76	0.45
Distance to Broadway squared (miles sq.)	0.058	0.227	0.26	0.80
Distance to closest core (miles)	0.090	0.058	1.57	0.12
CoStar dummy	0.541	0.126	4.30	0.00
Number of El stops within half mile	0.022	0.028	0.81	0.42
Year 1951	−0.425	0.141	−3.01	0.00
Year 1952	−0.097	0.137	−0.71	0.48
Year 1953	−0.318	0.106	−3.00	0.00
Year 1954	−0.166	0.101	−1.65	0.10
Year 1955	−0.247	0.129	−1.91	0.06
Year 1956	0.053	0.142	0.37	0.71
Year 1957	−0.247	0.188	−1.32	0.19
Year 1958	0.150	0.154	0.98	0.33
Year 1959	−0.118	0.172	−0.68	0.50
Year 1960	−0.146	0.195	−0.75	0.46
Year 1961	−0.014	0.251	−0.06	0.96
Year 1962	−0.194	0.173	−1.12	0.26
Year 1963	0.049	0.307	0.16	0.87
Year 1964	0.281	0.217	1.29	0.20
Year 1965	0.255	0.270	0.94	0.35
Year 1966	0.037	0.268	0.14	0.89
Year 1967	0.058	0.366	0.16	0.88
Year 1968	0.494	0.186	2.66	0.01
Year 1971	0.531	0.365	1.46	0.15
Year 1972	0.410	0.305	1.34	0.18
Year 1974	−0.891	0.160	−5.56	0.00
Year 1976	−0.674	0.226	−2.98	0.00
Year 1977	−0.869	0.238	−3.65	0.00
Year 1978	−0.449	0.360	−1.25	0.22
Year 1979	−0.759	0.295	−2.57	0.01
Year 1980	−0.676	0.207	−3.26	0.00
Year 1982	0.222	0.255	0.87	0.39
Year 1984	0.017	0.245	0.07	0.95
Year 1985	0.227	0.258	0.88	0.38
Year 1986	1.479	0.273	5.43	0.00
Year 1987	0.836	0.315	2.65	0.01
Year 1988	1.737	0.272	6.39	0.00
Year 1989	1.336	0.405	3.30	0.00
Year 1990	1.281	0.328	3.91	0.00
Year 1991	1.146	0.367	3.12	0.00

Appendix Table BB.3 Continued

Variable	Coef.	Robust std. err.	t-stat.	P > |t|
Year 1992	0.529	0.270	1.96	0.05
Year 1993	0.248	0.359	0.69	0.49
Year 1994	0.594	0.227	2.62	0.01
Year 1995	0.663	0.280	2.36	0.02
Year 1996	0.631	0.199	3.17	0.00
Year 1997	0.895	0.266	3.37	0.00
Year 1998	1.509	0.219	6.89	0.00
Year 1999	1.538	0.231	6.65	0.00
Year 2000	1.712	0.220	7.79	0.00
Year 2001	1.738	0.181	9.59	0.00
Year 2002	1.805	0.222	8.12	0.00
Year 2003	2.239	0.233	9.62	0.00
Year 2004	2.436	0.207	11.74	0.00
Year 2005	2.875	0.177	16.23	0.00
Year 2006	2.905	0.194	14.97	0.00
Year 2007	3.580	0.225	15.92	0.00
Year 2008	3.368	0.222	15.20	0.00
Year 2009	3.005	0.336	8.95	0.00
Year 2010	3.184	0.253	12.61	0.00
Year 2011	3.037	0.298	10.21	0.00
Year 2012	3.406	0.174	19.61	0.00
Year 2013	3.522	0.232	15.19	0.00
Constant	−1.802	1.368	−1.32	0.19
SD Fixed Effects P-value = 0.00				

Source: See Barr, Smith, and Kulkarni (2015).

APPENDIX CC

In order to test for Granger causality between land values and measures of skyscraper height, several tests were performed. In particular, I looked at the time series relationships between the *ln(1+total height)* and the *ln(land values index)*, and height (in feet) of the tallest completed building each year (*max*) and the *ln(land value index)*. Here I give a summary of the tests and results; the table below shows the results of the Granger causality tests. All of the other test results are available from the author. Also note that in all tests or vector auto-regression models, an exogenous time trend was included. For details on the theory and tests related to time series models, see Greene (2008).

First, I tested to see if each of the three times series has a unit root. The results of these tests show that neither height measure contains a unit root, but the land value index does. Next, I tested for co-integration between the height measures and the land values index. In each of these cases the Johansen tests for co-integration suggests that for each of the two pairwise tests (total height and land values, and tallest building and land values) each has one co-integrating vector. Next I ran vector error correction (VEC) models for the two pairs of times series. In both cases, the normalized coefficient in the co-integrating equation was not statistically different than zero; this suggests that a VEC model was not necessary.

Then, I ran vector autoregression (VAR) models for *ln(total height)* and change in *d.ln(land value index)* (the change in the land value index), and *max* and *d.ln(land value index)*. Before that, however, I ran selection-order tests to see how many lags to include in the VAR. For total height and land values index, all the selection criteria tests showed one lag was correct. For the max and land values index, the results suggested either one or two lags was correct. Two lags were chosen. Then the VARs were run and Granger causality (GC) tests were performed. The results of the GC tests are given in appendix table CC.

Appendix Table CC Results of Granger Causality Wald Tests for Measures of Skyscraper Height and Land Values

Note that probability values less than 0.1 suggest Granger causality. The upper part of the table shows that land value growth Granger causes total height, but not vice versa. The bottom part of the table suggests that land value growth Granger causes the height of the tallest completed building each year, but not vice versa. This suggests that skyscraper height is a response to land value growth, but not the other way around. Note both tests are for times series from 1890 to 2013

Equation	Excluded	chi2	df	Prob > chi2
ln(1+Total Height)	Δln(Land Value Index)	3.40	1	0.065
Δln(Land Value Index)	ln(1+Total Height)	0.13	1	0.718

Equation	Excluded	chi2	df	Prob > chi2
Max Height	Δln(Land Value Index)	5.14	2	0.077
Δln(Land Value Index)	Max Height	3.50	2	0.174

Sources: See Barr (2013); Fred Smith, Davidson College; reports by the New York City Tax Department; and Barr, Smith, and Kulkarni (2015).

Notes

Introduction

1. O'Leary (2012).
2. Ironically, the World Trade Center, as the ultimate symbol of American capitalism, was conceived of and built by government agencies to revitalize Lower Manhattan; the Port Authority of New York and New Jersey was the lead developer (Darton 1999).
3. Krugman (1996).
4. Arthur (1994); Marshall (2012).
5. Schumpeter (1950).
6. Glaeser (2011).
7. Jackson (1995).
8. Mankiw (2012).
9. The skyscraper is place of economic activity. In it, corporations make production, distribution, and marketing decisions, and food markets are certainly one is part of this. Regarding clothing, in the 1920s, the Garment District in Manhattan was the country's leading location for the production, distribution, and marketing of men's and lady's garments in the United States. Clearly the skyscraper is shelter to millions.
10. For excellent textbook treatments on real estate economics, see DiPasquale and Wheaton (1996) and Ball et al. (1998). For excellent works on urban economics, see O'Flaherty (2009) and O'Sullivan (2007).
11. Adams ([1931] 1974).
12. Mayor Bloomberg in 2013, for example, proposed a rezoning of Midtown East to allow for taller buildings. His plan was deemed too controversial, and it failed pass in the City Council. As of this writing, the de Blasio administration is reviving it and attempting to see it into law.
13. Gilbert (1900).

Chapter 1

1. Juet (1625).
2. Cantwell and diZerega Wall (2003).
3. Ibid., 120.
4. Sanderson (2009); Hill and Waring (1897).
5. Albion (1939).
6. Isachsen et al. (2000, 164).
7. This map was created by Jan Olechowski and Dimitrios Ntarlagiannis for this book, based on over 4,600 bedrock depth points from geologic maps of Manhattan. While there are

several maps and reports documenting bedrock depths. To the best of my knowledge this is the first digital bedrock map in existence.

8. Gates (2000).

9. Tamaro et al. (2000).

10. Moss (2012).

11. Note that other later orogenies further "jumbled" Manhattan's rock (Isachsen et al. 2000, chapter 5). Also note that the bedrock of Manhattan, the Bronx, and parts of Westchester County is part of a geological territory known as the New England Upland region, comprised mostly of metamorphic rocks. The geological characteristics of Manhattan's rocks have some differences relative to the larger New England province, and thus are referred to as the Manhattan Prong, which is sandwiched in between two other geological regions. To the west of the Hudson River in New Jersey is Triassic Lowlands, which includes the Palisades cliffs, running from New York Harbor to Nyack, New York. These cliffs are made from volcanic rock, which formed during the Triassic period. Long Island's geological territory is part of the Coastal Plain. Geologically speaking, the Coastal Plains are quite young and are comprised of sediments, such as clay, silt, sand, and gravel.

12. Baskerville (1982).

13. Merguerian and Merguerian (2004); Merguerian and Moss (2006).

14. http://www.wnyc.org/shows/lopate/series/story-new-york-10-objects/; http://www.wnyc.org/story/190000-object- 9-manhattan-schist/.

15. Moss (2010).

16. Cozzens (1843, 14).

17. Manhattan contains a surprising array of other rock types. For example, intrusions of igneous rock have left pockets of granite and other minerals. Over the centuries, gem hunters have found a variety of crystals, some of them perfectly clear-colored and precious, including aquamarine, smoky quartz, golden beryl, topaz, black tourmalines, and dark red garnets (Crewdson and Mittelback 2002).

18. Early attempts to open a marble quarry in the Bronx were a failure. In 1834, Cozzens (1843) writes, "A quarry was opened at Kingsbridge some years ago, which proved unprofitable. Lime has been burnt from this Limestone, but as it will not slack as quickly, but first crumbles up in small grains, it has been discontinued for fine work." He adds in a footnote, "When time is allowed, for lime made from this marble to slack perfectly, it answers well for strong work, and it has also, been extensively used for agricultural purposes" (16).

19. Merguerian and Moss (2006).

20. *New York Times* (1940).

21. Buder (1963).

22. Parsons (1976).

23. Cheryl Moss, email correspondence, September 2013.

24. Tantala, Nordenson, Deodatis, and Jacob (2008).

25. Shah et al. (2006); Sykes et al. (2008).

26. *New York Times* (1915b).

27. Hood (1993).

28. Isachsen et al. (2000, 163); Moss and Merguerian (2009). Note that the Ice Age ended 10,000 years ago, but locally the ice started to retreat from the area about 20,000 years ago and was gone from New York by about 15,000 years ago.

29. Moss and Merguerian (2008).

30. Only the Harbor Hill directly crosses New York, as the Ronkonkoma was run over by the Harbor Hill ice. Both the Harbill Hill and Ronkonkoma moraines are present on Long Island.

31. Merguerian (2003).
32. Moss and Merguerian (2005).
33. Merguerian (2003).
34. However, it is not clear how much of this layer is lake bottom and how much is new river bottom sand.
35. Smith (1938).
36. Kemp (1887).
37. A more detailed version of the map can be found in Sanderson (2009).
38. Sanderson (2009, 158).
39. Personal conversation with Richard K. Shaw, State Soil Scientist, USDA-NRCS, June 2014.
40. Sanderson (2009); Sanderson and Brown (2007).
41. Sanderson (2009).
42. Sanderson (2009); Sanderson and Brown (2007).
43. Sanderson and Brown (2007).
44. Sanderson's map of water courses and wetlands is one of several. Sanderson recreates his map mostly from the British Headquarters map of 1782. Perhaps the most famous is the Viele map of 1865 (figure 2.3). Another frequently cited one is by McCoun (see Merguerian and Merguerian 2004). Hill and Waring (1897) produce a simplified version of the Viele map as well.
45. Hill and Waring (1897, 195–196) write, "They were attracted, to a greater or less degree, by the low fertile plains, intersected with streams and tidal inlets, which resembled their native land and which invited the construction of canals."
46. Yamin and Schuldenrein (2007).
47. Hill and Waring (1897, 194).
48. Valentine (1856), "Lispenard's Meadows."
49. Anbinder (2001).
50. Hill and Waring (1897).
51. Ibid., 203.
52. Ibid., 215.
53. Ibid., 243.
54. Ibid., 200–201.
55. Ibid.
56. Perlmutter and Arnow (1953).
57. Koeppel (2000).
58. See Koeppel (2000) for how Aaron Burr established the Manhattan Water Company in 1799 to provide freshwater to the city but used the funds mostly for banking. Ironically, the fact that Burr and his colleagues were able to profit at the expense of the city lead to the creation of the Croton Aqueduct water system, one of the greatest engineering achievements of the early republic, and the reason for New York City's high water quality today.

Chapter 2

1. Albion (1939, appendices II and III). Also see Glaeser (2005).
2. Land, as I define it, is the ability to gain some direct benefit out of a particular location. This particularly applies to urban areas. Forests and other natural places can have an existence value, where there is generally no access, but we derive a certain psychic benefit knowing that they exist (Krutilla 1967), and, given climate change, inaccessible forests can also provide a value in stabilizing earth's climate and ecology.

3. Marshall (2012).
4. See Saiz (2010) on how land-constrained cities have higher housing prices.
5. Blackmar (1989).
6. Hartog (1983).
7. Buttenwieser (1987).
8. To this day, there are many lots in Manhattan that are owned by a different party than the building owner. These cases remain holdovers from the days when the Hybrid Model was the norm. Today, these landowners generally issue 99-year or 150-year ground leases to the building owner. Examples of this include the land beneath the Chrysler Building, which is owned by the Cooper Union; the land beneath Rockefeller Center had been owned by Columbia University but was sold to the Rockefeller Group in 1985 (Dowd 1985). I have not seen any data on how many plots still have ground leases, though I would guess it to be a relatively small fraction of the land market.
9. Blackmar (1989); Margo (1996).
10. Gandy (2003); Marshall (2012).
11. Rink (1986); Shorto (2004).
12. Juet (1625).
13. Stokes (1967, 1:6).
14. Rink (1986).
15. Shorto (2004, 40).
16. Valentine (1853).
17. Stokes (1967, 8).
18. Pound (1935).
19. There is some controversy about the first year of New York's founding. The official seal of New York puts it at 1625; 1624 is the year of settlement on Governors Island; 1626 is when they moved to Manhattan. See Roberts (2008).
20. Valentine (1853); Hill and Waring (1897, 195). This claim has been made in historical accounts, but no reference to original documents is given.
21. Philbrick (2006).
22. Imagine, for example, that the Puritans settled what is today New York, and the Dutch settled what is today New England. One cannot but help speculate that a much different national history would have occurred. Perhaps today's New England would have remained New Netherlands, and thus generated a binational country like Canada.
23. Kammen (1975); Kraft (1986); Shorto (2004).
24. O'Callaghan (1846). See the letter at: http://www.thirteen.org/dutchny/interactives/manhattan-island/.
25. Rosenwaike (1972).
26. Kammen (1975).
27. Shorto (2004).
28. Cantwell and diZerenga Wall (2003, 124).
29. Stokes (1967, 1:11).
30. Stokes (1967, 1:13); Landmarks Preservation Commission (1983).
31. Landmarks Preservation Commission (1983); Janvier (2000, 7–8).
32. Hill and Waring (1897, 198).
33. Ibid.
34. Valentine (1853); Stokes (1967, 2:359–411); Haley (1972); Shorto (2004).
35. Stokes (1967, 1:56). Also see Stokes (1967, vols. 2 and 6) for details on land grants.

36. Valentine (1853, 307).

37. Stokes (1967, 1:26).

38. Ibid., 33–34, 37.

39. Shorto (2004). New Amsterdam was likely the first municipality in the United States (Pound 1935).

40. Stokes (1967, 1:39).

41. Ibid., 58.

42. Valentine (1853).

43. For a history of Valentine's life and the *Manuals* he wrote, see *New York Times* (1895). For town lot grants, see Valentine (1857).

44. Dongan Charter of the City of New York (1686).

45. Quote is taken from Buttenwieser (1987).

46. Black (1897); Steinberg (2014).

47. Hartog (1983, 44).

48. Buttenwieser (1987, 31).

49. Ibid., 37.

50. Hartog (1983).

51. Hartog (1983); Buttenwieser (1987).

52. Council of Hygiene and Public Health (1866).

53. The most recent infill was the creation of Battery Park City in the 1970s. See Sanderson and Brown (2007) on total increase of Manhattan, and Buttenwieser (1987, 21), on Lower Manhattan. Kardas and Larrabee (1980) claim 50% increase below Chambers Street. Also see Walsh and LeFluer (1995).

54. McKay (1971).

55. Moss and Merguerian (2008).

56. Steinberg (2014).

57. Hill and Waring (1897).

58. Valentine (1853, 285).

59. Yamin (2000).

60. Stokes (1967, 5:1405).

61. Cozzens (1843).

62. Yamin and Schuldenrein (2007).

63. I use the 25 x 100 square foot plot as a convenient reference; most plots were not in fact 25 feet across, but less than that. Twenty-five feet of frontage was relatively large, and most likely to be demanded only by upper income households. Eighteen or 20 feet across would be more affordable for the middle classes. See Lockwood (1972).

64. Plunz (1990); Friedman personal conversation, November 2013.

65. Ballon (2012).

66. To investigate the relationship between early lot size and distance from the fort, each lot area was estimated from the map in figure 2.2 in millimeters square; distance to the fort was estimated in millimeters. Distance was converted to miles using Google maps. Areas in square feet were estimated by taking the entire areas of two blocks today that have the same size as in the map. Then the ratio of square feet area to millimeter area was taken for each, and the average value of this ratio was used, which turns out to be 100. To estimate the effects of distance on area, I ran a regression of ln(Area) on distance to the fort. The sample regression line is $Predicted Ln(Area) = 7.9 + 10.7 * distance$. Both estimated coefficients are statistically significant at greater than 99%. $R^2 = 0.396$.

67. Valentine (1860, 536).

68. Valentine (1860). Note that each colony had its own currency, denominated in pounds. The exchange rate between New York and British pounds varied over the colonial period, but Valentine (1860) uses $2.50 per pound to convert New York pounds to dollars. See McCusker (1992).

69. To create the index, I collected data from 146 transactions between 1667 and 1773 as given in Valentine (1860). The data set includes prices in New York pounds, approximate address, approximate lot area, whether it had a house or not, and whether it was a corner parcel. Using the approximate address, I determined the latitude and longitude coordinates from http://itouchmap.com/latlong.html. Then I calculated the Cartesian distance to the fort. Real lot prices were determined by dividing the nominal price by the Schumpter-Gillboy index given in McCusker (1992, table B-1, column 2). For the regression, I regressed *ln(real lot prices)* on distance to the fort, lot size, a dummy variable if a house was on the lot, a dummy variable if the lot was on a corner, and year dummy variables, with 1667 as the omitted year. Regression results are given in the appendix C. The index was formed by evaluating $100 * \exp(\hat{\beta}_t)$, which are the year dummy variable coefficients. Since 1667 was omitted, its index value is 100. Then averages and standard deviations for each decade were calculated to create figure 2.7.

70. Valentine (1853, 278) notes that lots in the Shoemakers' Pasture, north of Maiden Lane typically went for about £30 from 1700 to 1730.

71. Kammen (1975, 161).

72. Burrows and Wallace (1999, 168–171).

73. Ibid., 168–171.

74. Valentine (1860, 528).

75. To determine the growth in the general price level, I first used McCusker's (1992) Composite Consumer Price from 1770 to 1991 (table B-1, column 4), and then used the CPI-U-RS values to 2013. Index values were adjusted to 2013 dollars. Caution must be used when interpreting changes in prices over time, given how much the quality and quantity of goods and services have changed since the colonial period.

76. Wilkenfeld (1978).

77. Water lot sales data is given in Petersen and Edwards (1917) and Black (1897).

78. For example, Alexander Hamilton's summer home, the Grange, was part of his 32 acre estate, which was located at 287 Convent Avenue in Upper Manhattan. John Jacob Astor's country seat was along the East River, near 86th Street. This property was a mere 11 acres (see Sackersdorff 1868).

79. Spann (1988).

80. Spann (1988); Ballon (2012).

81. Ballon (2012).

82. Hartog (1983).

83. Randel (1864, 848).

84. Ballon (2012).

85. Randel (1864, 856). Emphasis in original.

86. Randel (1864, 848). Emphasis in original.

87. Morris, De Witt and Rutherford (1866).

88. Hurd (1903); Morris (1972); Kostof (1991).

89. Hurd (1903).

90. Baskerville (1982, 96).

91. Moehring (1981).
92. Valentine (1857).
93. Viele (1866, 10).
94. Morris, De Witt and Rutherford (1866).
95. Hoyt ([1933] 2000).
96. Spann (1988).
97. Hill and Waring (1897, 241).
98. Marcuse (1987, 288).
99. Spann (1988, 27).
100. Randel (1864, 848). Emphasis in original.
101. Reps (1965, 299).
102. Hoyt (1933).
103. Rose-Redwood and Li (2011).
104. The data was created by taking block-level amalgamations of the data created by Eric Sanderson for his Mannahatta Project and comparing it to current elevation levels. See Barr and Ort (2014) for more details about the data. Mannahatta data can be found at https://welikia.org/ and is used courtesy of Eric Sanderson, The Mannahatta Project, Wildlife Conservation Society. Also see Rose-Redwood (2011) for a similar analysis.
105. The regression results are given in the appendix E. The dependent variable is the average elevation change in feet for 3,180 blocks on Manhattan between 1609 and 2012. Controls included the average elevation in 1609 and a series of Mannahatta dummy variables (1 if the feature was present in 1609, 0 otherwise), such as if the block was below sea level in 1609, if it had a pond, stream, freshwater wetland, saltwater wetland, tulip tress, and the location of Collect Pond, respectively. Other geographic data included the distance to the tip, the distance to the closest shore, the distance to the central spine, and measures of miles north of the tip and miles east or west of Fifth Avenue. These additional controls were included to account for elements of the natural environment that might influence elevation changes over time. Mannahatta data can be found at https://welikia.org/ and is used courtesy of Eric Sanderson, The Mannahatta Project, Wildlife Conservation Society.
106. O'Grady (2013).
107. Randel (1864); Ballon (2012).
108. Wallace (2007).
109. It also seems that the construction of the Croton Aqueduct and sewage lines were not the reason for increasing land values above the demarcation line, given the ad hoc nature of how the pipes were laid down throughout the city. See Union History Company (1899); Moehring (1981); and Goldman (1997).
110. Willis (1995, 36).
111. Alpern and Durst (1984).
112. Samuels (1997).
113. Barr (2013) compares skyscraper heights across New York and Chicago. Although that article does not compare lot sizes directly, further work by the author using this data does not show statistically significant differences across the city in regard to lots used for skyscrapers.

Chapter 3

1. Riis (1890).
2. Jackson (1985).

3. It was the automobile and the system of highways which has made sprawl a pressing issue. But my point is that the tendency for a city or metropolitan area to see a rapidly expanding footprint is a product of mass transit, combined with the preference for suburban living.

4. In Spanish, the word "suburbio," specifically refers to the poor, often slum-like residential areas around central core and has the opposite connotation to "suburbia" in the United States.

5. Folkerts (1997).

6. See Sanderson (2009) for more information on soil types. Richard Shaw, State Soil Scientist, USDA-NRCS, confirmed my conclusions. However, he also would add Wotalf and Leicester, since they are freshwater wetland soils, but given their location in the "heart" of the rocky Upper West Side, they were excluded from fertile Manhattan. Shaw is the source about the culturally sensitive soils (email and phone correspondence, June 2014).

7. Stokes (1967, 2:181).

8. Bancker (1917).

9. Sanderson and Brown (2007).

10. Bisland (1897, 256).

11. Landmarks Preservation Commission (1969).

12. Valentine (1853, 573). Stuyvesant is buried in a vault on the grounds. In an ironic twist of history, St. Mark's Place today is known for its tattoo parlors and bohemian culture, in direct contrast to Stuyvesant's Calvinistic views.

13. Stokes (1967, 1:167).

14. Valentine (1866, 586).

15. Pierce, Toler, and Nutting (1903).

16. Ibid.

17. As Pierce, Toler, and Nutting (1903) indicate, that loss of autonomy was met with some bitterness by Harlem residents.

18. Brueckner (1987).

19. In this model, we assume that the landowner is different than the land user, though that does not alter the conclusions of the model. If the owner and the user are the same, we just assume that they wear two separate hats: the landlord-as-investor hat, and owner-as-user hat; the user has an implicit price that he pays to the owner, rather than explicit price.

20. Abbott (1974).

21. Ibid., 36.

22. Ibid.

23. Ibid.

24. See chapter 2 for more details about the data.

25. Jackson (1985).

26. Jackson (1985) argues that the year 1815 was when the walking city ended, since it was the introduction of steam ferry service to Brooklyn, allowing merchants to commute to work from Brooklyn Heights. However, mass transit options within Manhattan were introduced a few decades later.

27. Jackson (1985, 35).

28. Condit (1980, 24).

29. Ibid.

30. Jackson (1985).

31. Durst (1898).

32. The 1827 names were taken from *Longworth's American Almanac, New-York Register, and City Directory*. The 1849 names were culled from *Doggett's New York City Directory*. Every attempt was made to use all people in their respective jobs. The addresses were then geocoded using an address locater created from 1852 Perris Maps of the city of New York.

33. Claghorn (1901).

34. Rosenwaike (1972).

35. Ernst (1949, table 27).

36. Rosenwaike (1972, 44).

37. Ernst (1949, table 27).

38. Yamin (2001).

39. See Anbinder (2001) for neighborhood boundaries. He presents a more balanced history of the neighborhood.

40. McCormack (2009).

41. Anbinder (2001).

42. Glaeser (2011) make a similar point for the favelas of Brazil.

43. For population changes in Harlem and the rest of New York from 1910 to 1960, see Beveridge (2008).

44. Milne (2000).

45. Ibid.

46. Popper (1955) studies this case for Newark.

47. Attempts to beautify the pond and clean it up in the early 1800s were unsuccessful, and as a result the city chose to fill it in rather than use it as park space or create a canal from the Hudson to the pond.

48. Milne (2000, 26–27).

49. Yamin (2000).

50. Ibid.

51. Yamin (2001).

52. Anbinder (2001).

53. Ibid., 356.

54. Ibid., 382.

55. DiPasquale and Wheaton (1996); Glaeser et al. (2005).

56. Stott (1990, 56, 143); Wilentz (1984, figure 5).

57. This conclusion is based on several strands of evidence. First, see Stott (1990), table 16 shows that average rent payments comprised 23.7% of household's budgets for New York City workers. Further, Margo (1996) calculates 29% for housing New York City workers. Rental data is from two sources. First, Anbinder (2001, 102) cites statistics collected from the 1850s, which show average rents in Five Points ranged from $4.50 to $7.00, depending on the quality of the unit. Margo (1996) has collected an extensive data set on rents in New York from 1830 to 1860. Using his data, I ran a regression of the average monthly rent on a series of control variables that he collected, and I predict weekly rents for apartments one-third of a mile away, Collect Pond on the third floor, with two rooms and an apartment quality about average for the Five Point neighborhoods (the index from this is given in figure 3.10). From this analysis, I find weekly rents to be plus or minus $5.00 through the period.

58. Using Margo's (1996) index numbers, I first converted them to real numbers using the national consumer price index from the time (Officer and Williamson 2015) and then I normalized the values so that 1855 had a rent index value set to $6.50, given that is what Anbinder (2001) cites for the weekly rent for a two-room apartment in Five Points.

Margo's index was created on the assumption that the market values specific quality measures remained the same over time. It represents a first estimate for the value of housing in Antebellum New York.

59. Population data are from Ernst (1949). Wages tended to fall and rise with the business cycle but showed a net gain over the period. For example, construction laborer wages rose from $0.87 in 1851 to $0.97 by 1860. Wages spiked during the Civil War to $1.51 in 1866 (*Engineering News Record*, May 27, 1948).

60. The graph was generated by estimating the monthly wages of laborers and dividing it by the estimated cost of housing, as presented in figure 3.10A. Wage data for 1832 and 1835 to 1846 were taken from Wilentz (1984, figure 4). Wages from 1851 to 1860 are from *Engineering News Record* (1948). Data for missing years were interpolated from table Ba4254 (daily laborer wages in the northeast), in *Historical Statistics of United States* (2014). To convert the northeast values to New York figures, a regression was first run of New York wages on northeast wages for the overlapping years, and then northeast wages were converted to New York wages using the OLS-derived formula estimated. *Predicted New York Wage* = $0.761 + 0.191 * Northeast wage$. Daily wages were converted to weekly wages by multiplying by 5.5 and then converted to monthly wages by multiplying by four.

Chapter 4

1. *Real Estate Record and Builders' Guide* (1912c).
2. In chapters 8 and 9, I will demonstrate that this relationship is causal and not due to some other, omitted variable.
3. Lazarus (1883).
4. See Angel and Lamson-Hall (2014) for a very detailed treatment of Manhattan's population density from 1800 to 2010.
5. In this chapter, I keep the theory relatively simple. There is a large literature on the theory of spatial structure as it relates to housing. For more details, see Muth (1969); Brueckner (1987); Brueckner et al. (1999); and Barr and Ort (2014). This paper discusses how income, preference, and amenity differences can alter prices and urban density patterns.
6. Anas et al. (1998).
7. Claghorn (1901, 477).
8. Muth (1969); Brueckner (1987).
9. Wilson (1987) discusses these concentration effects for cities after World War II.
10. For this discussion, I assume that neighborhood amenities are exogenous, or exist before people decide to move into the neighborhood. Of course, amenities can be endogenous in the sense that groups already living in the neighborhood can choose to construct amenities that further attract more of that particular group. If only rich neighborhoods can pay for sewage removal, then only rich neighborhoods will have them. However, investigating this complication is left for future research. See Brueckner et al. (1999).
11. Tenement House Department (1903).
12. See Barr and Ort (2014) for more information about the data.
13. Tables 32 and 34, Statistics of Population, 1900 Census, Volume 1.
14. On the Germans, see Nadel (1990). On Jews and Italians, see Kessner (1977).
15. Eric Sanderson, personal conversation, January 2013.

16. In 1866 the Council on Hygiene reported that neighborhoods around the former Lispenard Meadows had sewer line laid at the wrong elevations, so that during high tide water from the Hudson River would fill up the lines and well up into the streets.
17. Durst (1898).
18. Living close to an El line can create noise and pollution. I do not explore this, since I only investigate the distance to each stop, rather than a particular line. Further, the nuisances were likely to be greater for front-facing apartments and I do not have data at the apartment level.
19. Pratt (1911).
20. Bromley and Bromley (1899).
21. Regression results and more information about the data can be found in Barr and Ort (2014).
22. One celebrated tulip tree still lived in Inwood Park as late as 1912. See *New York Times* (1912). For the distribution of tree types in Manhattan as of 2006, see NYC Parks (2006). Today, tulip trees, if present at all, are extremely rare.
23. Villarreal (2012) finds that, controlling for quality, apartment prices in the nineteenth and early twentieth century were lower near Manhattan's historical marshlands. His findings suggest too that people avoided areas with poor environmental amenities and that this avoidance persisted over time.
24. Tenement House Committee (1895).
25. Technically, three-stage regressions were run. See Barr and Ort (2014) for more information about the data and statistical methods.
26. Bender (2004).
27. Veiller (1903a).
28. Plunz (1990).
29. Claghorn (1901).
30. Veiller (1900).
31. Ibid, 18.
32. Veiller (1936).
33. Veiller (1900, 27).
34. Lubove (1961); Jackson (1976).
35. *Real Estate Record and Builders' Guide* (1908); Jackson (1976).
36. Council on Hygiene (1866); Veiller (1900).
37. Veiller (1903b).
38. Bremner (1958); Jackson (1976).
39. Veiller (1903c). An 1894 report suggests the return to tenements without a mortgage was 8% to 10% (Reynolds 1895).
40. Veiller (1903c, 370).
41. Ibid., 373–374.
42. Ibid., 375.
43. Smith (1776).
44. Veiller (1903d).
45. Lubove (1961).
46. Based on the block-level data collected by the Tenement House Department (1903).
47. Among the tenements, there were 264 water closets, and there were no stationary bathtubs. Forty apartments had hot running water (Lubove 1961).
48. Weise (2014).

49. *Engineering News Record* (1948), May 27, 143. Manufacturing jobs paid between $12 and $20 per week in 1905 wages (Pratt 1911). Officer and Williamson (2015), "Annual Wages in the United States, 1774-Present."

50. Flagg (1894, 108).

51. Historians frequently point out that the vestiges of Dutch New York have all been wiped out, but perhaps the 25 x 100 square foot lot remains one lasting effect.

52. http://www.demographia.com/db-state1900.htm.

Chapter 5

1. *New York Times* (1905).

2. Land value data is from three sources: Fred Smith, *Record and Guide* (1898), and Jeremy Atack and Robert Margo, which is detailed in Atack and Margo (1998). Their data was geocoded by Carlos Villarreal.

3. Gray (1996); Landau and Condit (1996).

4. Clark and Kingston (1930); Willis (1995).

5. We could use 163 stories, since the Burj Khalifa's top 46 stories are for equipment. Either way, a roughly 2% growth rate still applies.

6. See Linn (n.d.) about Frank Lloyd Wright's drawing for a mile-high building.

7. Koster et al. (2014).

8. This notion of "best" is called Pareto Efficiency. It means that any reallocation of resources from efficiency will only benefit one person if it harms another, without any net gain to society.

9. This discussed in Tauranac (1995) and demonstrated with statistical data in Barr (2012b).

10. The quality-of-life issue is no doubt incredibly important, but it is beyond the scope of this work. See Jacobs (1961) and Washburn (2013).

11. Weisman (1953); Webster (1959); Landau and Condit (1996).

12. Shultz and Simmons (1959).

13. Landau and Condit (1996).

14. Condit (1952, 84–85).

15. *New York Times* (1899); Peterson (1986).

16. Landau and Condit (1996, 166).

17. Condit (1988, 22).

18. *Historical Statistics of the U.S.*, Millennial Edition (2014, table Dg256).

19. *Phillips Business Directory* (1882).

20. Wallace (2006).

21. Ibid., 179.

22. Landau and Condit (1996).

23. Ibid.

24. Ibid.

25. Real estate cycles with overbuilding are not uncommon, and the underlying reasons are still somewhat mysterious and debatable. Economists have proposed several reasons for overbuilding, including changes in tax policy (Owens 1994); myopic expectations and long construction lags (Wheaton 1987, 1999); easy credit (Goetzmann and Newman 2010); developer competition (Helsley and Strange 2008); development cascades (Grenadier 1996); and overoptimism (McNulty 1995). See Kaiser (1997) and Glaeser (2013) for a review of real estate booms in American history.

26. Lueck (1989b).
27. Sabbagh (1989); Coonan (2015).
28. Wermiel (2006).
29. See http://www.nyc.gov/html/dob/html/development/permits_howto.shtml for all the steps currently required to receive a building permit.
30. Arzaghi and Henderson (2008); Rosenthal and Strange (2008).
31. Colin Buchanan and Partners (2008).
32. These results are from data that I collected on office rents and condo prices.
33. Jung et al. (2011).
34. Salvadori (1990).
35. Morgenstern (1995).
36. Sabbagh (1989, 12–13).
37. Ishii (1994); Sev and Özgen (2009).
38. Clark and Kingston (1930).
39. Dunlap (2009). My calculation, based on ln(3543/700)/(2010 – 1913).
40. Higgins (1980).
41. Note the asking rents are collected from publicly available sources, such as Kelly (2002) and industry reports, such as those by Cushman Wakefield. The Turner Index is published on Turner Construction Company's website and historical values are available from the *Historical Statistics of the United States*, Millennial Edition (2014, table Dc225). Note the Skyscraper Profit Index is determined by first taking the ratio of annual Midtown asking rents and dividing it by the annual Turner Index value. Next, I normalize the index so that 1960 = 1.0. Then I take a three-year moving average of the index and the number of skyscraper completions. The graphs show the Profit Index lagged two years and the completions count is the moving average of the number each year.
42. Zoning rules, of course, dictate what types of skyscrapers will be built where, since they largely determine which districts are for residences and which are for offices and hotels. However, I would argue that first, zoning follows prior use, so that residents create the spatial distribution of activity and the zoning rules codify it; second, over time there can be rezoning and readjustments of use based on the relative profitability of different types of projects. Take, for example, the rezoning of Long Island City and LIRR yards (Hudson Yards), which are now open to large-scale redevelopment.
43. Barr (2012b).
44. Condo prices from Case-Shiller condo price index for New York.
45. Hudson Yards Development Corp. (2015).
46. Willis (1995).
47. Huxtable (1984).
48. *New York Times* (1910).
49. Willis (1995, 26–27).
50. Quoted from Clark and Kingston (1930, 12).
51. Revell (1992).
52. Ibid., 26.
53. http://www.nber.org/cycles.html.
54. The term "Art Deco" originated from the 1925 Paris Exposition des Arts Decoratives et Industrielles, which introduced the world to the style.
55. Bassett (1913, 60).
56. Bassett (1913, figure 6); Revell (1992).

57. *New York Times* (1926b).

58. Willis (1995).

59. Using my data, I compared plot sizes of skyscrapers before and after 1916, and I do not find strong evidence of a big increase in their average sizes after 1916.

60. Weiss (1992).

61. *New York Times* (1926b).

62. Bertaud and Brueckner (2005).

63. See Le Corbusier (1931) section entitled, "Third Reminder: The Plan."

64. Harrison, Ballard, & Allen (1950).

65. This report states that if all areas in the city were built to maximum bulk it would be able to hold 70 million residents and 300 million workers. This contrasts with the figure of 55.6 million residents that is more frequently cited (Bennett 1960). The 1961 zoning code was designed to house a maximum of 12.3 million.

66. Harrison, Ballard, & Allen (1950, 9).

67. Goldberger (1977).

68. Fried (1967).

69. Fried (1968).

70. Goldberger (1981).

71. Kayden (1978).

72. Kayden (2000).

73. NYU Furman Center (2013).

74. Barr (2012b).

75. Scardino (1986).

76. Finn (2013); Morris (2014); Pincus (2014).

77. Bagli (1998); The Real Deal (2012).

78. Bagli (1998).

79. Finn (2013).

80. Clark and Kingston (1930, 11). Emphasis in original. Note they use these words in quotes as well.

81. A few notes are in order. First, to simplify my analysis, I only "costed" buildings that were 8, 15, 30, 50, 65, and 85 stories, which are a few buildings less than Clark and Kingston (CK) (1930). My analysis assumes as-of-right construction and no negotiations with the city. I did not consider any subsidies or tax breaks that might be available to the modern developer, though I did assume a developer could purchase air rights to go above the FAR limits. See Barr (2016) for more information. Lastly, CK had a team of architects, engineers, and brokers to help them in their analysis. My data comes from publicly available sources or statistical data provided by real estate companies. My results are based on my analysis alone, and as such, they represent a first attempt to estimate the returns to modern office construction in the Grand Central neighborhood; further research is needed in this area.

82. As of this writing SL Green Realty is planning to construct a sixty-five-story skyscraper across the street from Grand Central Station. The economics appear to work in their favor because they seem to have bet that they could negotiate with the city to get a tremendous FAR bonus (to get to a total FAR of 30). When they purchased the buildings on the block, it is likely the sellers were offering the buildings at prices that assumed the standard FAR limits for the block of 18 (15 plus amenity bonus). As such, it is likely that the returns from

the project are coming from the "gamble" taken by SL Green that they could get a much higher FAR than for which the land market was pricing.

83. To calculate this I take the Turner Construction Cost Index from 1929 to 2013 and divide it by both the GDP Deflator and the New York City CPI, and both numbers show a real increase above 200% (293% using the Deflator and 223% using the CPI). Looking at the ENR Building Cost Index divided by the price measures also shows similar results.

84. Sabbagh (1989, 23).

85. Holusha (2002).

86. Heath et al. (2000).

87. Bagli (2011).

88. Fenske (2008).

Chapter 6

1. This chapter is based on Barr (2010), where more details on the modeling and data can be found.

2. Barr (2010, 2013). Buildings data is from http://www.Emporis.com and http://www.sky-scraperpage.com.

3. For new skyscraper technology, see Gluckman (2003). For a history of energy usage in buildings, see Oldfield et al. (2009).

4. The first building to surpass the 295-feet/90-meter cutoff was completed in 1890; it was the World Building at 308 feet.

5. Weisman (1953).

6. For the skyscraper calculation, I first multiply the number of floors for each building times the lot size, which gives the sum of possible gross building area. Using the MapPLUTO (2014) file from the New York City Department of City Planning, I divided building floor area by plot size times the number of floors for all buildings in the data set for buildings that were twenty stories or higher. The average value comes 55%. Thus, I multiply 0.55 times lot area times the total floor count to get an estimate of usable square footage and then I convert it to square miles. For all buildings I added the total floor area for the Manhattan from MapPLUTO (2014) (excluding non-Manhattan properties such as Governors Island and Roosevelt Island).

7. National Bureau of Economic Research (2015).

8. Average growth rates are determined by running a regression of the skyscraper measures on a time trend.

9. Data is from US Census Bureau (downloaded from Wikipedia). For this analysis, the New York metropolitan area includes New York City, Westchester, Nassau, and Suffolk Counties in New York, and Hudson and Bergen Counties in New Jersey.

10. Kelly (2002, chapter 5).

11. For example, if the owner of the building is the City of New York, as in the case of the forty-story Municipal Building, B is an implicit number. In this case, each department will have a budget about how much "rent" they must pay to the city, but since the rent money comes from the city anyway, B is an accounting figure that represents the value of the space, while the money to maintain it flows from the tax coffers filled by the residents of the city.

12. Glaeser (2013).

13. Colin Buchanan and Partners (2008).

14. Performing the analysis with the number of completions each year produces very similar results.
15. Barr (2010).
16. Note in Barr (2012b) I find that the Empire State Building is too tall by 100%. The difference in the findings is due to the fact that I use different data sets. I leave for future work a better reconciliation of the two results.
17. One note is in order. The statistical analysis revealed that the number of variables that seem to affect the total height measure and the max height are different. In particular, the *max* variable had fewer statistically significant explanatory variables. This suggests that the determinants of the *max* variable are somewhat more idiosyncratic than the total height measure.
18. The five boroughs of New York were created in 1898, but I include all of them as part of the city prior to that year. Regarding the surrounding counties, adding other counties does not affect the results or conclusions. Also note, I did not subtract out the NYC metropolitan population from the national population. Finally, for simplicity, I did not include measures of the global or international population.
19. I do not include measures of wages cost estimates, since a New York specific time series is nearly impossible to get for 125 years. Using a national index for unskilled workers proved not to be a useful variable for this exercise.
20. Old space is increasingly attractive to the growing Internet-related businesses in the city. Evidently, the younger employees in these companies prefer the aesthetics of the older space, and to some degree, reject the aesthetics of shining corporate towers as being at odds with the youth culture associated with Internet software companies, such as Google, Twitter, and so on
21. This comes from my data set on skyscrapers used for this chapter.
22. MapPLUTO (2013) file from the New York Department of City Planning.
23. These are called "dummy variables" in economics.
24. The effect of tax rates on skyscraper height remains underexplored and more work is needed to investigate their true relationship.
25. Note that for the tallest building regression the trend becomes insignificant when I include One World Trade Center in the analysis. But I exclude this from this discussion because it was built as replacement for the Twin Towers and with little regard for economic considerations.
26. Jonnes (1981).
27. Marshall (2006b), (2013).
28. Veblen (1899).
29. Saez (2014, table A3 "Top fractiles income shares (including capital gains) in the U.S.").
30. Filler (2015).
31. Inequality and the ego are linked in the sense that an abundance of wealth frees the individual or corporate leaders from his or her need to operate on a tight budget. Squandering limited resources can lead to penury, and even death. But, if luck and pluck releases one from these concerns, the primal instincts to "show off" are now released into the public sphere.
32. Gilbert (1900, 624).
33. See Sutton (2013).
34. Helsley and Strange (2008); Barr et al. (2015).
35. A few notes are in order. First in this analysis Bank of Manhattan Trust Building is excluded. These results are somewhat different than in Barr (2012b); the difference again being affected

by the data sets. Also the reason why Two World Trade Center (1973) is lower on the list is because it followed the first one, completed in the prior year. As a result because of the regression equation, it would predict a higher height, and thus a smaller residual (this is discussed in the next section on height competition).

36. Certainly, builders can adjust their heights to some degree during the construction phase; and they may feel compelled to do so if they maintain a competitive spirit. See Barr (2013) for New York versus Chicago developers.

37. Barr (2010, 2013).

38. This result holds up even if we run the regression prior to the Twin Towers, since one tower was completed in 1972 and the other in 1973.

39. Barr, Mizrach, and Mundra (2015).

40. Reference to Midtown rents at a minimum of $2.50 are given in *New York Times* (1929). Also see Keast and Randall (1930, graph 7), which shows average rents for new buildings ranging from about $2.50 to $4.00 per square foot. Raskob and Smith estimated rents of $3.50 for most of the building and $4.00 for the tower (Friedman 1998). See chapter 5 for the source of the Turner Construction Cost Index and the Skyscraper Profit Index.

41. Kelly (2002).

42. The sales prices come from the New York City Real Estate Rolling File found on the New York City Department of Finance's website. I look at office buildings sold in 2013 that were in the "Midtown CBD" neighborhood.

43. Per square construction costs come from data privately shared by Cushman Wakefield. For average land costs in Manhattan, see Hughes (2015). For average office rents, see Voien (2013); Miller Samuel (2014).

44. For average condo prices, see Miller Samuel (2014) and Clark (2014).

Chapter 7

1. The architecture of European bell towers would inspire early skyscraper architects. For example, the Metropolitan Life Insurance Tower (1909) at Madison Square Park is a fifty-story version of the Campanile in St. Mark's Square in Venice. At the northern corner of that park also stood the 300-foot tower of Madison Square Garden (1890), inspired by the Giralda of Seville.

2. Roth (1993).

3. Levy and Salvadori (1992).

4. Ibid.

5. Marshall (2006a); Johnson (2011).

6. Goodspeed Publishing Co. (1891); Peck (1948).

7. US Geological Survey (2006).

8. Personal conversation with Donald Friedman, November 2013.

9. Deutsch (1907).

10. *New York Times* (1915a).

11. Deutsch (1907).

12. Ibid., 188. Note that Deutsch seems to have overstated the depth of the quicksand throughout Lower Manhattan, especially south of Wall Street. As discussed in chapter 1, at Wall Street and Broadway, for example, the elevation of the ground relative to sea level is about 20 feet; while the bedrock is about 21 feet below sea level, suggesting a maximum possibility of 41 feet of wet subsoil, though much likely closer to 21 feet.

13. Oser (1999).
14. Schuberth (1968, 81–82).
15. Also note that the depth to bedrock around Washington Square does not appear to drop to several hundred feet below the surface. Schuberth's (1968) characterization of the bedrock seems to be a bit of an overstatement.
16. There have been a few voices pointing out that other factors besides bedrock were at work. See Willis (1995); Landau and Condit (1996); and Marshall (2007). However none of them have presented evidence beyond anecdotal. Furthermore, people typically point to Grand Central Station as the reason for Midtown. Chapter 8 will show how, this too, is wrong.
17. Donald Friedman, email correspondence, April 2014.
18. *New York Times* (1897, 1907b).
19. *New York Times* (1907b, 1925).
20. *New York Times* (1897).
21. Ibid.
22. Equitable was influential in several respects. Besides their first tall building, their 1915 building become legendary for illustrating the problems from building tall without any height regulations. See chapter 5 and Landmarks Preservation Commission (1996).
23. Landau and Condit (1996).
24. Ibid., 66.
25. *New York Times* (1907b).
26. Landmarks Preservation Commission (1999).
27. Irish (1989).
28. Email correspondence with Gideon Sorkin, August 2009.
29. *New York Times* (1897).
30. *Real Estate Record and Builders' Guide* (1912b).
31. *New York Times* (1907a).
32. Fenske (2008, 191).
33. Ibid.
34. *Washington Post* (1911).
35. Kidder (1920).
36. Semsch (1908); Kidder (1920).
37. Semsch (1908, 12).
38. *Real Estate Record and Builders' Guide* (1909, 1912a).
39. *New York Times* (1911); Fenske (2008, 190).
40. Peck (1948).
41. Ibid.
42. Much of the results given in the rest of the chapter are based on Barr, Tassier, and Trendafilov (2010). See that article for more information on the data sources and preparation.
43. See Barr et al. (2010) for data sources.
44. Using the GDP deflator to adjust prices.
45. MapPLUTO file from New York City Department of City Planning (2013).
46. Kidder (1920, 75).
47. Clark and Kingston (1930).
48. In fact, the correlation coefficient between the two is 0.01.
49. See Barr (2012b).
50. Rosenthal and Strange (2004).

51. Myers (1931); Robbins and Terleckyi (1960).
52. This section is taken from Barr, Tassier, and Trendafilov (2010).
53. Also there may be some concern that the measure of factory workers in each assembly district is endogenous for some years. However, these districts were established before 1890, and therefore land use in 1905 is strongly correlated with past decisions about land use. Thus, the presence of factory workers is likely to be exogenous to the presence of skyscrapers constructed shortly after 1890.
54. Billings (1894).
55. Willis (1995).
56. Ibid.
57. This data was from land values maps produced by the City of New York in 1909 (and are given in dollars per linear front foot). Ideally, we would like to have land values for a period prior to initial skyscraper construction, such as 1890, but these data were not obtainable for this chapter. See Barr et al. (2010) for more discussion of this issue.
58. To do this requires a form of statistical analysis called a "probit" regression. See Wooldridge (2012).

Chapter 8

1. This chapter is based on the work presented in Barr and Tassier (2015) and which includes more details about the data.
2. Cushman & Wakefield (2013).
3. See Ford (1998) for typology of different types of "midtowns."
4. McKay (1971); Lockwood (1976).
5. Myers (1931).
6. Quante (1976).
7. Robbins and Terleckyi (1960); O'Flaherty (2009).
8. See Epilogue.
9. Marshall (2007); Chaban (2012).
10. Condit (1980).
11. Here a skyscraper is defined as building that is 262 feet (80 meters) or taller. See Barr, Tassier, and Trendafilov (2010).
12. Durst (1898).
13. Metlife (2014).
14. Beauregard (2006).
15. US Census data (taken from Wikipedia).
16. Essex, Union, Passaic, Hudson, and Bergen counties in New Jersey and Westchester, Suffolk, and Nassau counties. See Hoover and Vernon (1959).
17. US Census data (taken from Wikipedia).
18. Quante (1976).
19. New York Department of Health and Mental Hygiene (2010).
20. Folsom (1961b).
21. Folsom (1961a).
22. McMillen (1996); Anas et al. (1998); McMillen and Smith (2003).
23. Krugman (1996).
24. Hurd (1903); Ellison and Glaeser (1999); Davis and Weinstein (2002); Burchfield et al. (2006); Bleakley and Lin (2012).

25. Albion (1939).
26. Hoyt (1933).
27. Cronon (1991).
28. Garreau (1991).
29. Helsley and Sullivan (1991).
30. Krugman (1996).
31. Moehring (1981).
32. Valentine (1857).
33. Fujita and Ogawa (1982).
34. White (1988); DiPasquale and Wheaton (1996).
35. Garreau (1991).
36. Anas and Kim (1996).
37. Rosenwaike (1972).
38. Randel (1864); Geismer (2005).
39. The quote is given in Geismer (2005), 26, but it is taken from the minutes of the Common Council of 1808.
40. Simon (1978).
41. Valentine (1857); Lockwood (1976); Burrows and Wallace (1999).
42. Valentine (1857); Presa (1996, 2).
43. Presa (1996).
44. Similarly, where Broadway connected with Sixth Avenue would one day emerge as Herald Square in 1890.
45. Postal (2001).
46. Ibid., 6.
47. Ibid., 7, quoted from King's *Handbook* (1893).
48. Postal (2001).
49. Landmarks Preservation Commission (1989).
50. Cromley (1999).
51. Landmarks Preservation Commission (1989, 7).
52. Condit (1980, 24).
53. Ibid.
54. The station likely had an effect of drawing more business to the Madison Square neighborhood. However, as best I can tell, it was more like a waystation and warehouse. The larger aim of the railroad was to deliver people from Lower Manhattan to Harlem, and, as such, its effect on the neighborhood was probably more limited; it was not a terminal like the rebuilt Grand Central Station of 1913. See Condit (1980).
55. Ibid., 86.
56. Ibid., 87–89.
57. Ibid., 89.
58. This section is based the work in Barr and Tassier (2015), which presents much more information about the data, including tables about employment types and locations.
59. See Barr and Tassier (2015) for an analysis for 1892 for two different samples—those with both addresses and only those with home addresses.
60. These statistics are for people working in Manhattan but living anywhere, including Brooklyn, Bronx, and New Jersey.
61. *Real Estate Record and Builders' Guide* (1890).
62. Robbins and Terleckyi (1960).

63. A regression of distance of job to tip on distance of home to dip and year dummies for those who work south of Chambers Street yields a statistically insignificant coefficient for the distance to home variable.

64. More statistics are given in Barr and Tassier (2015).

65. Appendix V demonstrates this graphically, but I also ran a regression of the degrees latitude of buildings in Midtown on the year and year squared. Solving for the maximum reveals that northern most point of Midtown's northward movement was hit in 1991.5. The estimated regression is *Predicted latitude = 35.477 + .0053* year − 1.33* 10^{-6} * year^2*. All coefficients are statistically significant at the 99% level. $R^2 = 0.22$.

66. Jackson (2013); Kimmelman (2013).

Chapter 9

1. Miller (2014).
2. Tauranac (1995); Bascomb (2004).
3. The building has 86 occupiable stories, but the spire raises the building to 102 stories.
4. Willis (1995).
5. Shiller (2005).
6. Barr, Mizrach, and Mundra (2015).
7. Shiller (2008); Glaeser (2013).
8. *New York Times* (1930b); Tauranac (1995); Friedman (1998).
9. *New York Times* (1930e).
10. *New York Times* (1928d).
11. *New York Times* (1873).
12. In 1919, Walter Chrysler moved to New York to oversee the Willys-Overland Company, which made automobiles in Elizabeth, New Jersey. In the early 1920s, Chrysler branched out on his own to manufacture and sell automobiles; by 1925 the Chrysler Motor Company was born, and on its way to becoming one of America's largest corporations. Operating out of New York, Chrysler was able to be close to the bankers, marketers, and engineers who made his products successful. See *New York Times* (1928c); Curcio (2001); Fiat Chrysler Automobiles (2014).
13. Johnson (1936a); Goetzmann and Newman (2010).
14. Halliburton (1939); Rayden (2007).
15. Soule (1968, 110).
16. This was true after the Great Recession, when the Federal Reserve lowered interest rates to near zero, but did not stimulate lending by banks in the short term, since there was little demand for loans, even at this low rate.
17. Glaeser (2013) performs a real estate analysis based on data collected by Nicholas and Scherbina (2013) as well as Clark and Kingston (1930). His conclusion is that real estate prices, while on the high side, were consistent with the overall health of the economy; investors were not irrational in what they were willing to pay. However, he does not explore the underlying dynamics influencing the price movements.
18. These recessions were from January 1920 to July 1921 (18 months), May 1923 to July 1924 (14 months), and October 1926 to November 1927 (13 months). *Source:* NBER (2014).
19. The evidence does suggest that other cities were more susceptible to the easy credit problem, such as Detroit.
20. *New York Times* (1927d).

21. Green (1997).
22. Research that I performed on this form of strategic behavior throughout the twentieth century indicates that during the peak year, developers were adding about ten stories, on average, to their projects in order to rise above the rest (Barr 2010).
23. Soule (1968).
24. Ibid., 129.
25. Ibid., 121.
26. Ibid., 122–123.
27. Ibid., 123.
28. Ibid. 124.
29. Ibid., 164.
30. Gibson (1998), Pushkarev (1981).
31. Condit (1980, 348).
32. From building permit reports from the New York City Department of Buildings.
33. *New York Times* (1920a); Soule (1968, 170).
34. In June 1920, the ENR Construction Cost Index peaked at 273.8 (1913 = 100), by March 1922 the index fell to 164.62 (*Engineering News Record* 1948).
35. Shultz and Simmons (1959).
36. Ibid., 160–161.
37. *New York Times* (1926a).
38. *New York Times* (1927a).
39. *New York Times* (1928d).
40. Ibid.
41. Demorest (1929).
42. Armstrong and Hoyt (1941); MacDonald (1952).
43. *New York Times* (1930d).
44. *Wall Street Journal* (1931).
45. Armstrong and Hoyt (1941).
46. Shultz and Simmons (1959, 154).
47. Results from a regression of % office growth on 1935 vacancy rates for twenty US cities. Data is from Shultz and Simmons (1959, 162).
48. Regression of 1930 vacancy on 1925 vacancy rates, ln (Pop1930) and % office growth. Data from Shultz and Simmons (1959, 160–161).
49. The tower is still there, but it is covered in billboards and is unrecognizable as the structure that created Times Square.
50. Eliot (2002).
51. Condit (1981).
52. Ibid., 7.
53. Schlichting (2001, 2012).
54. *New York Times* (1909).
55. Ibid.
56. *New York Times* (1913).
57. Ibid.
58. See Jonnes (2007, 13), for other railroads into and out of New Jersey.
59. *New York Times* (1903).

60. Ibid.
61. Ballon (2002).
62. Hoover and Vernon (1959, 64–65); Dolkart (2012).
63. *New York Times* (1927c).
64. *New York Times* (1931).
65. Willis (n.d.).
66. Rayden (2007).
67. Ibid., 31 n. 23.
68. Halliburton (1939).
69. Raydon (2007).
70. Goetzmann and Newman (2010).
71. *Real Estate Record and Builders' Guide* (1927).
72. Johnson (1936a).
73. Goetzmann and Newman (2010, 3). This claim might not, in fact, be true. Based on my data, the 1980s had even more buildings, at least at the 295-feet (90 meter) or greater level.
74. The figure is based on a comparison of the data provided from two sources. The bond data is from Johnson (1936b), and the office construction data is from Shultz and Simmons (1959). There were seven cities that overlapped in both samples.
75. A comparison of the residuals from the change in vacancy regressions in the "Vacancy across America" section also show that there is no relationship between the size of the residual and the dollar issuance per million people.
76. Note that one of the buildings, the Downtown Athletic Club, was built by the Club itself.
77. Ennis (1958).
78. *New York Times* (1930c).
79. Willis (n.d.).
80. Ennis (1958).
81. *New York Times* (1947).
82. Rayden (2007, 52).
83. *New York Times* (1930a).
84. *Wall Street Journal* (1929).
85. Grebler (1955).
86. Board of Governors (1959).
87. Consider that the average long-run annual growth in the index has been about 6% (Shiller 2014).
88. *Historical Statistics of the United States*, Millennial Edition (2014, table Cb53).
89. Galbraith (1961).
90. *Real Estate Record and Builders' Guide* (1929).
91. Given the use of annual data, it is hard to estimate the effects of the run up in 1929, since the crash in October caused prices and volume to steeply drop.
92. *Historical Statistics of the United States*, Millennial Edition (2014, table Cc244).
93. Data was provided by the Skyscraper Museum and Columbia University Avery Library, which holds the records of several construction companies and the costs of their respective projects.
94. See Barr (2012a).

Chapter 10

1. George (1879).
2. Likely at the time of George's writing, he saw the rentier class as the landowners and the working classes as the renters. See Blackmar (1989).
3. Jackson (1985).
4. O'Sullivan (2007); O'Flaherty (2009).
5. Hurd (1903).
6. NYU Furman Center (2014).
7. Hurd (1903); Hoyt (1933).
8. The 1866 to 1900 data was provided by Professor Fred Smith of Davidson College. He collected vacant land transactions that were published in New York newspapers. For 1900 to 1950, I used the total value of assessed land in Manhattan (including exempt properties). I adjusted the assessed values by the equalization rates produced by New York State. The assessed values were from tax reports from Department of Finance or the agencies that preceded it, and published in the reports of the Tax Department and the Tax Commissioners (for more information, see Barr 2010). See Barr, Smith, and Kularni (2015) for more information about data from 1950 to 2013. These data were also vacant land sales.
9. The city reports assessed values based on the fiscal year, which ends on the last day of June. Thus, part of the lag in the data set is artefactual because it is presented as if it was reported at the end of the calendar year. This is done to more easily join the data with the vacant land sales series before 1901 and after 1949.
10. History and politics of the urban assessment process is obviously a complex one and describing this process for New York is beyond the scope of the book. Starting in 1906, however, each year the City Department of Taxation would publish land value maps; by and large they were deemed accurate maps of the city. As best I can tell, the assessment data is relatively accurate and has been used as measures of real estate values in the large body of research on New York history (see Arner 1922). Clearly, assessments are not free of politics, and I recognize they may be imperfect measures of land values.
11. Equalization rates pre-1950 were published in the annual reports of the New York City Tax Department and the Tax Commissioners.
12. Scafidi et al. (1998).
13. The late 1970s and early 1980s saw a new genre of film about the horrors of New York life, such as *Taxi Driver* (1976), *Fort Apache the Bronx* (1981), and *Escape from New York* (1981).
14. This was done by regressing *ln(Real Index)* on the year.
15. Glaeser (2005).
16. *Real Estate Record and Builders' Guide* (1898).
17. Ibid.
18. Ibid., 59.
19. Ibid., 71.
20. Ibid.
21. Ibid., 56.
22. Ibid., 113.
23. Ibid., 121.
24. Ibid., 120.
25. Hammack (1982); Burrows and Wallace (1999).

26. Kirschling (2012).
27. *Real Estate Record and Builders' Guide* (1908).
28. Soule (1968).
29. Officer and Williamson (2015).
30. Spengler (1930).
31. Starr (1985); Beauregard (2006).
32. Employment numbers of NYS Department of Labor. Ehrenhalt (1981); Klebaner (1981).
33. Horsley (1977).
34. Morris (1980).
35. Morris (1980); David (2012).
36. This practice of borrowing to fund day-to-day operations began under Lindsay's predecessor Mayor Robert F. Wagner Jr. But it was Lindsay who increased the practice to what ultimately became unsustainable levels.
37. Auletta (1975); Morris (1980); Starr (1985, 225).
38. King (2013).
39. David (2012).
40. See the special issue on the New York City crime drop in *Justice Quarterly* (2014), 31(1).
41. Schwartz, Susin, and Voicu (2003).
42. Note that Mayor Bloomberg in 2004 introduced a ten-year housing affordability plan with the aim of preserving or constructing over 160,000 affordable units (City of New York 2004). In March 2014, Mayor De Blasio proposed an updated ten-year plan with a more ambitious goal. Neither plan has helped stem the tide of rising housing prices.
43. Using MapPLUTO file (2014), for Manhattan, I estimate that about 14% of all developable land (i.e., those not in parks) are either in a historic district or hold a landmarked structure
44. See Barr, Smith, and Kularni (2015) for details about the predicted values and developable land calculations.
45. Forbes (2015).
46. Shiller (2015); Officer and Williamson (2015).
47. Adams ([1931] 1974, chapter 6).
48. *New York Times* (1945); Bagli (2011).
49. Feld (1926); Clark and Kingston (1930).
50. Bassett et al. (1913, 13).
51. *New York Times* (1910b).
52. *New York Times* (1928e).
53. Lawrence (2012, 1). See Barr (2012a) and Barr, Mizrach, and Mundra (2015) for a rebuttal of this claim, which provides detailed statistical results that show one cannot predict the timing of a financial crises by looking at the construction of the world's tallest building.
54. Granger (1988).
55. Gilbert (1900).

Epilogue

1. For statistics on new housing construction in New York, see Rent Guidelines Board (2014). This data gives the number of units constructed in each borough since 1960. Between 2000 and 2013, 76,766 units of housing in Manhattan were built. Let's assume that 75% are for residents and are not pieds-à-terre (Satow 2014, 2015). Let's further assume that each locally occupied unit holds two people, on average. This means that enough units were

built to accommodate 122,826 residents. However, since 2000, 2,171 buildings have been demolished in Manhattan, though the city does not track their type at time of demolition. Let's say 65% were residential (this is based on the fraction of 5+ unit apartment buildings demolished between 1985 and 1994, as given in the report cited above), so that 1,408 apartment buildings were demolished. Further, let's assume they were all five-story walkups with ten units and two people per unit. This suggests a loss of units for 28,169 people. So, on net, based on these assumptions, the city has added 94,657 new units. Between 2000 and 2013 the population of Manhattan increased by 89,000 people. This means housing additions were 6% greater than the population. However, as incomes have risen, we would expect a loss of units through the combining of units or removal of units for non-residential purposes; if this is greater than 6% of the housing stock, then Manhattan likely experienced a net loss in total rentable units for residents since 2000.

2. Glaeser, Gyourko, and Saks (2005).
3. On epidemics, see Rosner (1995) and New York Department of Health and Hygiene (2010). On crime, see Zimring (2011). On fire, see Wermiel (2000).
4. Glaeser (2011).
5. I want to stress that this statement is about a matter of balance. The point is this: if policies do not change to reflect the realities of the twenty-first century, New York's success and well-being are in jeopardy. As my policy recommendations demonstrate, my belief is that change and growth should be more organic at the neighborhood level, except where greater centralization is necessary. Policies also need to be democratically implemented, but NIMBYism should not stop needed construction that serves the greater good.
6. Boden, Marland, and Andres (2010).
7. We know that civilizations and societies are prone to rise and collapse (Diamond 2005); we have yet to see if modern, Western-style democratic-capitalism culture is capable of such a thing.
8. Office of the Comptroller (2014).
9. On density and carbon emissions, see Glaeser and Kahn (2010). On urban density and fossil fuel usage, see Newman and Kenworth (1989). Also see Washburn (2013) on how to design resilient cities.
10. Municipal Arts Society of New York (2013).
11. Been et al. (2014).
12. The proposal to add to Manhattan is not new. Over the decades several proposals have been floated. See Satow (2011); *New York Times* (1921, 1923).
13. On sea level rise, see National Oceanic and Atmospheric Administration (2015). For future predictions, see Phys.org (2015) and Phys.org (2006).
14. NYU Furman Center (2006); Office of the Comptroller (2014).
15. New York City Rent Guidelines Board (2014); Perlberg (2014).
16. Downs (1988).
17. Fischel (2004).
18. Jonnes (1981).
19. 2013 employment in manufacturing was 76,300; total employment was 3.967 million (NYS Department of Labor 2014).
20. New York City Department of City Planning (2011). If a developer wants to build housing that is currently not zoned for it, he must undergo the Uniform Land Use Review Procedure (ULURP) in order for the property to be rezoned. This serves only to increases costs and delay construction.

21. Jacobs (1961).
22. MapPLUTO file from NYC Department of City Planning (2014). I added up land areas for buildings that are landmarked or in historic districts in Manhattan. I removed lots that were in parks, such as Castle Clinton.
23. Been, Infranca, and Madar (2012).
24. If the city were fully built out to hit this bubble, it could hold about 12.3 million residents, an increase of 3.8 million people over its current population.
25. Dunlap (2013).
26. This is a common policy recommendation in urban economics. See Brueckner (2011).
27. Real Estate Board of New York (1992).
28. For example, coop and condo owners receive tax abatements. Other properties can qualify for a 421a tax exemption if owners provide affordable units. As of 2013, nearly 21,000 units in Manhattan qualify under the program (Rent Guidelines Board 2014).
29. Department of Finance (2014).
30. Ibid.
31. Smith (2014). The work was done by the non-partisan government agency the Independent Budget Office.
32. Department of Finance (2000).
33. Tax rate and AVs were collected from annual tax volumes published by the New York Department of Finance and the departments that preceded it. I used the GDP deflator to adjust the figures for inflation.
34. What I am proposing is not new. It was originally advocated for cities by Henry George in his 1879 book, *Progress and Poverty.* See Dye and England (2009) for more on the economics of land value taxation.
35. Dye and England (2009).
36. Caro (1974); Hood (1993); Kirschling (2012).
37. Those counties are the five boroughs of New York City and Essex, Union, Passaic, Hudson, and Bergen Counties in New Jersey and Westchester, Suffolk, and Nassau Counties in New York.
38. The difficulty of this is illustrated by Governor Chris Christie's decision in 2012 to cancel the so-called ARC Tunnel project, which would have created a new commuter rail tunnel from New Jersey to New York, in order to relieve train congestion. Credit for thinking regionally must be given to the RPA, who over the last century has produced many valuable studies and reports discussing how the region can best coordinate its economic activity. See Schrag (2014) on how Washington, DC, solved this problem with its Metro.
39. Of course, more specific details need to be worked out. Riders have to be given options and flexibility and prices cannot rise so much as to unfairly gouge the hapless traveler. Price changes over the day need to happen in say 15-minute intervals and cannot change by, say, more than 10% per interval to provide some protections to riders from finding that a good decision at one time becomes a bad one within a matter of minutes.
40. Smith (2014).
41. Hood (1993).
42. 2014 MapPLUTO file from the New York City Department of City Planning.
43. Consider that a significant fraction of residential units are pieds-à-terre or secondary homes. The IBO estimates that about a quarter of condos or coops are not primary residents. Condos and coops are about 36% of the housing stock in Manhattan, which suggests

that about 9% of all residential units in Manhattan are not occupied by the owner—though a large fraction is sublet to renters. If we assume that half are sublet, then about 4% to 5% of units are "idle" in Manhattan. See Satow (2015). For this section, I ignore this issue; the point here is to demonstrate that even under current zoning and landmarking rules, a significant population increase is allowable.

44. NY Furman Center (2012) shows fraction of units in 2011 that are rent controlled.
45. US Census (2010).
46. Manhattan is 22.7 square miles; assume that 8 square miles is devoted to fifty-story buildings; each of which has a 10,000 square foot footprint. This gives a total of 22,302 buildings. Each building is assumed to house 800 people (two people per household, on average, with ten apartments per floor of 900 square feet per apartment, on average), which gives sixteen people per floor times fifty floors, which is 800 people per building). 22,302 x 800 is 17.8 million people.
47. Hallegatte et al. (2013).

Bibliographic Note

This bibliographical note provides a general overview of the related literature and does not attempt a comprehensive review. Since this book aims to fill a gap in what might be termed "skyline economics," there is little that is directly comparable.

Carol Willis's (1995) *Form Follows Finance: Skyscrapers and Skylines in New York and Chicago* is an important work that discusses the relationship between skyscraper architecture and economics. Willis, an architectural historian, focuses on the architectural dimensions and the form of skyscrapers in New York and Chicago. She demonstrates how the early shape and layout of buildings were based on the need of developers, architects, and engineers to design them to maximize profits, given the institutions and real estate regulations in each place.

Another excellent book is *Rise of the New York Skyscraper: 1865-1913* by Sarah Landau and Carl Condit (1996). This book focuses on the important engineering developments in the creation of the skyscraper. As much as people may demand a tall building, it would be impossible without an army of architects and engineers to solve the problems related to their design and construction. Landau and Condit discuss the key innovations that made the skyscraper possible in New York, and the architectural achievements that accompanied them.

Regarding the economics of skyscrapers, one important early work is that of W. C. Clark and J. L. Kingston (1930), *The Skyscraper: A Study in the Economic Height of Modern Office Buildings.* Written at the height of the 1920s building boom, they provide an inside look at the economics of the tall building. The book chronicles, in minute detail, all of the elements that go into the decision about how tall to build—the rental income, the costs of construction and land, and the costs of operating and maintaining the structure. It offers a kind of window into the head of a hypothetical developer. As such, it gives a unique glimpse into the economics of the skyscraper. E. Shultz and W. Simmons (1959), *Offices in the Sky*, present a history of high-rise office buildings throughout the United States and give a descriptive account of their economics.

More recently, there are only a handful of academic works that study the economics of skyscrapers. R. W. Helsley and W. C. Strange (2008) provide a theoretical model to understand why some buildings may be economically too tall. In particular, in their model, builders are competing to claim the prize of "tallest building," and this requires them to add extra floors against rivals, who might be doing the same.

Statistical work includes H. R. Koster et al. (2014), who demonstrate that in the Netherlands, companies renting space in taller buildings are willing to pay a premium; they conclude that it is due to the "landmark effect," which presumably confers higher social status on the renters. Work by G. M. Ahlfeldt and D. P. McMillen (2015) investigates the relationship between land values and building height in Chicago, and they find, as expected, that buildings become taller as land values rise.

Other writings on the skyscraper tend to be of either the historical or architectural variety. There are myriad of "biographies" of particular buildings, such as John Tauranac's (1995) book on the Empire State Building or Eric Darton's (1999) work on the Twin Towers. Many of these writings are personality-driven in that they focus on individuals, their beliefs, and their attempts to achieve specific goals.

Similarly, works in the history of architecture focus on the architecture of specific skyscrapers. For New York, Ada Louise Huxtable's (1984) *The Tall Building Artistically Reconsidered* is a good example (also see Goldberger 1981). She focuses on the search for the proper form of the skyscraper among architects. The first generation of builders had no direct architectural precedents and, little by little, through experimentation and debate, created designs that constituted aesthetically successful buildings. Since the turn of the twentieth century, there have been several key styles, including the classical, the Art Deco tower, the glass box, and the postmodern structure; and each period reflected an artistic response to the period that preceded it.

Another set of writings, mostly by architectural historians, focuses on the cultural elements of the tall building, attempting to discover what they say about a society's values or how they influence shared cultural experiences (such as Moudry 2005; Flowers 2009). Little, again, is said about the market that makes these buildings and styles possible. Finally, another set of books focuses on how skyscrapers relate to urban design and the quality of life (see Yeang 1997; Al-Kodmany and Ali 2013). These works tend to focus on their engineering or architectural dimensions in the modern city, and less is said about the economic or historical context.

Bibliography

Books

Albion, RG 1939, *Rise of New York port 1815-1860*, Charles Scribner's Sons, New York.

Al-Kodmany, K & Ali, MM 2013, *The future of the city: tall buildings and urban design*, WIT Press, Billerica.

Alonso, W 1964, *Location and land use: toward a general theory of land rent*, Harvard University Press, Cambridge.

Alpern, A & Durst, SB 1984, *Holdouts!* McGraw-Hill, New York.

Anbinder, T 2001, *Five Points: the nineteenth-century New York City neighborhood that invented tap dance, stole elections, and became the world's most notorious slum*, Penguin Putnam Inc., New York.

Armstrong, RH & Hoyt, H 1941, *Decentralization in New York City*, Urban Land Institute, New York.

Armstrong, W 1891, *Industrial Chicago: the building interests*, Goodspeed Pub. Co., Chicago.

Arthur, B 1994, *Increasing returns and path dependence in the economy*, University of Michigan Press, Ann Arbor.

Ashbury, H 1927, *Gangs of New York: an informal history of the underworld*, Alfred A. Knopf, Inc., New York.

Auletta, K 1975, *The streets were paved with gold: the decline of New York, an American tragedy*, Random House, New York.

Ball, M, Lizieri, C & MacGregor, BD 1998, *The economics of commercial property markets*, Routledge, New York.

Ballon, H 2002, *New York's Pennsylvania stations*, WW Norton & Company, New York.

Ballon, H 2012, *The greatest grid: the master plan of Manhattan, 1811-2011*, Columbia University Press, New York.

Bascomb, N 2004, *Higher: a historic race to the sky and the making of a city*, Random House LLC, New York.

Beauregard, RA 2006, *When America became suburban*, U of Minnesota Press, Minneapolis.

Bender, DE 2004, *Sweated work, weak bodies: anti-sweatshop campaigns and languages of labor*, Rutgers University Press, New Brunswick.

Black, GA 1897, *The history of municipal ownership of land on Manhattan Island to the beginning of sales by the commissioners of the sinking fund in 1844*, 2nd edn, Columbia University Press, New York.

Blackmar, E 1989, *Manhattan for rent, 1785-1850*, Cornell University Press, Ithaca.

Board of Governors of the Federal Reserve System 1959, *All-Bank Statistics United States 1896-1955*, Federal Reserve System.

Bromley, GW & Bromley, WS 1899, *Atlas of the city of New York, borough of Manhattan*, Bromley & Bromley, Philadelphia.

Brueckner, JK 2011, *Lectures on urban economics*, MIT Press, Cambridge.

Burrows, EG & Wallace, M 1999, *Gotham: a history of New York City to 1898*, Oxford University Press, New York.

Buttenwieser, AL 1987, *Manhattan water-bound: Manhattan's waterfront from the seventeenth century to the present*, Syracuse University Press, New York.

Cantwell, AME & diZerega Wall, D 2003, *Unearthing Gotham: the archaeology of New York City*, Yale University Press, New Haven.

Caro, RA 1974, *The power broker: Robert Moses and the fall of New York*, Vintage, New York.

Carter, SB & Sutch, R (eds) 2014, *Historical statistics of the United States*, millennial edition online, Cambridge University Press, Web.

Clark, WC & Kingston, JL 1930, *The skyscraper: a study in the economic height of modern office buildings*, American Institute of Steel Construction, Inc., New York.

Committee on the Regional Plan of New York and Its Environs 1931. *Regional survey of New York and its environs*, vol. 1, *Major economic factors in metropolitan growth and arrangement*, Committee on the Regional Plan of New York and Its Environs, New York.

Condit, C 1952, *The rise of the skyscraper*, University of Chicago Press, Chicago.

Condit, C 1980, *The port of New York: a history of the rail and terminal system from the beginnings to Pennsylvania Station*, University of Chicago Press, Chicago.

Condit, C 1981, *The port of New York: a history of the rail and terminal system from the Grand Central electrification to the present*, University of Chicago Press, Chicago.

Corbusier, L 1931, *Towards a new architecture*, John Rodker, London.

Council on Hygiene and Public Health 1866, *Report of the Council of Hygiene of the Citizens' Association of New York upon the Sanitary Condition of the City*, 2nd edn, D. Appleton and Company, New York.

Cozzens, I 1843, *A geological history of Manhattan or New York Island*, Dean, New York.

Cromley, EC 1999, *Alone together: a history of New York's early apartments*, Cornell University Press, Ithaca.

Cronon, W 1991, *Nature's metropolis: Chicago and the great west*, WW Norton & Company, New York.

Curcio, V 2001, *Chrysler: the life and times of an automotive genius*, Oxford University Press, New York.

Darton, E 1999, *Divided we stand: a biography of New York's World Trade Center*, Basic Books, New York.

David, G 2012, *Modern New York: the life and economics of a city*, Palgrave Macmillan Trade, New York.

Day, JN 1999, *Urban castles: tenement housing and landlord activism in New York City, 1890-1943*, Columbia University Press, New York.

DeForest, RW & Veiller, L 1903, *The tenement house problem*, MacMillen Company, New York.

Diamond, J 2005, *Collapse: how societies choose to fail or succeed*, Penguin, New York.

DiPasquale, D & Wheaton, WC 1996, *Urban economics and real estate markets*, vol. 23, no. 7, Prentice Hall, Englewood Cliffs.

Douglas, GH 1996, *Skyscrapers: a social history in America*, MacFarland and Company, Jefferson.

Durst, SB 1898, *Greater New York: its government, financial institutions, transportation facilities, and chronology*, Evening Post Publishing Company, New York.

Dye, RF & England, RW (eds) 2009, *Land value taxation: theory, evidence, and practice*, Lincoln Institute of Land Policy, Cambridge.

Edwards, R 1884, *New York's great industries*, Historical Publishing Company Publishers, New York.

Eliot, M 2002, *Down 42nd Street: sex, money, culture, and politics at the crossroads of the world,* Warner Books, New York.

Ernst, R 1949, *Immigrant life in New York City 1825-1863,* Syracuse University Press, Syracuse.

Fenske, G 2008, *The skyscraper and the city: the Woolworth Building and the making of modern New York,* University of Chicago Press, Chicago.

Fitch, M & Waite, DS 1974, *Grand Central terminal and Rockefeller Center: a historic-critical estimate of their significance,* New York State Parks & Recreation Division of Historic Preservation, New York.

Flowers, BS 2009, *Skyscraper: the politics and power of building New York City in the twentieth century,* University of Pennsylvania Press, Philadelphia.

Galbraith, JK 1961, *The great crash 1929,* Pelican, New Orleans.

Gandy, M 2003, *Concrete and clay: reworking nature in New York City,* MIT Press, Cambridge.

Garreau, J 1991, *Edge city: life on the new frontier,* Anchor Books, New York.

George, H 1879, *Progress and poverty: an inquiry into the cause of industrial depressions and of increase of want with increase of wealth; the remedy,* Modern Library, New York.

Glaeser, EL 2011, *Triumph of the city: how our greatest invention makes us richer, smarter, greener, healthier, and happier,* Penguin Press, New York.

Goldberger, P 1981, *The skyscraper,* Knopf, New York.

Goldman, JA 1997, *Building New York's sewers: developing mechanisms of urban management,* Purdue University Press, Lafayette.

Goodspeed Publishing Co 1891, *Industrial Chicago: the building interests,* vol. 1, Goodspeed Publishing Company, Chicago.

Gratacap, LP 1909, *Geology of the city of New York,* Henry Holt and Company, New York.

Grebler, L 1952, *Housing market behavior in a declining area: long-term changes in inventory and utilization of housing on New York's lower east side,* Columbia University Press, New York.

Grebler, L 1955, *Experience in urban real estate: an interim report based on New York City properties,* Columbia University Press, New York.

Greene, WH 2008, *Econometric analysis,* Granite Hill Publishers, La Jolla.

Haley, KH 1972, *The Dutch in the seventeenth century,* Harcourt Brace Jovanovich, New York.

Halliburton, RA 1939, *The real estate bond house: a study of some of its financial practices,* Edwards Brothers, New York.

Hammack, DC 1982, *Power and society: greater New York at the turn of the century,* Russell Sage Foundation, New York.

Hartog, H 1983, *Public property and private power: the corporation of the city of New York in American law, 1730-1870,* Cornell University Press, Ithaca.

Homburger, E 1994, *The historical atlas of New York City: a visual celebration of 400 years of New York City's history,* Henry Holt and Company Inc., New York.

Hood, C 1993, *722 miles: the building of the subways and how they transformed New York,* Simon & Schuster, New York.

Hoover, EM & Vernon, R 1959, *Anatomy of a metropolis: the changing distribution of people and jobs within the New York metropolitan region,* Harvard University Press, Cambridge.

Hoyt, H [1933] 2000, *One hundred years of land values in Chicago: the relationship of the growth of Chicago to the rise of its land values, 1830-1933,* Beard Books, New York.

Hurd, RM 1903, *Principles of city land values,* Real Estate Record and Builders' Guide, New York.

Huxtable, AL 1984, *The tall building artistically reconsidered: the search for a skyscraper style,* Pantheon Books, New York.

Isachsen, YW et al. 2000, *Geology of New York: a simplified account*, New York State Museum/ Geological Survey, State Education Department, University of the State of New York, Albany.

Jackson, A 1976, *A place called home: a history of low-cost housing in Manhattan*, MIT Press, Cambridge.

Jackson, KT 1985, *Crabgrass frontier: the suburbanization of the United States*, Oxford University Press, New York.

Jackson, KT (ed.) 1995, *The encyclopedia of New York City*, Yale University Press, New Haven.

Jacobs, J 1961, *The death and life of great American cities*, Random House Inc., New York.

Janvier, TA 2000, *In old New York: a classic history of New York City*, St. Martin's Press, New York.

Jonnes, J 2007, *Conquering Gotham: building Penn Station and its tunnels*, Penguin Books, New York.

Juet, R 1625, *Juet's journal of Hudson's 1609 voyage*, 2006, New Netherland Museum.

Kammen, M 1975, *Colonial New York: a history*, Charles Scribner's Sons, New York.

Kayden, JS 2000, *Privately owned public space: the New York City experience*, John Wiley & Sons, Hoboken.

Kessner, T 1977, *The golden door: Italian and Jewish immigrant mobility in New York City 1880–1915*, Oxford University Press, New York.

Kidder, FE 1920, *Building construction and superintendence*, WT Comstock, New York.

King, M 1893, *King's handbook of New York City*, M King.

Klebaner, BJ (ed.) 1981, *New York City's changing economic base*, Universe Pub, Milford.

Koeppel, GT 2000, *Water for gotham: a history*, Princeton University Press, Princeton.

Koolhass, R 1978, *Delirious New York: a retroactive manifesto for Manhattan*, Monacelli Press, LLC, New York.

Kostof, S 1991, *The city shaped: urban patterns and meaning throughout history*, Bulfinch, Boston.

Kraft, HC 1986, *The Lenape: archaeology, history, and ethnography*, New Jersey Historical Society, Newark.

Krugman, PR 1996, *The self-organizing economy*, Blackwell Publishers, Cambridge.

Kurlansky, M 2007, *The big oyster: history on the half shell*, Random House Trade Paperbacks, New York.

Landau, SB & Condit, CW 1996, *Rise of the New York skyscraper: 1865–1913*, Yale University Press, New Haven.

Levinton, JS & Waldman, JR (ed.) 2006, *The Hudson River estuary*, Cambridge University Press, Cambridge.

Levy, M & Salvadori, M 1992, *Why buildings fall down*, WW Norton & Company, New York.

Lockwood, C 1972, *Bricks & brownstone: the New York row house, 1783–1929, an architectural & social history*, McGraw-Hill, New York.

Lockwood, C 1976, *Manhattan moves uptown: an illustrated history*, Houghton Mifflin Company, Boston.

Mankiw, NG 2012, *Principles of microeconomics*, 7th edn, Thomson/South-Western, Manson.

Marshall, A 2006a, *Beneath the metropolis: the secret lives of cities*, Caroll and Graph Publishers, New York.

Marshall, A 2012, *The surprising design of market economies*, University of Texas Press, Austin.

Mayne, AJ & Murray, T 2001, *The archaeology of urban landscapes: explorations in Slumland*, Cambridge University Press, Cambridge.

McKay, RC 1971, *South street: a maritime history of New York*, Haskell House Publishers, New York.

Miller, D 2014, *Supreme city: how jazz age Manhattan gave birth to modern America*, Simon & Schuster, New York.

Miller, J 1865, *Miller's New York as it is; or stranger's guide-book to the cities of New York, Brooklyn and adjacent place*, James Miller, New York.

Moehring, EP 1981, *Public works and the patterns of urban real estate growth: real estate in Manhattan, 1835–1894*, Arno Press, New York.

Morris, AEJ 1972, *History of urban form: prehistory to the Renaissance*, George Godwin Limited, London.

Morris, CR 1980, *The cost of good intentions: New York City and the liberal experiment, 1960–1975*, Norton, New York.

Moudry, R 2005, *The American skyscraper: cultural histories*, Cambridge University Press, New York.

Muth, RF 1969, *Cities and housing: the spatial pattern or urban residential land use*, University of Chicago Press, Chicago.

Myers, MG 1931, *The New York money market: origins and development*, vol. 1, Columbia University Press, New York.

Nadel, S 1990, *Little Germany: ethnicity, religion, and class in New York City, 1845–80*, University of Illinois Press, Urbana and Chicago.

Newman, PG & Kenworthy, JR 1989, *Cities and automobile dependence: an international source-book*, Gower Publishing, Brookfield.

New York (N.Y.) Board of Health 1867, *Annual report of the metropolitan board of health*, vol. 2, Union Printing House, New York.

Norcross, FW 1901, *A history of the New York swamp*, Chiswick Press, New York.

O'Callaghan, EB 1846, *History of New Netherland; or, New York under the Dutch*, D. Appleton, New York.

O'Flaherty, B 2009, *City economics*, Harvard University Press, Cambridge.

O'Sullivan, A 2007, *Urban economics*, McGraw-Hill/Irwin, New York.

Petersen, AE & Edwards, W 1917, *New York as an eighteenth century municipality*, Longman, Greens & Company, New York.

Philbrick, N 2006, *Mayflower: a story of courage, community, and war*, Penguin Group, New York.

Pierce, CH, Toler, WP & Nutting, HDP 1903, *New Harlem past and present: the story of an amazing civic wrong, now at last to be righted*, New Harlem Publishing Company, New York.

Plunz, R 1990, *A history of housing in New York City*, Columbia University Press, New York.

Pound, A 1935, *The golden earth: the story of Manhattan's landed wealth*, Macmillan, New York.

Pratt, EE 1911, *Industrial causes of congestion of population in New York City*, Columbia University Press, New York.

Quante, W 1976, *The exodus of corporate headquarters from New York City*, Praeger Publishers, New York.

Rayden, A 2007, *The people's city: a history of the influence and contribution of mass real estate syndication in the development of New York City*, BookSurge Publishing, New York.

Real Estate Board of New York 1992. *Open Market Sales*, Real Estate Board of New York, New York.

Real Estate Record and Builders' Guide 1898, *A History of real estate, building, and architecture in New York City during the last quarter of a century*, Real Estate Record and Builders' Guide, New York.

Reps, JW 1965, *The making of urban America: a history of city planning in the United States*, Princeton University Press, Princeton.

Riis, J 1890, *How the other half lives*, Charles Scribner's Sons, New York.

Rink, OA 1986, *Holland on the Hudson: an economic and social history of Dutch New York*, Cornell University Press, Ithaca.

Robbins, SM & Terleckyi, N 1960, *Money metropolis: a locational study of financial activities in the New York region*, Harvard University Press, Cambridge.

Rosenwaike, I 1972, *Population history of New York City*, Syracuse University Press, Syracuse.

Rosner, D (ed.) 1995, *Hives of sickness: public health and epidemics in New York City*, Rutgers University Press, New Brunswick.

Roth, LM 1993, *Understanding architecture: its elements, history, and meaning*, Westview Press, Boulder.

Sabbagh, K 1989, *Skyscraper: the making of a building*, Penguin Books, New York.

Salvadori, M 1990. *Why buildings stand up: the strength of architecture*, WW Norton Company, New York.

Sanderson, EW 2009, *Mannahatta: a natural history of New York City*, Abrams, New York.

Schlichting, KC 2001, *Grand central terminal: railroads, engineering, and architecture in New York City*, Johns Hopkins University Press, Baltimore.

Schlichting, KC 2012, *Grand central's engineer: William J. Wilgus and the planning of modern Manhattan*, Johns Hopkins University Press, Baltimore.

Schrag, ZM 2014, *The great society subway: a history of the Washington metro*, Johns Hopkins University Press, Baltimore.

Schuberth, CJ 1968, *The geology of New York City and environs*, American Museum of Natural History, Garden City.

Schumpeter, JA 1950, *Capitalism, socialism, and democracy*, 3rd edn, Harper, New York.

Semsch, OF (ed.) 1908, *A history of the Singer building construction: its progress from foundation to flag pole*, Trow Press, New York.

Shiller, RJ 2005, *Irrational exuberance*, Random House LLC, New York.

Shorto, R 2004, *The island at the center of the world: the epic story of Dutch Manhattan and the forgotten colony that shaped America*, Doubleday, New York.

Shultz, E & Simmons, W 1959, *Offices in the sky*, Bobbs-Merrill Company, Indianapolis.

Simon, K 1978, *Fifth avenue: a very social history*, Harcourt, New York.

Smith, A 1776, *An inquiry into the nature and causes of the wealth of nations*, Canaan edn, Random House Inc., London.

Smith, JR 1938, *Springs and wells of Manhattan and the Bronx, New York City, at the end of the nineteenth century*, New-York Historical Society, New York.

Soule, G 1968, *Prosperity decade: from war to depression, 1917–1929*, Harper & Row, New York.

Spengler, EH 1930, *Land values in New York in relation to transit facilities*, Columbia University Press, New York.

Starr, R 1985, *The rise and fall of New York City*, Basic Books, New York.

Starrett, WA 1928, *Skyscrapers and the men who build them*, Charles Scribner's Sons, New York.

Starrette, P & Waldron, W 1939, *Changing the skyline*, Whittlesey House, New York.

Steinberg, T 2014, *Gotham unbound: the ecological history of greater New York*, Simon and Schuster, New York.

Stokes, INP 1967, *The iconography of Manhattan Island 1498–1909*, Arno Press, New York.

Stott, RB 1990, *Workers in the metropolis: class, ethnicity, and youth in antebellum New York City*, Cornell University Press, Ithaca.

Tauranac, J 1995, *The Empire state building: the making of a landmark*, Scribner, New York.

Tenement House Committee 1895, *Report as Authorized by Chapter 479 of the Laws of 1894*. New York State, Albany.

Tenement House Department of the City of New York 1902–1903, *First Report*, vols. 1 & 2. New York City, New York.

Tishman, JL & Shactman, T 2011, *Building tall: my life and the invention of construction management*, University of Michigan Press, Ann Arbor.

Trow's *(formerly Wilson's) Business Directory* 1898, *Trow's business directory of the boroughs of Manhattan and the Bronx, City of New York*, Trow Directory Printing & Bookbinding Co, New York.

Trow's *New York City Directory* 1861, 1879, 1892, 1905, 1906, John F. Trow Publisher, New York.

Union History Company 1899, *History of architecture and the building trades of greater New York*, vol. 1, Union History Company, New York.

Valentine, DT 1851, *Manual of the corporation of the City of New York*, Common Council, New York.

Valentine, DT 1853, *History of the City of New York*, GP Putnam, New York.

Valentine, DT 1856, *Manual of the corporation of the City of New York*, Common Council, New York.

Valentine, DT 1857, *Manual of the corporation of the City of New York*, Common Council, New York.

Valentine, DT 1860, *Manual of the corporation of the City of New York*, Common Council, New York.

Valentine, DT 1866, *Manual of the corporation of the City of New York*, Common Council, New York.

Veblen, T 1899, *The theory of the leisure class*, Dover, New York.

Veiller, L 1900, *Tenement house reform in New York, 1834–1900*, Evening Post Job Printing House, New York.

Viele, EL 1865, *The topography and hydrology of New York*, Robert Craighead Printer, New York.

Walton, FL 1953, *Tomahawks to textiles: the fabulous story of Worth Street*, Appleton-Century-Crofts Inc., New York.

Ward, D & Zunz, O 1992, *The landscape of modernity: New York City, 1900–1940*, Johns Hopkins University Press, Baltimore.

Washburn, A 2013, *The nature of urban design: a New York City perspective on resilience*, Island Press, Washington.

Wermiel, S 2000, *The fireproof building: technology and public safety in the nineteenth-century American city*, Johns Hopkins University Press, Baltimore.

Wilentz, S 1984, *Chants democratic: New York City and the rise of the American working class, 1788–1850*, Oxford University Press, New York.

Wilkenfeld, BM 1978, *The social and economic structure of the city of New York, 1695–1796*, Arno Press, New York.

Willis, C 1995, *Form follows finance: skyscrapers and skylines in New York and Chicago*, Princeton Architectural Press, New York.

Wilson, WJ 1987, *The truly disadvantaged: The inner city, the underclass, and public policy*, University of Chicago Press, Chicago.

Wooldridge, JM 2012, *Introductory econometrics: a modern approach*, 5th edn, Cengage Learning, Boston.

Yamin, R. (ed.) 2000, *Tales of Five Points: working-class life in nineteenth-century New York*, John Milner Associates, West Chester.

Yeang, K 1997, *The skyscraper bioclimatically considered*, Wiley-Academy, Hoboken.

Zimring, FE 2011, *The city that became safe: New York's lessons for urban crime and its control*, Oxford University Press, New York.

Chapters in Edited Volumes

Adams, T [1931] 1974, "The character, bulk & surroundings of buildings" in *Buildings: their uses and the spaces about them. Regional Survey*, vol. 4, Regional Plan of New York and Its Environs, reprinted by Arno Press, New York.

Baskerville, CA 1982, "The foundation geology of New York City" in *Geology under cities*, Geological Society of America Inc., Boulder.

Bisland, E 1897, "Old Greenwich" in *Historic New York: being the first series of the Half Moon papers*, ed MW Goodwin, GP Putnam's Sons, New York.

Brueckner, JK 1987, "The structure of urban equilibria: A unified treatment of the Muth-Mills model" in *Handbook of regional and urban economics*, vol. 2, North Holland, Netherlands.

Condit, CW 1988, "The two centuries of technical evolution underlying the skyscraper" in *Second century of the skyscraper council on tall buildings and urban habitat*, ed LS Beedle, Van Nostrand Reinhold Co, New York.

Dolkart, AS 2012, "From the rag trade to riches" in *Chosen capital: the Jewish encounter with American capitalism*, ed R Kobrin, Rutgers University Press, New Brunswick.

Downs, A 1988, "Background theory and empirical findings" in *Residential rent controls: an evaluation*, Urban Land Institute, Washington DC.

Ehrenhalt, SM 1981, "Some perspectives on the New York City economy in a time of change" in *New York City's changing economic base*, ed BJ Klebaner, Universe Pub, Millford.

Fenske, G & Holdsworth, D 1992, "Corporate identity and the New York office building" in *The landscape of modernity: New York, 1900–1940*, Johns Hopkins University, Baltimore.

Friedman D 1998, "A story a day: engineering the work" in *Building the empire state*, ed D Friedman & C Willis, WW Norton & Company, New York.

Gates, AE 2000, "Continents adrift: the plate tectonic history of New York state" in *Geology of New York: a simplified Account*, New York State Geological Survey, New York State Museum, Cultural Education Center, Albany.

Gould, ERL 1908, "Financial aspects of recent tenement house operations in New York" in *The tenement house problem*, MacMillan Company, New York.

Green, N 1997, "Sweatshop migrations: the garment industry between home and shop" in *The landscape of modernity: New York City 1900–1940*, ed D Ward & O Zunz, Johns Hopkins University Press, Baltimore.

Hill, GE & Waring, GE 1897, "Old wells and watercourses of the island of Manhattan" in *Historic New York: being the first series of the Half Moon papers*, ed MW Goodwin, GP Putnam's Sons, New York.

Kemp, JF 1887, "The geology of Manhattan island" in *Transactions of the New York academy of sciences*, vol. 6, Academy of Sciences, New York.

Kenny, GJ & Bro 1908, "Appendix to report on speculative building of tenement houses" in *The Tenement House Problem*, MacMillan Company, New York.

Klebaner, BJ (ed.) 1981, "Introduction: the decline and testing of New York City's economy" in *New York City's changing economic base*, Universe Pub, Milford.

McCusker, JJ 1992, "How much is that in real money?: A historical price index for use as a deflator of money values in the economy of the United States" in *Proceedings of the American Antiquarian Society*, Worchester.

Milne, C 2000, "'Slaughterhouses in which I labored': industry, labor, and the land from colonial times to 1830" in *Tales of Five Points: working class life in nineteenth-century New York*, John Milner Associates, Inc., West Chester.

Morris, G, De Witt, S & Rutherford, J 1866, "Remarks of the commissioners for laying out streets and roads in the city of New New York, under the act of April 3,1807" in *Manual of the corporation of the City of New York*, Edmund Jones & Co., New York.

Pushkarev, BS 1981, "The future of Manhattan" in *New York City's changing economic base*, ed BJ Klebaner, Universe Pub, Milford.

Randel, J 1864, "City of New York, north of Canal Street, in 1808 to 1821" in *Manual of the corporation of the City of New York*, Edmund Jones & Co., New York.

Revell, KD 1992, "Regulating the landscape: real estate values, city planning, and the 1916 zoning ordinance" in *The landscape of modernity: New York City, 1900–1940*, Johns Hopkins University Press, Baltimore.

Reynolds, A 1895, "Supplement no. 7: report on rentals and savings" in *Report of the tenement house committee as authorized by chapter 479 of the laws of 1894*, New York State.

Rosenthal, SS & Strange, WC 2004, "Evidence on the nature and sources of agglomeration economies" in *Handbook of Regional and Urban Economics*, vol. 4, North Holland, Netherlands.

Spann, EK 1988, "The greatest grid: the New York plan of 1811" in *Two centuries of American planning*, ed D Schaffer, Mensell Publishing Ltd, London.

Veiller, L 1903a, "A statistical study in New York's tenement problem" in *The tenement house problem*, MacMillen Company, New York.

Veiller, L 1903b, "Financial aspects of recent tenement house operations in New York" in *The tenement house problem*, MacMillen Company, New York.

Veiller, L 1903c, "The speculative building of tenement houses" in *The tenement house problem*, MacMillan Company, New York.

Veiller, L 1903d, "Appendix IX tenement house rentals" in *The tenement house problem*, vol. 2, MacMillan Company, New York.

Veiller, L 1936, "The period of tenement house reform" in *Ford, slums and housing, with special reference to New York City: history, conditions, policy*, Harvard University Press, Cambridge.

Wang, E, Roberts, R, Hsia, L & Osbourne, C 2005, "Geotechnical investigation program for the no.7 subway line extension" in *Underground space use: analysis of the past and lessons for the future*, two volume set, ed Y Erdem & T Solak, Taylor and Francis, Istanbul.

Wermiel, SE 2006, "Norcross, Fuller, and the rise of the general contractor in the United States in the nineteenth century" in *Proceedings of the second international congress on construction history*, Construction History Society, Cambridge.

Yamin, R 2000, "The rediscovery of Five Points" in *Tales of Five Points: working-class life in nineteenth-century New York*, vol. 1, *a narrative history and archaeology of block 160*, John Milner Associates, West Chester.

Yamin, R 2001, "Alternative narratives: respectability at New York's Five Points" in *The archaeology of urban landscapes: explorations in slumland*, Cambridge University Press, Cambridge.

Yamin, R & Schuldenrein, J 2007, "Landscape archeology of Lower Manhattan: the collect pond as an evolving cultural landmark in early New York City" in *Envisioning landscape situations and standpoints in archaelogy and heritage*, Left Coast Press Inc., Walnut Creek.

Abbott, C 1974, "The neighborhoods of New York, 1760–1775," *New York History*, vol. 55, pp. 35–54.

Ahlfeldt, GM & McMillen, DP 2015, "The vertical city: the price of land and the height of buildings in Chicago 1870–2010," SERC Discussion Paper 180.

Anas, A, Arnott, R & Small, KA 1998, "Urban spatial structure," *Journal of Economic Literature*, vol. 36, no. 3, pp. 1426–1464.

Anas, A & Kim, I 1996, "General equilibrium models of polycentric urban land use with endogenous congestion and job agglomeration," *Journal of Urban Economics*, vol. 40, pp. 232–256.

Anbiner, T 2002, "From famine to Five Points: Lord Lansdowne's Irish tenants encounter North America's most notorious slum," *American Historical Review*, vol. 107, no. 2, pp. 351–387.

Angel, S & Lamson-Hall, P 2014, "The rise and fall of Manhattan's densities 1800–2010," New York University Working Paper.

Arner, GBL 1922, "Land values in New York City," *Quarterly Journal of Economics*, vol. 36, no. 4, pp. 545–580.

Arzaghi, M & Henderson, JV 2008, "Networking off Madison Avenue," *Review of Economic Studies*, vol. 75, no. 4, pp. 1011–1038.

Atack, J & Margo, RA 1998, "'Location, location, location!' the price gradient for vacant urban land: New York, 1835 to 1900," *Journal of Real Estate Finance and Economics*, vol. 16, no. 2, pp. 151–172.

Bancker, E 1917, "List of farms in New York island 1780," *New York Historical Society Quarterly*, vol. 1, no. 1, pp. 8–12.

Barr, J 2010, "Skyscrapers and the skyline: Manhattan, 1895–2004," *Journal of Real Estate Economics*, vol. 38, no. 3, pp. 567–597.

Barr, J 2012b, "Skyscraper height," *Journal of Real Estate Finance and Economics*, vol. 45, no. 3, pp. 723–753.

Barr, J 2013, "Skyscrapers and skylines: New York and Chicago, 1885–2007," *Journal of Regional Science*, vol. 53, no. 3, pp. 369–391.

Barr, J 2016, "A study of the economic height of modern office buildings: revisiting Clark and Kingston," Unpublished manuscript.

Barr, J, Mizrach, B & Mundra, K 2015, "Skyscraper height and the business cycle: separating myth from reality," *Applied Economics*, vol. 47, no. 2.

Barr, J & Ort, T 2014, "Density across the city: the case of 1900 Manhattan," Rutgers University-Newark, Working Paper.

Barr, J, Smith, F & Kulkarni, S 2015, "What's Manhattan worth? A land value index from 1950 to 2014," Rutgers University, Working Paper #2015-001.

Barr, J & Tassier, T 2015, "The dynamics of subcenter formation: Midtown Manhattan, 1861–1906," Rutgers University-Newark, Working Paper #WP2014-002.

Barr, J, Tassier, T & Trendafilov, R 2010, "Depth to bedrock and the formation of the Manhattan skyline, 1890–1915," *Journal of Economic History*, vol. 71, no. 4, pp. 1060–1077.

Been, V, Ellen, IG, Gedal, M, Glaeser, E & McCabe, BJ 2014, "Preserving history or hindering growth? The heterogeneous effects of historic districts on local housing markets in New York City," National Bureau of Economic Research, Working paper no. 20446.

Been, B, Infranca, J & Madar, J 2012, "The Market for TDRs in New York City". 1 November. Unpublished manuscript.

Been, V, Madar, J & Ellen, IG 2009, "Underused lots in New York City" Working paper, Lincoln Institute of Land Policy, Working paper no. WP09VB1.

Berkey, CP 1909, "Areal and structural geology of southern Manhattan island," *Annals of the New York Academy of Sciences*, vol. 19, no. 1, pp. 247–282.

Bertaud, A & Brueckner, JK 2005, "Analyzing building-height restrictions: predicted impacts and welfare costs," *Regional Science and Urban Economics*, vol. 35, no. 2, pp. 109–125.

Bleakley, H & Lin, J 2012, "Portage and path dependence," *Quarterly Journal of Economics*, vol. 127, no. 2, pp. 587–644.

Bremner, RH 1958, "The big flat history of a New York tenement house," *American Historical Review*, vol. 64, no. 1, pp. 54–62.

Brueckner, JK, Thisse, JF & Zenou, Y 1999, "Why is central Paris rich and downtown Detroit poor?: An amenity-based theory," *European Economic Review*, vol. 43, no. 1, pp. 91–107.

Burchfield, M, Overman, HG, Puga, D & Turner, MA 2006, "Causes of sprawl: a portrait from space," *Quarterly Journal of Economics*, vol. 121, no. 2, pp. 587–633.

Davis, DR & Weinstein, DW 2002, "Bones, bombs and break points: the geography of economic activity," *American Economic Review*, vol. 92, pp. 1269–1289.

Ellison, G & Glaeser, EL 1999, "The geographic concentration of industry: does natural advantage explain agglomeration?" *American Economic Review*, vol. 89, no. 2, pp. 311–316.

Fischel, WA 2004, "An economic history of zoning and a cure for its exclusionary effects," *Urban Studies*, vol. 41, no. 2, pp. 317–340.

Folkerts, J 1997, "The failure of West Indian Company farming on the island of Manhattan," History from Revolution to Construction and Beyond. Available from <http://www.let.rug.nl/usa/essays/before-1800/the-failure-of-west-indian-company-farming>.

Ford, LR 1998, "Midtowns, megastructures, and world cities," *Geographical Review*, vol. 88, no. 4, pp. 528–547.

Fujita, M & Ogawa, H 1982, "Multiple equilibria and structural transition of non-monocentric urban configurations," *Regional Science and Urban Economics*, vol. 12, no. 2, pp. 161–196.

Gilbert, C 1900, "The financial importance of rapid building," *Engineering Record*, vol. 41, p. 624.

Glaeser, EL 2005, "Urban colossus: why is New York America's largest city?" National Bureau of Economic Research, Working paper no. w11398.

Glaeser, EL 2013, "A nation of gamblers: real estate speculation and American history," *American Economic Review*, vol. 103, no. 3, pp. 1–42.

Glaeser, EL, Gyourko, J & Saks, R 2005, "Why is Manhattan so expensive? Regulation and the rise in housing prices," *Journal of Law and Economics*, vol. 48, no. 2, pp. 331–369.

Glaeser, EL & Kahn, ME 2010, "The greenness of cities: carbon dioxide emissions and urban development," *Journal of Urban Economics*, vol. 76, no. 3, pp. 404–418.

Goetzmann, WN & Newman, F 2010, "Securitization in the 1920's," National Bureau of Economic Research, Working paper no. w15650.

Granger, CW 1988, "Some recent development in a concept of causality," *Journal of Econometrics*, vol. 39, no. 1, pp. 199–211.

Grenadier, SR 1996, "The strategic exercise of options: development cascades and overbuilding in real estate markets," *Journal of Finance*, vol. 51, no. 5, pp. 1653–1679.

Hallegatte, S, Green, C, Nicholls, RJ & Corfee-Morlot, J 2013, "Future flood losses in major coastal cities," *Nature Climate Change*, vol. 3, pp. 802–803.

Heath, T, Smith SG & Lim, B 2000, "Tall buildings and the urban skyline: the effect of visual complexity on preferences," *Environment and Behavior*, vol. 32, no. 4, pp. 541–556.

Helsley, RW & Strange, WC 2008, "A game-theoretic analysis of skyscrapers," *Journal of Urban Economics*, vol. 64, no. 1, pp. 49–64.

Helsley, RW & Sullivan, AM 1991, "Urban subcenter formation," *Regional Science and Urban Economics*, vol. 21, no. 2, pp. 255–275.

Irish, S 1989, "A machine that makes the land pay," *Technology and Culture*, vol. 30, no. 2, pp. 367–397.

Ishii, T 1994, "Elevators for skyscrapers," *Spectrum, IEEE*, vol. 31, no. 9, pp. 42–46.

Johnson, EA 1936a, "The record of long-term real estate securities," *Journal of Land and Real Estate Economics*, vol. 12, no. 1, pp. 44–48.

Johnson, EA 1936b, "The record of long-term real estate securities: by cities of issue," *Journal of Land and Real Estate Economics*, vol. 12, no. 2, pp. 195–197.

Jung, K et al. 2011, "Effects of floor level and building type on residential levels of outdoor and indoor polycyclic aromatic hydrocarbons, black carbon, and particulate matter in New York City," *Atmosphere*, vol. 2, no. 2, pp. 96–109.

Kaiser, RW 1997, "The long cycle in real estate," *Journal of Real Estate Research*, vol. 14, no. 3, pp. 233–257.

Keast, WRM & Randall, AB 1930, "The minimum building for varying land values," *Architectural Record*, vol. 67, no. 4, pp. 376–395.

Koster, HR, van Ommeren, J & Rietveld, P 2014, "Is the sky the limit? High-rise buildings and office rents," *Journal of Economic Geography*, vol. 14, no. 1, pp. 125–153.

Krutilla, JV 1967, "Conservation reconsidered," *American Economic Review*, vol. 57, no. 4, pp. 777–786.

Lubove, R 1961, "Lawrence Veiller and the New York state tenement house commission of 1900," *Mississippi Valley Historical Review*, pp. 659–677.

Marcuse, P 1987, "The grid as city plan: New York City and laissez-faire planning in the nineteenth century," *Planning Perspectives*, vol. 2, no. 3, pp. 287–310.

Margo, RA 1996, "The rental price of housing in New York City, 1830–1860," *Journal of Economic History*, vol. 56, no. 3, pp. 605–625.

McMillen, DP 1996, "One hundred fifty years of land values in Chicago: a nonparametric approach," *Journal of Urban Economics*, vol. 40, no. 1, pp. 100–124.

McMillen, DP & Smith, SC 2003, "The number of subcenters in large urban areas," *Journal of Urban Economics*, vol. 53, no. 3, pp. 321–338.

McNulty, JE 1995, "Overbuilding, real estate lending decisions, and the regional economic base," *Journal of Real Estate Finance and Economics*, vol. 11, no. 1, pp. 37–53.

Merguerian, C 2003, "The Narrows flood—Post-woodfordian meltwater breach of the Narrows channel, NYC," Tenth Annual Conference on Geology of Long Island and Metropolitan, 12 April 2003, State University of New York at Stony Brook, NY, Long Island Geologists Program with Abstracts.

Merguerian, C & Merguerian, M 2004, "Geology of Central Park—from rocks to ice" in *Eleventh Annual Conference on Geology of Long Island and Metropolitan New York*, 17 April 2004, State University at Stony Brook, NY, Long Island Geologists Program with Abstracts, p. 24.

Merguerian, C & Moss, CJ 2006, "Structural implications of Walloomsac and Hartland rocks of southern Manhattan Island," *Geological Society of America Abstracts with Programs*, vol. 38, no. 7, p. 20.

Merguerian, C & Sanders JE 1991, "Geology of Manhattan and the Bronx: guidebook for on-the-rocks-1990-91 fieldtrip series, trip 16," 21 April 1991, *Section of Geological Sciences*, New York Academy of Sciences, p. 141.

Moss, C 2010, "Newly mapped Walloomsac formation in lower Manhattan and New York Harbor and the implications for engineers," Seventeenth Conference on Geology of Long Island and Metropolitan New York, Long Island Geologists Program with Abstracts.

Moss, C 2012, "Evidence of two Wisconsin age glacial advances in a bedrock valley below the new Yankee Stadium, Bronx, New York," Nineteenth Annual Conference on Geology of Long Island and Metropolitan New York, Long Island Geologists Program with Abstracts.

Moss, CJ & Merguerian, C 2005, "Loading patterns in varved Pleistocene sediment in the NYC area," Twelfth Annual Conference on Geology of Long Island and Metropolitan New York, 16 April 2005, State University of New York at Stony Brook, NY, Long Island Geologists Program with Abstracts.

Moss, CJ & Merguerian, C 2008, "Bedrock control of a boulder-filled valley under the World Trade Center site," Fifteenth Annual Conference on Geology of Long Island and Metropolitan New York, 12 April 2008, State University of New York at Stony Brook, NY, Long Island Geologists Program with Abstracts.

Moss, CJ & Merguerian, C 2009, "50 ka till-filled Pleistocene plunge pools and potholes found beneath the World Trade Center Site, New York, NY," Sixteenth Annual Conference on Geology of Long Island and Metropolitan New York, 28 March 2009, State University of New York at Stony Brook, NY, Long Island Geologists Program with Abstracts.

Murphy, JJ & Fluhr, TW 1944, "The subsoil and bedrock of the borough of Manhattan as related to foundations," *Municipal Engineers Journal*, vol. 30, no. 4, pp. 119–157.

Nicholas, T & Scherbina, A 2013, "Real estate prices during the Roaring Twenties and the Great Depression," *Real Estate Economics*, vol. 41, no. 2, pp. 278–309.

Oldfield, P, Trabucco, D & Wood, A 2009, "Five energy generations of tall buildings: an historical analysis of energy consumption in high-rise buildings," *Journal of Architecture*, vol. 14, no. 5, pp. 591–613.

Owens, RE 1994, "Commercial real estate overbuilding in the 1980's: beyond the hog cycle," Federal Reserve Bank of Richmond, Working paper, pp. 94–96.

Parsons, JD 1976, "New York's glacial lake formation of varved silt and clay," *Journal of the Geotechnical Engineering Division*, vol. 102, no. 6, pp. 605–638.

Peck, RB 1948, "History of building foundations in Chicago," *University of Illinois Bulletin*, vol. 45, no. 29, pp. 1–61.

Rosenthal, SS & Strange, WC 2008, "The attenuation of human capital spillovers," *Journal of Urban Economics*, vol. 64, no. 2, pp. 373–389.

Rose-Redwood, R & Li, L 2011, "From island of hills to cartesian flatland? Using GIS to assess topographical change in New York City, 1819–1999," *Professional Geographer*, vol. 63, no. 3, pp. 392–405.

Saiz, A 2010, "The geographic determinants of housing supply," *Quarterly Journal of Economics*, vol. 125, no. 3, pp. 1253–1296.

Sanderson, EW & Brown, M 2007, "Mannahatta: an ecological first look at the Manhattan landscape prior to Henry Hudson," *Northeastern Naturalist*, vol. 14, no. 4, pp. 545–570.

Scafidi, BP, Schill, MH, Wachter, SM & Culhane, DP 1998, "An economic analysis of housing abandonment," *Journal of Housing Economics*, vol. 7, no. 4, pp. 287–303.

Schwartz, AE, Susin, S & Voicu, I 2003, "Has falling crime driven New York City's real estate boom?" *Journal of Housing Research*, vol. 14, no. 1, pp. 101–136.

Sev, A & Özgen, A 2009, "Space efficiency in high-rise office buildings," *METU JFA*, vol. 26, no. 2, pp. 69–89.

Shah, A, Cahkraborty, S & Kim, K 2006, "The geological setting of New York City and the geotechnical challenges in urban construction," *IAEG*, New York.

Shiller, RJ 2008, "Historic turning points in real estate," *Eastern Economic Journal*, vol. 34, no. 1, pp. 1–13.

Sykes, LR, Armbruster, JG & Won-Young Kim, LS 2008, "Observations and tectonic setting of historic and instrumentally located earthquakes in the greater New York City-Philadelphia area," *Bulletin of the Seismological Society of America*, vol. 98, no. 4, pp. 1696–1719.

Syrett, HC 1954, "Private enterprise in New Amsterdam," *William and Mary Quarterly*, vol. 11, no. 4, pp. 536–550.

Tamaro, GJ, Kaufman, JL & Azmi, AA 2000, "Design and construction constraints imposed by unique geological conditions in New York City," Deep Foundations Institute 25th Annual Meeting and 8th International Conference, New York.

Tantala, MW, et al. 2008, "Earthquake loss estimation for the New York City metropolitan region," *Soil Dynamics and Earthquake Engineering*, vol. 28, no. 10, pp. 812–835.

Villarreal, C 2012, "The persisting influence of historical marshes on the rental price of housing in New York City 1830–1940," Working paper.

Wallace, A 2006, "A height deemed appalling: nineteenth-century New York newspaper buildings," *Journalism History*, vol. 31, no. 4, pp. 178–189.

Walsh, DC & LaFleur, RG 1995, "Landfills in New York City: 1844–1994." *Groundwater*, vol. 33, no. 4, pp. 556–560.

Webster, JC 1959, "The skyscraper: logical and historical considerations," *Journal of the Society of Architectural Historians*, vol. 18, no. 4, pp. 126–139.

Weisman, W 1953, "New York and the problem of the first skyscraper," *Journal of the Society of Architectural Historian*, vol. 12, no. 1, pp. 13–21.

Weiss, MA 1992, "Skyscraper zoning: New York's pioneering role," *Journal of the American Planning Association*, vol. 58, no. 2, pp. 202–212.

Wheaton, WC 1987, "The cyclic behavior of the national office market," *Real Estate Economics*, vol. 15, no. 4, pp. 281–299.

Wheaton, WC 1999, "Real estate 'cycles': some fundamentals," *Real Estate Economics*, vol. 27, no. 2, pp. 209–230.

Wheaton, WC, Barnaski, MS & Templeton, CA 2009, "100 years of commercial real estate prices in Manhattan," *Real Estate Economics*, vol. 37, no. 1, pp. 69–83.

Other References

Architectural Record, "Mile High Illinois: Frank Lloyd Wright," Architectural Record: Innovation. Available from <http://archrecord.construction.com/innovation/2_features/0411history.asp>.

Bagli, CV 1998, "Trump starts a new tower near the U.N.," *New York Times* 16 October, p. A1.

Bagli, CV 2011, "Nice view, and the profits surpass all horizons," *New York Times* 24 December.

Baskerville, CA 1994. Bedrock and Engineering Geologic Maps of New York County and Parts of Kings and Queens Counties, New York and Parts of Bergen and Hudson Counties, New Jersey. IMAP, I-2306A, I-2306B, 1:24000, U.S Geological Survey, New York.

Bassett, EM et al. 1913, "Report of the Heights of Buildings Commission to the Committee on the Height, Size and Arrangement of Buildings of the Board of Estimate and Apportionment of the City of New York," MB Brown Print and Binding Company, New York.

Barr, J 2012a, "The myth of the skyscraper index," *History News Network* 17 December. Available from <http://historynewsnetwork.org/article/149784>.

Bennett, CG 1960, "New zoning law adopted by city," *New York Times*, 16 December, p. 1.

Beveridge, A 2008, "An affluent, white Harlem?" *Gotham Gazette* 27 August. Available from <http://www.gothamgazette.com/index.php/demographics/4062-an-affluent-white-harlem>.

Billings, JS 1894, "Vital statistics of New York and Brooklyn: covering a period of six years ending in May 31, 1890," US Census Bureau, Washington.

Boden, TA, Marland, G & Andres, RJ 2010, "Global, regional, and national fossil-fuel CO2 emissions," Carbon Dioxide Informational Analysis Center, Oak Ridge National Laboratory, U.S. Department of Energy, Oak Ridge, Tenn., USA. Available from <http://cdiac.ornl.gov/trends/emis/tre_glob.html>.

Brown, E 2014, "Office rents cut at one world trade: the tallest tower at the world trade center is 55% leased," *Wall Street Journal* 27 May.

Buder, L 1963, "Hidden stream at school site causes $100,000 delay in work," *New York Times* 14 October, p. 1.

Buis, A 2014, "NASA finds good news on forests and carbon dioxide," NASA, 29 December. Available from <http://www.nasa.gov/jpl/nasa-finds-good-news-on-forests-and-carbon-dioxide/#.VQxuyPnF-Rp>.

Chaban, M 2012, "Paul Goldberger and skyscraper economist Jason Barr debate the Manhattan skyline," *New York Observer* 25 January. Available from < http://observer.com/2012/01/paul-goldberger-and-skyscraper-economist-jason-barr-debate-the-manhattan-skyline/#ixzz3Nhe77p00>.

City of New York, Department of Finance 2000, "Annual report on the NYC property tax," City of New York. Available from <http://www1.nyc.gov/assets/finance/downloads/pdf/99pdf/rptsum00.pdf>.

City of New York, Department of Finance 2014, "Annual report on the NYC property tax," City of New York. Available from <http://www1.nyc.gov/assets/finance/downloads/pdf/reports/reports-property-tax/nyc_property_fy14fmvandav.pdf>.

Claghorn, KH 1901, "The foreign immigrant in New York City," *Reports of the Industrial Commission*, vol. 15, pp. 465–492.

Clark, K 2014, "Ranking new condos—from Barnett's One57 to Rudin's Greenwich Lane—per-square-foot prices," *The Real Deal* 1 Feb. Available from <http://therealdeal.com/issues_articles/ranking-new-condos-from-barnetts-one57-to-rudins-greenwich-lane-by-per-square-foot-prices/>.

Colin Buchanan and Partners 2008, "The economic impact of high density development and tall buildings in central business districts," British Property Federation.

Coonan, C 2015, "Skyscraper 57 storeys tall built in 19 days in Chinese city," *Irish Times* 23 March.

Crewdson, M & Mittelbach, M 2002, "Scratch Manhattan, and it's a big jewel box," *New York Times* 7 June, p. E33.

Cushman & Wakefield 2013, "Marketbeat office snapshot: Asia Pacific," Cushman & Wakefield Research, New York.

Demorest, WJ 1929, "Millions of feet of office space added to Grand Central zone," *New York Times* 20 January, p. RE1.

Deutsch, M 1907, "Foundations of high buildings," *Real Estate Record and Builders' Guide*, pp. 187–188.

Dowd, M 1985, "Columbia is to get $400 million in Rockefeller Center land sale," *New York Times* 6 February, p. A1.

Dunlap, DW 2009, "World Trade Center's elevators to be among the world's fastest," *New York Times* 26 February.

Dunlap, DW 2013, "Bloomberg's plan for bigger east midtown towers is 'zoning for dollars,' group says," *New York Times* 27 August.

Engineering News Record 1948, "Construction wage rates, skilled labor for United States," 27 May.

Ennis, T 1958, "Skyscraper builders of yesteryear give way to the new," *New York Times* 12 April, p. R1.

Feld, RC 1926, "Now the skyscraper is sharply attacked: it breeds congestion," *New York Times* 4 July, p. XX3.

Fiat Chrysler Automobiles 2014, "Chrysler Heritage—1800s," 1 June. Available from < http://30079.bbnc.bbcust.com/page.aspx?pid=421 >.

Filler, M 2015, "New York: conspicuous construction," *New York Review of Books* 2 April. Available from <http://www.wsj.com/articles/SB100014240527023039033045795862700704200060>.

Finn, R 2013, "The great air race," *New York Times* 22 February.

Flagg, E 1894, "The New York tenement-house evil and its cure," *Scribner's Magazine,* vol. 16, no. 1, pp. 108–117.

Folsom, M 1961a, "More businesses go to suburbs hunting space, but some return," *New York Times* 5 September, p. 1.

Folsom, M 1961b, "Move to Armonk planned by I.B.M: shift of headquarters from Madison Ave. due in '63," *New York Times* 21 December, p. 20.

Forbes 2015, "The world's billionaires," *Forbes.* Available from <http://www.forbes.com/billionaires/list/>.

Fried, JP 1967, "Landmark on lower Broadway to go: end near for Singer Building, a forerunner of skyscrapers," *New York Times* 22 August, p. 41.

Fried, JP 1968, "U.S. steel to erect a 54-story skyscraper here: lower Broadway," *New York Times* 5 April, p. 37.

Geismer, J 2005, "Washington Square Park phase 1A archaeological assessment," Report for NYC Department of Parks and Recreation, Thomas Balsley Associates.

Gibson C 1998, "Population of the 100 largest cities and other urban places in the United States," U.S. Bureau of the Census, June. Avaliable from <https://www.census.gov/population/www/documentation/twps0027/twps0027.html>.

Gluckman, R 2003, "How high will they build? World-beating skyscraper engineering isn't dead. Across the Pacific, new technology is feverishly being deployed to set records," *Popular Science* 6 February.

Goldberger, P 1977, "Energy crisis is expected to alter building design," *New York Times* 22 May, p. 48.

Gray, C 1996, "Streetscapes/The tower building, the idea that led to New York's first skyscraper," *New York Times* 5 May, p. RNJ7.

Harrison, Ballard & Allen 1950, "Plan for rezoning the City of New York: a report submitted to the city planning commission," City Planning Commission, New York.

Higgins, R 1980, "Office builders feel impact of prime rate: commercial builders are feeling impact of rise in prime rate," *New York Times* 20 April, p. R1.

Hobbs, WH 1905, "The configuration of the rock floor of greater New York," Government Printing Office, United States Geological Survey, Washington.

Holusha, J 2002, "Commercial real estate: 6-year quest for land on east side pulling together the sites for a building can take years of work," *New York Times* 16 January, p. C10.

Horsley, CB 1977, "Will values of prime city land climb all the way back?" *New York Times* 20 November, p. R1.

Hudson Yards Development Corp 2015, "Hudson yards," Hudson Yards Development Corporation, City of New York. Available from <http://www.hydc.org/html/home/home.shtml>.

Hughes, CJ 2015, "The dirt on NYC land values: with condo prices filing to keep pace, industry experts worry land prices will hit 'point of no returns'" *The Real Deal* 6 April. Available from <http://therealdeal.com/blog/2015/04/06/the-dirt-on-nycs-soaring-land-values/>.

Jackson, KT 2013, "Gotham's towering ambitions," *New York Times* 29 August.

Johnson, T 2011, "Mexico City copes with that sinking feeling," *Seattle Times* 24 September.

Jones, AF 1925, "Old Trinity gets new foundation: steel casings support building weakened by nearby city excavations," *New York Times* 23 August, p. XX6.

Jonnes, J 1981, "City's zoning: a tough game that few play," *New York Times* 12 July, p. R1.

Kardas, S & Larrabee, EM 1980, "Landmaking in Lower Manhattan," *Seaport Magazine*, vol. 14, no. 3, pp. 15–19.

Kayden, JS 1978, "Incentive zoning in New York City: a cost-benefit analysis," Lincoln Institute of Land Policy.

Kelly, H 2002, "The New York regional and downtown office market: history and prospects after 9/11," report prepared for the Civic Alliance.

Kimmelman, M 2013, "The plan to swallow Midtown," *New York Times* July 24.

King, R 2013, "217 year of homicide in New York," *Quartz* 31 December. Available from <http://qz.com/162289/217-years-of-homicide-in-new-york/>.

Kirschling, KM 2012, "An economic analysis of rapid transit in New York, 1870–2010," Master's thesis, Columbia University.

Landmarks Preservation Commission 1969, "Greenwich Village historic district designation report," Landmarks Preservation Commission.

Landmarks Preservation Commission 1983, "Street plan of New Amsterdam and colonial New York," Landmark Preservation Commission, 14 June, Designation List 165 LP-1235.

Landmarks Preservation Commission 1989, "Ladies Mile district designation report," Landmarks Preservation Commission.

Landmarks Preservation Commission 1996, "Equitable building," Landmarks Preservation Commission, 25 June, Designation List 273, LP-1935.

Landmarks Preservation Commission 1999, "American tract society building," Landmarks Preservation Commission, 15 June, LP-2038.

Lawrence, A 2012, "Skyscraper index," Barclays Capital Equity Research Report 12 January.

Lazarus, E 1883. "The new colossus." Available from <http://www.poetryfoundation.org/poem/175887>.

Linn, C (n.d.), "Tall tales," Architectural Record Innovation. Available from <http://archrecord.construction.com/innovation/2_features/0411history.asp>.

Lueck, TJ 1989a, "Condo boom by investors outside U.S.," *New York Times* 20 March, p. B1.

Lueck, TJ 1989b, "A skyscraper-high office space surplus," *New York Times* 22 October, p. R1.

MacDonald, GD 1953, "Office building construction, Manhattan, 1901–1953," Real Estate Board of New York, Inc., Research Dept.

Marshall, A 2006b, "The commanding heights," RPA Spotlight on the Region, 1 December. Available from <http://www.rpa.org/spotlight/commanding-heights>.

Marshall, A 2007, "Rail matters more than rock," *RPA Spotlight on the Region*, vol. 6, no. 5.

Marshall, A 2013, "Tall and out of reach: skyscrapers seem to be growing along with income inequality," Governing, December, pp. 24–25.

McCormack, M 2009, "Shanty town, New York," New York State Board of the Ancient Order of Hibernians, 21 February. Available from <http://www.nyaoh.com/2009/02/21/91/>.

MetLife 2014, "MetLife begins," MetLife. Available from <https://www.metlife.com/about/corporate-profile/metlife-history/metlife-begins/index.html>.

Miller Samuel 2014, "Manhattan sales: quarterly survey of co-ops & condo sales," Elliman Report 1Q-2014, Douglass Elliman Real Estate, New York. Available from <http://www.millersamuel.com/files/2014/04/Manhattan_1Q_2014.pdf>.

Morgenstern, J 1995, "The fifty-nine story crisis," New Yorker 29 May, pp. 45–53.

Morris, K 2014, "Sky is limit for air rights in Manhattan: average price paid for space above a building rose 47% last year," Wall Street Journal 23 April.

Municipal Arts Society of New York 2013, "50 years after the demolition of Penn Station," Municipal Arts Society of New York, 31 October. Available from <http://www.mas.org/50-years-after-the-demolition-of-penn-station/>.

Murphy, JJ 1940. Rock data map of Manhattan, third edition, 1:7200, Borough of Manhattan Topographical Bureau, New York City.

National Bureau of Economic Research 2014, "US business cycles and contractions," National Burueau of Economic Research. Available from <http://www.nber.org/cycles.html>.

National Oceanic and Atmospheric Administration 2015, "Mean sea level trend," Available from <http://tidesandcurrents.noaa.gov/sltrends/sltrends_station.shtml?stnid=8518750>

New York City 2005, "The new housing marketplace plan: creating housing for the next generation, 2004–2013." Available from <http://www.berkeleyprize.org/downloads/files/global/10year%20New%20Housing%20Marketplace%20plan.pdf>.

New York City Department of City Planning 2011, "Zoning handbook," Department of Planning, NYC. Available from <http://www.nyc.gov/html/dcp/html/pub/zonehand.shtml>.

New York City Department of Health and Hygiene 2010, "Summary of vital statistics 2010," The City of New York, New York.

New York City Department of Health and Hygiene 2011, "Summary of Vital Statistics 2010: Population and Mortality." Available from <http://www.nyc.gov/html/doh/downloads/pdf/vs/vs-population-and-mortality-report.pdf>.

New York City Department of Parks & Recreation 2005–2006, "2005–2006 Trees count! Street tree census." Available from <http://www.nycgovparks.org/trees/tree-census/2005-2006>.

New York City Rent Guidelines Board 2014, "2014 Housing supply report," New York City Rent Guidelines Board. Available from <http://www.nycrgb.org/downloads/research/pdf_reports/14HSR.pdf>.

New York State Department of Labor 2014, "Major areas, current employment estimates," Labor Statistics. Available from <http://labor.ny.gov/stats/lscesmaj.shtm>.

New York Times 1873, "Leather and jewelry: the leading manufactures of the city of Newark," New York Times 6 January, p. 2.

New York Times 1895, "He noted city history: David T. Valentine's work on the common council manuals," New York Times 28 April, p. 21.

New York Times 1897, "FAULTS OF PILE FOUNDATION: contractor Sooysmith explains why his new buildings will rest on the bed rock," New York Times 13 August, p. 8.

New York Times 1899, "Disputes of architects," New York Times 19 August, p. 12.

New York Times 1901, "Macy's new store site," New York Times 16 May, p. 10.

New York Times 1902, "New locality for trade at Broadway and thirty-fourth street," *New York Times* 9 November, p. 24.

New York Times 1903, "SITE OF NEW POST OFFICE: government likely to accept Pennsylvania railroad's offer," *New York Times* 21 February, p. 1.

New York Times 1905, "The birth of the New York skyscraper—a romance of architecture," *New York Times* 21 May, p. X6.

New York Times 1907a, "Great works and their cost in human life," *New York Times* 9 June, p. SM6.

New York Times 1907b, "The increasing marvels of lower Manhattan," *New York Times* 6 October, p. SM3.

New York Times 1909, "The new terminal of the 'Grand Central'," *New York Times* 12 September, p. SM9.

New York Times 1910a, "New top on Macy's store," *New York Times* 7 July, p. 12.

New York Times 1910b, "New Woolworth Building on Broadway will eclipse Singer Tower," *New York Times* 13 November, p. RE1.

New York Times 1911, "OBTAINS $8,000,000 FOR BIG SKYSCRAPER: Gillespie finds abroad the balance of $13,000,000 for 55-story Woolworth Building," *New York Times* 2 August, p. 1.

New York Times 1912, "Giant Tulip that is 225 years old showers leaves in benediction of its admirers," *New York Times* 31 October, p. 22.

New York Times 1913, "New grand central terminal opens its doors open," *New York Times* 2 February, p. T1.

New York Times 1915a, "SINKS IN QUICKSAND FAR BENEATH STREET," *New York Times* 9 July, p. 20.

New York Times 1915b, "Manhattan Island, the world's greatest mine," *New York Times* 17 October, p. SM18.

New York Times 1920a, "The 25 per cent increase," *New York Times* 2 April, p. 14.

New York Times 1920b, "New home for Fred F. French Co.," *New York Times* 4 April, p. RE2.

New York Times 1921, "Plan to extend Manhattan Island six miles down the bay discussed by its promoters," *New York Times* October 30, p. 102.

New York Times 1923, "New York City can be extended nine miles into the bay," *New York Times* 24 June, p. 21.

New York Times 1925, "Stones 40,000 years old found under Trinity: dug up while bracing church underpinning," *New York Times* 28 July, p. 3.

New York Times 1926a, "Metropolitan Life controller discusses over appraisals and overbuilding," *New York Times* 24 January, p. RE1.

New York Times 1926b, "Overappraisals and overproduction declared menace to realty interests," *New York Times* 12 September, p. RE1.

New York Times 1927a, "Survey shows firm market conditions," *New York Times* 15 April, p. 37.

New York Times 1927b, "Building managers condemn freaks," *New York Times* 28 August, p. RE2.

New York Times 1927c, "Lefcourt announces list of new tenants," *New York Times* 20 November, p. RE2.

New York Times 1927d, "Abraham Bricken honored at dinner," *New York Times* 22 December, p. 42.

New York Times 1928a, "Building outlook for new year good," *New York Times* 1 January, p. RE1.

New York Times 1928b, "See the investor dominating in 1928," *New York Times* 29 January, p. 160.

New York Times 1928c, "W.P. CHRYSLER BEGAN LIFE AS A FARM BOY: first job in Kansas railroad," *New York Times* 3 June, p. N11.

New York Times 1928d, "Skyscraper need in midtown seen," *New York Times* 15 July, p. RE2.

New York Times 1928e, "Huge home opened by New York Life: new home of New York Life Insurance, Co.," *New York Times* 13 December, p. 16.

New York Times 1929, "Big office space in new buildings," *New York Times* 14 July, p. RE1.

New York Times 1930a, "Five av. values always advancing," *New York Times* 23 March, p. RE6.

New York Times 1930b, "Bank of Manhattan built in record time," *New York Times* 6 May.

New York Times 1930c, "Thirty-one commercial buildings erected by A. E. Lefcourt in two decades," *New York Times* 18 May, p. RE2.

New York Times 1930d, "Dearth of tenants hits skyscrapers," *New York Times* 16 August, p. 26.

New York Times 1930e, "Smith lays stone for tallest tower," *New York Times* 10 September, p. 27.

New York Times 1931, "Broadway building open," *New York Times* 6 January, p. 53.

New York Times 1934, "Nelson tower offered: forty-five-story building on 7th Ave. to be put up at auction," *New York Times* 22 December, p. 29.

New York Times 1940, "GOING DOWN TO BEDROCK: builders to need 60-foot concrete piles for west side house," *New York Times* 20 October, p. 154.

New York Times 1945, "Few reach work in empire state," *New York Times* 25 September, p. 15.

New York Times 1947, "Abraham Bricken, builder, 63, dead," *New York Times* 8 July, p. 24.

New York University Furman Center 2006, "Recent homeownership trends in New York City," NYU Furman Center. Available from <http://furmancenter.org/files/sotc/SOC2006_ownershiptrends06_000.pdf>.

New York University Furman Center 2012, "Rent stabilization in New York City," Furman Center for Real Estate & Urban Policy. Available from <http://furmancenter.org/files/publications/HVS_Rent_Stabilization_fact_sheet_FINAL_4.pdf>.

New York University Furman Center 2013, "Buying sky: the market for transferable development rights in New York City," NYU Furman Center, October 2013, pp. 1–20.

New York University Furman Center 2014, "Profile of rent-stabilized units and tenants in New York City," NYU Furman Center, June 2014, pp. 1–8.

Office of the Comptroller of the City of New York 2014, "The growing gap: New York City's housing affordability challenge," Office of the Comptroller of the City of New York, April. Available from <http://comptroller.nyc.gov/wp-content/uploads/documents/Growing_Gap.pdf>.

Officer, LH & Williamson, SH 2015, "The annual consumer price index for the United States, 1774-2014," MeasuringWorth. Available from <http://www.measuringworth.com/uscpi/>.

O'Grady, T 2013, "Spatial institutions in urban economies: how city grids affect development," Dissertation chapter, University of California, Santa Barbara.

O'Leary, A 2012, "Everybody inhale: how many people can Manhattan hold?" *New York Times* 1 March.

Oser, AS 1999, "How to build with a firm foundation: avoiding high water tables," *New York Times* 31 January, p. RE1.

Perlberg, H 2014, "Manhattan apartment rents jump as vacancies rate tumbles," Bloomberg, 10 July. Available from <http://www.bloomberg.com/news/articles/2014-07-10/manhattan-apartment-rents-jump-as-vacancies-rate-tumbles>.

Perlmutter, N & Arnow, T 1953, "Ground water in Bronx, New York, and Richmond Counties with summary data on Kings and Queens Counties, New York City, New York" Bulletin GW-32, New York State Water Power and Control Commission, Albany.

Peterson, I 1986, "Off the beat: the first skyscraper," *Science News*, vol. 129, no. 14, pp. 218–219.

Phys.org 2006, "NASA looks at sea level rise, hurricane risks to New York City," Phys.org, 25 October. Available from <http://phys.org/news81007489.html>.

Phys.org 2015, "Flood risk on rise for New York City and New Jersey coast, study finds," Phys.org, 28 September. Availible from < http://phys.org/news/2015-09-nyc-future-hurricanes.html>.

Pincus, A 2014, "City construction costs break $1,000 per foot barrier," *The Real Deal* 1 October. Available from <http://therealdeal.com/issues_articles/nycs-construction-craze/>.

Popper, SH 1955, "Newark, NJ, 1870–1910: chapters in the evolution of an American metropolis," Ph.D. dissertation, New York University.

Postal, MA 2001, "Madison Square north historic district designation," New York City Landmarks Preservation Commission, New York.

Presa, D 1996, "Designation list 271 union square savings bank," New York Landmarks Preservation Commission, Report #LP-1945.

The Real Deal 2012, "Developers vie for 'tallest' designation next to residential towers," *The Real Deal Magazine* 18 May. Available from <http://therealdeal.com/blog/2012/05/18/developers-vie-for-tallest-designation-next-to-residential-towers/>.

The Real Deal 2014, "NYC's construction craze," *The Real Deal Magazine* 1 October. Available from <http://therealdeal.com/issues_articles/nycs-construction-craze/>.

Real Estate Record and Builders' Guide 1890, "Entered at the post office at New York, N.Y., as second-class matter," *Real Estate Record and Builders' Guide* 4 January, vol. 45, no. 1138.

Real Estate Record and Builders' Guide 1908, "The real estate market in 1907," *Real Estate Record and Builders' Guide* 4 January, vol. 31, no. 2077, p. 1.

Real Estate Record and Builders' Guide 1909, "Price per year in advance eight dollars," *Real Estate Record and Builders' Guide* 25 December, vol. 84, no. 2180, pp. 1157–1200.

Real Estate Record and Builders' Guide 1912a, "Court of appeals decision causes a stir: it removes apartment houses from the jurisdiction of the tenement department and causes and emergency bill to be introduced at Albany," *Real Estate Record and Builders' Guide* 24 February, vol. 89, no. 2293, p. 365.

Real Estate Record and Builders' Guide 1912b, "Prospect park west shows marked improvement," *Real Estate Record and Builders' Guide* 4 May, vol. 89, no. 2303.

Real Estate Record and Builders' Guide 1912c, "Economic causes of the growth of Brooklyn: a marvelous increase of population and industry, which will be accelerated by improved transportation—how dependence on Manhattan influences real estate," *Real Estate Record and Builders' Guide* 11 May, vol. 89, no. 2304, p. 1002.

Real Estate Record and Builders' Guide 1927, "To study realty bond marketing," *Real Estate Record and Builders' Guide* 19 February, p. 5.

Real Estate Record and Builders' Guide 1929, "Survey shows increasing migration of large business institution," *Real Estate Record and Builders' Guide* 13 April, p. 8.

Roberts, S 2008, "Hot History Debate: 1624 or 1625?" *New York Times* 24 July. Available from <http://cityroom.blogs.nytimes.com/2008/07/24/hot-history-debate-1624-or-1625/?_php=true&_type=blogs&_php=true&_type=blogs&_r=1>.

Rose-Redwood, RS 2002, "Rationalizing the landscape: superimposing the grid upon the island of Manhattan," Masters thesis, Pennsylvania State University.

Sackersdorff, O 1868. "Maps of Farms: Commonly Called the Blue Book, 1815." Office of City Surveyor.

Saez, E 2014, "Income inequality in the US tables." Available from <http://eml.berkeley.edu/~saez/TabFig2013prel.xls>.

Samuels, D 1997, "The real-estate royals: end of the line?" *New York Times* 10 August, p. SM36.

Satow, J 2011, "Visions of a development rising from the sea," *New York Times* 22 November.

Satow, J 2014 "Pied-a-Neighborhood," *New York Times* 24 October.

Satow, J 2015 "Why the doorman is lonely," *New York Times* 9 January.

Scardino, A 1986, "Trading air to build towers," *New York Times* 21 February, p. D1.

Shiller R 2014, "U.S. Stock Markets 1871–Present and CAPE Ratio." Availible from <http:// www.econ.yale.edu/~shiller/data.htm>. [Accessed December 2014]

Shiller, R 2015, "Standard & Poor's/Case-Shiller Home Price Indices," S&P Dow Jones Indices. Available from <http://www.spindices.com/index-family/real-estate/sp-case-shiller>.

Sinking Mexico City. Holt CNN Math Activities. Available from <http://go.hrw.com/math/ cnn/course3/3_1_Sinking/3_1_Sinking.htm>.

Smith, G 2013, "New York City property tax system favors the rich, hits lower classes harder, News investigation finds," *New York Daily News* 28 September. Available from <http://www.nydaily-news.com/new-york/higher-income-areas-taxes-poorer-counterparts-article-1.1470735>.

Smith, SJ 2014, "Congestion pricing in New York may come back from the dead," *Next City* 25 March. Available from <http://nextcity.org/daily/entry/congestion-pricing-in-new-york-may-come-back-from-the-dead>.

Sutton, P 2013, "The Woolworth building: the cathedral of commerce," New York Public Library, 22 April. Available from <http://www.nypl.org/blog/2013/04/22/woolworth-building-cathedral-commerce>.

US Census 2010, "Quick facts." Available from <http://quickfacts.census.gov/qfd/states/ 36/36061.html>.

US Geological Survey 2006, "Liquefaction in past earthquakes." Available from <http://geo-maps.wr.usgs.gov/sfgeo/liquefaction/effects.html>.

Valentino, S 2012, "Object #9: Manhattan Schist." The Lodown, WNYC, 1 March. Available from <http://www.wnyc.org/story/190000-object-9-manhattan-schist/>.

Venables, R 1983, "Street plan of New Amsterdam and colonial New York," Landmark Preservation Commission New York, Report # LP-1253.

Voien, G 2013, "Manhattan leasing strong in Q3; Midtown market stratifies," *The Real Deal* 1 October. Available from <http://therealdeal.com/blog/2013/10/01/ manhattan-leasing-strong-in-q3-midtown-market-stratifies/>.

Young, JC 1926, "New York rebuilds itself on a huge scale," *New York Times* 27 June, p. XX5.

Wallace, M 2007, "The grid, yellow fever and real estate," *New York Times* 20 June.

Wall Street Journal 1929, "Equitable bldg. best year seen," *Wall Street Journal* 11 September, p. 1.

Wall Street Journal 1931, "Office vacancy not abnormal," *Wall Street Journal* 20 June, p. 3.

Washington Post 1911, "Fire far underground," *Washington Post* 19 December, p. 1.

Weise, K 2014, "Housing's 30-Percent-of-Income Rule is Nearly Useless." *Bloomberg Business* 14 July. Available from < http://www.bloomberg.com/bw/articles/2014-07-17/housings-30-percent-of-income-rule-is-near-useless>.

Willis, C (n.d.), "Urban fabric: building New York's Garment District" and "Installation Walkthrough." Skyscraper Museum. Available from <http://www.skyscraper.org/ EXHIBITIONS/URBAN_FABRIC/walkthrough_intro.php>.

Zerba, A 2014, "Notable fires in the New York City area," *New York Times* 20 June.

Index